*Oracle Press*™

Oracle Database 11g & MySQL 5.6 Developer Handbook

About the Author

Michael McLaughlin is a professor of Computer Information Technology at Brigham Young University–Idaho. He is also an Oracle ACE. Michael has worked with the Oracle product stack for 20 years as a developer, DBA, and E-Business Suite Applications DBA.

Michael left Oracle as the Senior Upgrade Manager in Release Engineering for the Oracle Applications Division. He worked at Oracle for more than eight years in consulting, support, and development. He is the inventor of the ATOMS transaction architecture (U.S. Patents #7,206,805 and #7,290,056). The patents are assigned to Oracle Corporation.

He is the author of six books on Oracle technology, including *Oracle Database 11g PL/SQL Programming* and *Oracle Database 10g PL/SQL Programming*.

Michael and his wife, Lisa, have been married for more than 20 years and they have nine children. They live in Idaho near Yellowstone National Park.

About the Technical Editor

A. Scott Mikolaitis is an applications architect at Oracle Corporation and has worked at Oracle for more than ten years. He works on prototyping and standards development for the SOA technology in Oracle Fusion.

Scott also enjoys working with web services in Java as well as Jabber for human and system interaction patterns. He spends his spare time on DIY home improvement and gas-fueled RC cars.

Oracle Press™

Oracle Database 11g & MySQL 5.6 Developer Handbook

Michael McLaughlin

New York   Chicago   San Francisco
Lisbon   London   Madrid   Mexico City   Milan
New Delhi   San Juan   Seoul   Singapore   Sydney   Toronto

The McGraw·Hill Companies

Cataloging-in-Publication Data is on file with the Library of Congress

McGraw-Hill books are available at special quantity discounts to use as premiums and sales promotions, or for use in corporate training programs. To contact a representative, please e-mail us at bulksales@mcgraw-hill.com.

Oracle Database 11g & MySQL 5.6 Developer Handbook

1 2 3 4 5 6 7 8 9 0   DOC DOC   1 0 9 8 7 6 5 4 3 2 1

ISBN   978-0-07-176885-6
MHID   0-07-176885-8

Sponsoring Editor Wendy Rinaldi	**Technical Editor** A. Scott Mikolaitis	**Composition** Cenveo Publisher Services
Editorial Supervisor Patty Mon	**Copy Editor** Lisa Theobald	**Illustration** Cenveo Publisher Services
Project Manager Sandhya Gola, Cenveo Publisher Services	**Proofreader** Bev Weiler	**Art Director, Cover** Jeff Weeks
Acquisitions Coordinator Stephanie Evans	**Indexer** Ted Laux	**Cover Designer** Pattie Lee
	Production Supervisor George Anderson	

To Lisa, my eternal companion, inspiration, wife, and best friend; and to Sarah, Joseph, Elise, Ian, Ariel, Callie, Nathan, Spencer, and Christianne, who supported me like the champions they are throughout the writing process.

Contents at a Glance

Contents

PART I
Development Components

PART II
SQL Development

Acknowledgments

Many thanks go to Wendy Rinaldi and Stephanie Evans at McGraw-Hill for their tireless work on this project, and their support throughout the project.

Special thanks go to Ian McLaughlin, who proofread for me. Thanks to Kent Jackson for looking over outlines; Michael Stokes, Benjamin Benson, and William Graham for editing and testing code components; Rex Barzee for letting me brainstorm organizational ideas; and Art Ericson, my CIT Department Chair, for his support on the project.

Finally, no acknowledgment would be complete without thanking the production department for their conscientious attention to detail and hard work in putting all the pieces together. I'd like to thank Lisa Theobold for smoothing my writing, Bev Weiler for finding errors of omission and commission and tuning the organization of content, and Sandhya Gola for keeping things organized through copy edit, proof edit, and final book preparation.

Introduction

The Introduction is always the last thing you write, and I've sometimes thought it should be the first thing you write. This time I drafted the introduction before writing and it helped me make sure I stayed a planned course. The production staff also helps clear up what I write, and you can check my acknowledgment page recognizing them and their talents, which are critical to bring a quality book into print.

This introduction covers the following:

- The "Book Outline" section summarizes each chapter in a sentence or two and should be worth a quick look.

- The "Lexicon" section gives you the rationale for variable naming conventions in the book, and my recommendations for saving you time debugging your code.

- The "Data Model" section describes the basis for the examples and tells you where to find the code that creates and seeds the student database.

Book Outline

The book has three parts: "Development Components," "SQL Development," and "Stored Program Units." Each chapter within these three parts covers a set of fundamentals and includes a mastery check at the end. Each mastery check contains ten true or false questions and five multiple-choice questions.

Part I: Development Components

- Chapter 1, "Architectures," explains the Oracle 11*g* and MySQL 5.6 development architectures and highlights the comparative aspects of both client and server environments.

- Chapter 2, "Client Interfaces," explains and demonstrates the basics of how you use SQL*Plus and MySQL Monitor client software.

- Chapter 3, "Security," explains the security barriers for database servers and Data Control Language (DCL) commands that let you manage user and account privileges in the database servers.

- Chapter 4, "Transactions," explains the nature of ACID-compliant transactions and the Two-phase Commit (2PC) process demonstrated by INSERT, UPDATE, and DELETE statements.

- Chapter 5, "Constraints," explains the five primary database-level constraints and covers the check, not null, unique, primary key, and foreign key constraints.

Part II: SQL Development

- Chapter 6, "Creating Users and Structures," explains how you can create users, databases, tables, sequences, and indexes.

- Chapter 7, "Modifying Users and Structures," explains how you modify users, databases, tables, sequences, and indexes.

- Chapter 8, "Inserting Data," explains how you insert data into tables.

- Chapter 9, "Updating Data," explains how you update data in tables.

- Chapter 10, "Deleting Data," explains how to delete data from tables.

- Chapter 11, "Querying Data," explains how you query data from a single table, from a join of two or more tables, and from a join of two or more queries through set operators.

- Chapter 12, "Merging Data," explains how you import denormalized data from external tables or source files and insert or update records in normalized tables.

Part III: Stored Program Development

- Chapter 13, "PL/SQL Basics," explains the basics of using PL/SQL to write transactional blocks of code.

- Chapter 14, "SQL/PSM Basics," explains the basics of using SQL/PSM to write transactional blocks of code.

- Chapter 15, "Triggers," explains how to write database triggers in Oracle and MySQL databases.

- The appendix covers the answers to the mastery questions at the end of the chapters.

Lexicon

There are many ways to write programs, and they generally differ between programming languages. SQL, PL/SQL, and SQL/PSM code share that commonality: they are different languages and require different approaches.

SQL Lexicon

My recommendation on SQL statements is that you align your keywords on the left. That means placing SELECT list commas and WHERE clause logical AND [NOT] or OR [NOT] syntax on the left, because it allows you to sight read your code for errors. Those recommendations are easy, but my recommendations on how to write *join-syntax* are more complex, because you can write joins that use ANSI SQL-89 or ANSI SQL-92. ANSI SQL-89 lets you organize tables as comma delimited lists, whereas ANSI SQL-92 has you specify the type of join using keywords.

These are my suggestions on join syntax:

- Always use table aliases, because they ensure that you won't run into an ambiguous column error when the SELECT list can return two or more columns with the same name. This can happen when you join tables that share the same column name. It's also a good practice to use aliases when you write a query from a single table, because you might subsequently add another table through a join. Chapter 11 covers the SELECT statement and syntax that supports this recommendation.

- When using ANSI SQL-89 and comma-delimited tables, place each table on its own line and the separating columns on the left, like SELECT list columns. This lets you sight read your programs. This doesn't apply to multiple-table UPDATE and DELETE statements found in Chapters 9 and 10, respectively, and you should refer to those chapters for examples.

- When using ANSI SQL-92, you put the join conditions inside the FROM clause by using either the ON or USING subclauses. Two common approaches seem to work best for most developers inside the FROM clause with the ON or USING subclauses. In small two, or at maximum three table joins, place the ON or USING subclause after the join on the same line. In large joins of three or more, place the ON or USING subclause on the line below the joining statement. When joins involve multiple columns, left-align logical AND [NOT] or OR [NOT] syntax to allow you to sight read your code.

- When using ANSI SQL-89 includes join statements in the WHERE clause of queries, it's a good idea to place joins as the first statements in the clause. The ANSI SQL-89 WHERE clause also includes statements that filter result sets, while the ANSI SQL-92 WHERE clause only contains filtering statements. Statements in the WHERE clause are joined by logical AND [NOT] or OR [NOT] syntax. The AND logical operator takes precedence over the OR logical operator unless you use parentheses to change the order of operation. You should left-align logical AND [NOT] or OR [NOT] syntax to allow you to sight read your code.

- ANSI SQL-92 lets you use fully descriptive keywords or use only required keywords. Although most of us would like to type the least amount of words possible, ultimately, our code goes to support staff, and its clarity can help avoid frivolous bug reports. Therefore, consider using INNER JOIN instead of JOIN; LEFT OUTER JOIN or RIGHT OUTER JOIN instead of LEFT JOIN and RIGHT JOIN; and FULL OUTER JOIN instead of FULL JOIN. I've shortened syntax in the book solely because of the required 67-character limit on code lines (or they shrink the font and make it less readable) to make them fit on the printed page.

A Word on Tools

Although this book focuses on writing SQL at the command line because that's how it'll work inside your C++, C#, Java, or PHP programs, CASE (Computer-aided Software Engineering) tools are effective when working interactively with the database. They help you discover syntax and possibilities, provided you don't use them as a crutch.

In short, use a tool to learn; don't become a slave to it. Always ask why something works and how it might work better. If you do, you'll find CASE tools a blessing for getting your job done and not a career limiting curse.

Now that I've written that, let me share my experience at not following syntax advice. My instructor at IBM's Santa Teresa Lab (now IBM's Silicon Valley Lab) taught me how to write SQL (actually SQL/DS [Structured Query Language/Data System]) in 1985. He told me to put the commas on the left to save myself hours of hunting for missing commas. I ignored the advice and put them on the right, at the end of the line, for a couple months before realizing he was right. His mantra that week was, "Good programming follows simple principles."

At school now, I emphasize this advice term after term. Some students accept it and use it, and some don't. Those students who don't accept it struggle with the syntax throughout the course, because they're always trying to find that missing comma or component in their SQL statement. SQL's not an easy thing to learn, because it requires creating a spatial map of data, which isn't a skill all developers possess immediately. Sometimes it takes quite a while to sort through seeing the relationships between data in a relational database. It becomes easier with practice, provided you strive to maintain the clarity of your statements, the consistencies of your approach, and consistent choice of using portable SQL syntax.

PL/SQL and SQL/PSM Stored Programs

PL/SQL and SQL/PSM are fully fledged programming languages. They allow you to write programs stored in the database that manage collections of SQL statements as a complete transaction.

Chapters 13, 14, and 15 deal with stored programming languages, and they include various types of variables. Variable naming conventions can be controversial in some organizations, because many developers believe variables should be semantically meaningful, which means their names should describe their use or purpose. The argument against naming conventions is that the conventions, such as prefixes, decrease code readability. This argument is like anything else in life, however—a conflict of ideas. There's merit on both sides of the argument, and a right time to do one over the other. From my perspective, the key is finding balance between what adds stability to the company or corporate enterprise while providing meaningful variable names.

Here in the book, I've tried to be consistent and use prefaces. In some places, I've opted for semantic clarity in variable names (such as the Oracle session or bind variable :whom in Chapter 2). I believe that using prefaces increases readability in your code, and I suggest you use the prefaces in Table 1, which map between Oracle and MySQL databases.

Prefix	Example	Description
cv	cv_input_var	Represents cursor parameter variables. These are pass-by-value input parameters to cursors in PL/SQL stored programs. Unfortunately, SQL/PSM stored programs don't support cursor parameters.
lv	lv_target_var	Represents local variables defined inside PL/SQL or SQL/PSM stored programs.
pv	pv_exchange_var	Represents parameters to PL/SQL and SQL/PSM stored functions and procedures. They're not exclusively input parameters because PL/SQL supports input and output parameters in both stored functions and procedures, and SQL/PSM supports input and output parameters in stored procedures (not functions as qualified in Chapter 14).
bv sv	bv_global_var or sv_global_var	Represents session, or Oracle's *bind* variables; they act as global variables for the duration of a client connection to the database. Oracle lets you share the values in these variables between anonymous blocks using a colon before the variable name (:sv_global_var) inside the block, and they're called bind variables (hence the alternative :bv_global_var). MySQL lets you reference them in named blocks and requires an @ symbol to appear before the variable name: @sv_global_var. More on MySQL session variables is found in Chapters 2 and 14.

TABLE 1. *PL/SQL Variable Prefixes*

Some advanced variable data types, known as composite variables, require both prefixes and suffixes. The suffix identifies the type of composite variable. These requirements are unique to the Oracle database. Table 2 qualifies my recommended suffixes (with a lead-in underscore) for Oracle composite data types. Table 2 shows you long and short name versions for the suffixes.

It's generally an accepted practice to use suffixes for composite data types, because these are user-defined types (UDTs). However, it isn't a rule or requirement in the PL/SQL programming language. The details of the PL/SQL programming language are summarized in Chapter 13 or available in a more complete fashion in *Oracle Database 11g PL/SQL Programming* (Oracle Press/McGraw-Hill, 2008).

	Suffix	
Long	**Short**	**Description**
_ATABLE _AARRAY	_ATAB, _AA	_ATABLE, _AARRAY, _ATAB, and _AA are used to describe associative arrays in PL/SQL. My preference is the _ATABLE or _ATAB suffix, because the other suffixes aren't intuitively obvious and require documentation in your code.
_CURSOR	_CUR _C	_CURSOR, _CUR, and _C are used to describe variables based on a cursor structure defined in a local declaration block or a package specification in PL/SQL. My preference is the _CURSOR or _C suffix. You can also declare a cursor structure, which is covered in Chapter 13.
_EXCEPTION	_EXCEPT _EX _E	_EXCEPTION, _EXCEPT, _EX, and _E are used to describe user-defined exceptions in PL/SQL. My preference is the _EXCEPTION or _E suffix.
_OBJECT	_OBJ _O	_OBJECT, _OBJ, and _O are used to describe UDTs in both SQL and PL/SQL. Object types can act like PL/SQL RECORD data types, which are record data structures. They differ because they're schema-level SQL UDTs and not exclusively PL/SQL UDTs. Object types can also be instantiable objects such as C++, C#, and Java classes, but you should refer to *Oracle Database 11g PL/SQL Programming*. My preference is the _OBJECT or _O suffix.
_NTABLE _TABLE	_NTAB _TAB	_NTABLE, _TABLE, _NTAB, and _TAB are used to describe nested tables, which are collection types in SQL and PL/SQL. They act like lists because they've no upward limit on how many elements can be in the collection. My preference is the _TABLE or _TAB suffix because a nested table is the collection most like a list in other programming languages.
_RECORD	_REC _R	_RECORD, _REC, and _R are used to describe UDTs exclusively in PL/SQL. They are a PL/SQL implementation of a record data structure. They can be elements of PL/SQL collections but not of SQL collections. My preference is the _RECORD or _R suffix because both are fully descriptive or shorthand, but many developers opt for _REC.

TABLE 2. *PL/SQL Variable Suffixes*

Suffix		
Long	**Short**	**Description**
_TYPE	_T	_TYPE, _T are used to describe UDTs, like subtypes of normal scalar data types described in Chapter 13. Either of these suffix works for me but _TYPE seems more frequent in code repositories.
_VARRAY	_VARR _VA	_VARRAY, _VARR, _VA are used to describe the VARRAY (my mnemonic for this Oracle data type is a virtual array). The VARRAY is the collection most like a standard array in programming languages, because it has a maximum size and must always have sequential index values. It can be used to define SQL and PL/SQL collections. My preference is the _VARRAY or _VA suffix because _VARR is too close to generic variable shorthand.

TABLE 2. *PL/SQL Variable Suffixes*

PL/SQL is a strongly typed language, and both PL/SQL and SQL/PSM programs are blocked programs. Blocked programs use keywords to start and end program units as opposed to curly braces found in C++, C#, Java, or PHP. As found in the GeSHi (Generic Syntax Highlighter) libraries, PL/SQL and SQL/PSM block keywords appear as uppercase letters, and I've adopted that convention throughout the book.

Other Conventions

Sometimes code blocks need clarity. Line numbers are provided throughout the examples for Oracle, because they're a display feature of the SQL*Plus environment. While I was tempted to add them for the MySQL programs, they're not part of the MySQL Monitor display and were omitted except in certain cases where they bring clarity to describing how the code works.

The text conventions for the book cover highlighting, italicizing, and separating syntax. They are qualified in Table 3. Hopefully, these conventions make reading the book easier.

Convention	Meaning
Boldface	Focuses attention on specific lines of code in sample programs.
Italics	Focuses attention on new words or concepts.
Monospaced	All code blocks and bits of code in text are monospaced.
UPPERCASE	Denotes keywords used in SQL and PL/SQL.
lowercase	Denotes the names of user-defined tables, views, column, function, procedure, package, and types.
[]	Square brackets designate optional syntax and appear in the prototypes.
{}	Curly braces group lists of options, which are separated by a single pipe symbol (|).
|	The single pipe symbol indicates a logical OR operator between option lists.
. . .	Ellipses indicate that content repeats or was removed for space conservation.

TABLE 3.   *Text Conventions*

Data Model

The data model is a small video store. The source code to create and seed the data model for Oracle and MySQL is found on the publisher's web site for the book, which at the time of writing is: http://www.mhprofessional.com/product.php?isbn=0071768858.

Figure 1 shows the basic, or core, tables used in the example programs. The drawing was rendered by using MySQL Workbench 5.2 and reverse engineering of the physical schema. If you're unfamiliar with MySQL Workbench, I'd recommend you become acquainted with it, because it's a great tool that effectively supports data modeling and design against the MySQL database.

One table in the model might require some explanation, and that's the common_lookup table. The common_lookup table is a table of tables, as shown in Figure 2.

A set of attributes (columns) that uniquely identify rows is the natural key. It consists of the table and column name plus the type. Types are uppercase strings joined by underscores that make querying these lookup sets easier. (In Oracle, all metadata strings are stored in uppercase text, whereas MySQL stores metadata in lowercase text strings.) The meaning column provides the information that you'd provide to an end user making a choice in a drop box.

The primary key of the common_lookup table is a surrogate key column, common_lookup_id (following the practice of using the table name and a _id suffix for primary key column names). A copy of this value is stored in the table and column, such as item and item_type. With this type of design, you can change the display value of *XBOX* to *Xbox* in a single location, and all code modules and table values would be unchanged. It's a powerful modeling device, because it prevents placing components such as gender, race, or yes/no answers in web forms (embedded options), and it reduces management costs of your application after deployment.

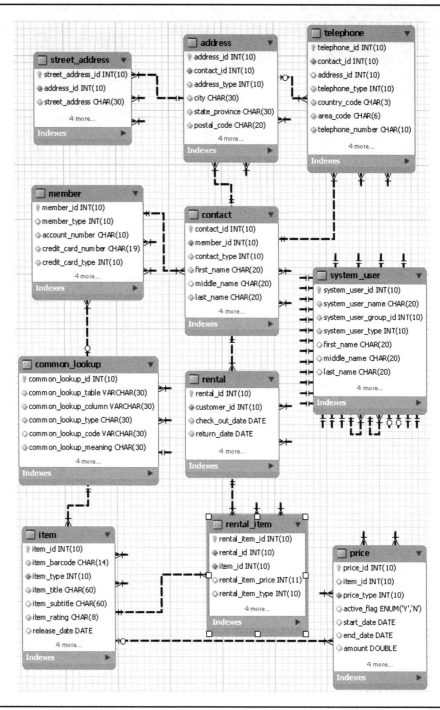

FIGURE 1. *Video store Entity Relation Diagram (ERD)*

common_lookup_id	common_lookup_table	common_lookup_column	common_lookup_type	common_lookup_meaning
1	SYSTEM_USER	system_user_id	SYSTEM_ADMIN	System Administrator
2	SYSTEM_USER	system_user_id	DBA	Database Administrator
3	CONTACT	CONTACT_TYPE	EMPLOYEE	Employee
4	CONTACT	CONTACT_TYPE	CUSTOMER	Customer
5	MEMBER	MEMBER_TYPE	INDIVIDUAL	Individual Membership
6	MEMBER	MEMBER_TYPE	GROUP	Group Membership
7	MEMBER	CREDIT_CARD_TYPE	DISCOVER_CARD	Discover Card
8	MEMBER	CREDIT_CARD_TYPE	MASTER_CARD	Master Card
9	MEMBER	CREDIT_CARD_TYPE	VISA_CARD	VISA Card
10	ADDRESS	ADDRESS_TYPE	HOME	Home
11	ADDRESS	ADDRESS_TYPE	WORK	Work
12	ITEM	ITEM_TYPE	DVD_FULL_SCREEN	DVD: Full Screen
13	ITEM	ITEM_TYPE	DVD_WIDE_SCREEN	DVD: Wide Screen
14	ITEM	ITEM_TYPE	NINTENDO_GAMECUBE	Nintendo GameCube
15	ITEM	ITEM_TYPE	PLAYSTATION2	PlayStation2
16	ITEM	ITEM_TYPE	XBOX	XBOX
17	ITEM	ITEM_TYPE	VHS_SINGLE_TAPE	VHS: Single Tape
18	ITEM	ITEM_TYPE	VHS_DOUBLE_TAPE	VHS: Double Tape
19	TELEPHONE	TELEPHONE_TYPE	HOME	Home
20	TELEPHONE	TELEPHONE_TYPE	WORK	Work
21	PRICE	ACTIVE_FLAG	YES	Yes
22	PRICE	ACTIVE_FLAG	NO	NO

FIGURE 2. *Common lookup table (table of tables)*

PART
I

Development Components

CHAPTER
1

Architecture

atabase architecture has two parts: One part qualifies how the database server works; the other part explains how the developer interacts with the database server. The latter part is *client-server computing*.

The client software provides the interface to the engine, like the steering wheel, brakes, and dashboard of a car. The engine is the server software. Server software includes an engine that stores and processes data, a transmission that governs transactions, and an enhanced odometer that logs what the system does to files. It also includes tires, body parts, seat cushions, and bumpers, which are support programs that manage the system's content integrity.

This chapter discusses client-server architecture for the Oracle and MySQL databases. It describes how they work together in general and explains how their client and server components work together. The chapter covers the following:

- General client-server computing model
- Oracle Database 11*g*

  - Client software: SQL*Plus

  - Oracle server software
- Oracle MySQL 5.6

  - Client software: MySQL Monitor

  - MySQL server software

These two databases have many similarities and some big differences. Any comparative comments are included here only once, where they make sense. Rather than repeat them in subsequent sections, you're asked to refer back to the prior comment. These comments should help you develop a solid understanding about how both databases work and the differences between the two.

General Client-Server Computing Model

Let's start with a brief discussion of how client and server software works before we examine how the Oracle or MySQL databases work. Client-server computing is a model whereby two computers share resources across a network. The sharing pattern involves a client that originates requests and a server that receives them. Like a mailbox in front of your home, a recipient in this model is a running process that actively listens for incoming requests and forwards them to the database. That process is called the *listener*.

The following illustration shows a view of how the two software components work in client-server computing. Oracle and MySQL implement these concepts differently, as you will see.

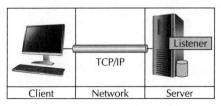

The client software component provides an interactive and batch interface that lets you and your programs interact with the database. Both MySQL and Oracle provide client interface software to manipulate database structures, and both query and modify data. These are command-line interfaces. Oracle implements its client as Oracle SQL*Plus and MySQL Server implements its client as MySQL Monitor.

Command-line tools are necessary in this computing model but can be discouraging to most beginning developers, because it takes time to learn how to use them. You can find instructions on using command-line tools in Chapter 2. Developers expect friendlier tools, known as *Computer-Aided Software Engineering (CASE)* tools, which generally provide a graphical user interface (GUI) to command-line–based client software.

Oracle SQL Developer and Oracle MySQL Workbench are the current vendor development tools. Many others exist, such as Quest's Toad. Although it was tempting to throw in a chapter on using these GUI CASE tools, the interface could change between writing and publishing this book. Because writing SQL and stored programs prepares you to develop database-centric applications, this book focuses on the command-line tools that you'll likely use in writing your code.

The Oracle and MySQL server-side software supports a relational database management system (RDBMS). You install local copies of both the client- and server-side software when you install either database product on any platform. As mentioned, the client-side software is a command-line console. It submits requests to the server-side engine and the engine returns result sets or acknowledgments of success or failure.

These requests are written in SQL (pronounced *sequel* by IBM engineers) statements. SQL stands for Structured Query Language and originally stood for Structured English Query Language (SEQUEL). SEQUEL as a name ran afoul of an existing British trademark and was shortened by IBM to SQL. Although SQL is often labeled as a nonprocedural programming language, that's *technically* inaccurate. Nonprocedural languages are typically event-driven languages, such as Java.

Instead, *SQL is a set-based declarative language*. Declarative programming languages let developers state what a program should do without qualifying how it will accomplish this. Declarative languages are much like an automatic transmission in a car. High-level instructions map to detailed activities hidden from the driver, such as accelerating and decelerating without bothering to change gears.

Like the throttle or gas pedal, SQL statements submit requests to database engines. The engine receives the request, determines the sequence of actions required to accomplish the task, and performs the task. Internally, the engines support *imperative languages*. The imperative languages change the state of variables and sets of variables for any assigned task.

SQL lets you interact with data, but it also lets you define and configure data structures without dealing with the specific mechanics of operation. The SQL statement engine processes all SQL statements. All means *all*, with no exceptions. SQL statements are *events* and fall into categories: they can be *Data Definition Language (DDL)*, *Data Manipulation Language (DML)*, *Data Control Language (DCL)*, and *Transaction Control Language (TCL)*.

Although there are many variations of how you use SQL commands, only 16 basic commands exist. The DDL commands let you create and modify structures in the database via `CREATE`, `ALTER`, `DROP`, `RENAME`, `TRUNCATE`, and `COMMENT` statements. DML commands let you query, add, modify, or remove data from structures via `SELECT`, `INSERT`, `UPDATE`, and `DELETE` statements. You also have a hybrid `MERGE` statement in the DML family of commands, which lets you insert or update rows based on logic you embed in the statement. When you transact across more than a single table, you use TCL commands `SAVEPOINT`, `ROLLBACK`, and `COMMIT`. Lastly the `GRANT` and `REVOKE` DCL commands let you give and retrieve privileges to act in the database.

Procedural Language Extensions

PL/SQL (Procedural Language/SQL) was defined by Oracle before database standards were provided for stored programs. They were added because SQL by itself couldn't do everything required of database-centric applications. MySQL 5.0 and newer versions implement SQL/PSM (SQL/Persistent Stored Module). This implementation owes its approach to the ISO/IEC 9075-4:2003 (more or less the ANSI SQL:2003) standard.

These are both procedural languages, which means they are imperative programming languages that use procedures or subroutines. The strength of both implementations is their recursive ability to allow SQL to call stored programs and stored programs to run SQL statements.

Essential elements of modern databases exist because of procedural language extensions, such as database triggers. Triggers are event-driven components defined by SQL and implemented by PL/SQL or SQL/PSM.

Set-based declarative languages such as SQL don't accomplish all that databases need to do. As a result of that failure, most commercial databases have implemented procedural programming language extensions called *modularized* imperative programming languages. *Modularized* means that they include subroutines and *procedural* comes from the label of subroutines as functions or procedures. Although they are subroutines, both require different semantics and interface paradigms.

Server-side software provides the management infrastructure for databases. It provides the SQL statement processor, which parses and runs statements. It also provides a subordinate engine for processing blocks of SQL, which may be a SQL statement, a set of SQL statements, or blocks of Oracle PL/SQL or MySQL SQL/PSM code.

As a developer, you must understand how the client software speaks with the server. It isn't adequate, in and of itself, to say *client-server computing is where two computers share resources across the network*. The client sends requests to the server and the server replies to the client through process communication. Process communication can occur through either an operating system pipe or a network socket. The former works only on a single machine, while the latter works on a single machine or set of machines connected by a network.

Beyond resolving their network addresses, the server software needs to start a process that *listens* for incoming requests. As mentioned, these types of processes are called *listeners*.

Although listener processes are part of the server software, their implementations often differ. Some of the differences are tied to how they implement user security.

A *schema* in an Oracle database is a discrete work area and equivalent to a database in the MySQL database except for one difference: the relationship between the user and work area. A *user* is synonymous with a schema in Oracle Database 11*g*, and there's a one-to-one map between user and schema. This makes an Oracle schema a private work area of a designated user.

MySQL users are separate from databases and the super user must grant privileges on a database to the user. A user has equivalent permissions to an Oracle user in their schema when the `root` user grants all privileges on that database to the user.

A data *repository* is a database or database instance. Database management systems create and maintain databases, just like Microsoft Word creates and maintains Word documents. The principal difference between a simple Word document and a database lies in the *data catalog*. The data catalog is a set of two-dimensional tables that define all data types, structures, and

Process Communication

An operating system pipe is an operator that lets the standard out (`stdout`) from one program feed into the standard in (`stdin`) of another program. You can use the pipe (`|`) operator to pipeline communication between two programs, or you can define a named pipe, which is a specialized file or FIFO (first in, first out) queue in Linux. That's why developers call them local sockets or Inter-Process Communication (IPC).

Network sockets are like named pipes. They take a request from a client program and forward it to the server program. Network sockets typically use the Transmission Control Protocol (TCP) to communicate between computers. Internet Protocol (IP) addresses support this type of connection between computers; that's why developers call network sockets TCP/IP communication.

Unlike named pipes, network sockets don't define an intermediary, because the network TCP/IP stack provides the communication plumbing between client and server machines. Network sockets require a program that's awake and ready to receive requests from client software. These awake and ready programs are listeners.

A listener program listens on an *ephemeral* (fancy word for *short-lived*) port. The word *ephemeral* in this context actually means a temporary address. Ports act like post office boxes to the server. When you start a program listening on a port, it acts like a FIFO queue, processing requests as they arrive.

processes. A data catalog is defined when you initially create a database, and it contains the default values that become building blocks for your database. As you use these building blocks, they write more data into the data catalog. The data catalog is a repository for *metadata*—data about data.

The building blocks also define basic data types and the rules for creating and running stored programs. You implement these as PL/SQL or SQL/PSM programs. You also have an option of

Database or Schema?

Is a discrete work area different when we call it a database or schema? The short answer is *yes*! They're not the same thing.

The long answer is more difficult, because *schema* is, since MySQL 5.0.2, an alias for *database* in Oracle MySQL 5.6. That might give you the impression that they're exactly the same, but they're not.

A MySQL database is a discrete work area. It is not directly and exclusively tied to a user as the owner of the work area. For example, a super user (`root`) in a MySQL database must grant privileges to a user to work in a database. Users by default have no designated or default work area. In fact, many users may be granted access to work in the same database.

On the other hand, an Oracle schema is a discrete work area owned by a single user account. When a super user (typically `SYS` or `SYSTEM`) creates users, it also creates the discrete work area owned by the user. Together, the user and work area create a schema in an Oracle database. However, any user may grant privileges to another user to work in their schema, and super users may do likewise.

creating anonymous or named block programs in PL/SQL but not SQL/PSM. You'll read more about PL/SQL in Chapter 13.

The next sections show you how the client, listener, and sever software work together and what they do in the two RDBMSs. Examples in Chapter 2 will show you how to interact through the SQL command-line interface of both databases. The following section describes the implementation of the database server architectures.

Oracle Database 11g

The Oracle Database 11g architecture has three components: the client, server, and listener software. Here we'll define, demonstrate, and explore the client and server software components of the Oracle database.

Next, we'll cover the Oracle Database 11g client, server, and listener software. These subsections describe the following:

- The general purpose of the command-line client software
- How to start, stop and configure the listener
- How to find and use the data dictionary

The data dictionary, or data catalog, keeps track of all structures and data. Ultimately, each data structure is stored by a *unique identifier (UID)* that is numeric. Structures also have a label or alias assigned to them, such as a table or column name. Using SQL, you can change that alias at any time, but changes to the table or column name won't alter the UID of those structures.

Client Software: SQL*Plus

SQL*Plus is the client software for Oracle. It was originally written as an interactive and batch development environment and SQL report writer in the 1980s. As a result, the client software also includes a set of well-designed formatting extensions to SQL. These extensions let you format, aggregate, and manipulate breaks for output from queries.

Converting from MySQL

Keep in mind the following when you're converting from a MySQL database to an Oracle database:

- Oracle SQL*Plus replaces the MySQL Monitor.
- The Oracle listener is a separately configurable server-side component, and a single listener can support multiple listening ports.
- Users map to a single schema, and they are synonymous for the purpose of definer rights models, covered in Chapter 3.
- All database users have permissions to connect via IPC or TCP/IP sockets because that's how they're configured in the default `listener.ora` and `sqlnet.ora` files.
- Grants of privileges to schema are effectively grants of permissions to users.

Advanced Friendly Interface

SQL*Plus was originally labeled as the Advanced Friendly Interface (AFI). That should debunk the rumor that the temporary `afiedt.buf` buffer file stood for *a file editor buffer*. Although you might not see it as *advanced* or *friendly* by today's standards, it certainly was back in the day.

Chapter 2 shows you how to use the SQL*Plus client software. Specifically, it shows you how to connect, write log files, save statements, edit statements from the SQL prompt, abort statements, call script files, and call and run statements.

NOTE
*You can find more information on SQL*Plus in the SQL*Plus User's Guide and Reference, Oracle documentation that is downloadable from Oracle's web site.*

Oracle 11*g* Server Software

This section covers the basics of how the Oracle Database 11*g* works. It also describes how users, scheme (schemas), and privileges work. These components are important because they support the design and development of database-centric applications.

Figure 1-1 shows a conceptual view of how the Oracle Database 11*g* client and server software interact. It also shows a breakaway view of the database session. Every session includes at a minimum one SQL*Plus environment, a SQL statement engine, and a PL/SQL engine that all interact with each other.

The inputs are straightforward in the figure because they are SQL statements that you enter or send to the SQL*Plus client software. Client software can process these statements interactively or through batch submission. You create a batch operation by grouping a series of SQL statements into a single file. This type of file is a *script* or *batch* file. There are also batch operations or programs.

Batch files should be rerunnable programs. Rerunnable programs don't raise exceptions or errors unless failures are critical. That means they conditionally process SQL statements that add, drop, or alter structure, and they insert, update, and delete data with statements that conform to the definitions of tables. The command-line syntax for running batch programs is shown in the "Batch Submission" section of Chapter 2.

At the bottom right in Figure 1-1, you can see external input and output files. These may be plain text or program units. When they're program units, they present alternative ways for submitting SQL statements to the database. They may use the Open Database Connectivity (ODBC) or Java Database Connectivity (JDBC) libraries.

At the top of Figure 1-1, outputs are returned to the console. The output results can support interactive statements through session variables. Alternatively, output results may simply write a log file. At least, that's the case when the *SQL statement engine* returns outputs to the calling session. There's a *buffer* between the SQL*Plus environment and the PL/SQL engine. That buffer

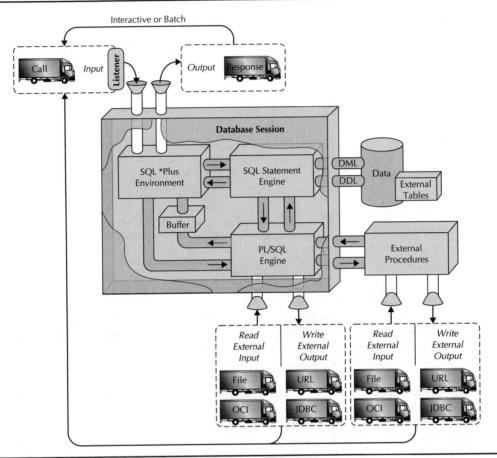

FIGURE 1-1. *Oracle Database 11g processing architecture*

is closed by default, which means comments echoed out by PL/SQL programs are blocked from display. You'll learn how to open the buffer and capture results in Chapter 2.

Reading and writing files appears straightforward, but it isn't. You have the option of reading external file data through (a) externally organized tables (covered in Chapter 6), (b) the Oracle's UTL_FILE package, (c) Java libraries inside the database, or (d) external procedures. Check the *Oracle Database 11g PL/SQL Packages and Types Reference* for the UTL_FILE package. You can find examples on embedded Java in Chapter 15 of *Oracle Database 11g PL/SQL Programming*.

The UTL_FILE package and Java libraries are the most secure approaches to reading and writing external files, because grants to these external locations are stored within the data catalog. External procedures call external C-callable libraries. These procedures pose a security risk to the database simply because anyone with access to the file system may access these libraries. These libraries can contain code that lets you establish a network socket for outgoing transmissions. As a result of that risk, many DBAs choose not to grant the CREATE LIBRARY privilege to protect against a security breach of confidential company and customer data.

Oracle Database Management System

The Oracle database management system comprises two major components: the data repository and a set of programs. The set of programs represent the library of code and APIs that implement Oracle Database 11*g*. The set of programs also lets you start a database instance. They allocate a shared memory realm where other programs process SQL statements. This shared memory realm is the active database instance.

In addition to implementing an RDBMS, the set of programs provides background processes that run the components that support the database. They're also programs that provide APIs for integration, backup and recovery resources, and configuration utilities and wizards. Some background processes run by default when you start an Oracle instance, while others require an administrator to configure and start them separately.

By way of an example, the optional *Archiver (ARCn)* process is critical to recovering databases. When an Oracle database is in archive mode, the Archiver mirrors writes to the redo log file. The Archiver writes those changes to the archive log files as the database switches from one redo log file to another. You can configure a number of other optional background processes. Refer to the *Oracle Database Administrator's Guide 11*g for more information on optional processes.

Together, the set of programs also provides a Multiversion Concurrency Control (MVCC), which ensures that one user won't inadvertently destroy another user's change. It does this by guaranteeing all changes to data are ACID-compliant (as described in the following discussion), which ensures the integrity of concurrent operations on data transactions.

ACID-compliant transactions meet four conditions: atomicity, consistency, isolation, and durability:

- *Atomic* means they complete or fail while undoing any partial changes.
- *Consistent* means they change from one state to another the same way whether or not the change is made through parallel or serial actions.
- *Isolated* means partial changes are never seen by other users or processes in the concurrent system.
- *Durable* means they are written to disk and made permanent when completed.

Object Relational Database Management System

Oracle is more than an ordinary RDBMS. The Oracle database is actually an object relational database management system (ORDBMS) because it supports collapsed objects inside the data repository. A *collapsed object* (also a flattened object) is a text string representing an object type and a call parameter list to the object, such as this:

```
some_object_type(call_param1, call_param2, call_param3)
```

The database holds the definitions of object types in the program source component of the database catalog. You can query its contents from the USER_SOURCE view (provided it's not *wrapped,* or obfuscated, to hide the source). Likewise, you can discover its constructors, functions, and procedures by describing it. Chapter 2 shows you how to describe tables. All you need to do is substitute the object name for the table name to make it work for object types.

Oracle manages ACID-compliant transactions by writing them to disk first, as redo log or redo and archive log files. Then it writes them to the database. This multiple step process with logs ensures that Oracle's buffer cache (part of the instance memory) isn't lost from any completed transaction. Log writes occur before acknowledgement of the transaction process occurs.

Oracle has five core background processes. Together, they ensure the successful operation and maintenance of an Oracle database instance. They are:

- **Process Monitor (PMON)**   Cleans up the instance after failed processes by rolling back transactions, releasing database locks and resources, and restarting deceased processes.

- **System Monitor (SMON)**   Manages system recovery by opening the database, rolling forward changes from the online redo log files, and rolling back uncommitted transactions. SMON also coalesces free space and deallocates temporary segments.

- **Database Writer (DBWR)**   Writes data to files when any of the following occur: checkpoints are reached, dirty buffers reach their threshold or no buffers are free, timeouts occur, Real Application Cluster (RAC) ping requests are made, tablespaces are placed in OFFLINE or READ ONLY state, tables are dropped or truncated, and tablespaces begin backup processing.

- **Log Writer (LGWR)**   Writes at user commits or at 3-second intervals, whichever comes first; when one-third of the log is full or 1 MB of redo instructions exists; and before the DBWR writes.

- **Checkpoint (CKPT)**   Signals the DBWR at checkpoints and updates the file header information for database and control files at checkpoints. The checkpoint process synchronizes buffer cache information from the shared memory segment with database disks.

If you're a MySQL regular, you'll notice Oracle has included several additional processes for managing different responsibilities of the database. Although MySQL doesn't implement these processes directly, the responsibilities held by theses processes are delegated to the MySQL engines. MySQL 5.6 implements the InnoDB engine as the default engine, which provides services similar to those of an Oracle database.

Oracle Work Areas

The work area for an application is where you create and maintain tables, and insert, update, and delete data. The work area is a *database* in MySQL and a *schema* in Oracle Database 11*g*. An Oracle database instance often has many schemas. Although they can exist to support discrete applications, they often support designs known as *definer* and *invoker rights* models.

The definer rights model qualifies who defines or owns an object in the database, such as a table or view. The invoker rights model qualifies who may invoke a stored program. In a nasty twist with invoker rights programs, the invoker must have a local place to store any data inserted or updated and likewise a local place from which to delete data. Unfortunately, this generally results in duplicating tables in schemas granted invoker right privileges on stored programs.

Grants to the tables owned by the schema that defined the stored programs are impractical. If the schema needs to provide access to the programs and local tables, it uses the default definer rights model. The principal advantage of invoker rights is that they distribute the data in the tables.

The definer rights model in Oracle holds that the user/schema is always the definer; they cannot be disassociated. Although the super users SYS and SYSTEM hold a specialized privilege to CREATE ANY TABLE, users may create tables only in their own schema by default. Naturally, super users may grant super privileges to other users, but that is a bad idea unless those accounts are crafted to administer the database. Definer rights models are discussed further in Chapter 3.

The next section builds on your basic understanding of how a database management system works. It describes the Oracle Listener service and some basic configuration elements.

Listener

The Oracle Listener is a separate configurable component for any Oracle database. A single listener can support multiple databases.

The listener can be configured to listen for local traffic only, such as IPCs. It is generally configured to support IPCs and network sockets across TCP/IP. The default configuration of the listener traditionally mixes the IPC traffic and TCP/IP traffic through the same net service name. This type of configuration causes external procedures to fail. You must create distinct listeners when you implement external procedures to avoid failure of the procedures at runtime. The instructions to modify the listener file for external procedures can be found in Chapter 13 of *Oracle Database 11g PL/SQL Programming*. You can also find them in the *Oracle Database Advanced Application Developer's Guide, 11g Release*.

You typically configure two files, listener.ora and tnsnames.ora, to change how the Oracle Listener works. Sometimes you need to modify the sqlnet.ora file, too. These files can be found in the network/admin subdirectory of the Oracle home.

The listener.ora file contains the configuration instructions for starting and running the Oracle Listener process. The tnsnames.ora file contains the mapping between net service names, such as orcl or xe, and fully qualified Transparent Network Substrate (TNS) addresses. Aliases simplify the parameters a user needs to provide to connect the client to the server. The sqlnet.ora file provides configuration instructions for tracing connections, network domain limitations, and encryption.

The default listener.ora file for Oracle Database 11g should look more or less like this:

```
-- This is an example of a default listener.ora file.

LISTENER =
  (DESCRIPTION_LIST =
    (DESCRIPTION =
      (ADDRESS = (PROTOCOL = IPC)(KEY = EXTPROC1))
      (ADDRESS = (PROTOCOL = TCP)(HOST = hostname)(PORT = port_number))
    )
  )


SID_LIST_LISTENER =
  (SID_LIST =
    (SID_DESC =
      (SID_NAME = PLSExtProc)
      (ORACLE_HOME = oracle_product_home_directory)
      (PROGRAM = extproc)
    )
  )
```

The `listener.ora` file is taken from the standard installation of a sample Oracle Database 11*g* installation. The default name of the listener is `LISTENER` and it holds references to the hostname and listening port. The `SID_LIST_{listener_name}` uses `LISTENER`. For every listener, there is an `SID_LIST_{listener_name}` because this list holds the Oracle Server home directory and any libraries used by external programs. Only the actual hostname, port number, and Oracle product home directory have been removed and replaced with generic comments. Notice that both an IPC and a TCP address exist in the `DESCRIPTION` section of the listener. This type of configuration file lets a single listener handle both protocols. It's convenient and it's the default file with the sample databases.

Oracle Listeners let users connect through either a local IPC or TCP/IP socket to a database instance. They do this by referencing a TNS alias for the listener. TNS implements the session, presentation, and application layers of the Open Systems Interconnection (OSI) model. Moreover, it maps a net service name to a physical address. Definitions for how this map works are found in the `listener.ora` file. The settings are configurable by the database administrator (DBA).

A default `tnsnames.ora` file for the same release should look similar to this:

```
-- This is an example of a default tnsnames.ora file.

ORCL =
  (DESCRIPTION =
    (ADDRESS = (PROTOCOL = TCP)(HOST = hostname)(PORT = port_number))
    (CONNECT_DATA =
      (SERVER = DEDICATED)
      (SERVICE_NAME = ORCL)
    )
  )

EXTPROC_CONNECTION_DATA =
  (DESCRIPTION =
    (ADDRESS_LIST =
      (ADDRESS = (PROTOCOL = IPC)(KEY = EXTPROC1521))
    )
    (CONNECT_DATA =
      (SID = PLSExtProc)
      (PRESENTATION = RO)
    )
  )
```

Look at the entry in the `tnsnames.ora` file and you can see that `ORCL` is the net service name for a connection, which is an alias for the full connect string. Because an Oracle Listener can connect to multiple databases, a `SERVICE_NAME` = ORCL value is also included. The `SERVICE_NAME` is an alias to an instance or several instances when you work with clustered databases and is separate from the net service name. You should also know that the NETCA (Oracle Net Services Configuration) utility provides a GUI interface tool and wizard for most network configuration steps.

TIP
In Linux or UNIX, the net service name is case-sensitive.

You could change the net service name from ORCL to a name more appropriate for your system (RUMBA in the example below), stop and start the listener, and then connect using this:

```
sqlplus some_user@RUMBA
```

Here's the command-line syntax to start the listener:

```
lsnrctl start
```

Getting the listener's status is straightforward: replace the word start with status, like this:

```
lsnrctl status
```

You stop the listener with this:

```
lsnrctl stop
```

The lsnrctl command works at the command line in Windows or Linux. The listener is also a service in Microsoft Windows. You can start or stop the listener at the command line or through the service, because the service calls the same command.

If you can't reach the Oracle Listener, you can use an Oracle utility to check the network. The tnsping utility is similar to the ping utility. Assuming the preceding tnsnames.ora file and net service name ORCL, you can check whether the listener is reachable and available using this syntax:

```
tnsping orcl
```

You would see the following type of reply:

```
TNS Ping Utility for 64-bit Windows: Version 11.1.0.7.0 - Production on ...
Copyright (c) 1997, 2008, Oracle.  All rights reserved.
Used parameter files:
C:\app\McLaughlin-7x64\product\11.1.0\db_1\network\admin\sqlnet.ora
Used TNSNAMES adapter to resolve the alias
Attempting to contact (DESCRIPTION = (ADDRESS = (PROTOCOL = TCP)(HOST =
McLaughlin7x64)(PORT = 1521)) (CONNECT_DATA = (SERVER = DEDICATED) (SERVICE_
NAME = orcl)))
OK (10 msec)
```

Potential Laptop Configuration Issue

A failure can occur when you install Oracle on any computer without a static IP address. It shows itself when you can't connect through a network socket but can connect through IPC. This problem is most likely caused by Oracle substituting the IP address at the time of installation for a hostname value in both the listener.ora and tnsnames.ora files.

Make sure that the hostname matches your machine's hostname, not the assigned IP address. You can do this by checking the hosts file, found in the C:\WINDOWS\System32\drivers\etc directory on Windows and in the /etc directory on Linux or UNIX. You may need to disable Microsoft's User Account Controls (UAC) to access the hosts file on Windows Vista and Windows 7.

The Oracle Listener is a convenient architecture, because it provides a number of configuration options. However, if your database is running when the listener is down, or vice versa, you won't be able to connect to the database through the network layer and you'll have two components to check and potentially fix.

Oracle's security model allows connections from all authorized users. It doesn't check their network origin unless you configure advanced networking options. Chapter 6 shows steps that let you configure network access rights in the `sqlnet.ora` file. That's because the Oracle Listener doesn't disambiguate `localhost` and network access across network sockets. This differs from the MySQL security model. By default, Oracle supports IPC communication when you opt not to include the net service name in your call to SQL*Plus, which is also known as a connect string. A connect string is a string used to identify and connect to a remote database. Connect strings are defined in a local `tnsnames.ora` file, Oracle Names Server or OID directory.

The biggest difference between how Listeners work is their role in the server software. Oracle Database 11*g* implements a single listener process that can listen for multiple database instances, whereas Oracle MySQL 5.6 (and its predecessors) has a listener process for each MySQL installation. The former scales better but the latter is simpler to administer for novices.

Oracle Data Dictionary

The Oracle data dictionary is stored in the `SYS` schema. It is a complex design, and you should not change data there without the explicit guidance and direction of Oracle Support. The dictionary houses the structure, definition, declaration, and access control attributes for all the objects in the database.

Names of data objects (tables) in the data dictionary end with a dollar ($) sign. Oracle does not publish a way to map these tables, and it does not provide an Entity Relation Diagram (ERD) or map of the data dictionary. Your sole interface to these objects should be SQL commands.

Oracle does provide administrative views that let you examine objects you've created and built-in objects in the database. These views start with `ALL_`, `DBA_`, `USER_`, and denote access levels to the internally defined objects. You can find a comprehensive list of these administrative views in the Oracle Database Reference 11*g* online. Many chapters show you how to use these administrative views to solve particular problems.

Oracle MySQL 5.6

Like Oracle Database 11*g*, the Oracle MySQL 5.6 architecture has two direct components: client and server software. Notably different from Oracle Database, MySQL embeds the listener software inside the server component. This means when you start the MySQL daemon, `mysqld` process, you start the database server and listener.

The following sections define, demonstrate, and explore the client and server software components of the MySQL database. These sections cover the Oracle MySQL 5.6 client, server, and listener software. They describe the general purpose of the command-line client software; how to start, stop, and configure the listener; and how to find and use the data dictionary.

Client Software: The MySQL Monitor

The *MySQL Monitor* is the command-line SQL interface for the MySQL 5.6 database. MySQL Monitor processes SQL statements, which it does well.

Converting from Oracle

Keep in mind the following when you're converting from an Oracle database to a MySQL database:

- Oracle MySQL Monitor replaces Oracle SQL*Plus and doesn't offer any formatting features or extended SQL aggregation behaviors.

- The Oracle MySQL listener is part of the database server. You must have a unique listener for each installation of the MySQL database. All you can configure is the listening port.

- Oracle MySQL users are distinct from any schema or database.

- MySQL users connect via TCP/IP sockets when defined by a domain, a partial domain, or as anywhere (%), unless you shut down network connections by configuring the my.ini file.

- Grants of privileges are made to users and never to databases.

There are two big differences between the MySQL Monitor and Oracle SQL*Plus environments. One is that the error messages are much less meaningful and in many cases not actionable. The second difference is that MySQL Monitor processes SQL and SQL/PSM call statements only. SQL report writing is left to other tools that you can purchase or implement.

Errors are less meaningful in MySQL, because MySQL provides two levels of error handling: error and warning messages. You generally need to check the warning messages in MySQL before you start solving problems. Chapter 2 shows you how to use the MySQL Monitor.

MySQL Server Software

Like the server section for the Oracle database, this section covers the Oracle MySQL database. You'll learn about the organization of users and databases, as well as the security privileges that link them together.

The root user is the super user in a MySQL Database. Likewise, SYS is the super user in Oracle and equivalent to the root user in a MySQL database.

Note that a database in MySQL is a *logical* repository, not a *physical* one. This means that you create and maintain things in a logical work area, or database. Database engines manage the physical storage of data.

Figure 1-2 shows a conceptual view of how the MySQL client and server software interact. It also shows a breakaway view of a session, which includes how the MySQL Monitor, SQL statement engine, and SQL/PSM engine interact with each other. Note that MySQL doesn't include the equivalent of Oracle Database 11*g* external procedures.

Reading and writing files is performed by SQL statements processed in the MySQL Monitor. This differs from Oracle Database 11*g*, where they're managed by the PL/SQL engine. You can input or output files, and you can choose how the outputted files are formatted. Beginning with Oracle MySQL 5.6, you can natively read and write XML files.

SQL/PSM stored programs can return data to the console when you select the information inside stored procedures. The data selected can be as simple as debugging comments or as complex as large return sets from complex queries, but only stored procedures can return the data to the console. Functions cannot return data because they run as contained units. All their internal behaviors are encapsulated, and they can't echo content to the current session. Functions return only values defined by their return types. Chapters 13 and 14 show how you work with functions and procedures.

MySQL Database Management System

The MySQL database management system has three major components. Two are similar to the Oracle database's data repository and its set of programs, but they're not exactly the same.

The MySQL data repository isn't a single entity as in Oracle. It is a series of repositories organized by the logical database that owns the table definitions. Likewise, the set of programs is more complex. Some programs exist at the MySQL level and key transactional programs exist at the engine level. Moreover, these sets of programs mimic the set of programs in an Oracle database.

Together they maintain Multiversion Concurrency Control (MVCC) in most cases. MVCC prevents one user from inadvertently destroying another user's work. These sets of programs fail to maintain MVCC rules when some of the data is stored and managed by one processing engine

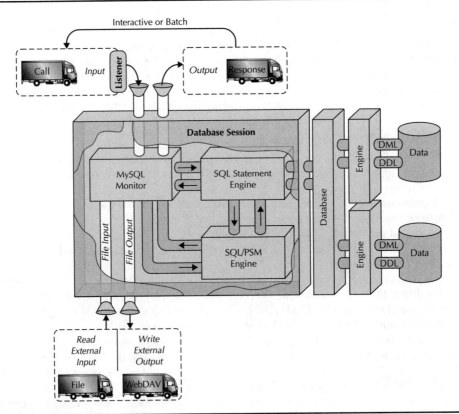

FIGURE 1-2. *MySQL database processing architecture*

and the rest is managed by another processing engine. Unfortunately, only the default InnoDB engine supports the X/Open XA distributed transaction model.

Distributed transactions require agreement between all parties before writing data permanently. One party may write data with the mistaken belief that the other parties' data is in agreement. The result is that the transaction state is incomplete as a whole. This possibility breaks the guarantee of ACID-compliant transactions in a distributed transaction. The behavior causes data inconsistencies between data stored in two or more repositories when they're managed by different MySQL engines.

Database users with the create table privilege may create tables in one database that use different engines. This introduces a major design and management issue, however, because tables defined in an engine are stored in that engine's repository. There is no way to guarantee ACID-compliant transactions across different repositories, because the X/Open XA protocol is deployed only by one engine, and both engines are needed to support the XA protocol. At present, the best thing to do for transactional data is store the tables exclusively in the InnoDB engine.

For example, suppose a table that contains rows of data for orders uses one engine, while another table containing binary images of scanned shipping labels uses another. It's presently impossible to update both tables with a guarantee that both will be changed. That's because this involves a distributed transaction, and agreement to write may result in one completed update without the other.

You should implement transactional data only in a single engine. That engine should support the full spectrum of transactional mechanics.

Engines

As mentioned, Oracle MySQL supports multiple engines. Each engine has distinct features but *only* InnoDB enforces referential integrity and the full X/Open XA protocol for distributed transactions.

InnoDB is the *default* engine for Oracle MySQL 5.6 for all but the `mysql` and `information_` `schema` databases. These two databases store and manage data using the MyISAM database engine. MyISAM was the default engine for earlier versions of the MySQL database. You can find the available engines in any release by typing the following from the command line:

```
help engines
```

Engines own the processes governing the integrity of data in their repositories. They also determine the physical structure of data and provide APIs that map those physical data structures to the logical structures of the data dictionary or catalog.

InnoDB maintains logs much like Oracle Database 11*g*. It uses those logs to ensure the integrity of transactions and to limit the cost of committing transactions. The engine does this by logging transactions rather than flushing the buffer pool after every commit. The InnoDB log management shifts random I/O into sequential I/O and provides effective transaction management, including *savepoint* and *rollback* behaviors. Chapter 4 qualifies the definition and use of savepoints and rollbacks in transaction management.

Chapter 6 shows you how to define tables that use the default or an override engine. Oracle MySQL Database 5.6 uses the following engines:

- **InnoDB**   A transaction safe or ACID-compliant database engine

- **MyISAM**   A non-transaction safe database engine, and previous default engine for earlier releases of the MySQL database

- **Memory**   An in-memory database engine that stores all data in physical or virtual memory

- **Merge** A non-transaction database engine that lets you group identical MyISAM tables as one entity; key infrastructure element of many Very Large Databases (VLDB)
- **Archive** An engine that lets you archive seldom-used data
- **Federated** An engine that allows you to link several MySQL servers into one logical database from many physical servers; often used when servicing data marts
- **CSV** A non-transactional database engine that lets you store data in a comma-separated values (CSV) format, which makes interchanges easier when using other CSV-enabled tools
- **Blackhole** A non-transactional database that accepts but doesn't store data; used as an engine for external replication of the database
- **Example** A stub provided to developers to help them understand how to link engines into MySQL databases

Like Oracle, the InnoDB engine transforms MySQL 5.6 into a transaction database. InnoDB provides ACID-compliant transactions, row-level locking, Oracle-style nonlocking reads, and referential integrity through foreign keys. Changing the MySQL 5.6 default InnoDB engine means you switch from a transactional engine to a non-transactional engine.

Listener

The listener is started by the MySQL daemon (`mysqld`) when that process starts. The MySQL listener is a subordinate process of the server process, and it runs on the `[mysqld]` port number you specify in the `mysql.ini` configuration file. By default, the port number for the listener is 3306.

You can verify whether or not it's running by checking the Windows Services (`services.msc`), or you can check at the MS-DOS command line with the following syntax:

```
netstat -a | findstr /C:LISTENING | findstr /C:3306
```

It should report something similar to this:

```
TCP    0.0.0.0:3306         McLaughlin7x64:0      LISTENING
```

The port number will change after you modify the `my.ini` file and reboot the MySQL service. Any changes made in the `my.ini` file are visible only after you restart the service (Windows) or process (Linux).

MySQL's security model does distinguish users according to their point of origin. Users defined within MySQL have a three-part authentication token: user name, password, and host. Users have three possible host values:

- **`localhost`** Can connect only from the same machine as the MySQL server
- **IP, subdomain, or domain** Can connect only from an IP or partially qualified subdomain or domain address
- **`%`** Can connect from anywhere; basically a *wildcard* host operator across the network

MySQL databases generally let you connect through a TCP/IP socket, but you can define the `mysql.ini` file to allow IPC communication. You disable TCP communication when you enable

IPC communication in MySQL. As a result, you usually use IPC communication only while performing system maintenance.

MySQL Data Dictionary

The MySQL data dictionary is stored in the `mysql` database. A view-only copy is also stored in the `information_schema` database. It is a fairly straightforward set of tables. Although you can make changes to the MySQL data dictionary, you should be very careful about what you do. If you're using the Community Edition, you're responsible for any changes you make that lead to catastrophic failures. If you're using the Enterprise Edition of MySQL, you should not change data without the explicit guidance and direction of Oracle Support.

All objects in the `mysql` database are tables. The equivalent objects in the `information_schema` database are non-updateable views. MySQL doesn't provide administrative views as does Oracle Database 11*g*.

Summary

There are many similarities and notable differences between the Oracle Database 11*g* and Oracle MySQL 5.5 databases. Primarily, Oracle databases map each user account to a given schema of the same name, while MySQL databases grant permissions to user accounts to access independent databases. MySQL databases can store data in one or more repositories, which may not be transaction safe.

Transactions across repositories in MySQL databases aren't ACID-compliant unless both engines support the X/Open XA distributed transaction protocol. At this time, only InnoDB is transaction safe and implements X/Open XA transactions. On the other hand, Oracle Database 11*g* stores data in a single transaction-safe repository.

The two-tier client-server model works in both databases. The features of client-side SQL*Plus and MySQL Monitor software are different from the perspective of available features. Servers differ in how they enforce ACID-compliance. MySQL's ability to log and maintain files differs by the engine you use. InnoDB is the default engine for MySQL 5.5, and it runs very much like Oracle by maintaining sequential log files.

Mastery Check

The mastery check is a series of true or false and multiple choice questions that let you confirm how well you understand the material in the chapter. You may check the Appendix for answers to these questions.

1. **True** ☐ **False** ☐ Databases implement a two-tier client-server model.
2. **True** ☐ **False** ☐ Client software provides only an interactive method for running SQL statements.
3. **True** ☐ **False** ☐ SQL statements can be grouped into categories.
4. **True** ☐ **False** ☐ You must interact with all databases across a network socket.
5. **True** ☐ **False** ☐ Distributed transactions occur by default in MySQL when you store data in two or more tables using different engines.
6. **True** ☐ **False** ☐ You can connect to MySQL database only through a network socket.

7. **True** ☐ **False** ☐ You can connect to an Oracle database only through a network socket.

8. **True** ☐ **False** ☐ The MVCC model for Oracle Database 11*g* maps with some small exceptions to the MVCC model of a MySQL database transactional engine such as InnoDB.

9. **True** ☐ **False** ☐ Any Oracle user is synonymous with the schema of the same name.

10. **True** ☐ **False** ☐ Sequential log files are maintained by programs in MySQL databases as they are for Oracle databases, notwithstanding the engine of implementation.

11. Which of the following isn't a valid engine in a MySQL database instance?

    A. Blackhole

    B. CSV

    C. TSV

    D. Memory

    E. MyISAM

12. Which of the following isn't a valid SQL category?

    A. Data Query Language (DQL)

    B. Data Control Language (DCL)

    C. Data Manipulation Language (DML)

    D. Data Definition Language (DDL)

    E. Transaction Control Language (TCL)

13. Which of the following isn't a core background process for an Oracle Database 11*g* server?

    A. ARCn

    B. PMON

    C. SMON

    D. Checkpoint

    E. LGWR

14. Which of the following isn't a property of an ACID-compliant transaction?

    A. Atomic

    B. Consistent

    C. Isolated

    D. Durable

    E. None of the above

15. Which users have the same role and responsibility in Oracle Database 11*g* and MySQL 5.6, except for mapping to the data catalog?

A. The Oracle SYSTEM and MySQL root users

B. The Oracle SYS and MySQL root

C. The Oracle SYS, SYSTEM, and MySQL root

D. The Oracle SYS and MySQL super

E. The Oracle SYSTEM and MySQL super

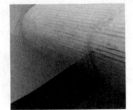

CHAPTER
2

Client Interface

evelopment can take many approaches, because many CASE tools are available for Oracle and MySQL databases. Oracle SQL Developer and Oracle MySQL Workbench are the current vendor CASE development tools. Many others exist, such as Quest's Toad for Oracle or Toad for MySQL Freeware.

Although it was tempting to demonstrate how to create and maintain tables with one or more of these CASE tools, that wouldn't help you script production solutions or write SQL to support web applications. So I've opted to explain how to use the SQL*Plus and MySQL Monitor, because these skills feed your abilities to develop database-centric applications.

This chapter describes how you connect to and disconnect from the environment; write, edit, save, and abort entry of SQL statements and log files; call and run script files, functions, and procedures; and set session variables for SQL*Plus and MySQL Monitor.

SQL*Plus

SQL*Plus is the client software for Oracle that runs SQL statements and anonymous block PL/SQL statements in an interactive and batch development environment. They're organized in the order that you generally encounter them as you start working with SQL*Plus or the MySQL Monitor.

Although Oracle supports large object types, you couldn't display more than 32,767 characters' worth of them in SQL*Plus prior to Oracle Database 10*g*. That's because the maximum size of a long data type was 32,767, and SQL*Plus displayed large objects using the LONG data type. From Oracle Database 10*g* forward, you can set the LONG environment variable as high as you want, and it works. The CLOB data type is displayed now by SQL*Plus, but the LONG environment variable hasn't changed yet. Likewise, you can see a billion bytes of a binary large object in SQL*Plus.

Connecting to and Disconnecting from SQL*Plus

After installing the product on the Windows OS, you access SQL*Plus from the command line. This works when the operating system finds the sqlplus executable in its path environment variable (on Windows that's %PATH% and on Linux $PATH). Linux installations require that you configure this manually. When sqlplus is in the path environment variable, you can access it by typing the following:

```
sqlplus some_username/some_password
```

The preceding connect string uses IPC to connect to the Oracle database. You can connect through the network by specifying a valid net service name, like this:

```
sqlplus some_username/some_password@some_net_service_name
```

While this works and many use it, you should simply enter your user name and let the database prompt you for the password. That way, it's not displayed as clear text, as shown in the following illustration.

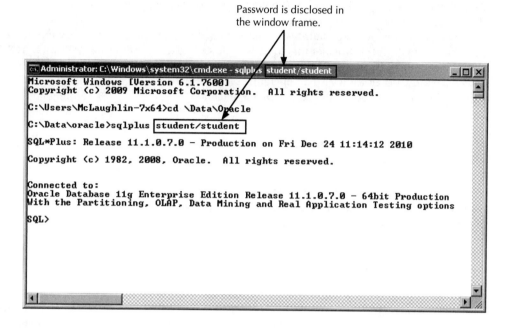

NOTE
Aside from the obvious security risks of the windows dialog, it is possible for others to snoop for passwords from command histories.

You should connect in this way to avoid displaying your password, which uses an IPC.

```
sqlplus some_username
```

Or you can connect using the network layer by using a net service name like this:

```
sqlplus some_username@some_tns_alias
```

You'll then see a password prompt. As you type your password, it is masked from prying eyes. The password also won't be visible in the window of the command session.

After you're connected as an authenticated user, you can switch to work as another user by using the following syntax that discloses your password to the screen but not the session window:

```
SQL> connect some_otheruser/some_password
```

Or you can connect this way to avoid displaying your password:

```
SQL> connect some_otheruser
```

As with the preceding initial authorization example, you are prompted for the password. Entering it this way also protects it from prying eyes.

If you try to run this and it fails with a message that it can't find the `sqlplus` executable, you must correct that. Check whether the `%ORACLE_HOME%\bin` (Windows) or `$ORACLE_HOME/bin` (Linux or UNIX) are found in the respective `%PATH%` or `$PATH` environment variable. Like `PATH`, the `ORACLE_HOME` is also an operating system environment variable. `ORACLE_HOME` should point to where you installed the Oracle database.

NOTE
Make sure your `%PATH%` or `$PATH` variable includes the Oracle executables, which are in the `bin` directory of the `ORACLE_HOME`.

You can use the following commands to check the contents of your path environment variable. Instructions for setting these are in the *Oracle Database Installation Guide* for your platform and release:

- Windows: `echo %PATH%`
- Linux or UNIX: `echo $PATH`

When you've connected to the SQL*Plus, you will see the `SQL>` prompt. If you haven't created your own user, you can connect with the `SYSTEM` user name and password and create one. The Oracle `root` account is the `SYS` user, but Oracle recommends that you use the `SYSTEM` user, which shares most administration rights and privileges. It provides insurance that you won't directly update the data dictionary, which is found in the `SYS` schema.

You set the password for the `SYS` and `SYSTEM` users when installing the Oracle Database. If you're new to Oracle, refer to the "Create a Default Oracle User" sidebar later in this chapter for instructions. If you didn't install the database, you can ask whoever did to create a user name for you. (Note that these instructions are also found in the book's introduction.)

After you create a user, you must grant the user privileges. Privileges let the user connect to the database and perform runtime tasks. You may also grant privileges as groups. This is done with *roles*, which are collections of privileges. The caveat with roles is that they change between releases. It is critical that you understand exactly what roles do before you grant privileges through them. For example, you should avoid granting the `CONNECT` and `RESOURCE` roles, because the Oracle Database 10*g* documentation announced that they will be deprecated in future versions.

NOTE
Oracle plans to legacy deprecate the `CONNECT` and `RESOURCE` roles and began letting customers know of this change in the Oracle Database 10g documentation.

The `CONNECT` and `RESOURCE` roles are overused in many sample and some production databases. Legacy roles can create unnecessary vulnerabilities by conveying more than necessary privileges to user accounts. You should always check what privileges come with any role before granting the role, which you'll learn about in Chapter 3. Acknowledging that caveat, roles are preferred to grants of individual privileges because they provide a layer of abstraction.

TIP
Granting the RESOURCE *role to a user automatically grants unlimited tablespace to that user, at least up to the physical size limit imposed on a tablespace by its physical files.*

The benefit of abstraction in roles is an added layer of security. Although users should understand what they can and can't do, a hacker shouldn't be able to query an administrative view and discover what they can do as that user. For example, when a hacker gains access to a database user, he will often query well-known views to determine the amount of control he can exert on the system. Granting privileges through roles obstructs a hacker's ability to query privileges from the USER_SYS_PRIVS administrative view in an Oracle database. The hacker would be able to see only the roles he's been granted directly through the USER_ROLE_PRIVS administrative view. That forces a user, or hacker acting as a non-super user, to experiment with syntax before he knows what he can or can't do. The delay may limit damage done by a hacker.

Create a Default Oracle User

In this sample code, you create a student Oracle user/schema with a minimum set of permissions. You or your DBA can perform the following steps to create the student account:

```
CREATE USER student IDENTIFIED BY student
DEFAULT TABLESPACE users QUOTA 50M ON users
TEMPORARY TABLESPACE temp;
```

This is a limited account, because you can consume only up to 50 megabytes of space in the users tablespace, which is available in all sample Oracle databases. A *tablespace* is a logical unit that can contain one or more users and physical data files where you read and write data. Tablespaces can include one to many physical files, and their size is constrained by the space available in these files. You can learn more about tablespaces in the *Oracle Database 11g DBA Handbook* (Oracle Press, 2007).

Next you should grant several privileges to the student user. The Data Control Language (DCL) provides the GRANT command to perform this task. The GRANT command lets an authorized user assign roles and privileges to other users. The following example uses privileges, which are provided as comma-separated lists:

```
GRANT create cluster, create indextype, create operator
,     create procedure, create sequence, create session
,     create table, create trigger, create type
,     create view TO sample;
```

The grant extends the permission to connect to the database through the CREATE SESSION privilege. It also provides you with the basic privileges you need to run the examples in the book.

Sometimes privileges convey permission to perform an overloaded behavior. The Oracle `CREATE PROCEDURE` or MySQL `CREATE ROUTINE` privilege is an example of that behavior. It allows you to create a function or procedure. Functions and procedures are stored blocks of executable code that return output back to the calling process (see Chapter 13). Although there are a number of differences between functions and procedures, the significant one is that a function's output can be assigned to a variable while a procedure's output can't. A procedure doesn't have a result that can serve as an expression, a call parameter, or as a right operand in an assignment.

A user can see her privileges in the `USER_SYS_PRIVS` administrative view. You can learn more about roles and privileges in Chapter 3.

Working in the SQL*Plus Environment

The SQL*Plus environment isn't limited simply to running SQL statements, like many counterpart client-software components. Originally, it was written as a SQL report writer. This means SQL*Plus contains a number of features to make it friendlier and more useful. (That's why SQL*Plus was originally known as an Advanced Friendly Interface [AFI]). Examples of these friendlier and useful features include a set of well-designed formatting extensions that let you work with formatting and aggregating result set data. SQL*Plus also lets you interactively edit files from the command line.

This section introduces you to three things: how you can dynamically configure your environment to suit your needs for each connection; configure SQL*Plus to remember settings for every connection; and discover features through the interactive help menus.

Configuring SQL*Plus Environment

You can configure your SQL*Plus environment in two ways: One requires that you configure it each time that you start a session. The other requires that you configure the `glogin.sql` file. The `glogin.sql` file is the first thing run after a user authenticates and establishes a connection with the database. The caveat with modifying the `glogin.sql` file is that any changes become universal for all users of the Oracle Database installation. Also, only the owner of the Oracle account can make these changes.

Dynamically Configuring SQL*Plus   Every connection to SQL*Plus is configurable. Some developers choose to put these instructions inside their script files and others prefer to type them as they go. Putting them in the script files means you have to know what options you have first. The SQL*Plus `SHOW` command lets you find *all* of them with the keyword `ALL`, like this:

```
SHOW ALL
```

The SQL*Plus `SHOW` command also lets you see the status of a given environment variable. The following command displays the default value for the `FEEDBACK` environment variable:

```
SHOW FEEDBACK
```

It returns the default value, unless you've altered the default by configuring it in the `glogin.sql` file. The Oracle user has the rights to make any desired changes in this file, but they apply to all users who connect to the database. The default value for `FEEDBACK` is

```
FEEDBACK ON for 6 or more rows
```

By default, an Oracle database shows the number of rows touched by a SQL command only when there are six or more. If you want to show feedback for zero to many rows, the following syntax resets the environment variable:

```
SET FEEDBACK ON
```

It returns 0 or the number of rows affected by any SQL statement. Setting these environment variables inside script files allows you to designate runtime behaviors, but you should also reset them to the default at the conclusion of the script. When they're not reset at the end of a script, they can confuse a user expecting the default behaviors.

Configuring the Default SQL*Plus Environment File The `glogin.sql` file is where you want to define override values for the environment variables. You might want to put many things beyond environment variable values into your `glogin.sql` configuration file. The most common is a setting for the default editor in Linux or UNIX, because it's undefined out of the box. You can set the default editor to the `vi` text editor in Linux by adding the following line to the `glogin.sql` file:

```
DEFINE _EDITOR=vi
```

The `DEFINE` keyword has two specialized uses in SQL*Plus. One lets you define substitution variables (sometimes called user variables) that act as session-level variables. The other lets you enable or disable the ampersand (`&`) symbol as a substitution variable operator. It is enabled by default because the `DEFINE` environment variable is `ON` by default. You disable the specialized role by setting `DEFINE` to `OFF`. SQL*Plus treats the ampersand (`&`) as an ordinary text character when `DEFINE` is `OFF`. You can find more on this use of the `DEFINE` environment variable in the "When to Disable Substitution Variables" sidebar later in this chapter.

Substitution variables are placeholder variables in SQL statements or session-level variables in script files. As placeholders, they are discarded after a single use when you precede the variable name with a single ampersand, and they are session-level variables when you precede them with two ampersands. Two ampersands (`&&`) make the assigned value of a substitution variable reusable. You can set a session-level variable with the `DEFINE` command shown previously with the `_EDITOR` variable or by using a double ampersand, as in the following:

```
SELECT '&&BART' FROM dual;
```

With two ampersands, the query prompts the user for a value for the `BART` session-level variable and sets the value as a session-level variable. A single ampersand would simply prompt, use it, and discard it. Assuming you enter *"Cartoon Character"* as the response to the preceding query, you see the value by querying it with a single or double ampersand:

```
SELECT '&BART' AS "Session Variable" FROM dual;
```

It displays:

```
Session Variable
----------------
Cartoon Character
```

Or you use the DEFINE command like this:

```
DEFINE BART
```

This displays the following:

```
DEFINE BART             = "Cartoon Character" (CHAR)
```

The scope of the session variable lasts throughout the connection unless you undefine it with the following command:

```
UNDEFINE BART
```

Although you can define substitution variables, you can use them only by preceding their name with an ampersand. That's because a single ampersand also lets you read the contents of substitution variables when they're set as session-level variables. Several user variables are reserved for use by the Oracle Database. These user variables can contain letters, underscores, or numbers in any order. Oracle-reserved use of these variables all start with an underscore, as is the case with the _EDITOR variable. Any reference to these variables is case-insensitive, although they're shown in uppercase in the book for clarity.

SQL*Plus checks the contents of the _EDITOR user variable when you type the EDIT command, often abbreviated as ED. The EDIT command launches the executable stored in the _ EDITOR user variable. The Windows version of the Oracle Database comes preconfigured with Notepad as the default editor. It finds the Notepad utility because it's in a directory found in the operating system path variable. If you choose another editor, you need to ensure that the executable is in your default path environment. In Windows, you should create a shortcut that points to the physical location of the new editor, and put it in the C:\Windows\System32 directory.

The DEFINE command also lets you display the contents of all session-level variables. There is no all option for the DEFINE command, as there is for the SHOW command. You simply type DEFINE without any arguments to get a list of the default values:

```
DEFINE _DATE            = "14-FEB-11" (CHAR)
DEFINE _CONNECT_IDENTIFIER = "orcl" (CHAR)
DEFINE _USER            = "STUDENT" (CHAR)
DEFINE _PRIVILEGE       = "" (CHAR)
DEFINE _SQLPLUS_RELEASE = "1101000700" (CHAR)
DEFINE _EDITOR          = "Notepad" (CHAR)
DEFINE _O_VERSION       = "Oracle Database 11g Enterprise Edition
DEFINE _O_RELEASE       = "1101000700" (CHAR)
```

The preceding user variables are set by Oracle during configuration or on connection. As explained, you can define the contents of other substitution variables.

Although substitution variables have many uses, their primary purpose is to support the SQL*Plus environment. For example, you can use them to reset the SQL> prompt. You can reset the default SQL*Plus prompt by using two predefined session-level variables, like this:

```
SET sqlprompt "'SQL:'_user at _connect_identifier>"
```

This would change the default prompt to look like this when the _user name is system and the _connect_identifier is orcl:

```
SQL: SYSTEM at orcl>
```

This type of prompt takes more space, but it tells you your current user and schema at a glance. It's a handy prompt to avoid making changes in the wrong schema or instance, which occurs too often in daily practice.

A number of possibilities exist for modifying your prompt beyond this example. The preceding example provided the syntax to set the prompt for the duration of the connection. If you want to modify the starting default prompt, you can edit the %ORACLE_HOME%\sqlplus\ admin\glogin.sql in Windows or its equivalent in Linux or UNIX.

Using Interactive Help in the SQL*Plus Environment   SQL*Plus also provides an interactive help console that contains an index of help commands. You can find the index of commands by typing the following in SQL*Plus:

```
SQL> help index
```

It displays the following:

```
Enter Help [topic] for help.
```

@	COPY	PAUSE	SHUTDOWN
@@	DEFINE	PRINT	SPOOL
/	DEL	PROMPT	SQLPLUS
ACCEPT	DESCRIBE	QUIT	START
APPEND	DISCONNECT	RECOVER	STARTUP
ARCHIVE LOG	EDIT	REMARK	STORE
ATTRIBUTE	EXECUTE	REPFOOTER	TIMING
BREAK	EXIT	REPHEADER	TTITLE
BTITLE	GET	RESERVED WORDS (SQL)	UNDEFINE
CHANGE	HELP	RESERVED WORDS (PL/SQL)	VARIABLE
CLEAR	HOST	RUN	WHENEVER OSERROR
COLUMN	INPUT	SAVE	WHENEVER SQLERROR
COMPUTE	LIST	SET	XQUERY
CONNECT	PASSWORD	SHOW	

You can discover more about the commands by typing help with one of the index keywords. The following demonstrates the STORE command, which lets you store the current buffer contents as a file.

```
SQL> help store
```

It displays the following:

```
STORE
-----
 Saves attributes of the current SQL*Plus environment in a script.

 STORE {SET} file_name[.ext] [CRE[ATE] | REP[LACE] | APP[END]]
```

This is one way to save the contents of your current SQL statement into a file. You'll see another, the SAVE command, shortly. You might want to take a peek in the next section if you're experimenting with capturing the results of the HELP utility by spooling the information to a log file.

As discussed, the duration of any SQL*Plus environment variable is from the beginning to the end of any session. Define them in the glogin.sql file when you want them to be available in all SQL*Plus sessions.

Shelling out of the SQL*Plus Environment

Sometimes you don't want to exit an interactive session of SQL*Plus. In those cases, you can leave the session (known as *shelling out*) and run operating system commands. The HOST command lets you do that, like so:

```
SQL> HOST
```

Anything that you do inside this operating system session other than modify files is lost when you leave it and return to the SQL*Plus session. The most frequent things that most developers do in a shelled-out session are checking the listing of files or renaming files. Sometimes, developers make small modifications to files, exit the subshell session, and rerun the file from SQL*Plus.

You exit the operating system shell environment and return to SQL*Plus by typing this:

```
EXIT
```

An alternative to shelling out is running a single operating system command from SQL*Plus. For example, you can type the following in Windows to see the contents of the directory from which you entered SQL*Plus:

```
SQL> HOST dir
```

Linux works with the HOST command, too. In Linux, you also have the option of a shorthand version of the HOST command—the exclamation mark (!). You use it like this:

```
SQL> ! ls -al
```

The difference between the ! and HOST commands is that you can't use substitution variables with the !. Also, the ! doesn't work when you're deployed on a Windows platform.

Exiting the SQL*Plus Environment

You use QUIT or EXIT to exit a session in the SQL*Plus program. Either command ends a SQL*Plus session and releases any session variables.

The next sections show you how to write, save, edit, rerun, abort, call, run, and pass parameters to SQL statements. Then you'll learn how to call PL/SQL programs and write SQL*Plus log files.

Writing SQL Statements with SQL*Plus

Writing a SQL statement depends on you having some knowledge of SQL. A quick query seems like a simple and direct way to demonstrate how you can write SQL statements in SQL*Plus. Queries use the keyword SELECT to list columns from a table and the FROM keyword to designate a table or set of tables.

The following query selects a string literal value from thin air with the help of the *pseudo table* dual. The dual pseudo table is a structure that lets you query one or more columns of data without accessing a table, view, or stored program. Oracle lets you select any type of column except a large object (LOB) from the dual table. The `dual` table returns only one row of data.

NOTE
The dual table exists in MySQL, but its use is optional in the equivalent syntax.

This selects "Hello World!"

```
SELECT 'Hello World!' FROM dual;
```

Notice that Oracle requires single quotation marks as delimiters of string literal values. Any attempt to substitute double quotes raises an `ORA-00904` error message, which means you've attempted to use an invalid identifier. For example, you'd generate the following error if you used double quotes around the string literal in the original statement:

```
SELECT "Hello World!" FROM dual
       *
ERROR at line 1:
ORA-00904: "Hello World!": invalid identifier
```

Back-Quoting in Oracle

The art of back-quoting is critical in many programming languages. You back-quote a character that has special purpose in a programming language when you want to use the character as ordinary text. The apostrophe (`'`) is a special character in Oracle's implementation of SQL.

When you have a string with a possessive quotation mark, you must back-quote the apostrophe with another apostrophe. Here's an example:

```
SELECT 'Ralph Malph is stealing Fonzie''s bike.' AS Statement
FROM dual;
```

The first apostrophe instructs the parser to treat the next character as an ordinary text character. This means that the second apostrophe is stored in a column or printed from the query. This syntax also works in the MySQL database. Here's the output from the query:

```
Statement
---------------------------------------
Ralph Malph is stealing Fonzie's bike.
```

Beginning with Oracle Database 10g, you have an alternative to back-quoting: an apostrophe. You may use the following syntax:

```
SELECT q'(It's a bird, no plane, it's Superman!)' AS trite

FROM dual;
```

Alternatives are nice. You should use the one that works best for you.

If you're coming from the MySQL world to work in Oracle databases, this may seem a bit provincial. MySQL works with either single or double quote marks as string delimiters but Oracle doesn't. No quote delimiters are required for numeric literals.

SQL*Plus places a query or other SQL statement in a special buffer when you run it. Sometimes you want to save these queries in files. The next section shows you how to do that.

Saving SQL Statements with SQL*Plus

Sometimes you want to save a SQL statement in a file. That's actually a perfect activity for the SAVE or STORE command rather than spooling a log file. Using the SAVE or STORE command lets you save your current statement to a file. Capturing these ad hoc SQL statements is generally important—after all, SQL statements ultimately get bundled into rerunnable script files before they ever move into production systems.

Use the following syntax to save a statement as a runnable file:

```
SAVE some_new_file_name.sql
```

If the file already exists, you can save the file with this syntax:

```
SAVE some_new_file_name.sql REPLACE
```

CAUTION
Note that SAVE and STORE commands that include a REPLACE option have no undo capability. That means any existing file with the same name is immediately unrecoverable. Use the REPLACE option with care.

Editing SQL Statements with SQL*Plus

You can edit your current SQL statements from within SQL*Plus by using EDIT. SQL*Plus preconfigures itself to launch Notepad when you type EDIT or the shorthand ED in any Windows installation of the Oracle Database.

Although the EDIT command points to Notepad when you're working in Windows, it isn't configured by default in Linux or UNIX. You have to set the editor for SQL*Plus when running on Linux or UNIX. Check back to the "Working in the SQL*Plus Environment" section earlier in the chapter for details about setting up the editor.

Assuming you've configured the editor, you can edit the last SQL statement by typing EDIT like this (or you can use ED):

```
SQL> EDIT
```

The temporary contents of any SQL statement are stored in the afiedt.buf file by default. After you edit the file, you can save the modified statement into the buffer and rerun the statement. Alternatively, you can save the SQL statement as another file.

Rerunning SQL*Plus SQL Statements from the Buffer

After editing a SQL statement, SQL*Plus automatically lists it for you and you can rerun it. Use a forward slash (/) to run the last SQL statement from the buffer. The semicolon at the end of your original SQL statement isn't stored in the buffer. It's replaced by a forward slash. If you add the semicolon back when you edit the SQL statement, you would see something like the following with the semicolon at the end of the last line of the statement:

```
SQL> EDIT
Wrote file afiedt.buf
  1* SELECT 'Hello World!' AS statement FROM dual;
```

A forward slash can't rerun this from the buffer because the semicolon is an *illegal character*. You would get an error like this:

```
SQL> /
SELECT 'Hello World!' AS statement FROM dual;
                                             *
ERROR at line 1:
ORA-00911: invalid character
```

To fix this error, you should re-edit the buffer contents and remove the semicolon. The forward slash would then run the statement.

Some SQL statements have so many lines that they don't fit on a single page in your terminal or shell session. In these cases, you can use the `LIST` command (or simply a lowercase `l` or uppercase `L`) to see only a portion of the current statement from the buffer. The `LIST` command by itself reads the buffer contents and displays them with line numbers at the SQL prompt.

If you're working with a long PL/SQL block or SQL statement, you can inspect ranges of line numbers with the following syntax:

```
SQL> LIST 23 32
```

This will echo back to the console the inclusive set of lines from the buffer when they exist. Another command line interface is used to edit line numbers. It's very cumbersome and limited in its utility, so you should simply edit the SQL statement in a text editor.

Aborting Entry of SQL Statements in SQL*Plus

When you're working at the command line, you can't just point the mouse to the prior line and correct an error; instead, you must abort a statement with typos or run it with the failure. SQL*Plus lets you abort statements with errors.

You can abort a SQL statement that you're writing interactively by pressing the RETURN key and typing a period (.) as the first character on a new line, followed by pressing the RETURN key. This aborts the statement but leaves it in the active buffer file in case you want to edit it.

TIP
The period (.) aborts the statement only when it's the first and only character in a line.

You can use the preceding instructions for the ed utility to edit the statement—that is, if it's easier than retyping the whole thing.

Calling and Running SQL*Plus Script Files

Script or batch files are composed of related SQL statements. They are the backbone of implementing new software and patches for old software. You use script files because others run them in production environments, and quality assurance departments want them to ensure code integrity.

Rerunnable scripts mean that they must manage preexisting conditions in the production database without raising errors. You must eliminate all errors because administrators might not be able to judge when some errors can be safely ignored. This means the script must perform conditional drops of tables and data migration processes.

Assuming you have a file named `create_data.sql` in a `C:\Data` directory, you can run it with the `@` (*at*) command in SQL*Plus. This script can be run from within SQL*Plus with either a relative or an absolute filename. A relative filename contains no path element because it assumes the present working path. An absolute filename requires a fully qualified path (also known as a canonical path) and filename.

The relative filename syntax depends on starting SQL*Plus from the directory where you have saved the script file. Here's the syntax to run a `create_data.sql` file:

```
@create_data.sql
```

Although the relative filename is easy to use, it limits you to starting SQL*Plus from a specific directory. That's not always possible, so the absolute filename syntax works regardless of where you start SQL*Plus. Here's an example for the Windows OS:

```
@C:\Data\create_data.sql
```

The `@` is also synonymous with the SQL*Plus command `START`. This means you can also run a script file based on its relative filename like this:

```
START create_data.sql
```

The `@` symbol reads the script file into the active buffer and then runs the script file. You use two `@@` symbols when you call another script file from one script file and they exist in the same directory. The combined `@@` symbols instruct SQL*Plus to look in the directory specified by the command that ran the calling script. This means that a call such as the following runs a subordinate script file *from the same directory*:

```
@@some_subordinate.sql
```

If you need to run scripts delivered by Oracle and they reside in the Oracle home, you can use a handy shortcut: the question mark (?). The question mark maps to the Oracle home. This means you can run a library script from the `\rdbms` subdirectory of the Oracle home with this syntax in Windows:

```
?\rdbms\somescript.sql
```

The shortcuts and relative path syntax are attractive during development but should be avoided in production. Using fully qualified paths from a fixed environment variable such as the `%ORACLE_HOME%` in Windows or `$ORACLE_HOME` in Linux is generally the best approach.

Passing Parameters to SQL*Plus Script Files

Writing and running static SQL statements or script files is important, but more important is writing and running SQL statements or script files that can solve dynamic problems. You use substitution variables to write dynamic scripts because they act like *placeholders* in SQL statements or scripts.

As mentioned, SQL*Plus supports two methods of interaction: interactive and batch modes. The method for interacting with SQL*Plus in external programming languages is covered in the "Batch Mode Parameter Passing" section.

Interactive Mode Parameter Passing

When you call a script that contains substitution variables, SQL*Plus prompts for values that you want to assign to the substitution variables. The standard prompt is the name of the substitution variable, but you can alter that behavior by using the ACCEPT SQL*Plus command.

For example, assume you wrote a script that looked for a table with a name that's some partial string, but you knew the search string would change. A static SQL statement wouldn't work, but a dynamic one would. The following dynamic script lets you query the database catalog for any table, based on your knowing only the starting part of the table name. The placeholder variable is designated using an ampersand (&) or two. A single ampersand tells SQL*Plus to make the substitution at runtime and forget the value immediately after the substitution. Two ampersands instruct SQL*Plus to make the substitution, store the variable as a session-level variable, and undefine the substitution variable.

```
SQL> SELECT    table_name
  2  ,          column_id
  3  ,          column_name
  4  FROM       user_tab_columns
  5  WHERE      table_name LIKE UPPER('&input')||'%';
```

The UPPER function on line 5 promotes the input to uppercase because Oracle stores all metadata in uppercase and performs case-sensitive comparisons of strings by default. The query prompts as follows when run:

```
Enter value for input: it
```

When you press the RETURN key, it shows the substitution of the value for the placeholder, like so:

```
old   5: WHERE    table_name LIKE UPPER('&input')||'%'
new   5: WHERE    table_name LIKE UPPER('it')||'%'
```

At least this is the default behavior. The behavior depends on the value of the SQL*Plus VERIFY environment variable, which is set to ON by default. You can suppress that behavior by setting the value of VERIFY to off:

```
SET VERIFY OFF
```

You can also configure the default prompt by using SQL*Plus formatting commands, like so:

```
ACCEPT input CHAR PROMPT 'Enter the beginning part of the table name:'
```

This syntax acts like a double ampersand assignment and places the input substitution in memory as a session-level variable.

When to Disable Substitution Variables

Substitution variables are important aspects of the SQL*Plus environment and should generally be enabled. However, you need to disable substitution variables when you create and compile a Java source. Java code uses the double ampersand (&&) as the *logical and* operator. Before attempting to create and compile a Java source file, you should disable the DEFINE environment variable:

```
SET DEFINE OFF
```

After you've created and compiled the Java source file, you should re-enable it with the ON option.

Batch Mode Parameter Passing

Batch mode operations typically involve a script file that contains more than a single SQL statement. The example uses a file that contains a single SQL statement because it successfully shows the concept and conserves space.

The trick to batch submission is the -s option, or the silent option. Script files that run from the command line with this option flag are batch programs. They suppress a console session from being launched and run, much like statements submitted through the Java Database Connectivity (JDBC) or Open Database Connectivity (ODBC) APIs. Batch programs must include a QUIT or EXIT statement at the end of the file or they will hang in SQL*Plus. This technique lets you create a file that can run from an operating system script file, also commonly known as a *shell script*.

The following sample.sql file shows how you would pass a parameter to a dynamic SQL statement embedded in a script file:

```
-- Disable echoing substitution.
SET VERIFY OFF

-- Open log file.
SPOOL demo.txt

-- Query data based on an externally set parameter.
SELECT    table_name
,         column_id
,         column_name
FROM      user_tab_columns
WHERE     table_name LIKE UPPER('&1')||'%';

-- Close log file.
SPOOL OFF

-- End session connection.
QUIT;
```

You would call the program from a batch file in Windows or a shell script in Linux. The syntax would include the user name and password, which presents a security risk. Provided you've secured your local server and you routinely purge your command history, you would call a `sample.sql` script from the present working directory like this:

```
sqlplus -s student/student @sample.sql it
```

You can also pass the user name and password as connection parameters, which is illustrated in the following sample:

```
SET VERIFY OFF
SPOOL demo.txt
CONNECT &1/&2
SELECT USER FROM dual;
SPOOL OFF
QUIT;
```

The script depends on the `/NOLOG` option to start SQL*Plus without connecting to a schema. You would call it like this, providing the user name and password:

```
sqlplus -s /NOLOG @create_data.sql student student
```

Although you've now seen the possibilities, there are risks to disclosing user names and passwords, because the information from the command line can be hacked from user history logs. Anonymous log-in or operating system user validation really should be used when you want to run scripts like these.

NOTE
You can learn how to configure the anonymous user account in Chapter 16 of Oracle Database 11g PL/SQL Programming *(Oracle Press, 2008) because it's a necessary component of working with the XDB Server. The* Oracle Database 11g DBA Handbook *shows you how to configure operating system user account validation in lieu of formal credentials.*

Calling PL/SQL Programs

PL/SQL (Procedural Language/SQL) provides capabilities required by database-centric applications missing from SQL. PL/SQL programs are stored programs that run inside a separate engine from the SQL statement engine. Their principal role is to group SQL statements and procedural logic to support transaction scopes across multiple SQL statements.

NOTE
Chapter 3 covers transactions and Chapter 13 covers basic PL/SQL operations. See Oracle Database 11g PL/SQL Programming *for a more complete treatment of the PL/SQL language. The* Oracle Database PL/SQL Language Reference *should also answer basic questions.*

PL/SQL supports two types of stored programs: anonymous blocks and named blocks, functions and procedures. MySQL SQL/Persistent Stored Modules (PSM) support only named block functions and procedures. PL/SQL also supports *packages*, which are groups of related functions and procedures. Packages support function and procedure overloading and provide many of the key utilities for Oracle databases.

Functions and procedures support pass-by-value and pass-by-reference methods available in other procedural programming languages. Functions return a value when they're placed as right operands in an assignment and as calling parameters to other functions or procedures. Procedures don't return a value or reference as a right operand and can't be used as calling parameters to other functions or procedures.

NOTE
You can find more details about functions and procedures in Chapter 13.

Sometimes you want to output diagnostic information to your console or formatted output from small PL/SQL programs to log files. This is frequently done in Oracle, because unlike named only blocks in MySQL PSMs, PL/SQL supports anonymous block program units.

Before you can receive output from a PL/SQL block, you must open the buffer that separates the SQL*Plus environment from the PL/SQL engine. This is done with the following SQL*Plus command:

```
SET SERVEROUTPUT ON SIZE UNLIMITED
```

You enable the buffer stream for display to the console by changing the status of the SERVEROUTPUT environment to ON. Although you can set the SIZE parameter to any value, the legacy parameter limit of 1 million no longer exists. That limit made sense in earlier releases because of physical machine limits governing console speed and network bandwidth. Today, there's really no reason to constrain the output size, and you should always use UNLIMITED when you open the buffer.

You'll learn how to call the various types of PL/SQL programs. Whether the programs are yours or built-ins provided by Oracle, much of the logic that supports features of Oracle databases rely on stored programs.

Executing an Anonymous Block Program

The following demonstrates a traditional "Hello World" program in an anonymous PL/SQL block. It uses a specialized stored program known as a *package*. Packages contain data types and shared variables, as well as cursors, functions, and procedures. You use the package name, a dot (the *component selector*), and a function or procedure name when you call package components.

You print "Hello World!" with the following anonymous block program unit:

```
SQL> BEGIN
  2    DBMS_OUTPUT.PUT_LINE('Hello World!');
  3  END;
  4  /
```

PL/SQL is a strongly typed language that uses declarative blocks as opposed to the curly braces you may know best from C, C#, C++, Java, Perl, or PHP. The execution block starts with the BEGIN keyword and ends with an EXCEPTION or END keyword. Since this sample program doesn't employ an exception block, the END keyword ends the program. All statements and blocks in PL/SQL end with a semicolon. The forward slash on line 4 executes the anonymous block program because the last semicolon ends the execution block. It prints "Hello World!" to the console, provided you opened the buffer by enabling the SQL*Plus SERVEROUTPUT environment variable.

Anonymous block programs are very useful when you need one-time procedural processing in the scope of a single batch or script file. Displaying results from the internals of the PL/SQL block is straightforward as discussed earlier in this section.

Setting a Session Variable Inside PL/SQL

Unlike substitution variables, Oracle databases also support session variables. *Session variables* act like global variables in the scope and duration of your connection, as do session-level substitution variables, but the former differs from substitution variables in two ways. Substitution variables are limited to a string data type, while session variables may have any of the following data types: BINARY_DOUBLE, BINARY_FLOAT, CHAR, CLOB, NCHAR, NCLOB, NUMBER, NVARCHAR2, REFCURSOR, or VARCHAR2. Session variables, more commonly referred to as *bind variables*, can't be assigned a value in SQL*Plus or SQL scope. You must assign values to session variables in an anonymous PL/SQL block.

Session variables, like session-level substitution variables, are very useful, because you can share them across SQL statements. You must define session variables with the VARIABLE keyword, which gives them a name and data type but not a value. As an example, you can define a bind variable as a 20-character-length string like so:

```
VARIABLE whom VARCHAR2(20)
```

You can assign a session variable with an anonymous PL/SQL block or a CALL to a stored function. Inside the anonymous block, you reference the variable with a colon preceding the variable name. The colon points to a session level scope that is external to its local block scope:

```
SQL> BEGIN
  2    :whom := 'Sam';
  3  END;
  4  /
```

After assigning a value to the session level variable, you can query it in a SQL statement or reuse it in another PL/SQL anonymous block program. The following query from the dual pseudo table concatenates string literals before and after the session level variable:

```
SELECT 'Play it again, ' || :whom || '!' FROM dual;
```

The colon appears in SQL statements, too. Both the anonymous block and SQL statement actually run in execution scopes that are equivalent to other subshells in operating system shell scripting. The query prints the following:

```
Play it again, Sam!
```

The dual pseudo table is limited to a single row but can return one to many columns. You can actually display 999 columns, which is the same as the number of possible columns for a table.

Executing a Named Block Program

Stored functions and procedures are known as named blocks, whether they're standalone or part of a package. You can *call* a named function into a session variable or return the value in a query. Procedures are different because you *execute* them in the scope of a session or block.

The following is a "Hello World!" function that takes no parameters:

```
SQL> CREATE OR REPLACE FUNCTION hello_function RETURN VARCHAR2 IS
  2  BEGIN
  3    RETURN 'Hello World!';
  4  END hello_function;
  5  /
```

A query of the function uses the dual pseudo table, like so:

```
SELECT hello_function FROM dual;
```

Calling a function that doesn't have defined parameters in a query lets you leave off the open and closing parentheses traditionally associated with function calls with no arguments. However, if you use the SQL*Plus CALL syntax, you must provide the opening and closing parentheses or you raise an ORA-06576 error message. Assuming that the return value of the function will be assigned to a bind variable of output, you need to define the session variable before calling the function value into the output variable.

This defines a session variable as a 12-character variable-length string:

```
VARIABLE my_output VARCHAR2(12)
```

The following statement calls the function and puts the result in the session variable :my_output. The colon preceding the session variable is the only way it can be accessed from SQL statements or anonymous PL/SQL blocks.

```
CALL hello_function AS INTO :my_output;
```

The lack of parentheses causes this statement to fail and raises an ORA-06576 error message. Adding the parentheses to the CALL statement makes it work:

```
CALL hello_world() AS INTO :my_output;
```

Procedures work differently and are run by the EXECUTE command. The following defines a stored procedure that echoes out the string "Hello World!" Procedures are easier to work with from SQL*Plus because you don't need to define session variables to capture output. All you do is enable the SQL*Plus SERVEROUTPUT environment variable.

This defines the "Hello World!" procedure:

```
SQL> CREATE OR REPLACE PROCEDURE hello_procedure IS
  2  BEGIN
  3    dbms_output.put_line('Hello World!');
  4  END hello_procedure;
  5  /
```

You can execute the procedure successfully like so:

```
EXECUTE hello_procedure;
```

Or you can execute the procedure with open and close parentheses, like so:

```
EXECUTE hello_procedure();
```

You should see "Hello World!" using either form. If it isn't displayed, enable the SQL*Plus SERVEROUTPUT environment variable. Remember that nothing returns to the console without enabling the SERVEROUTPUT environment variable.

All the examples dealing with calls to PL/SQL named blocks use a *pass-by-value* process, which means that values entering the program units, are consumed, and other values are returned. *Pass-by-reference* processes are covered in Chapter 13.

Writing SQL*Plus Log Files

When you're testing the idea of how a query should work and want to capture one that did, you can write it directly to a file. You can also capture all the activity of a long script by writing it to a log file. You can write log files in two ways: One captures only the *feedback* messages, such as "four rows updated." The other captures the statement executed and then the feedback message. The latter are called *verbose* log files.

You can write verbose log files by leveraging the SQL*Plus ECHO environment variable in SQL*Plus. You enable it with this command:

```
SET ECHO ON
```

Enabling the ECHO command splits your SQL commands. It dispatches one to run against the server and another *echoed* back to your console. This allows you to see statements in your log file before the feedback from their execution.

You open a log file with the following command:

```
SPOOL C:\Data\somefile.txt
```

This logs all output from the script to the file C:\Data\somefile.txt until the SPOOL OFF command runs in the session. The output file's extension is not required but defaults to .lst when not provided explicitly. As an extension, .lst doesn't map to a default application in Windows or Linux environments. It's a convention to use some file extension that maps to an editor as a text file.

You can append to an existing file with the following syntax:

```
SPOOL C:\Data\somefile.txt APPEND
```

Both of the foregoing syntax examples use an absolute filename. You can do the same thing in Linux by substituting a mount point for the logical drive (C:\) and changing the backslashes to forward slashes. You use a relative filename when you omit the qualified path and it writes the file to the directory where you launched SQL*Plus.

When using a relative path, you should know that it looks in the directory where you were when you launched sqlplus. That directory is called the *present working directory* or, by some old csh (C Shell) folks, the *current working directory*. In older Windows versions, a GUI version of SQL*Plus (that's deprecated in Oracle Database 11g) writes to the bin directory of the Oracle home.

You close a log file with the following command:

```
SPOOL OFF
```

No file exists until you close the buffer stream. Only one open buffer stream can exist in any session. This means you can write only to one log file at a time from a given session. Therefore, you should spool in only script files that aren't called by other script files that might also spool to a log file. You shouldn't attempt to log from the topmost script because then triaging errors among the programming units becomes more complex.

TIP
When you spool to a log file, avoid overwriting your script filename by making the log file extension something other than .sql.

A pragmatic approach to development requires that you log work performed. Failure to log your work can have impacts on the integrity of data and processes.

MySQL Monitor

The *MySQL Monitor* is the command-line SQL interface for the Oracle MySQL 5.5 database. It has far fewer features than the Oracle SQL*Plus environment, because it wasn't written to support SQL report processing. MySQL Monitor's purpose is to process SQL statements, which it does well.

There are three differences between the MySQL Monitor and Oracle SQL*Plus environments. One is that the error messages are divided into two types: errors that cause failures and warnings that signal implicit behaviors, such as data type conversions. Another is that the MySQL Monitor processes only SQL and SQL/PSM named blocks. The last difference is that SQL report writing isn't provided in the MySQL Monitor, and you must purchase or use other tools for report writing.

Connecting to and Disconnecting from MySQL Monitor

After installing the product, you access the MySQL Monitor from the command line by typing the following:

```
mysql -usome_username -psome_password
```

The -u designates the connecting user and the -p sets the password for the connection. If your %PATH% or $PATH environment variable isn't set when you try this command, you get this message in Windows:

```
'mysql' is not recognized as an internal or external command
```

Or you get this message in Linux:

```
mysql: is not found
```

Assuming the mysql client executable is found, this type of connection request displays your password as readable text on the screen and records it in the command-line buffer. It's much better to let the database request your password as an obfuscated string, which is the same rule covered for Oracle's SQL*Plus. When you don't protect your user credentials, you see them disclosed, as in the following console screen from Windows:

Password is disclosed
in the window frame.

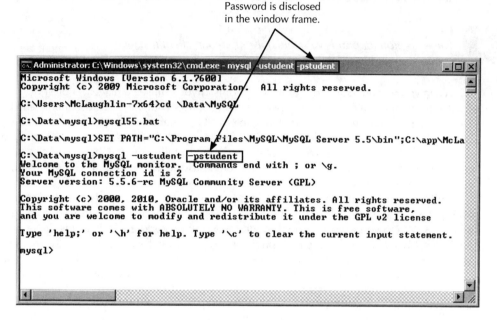

As mentioned, it is also possible that command histories can provide passwords to hackers. Avoid entering your password in clear text to improve the security of the work environment.

NOTE
MySQL Monitor connects through TCP/IP sockets by default unless you secure the server for maintenance.

You can use the following syntax to prevent disclosing your password to onlookers:

```
mysql -usome_username -p
```

An alternative way to write the connection statement provides a listening port other than the default 3306 port. The capital -P lets you specify a different listening port, whereas, the lowercase -p is the option for a password. You connect to MySQL through a 3307 listening port like this:

```
mysql -usome_username -p -P3307
```

If the database isn't listening on that port, you get the following error:

```
ERROR 2003 (HY000): Can't connect to MySQL server on 'localhost' (10061)
```

You can find the correct listening port by checking the my.ini configuration file. There are two port assignments in the file. One is for the client and it is in the [client] section of the configuration file. That's the default port the client attempts to *connect to* when you don't provide a -P option. The other is for the MySQL daemon, or server-side process. You can find it in the [mysqld] section of the configuration file. That's the port the MySQL server *listens on*.

TIP
The –P option for port is valuable only when one client instance connects to multiple database servers.

When you've connected to the MySQL Monitor, you will see a mysql> prompt.

If you haven't created your own user, you can connect with the root user name and password. You set the root password when installing the MySQL Database. The "Create a Default MySQL User" sidebar a bit later provides instructions for setting up a student user that can run all the code provided in the book. If you're not the one who installed the database, you can ask that person to create a user account for you. You should provide that superuser with the instructions from the sidebar.

Unlike Oracle, you can't grant roles. While MySQL Workbench gives you the impression that MySQL Server supports roles but it doesn't. MySQL Workbench maps its roles to a series of privileges. When you assign a role through the MySQL Workbench, it grants those mapped privileges. MySQL users can see their privileges by querying the user_privileges table in the public copy of the data catalog, which is the information_schema database. The lack of roles in MySQL means that you lose a level of security obfuscation (fancy word for *layered access*).

Privileges are distinct things that you grant to a user. They give permission to perform tasks, such as creating a table, view, or procedure. Sometimes privileges convey permission to perform overloaded behaviors. For example, the CREATE PROCEDURE privilege in MySQL 5.5 grants the right to create procedures or functions just like in Oracle Database 11*g*. Chapter 14 provides more information on functions and procedures, and you can learn more about roles and privileges in Chapter 3.

Configuring MySQL Monitor

You can change the session prompt, but doing so limits you to including only manual strings. There are no meta-options similar to Oracle's SQL*Plus _user. The session prompt is seldom customized by users, because they're generally running scripts at the command line when moving their work into a staging or production environment.

If you want to configure the MySQL prompt to include the same type of information as the Oracle SQL*Plus example, you would query the user and database and then use the results as arguments to the PROMPT command or shortcut \R command. A single query can get those values by referencing two built-in MySQL functions, like so:

```
SELECT user(), database();
```

The user() function returns the name and the location of current user information for the connection. The connection location identifies the location of the connected user. Its possible values are localhost, a physical IP address, a domain name, a partial domain name, or a wildcard (%). The database() function returns the name of the work area in which a user is working or a *null* before the user chooses a database with the USE command.

Create a Default MySQL User

This sample code depends on you creating a `student` MySQL user and `studentdb` database. Unlike for the Oracle user, you want to grant all permissions to the user to work in the `studentdb` database.

You or your DBA can create a `student` user and `studentdb` database using this syntax as the `root` user:

```
CREATE USER 'student'@'%' IDENTIFIED BY 'student';
```

This account has access to nothing at this point. All the user can do is *connect* to the database from anywhere. When the `localhost` replaces the % it restricts access to the same machine, and an IP address, domain, or subdomain restricts it to one or a set of TCP/IP addresses. The `%` lets the user connect from anywhere. A user with these permissions can see only the `information_schema` database with the following command:

```
SHOW DATABASES;
```

Such an enabled user can also use only the `information_schema` database. The `information_schema` database is a snapshot of the MySQL database instance. Any user with access to the `information_schema` database can query and discover information about databases that they can't see when they issue a `SHOW DATABASES;` command. This appears to be a security hole in MySQL 5.5 that Oracle will certainly fix in subsequent releases.

After creating the user, you should create a `studentdb` database. Here's the command syntax:

```
CREATE DATABASE studentdb;
```

Alternatively, an administrator can create a `SCHEMA` instead of a `DATABASE`. `SCHEMA` is a synonym for `DATABASE` as of MySQL 5.0.2.

This `GRANT` command gives all permissions on the `studentdb` to the `student` user:

```
GRANT ALL ON studentdb.* TO 'student'@'%';
```

Now the `student` user can use the `studentdb` database. The connection by itself does not connect the user to a work area. The `student` user must tell MySQL which database it wants to use, which connects the user to a work area. You do that with the following command:

```
USE studentdb
```

Note that the `USE` command doesn't require a semicolon. It's like a SQL*Plus command in an Oracle Database 11*g* instance. It's one of the exceptions because it doesn't require a semicolon but it works with one too. Using a semicolon doesn't raise an error in the MySQL Monitor but forgetting one when it is required does.

You can change databases at any time, but you must disconnect and reconnect when you want to change the user. This is less convenient than the Oracle solution, which lets you connect as another user without leaving the SQL*Plus environment.

Assuming that the query returns values for the user as student and database as studentdb, this would be the new prompt:

```
PROMPT mysql: STUDENT at STUDENTDB>
```

Resetting the prompt to the default can't be done with the PROMPT command, but must be done with the \R shortcut. For reference, there are no dynamic runtime metadata global values to set, as with the Oracle's SQL*Plus environment.

Using Interactive Help in the MySQL Monitor Environment

You can discover what's possible in the MySQL Monitor by checking the help menu. Type help, \h, or ? at the command prompt to see a help menu:

```
List of all MySQL commands:
Note that all text commands must be first on line and end with ';'
?         (\?) Synonym for 'help'.
clear     (\c) Clear the current input statement.
connect   (\r) Reconnect to the server. Optional arguments are db and host.
delimiter (\d) Set statement delimiter.
ego       (\G) Send command to mysql server, display result vertically.
exit      (\q) Exit mysql. Same as quit.
go        (\g) Send command to mysql server.
help      (\h) Display this help.
notee     (\t) Don't write into outfile.
print     (\p) Print current command.
prompt    (\R) Change your mysql prompt.
quit      (\q) Quit mysql.
rehash    (\#) Rebuild completion hash.
source    (\.) Execute an SQL script file. Takes a file name as an argument.
status    (\s) Get status information from the server.
tee       (\T) Set outfile [to_outfile]. Append everything into given
               outfile.
use       (\u) Use another database. Takes database name as argument.
charset   (\C) Switch to another charset. Might be needed for processing
               binlog with multi-byte charsets.
warnings  (\W) Show warnings after every statement.
nowarning (\w) Don't show warnings after every statement.

For server side help, type 'help contents'
```

You can view the server-side components by typing this:

```
mysql> help contents
```

It shows the following expanded list. You can drill down on these and others. Try using help for information about administration to experiment.

```
You asked for help about help category: "Contents"
For more information, type 'help <item>', where <item> is one of the
following categories:
   Account Management
```

```
Administration
Compound Statements
Data Definition
Data Manipulation
Data Types
Functions
Functions and Modifiers for Use with GROUP BY
Geographic Features
Help Metadata
Language Structure
Plugins
Table Maintenance
Transactions
User-Defined Functions
Utility
```

Shelling out of the MySQL Monitor Environment

Unlike the SQL*Plus host command, when operating in Linux or UNIX, you can only peek in the directory where you launched MySQL Monitor. You can run single operating system commands. For example, running MySQL in Linux lets you check the present working directory from which you launched the mysql client software. Type the following to peek at that directory:

```
SYSTEM pwd
```

A semicolon isn't required to run this environment command. Unfortunately, you must exit and reconnect in a new session when you need more than a single command.

Exiting MySQL Monitor

You can use either QUIT or EXIT to exit the MySQL Monitor.

```
mysql> QUIT;
```

Writing MySQL SQL Statements

Earlier in the chapter, you saw how to use the dual pseudo table for querying literal values. This capability lets you display values on the console and fabricate data from literals rather than table values. Chapter 11 contains more on data fabrication.

The same query statement mentioned earlier works in MySQL. Unlike Oracle Database 11*g*, Oracle MySQL works with or without a direct reference to the dual table. So, this works:

```
SELECT "Hello World!";
```

Or this more Oracle-like statement also works:

```
SELECT 'Hello World!' FROM dual;
```

Note that although Oracle requires single quotation marks as delimiters of string literal values, MySQL lets you use either single or double quotes. Like other relational Oracle databases, MySQL databases don't require delimiters for numeric literals.

NOTE
The dual *table exists in MySQL and should be used when you might
port your code to an Oracle or SQL Server database.*

The dual pseudo table is a structure that lets you query one row of data that might contain
one or more columns without accessing a table or view. MySQL lets you select any type of

---

Back-Quoting in MySQL

There's generally no need to back-quote in MySQL, but the backslash (\) and apostrophe or
single quote (') are the official back-quoting characters. If a literal value contains a single
quote, you can enclose the literal in double quotes, and vice versa. Here's an example of this:

```
SELECT "Hello there. It's John's" AS statement;
```

Alternatively, you can use the apostrophe and single quotes entirely, like so:

```
SELECT 'Hello there. It''s John''s' AS statement;
```

Both return the same result:

```
+--------------------------+
| statement                |
+--------------------------+
| Hello there. It's John's |
+--------------------------+
```

It becomes more complex when you've got a combination in a string, like this:

```
mysql> SELECT "Hello there, he said "It's John's" AS statement;
    "> ";
```

There are two problems with this statement. First, the mixture of double and single quotes is
unbalanced because there are three of them. Second, the last double quote instructs the
parser to expect a closing double quote. The result is that the semicolon is treated as an
ordinary text character inside a larger string. The " > prompt after the statement indicates
that a double quote must close an open string. The ' > prompt indicates a single quote must
close an open string.
   The easiest fix to the broken statement is back-quoting with the backslash (\) character.
At the same time, you should add the missing double quote for the quotation phrase, like
this:

```
SELECT "Hello there, he said \"It's John's\"" AS statement;
```

The nested double quotes are back-quoted by the backslash, which eliminates any
problems parsing and executing complex strings like the last one.

column at the command prompt, including a BLOB data type. The output isn't too useful since a BLOB is just a binary stream, but it is available.

You execute queries or other SQL statements with the delimiter defined in your MySQL Monitor. The delimiter is a semicolon (;) by default. You can also use the \g and receive the exact same output as you would when using the semicolon. When you want to display column names on the right and values on the left, you use the \G to execute the query.

You write a query with the \G when you want all columns from an order_item table displayed with column names on the right and values on the left:

```
SELECT * FROM order_item\G
```

Saving MySQL SQL Statements

You can't save SQL statements interactively as you can in Oracle SQL*Plus. Inside MySQL Monitor, you must mark and copy the contents from your terminal session, and paste them into a text editor or CASE development tool.

The steps for this terminal copy-and-paste operation are provided in the following illustrations for Windows 7, but they apply to Windows XP and Vista, too. Click the C:\ box in the upper-left corner of the command prompt dialog and choose Edit | Mark. Then highlight the desired content with your mouse to copy it to a text editor.

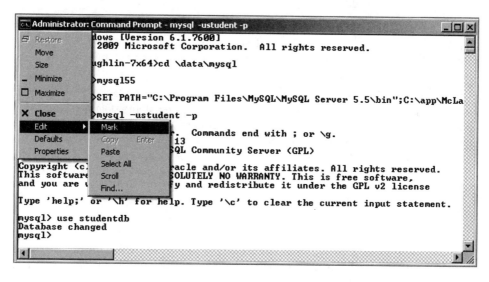

After you've highlighted the text, copy it into the copy buffer, which is the Windows operating system clipboard. Navigate back to the C:\ box and choose Edit | Copy to paste it into the code, as shown in the next illustration.

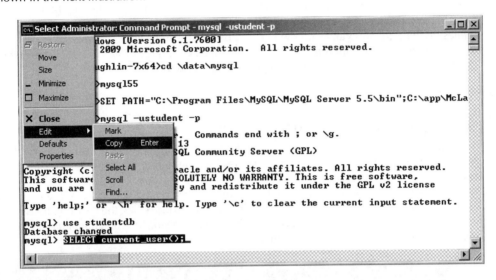

You can paste the contents of the SQL statement into a text editor or CASE tool of your choice. The terminal operations differ on Linux and UNIX but not by much.

Editing MySQL SQL Statements

At the completion of any SQL statement, MySQL doesn't recall the statement because there's no buffer in the MySQL Monitor. That's why it is important that you work with a CASE tool or text editor. Either can usually let you edit and run statements against MySQL Monitor without leaving the comfort of your editor or tool.

TIP
MySQL databases don't support typing a forward slash or semicolon to rerun a SQL statement from the buffer, because there's no buffer.

The closest thing you have to editing a file is the ability to change the default semicolon delimiter value. You can change the delimiter any time you want during your session. The following example changes the semicolon to a double dollar symbol ($$):

```
delimiter $$
```

Changing the delimiter is a necessary practice when you want to create stored programs in MySQL. If you're curious about this feature, you'll read more about it in Chapter 14.

You reset the delimiter to a semicolon after you create your stored programs (at least that's typically where you want to do it). The following shows how to reset it:

```
delimiter ;
```

It's interesting, that the delimiter string is an environment command, similar to SQL*Plus environment variables. The DELIMITER keyword is case-insensitive, and later in this chapter examples will show it in uppercase syntax. If you change the delimiter value to create a stored program unit and forget to reset it, you'll get errors when you try to run ad-hoc statements.

You can check the value of the delimiter environment variable by using the status command. The status command also provides much more information than just the delimiter's value. Here's an example of the output from the status command run on my Mac Pro:

```
--------------
mysql  Ver 14.14 Distrib 5.5.9, for osx10.6 (i386) using readline 5.1

Connection id:          3
Current database:
Current user:           student@localhost
SSL:                    Not in use
Current pager:          stdout
Using outfile:          ''
Using delimiter:        ;
Server version:         5.5.9 MySQL Community Server (GPL)
Protocol version:       10
Connection:             Localhost via UNIX socket
Server characterset:    latin1
Db       characterset:  latin1
Client characterset:    utf8
Conn.    characterset:  utf8
UNIX socket:            /tmp/mysql.sock
Uptime:                 5 hours 42 min 14 sec

Threads: 1  Questions: 6  Slow queries: 0  Opens: 33  Flush tables: 1
Open tables: 26  Queries per second avg: 0.0
--------------
```

The connection is across a UNIX socket (covered in Chapter 1), because incoming network connections are blocked and thereby disallowed on the machine. Enabling network connections, you would see changes in only the two lines shown here:

```
Connection:             localhost via TCP/IP
...
TCP port:               3306
```

The status command displays either the *UNIX socket* or *TCP port* line configured in the my.ini file in Windows or the my.cnf file in Linux.

Aborting MySQL SQL Statements

You can abort a SQL statement that you're writing interactively by typing a backslash and the letter c (\c). You can type it on a fresh line or at the end of any line: it stops the process of writing a SQL statement.

Calling and Running MySQL Script Files

As a developer, you often run your code interactively from development machines. You also probably make changes as you experiment with the code. But when you move your code into production, the rules change. The best way to store your SQL statements for later use is to put them in script files. Script files are text files that contain one or more SQL statements that are run in some sequence of operations. You can create and maintain these script files in any text editor.

Assuming you have a file named `create_data.sql`, you can run it from the MySQL Monitor interactively, like this:

```
source C:\Data\create data.sql
```

Or like this:

```
\. C:\Data\create_data.sql
```

MySQL treats the backslash character as a normal character rather than a back-quote operator when it appears as a parameter to the `source` command. MySQL also knows how to convert the backslashes to forward slashes for Windows platforms. This means you can use this alternative syntax on Windows:

```
source C:/Data/create_data.sql
```

Script files also create log files. Instructions for generating log files are covered in the "Writing MySQL Log Files" section later in this chapter.

Setting a Session Variable

As mentioned, *session variables* are valuable in a database environment. They act as global variables in the scope and duration of your connection. Session variables in MySQL are critical in their role of binding values into MySQL prepared statements.

Like Oracle session variables, MySQL session variables are available from when you declare them in an open session until you end the session. Unlike Oracle Database 11*g*, you can assign values without using a stored program unit procedure or function.

You can declare session variables in the MySQL Monitor in several ways. For example, you can define the variable inside or outside of a SQL statement, or inside a stored program. However, you can display session variables only in queries and stored procedures.

Define or Declare; That's the Question

Define and *declare* are two words that give grief to newbies. Let's qualify what they mean. *Define* means to give a variable a name and data type. *Declare* means to define a variable and assign it a value. Another word for assigning a value is *initializing* the variable.

You can't really define a variable in MySQL because it disallows this. You must declare session variables and they inherit their data type from the value you assign. That's because SQL and SQL/PSM are strongly typed languages and the semantic adopted doesn't allow explicit data type assignment.

This lets you declare a number and variable-length string:

```
SET @myint := 1;
SET @mystring := 'Hello World!';
```

You can also use a SELECT-INTO statement to declare these variables, like this:

```
SELECT 1 INTO @myint;
SELECT 'Hello World!' INTO @mystring;
```

The SELECT-INTO syntax is an assignment pattern that's very handy in MySQL. It can be used in both a SQL and SQL/PSM context, which is quite different from Oracle Database 11*g*. The SELECT-INTO syntax in Oracle can run only inside a PL/SQL block, and that limitation means session variables can only be assigned values in a PL/SQL context.

You can query session-level variables in any SELECT statement. These work against the dual pseudo table. The advantage in MySQL is that you don't have to type the dual keyword to use it. This SELECT statement queries two session-level variables:

```
SELECT @myint, @mystring;
```

It displays this:

```
+--------+--------------+
| @myint | @mystring    |
+--------+--------------+
|      1 | Hello World! |
+--------+--------------+
```

Calling SQL/PSM Programs

SQL/PSM provides two ways to call procedures and one way to call functions. Unlike Oracle's PL/SQL, SQL/PSM doesn't support anonymous block programs. You must define stored programs as functions or procedures.

Before defining sample functions and procedures, you must set the DELIMITER value to something other than the default semicolon (;). As mentioned, you can use the double dollar symbol ($$), because it doesn't interfere with anything else.

You reset the DELIMITER to $$ before attempting to place a stored program into the database, like this:

```
DELIMITER $$
```

With the delimiter reset, you can enter statements in SQL/PSM format. The "Hello World!" function uses semicolons to end statement lines and a double dollar symbol to execute the DDL that creates the function:

```
CREATE FUNCTION hello_function() RETURNS VARCHAR(12)
BEGIN
  RETURN "Hello World!";
END;
$$
```

After you create the function, it's good practice to reset the delimiter to the standard semicolon value. That way, your SQL statements work with the default execution operator. As shown earlier, you change it back with this syntax:

```
DELIMITER ;
```

Oracle hacks should notice immediately that there are two major differences in syntax for SQL/PSM functions. One is that the keyword is a plural `RETURNS`, not Oracle PL/SQL's singular `RETURN` identifier. The other is that the return data type has a physical size set when you define the function. Oracle doesn't fix size at definition but inherits size at runtime.

You can get the result by calling the function this way:

```
SELECT hello_function();
```

Or you can define a session variable and then assign the function result to it:

```
SET @my_output := '';
SELECT hello_function() INTO @my_output;
```

Then you can query the value from the session variable:

```
SELECT @my_output;
```

It prints this:

```
+--------------+
| helloworld() |
+--------------+
| Hello World! |
+--------------+
```

You create a procedure much as you did a function. The first step is to set the delimiter to a double dollar value. Then write the "Hello World!" procedure.

```
CREATE PROCEDURE hello_procedure()
BEGIN
  SELECT 'Hello World!';
END;
$$
```

You can call the procedure only with the `CALL` command:

```
CALL hello_procedure();
```

It returns the string literal "Hello World!" from the procedure and prints it to the console. Stored programs are powerful structures in MySQL and afford value when you develop ACID-compliant transactions across multiple tables. They also let you do interactive debugging without much effort, unlike stored functions. This is covered in more depth in Chapters 14 and 15.

Setting a Session Variable Inside SQL/PSM

Stored functions and procedures can use values from and reset values of externally set session variables. They can also define new session variables, which are available after the completion of a function or procedure call in any session.

Consider the following example function, casablanca(). It takes a no-input parameter but is dependent on the existence of a session variable. This type of behavior is actually a bad coding practice for anything other than an example. It's bad because it ties the behavior of the function to a session variable. It is also disallowed in Oracle, and trying to place a session-level (bind) variable in a named block program unit raises an error while trying to compile it.

The dependency doesn't require you to create the @piano session variable before the function, because line 11 places it in scope with a null value. However, it's a better practice to place the session variable in scope, like so:

```
SET @piano := 'Elsa';
```

You create the function with this syntax:

```
 1 CREATE FUNCTION casablanca() RETURNS VARCHAR(40)
 2 BEGIN
 3   /* Declare a local variable with a null value. */
 4   DECLARE lv_phrase VARCHAR(40);
 5
 6   /* Set internal variable. */
 7   SET @inside := "Inside Rick's, ";
 8
 9  /* Checking whether the session variable exists in scope, places
10     the session variable in scope. */
11  IF EXISTS (SELECT @piano) THEN
12    /* Assign a literal when the value is a zero length string. */
13    IF LENGTH(@piano) = 0 THEN
14      SELECT CONCAT(@inside,'Play it again$, Sam!')
15      INTO lv_phrase;
16    ELSE
17      SELECT CONCAT(@inside,'Play it again, ',IFNULL(@piano,'Sam'),'!')
18      INTO lv_phrase;
19    END IF;
20  END IF;
21
22   /* Return the local variable contents. */
23   RETURN lv_phrase;
24 END;
25 $$
```

Although MySQL doesn't generate line numbers, they are helpful here to step through the code. The casablanca() function has no formal parameters and returns a variable length string up to 40 characters long. As discussed, it also has a dependency on the @piano session variable found on lines 11 and 13. The session-level variable should be set before calling the function. To avoid returning a null value, the IFNULL() function in line 17 substitutes a default value for the @piano variable.

You can call the function like this:

```
SELECT casablanca();
```

When `Elsa` has been assigned in the session to the `@piano` variable, the call to the function returns this:

```
+-----------------------------------+
| casablanca()                      |
+-----------------------------------+
| Inside Rick's, Play it again, Sam! |
+-----------------------------------+
```

Although the `@inside` session variable is useful inside this function, the assignment of a value ends with the completion of the function call. You can query it like this after running the function:

```
SELECT @inside;
```

It returns the following:

```
+----------------+
| @inside        |
+----------------+
| Inside Rick's, |
+----------------+
```

This example shows the behaviors of MySQL Monitor session variables. If you need to use these features in a script, make sure you clear the values at the end of your file.

For reference, you can set a session variable to a zero-length string like this:

```
SET @inside := '';
```

Naturally, a better approach for the `casablanca()` function would be to pass a formal parameter value for the piano player. More about that in Chapter 14.

Writing MySQL Log Files

You can write log files when you run scripts, but the log files aren't too meaningful because you can't display SQL statements in a log file. That's because there's no `ECHO` command in MySQL.

Querying a string literal before each SQL statement is a best practice, or it should be a best practice, because it saves you time trying to pinpoint errors in log files. The syntax for a diagnostic query looks like this:

```
mysql> SELECT 'Some string' AS "Statement" FROM dual;
```

Or without the `FROM` clause, it looks like this:

```
mysql> SELECT 'Some string' AS "Statement";
```

Notice that the string literal value is delimited by single quote marks, but you can also use double quotes and get the same output. The column alias for the string literal is delimited by double quotes but they don't do anything unless you included a white space in the column alias. The double quotes on a two-word alias with a white space tell the server to treat the alias as a single string and ignore the white space as a word delimiter. The output that would be written in this case to your log file is shown here:

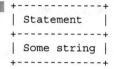

```
+-------------+
| Statement   |
+-------------+
| Some string |
+-------------+
```

You open a log file with the TEE command, which splits the output into two copies. One goes to the console and another goes to the log file. You would implement it like so:

```
TEE C:\Data\somefile.txt
```

This syntax uses an absolute filename. You can also write it with forward slashes. MySQL knows to convert them to backslashes for Windows:

```
TEE C:/Data/somefile.txt
```

You can do the same thing in Linux by substituting the logical drive (C:\) with a mount point and changing the backslashes to forward slashes. You use a relative filename when you omit the qualified path. The TEE command writes the log file to the directory where you launched MySQL Monitor.

NOTE
You can close a log file, but if you attempt to reuse the same filename in another script, it appends to the original file by default.

You close the log file by using the following:

```
NOTEE
```

You can write only one log file at a time from MySQL Monitor. That means if you write a script that calls other scripts, you should put the TEE commands in the lowest level scripts. You also can't reuse filenames unless you delete the files or want to append to existing file content. That's because MySQL Monitor appends new log materials to existing files.

Summary

Both SQL*Plus and MySQL Monitor support session variables with different syntax. Stored programs use dynamically sized return values in Oracle Database 11*g*, but presized return values are used in Oracle MySQL 5.5. Both client software environments let you run SQL statements, call stored programs, and develop robust batch programs.

Mastery Check

The mastery check is a series of true or false and multiple choice questions that let you confirm how well you understand the material in the chapter. You may check the Appendix for answers to these questions.

1. **True** ☐ **False** ☐ You can set a session variable in Oracle outside of an anonymous PL/SQL block.

2. **True** ☐ **False** ☐ Customizing the SQL*Plus and MySQL Monitor prompts is possible.

3. **True** ☐ **False** ☐ Oracle SQL*Plus maintains a buffer of the last SQL statement and allows you to edit its contents.

4. **True** ☐ **False** ☐ You run a script file in MySQL Monitor by using the source or \. command before the script name.

5. **True** ☐ **False** ☐ You can edit the last SQL statement from a native buffer file in MySQL.

6. **True** ☐ **False** ☐ You can connect to another database without exiting MySQL.

7. **True** ☐ **False** ☐ You can create log files by setting the ECHO environment in MySQL Monitor.

8. **True** ☐ **False** ☐ You can run script files (collections of related SQL statements) from the SQL*Plus or MySQL Monitor client software.

9. **True** ☐ **False** ☐ You back-quote apostrophes with another apostrophe in both Oracle and MySQL.

10. **True** ☐ **False** ☐ MySQL allows you to create log files and automatically overwrite any existing files with the same name.

11. Which of the following lets you run a command in the MySQL Monitor?

   a. `mysql> @script_name.sql`

   b. `mysql> @script_name`

   c. `mysql> \. script_name`

   d. `mysql> \. script_name.sql`

   e. `mysql> source script_name.sql`

12. Which of the following lets you run a command in Oracle database SQL*Plus?

   a. `SQL> @script_name.sql`

   b. `SQL> @script_name`

   c. `SQL> \. script_name`

   d. `SQL> \. script_name.sql`

   e. `SQL> source script_name.sql`

13. Which of the following isn't a supported data type in SQL*Plus?

    a. A BINARY_DOUBLE

    b. A CHAR

    c. A STRING

    d. A REFCURSOR

    e. A VARCHAR

14. Which of the following runs a function in an Oracle SQL*Plus environment (multiple possible answers)?

    a. A CALL statement

    b. An EXECUTE statement

    c. A SELECT function_name() FROM dual;

    d. A SELECT function_name();

    e. A SOURCE statement

15. You can use which special characters to back-quote in MySQL Monitor?

    a. The \

    b. The '

    c. The q|some_character|

    d. The "

    e. The /

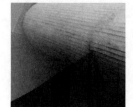

CHAPTER
3

Security Models

racle Database 11*g* offers many more facilities for securing the database than MySQL 5.5, including the Oracle Database Vault, Oracle Label Security, and Transparent Data Encryption. Refer to the *Oracle Database 2 Day + Security Guide* for more information.

MySQL doesn't support Virtual Private Databases (VPDs) such as traditional Oracle databases. A VPD allows you to stripe rows in a table, which lets you restrict access to them based on user privileges. Striping a row is easy: you just add a column that holds a key that specifies your access rights. You can create something similar to VPD in MySQL that requires careful design and you will own all the implementation details; Oracle VPDs, on the other hand, take care of much of the plumbing for you.

This chapter focuses on security barriers. The network, operating system, database configuration, user privileges, roles, and basic design models are the barriers that keep intruders at bay and data safe. It also covers security privileges and the two predominant design architectures, definer and invoker rights modules, which provide generalized patterns for building database-centric applications.

Security Barriers

Security barriers prevent unauthorized access to data, like a series of perimeter fences that keep intruders out. Security gates allow access through the barriers to the data. The gates have locks and keys; only authorized users should possess the keys, and the locks should always be latched. Unfortunately, sometimes gates are unlatched by guards (administrators) or left open by visitors (users). And sometimes developers leave holes in the fence.

Securing the Network

As a database administrator (DBA), before you start working with security privileges inside a database, you should secure the outer barriers. The first barrier is the *network*, and it has two components: the *Internet* and a *company intranet*. A firewall should block all but authorized Internet traffic and allow only secure tunneling into the company from the Internet. This type of firewall is called a *web application firewall (WAF)*, such as the `mod_security` module in PHP. The company intranet should also secure traffic to prevent internal hacking attacks. This type of security is called a *screened subnet*, a very important aspect of any company's governance policy.

Securing the Operating System

After the network has been secured as the first security barrier, your next step is to secure the operating system. The operating system provides a barrier to the local machine and controls how permissions limit access to files and directories. This is known as *host hardening*, and it is a critical element of system administration.

Connecting to the operating system provides any user with privileges that he or she can exploit to compromise a server. System administrators are responsible for planning, issuing, and maintaining users and their account privileges. If you are the system administrator, you should ensure that users can connect only through a secure shell connection. Likewise, you should limit the operating system user permissions only to those privileges that they require.

Securing the Database

After managing operating system access, the DBA has a few more tasks—specifically, to protect read, write, and execute permissions on the database user's files and directories.

Linux implements security at three levels: owner, group, and others. The owner should enjoy full (read, write, and execute) privileges on his or her files. The owner can then set permissions on these files to allow or disallow privileges. Although the system administrator controls group membership, he or she doesn't restrict users granting rights to group users. The account user should make sure that group members can access only what they need. The last group of users is the most difficult to manage, because it consists of all others who can connect to the operating system.

Those others may have accounts to access different applications that are co-resident on the same server. You should generally restrict these users only to read and execute permissions on key program files, and restrict their read access from database configuration, script, and data files. Unless the data files are encrypted, an internal hacker could try to see text fragments from data files. You should also restrict others' execute privileges on some or all of the Oracle or MySQL program files.

Microsoft Windows offers many types of permissions, but they can be generalized into two types of file privileges: *read and execute* and *read, write, and execute*. Although Windows supports groups, they function as groups of users with the same responsibilities. The Windows system administrator should try to isolate product installations with services that run without full system administrator responsibilities.

NOTE
Oracle Database 11g lets you encrypt *your data files. This prevents someone who breaches your operating system barrier from reading data in the data files. It's an awesome security feature that presently doesn't exist for MySQL 5.5.*

After you've secured the local operating system, your focus should turn to those users who can connect directly to your database without local operating system accounts. These users can connect to the database through TCP/IP sockets from remote machines, which should be restricted to operations inside the company's firewall. Authorized external connections such as these should be few in number. Any connection through the firewall must be managed by IP tunneling and typically involves Cisco client-software on the remote machine. You should weigh carefully how you implement these types of access and, where possible, manage them by a list of authorized IP addresses.

Web-based communication between customers and databases typically moves through layers. The layer model starts with a browser using HTTP (Hypertext Transport Protocol) sending a message to an Apache server, which forwards the request to an Apache module, which in turn communicates with the database server. Figure 3-1 shows the general architecture of those layers and illustrates how n-tier computing works.

Communication across the Internet starts with a uniform resource locator (URL) in a browser. A URL is the exposed part of a uniform resource indicator (URI). The URI contains the URL and name and value pairs representing headers and cookies. URLs connect a customer browser with an Apache server. You secure this portion of network barrier by implementing HTTPS (Hypertext Transport Protocol Secure) on your Apache server.

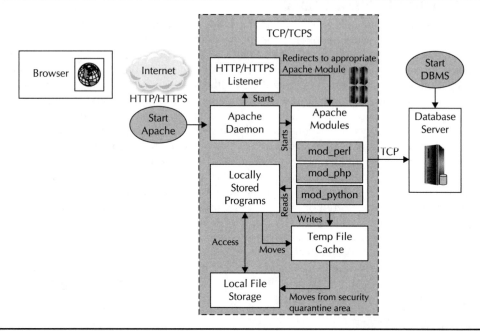

FIGURE 3-1. *N-tier computing model*

The Apache server inspects the URI and typically calls a server-side include (SSI) program for dynamic content. That call is typically made across a TCP/IP or TCPS/IP socket (see Chapter 1 for details on TCP/IP socket communication). TCPS sockets are an Oracle acronym for TCP/IP with SSL (Secure Socket Layer). These sockets are encrypted through Oracle's use of wallets and configuration of the `sqlnet.ora` file. You can read more about TCPS in the *Oracle Database Net Services Reference 11g*. Currently, Oracle uses port 1521 for both TCP and TCPS configurations, but the Oracle Database 11*g* documentation advises TCP will use port 2483 and TCP with SSL (TCPS) will use port 2484 in future releases. Both of these ports are registered for these uses through IANA (Internet Assigned Numbers Authority). You can also implement SSI programming in Java, C#, or scripting languages such as those shown in Figure 3-1.

Many companies believe that their intranets are secure and implement unsecured TCP behind the firewall. Others believe that man-in-the-middle attacks can be mounted from within and they implement TCPS between the Oracle listener and database servers. Oracle provides a TCPS facility with their proprietary Transparent Network Substrate (TNS) communication stack. You can find the details in the *Oracle Database Advanced Security Administrator's Guide*. MySQL implements Open Secure Socket Layer (OpenSSL), which is disabled by default in the Community Edition.

The choice of whether you use secured or unsecured TCP/IP inside your firewall contributes to or detracts from the strength of your network security barrier. You should, however, know that they are available and discuss them with your information security and database administration teams.

The next and last barrier is authenticating with the database. Database authentication requires that a user type in their user name and plain text password when attempting to connect to the database. The database encrypts the password string and then compares the user name and encrypted password against those values stored in the database catalog. MySQL 5.5 opens a connection and creates a session when an encrypted entry matches the stored value, and it disallows a connection when they don't match. Oracle Database 11*g* does this as well, but it also checks whether the user has been granted the *connect privilege*.

The user name and unencrypted password are *tokens*, and together they act as the *keys* to the last gate. These tokens should be protected. Protecting them is a constant process of vigilance. Although an organization can compel users to change their passwords regularly to keep these keys safe from theft, it is a good idea only when the process doesn't drive users to write down their passwords. Unauthorized individuals can find, see, borrow, and use these keys when they are written down because the password standards are too complex for average mortals to remember.

The next section discusses security privileges and introduces and qualifies how the Data Control Language (DCL) works in SQL.

Security Privileges

Security privileges are permissions granted to individual users to work in the database. Some privileges grant wide-ranging permissions and others grant narrowly defined rights. All privileges should be granted to users with care and only to support real business needs. Wide-ranging permissions offer more rights, such as CREATE ANY RESOURCE, which allows users to create any type of database object in their own or others' schemas. That degree of access, however, is probably a bad idea for anybody other than a DBA.

Designing database applications architecture requires making design decisions involving technology and security. These decisions must resonate at every level to support integration when the pieces of the application product are assembled. Security, a crucial component in application design, manages how users of the application interact with the data.

The super user account holds all privileges and grants database privileges to other users. Privileges provide permissions to perform a task or a series of tasks. Some databases support the concept of *roles*, or groups of related privileges. A role gives a user a series of bundled privileges. Roles are convenient when you understand what they do. They're dangerous, however, if you lack knowledge about what they do, because you can inadvertently grant privileges that you shouldn't.

There are two types of security privileges. One type contains system privileges and the other contains object privileges. System privileges don't relate to a specific object or schema/database. Object privileges provide specific permissions to work with individual objects or schemas/databases.

System privileges allow wide-ranging actions and should be restricted to specific administrative user accounts. They allow a user to administer a system, create new privileges, change the behavior of existing privileges, change the behavior of system resources, or manipulate any type of object, such as tables, views, indexes, and so forth. DBAs have system privileges, and these privileges are often frequently provided to developers in small test systems. When developers package their code for integration testing and deployment, DBA system privileges run their code.

Object privileges grant specific access to a single user or set of users. These privileges often allow the user to manipulate data objects such as tables or views: a user can select, insert, update, or delete data. They also grant privileges to run or execute stored programs, such as stored functions, procedures, and in object-relational databases, instantiable objects. Object privileges also are granted to the DBA during implementation, but they are key components of application architectures. They allow the application designer to segment sets of tables and programs into separate schemas. These schemas act like packages in object-oriented programming languages.

Both system and object privileges can be revoked by the grantor or other super user. Any work the user does to the data while he or she has access to the system remains unaltered when privileges are revoked. Therefore, privileges should be granted only where appropriate and their use should be monitored.

Both the Oracle and MySQL databases support statements that let you grant and revoke privileges. These commands are collectively called *Data Control Language (DCL) statements*.

Data Control Language

DCL is a category of SQL that consists of two SQL statements, GRANT and REVOKE. Using these two commands, you can provision security privileges. That's a fancy way of saying you provide users the permissions to manage objects in the database and to add, change, or remove data from the database.

The types of privileges you grant can be system or object privileges. As you know, system privileges provide administrators with generalized rights or permissions. Object privileges are specific to databases or objects inside databases.

Any user who can grant privileges can extend to the grantee of a privilege the right to grant that privilege to others. An administrative user can grant WITH ADMIN OPTION for system privileges and WITH GRANT OPTION for object privileges. Make sure that these grant options are made infrequently and in conjunction with your company's security policy. The grantor may also revoke a grant option without revoking privileges. The WITH ADMIN OPTION is unique to Oracle databases, while the WITH GRANT OPTION is shared across Oracle and MySQL databases.

System Privileges

An example of a system privilege would be the ability to create any table in any schema. Different syntaxes are used for Oracle Database 11*g* and Oracle MySQL for this type of system privilege. Table 3-1 compares system privileges of the two databases. Dozens of Oracle Database 11*g* permissions are excluded because there are no equivalents in MySQL.

NOTE
ANY is an optional keyword and provides wide-ranging permissions in Oracle. This privilege shouldn't be granted to anyone except a DBA.

NOTE
Global-level permissions in MySQL are server-wide permissions. Database permissions, on the other hand, are limited to a single work area.

The approach to using the GRANT and REVOKE statements differs between the two databases. The following sections show you how to grant and revoke a system privilege in both Oracle Database 11*g* and Oracle MySQL.

Oracle Grant System Privileges   To understand the generalized form of the syntax, recall that user and schema are synonymous. When you grant a system privilege to create any table, you include the keyword ANY in front of an object type, such as a table. The ANY keyword indicates that it is a generic privilege that may apply to any schema.

Level	MySQL Privilege	Oracle Privilege(s)
Global	ALTER	ALTER ANY CLUSTER, ALTER ANY SEQUENCE, ALTER ANY TABLE, COMMENT ANY TABLE
Global	ALTER ROUTINE	ALTER ANY PROCEDURE, DROP ANY PROCEDURE
Global	CREATE	CREATE ANY CLUSTER, CREATE ANY DATABASE, CREATE ANY DATABASE LINK, CREATE ANY TABLE, CREATE ANY SEQUENCE, COMMENT ANY TABLE
Global	CREATE ROUTINE	CREATE ANY PROCEDURE
Global	CREATE USER	CREATE USER
Global	CREATE VIEW	CREATE ANY VIEW
Global	DELETE	ALTER ANY TABLE, DELETE ANY TABLE, DROP USER
Global	DROP	DROP ANY CLUSTER, DROP ANY SEQUENCE, DROP ANY TABLE, DROP ANY VIEW
Global	EXECUTE	EXECUTE ANY PROCEDURE
Global	INDEX	ALTER ANY INDEX, CREATE ANY INDEX, DROP ANY INDEX
Global	INSERT	INSERT ANY TABLE
Global	LOCK TABLES	LOCK ANY TABLE
Global	SELECT	SELECT ANY TABLE
Global	SUPER	SELECT ANY TABLE
Global	UPDATE	UPDATE ANY TABLE
Global	USAGE	ALTER SESSION, CREATE SESSION, UNLIMITED TABLESPACE
Database	CREATE	CREATE CLUSTER, CREATE DATABASE LINK, CREATE SEQUENCE, CREATE TABLE
Database	CREATE ROUTINE	CREATE PROCEDURE
Database	CREATE VIEW	CREATE VIEW

TABLE 3-1. *System Privilege Comparison*

System privileges are granted to the user and stand independent of their private work area, or schema. As the SYSTEM user, you would grant the system privilege using the following syntax:

```
GRANT CREATE ANY TABLE TO student;
```

With this privilege, the student user can create a table in any schema provided adequate space is allotted. That's something a DBA would want to do without connecting as the schema/user.

The DBA would sign on to his or her normal work area and issue a command that would create an object in another schema.

Here's the syntax to create a table in another user schema:

```
CREATE TABLE otheruser.sample (sample_id NUMBER);
```

Note that certain system privileges grant extraordinary rights. The data catalog shows that the `otheruser` account is the owner of the `sample` table. It would appear to anyone inspecting the data catalog that the table was created by the `otheruser` user.

After creating this `sample` table, you should revoke the system privilege granted. You would use the following syntax as the `SYSTEM` user:

```
REVOKE CREATE ANY TABLE FROM student;
```

NOTE
Don't forget to drop the table from the `otheruser` database. It's always a good practice to clean up experiments as soon as you're done with them.

MySQL Grant System Privileges   In MySQL, understanding the disassociation between user and database helps you understand the syntax for granting a system privilege. You must specify as a target of the `ON` subclause all databases and all objects by substituting an asterisk (*) for both a database and an object. In MySQL, you grant privileges to the user, not the database.

The proper way to grant all privileges on a database includes the user's method of access, as qualified in Chapter 2. The following syntax shows the `student` user enclosed in single quotes and separated by the @ symbol from the connection access permission that is also embedded in single quotes. This authorization method limits the grant to a student user, who connects through a local server user account. A wildcard (%) symbol in lieu of the `localhost` access permission would allow the user to connect from any local account or remote server:

```
GRANT CREATE ON somedatabase.* TO 'student'@'localhost';
```

The following syntax is important to understand but risky, because it grants wide privileges to a user. Specifically, it grants the `create` privilege on any type of object in any database. It's a bad idea to make such a broad grant of permissions to anyone other than an application DBA. Here's the syntax for such a grant:

```
GRANT CREATE ON *.* TO 'student'@'localhost';
```

You can create a table in any database with this system privilege. It's not a privilege that should be granted to anything other than an administrator's account, however. The syntax to create a table doesn't require that you be using that database at the time you run the statement. Here's the syntax with this system privilege:

```
CREATE TABLE otheruser.sample (sample_id INT UNSIGNED);
```

You can revoke this system privilege grant with the following command:

```
REVOKE CREATE ON *.* FROM 'student'@'localhost'
```

NOTE
Be sure to drop this table from the `otheruser` *database. Cleanup is always important and best done close to the event. Also, never grant a privilege unless you need to do so.*

Object Privileges

Object permissions differ from system permissions, because they link to a concrete resource, such as a table, view, or stored program. They let you grant permissions to a user to perform a task. Table 3-2 displays comparative object privileges between the databases, but some are excluded because they don't have equivalents on one side or the other. Some privileges simply don't map to equivalents, but they're included to give you the broadest perspective.

Level	MySQL Privilege	Oracle Privilege(s)
Object	ALTER	ALTER SEQUENCE, ALTER TABLE, COMMENT TABLE
Object	ALTER ROUTINE	ALTER FUNCTION, ALTER PROCEDURE, DROP FUNCTION, DROP PROCEDURE
Object	CREATE	CREATE CLUSTER, CREATE DATABASE, CREATE DATABASE LINK, CREATE SEQUENCE, CREATE TABLE, COMMENT TABLE
Object	CREATE ROUTINE	CREATE FUNCTION, CREATE PROCEDURE
Object	CREATE USER	CREATE USER
Object	CREATE VIEW	CREATE VIEW
Object	DELETE	DELETE
Object	DROP	DROP CLUSTER, DROP SEQUENCE, DROP TABLE, DROP VIEW
Object	EXECUTE	EXECUTE PROCEDURE
Object	FILE	READ, WRITE
Object	INDEX	ALTER INDEX, CREATE INDEX, DROP INDEX
Object	INSERT	INSERT
Object	LOCK TABLES	LOCK TABLE
Object	SELECT	SELECT TABLE
Object	SHOW VIEW	CREATE VIEW
Object	TRIGGER	ALTER TRIGGER, CREATE TRIGGER, DROP TRIGGER
Object	UPDATE	UPDATE
Object	USAGE	CREATE SESSION

TABLE 3-2. *Object Privilege Comparison*

Oracle privileges to work in the default work area or schema are grants to maintain structures, define stored programs, transact against the data, and run the stored programs. The user receives privileges to create, alter, and drop objects such as tables, views, stored programs, or triggers. They also receive privileges to insert, update, delete, or select data, and to execute stored programs.

Oracle Object Privileges Object grants work on tables, views, indexes, and stored programs. You can grant privileges one at a time or grant ALL privileges with a single command. A super user makes the following grant of all privileges on a table in the lib schema:

```
GRANT ALL ON lib.sample TO student;
```

A grant of ALL provides ALTER, DEBUG, DELETE, FLASHBACK, INDEX, INSERT, ON COMMIT REFRESH, QUERY REWRITE, REFERENCES, SELECT, and UPDATE privileges on the sample table to the student user. These permissions generally provide the access to interact with previously created tables. Tools such as Quest's Toad or Oracle SQL Developer let you discover these with a few mouse clicks. You can also query the user_tab_privs administrative view of the data catalog for this information.

A query such as the following that is run from the student schema discovers which privileges the student user holds on the sample table in the lib schema. This sample query would run from the SQL*Plus environment introduced in Chapter 2. The column commands allow you to format the output, with A*nn* meaning an alphanumeric left aligned string.

```
COLUMN OWNER        FORMAT A6
COLUMN TABLE_NAME   FORMAT A10
COLUMN GRANTEE      FORMAT A8
COLUMN PRIVILEGE    FORMAT A18
COLUMN GRANTABLE    FORMAT A10

SQL> SELECT    utp.owner
  2  ,          utp.table_name
  3  ,          utp.grantee
  4  ,          utp.privilege
  5  ,          utp.grantable
  6  FROM       user_tab_privs utp
  7  WHERE      utp.table_name = 'SAMPLE';
```

The column formatting is a SQL report writing feature available in SQL*Plus. The script returns the following data for the sample table:

```
OWNER   TABLE_NAME  GRANTEE   PRIVILEGE           GRANTABLE
------  ----------  --------  ------------------  ----------
LIB     SAMPLE      STUDENT   ALTER               NO
LIB     SAMPLE      STUDENT   DELETE              NO
LIB     SAMPLE      STUDENT   INDEX               NO
LIB     SAMPLE      STUDENT   INSERT              NO
LIB     SAMPLE      STUDENT   SELECT              NO
LIB     SAMPLE      STUDENT   UPDATE              NO
LIB     SAMPLE      STUDENT   REFERENCES          NO
LIB     SAMPLE      STUDENT   ON COMMIT REFRESH   NO
LIB     SAMPLE      STUDENT   QUERY REWRITE       NO
LIB     SAMPLE      STUDENT   DEBUG               NO
LIB     SAMPLE      STUDENT   FLASHBACK           NO
```

Notice that none of these privileges were granted WITH GRANT OPTION, which means the student user can't grant them to another user. If these privileges had been made through a role, you would query the user_role_privs administrative view. A role grant fails to write any information to the user_tab_privs view.

NOTE
Understanding which permissions are granted through roles is critical before assigning them to users. Decisions made about whether to use a role or collection of privileges rests with the DBA.

An alternative syntax could grant a subset of these privileges, like so:

```
GRANT SELECT, INSERT, UPDATE, DELETE ON lib.sample TO student;
```

The student schema can now transact against the lib.sample table, but it must reference the table by its schema first. Generally, an administrator wouldn't grant these privileges. The lib user would grant the privileges to the student user. Oracle provides a synonym that acts like an alias assignment. It's unique to Oracle, and there's no equivalent in a MySQL database. A synonym removes the required reference by placing a map of the full reference inside the data catalog. This makes the synonym a database catalog shortcut to a fully qualified path within the database.

When the student user holds the CREATE SYNONYM privilege, the student user can create a synonym with the following syntax:

```
CREATE SYNONYM sample FOR lib.sample;
```

Synonyms translate an alias to a fully qualified object address, such as the schema name, a component selector (the period), and a table name: lib.sample. The synonym can fail to translate when the grant is revoked or the remote object is deleted.

You can also revoke the previous grants. The next statement revokes the early grant of SELECT, INSERT, UPDATE, and DELETE from the student user on the sample table in the lib database:

```
REVOKE SELECT, INSERT, UPDATE, DELETE ON lib.sample FROM student;
```

A user can also grant the EXECUTE privilege on stored programs to other users. Those users, in turn, can create synonyms to reference the stored programs as if they were locally defined in the same schema.

MySQL Grant Object Privileges   MySQL grants object privileges on databases/schemas or tables. Like Oracle Database 11*g*, grants are made to users. You can grant wide-ranging privileges by specifying all objects with an asterisk (*). Security levels in MySQL differ from levels in Oracle, because user access permissions may be left open to all sources or they may be restricted by localhost, physical IP address, subdomain, or domain. Another substantial difference between Oracle and MySQL is that you must place single quote marks around the user name and the host access. Chapter 6 provides you with several configuration options for users with different privileges when they connect from different hosts.

You would grant all privileges on the lib database/schema to the student user with the following syntax:

```
GRANT ALL ON lib.* TO 'student'@'%';
```

The `student` user can now query and change data found in the `lib` database's tables and views. This grant information is stored in the MySQL database's catalog, which is found in the `mysql` database. A query-only copy of the database catalog exists in the `information_schema` database.

Although you could use MySQL Workbench or PHP MyAdmin to find this information, a query against the data catalog can be made as follows:

```
mysql> SELECT    sp.table_schema
    -> ,         sp.privilege_type
    -> ,         sp.grantee
    -> FROM      information_schema.schema_privileges sp
    -> WHERE     sp.table_schema = 'lib'
    -> AND       sp.grantee REGEXP '.*student.*';
```

The regular expression operator is the easiest way to match the grantee name, because it's stored with delimiting single quotes and a hostname. The query would return the following:

```
+--------------+-------------------------+----------------+
| table_schema | privilege_type          | grantee        |
+--------------+-------------------------+----------------+
| lib          | SELECT                  | 'student'@'%'  |
| lib          | INSERT                  | 'student'@'%'  |
| lib          | UPDATE                  | 'student'@'%'  |
| lib          | DELETE                  | 'student'@'%'  |
| lib          | CREATE                  | 'student'@'%'  |
| lib          | DROP                    | 'student'@'%'  |
| lib          | REFERENCES              | 'student'@'%'  |
| lib          | INDEX                   | 'student'@'%'  |
| lib          | ALTER                   | 'student'@'%'  |
| lib          | CREATE TEMPORARY TABLES | 'student'@'%'  |
| lib          | LOCK TABLES             | 'student'@'%'  |
| lib          | EXECUTE                 | 'student'@'%'  |
| lib          | CREATE VIEW             | 'student'@'%'  |
| lib          | SHOW VIEW               | 'student'@'%'  |
| lib          | CREATE ROUTINE          | 'student'@'%'  |
| lib          | ALTER ROUTINE           | 'student'@'%'  |
| lib          | EVENT                   | 'student'@'%'  |
| lib          | TRIGGER                 | 'student'@'%'  |
+--------------+-------------------------+----------------+
```

When you don't want to grant complete privileges on a database/schema, you can grant privileges on individual tables or views. A grant to the `sample` table in the `lib` database would be made with the following syntax:

```
GRANT ALL ON lib.sample TO 'student'@'%';
```

The grant of these permissions is found in the `table_privileges` view of the `information_schema` and is accessible with this modified query:

```
mysql> SELECT    tp.table_schema
    -> ,         tp.table_name
    -> ,         tp.privilege_type
```

```
    -> ,           tp.grantee
    -> FROM        information_schema.table_privileges tp
    -> WHERE       tp.table_schema = 'lib'
    -> AND         tp.table_name = 'sample'
    -> AND         tp.grantee REGEXP '.*student.*';
```

This query returns the following:

```
+---------------+------------+----------------+---------------+
| table_schema  | table_name | privilege_type | grantee       |
+---------------+------------+----------------+---------------+
| lib           | sample     | SELECT         | 'student'@'%' |
| lib           | sample     | INSERT         | 'student'@'%' |
| lib           | sample     | UPDATE         | 'student'@'%' |
| lib           | sample     | DELETE         | 'student'@'%' |
| lib           | sample     | CREATE         | 'student'@'%' |
| lib           | sample     | DROP           | 'student'@'%' |
| lib           | sample     | REFERENCES     | 'student'@'%' |
| lib           | sample     | INDEX          | 'student'@'%' |
| lib           | sample     | ALTER          | 'student'@'%' |
| lib           | sample     | CREATE VIEW    | 'student'@'%' |
| lib           | sample     | SHOW VIEW      | 'student'@'%' |
| lib           | sample     | TRIGGER        | 'student'@'%' |
+---------------+------------+----------------+---------------+
```

You can opt to grant only individual or comma-delimited privileges on an object with the following syntax:

```
GRANT SELECT, INSERT, UPDATE, DELETE ON lib.sample TO 'student'@'%';
```

This would grant only the four privileges to the `student` user on the `sample` table in the `lib` database. The previous query against the `table_privileges` table would return only the four rows, provided that the prior grant had been revoked first.

Unlike Oracle Database 11*g*, the Oracle MySQL 5.5 database doesn't support synonyms. You can *mimic synonyms* by creating a view of the same name in another database/schema. This practice works when the user has privileges to work in each database.

You can create a `sample` view in the `app` database that queries the qualified location of the `sample` table in the `lib` database like so:

```
mysql> CREATE OR REPLACE VIEW sample AS
    -> SELECT * FROM lib.sample;
```

You can also undo grants with the `REVOKE` statement, which lets you remove the privileges from the `student` user held on the `lib.sample` table. You can revoke a single privilege, such as selecting data, like so:

```
REVOKE SELECT ON lib.sample FROM 'student'@'%';
```

Alternatively, you can revoke a bundle of privileges using the following syntax:

```
REVOKE INSERT, UPDATE, DELETE ON lib.sample FROM 'student'@'%';
```

Grants are effective in managing security because they create contained compartments. Two patterns demonstrate the use of contained compartments, and they are commonly deployed for database-centric applications: the *definer* and *invoker rights* models.

Definer and Invoker Rights

The definer rights model is the default for Oracle Database 11*g* and Oracle MySQL 5.5 databases. Both databases also support the invoker rights model. Although the same general principals apply to these models, some differences exist between the implementations. Most are syntax related and of little consequence, but one key difference is important to note. MySQL doesn't support synonyms. The workaround is to create views for tables and wrapper subroutines for subroutines. Views were covered earlier in the "Security Privileges" section. Chapter 15 shows you how to write MySQL wrappers.

Definer Rights

A centralized data repository is synonymous with the definer rights model. The definer owns all objects that it creates and holds the right to query and transact with them. A definer can also grant rights on the tables, views, and stored programs to other users. Stored programs run with the same privileges as the definer. This is the application design pattern that supports VPDs. Effectively, every table becomes like an apartment building or a multiple tenancy building: some rows in the table belong to one user or privileged group while others belong to another user.

A definer rights model offers two advantages. The first lets you stripe your tables and wrap them in views so that only certain rows can be seen by specific users. The second lets you wrap access to the tables behind a series of stored functions and procedures, which provides an additional security barrier.

Opting to stripe tables requires that you add a column to them that stores a unique ID or name. A view implements a filtering clause that checks whether the current user or database matches the striped column value. This limits access to rows of data to information recorded during the session—the duration of a connection. It's similar to assigning apartment numbers to tenants in a large building.

The strategy of separating tables from connections is powerful. It compels programmers to use an application programming interface (API) rather than query and transact directly against the data. You can also set session-level variables with key data. For example, many business applications connect all users to the database with the same user name, password, and database name, but then validate against an Access Control List (ACL) stored in a table. Heading back to the analogy of a multiple tenant apartment building, every tenant has the same key to unlock the building's external door. Each tenant has a unique key to access his or her apartment. An ACL is a cabinet where spare keys to all the apartments are stored, indexed by apartment tenant.

When APIs wrap access to tables, they filter queries to a restricted list of rows. The APIs identify requestors by inspecting the ACL, determining their rights of access to rows, and filtering their access to those rows. APIs also provide another barrier to wide-open access to data tables. The parameters for the APIs guarantee access rules. APIs also let you control parameters by using prepared statements, which help minimize the possibility of SQL injection attacks.

Restricting web-based program components from directly accessing tables also provides a way to vet (audit and verify) parameters for SQL injection attacks. Using stored programs also gives you control over the scope and integrity of transactions, which presumes good development always uses transaction databases. Although individual DML statements are individually ACID-compliant and naturally Multiversion Concurrency Control (MVCC)–safe, stored programs extend those protections to sets of DML statements. This lets a complete business process have the same guarantee provided by individual DML statements.

The definer rights model also gives you control over table to table relationship designs, because the stored programs constitute an additional barrier to your data. They abstract or hide the internal structure of your tables and their relationships. This means that the design of tables, views, and relationships can change independently of web-based or other interfaces.

Overall, the definer rights model offers extremely strong benefits. The model doesn't offer good support for distributed data sets, however. The definer rights model isn't a good fit when the business requires independent database instances and consolidation models at fixed financial periods, such as weekly, monthly, quarterly, or yearly. Those types of models fit better with the invoker rights model, covered next.

Invoker Rights

Invoker rights models use distributed data repositories and a common code base. This means that all stored programs run with the rights of the invoker, or caller, of the programs. Therefore, the invoker must have access to any tables or views that the stored programs use, or the invoker must have his or her own copies. Typically, this requires that duplicate copies of the tables and views be deployed into every invoker's work area.

Adopting an invoker rights model inherently separates data into discrete work areas. This model is desirable when the business model supports franchisees that operate as separate business entities. In a franchisee model, application software helps the franchises operate the same way and collect critical information for consolidation. It also lets the central franchising operation control the look, feel, and integrity of data over which it doesn't have direct control.

Invoker rights also can parallel the idea of multiple tenancy housing, as discussed in the context of definer rights. It is a decidedly different model, however, because the tenants reside in different buildings in a complex, and each building has its own external door. Tenants in building A hold keys for building A and tenants in building B hold keys for building B, but both have keys to the common area. This is a model of a distributed database.

Years ago, the separate franchisees might operate on separate servers, but today these types of operations exist in virtual clouds. They often share a single deployment but retain control over their data. This type of model is used in many hosting companies around the world.

Invoker rights models don't prevent the striping of data, as discussed earlier, but they may disclose how that security information is managed. Note that the most effective implementations of invoker rights models define key parts of their solutions as definer rights components. Separation is critical in hiding how they manage security. Otherwise, disclosure to one franchisee may expose others to educated and directed hacking exploits. Therefore, the combination of both approaches makes for a stronger security deployment when the security component is implemented in a definer rights model.

Summary

This chapter covered security barriers and privileges and explored definer and invoker rights models. Security barriers are applied to various situations, from company firewalls, to account authentication, and each barrier should be secured in turn. Privileges exist for system and object components, and the syntax should be carefully examined, because these components are the key barriers to the company's crown jewels: its data.

The definer rights model is the default design paradigm and best suited to consolidated repositories. It offers options that can create an additional security barrier after database authentication. The invoker rights model lets you share a common code repository while replicating data into separately maintained databases.

Mastery Check

The mastery check is a series of true or false and multiple choice questions that let you confirm how well you understand the material in the chapter. You may check the Appendix for answers to these questions.

1. **True** ☐ **False** ☐ You start securing security barriers by setting object privileges inside the database and working outward.

2. **True** ☐ **False** ☐ The database stores encrypted passwords in the database.

3. **True** ☐ **False** ☐ Oracle validates only user name and encrypted password to start a database session.

4. **True** ☐ **False** ☐ Roles don't impede a hacker's discovery process after the hacker has connected to the database.

5. **True** ☐ **False** ☐ You can grant ALL privileges on a database or a schema to a user.

6. **True** ☐ **False** ☐ You can grant roles and privileges to a user.

7. **True** ☐ **False** ☐ Roles can contain one to many privileges.

8. **True** ☐ **False** ☐ The CONNECT and RESOURCE roles are recommended as best practices in Oracle Database 11*g* forward.

9. **True** ☐ **False** ☐ Oracle MySQL 5.5 was the first version to support roles.

10. **True** ☐ **False** ☐ MySQL's inability to create synonyms prevents you from creating a definer rights model that isolates access from code and data.

11. Which of the following isn't a security barrier that you should secure?

    A. The network

    B. The intranet

    C. File system permissions

    D. Uniform Resource Indicator (URI)

    E. Operating system accounts

12. Which of the following Oracle privileges are equivalent to the MySQL CREATE privilege?

    A. CREATE ANY TABLE

    B. CREATE ANY SEQUENCE

    C. CREATE ANY DATABASE LINK

    D. CREATE ANY CLUSTER

    E. CREATE ANY COMMENT

13. Which of the following are Data Control Language (DCL) statements?

     A. A `PRIVILEGE` statement

     B. A `ROLE` statement

     C. A `GRANT` statement

     D. A `REVOKE` statement

     E. A `PERMISSION` statement

14. Which of the following are the two types of privileges?

     A. System privileges

     B. Database privileges

     C. Table privileges

     D. Object privileges

     E. Resource privileges

15. Which clause lets you grant the right to grant system privileges?

     A. The `WITH ADMINISTRATOR OPTION`

     B. The `WITH GRANT OPTION`

     C. The `WITH GRANTOR OPTION`

     D. The `WITH ADMIN OPTION`

     E. The `WITH GRANTING OPTION`

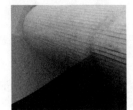

CHAPTER
4

Transaction Models

ransaction models depend on transactions, which are *ACID-compliant* blocks of code. Flip back to Chapter 1 for more detail on the properties of ACID-compliant transactions. This chapter defines common transactions and demonstrates how they work. We'll focuses on how ACID-compliant transactions work in a Multiversion Concurrency Control (MVCC) system, such as a commercial database. MVCC prevents one user from inadvertently interfering with or harming another user's work.

The smallest transaction in a database is a single SQL statement that inserts, updates, or deletes rows. SQL statements can also change values in one or more columns of a row in a table. Each SQL statement is by itself an ACID-compliant and MVCC-enabled transaction when managed by a transaction-capable database engine. The Oracle database is always a transaction-capable system, while MySQL is transaction-capable only when all tables are defined by the InnoDB engine. Transactions are typically a collection of SQL statements that work in close cooperation to accomplish a business objective. They're often grouped into stored programs, which are functions, procedures, or triggers. Triggers are specialized programs that audit or protect data. They enforce business rules that prevent unauthorized changes to the data.

This chapter covers the following:

- SQL statements
- Stored programs
- Triggers

SQL statements and *stored programs* are foundation elements for development of business applications. They contain the interaction points between customers and the data and are collectively called the Application Programming Interface (API) to the database. User forms (typically web forms today) access APIs to interact with the data. In well-architected business application software, the API is the only interface that the form developer touches.

Database developers, such as you and I, create these code components to enforce business rules while providing options to form developers. In doing so, database developers must guard a few things at all cost. For example, some critical business logic and controls must prevent changes to the data in specific tables, even changes in API programs. That type of critical control is often written in database triggers. *Triggers* are blocks of code that run when an event fires them. SQL statements are events that add, modify, or delete data. Triggers guarantee that API code cannot make certain additions, modifications, or deletions to critical resources, such as tables. Triggers can run before or after SQL statements. Their actions, like the SQL statements themselves, are temporary until the calling scope sends an instruction to commit the work performed.

For example, a database trigger can intercept values before they're placed in a column, and it can ensure that only certain values can be inserted or updated into a column. A trigger overrides an `INSERT` or `UPDATE` statement value that violates a business rule and either raises an error and aborts the transaction or changes the value before it can be inserted or updated into the table. Chapter 16 offers examples of both types of triggers in Oracle and MySQL databases.

Data Transactions

Data Manipulation Language (DML) commands are the SQL statements that transact against the data. They are principally the `INSERT`, `UPDATE`, and `DELETE` statements, and, respectively, add, change, or remove rows of data from tables. You'll learn more about these DML statements in Chapters 7, 8, and 9.

The Oracle MERGE and MySQL REPLACE INTO statements transact against the data by providing a conditional insert or update feature. Chapter 13 covers merging data with the MERGE and REPLACE INTO commands. Oracle also provides a conditional INSERT ALL statement that lets you insert into multiple tables from the same data source. Chapter 8 covers the INSERT ALL statement.

The INSERT statement adds new rows in a table. The UPDATE statement modifies columns in existing rows. The DELETE statement removes a row from a table. The MERGE statement lets you add new rows when they don't exist or change column values in rows that do exist. All of these statements are transactions by themselves, like the INSERT, UPDATE, and DELETE statements.

Inserting data seldom encounters a conflict with other SQL statements, because the values become a new row or rows in a table. Updates and deletes, on the other hand, can and do encounter conflicts with other UPDATE and DELETE statements. INSERT statements that encounter conflicts occur when columns in a new row match a pre-existing row's uniquely constrained columns. The insertion is disallowed because only one row can contain the unique column set.

These individual transactions have two phases in transactional databases, such as Oracle and MySQL with an InnoDB engine. The first phase involves making a change that is visible only to the user in the current session. The user then has the option of committing the change, which makes it permanent, or rolling back the change, which undoes the transaction. Developers use Data Control Language (DCL) commands to confirm or cancel transactions. The COMMIT statement confirms or makes permanent any change, and the ROLLBACK statement cancels or undoes any change.

Figure 4-1 shows a generic transaction lifecycle for a two-table insert process. The business rule requires that both INSERT statements work or neither works. If the first INSERT statement fails, the second INSERT statement never runs. If the second INSERT statement fails, the first INSERT statement is undone by a ROLLBACK statement to a SAVEPOINT. After a failed transaction is unwritten, good development practice requires that you write the failed event(s) to an error log table. The write succeeds because it occurs after the rollback but before the COMMIT statement.

An SQL statement followed by a COMMIT statement is called a *transaction process*, or a *two-phase commit (2PC)* protocol. ACID-compliant transactions use a 2PC to manage one SQL statement or collections of SQL statements. In a 2PC model, the INSERT, UPDATE, MERGE, or DELETE DML statement starts the process and submits changes. These DML statements can also act as events that fire database triggers assigned to the table being changed.

Transactions become more complex when they include database triggers, because triggers can inject an entire layer of logic within the transaction scope of a DML statement. For example, database triggers can do the following:

- Run code that verifies, changes, or repudiates submitted changes
- Record additional information after validation in other tables (they can't write to the table being changed—or, in database lexicon, mutate)
- Throw exceptions to terminate a transaction when the values don't meet business rules

As a general rule triggers can't contain a COMMIT or ROLLBACK statement, because they run inside the transaction scope of a DML statement. Oracle databases give developers an alternative to this general rule, because they support *autonomous transactions*. Autonomous transactions

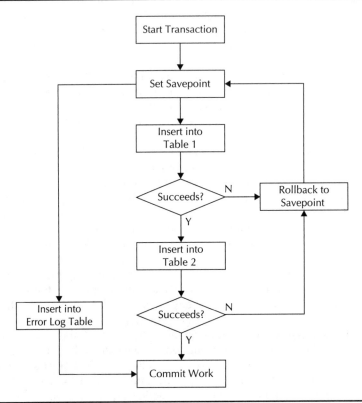

FIGURE 4-1. *Transaction lifecycle*

run outside the transaction scope of the triggering DML statement. They can contain a COMMIT statement and act independently of the calling scope statement. This means an autonomous trigger can commit a transaction when the calling transaction fails. This advanced behavior is covered in the "Triggers" section later in this chapter.

As independent statements or collections of statements add, modify, and remove rows, one statement transacts against data *only* by locking rows: the SELECT statement. A SELECT statement typically doesn't lock rows when it acts as a *cursor* in the scope of a stored program. A *cursor* is a data structure that contains rows of one to many columns in a stored program. This is also known as a list of record structures.

NOTE
The ability to lock rows for pending transaction statements is why the SELECT *statement is considered a DML command. That's generally accomplished by appending a* FOR UPDATE *clause in Oracle or MySQL.*

Cursors acts like ordinary SQL queries, except they're managed by procedural programs row-by-row. There are many examples of procedural programming languages. PL/SQL and SQL/PSM programming languages are procedural languages designed to run inside the database. C, C++, C#, Java, Perl, and PHP are procedural languages that interface with the database through well-defined interfaces, such as Java Database Connectivity (JDBC) and Open Database Connectivity (ODBC).

Cursors can query data two ways: One way locks the rows so that they can't be changed until the cursor is closed; closing the cursor releases the lock. The other way doesn't lock the rows, which allows them to be changed while the program is working with the data set from the cursor. The safest practice is to lock the rows when you open the cursor, and that should always be the case when you're inserting, updating, or deleting rows that depend on the values in the cursor not changing until the transaction lifecycle of the program unit completes.

Loops use cursors to process data sets. That means the cursors are generally opened at or near the beginning of program units. Inside the loop, the values from the cursor support one to many SQL statements for one to many tables.

Stored and external programs create their *operational scope* inside a database connection when they're called by another program. External programs connect to a database and enjoy their own operational scope, known as a *session scope*. The session, as covered in Chapter 1, defines the programs' operational scope. The operational scope of a stored program or external program defines the *transaction scope*. Inside the transaction scope, the programs interact with data in tables by inserting, updating, or deleting data until the operations complete successfully or encounter a critical failure. These stored program units commit changes when everything completes successfully, or they roll back changes when any critical instruction fails. Sometimes, the programs are written to roll back changes when *any* instruction fails.

In both Oracle and MySQL databases, the most common clause to lock rows is the FOR UPDATE clause, which is appended to a SELECT statement. An Oracle database also supports a WAIT *n* seconds or NOWAIT option. The WAIT option is a blessing when you want to reply to an end user form's request and can't make the change quickly. Without this option, a change could hang around for a long time, which means virtually *indefinitely* to a user trying to run your application. MySQL doesn't support this *wait* or *no wait* feature. The default value in an Oracle database is WAIT without a timeout, or wait indefinitely. You should avoid this default behavior when developing program units that interact with customers, and use NOWAIT or WAIT n (where n is a number of seconds).

MySQL does support the LOCK IN SHARE MODE clause for cursors. There is no equivalent implemented by Oracle at the SQL statement level. Oracle supports a full table lock with the SQL LOCK TABLE command, but you would need to embed the command inside a stored or external program's instruction set.

I've avoided actual code samples in the following sections because you haven't yet been introduced to the SQL statement syntax. Syntax at this point could serve as a distraction to learning how and why transactions work. Rather than code, process flow charts capture how SQL statements interact with tables in the database. The process flows and text highlight the nature of ACID-compliant transactions and MVCC management.

ACID-compliant SQL Statements

Any INSERT, UPDATE, MERGE, or DELETE SQL statement that adds, updates, or deletes rows in a table locks rows in a table and hides the information until the change is committed or undone (that is, rolled back). This is the nature of ACID-compliant SQL statements. Locks prevent other sessions from making a change while a current session is working with the data. Locks also restrict other sessions from seeing any changes until they're made permanent. The database keeps two copies of rows that are undergoing change. One copy of the rows with pending changes is visible to the current session, while the other displays committed changes only.

ACID-compliance relies on a 2PC protocol and ensures the current session is the only one that can see new inserts, updated column values, and the absence of deleted rows. Other sessions run by the same or different users can't see the changes until you commit them.

INSERT, UPDATE, and DELETE SQL statements each present a unique use case for inserting, updating, and deleting data. Another DML statement, MERGE, acts like a decision tree statement. You insert new data and update old data using a MERGE statement. MERGE statements are covered in depth in Chapter 12.

Each use case is represented by a flow chart that captures ACID-compliance properties and the steps in a 2PC protocol. Not all details are provided on triggers here, because they are more complex and covered fully in Chapter 16.

The following sections examine the three use cases: inserting, updating, and deleting data. Only the "INSERT Statement" section describes a use case that includes a database trigger, but the same trigger logic also applies to UPDATE and DELETE statements.

INSERT Statement

The INSERT statement adds rows to existing tables and uses a 2PC protocol to implement ACID-compliant guarantees. (Chapter 8 provides full coverage on the syntax and use of the INSERT statement.)

The SQL INSERT statement is a DML statement that adds one or more rows to a table. Oracle and MySQL support a VALUES clause when adding a single row and a subquery when adding one to many rows. MySQL also supports a VALUES clause that lets you add multiple rows as values, while Oracle doesn't. You can find syntax examples in Chapter 8.

Figure 4-2 shows a flow chart depicting an INSERT statement. The process of adding one or more rows to a table occurs during the first phase of an INSERT statement. Adding the rows exhibits both *atomic* and *consistent* properties. Atomic means all or nothing: it adds one or more rows and succeeds, or it doesn't add any rows and fails. Consistent means that the addition of rows is guaranteed whether the database engine adds them sequentially or concurrently in threads.

Concurrent behaviors happen when the database parallelizes DML statements. This is similar to the concept of threads as lightweight processes that work under the direction of a single process. The parallel actions of a single SQL statement delegates and manages work sent to separate threads. Oracle supports all ACID properties and implements threaded execution as parallel operations. All tables support parallelization, as you will see in Chapter 6.

After adding the rows to a table, the *isolation property* prevents any other session from seeing the new rows—that means another session started by the same user or by another user with access to the same table. The atomic, consistent, and isolation properties occur in the first phase of any INSERT statement. The durable property is exclusively part of the second phase of an INSERT statement, and rows become durable when the COMMIT statement ratifies the insertion of the new data.

Databases also support specialized code blocks that validate the authority, or the values of DML statements. These code blocks are database triggers. Triggers run once per statement or once per row processed by a statement. They're fired by INSERT, UPDATE, and DELETE

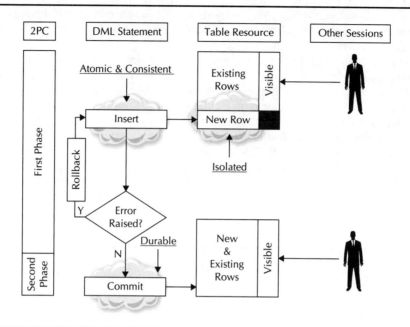

FIGURE 4-2.   *A 2PC INSERT statement*

Processes and Threads

A process is a running program. In most cases, an operating system allocates physical memory, disk space, and security permissions to let you run a process. A process can run sequentially or concurrently. A sequential process works through program instructions step-by-step, which is like swimmers in a relay race where one starts and ends before the next enters the pool, until the last enters and finishes the race. Processes that run concurrently have two scenarios. One scenario lets a process divide the program instructions into sets and then forks (starts) new processes to run subsets of program instructions. Forking launches a new process, which requires the allocation of new physical memory and disk space. Forked processes run with the same security permissions as their forking (or parent) process. Think of this as a swimmer who starts a workout in one pool, moves to another pool to swim some laps, and then returns to finish the workout in the original pool.

A second scenario lets a process divide a task into sets of instructions and allocate portions of its own resources to process the subtasks. These subtasks are threads, or lightweight processes. They can read and write to the memory area allocated to the parent process. Like small functions or methods, they can also read and write to local variables in their segment of the process memory. Because they share access to parts of a common process, they're not completely independent. That's why they're called lightweight processes. Think of a process as a pool of resources and threads as swimmers delegated to swim in specific lanes in the pool until they've collectively swam 100 laps.

statements. Developers deploy triggers by writing the program logic and then deploying them against specific tables. Not all tables have database triggers assigned to them. Chapter 16 provides full coverage on database triggers.

Every standalone INSERT statement adds one or more rows to a table, but not every statement fires a database trigger, even when one exists. When an ON INSERT trigger exists, an insertion to the table fires the trigger. The database triggers run during the first phase of 2PC protocol, between the DML statement and DCL COMMIT or ROLLBACK statement.

Figure 4-3 shows how an ON INSERT trigger runs between the INSERT statement and database tables. Because a row-level triggers act like an instruction inside a loop, it is repeated as long as there are rows to insert. (That iteration loop is excluded from the figure to simplify it.)

The figure also excludes the behavior of autonomous transactions, because they are discussed in the "Triggers" section later in this chapter. (You can flip there to see an explanation of the concept.)

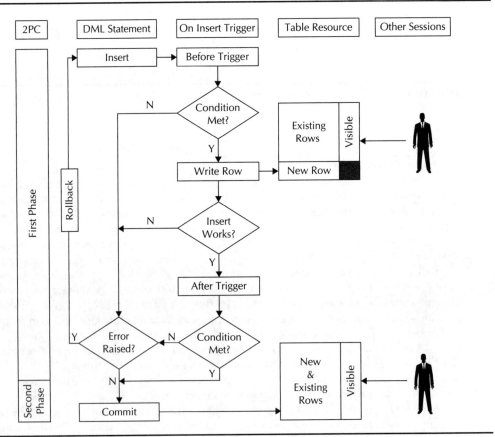

FIGURE 4-3. *2PC* INSERT *statement with a database trigger*

Surrogate, Natural, and Primary Keys

A *surrogate* key is an artificial numbering sequence that uniquely identifies every row in a table externally to other tables. A *natural* key is one or more columns in a table that uniquely identifies every row, and it allows you to find any row inside a table. Natural keys are also called unique keys. It is a good practice to ensure that a surrogate key matches each unique or natural key. Failure to ensure that match means you invite insertion, update, and deletion anomalies because the design fails to achieve a minimum of third-normal form (3NF).

3NF is the third level of the eight levels in the normalization process, which organizes data in relational models. 3NF requires two things: no transitive dependencies should exist between attributes—that is, no dependency exists between non-key columns; and the table must already be in second-normal form (2NF). 2NF also requires two things: All non-key attributes must depend on all of the *natural* key, which means a natural key defines uniqueness for all rows in a table. Also, the table should already be in first-normal form (1NF). 1NF is the basic foundation layer of normalization and requires that all columns together uniquely define an instance of the table, or row, and that every column is atomic. Atomic columns have a single data type and no more than one value of that data type.

Both surrogate and natural keys become candidates for selection as the *primary* key because they guarantee unique row selection. You should choose the surrogate key as the primary key because its role is external identification, which supports join operations to other tables. Then, you create an index (covered in Chapter 6) composed of the surrogate key and natural key to help the database engine find rows in the table more quickly than it could with a full table scan.

This practice is important for normalization, because occasionally design teams can evolve their understanding of the natural key. When you've based joins on a surrogate key and index, you can simply drop and re-create the index with the new knowledge. However, joins based on the natural key often require rewriting all SQL join statements between tables. The latter is simply too expensive and can be avoided by the use of surrogate keys. You can find more on joins in Chapter 11.

UPDATE Statement

An UPDATE statement changes column values in one-to-many rows. With a WHERE clause, you update only rows of interest, but if you forget the WHERE clause, an UPDATE statement would run against all rows in a table. Although you can update any column in a row, it's generally bad practice to update a primary or foreign key column because you can break referential integrity. You should only update *non-key data* in tables—that is, the data that doesn't make a row unique within a table.

Changes to column values are atomic when they work. For scalability reasons, the database implementation of updates to many rows is often concurrent, in threads through parallelization. This process can span multiple process threads and uses a transaction paradigm that coordinates changes across the threads. The entire UPDATE statement fails when any one thread fails.

Similar to the INSERT statement, UPDATE statement changes to column values are also hidden until they are made permanent with the application of the *isolation property*. The changes are hidden from other sessions, including sessions begun by the same database user.

It's possible that another session might attempt to lock or change data in a modified but uncommitted row. When this happens, the second DML statement encounters a lock and goes into a wait-state until the row becomes available for changes. If you neglected to set a timeout value for the wait-state, the FOR UPDATE clause waits until the target rows are unlocked:

```
WAIT n
```

As Figure 4-4 shows, actual updates are first-phase commit elements. While an UPDATE statement changes data, it changes only the current session values until it is made permanent by a COMMIT statement. Like the INSERT statement, the atomic, consistent, and isolation properties of an UPDATE statement occur during the first phase of a 2PC process. Changes to column values are atomic when they work. Any column changes are hidden from other sessions until the UPDATE statement is made permanent by a COMMIT or ROLLBACK statement, which is an example of the *isolation property*.

Any changes to column values can be modified by an ON UPDATE trigger before a COMMIT statement. ON UPDATE triggers run inside the first phase of the 2PC process. A COMMIT or ROLLBACK statement ends the transaction scope of the UPDATE statement.

The Oracle database engine can dispatch changes to many threads when an UPDATE statement works against many rows. UPDATE statements are consistent when these changes work in a single thread-of-control or across multiple threads with the same results.

As with the INSERT statement, the atomic, consistent, and isolation properties occur during the first phase of any UPDATE statement, and the COMMIT statement is the sole activity of the second phase. Column value changes become durable only with the execution of a COMMIT statement.

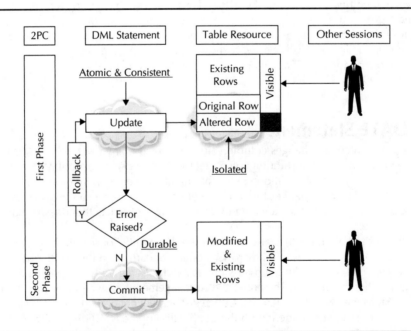

FIGURE 4-4. *2PC UPDATE statement*

DELETE Statement

A DELETE statement removes rows from a table. Like an UPDATE statement, the absence of a
WHERE clause in a DELETE statement deletes all rows in a table. Deleted rows remain visible
outside of the transaction scope where it has been removed. However, any attempts to UPDATE
those deleted rows are held in a pending status until they are committed or rolled back.

You delete rows when they're no longer useful. Deleting rows can be problematic when rows
in another table have a dependency on the deleted rows. Consider, for example, a CUSTOMER
table that contains a list of cell phone contacts and a table ADDRESS that contains the addresses
for some but not all of the contacts. If you delete a row from the CUSTOMER table that still has
related rows in the ADDRESS table, those ADDRESS table rows are now *orphaned* and useless.

As a rule, you delete data from the most dependent table to the least dependent table, which
is the opposite of the insertion process. Basically, you delete the child record before you delete
the parent record. The parent record holds the primary key value and the child record holds the
foreign key value. You drop the foreign key value, which is a copy of the primary key, before you
drop the primary key record. For example, you would insert a row in the CUSTOMER table before
you insert a row in the ADDRESS table; and you delete rows from the ADDRESS table before you
delete rows in the CUSTOMER table.

Figure 4-5 shows the logic behind a DELETE statement. Like the INSERT and UPDATE
statements, atomic, consistent, and isolation properties of the ACID-compliant transaction are
managed during the first phase of a 2PC. The durability property is managed by the COMMIT or
ROLLBACK statement.

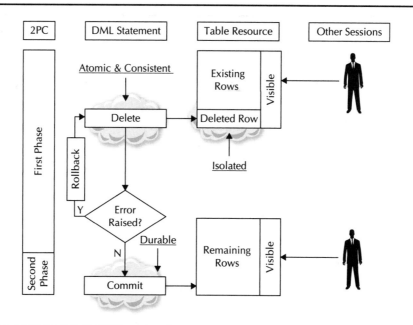

FIGURE 4-5. *2PC DELETE statement*

Stored Programs

Several varieties of stored programs can be used in Oracle and MySQL databases, but the basic types of programs are *procedures* and *functions*. Procedures are subroutines that don't return a value as an expression, which means you can't assign their results to a local variable. Functions are subroutines that return a value as an expression. This means you can assign their results to a local variable and use the return from a function as a call parameter to another function or procedure.

Stored programs are subroutines that group related DML statements into cohesive processing units. They provide programmers with APIs that perform complex tasks, such as taking a single stream of inputs and adding some of the inputs to one table and other inputs to another table. For example, you could send all the information to the subroutine to create a new customer, and inside the subroutine you would insert data to different tables. All inserts would need to work before you commit the changes, or you would undo all changes.

Such subroutines manage INSERT statement groups as a single transaction context and guarantee an all-or-nothing transaction lifecycle. They also hide the complexity of leveraging surrogate keys (sequences). Sequences are automatic numbering structures in databases and are covered in Chapters 6 through 8.

The key aspect of stored programs is that they interact generally with more than a single table and more than one DML statement. These stored programs also contain Data Control Language (DCL) commands to manage transactional integrity across a set of tables. This type of control is necessary because application integrity requires that all DML statements succeed or fail as a unit. Figure 4-6 shows the logic of how they ensure ACID-compliant transactions across several tables.

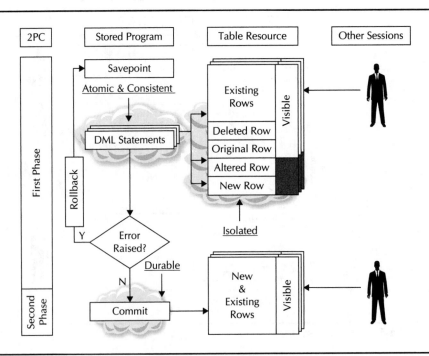

FIGURE 4-6. *Stored program transaction flow*

Transactions often perform many changes to different records, such as creating a new customer, defining a new address for that customer, and then creating an order for merchandise. Although each of these individual steps as a transaction is unique, and they're considered a transaction when they act as a group. Individual SQL statements can fail or succeed independently of each other, but when one fails, they all fail in the scope of a transaction.

To this end, stored procedures start with a `SAVEPOINT` statement, which sets a milestone in the scope of a connected session with the database. You set a `SAVEPOINT` by giving it a name, like this:

```
SAVEPOINT someSavepointName;
```

A `COMMIT` statement makes permanent, or durable, all changes in the stored program when everything happens correctly. A `ROLLBACK` statement undoes all changes when any one of the DML statements fails before *all of them* have completed normally. The rollback process has two options: One option rolls back to the beginning of the session or the last `COMMIT` statement in the session; the other option rolls back to a `SAVEPOINT` name. Here's the syntax for a rollback to a savepoint:

```
ROLLBACK TO someSavepointName;
```

CAUTION
SQL DDL statements, like ALTER, CREATE, or
DROP can create implicit commit points.

You might be wondering where to place DCL commands. One approach would be to include them in every stored program, and another approach would be to include them only in published API procedures. You must prevent independent calls to the other procedures when you place the DCL commands in only the published APIs. As a rule, I'd recommend this approach, because it affords you the most control over your application logic. Many strategies to organize stored programs to support this recommendation are covered in Chapter 15.

Stored programs generally run inside the transaction scope of a session. In this scenario, the calling scope program or DML statement *waits on completion* of the stored program. A more complex alternative exists in the Oracle database: you can call stored programs in a separate scope. This separate scope operates like an operating system process that forks another process. These independent scope stored programs are called *autonomous transactions* in an Oracle database, and they are *no-wait* operations. Autonomous transactions run outside the transaction scope of a session, which means they can commit their work when the calling scope fails to make permanent any work. Moreover, while autonomous procedures can raise exceptions, they have only a local impact, because they're run outside the calling scope.

In a no-wait operation, the calling scope program doesn't wait to find out if the called program worked or failed. It is a form of "optimistic processing," which means the calling scope program assumes it worked and chooses to take no action if it failed. This type of logic can be implemented with an autonomous stored procedure when all values are passed by value (see Chapters 13 and 14 for more on parameter modes), because the calling scope doesn't need to wait for its completion. It can't be implemented with an autonomous stored function, because a function must return a value on completion, and the calling scope program must handle the returned value from the function.

The next section expands coverage to discuss the basic purpose of database triggers in the scope of transaction management. A broader discussion of the specific syntax and approaches for triggers is in Chapter 16.

Triggers

Database triggers implement logic to control transactions, such as INSERT, UPDATE, and DELETE statements. Triggers are event-driven programs fired by DML statements and include ON INSERT, ON UPDATE, and ON DELETE triggers, as well as combination event triggers in both Oracle and MySQL databases. Some triggers fire once for a statement and others fire for each row inserted, updated, or deleted by a DML statement.

Triggers that fire once per statement are called *statement-level* triggers. Triggers that fire once per row are called *row-level* triggers. Row-level triggers can override values inserted or updated. Row-level triggers can also take copies of individual column values for INSERT, UPDATE, and DELETE statements and store them in another logging table. You would log values when security rules require that you monitor the tasks performed by authorized users. For example, you might want to record information about new loans greater than $50,000 when security rules allow a loan officer to make a car loan up to $100,000, but they should generally make loans of less than $50,000. It's a proactive way to give responsible employees some autonomy while maintaining audit controls to review some actions.

Triggers always occur during the first phase of a 2PC process. They run before or after a DML statement and they have the power to maintain business rules by raising an exception when they're violated—at least, they usually have that power. The exception to the rule is an autonomous trigger in an Oracle database. Like an autonomous procedure, an autonomous trigger can't raise an exception to signal failure because it is outside of the calling scope.

Autonomous transactions let you log activity that shouldn't occur without letting the end user know that the activity was observed. They're often used to monitor financial transactions for which users shouldn't attempt disallowed behaviors.

Database triggers are written in stored programming languages, such as PL/SQL or SQL/PSM. You also have the option in Oracle of writing database triggers in Java or any C-callable programming language.

Summary

Transaction models support ACID-compliant blocks of code. They can be individual DML statements, such as INSERT, UPDATE, and DELETE statements, or they can be stored programs. All ACID-compliant blocks of code run in 2PC protocol. The database engine ensures the atomicity, consistency, and isolation of individual DML statements between concurrent sessions. This control is known as Multiple Version Concurrency Control (MVCC).

Individual DML statements, such as INSERT, UPDATE, and DELETE statements, are the first phase of any transaction. The DCL COMMIT command makes changes permanent, and this occurs in the second phase of a transaction. The ROLLBACK command undoes transaction changes.

Stored programs operate as organized blocks of DML statements. They manage the set of DCL commands to ensure that all or none of them succeed or fail.

Database triggers provide event-driven controls that are fired by individual DML statements. They operate inside the first phase of the 2PC protocol.

Mastery Check

The mastery check is a series of true or false and multiple choice questions that let you confirm how well you understand the material in the chapter. You may check the Appendix for answers to these questions.

1. **True** ☐ **False** ☐ An INSERT statement is always ACID-compliant.

2. **True** ☐ **False** ☐ An UPDATE statement runs in the second phase of a two-phase commit.

3. **True** ☐ **False** ☐ A DELETE statement leaves deleted rows visible to all sessions until the COMMIT statement runs in another session.

4. **True** ☐ **False** ☐ You can create a single trigger that applies to multiple tables.

5. **True** ☐ **False** ☐ The industry uses 2PC as an acronym for two-phase commit.

6. **True** ☐ **False** ☐ A SELECT statement isn't a DML statement because it doesn't lock or change any data in tables.

7. **True** ☐ **False** ☐ You append the FOR UPDATE clause to DELETE statements when you want to lock the changes away from other sessions.

8. **True** ☐ **False** ☐ A MERGE statement provides INSERT or UPDATE behaviors.

9. **True** ☐ **False** ☐ MySQL supports a WAIT *n* seconds feature on SELECT statements used as cursors.

10. **True** ☐ **False** ☐ A lightweight process is part of a thread.

11. Which of the following lets you lock a subset of rows in a table in Oracle (multiple answers possible)?

    A. The FOR UPDATE clause

    B. The LOCK TABLE SQL command

    C. The LOCK IN SHARE MODE clause

    D. The LOCK IN EXCLUSIVE MODE clause

    E. The FOR LOCK clause

12. Which of the following lets you lock a subset of rows in a table in MySQL (multiple answers possible)?

    A. The FOR UPDATE clause

    B. The LOCK TABLE SQL command

    C. The LOCK IN SHARE MODE clause

    D. The LOCK IN EXCLUSIVE MODE clause

    E. The FOR LOCK clause

13. Which isn't a valid Data Control Language (DCL) statement in Oracle or MySQL?

    A. `COMMIT`

    B. `COMMIT IMMEDIATE`

    C. `SAVEPOINT savepointName`

    D. `ROLLBACK`

    E. `ROLLBACK TO savepointName`

14. Inside a stored program unit, what is the correct order for DCL statements?

    A. `SAVEPOINT sName, COMMIT IMMEDIATE, ROLLBACK`

    B. `SAVEPOINT sName, COMMIT NO WAIT, ROLLBACK`

    C. `SAVEPOINT sName, COMMIT NOWAIT, ROLLBACK`

    D. `SAVEPOINT sName, COMMIT, ROLLBACK TO sName`

    E. `SAVEPOINT sName, COMMIT IMMEDIATE, ROLLBACK TO sName`

15. You can use an `UPDATE` statement to perform which of the following?

    A. Update any column not in a unique index

    B. Update any column regardless of its role in the design

    C. Update only columns that aren't in the surrogate or natural key

    D. Update only columns that are in the surrogate or natural key

    E. Update only columns that are numeric, text, or dates

CHAPTER
5

Constraints

onstraints are critical components in databases. They *restrict* (constrain) what you can add, modify, or delete from tables with `INSERT`, `UPDATE`, and `DELETE` statements. Constraints let you restrict what can be placed in columns, rows, tables, or relationships between tables. That's a tremendously broad statement that requires some qualification. So what are these restrictions and why are they important?

As with the prior chapter, this chapter develops what and why before delving into the SQL implementation of database constraints that work with columns, tables, and relationships, which are covered in Chapters 6 and 7. Those chapters show you, respectively, how to implement constraints as you create new structures or modify them through maintenance activities. Chapters 6 and 15 cover constraints that restrict row behaviors, which include the `CHECK` constraint in an Oracle database and triggers in both Oracle and MySQL databases.

This chapter covers the following database constraints; database triggers are also included, because they hold the keys to advanced constraints:

- `NOT NULL`
- `UNIQUE`
- Primary key
- Foreign key
- `CHECK`
- Trigger

A preliminary understanding of constraint capabilities should help you focus on their respective roles as you read this chapter. Two types of constraints are used: column and table constraints. A column constraint applies to a single column. You define it in-line by adding it to the same line in which you define the column. In-line constraints don't require an explicit reference to the column because they apply to the column that shares the line. You can also define a column constraint after defining of all column values in both an Oracle and MySQL database. Constraints that follow the definition of columns are out-of-line constraints, because they are not placed on the same line as their column definition.

You create tables with the `CREATE` statement, covered in Chapter 6. The generalized definition of a `CREATE TABLE` statement is as follows:

```
CREATE TABLE table_name
( column_name data_type [inline_constraint] [, ...]
[, out_of_line_constraint [, ...]);
```

Some constraints involve more than a single column. Multiple-column constraints are *table constraints*. Table constraints are always defined after the list of columns as you create a table, because they depend on the column definitions. Alternatively, table constraints can be added to a table definition with an `ALTER TABLE` statement. Chapter 7 covers the syntax for maintenance activities such as the `ALTER TABLE` statement.

Figure 5-1 provides a matrix that compares constraints against the behaviors they can restrict: columns, rows, tables, and external relationships between tables.

Column-level constraints let you restrict whether a column can be empty or must contain a value. They also let you restrict the values that can be inserted into a column, such as only a *Yes* or *No* string, and restrict the values to a list of values found in another table (that's the role of a foreign key, as you'll discover later in this chapter).

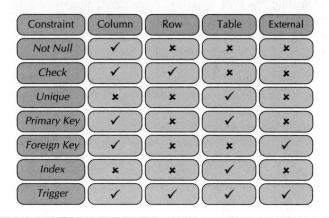

Constraint	Column	Row	Table	External
Not Null	✔	✘	✘	✘
Check	✔	✔	✘	✘
Unique	✘	✘	✔	✘
Primary Key	✔	✘	✔	✘
Foreign Key	✔	✘	✘	✔
Index	✘	✘	✔	✘
Trigger	✔	✔	✔	✔

FIGURE 5-1. *Constraint matrix*

Row-level constraints let you restrict the behavior of one or a group of column values in the same row. For example, you could constrain one column's value based on another column's value.

Table-level constraints let you restrict the behavior between rows in a table. A unique constraint on one or a group of columns prevents more than one row from having the same value for that column or group of columns.

External constraints are trickier, because they involve relationships between tables. They limit the value list of a column or a group of columns (foreign key) to those values already found in another column or group of columns (primary key) in another table or a copy of the same table. This type of constraint is known as a *referential integrity constraint* because it ensures that a reference in one table can be found in another.

The following sections qualify not null, unique, primary key, foreign key, and database trigger constraints. The sections describe differences between constraints in Oracle and MySQL databases.

NOT NULL Constraints

A NOT NULL constraint applies to a single column only, as shown in Figure 5-1. It restricts a column by making it mandatory, which means you can't insert a row without a value in the column. Likewise, you can't update a mandatory column's value from something to a null value. Optional columns are nullable or null-allowed. This means you can enter something or nothing, where nothing is a null value. Null values also differ from empty strings in MySQL.

In MySQL, the CREATE TABLE statement lets you assign a NOT NULL column constraint as in-line or out-of-line constraints. Oracle requires that you define NOT NULL constraints in-line. There's no option to add a NOT NULL constraint as a table constraint in an Oracle CREATE TABLE statement. You can, however, use the ALTER TABLE statement to add a NOT NULL constraint to an existing table's columns in both Oracle and MySQL databases.

NOT NULL constraints impose a minimum cardinality of 1 on a column, which typically makes the column's cardinality [1..1] (one-to-one). This is a Unified Modeling Language (UML) notation for cardinality. The UML notation assigns the minimum cardinality constraint to the number on the left and the maximum cardinality constraint to the number on the right. The two dots in the middle indicate a range.

Maximum cardinality is always considered one, because each column has one data type and one value in a relational model. The rule applies to all scalar data types.

The maximum cardinality rule changes in an object relational database management system (ORDBMS), such as an Oracle database. That's because it supports collection data types. In an ORDBMS, the maximum cardinality can be one to many, depending on what you measure. It is one when you measure whether a column contains a collection data type or not; and it's many when you measure the number of elements in a collection data type. Another twist is some arbitrary number between one and many, which happens with a VARRAY data type in an Oracle database. The VARRAY has a fixed maximum size like ordinary arrays in programming languages.

Some implementation differences exist between NOT NULL constraints in the Oracle and MySQL databases. The differences qualify where you can define them and how and when you can name them.

Cardinality

Cardinality comes from set mathematics and simply means the number of elements in a set. For example, in an arbitrary set of five finite values, a cardinality of [1..5] qualifies the minimum of 1 and the maximum of 5. This set expresses a range of five values.

In databases, cardinality applies to the following:

- The number of values in an unconstrained column within a row has a default cardinality of [0..1] (zero-to-one) for nullable columns. (The minimum cardinality of zero applies only to nullable columns.)

- The number of values in a NOT NULL constrained column within a row has a cardinality of [1..1] (one-to-one).

When there's no upward limit on the number of values in a column, it holds a *collection*. Collections typically contain [1..*] (one-to-many) elements and their cardinality is [0..*] (zero-to-many) in an unconstrained column.

Developers often describe the frequency of repeating values in a table as having low or high cardinality. *High cardinality* means the frequency of repeating values is closer to unique, where unique is the highest cardinality. *Low cardinality* means values repeat many times in a table, such as a gender column where the distribution is often close to half and half. A column that always contains the same value, which shouldn't occur, is in the lowest cardinality possible.

Cardinality also applies to binary relationships between tables. Two principal physical implementations of binary relationships exist: one-to-one and one-to-many. The one-to-many relationship is the most common pattern. In this pattern, the table on the one side of the relationship holds a primary key and the table on the many side holds a foreign key. In a one-to-one relationship, you choose which table holds the primary and foreign key.

Oracle NOT NULL Constraints

Oracle lets you create NOT NULL columns when you create tables and modify a column in an existing table to make it a NOT NULL or null-allowed column. You perform the former with the CREATE TABLE statement and the latter with the ALTER TABLE statement. Chapters 6 and 7 show you how to use the CREATE TABLE and ALTER TABLE statements.

All rows must be empty or contain data in the target column before you can add a NOT NULL constraint. You can remove a NOT NULL constraint from a column by using an ALTER TABLE statement.

You can mimic the behavior of a NOT NULL constraint by adding a CHECK constraint after the table is created. NOT NULL and CHECK constraints are stored exactly alike in the data catalog. Unfortunately, a NOT NULL restriction on a CHECK constraint isn't displayed when you describe the table. Using a CHECK constraint to mimic a NOT NULL constraint is not a good idea, because it can be misleading to other developers and disguise business rules.

You can also give meaningful names to NOT NULL constraints in an Oracle database when you create tables. These meaningful names help diagnose runtime violations of the constraint more easily than working with system-generated names.

NOTE
Chapter 6 shows syntax examples for creating columns with or without a NOT NULL constraint. Chapter 7 shows how to add and remove a NOT NULL constraint to or from an existing column.

Finding the name of a NOT NULL constraint is more difficult if you didn't assign a constraint name. You can also find the columns of a NOT NULL or CHECK constraint in the ALL_, DBA_, or USER_CONSTRAINTS and USER_CONS_COLUMNS view. You can use the following query to discover information about constraints:

```
COLUMN owner             FORMAT A10
COLUMN constraint_name FORMAT A20
COLUMN table_name        FORMAT A20
COLUMN position          FORMAT 9
COLUMN column_name       FORMAT A20
SELECT   ucc.owner
,        ucc.constraint_name
,        ucc.table_name
,        ucc.column_name
,        ucc.position
FROM     user_constraints uc INNER JOIN user_cons_columns ucc
ON       ucc.owner = uc.owner
AND      ucc.constraint_name = uc.constraint_name
WHERE    uc.constraint_type = 'C';
```

The same query works to return CHECK constraints, because NOT NULL constraints are variations on CHECK constraints in the data catalog.

MySQL NOT NULL Constraints

MySQL lets you create a table with NOT NULL columns. As with the Oracle database, MySQL lets you add and remove NOT NULL constraints to or from a column in an existing table. You can add a NOT NULL constraint when data exists in the table, provided no null values exist in the target column. There's no need to discuss why you should avoid a CHECK constraint, because they don't exist in MySQL.

UNIQUE Constraints

A UNIQUE constraint is a table-level constraint, because it makes the value in a column or set of columns unique within the table. Table-level constraints apply to relationships between columns, sets of columns, or all columns in one row against the same columns in other rows of the same table. UNIQUE constraints are out-of-line constraints set after the list of columns in a CREATE statement. Alternatively, you can add them through an ALTER statement after creating a table.

Every well-designed table should have a minimum of two unique keys: natural (covered in Chapter 4) and surrogate keys. The *natural key* is a column or set of columns that describes the subject of the table and makes each row unique. You can search a table for a specific record by using the natural key in a WHERE clause (see Chapter 11 for more on queries), which makes them internal identifiers within the set of data in a table. Natural keys are rarely a single column.

All *surrogate keys* are uniquely indexed as a single column. Surrogate keys are ID columns. They're generally produced from automatic numbering structures known as *sequences*. Chapter 6 describes sequences in detail. Surrogate keys don't describe anything about the data in the table. They do, however, provide a unique identifier that can be shared with other related tables. Then those related tables can link their data back to the table where the surrogate keys are unique.

The natural and surrogate keys are potential candidates to become the primary key of a data table. As such, they're also *candidate* keys. The primary key uniquely identifies rows in the table and must contain a unique value, as opposed to a null value. As a rule, you should choose the surrogate key as the primary key, because all joins will use the single column. This makes writing joins in SQL statements easier and less expensive to maintain over time, because surrogate keys shouldn't change or be reused. By itself, a surrogate key, a sequence-generated value, doesn't provide optimal search performance when you have lots of data. That's accomplished by a unique index made up of the surrogate key and the natural key. That type of index helps optimize databases to find and retrieve rows faster.

A UNIQUE constraint can apply to either a single column or a set of columns. You can create a UNIQUE constraint in Oracle or MySQL when you create or alter a table. The UNIQUE constraint automatically creates an index to manage the constraint. After all, it is a table constraint, and when you attempt to add a row that duplicates a unique column or set of columns, there must be a reference against which it can make a comparison to prevent it. Those reference points are *indexes*, and they're organized by a *B-Tree*, an inverted tree structure that expedites finding a matching piece of data. It brackets elements in groups and then subgroups until it arrives at the basic elements of data, which are the column or columns of data qualified as unique.

The next two sections qualify where you can find UNIQUE constraints. They also qualify some rules that govern how you can interact with them during creation and removal with the CREATE TALBE and DROP INDEX statements, respectively.

Oracle UNIQUE Constraints

As mentioned, you can create a table with a UNIQUE constraint or alter an existing table to add a UNIQUE constraint. Creating a UNIQUE constraint implicitly adds a unique index. The UNIQUE constraint is visible in the ALL_, DBA_, or USER_CONSTRAINTS administrative view of the database catalog. You can also find the columns of the UNIQUE constraint in a join of the ALL_, DBA_, or USER_CONSTRAINTS and USER_CONS_COLUMNS views. Likewise, you can find another entry for the UNIQUE constraint in the ALL_, DBA_, or USER_INDEXES and USER_IND_COLUMNS views.

The following query shows you how to check the Oracle database catalog for UNIQUE constraints:

```
COLUMN owner            FORMAT A10
COLUMN constraint_name  FORMAT A20
COLUMN table_name       FORMAT A20
COLUMN position         FORMAT 9
COLUMN column_name      FORMAT A20
SQL> SELECT    ucc.owner
  2  ,          ucc.constraint_name
  3  ,          ucc.table_name
  4  ,          ucc.position
  5  ,          ucc.column_name
  6  FROM       user_constraints uc INNER JOIN user_cons_columns ucc
  7  ON         ucc.owner = uc.owner
  8  AND        ucc.constraint_name = uc.constraint_name
  9  WHERE      uc.constraint_type = 'U';
```

The query returns a list of all UNIQUE constraints from the data catalog, and each UNIQUE constraint creates a UNIQUE INDEX. You cannot drop this implicitly created index because the UNIQUE constraint is dependent on it. An attempt to drop an implicitly created unique index results in an ORA-02429 exception. This exception's error message text aptly says that you cannot drop an index used for enforcement of a unique/primary key. However, you can alter the table and drop the UNIQUE constraint. The command also implicitly drops the supporting index.

NOTE
Chapters 6 and 7 contain sample SQL statements that let you create UNIQUE constraints in and drop UNIQUE constraints from tables. Chapter 7 also demonstrates how you can modify constraints within the ALTER TABLE statement.

MySQL UNIQUE Constraints

MySQL differs from Oracle in that no separate data catalog tables separate a UNIQUE constraint from a unique index. Like Oracle, the MySQL database lets you create a table with or modify a table to include a UNIQUE constraint. It is made visible only with the following command:

```
SHOW INDEXES { IN | FROM } table_name;
```

The IN or FROM keywords are synonymous. This provides a list of all unique and non-unique indexes that operate against a table.

The `information_schema` allows you visibility into the data catalog. You can find the `UNIQUE` constraints with the following query:

```
SELECT    tc.constraint_name
,         tc.constraint_type
,         kc.table_name
,         kc.ordinal_position
,         kc.column_name
FROM      table_constraints tc JOIN key_column_usage kc
ON        kc.constraint_schema = tc.constraint_schema
AND       kc.constraint_name = tc.constraint_name
AND       kc.table_schema = tc.table_schema
AND       kc.table_name = tc.table_name
WHERE     tc.constraint_type = 'UNIQUE'
ORDER BY 1,2,3,4;
```

The query returns a list of all `UNIQUE` keys and indexes with the participating columns in order. This gives you a snapshot of all `UNIQUE` constraints in the MySQL server.

Although there's no way to drop any index directly, both indexes and `UNIQUE` constraints are removed by altering the table and dropping the `UNIQUE` constraint or index from the table. `UNIQUE` constraints are dropped by using the `KEY` keyword, and indexes are dropped by using the `INDEX` keyword. Chapter 6 and 7 also contain examples to create and drop `UNIQUE` constraints in MySQL.

Unique Indexes

It is possible to create a unique index that stands apart from a `UNIQUE` constraint in both the Oracle and MySQL databases. These indexes maintain the same restriction as a `UNIQUE` table-level constraint because they create indexes to maintain uniqueness among rows in the table. The next two sections qualify the implementation specific details of unique indexes in Oracle and MySQL databases.

Oracle Unique Indexes

You can create an index as a standalone object in an Oracle database. Indexes behave differently than constraints. For example, there is no `UNIQUE` constraint visible in the `USER_CONSTRAINTS` administrative view of the database catalog or in the super user views of `ALL_` and `DBA_` `CONSTRAINTS`. However, you can find entries for unique indexes in the `ALL_`, `DBA_`, or `USER_` `INDEXES` and `USER_IND_COLUMNS` views.

This is similar to the query that finds `UNIQUE` constraints but it uses different views. It finds all unique and non-unique indexes:

```
COLUMN table_owner      FORMAT A10
COLUMN index_name       FORMAT A20
COLUMN table_name       FORMAT A20
COLUMN column_position  FORMAT 9
COLUMN column_name      FORMAT A20
SQL> SELECT    ui.table_owner
  2  ,          uic.index_name
  3  ,          ui.uniqueness
  4  ,          uic.table_name
```

```
 5  ,           uic.column_position
 6  ,           uic.column_name
 7  FROM        user_indexes ui JOIN user_ind_columns uic
 8  ON          uic.index_name = ui.index_name
 9  AND         uic.table_name = ui.table_name
10  WHERE       ui.uniqueness = 'UNIQUE';
```

You would find the non-unique indexes with the following change of line 10:

```
10  WHERE       ui.uniqueness = 'NONUNIQUE';
```

You also have the right to drop (or remove) indexes without modifying the table that the indexes organize. This is possible because no UNIQUE constraint is dependent on the unique index.

MySQL Unique Indexes

A MySQL unique index is indistinguishable from a UNIQUE constraint. In fact, you use virtually the same syntax to create or drop the index. Chapter 6 shows you how to create indexes and Chapter 7 shows you how to drop unique indexes. Feel free to flip there if you want to see the syntax now, but the differences are in the words KEY and INDEX. A CREATE statement that adds a UNIQUE table constraint excludes the word INDEX, while a constraint of a unique index uses the word INDEX.

You can use the query from the "MySQL UNIQUE Constraints" section because keys and indexes are stored in the same tables.

Primary Key Constraints

As mentioned, primary keys uniquely identify every row in a table. Primary keys are also the published identifier of tables. As such, primary keys are the point of contact between data in one table and that in other tables. Primary keys also contain the values that foreign key columns copy and hold. When using referential integrity, the primary and foreign keys shared values let you link data from different tables together through join operations.

Primary keys can be column or table constraints. They're column constraints when they apply to a single column, such as a surrogate key. They're generally table constraints when they apply to a natural key because natural keys usually contain more than one column. Natural keys often contain multiple columns, because that is generally how you qualify uniqueness in a record set.

A single column primary key exhibits two behaviors; these are *not null* and *unique*. A multiple column primary key can have a set of behaviors different from those of a single column primary key. Although the collection of columns must be not null and unique in the set, it is possible that one or more, but not all, columns can contain a null value. This rule is *not* consistently enforced across relational databases in the industry.

The next two sections qualify implementation rules for primary keys in Oracle and MySQL databases. They also show you how to query the status of constraints in the data catalog.

Oracle Primary Key Constraints

Oracle implements all primary keys as NOT NULL and UNIQUE. This means all columns in a single or multiple column primary key are *mandatory* columns. Any attempt to insert a null value in a column of a primary key generates an ORA-01400 error. The error message tells you that you cannot insert NULL into the primary key.

You can assign a meaningful name to primary key constraints, but Oracle assigns a system-generated name when you don't. It is much more difficult to trace back errors on primary key constraints unless you give them meaningful names. You can look up the definition of primary keys in the ALL_, DBA_, or USER_CONSTRAINTS and USER_CONS_COLUMNS administrative views. Primary keys always have a 'P' in the constraint_type column.

Here's the syntax for this query:

```
COLUMN owner           FORMAT A10 HEADING "Owner"
COLUMN table_name      FORMAT A20 HEADING "Table Name"
COLUMN constraint_name FORMAT A20 HEADING "Constraint Name"
COLUMN column_name     FORMAT A20 HEADING "Column Name"
COLUMN constraint_type FORMAT A1  HEADING "Primary|Key"

SQL> SELECT    ucc.owner
  2  ,          ucc.constraint_name
  3  ,          ucc.table_name
  4  ,          ucc.position
  5  ,          ucc.column_name
  6  FROM      user_constraints uc INNER JOIN user_cons_columns ucc
  7  ON        ucc.owner = uc.owner
  8  AND       ucc.constraint_name = uc.constraint_name
  9  WHERE     uc.constraint_type = 'P';
```

MySQL Primary Key Constraints

MySQL implements primary keys differently based on the type of engine that creates the table. Chapter 1 qualifies that MySQL 5.5 uses the InnoDB engine by default, because it is transactional. The InnoDB engine implements single and multiple column primary keys as UNIQUE and NOT NULL constrained. However, there's a twist to that implementation. An empty or zero length string isn't considered a null in MySQL. This makes it possible to insert an empty string in a character column when the column is part of or the only column in a primary key.

```
SELECT    tc.constraint_name
,          tc.constraint_type
,          kc.table_name
,          kc.ordinal_position
,          kc.column_name
FROM      table_constraints tc JOIN key_column_usage kc
ON        kc.constraint_schema = tc.constraint_schema
AND       kc.constraint_name = tc.constraint_name
AND       kc.table_schema = tc.table_schema
AND       kc.table_name = tc.table_name
WHERE     tc.constraint_type = 'PRIMARY KEY'
ORDER BY 1,2,3,4;
```

You can't assign a meaningful name to a primary key constraint in MySQL because it's always PRIMARY by default. The primary key is maintained just like other constraints. You also see a 'PRI' (abbreviation) in the KEY column when you describe a table.

Foreign Key Constraints

A foreign key constraint is both a column-level and external constraint. The column-level constraint restricts the list of values to those found in a primary key column or set of columns. The primary key column(s) generally exist in another table, which is why an external constraint exists. A self-referencing relationship occurs when the foreign key points to a primary key in the same table. In a self-referencing relationship, the primary and foreign keys are different columns or different sets of columns.

A foreign key constraint basically instructs the database to allow only the insertion or update of a column's value to a value found in a referenced primary key. Foreign keys always contain the same number of columns as the primary key, and the data types of all columns must match. The column and data type matching criteria is the minimum matching criteria. The values in the foreign key column(s) must match the values in the primary key column(s). More or less, foreign keys impose a boundary range of values on foreign key column(s).

The matching values in the foreign and primary key columns allow you to join rows found in one table to those found in another table. Joins between primary and foreign keys are made on the basis of equality of values between two columns or two sets of columns. These are called *equijoins*. (Check Chapter 11 for join possibilities and syntax.)

Foreign key constraints make the database responsible for enforcing cross-referencing rules. This cross-referencing is *referential integrity*, which means that a constraint reference guarantees a foreign key value must be found in the list of valid primary key values. Many commercial database applications don't impose referential integrity through constraints because companies opt to enforce them through stored programs. A collection of stored programs that protects the integrity of relationships is an application programming interface (API). The benefit of an API is that it eliminates the overhead imposed by foreign key constraints. This also means DML statements run faster without database-level constraint validation.

The downside of foreign key constraints is minimal but important to understand. Although foreign key constraints guarantee referential integrity of data, they do so at the cost of decreased performance. A nice compromise position on foreign keys deploys them in the stage environment (pre-production) to identify any referential integrity problems with your API.

NOTE
A stage environment is where stable information technology companies conduct end user and final integration testing.

Foreign key constraints are useful tools for Electronic Data Processing (EDP) auditors regardless of whether they're deployed to maintain referential integrity. For example, an EDP auditor can attempt to add a foreign key constraint to verify whether the API does actually maintain the

Mandatory or Optional Foreign Keys

A mistaken belief among some database developers is that a foreign key constraint restricts a column's cardinality such that it must have a value. A foreign key constraint does not implement a `NOT NULL` constraint. You must assign a `NOT NULL` constraint when you want to prevent the insertion or update of a row without a valid foreign key value.

integrity of relationships. An EDP auditor knows there's a problem with an API when a foreign key can't be added. That type of failure occurs because the data doesn't meet the necessary referential integrity rules. Likewise, an EDP auditor verifies the referential integrity of an API when foreign key constraints can be added to a primary-to-foreign key relationship. Such experimental foreign key constraints are removed at the conclusion of an EDP audit.

There are differences between foreign keys in Oracle or MySQL. The next sections discuss those differences and how to discover foreign key constraints.

Oracle Foreign Key Constraints

An Oracle foreign key constraint is very robust and can have three possible implementations:

- The default implementation prevents the update or deletion of a primary key value when a foreign key holds a copy of that value.

- Another implementation lets you delete the row but not update the primary key column or set of column values. This is accomplished by appending an ON DELETE CASCADE clause when creating or modifying the foreign key constraint.

- Another implementation updates the foreign key value to a null value when the row containing the primary key is deleted. Like the other options, you can't update the primary key column value. This implementation doesn't work when a foreign key column has a column-level NOT NULL constraint. In that case, any attempt to delete the row holding the primary key raises an ORA-01407 error, which reports that the foreign key column can't be changed to a null value.

You can disable a foreign key constraint in an Oracle database. This would let a DELETE statement remove the row that has a primary key value with dependent foreign key values. Enabling the foreign key constraint after deleting the row with the primary key raises an ORA-02298 error. The error indicates that the database can't validate the rule that the constraint supports, which is that every foreign key value must be found in the list of primary keys.

The Oracle database also requires that you add foreign key constraints as out-of-line constraints when creating a table. This means that foreign key constraints are treated as table constraints. You can add self-referencing foreign key constraints during table creation, but inserting values requires that the first row insertion validates its foreign key against the primary key value in the same row. This means the first row must have the same value for the primary and foreign key column or set of columns.

You can also find foreign keys in the ALL_, DBA_, or USER_CONSTRAINTS and USER_CONS_COLUMNS administrative views.

```
COL constraint_source FORMAT A38 HEADING "Constraint Name:| Table.Column"
COL references_column FORMAT A38 HEADING "References:| Table.Column"

SELECT   uc.constraint_name||CHR(10)
||       '('||uccl.TABLE_NAME||'.'||uccl.column_name||')' constraint_source
,        'REFERENCES'||CHR(10)
||       '('||ucc2.TABLE_NAME||'.'||ucc2.column_name||')' references_column
FROM     user_constraints uc
,        user_cons_columns uccl
,        user_cons_columns ucc2
WHERE    uc.constraint_name = uccl.constraint_name
```

```
AND       uc.r_constraint_name = ucc2.constraint_name
AND       ucc1.POSITION = ucc2.POSITION
AND       uc.constraint_type = 'R'
ORDER BY ucc1.TABLE_NAME
,         uc.constraint_name;
```

This is similar to the other queries against the database catalog. The only difference is that the constraint type value narrows it to referential integrity.

MySQL Foreign Key Constraints

Foreign key constraints in MySQL require the InnoDB engine, which becomes the default engine beginning with the MySQL 5.5 database. The InnoDB engine is a fully transactional model that supports referential integrity. Other MySQL engines may implement foreign key relationships but don't have the capability of enforcing a database constraint.

MySQL lets you create tables with foreign key constraints. Like the Oracle database, MySQL requires that you use out-of-line or table constraints inside CREATE TABLE statements. You also have the option of adding a foreign key constraint after you have created the table. The ALTER TABLE statement lets you add a foreign key to any column.

Type mismatches on primary and foreign keys can occur frequently when you're new to MySQL. For example, new users know that a primary key should be a positive number, and they naturally assign an *unsigned integer* as the data type of a surrogate primary key column. The same new users don't know that a foreign key must match exactly so that a foreign key constraint works. This mistake typically involves assigning a signed integer as the data type of a foreign key rather than an unsigned integer.

NOTE
It's a practice in MySQL to use an unsigned integer as the data type for surrogate keys until their sequence values approach the limit of 4.294 billion rows. At that point, you should adopt an unsigned double as the data type.

A type mismatch between a foreign and primary key throws an error when you try to connect, typically an Error 1005. This error message isn't very helpful or actionable, but you can read the InnoDB logs for more information by using the SHOW ENGINE command:

```
SHOW ENGINE innodb STATUS;
```

You can see more detail by unfolding the complete log if you're interested in the details. The significant part of the log to solve this type of problem is shown here:

```
------------------------
LATEST FOREIGN KEY ERROR
------------------------
100130 17:16:57 Error IN FOREIGN KEY CONSTRAINT OF TABLE sampledb/#sql-
FOREIGN KEY(member_type)
REFERENCES common_lookup(common_lookup_id):
Cannot find an INDEX IN the referenced TABLE WHERE the
referenced COLUMNS appear AS the FIRST COLUMNS, OR COLUMN types
IN the TABLE AND the referenced TABLE do NOT MATCH FOR CONSTRAINT.
```

You should ensure that all tables use the default InnoDB engine when you want to enforce foreign key relationships by database constraints. Foreign key constraints can be ignored when a designer opts to maintain referential integrity through an API.

You can also discover foreign keys in the `information_schema` database. This query lets you see your foreign keys:

```
SELECT    CONCAT(tc.table_schema,'.',tc.TABLE_NAME,'.',tc.constraint_name)
,         CONCAT(kcu.table_schema,'.',kcu.TABLE_NAME,'.',kcu.column_name)
,         CONCAT(kcu.referenced_table_schema,'.',kcu.referenced_table_name
          ,'.',kcu.referenced_column_name)
FROM      information_schema.table_constraints tc JOIN
          information_schema.key_column_usage kcu
ON        tc.constraint_name = kcu.constraint_name
WHERE     tc.constraint_type = 'FOREIGN KEY'
ORDER BY  tc.TABLE_NAME
,         kcu.column_name;
```

CHECK Constraints

CHECK constraints let you verify the value of a column during an insert or update. A CHECK constraint can set a boundary, such as the value can't be less than, greater than, or between certain values. This differs from the boundary condition imposed by foreign key constraints because CHECK constraints qualify their boundaries rather than map them to dynamic values in an external table.

As mentioned earlier in the NOT NULL constraint discussion, you can use a CHECK constraint to guarantee not null behaviors (qualified as a bad practice). Boundary conditions on the value of a column are typically column-level constraints. You also have set membership conditions. This type of validation works against a set of real numbers, characters, or strings.

Beyond the column-level role of a CHECK constraint, there are boundary and set membership conditions where the comparison values are the values of other columns in the same row. When the boundaries are set by the values of other columns in the same row, a CHECK constraint becomes a row-level constraint.

A simple boundary or set element example can also apply to row-level constraints. A row-level CHECK constraint can disallow the insertion of a null value when another column in the same row would also contain a null value. (A business rule that illustrates this type of need would be a menu item table that has separate columns that classify whether an item belongs on the breakfast, lunch, or dinner menu.)

Beyond boundary and set membership CHECK constraints, you have complex business rule conditions that involve checking multiple other columns for sets of business rules. These complex CHECK constraints are powerful tools, and in some cases are relegated to database triggers because not all databases implement CHECK constraints. Row-level constraints must be implemented in database triggers when CHECK constraints aren't supported in a database management system.

Basketball scoring provides a nice business rule for illustrating a *row-level* CHECK constraint that is complex. When a player scores a field goal from a shooting position outside the 3-point boundary, the goal is worth 3 points. Any other basket is worth 2 points, unless it is a free throw.

Free throws are worth 1 point. Let's assume the table designed to record points during the game contains the following three columns:

- An optional column (that's null allowed) records whether the basket was made from beyond the 3-point boundary; you enter an X when the condition is met: a field goal.

- An optional column (again, null allowed) records whether a basket was a free throw; you enter an X when the condition is met.

- A mandatory column for the number of points is constrained by values in the optional columns for a field goal and free throws. When the field goal column contains an X, you enter a 3. When the free throw column contains an X, you enter 1. When neither contains an X, you enter 2.

A hidden rule in the foregoing business logic is that an X can be inserted or updated only into the 3-point boundary column when the free throw column is null, and vice versa. It's hidden because it doesn't change the entry of a value for the points scored, only the entry of the Xs in the same row. You would implement CHECK constraints on the field goal and free throw columns that would verify that the other was null before allowing the insertion of a value in their respective columns.

The big difference between Oracle and MySQL on CHECK constraints is that MySQL doesn't support them. MySQL does support custom data types that mimic the member of sets boundary constraint. The next sections discuss what each database supports.

Oracle CHECK Constraints

Oracle supports boundary constraints, set membership, and complex logic CHECK constraints. This means you can avoid writing database triggers for many row-level constraints, which makes implementation actions easier. You will find the basketball example in Chapter 7 where it is shown as part of an ALTER TABLE statement.

The query for a NOT NULL constraint works for all CHECK constraints. You can find the rule enforced by a CHECK constraint in the search_condition column of the ALL_, DBA_, or USER_CONSTRAINTS view.

MySQL CHECK Constraints

MySQL doesn't support CHECK constraints. This means that you must implement row-level constraints inside database triggers. MySQL does support two data types that mimic the set membership condition of CHECK constraints: the ENUM and SET data types.

ENUM Data Type

The ENUM data type supports a set membership condition that is like a CHECK constraint. When you define a column with an ENUM data type, you list the possible elements in the set and any insert or update to the column must be found in the list. What's actually stored in the column is an index value that points to one of the elements in the list. The list is stored as a property of the column in the table definition of the database catalog.

An ENUM data type lets you choose one of the values from the list or a null, which makes its default cardinality [0..1] (zero-to-one). You can also place a NOT NULL constraint on a column using an ENUM data type, which makes its cardinality [1..1] (one-to-one). The ENUM data type restricts you to an exclusive choice between available values defined for the column. That means that you can enter the index of only one element from the list of possible values for the ENUM data type.

SET Data Type

The SET data type also supports a set membership condition and thus mimics a CHECK constraint. You are limited to 64 possible values in a SET data type. Like the ENUM data type, a SET data type stores an indexed table of values as a property of the column. A SET data type holds a series of strings.

Insertions and updates to a column with a SET data type can hold more than one reference index. This makes a SET data type an inclusive choice, which means you can enter from 1 to a maximum of 64 elements in a single column. This means that the SET data type lets you store an array of potential values in any column that uses the data type.

The default cardinality of a SET data type column is [0..64] (zero-to-sixty-four). A SET data type column that is NOT NULL constrained has a [1..64] (one-to-sixty-four) cardinality.

Trigger Constraints

Database triggers let you implement logic that enforces behaviors like database constraints. They let you restrict column-level and row-level behaviors and allow you to implement external constraints. These external constraints aren't limited to referential integrity through foreign key constraints.

Database triggers also don't let you perform table-level constraints, because they're run after a DML statement begins a transaction against a table. DML statements change the content of tables and fire triggers in the first phase of a two-phase commit (2PC) operation. DML statements also leave the change in an uncommitted state, which means the table is mutating, or undergoing change.

You define triggers to run when an event occurs against a table. Two types of triggers can be defined: statement- and row-level triggers. Triggers have limited options that govern how they act against data in their assigned table. Statement-level triggers can't do anything to the data inside their assigned tables, but row-level triggers can perform the following:

- Column-level validation, substitution, and in validation; that means they can see the proposed change and allow it or substitute values for it.

- Row-level validation, substitution and invalidation; that means they can see all proposed changes to columns and allow them or substitute all or part of them.

- Table-level validation, substitution, and invalidation; that means they can see all proposed changes to columns while exploring values in the same or different tables before making decisions to allow or disallow changes. They can also make substitutions where the values come from other tables.

Triggers are covered in this chapter because they're an option to database constraints. Triggers can be used to add row-level behaviors to any database regardless of whether it supports CHECK constraints.

Although triggers work differently in Oracle than they do in MySQL, the different performance characteristics are best left to Chapter 15. You have some foundational knowledge to acquire before you explore the details of how triggers work.

Summary

Database constraints provide you with the ability to restrict the behavior of DML statements at the column, row, and table levels. They also let you enforce external relationship constraints that restrict values from being added, changed, or removed from tables.

This chapter has covered NOT NULL, UNIQUE, primary key, CHECK, and foreign key database constraints, and it provided an introduction to the role of database triggers in restricting or modifying the behavior of DML statements. You have also been exposed to the Oracle and MySQL database implementation differences between these constraints.

Mastery Check

The mastery check is a series of true or false and multiple choice questions that let you confirm how well you understand the material in the chapter. You may check the Appendix for answers to these questions.

1. **True** ☐ **False** ☐ A database constraint can determine whether a column is mandatory or optional.

2. **True** ☐ **False** ☐ A database constraint can determine whether a row is unique in a table.

3. **True** ☐ **False** ☐ A database constraint can only accept or reject values for a column based on boundary conditions.

4. **True** ☐ **False** ☐ You can't add any database constraint during a CREATE TABLE statement.

5. **True** ☐ **False** ☐ You can implement referential integrity through database constraints.

6. **True** ☐ **False** ☐ Creating a UNIQUE constraint is straightforward and doesn't create any other dependent structures in the database catalog.

7. **True** ☐ **False** ☐ A mutating table doesn't prevent a database trigger from changing the input values of an INSERT statement.

8. **True** ☐ **False** ☐ Assigning an ENUM data type to a column acts like a CHECK constraint.

9. **True** ☐ **False** ☐ MySQL supports referential integrity in the MyISAM database engine.

10. **True** ☐ **False** ☐ A foreign key works when it has a signed int data type, while the primary key has an unsigned int data type.

11. Which of the following behaviors is/are supported by a primary key constraint (multiple answers possible)?

    A. A column-level behavior

    B. A row-level behavior

    C. A table-level behavior

    D. A mutating table behavior

    E. An external relationship behavior

12. Which of the following behaviors isn't supported by a database trigger?

    A. A column-level behavior

    B. A row-level behavior

    C. A table-level behavior

    D. A mutating table behavior

    E. An external relationship behavior

13. Which of the following constraints isn't supported by both Oracle and MySQL?

    A. A NOT NULL constraint

    B. A CHECK constraint

    C. A UNIQUE constraint

    D. An index constraint

    E. A foreign key constraint

14. Which of the following constraints are engine-dependent in MySQL?

    A. A NOT NULL constraint

    B. A CHECK constraint

    C. A primary key constraint

    D. A foreign key constraint

    E. A UNIQUE constraint

15. What types of conditions aren't supported by CHECK constraints?

    A. A boundary condition

    B. A set membership condition

    C. A nullable condition

    D. A unique condition

    E. A complex business rule based on multiple columns in the same row

PART
II

SQL Development

CHAPTER
6

Creating Users and Structures

n this chapter, you'll learn how to create users, databases, tables, indexes, constraints, sequences, and views in Oracle and MySQL databases. The chapter is organized by the following topics:

- Users
- Databases
- Tables
- Indexes

Users are synonymous with *schemas* in an Oracle database, but they are distinct from databases in MySQL databases. A *database* or *schema* is a private work area, but it is also a container of tables. *Tables* are two-dimensional containers of data, and *views* are logical filters to access subsets or supersets of tables. *Sequences* are structures that support automatic numbering of ID columns for tables. Sequences are described and explained in the "Tables" section in this chapter, because although they're independent data structures in an Oracle database, they're properties of tables in the MySQL database. *Constraints* are structures that restrict the type of data you can put in tables. Tables and constraints are also discussed in the "Tables" section.

Indexes are structures that hold search trees that help SQL statements find rows of interest faster. These search trees can be Balanced Trees (B-Trees), hash maps, and other mapping data structures.

Views are covered in Chapter 11, because that's where queries reign supreme; views are nothing more than named queries. Two types of views are used for reference: a *subset* view with a `SELECT` statement that filters data from a table, and a *superset* view with a `SELECT` statement that joins data from two or more tables.

If you wonder why stored programs aren't discussed in this chapter, it is because stored programs and triggers aren't data containers. Stored programs let you implement database-centric transaction management logic and APIs. As such, they are program logic containers. Stored programs are covered in Chapters 13–14 and database triggers are covered in Chapter 15.

The following sections introduce the generic behaviors of users, databases, tables, sequences, and views before qualifying the details of their implementation in Oracle and MySQL. The focus is on the things a developer needs to know.

Users

Users hold privileges to work in the database. Each database designates at least one default *super user*. The super user enjoys *all* privileges in the database. The following sections cover the behaviors of super users in Oracle and MySQL databases.

Oracle Users

The Oracle database defines two super users, `SYS` and `SYSTEM`, and follows the ANSI-SPARC architecture's three-tiered model. This architectural model divides the internal, conceptual, and external view of schemas or databases.

The *internal* view consists of the physical reality of how data is organized, which is specific to any DBMS. The internal view also contains the editable data catalog that maintains all the data about data, or *metadata*. This metadata contains all the definitions of users, databases, tables, indexes, constraints, sequences, data types, and views. Inside the internal view and with the proper credentials, a super user can alter the contents of the data catalog with Data Manipulation Language (DML) statements. That means an authorized user could use an `INSERT`, `UPDATE`, or `DELETE` statement to change critical metadata outside the administrative barrier of system privileges and Data Definition Language (DDL) statements.

NOTE
You should never use DML statements to change the data catalog values without the express instruction of Oracle Support.

The *conceptual* view consists of the community view of data. The *community view* is defined by the users with access privileges to the database, and it represents an administrator's view of data from the perspective of SQL. This view of data provides administrator friendly views of data stored in the data catalog.

It isn't possible to change the contents of the metadata in the community view, except through DDL statements such as `ALTER`, `CREATE`, and `DROP` statements. Developers can use only these DDL statements against objects, or in the case of the `ALTER` statement, against system and database environment settings. These types of environment settings enable such things as database traces measuring behavior and performance. More on these types of DDL statements can be found in the *Oracle Database 11g DBA Handbook*.

Oracle implements the concept of a community view as a collection of *striped views*. Striped views detect the user and allow them to see only things they have rights to access. These views typically start with `ALL_`, `DBA_`, and `USER_` prefixes, and you access them as you would any other table or view through queries with a `SELECT` statement. The `ALL_` and `DBA_` prefixed views are accessible only to the Oracle super users: `SYS`, `SYSTEM`, and user-defined accounts granted super privileges.

Every user has access to the community views prefixed with `USER_`. Those views provide access to structures only in the user's schema or personal work area. This approach is more secure than the read-only `information_schema` made available for the same purpose to all users in the MySQL Server.

The *external* view consists of access to the user's schema or database, which is a private work area. Users typically have complete control over the resources of their schema or database, but in some advanced architectures, users can have restricted rights. In those models, the user may be able to perform only the following tasks:

- Create tables and sequences
- Create or replace stored program units
- Provide or rescind grants and synonyms
- Limit access to memory, disk space, or network connections

Oracle's super users (`SYS` and `SYSTEM`) are synonymous with the two schemas for the internal (`SYS`) and conceptual (`SYSTEM`) views.

The differences between the definition of the internal view and the privileges conveyed when connecting as `SYS` aren't immediately visible. You cannot change things in the `SYS` schema when you connect as the SYS user, unless you connect with the / AS SYSOPER (*system operator*) or / AS SYSDBA (*system DBA*) privilege. You have full privileges as the system DBA but only a subset of privileges as the system operator. Typically, the only thing you perform with either of these responsibilities is routine maintenance or granting of specialized privileges. Routine maintenance would include starting and stopping the database. Specialized privileges include granting a user wider privileges or revoking privileges already granted, and defining the internal Java permissions though the DBMS_JAVA package. You can find more about using the DBMS_JAVA package in Chapter 14 of the *Oracle Database 11g PL/SQL Programming* book.

Although you can create new users and grant them privileges like the super user, you shouldn't alter the predefined roles of the super users. The next sections describe how you create users and grant privileges to or revoke privileges from a user.

Creating an Oracle User

Creating a user is synonymous with creating a schema in an Oracle database. Because of this, the topic is covered twice in this chapter: here and later in the "Database" section. Here we'll focus on the aspects of authentication, profile, and account status for an Oracle database user.

The SQL prototype to create a user allows you to identify the user with a password, an external SSL-authenticated certificate name, or a globally identified user name based on a Lightweight Directory Access Protocol (LDAP) entry. The certificate is a SSL (Secure Sockets Layer) file. It lets you encrypt your database credentials to support secure data communication.

The following syntax (similar to that in Chapter 2) lets you create a student user that is identified by a local database password:

```
CREATE USER student IDENTIFIED BY student;
```

One alternative to a local password is an SSL-authenticated certificate name, which would look like this:

```
CREATE USER student IDENTIFIED EXTERNALLY AS 'certificate_name';
```

The LDAP alternative would look the same but use a different source.

```
CREATE USER student IDENTIFIED EXTERNALLY AS 'CN=miles,O=apple,C=US';
```

Any of the three syntax methods can be used to create a private student work area, which is a schema. A number of other options are available for the default and temporary tablespaces of the work area, and quota syntax is available to limit the space authorized for a schema. These clauses are covered in the "Database" section later in the chapter.

Another clause allows you to assign a profile to users when you create them. That clause generally follows any tablespace assignments and quota limits. An example that assumes default assignment of tablespaces and quota limits would look like this with a local password:

```
CREATE USER student IDENTIFIED BY student
PROFILE profile_name;
```

Profiles allow you to restrict the number of concurrent user sessions, amount of CPU per call, and so forth. Profiles also let you impose restrictions or overriding password functions. The latter allows you to enhance the base security provided by the Oracle database, like surrounding the castle gate with a moat.

You can also set a password as expired. With this setting, when the user signs on with a provided password, he or she will be prompted to change it immediately. This is the best practice for issuing user accounts. Accounts are unlocked by default, but sometimes an account should be locked. For example, you might need to create the schema to reference it in another schema before planned use of the schema. These clauses generally follow all of those previously discussed. A sample CREATE statement with these clauses would look like this:

```
CREATE USER student IDENTIFIED BY student
PROFILE profile_name
PASSWORD EXPIRE
ACCOUNT LOCK;
```

You can use an ALTER statement to unlock the user account when the time comes to activate it. Chapter 7 shows the ALTER statement syntax to unlock an account.

Restricting access through the Oracle Transparent Network Substrate (TNS) is accomplished by configuring the Oracle networking stack. This is different from the authentication model in the MySQL database, where the user's point of access is part of his or her unique identification. For example, you can configure the sqlnet.ora file to restrict connections within a domain.

The following shows how to enable or exclude client machine access. The parameter lines go into the sqlnet.ora file on the server.

```
tcp.validnode_checking = yes
tcp.invited_nodes = (192.168.0.91)
tcp.excluded_nodes = (192.168.0.129)
```

The first parameter allows you to check whether the IP address is authorized or not. The second line shows you how to authorize a client, and the third line shows you how to prohibit a client from connecting to the Oracle database server.

After the user connects to the database, you can provide fine-grain access control through SQL configuration. For example, you can restrict a user's access down to the column level, as with a MySQL database, but you must put the logic into a stored program. Then, you grant execute privileges on the program only to users who should have limited access privileges. Unlike the MySQL Server, Oracle Database 11*g* doesn't support grants of privileges at the column level.

You can find full documentation on Oracle networking in the *Oracle Database Net Services Reference 11*g.

This concludes the basics of setting up a new user account. You can explore more on the topic in the *Oracle Database 11*g *SQL Reference* manual online.

Granting Oracle Privileges

Creating an account in an Oracle database doesn't automatically enable it for use. First you must grant basic permissions to use the account. The SYSTEM user or an administrator account created with the CREATE ANY USER privilege should run these commands.

As presented in Chapter 2, these are the basic privileges that you would want to extend to a default user. There you saw the syntax to limit access to physical space. Chapter 3 covers system

Oracle Network Tracing

Sometimes you need to trace what's happening in the Oracle portion of the network communication stack. You do that by configuring the `sqlnet.ora` file. It is possible to set four levels of tracing: Oracle Worldwide Support (16), Administration (10), User (4), and Tracing Off (0).

When you add the following parameters to the `sqlnet.ora` file, you generate a server-side network trace file:

```
trace_level_server = 10
trace_file_server = server.trc
trace_directory_server = <path_to_trace_dir>
```

The `trace_level_server` value designates the desired level of tracing. The setting shown here provides values at the local administrator level.

An alternative to server-side tracing is client-side tracing, which can be accomplished by adding a parameter to the `sqlnet.ora` file on the client, like this:

```
trace_level_client = 10
trace_unique_client = on
trace_file_client = sqlnet.trc
trace_directory_client = <path_to_trace_dir>
```

Network tracing is a valuable tool when you're debugging your application stack. You might likewise need to debug the processing instruction sets, and that is included in Chapter 13, where you'll learn how to write stored programs.

and object privileges. However, privileges don't work when you create a user without a default and temporary tablespace clause, unless you also grant UNLIMITED TABLESPACE as shown here:

```
GRANT create cluster, create indextype, create operator
,       create procedure, create sequence, create session
,       create table, create trigger, create type
,       create view, unlimited tablespace TO sample;
```

This type of GRANT statement lets you create a user in a small, developer-only environment, but you shouldn't do this in a production database. It works because you avoid assigning default and temporary tablespaces by granting unlimited space rights. This is never a good thing to do, except on your laptop! Some might say that you shouldn't do it on your laptop either, but this is something for you to decide.

The ALTER statement also lets you assign a default and temporary tablespace after a user is created. Both the CREATE and ALTER statements let you assign quotas to the default tablespace, but you can no longer assign a quota to the temporary tablespace. Any attempt to do so raises an error. This change became effective with Oracle Database 10*g*. You can find the syntax for the ALTER statement in Chapter 7.

Most commercial databases define user profiles and assign them when creating new users. You can find out more about that in the *Oracle Database 11g DBA Handbook*.

NOTE
Beginning with Oracle Database 10g Release 2, you can no longer assign a temporary tablespace quota.

A sample grant of select privileges, typically made by a user for his or her own schema objects, would look like this:

```
GRANT SELECT ON some_tablename TO some_user;
```

Sometimes a user wants to grant privileges to another user with the privilege to extend that privilege to a third party. This is the infrequent pattern of grants reserved for setting up administrative users. You append a `WITH GRANT OPTION` clause to give another user the right to provide others with the privileges you've conveyed to them:

```
GRANT SELECT ON some_tablename TO some_user WITH GRANT OPTION;
```

Oracle also supports the concept of a *synonym*, which simplifies how another user can access your object. Without a synonym, the other user would need to put your user name and a dot (`.`) in front of the object before accessing it. The dot is called a *component selector*. A synonym creates an alias that maps the user name, component selector, and object name to a synonym (alias) name in the user's work area or schema.

You don't need to use a component selector on objects that you create in your schema. They're natively available to you. The `SYS` super user has access to every object in the Oracle Database 11*g* Server by simply addressing objects by their fully qualified location—schema name, component selector, and object name. This makes perfect sense when you recall that the user and schema names are synonymous.

You create a synonym like this:

```
CREATE SYNONYM some_tablename FOR some_user.some_tablename;
```

Typically, the local table name is the same as the table name in the other schema, but not always. You can also grant privileges on a table to a `PUBLIC` account, which gives all other users access to the table. Public synonyms also exist to simplify how those users access the table.

You would grant the `SELECT` privilege to the `PUBLIC` account with this syntax:

```
GRANT SELECT ON some_tablename TO PUBLIC;
```

After granting the privilege, you create a public synonym with this syntax:

```
CREATE PUBLIC SYNONYM some_tablename FOR some_user.some_tablename;
```

As a rule of thumb, use the `PUBLIC` account only when you're granting privileges to invoker rights stored programs. Chapter 3 discusses the default definer and invoker rights models. Chapter 13 shows you how to define stored programs that run under definer or invoker rights models.

Revoking Privileges

You can revoke any privilege from a user provided you or a peer super user made the grant. Let's say you just finished reading Chapter 7 on the `ALTER` statement and realized that you should remove the `UNLIMITED TABLESPACE` privilege from the `student` user. That command would look like this:

```
REVOKE unlimited tablespace FROM student;
```

The funny thing about this revocation is that it doesn't immediately disable a user from writing to the tablespace generally. That's because revocation only disallows the allocation of another extent to any table previously created by the user. An extent is a contiguous block of space inside a tablespace. Extents are added when an `INSERT` or `UPDATE` statement can't add anything more in the allocated space. The number of extents allocated to a table is a measure of the fragmentation of the table on disk. Chapter 7 examines how you can defragment storage.

You can revoke privileges from the `PUBLIC` account with the same type of syntax:

```
REVOKE SELECT ON some_tablename FROM PUBLIC;
```

When you revoke privileges that included a `WITH GRANT OPTION` clause, make sure you also revoke the granting option. There should be a routine process in place for validating the grants and privileges to ensure that they comply with your company's governance policy and appropriate laws, such as Sarbane-Oxley in the United States. This is referred to as hardening. You can find more about hardening in an application context in the book *Oracle E-Business Suite Security*.

MySQL Users

The MySQL database defines one `root` super user. MySQL, like Oracle, supports the ANSI-SPARC architecture's three-tiered model. As mentioned, that model divides responsibilities into the internal, conceptual, and external view of schemas or databases.

MySQL provides access to the internal view to the `root` super user. The internal view or data catalog is stored in the `mysql` database. It is possible to edit the catalog as the `root` super user with DML statements, such as `INSERT`, `UPDATE`, and `DELETE`. Although it's not a best practice, it is done by DBAs from time to time.

The conceptual view was added in MySQL 5 as the `information_schema` database. It is a read-only copy of the `mysql` database. At the time of writing, all users have read-only access to this database. It actually provides more access to the database catalog than minimally authorized users should have, because they can explore definitions of other databases. This access to the `information_schema` compromises the principle of information hiding.

Like an Oracle database user schema, MySQL databases are the external views. Users that hold permissions on user-defined databases can run DDL statements against the database's tables, constraints, indexes, and views; and they can run DML statements against tables and views.

Creating a MySQL User

MySQL users are defined by three key attributes: the user name, password, and access point of origin. The user name is stored as a plain text string. The password is stored as an encrypted string. The access point origin, known as `host`, designates the permitted origin of communication with the MySQL database. The options for hostname are `localhost`, `hostname`, IP address, domain or subdomain address, or a wildcard, which is the percent (`%`) character.

The most generic way to create a user in MySQL excludes reference to the access point of origin. You would use the following syntax to implicitly create a user that can connect from anywhere:

```
CREATE USER 'some_username' IDENTIFIED BY 'some_password';
```

Alternatively, you could create the same user by qualifying anywhere, like this:

```
CREATE USER 'some_username'@'%' IDENTIFIED BY 'some_password';
```

When you want to link an access point through a DNS server lookup, you would qualify the user with the following syntax. This is the easiest configuration when you know the hostname, and IP addresses are provided through DHCP licenses that can change over time.

```
CREATE USER 'some_username'@'hostname.company.com'
IDENTIFIED BY 'some_password';
```

You can exclude the hostname and substitute an IP address to accomplish the same task. That's possible when user machines are assigned static IP addresses.

```
CREATE USER 'some_username'@'192.168.1.124'
IDENTIFIED BY 'some_password';
```

Limiting connections to machines within your company's domain is a common configuration for limiting developer connections. You would substitute a % as the wildcard for hostname before the domain name as the access point of origin to accomplish this, like so:

```
CREATE USER 'some_username'@'%.company.com'
IDENTIFIED BY 'some_password';
```

Another option lets you limit access points of origin to a subdomain within a company. Two options are available for that. The first uses the % wildcard operation and the other the IP number and netmask. Here's the wildcard subnet syntax:

```
CREATE USER 'some_username'@'192.168.%'
IDENTIFIED BY 'some_password';
```

Here's the more complex IP number and netmask:

```
CREATE USER 'some_username'@'10.0.0.0/255.255.255.0'
IDENTIFIED BY 'some_password';
```

This matches the first 24 bits of its IP number, which maps to 10.0.0. It lets a specified user connect from any host in the subnet 10.0.0!

The most restrictive connection is `localhost`, which means the user can connect only from the server where the MySQL database is installed. A user with only `localhost` as an access point of origin can't connect through a web server. Here's the syntax for a server only connection:

```
CREATE USER 'some_username'@'localhost'
IDENTIFIED BY 'some_password';
```

It's important to know that the IDENTIFIED BY clause may be *excluded when you create a user*. That means the user can initially connect to the database without providing a password.

Creating users without a password is not a good practice, but you can do it, so you should know how to add a password.

The `root` super user can add a password once the user is connected with the following syntax:

```
SET PASSWORD FOR 'some_username'@'%' = PASSWORD('some_password');
```

It is also possible for a connected user to set his or her own password. The syntax is virtually the same. Only the `FOR 'some_username'@'%'` clause is excluded, like this:

```
SET PASSWORD = PASSWORD('some_password');
```

Other, more advanced ways of creating users can be used as well. Specifically, it's possible in MySQL to create a user with the same name but different hosts and passwords. When you choose to do this, it means all subsequent grants of privileges must include the user, password (through the `IDENTIFIED BY` clause), and host.

At this point, a user is capable of connecting to the MySQL database but he or she can't do anything meaningful. A MySQL user enjoys more access than an Oracle user connecting with the /NOLOG option as demonstrated in Chapter 2. This appears as a security weakness that Oracle will fix eventually, but at the time of writing, a user without any permission can see the `information_schema` and connect to it. This means that once a nonprivileged user is connected, he can explore the information about databases that he can't see with the `SHOW` command.

Two-Face User

Sometimes you want to create a user who has different levels of access when they're working through different types of connections to the database. You can do this in the MySQL database, because users are uniquely resolved by a combination of their user name, password, and host connection designator.

Let's say you want a developer to have full control when she is working on the database server and only limited control when she is connecting through the network from a client. You define two instances of the user account. The first lets the `two_face` user connect from the server that's hosting the MySQL database, like this:

```
CREATE USER 'two_face'@'localhost'
IDENTIFIED BY 'some_password';
```

The second `two_face` user connects from somewhere in the company domain, like this:

```
CREATE USER 'two_face'@'hostname.company.com'
IDENTIFIED BY 'some_password';
```

Now you can grant different privileges to the `two_face` user based on where she is when she connects to the database server. The only catch is that all `GRANT` statements must include the user's unencrypted password. Naturally, this means you'll need to create a trivial password while managing the grants. You can reset the password later with the `SET PASSWORD` command, and the grants migrate to the correct user.

Granting MySQL Privileges

Granting privileges in MySQL differs slightly from how it's done in Oracle. Specifically, users are created separately from databases. This means users don't have private work areas when you create them. You have to create a user and a database, and then grant privileges on the database to the user. The "Databases" section of this chapter shows you how to create databases, but for this discussion you don't need to know that syntax.

Chapter 3 lists the privileges that you can grant. You have the option of granting all privileges or individual privileges. If you want to provide a user the equivalent privileges that an Oracle user enjoys, you grant all privileges on a database.

The syntax to grant all privileges on all objects uses the name of a database, a period, and a * (wildcard operator that represents any table or subroutine). Here's an example of the syntax:

```
GRANT ALL ON some_database.* TO some_username;
```

You can also grant limited privileges to a table, column of a table, or stored programs (also called a routine). The following syntax is used to grant privileges to query, update, and delete anything from a table:

```
GRANT ALL ON some_database.some_table TO some_username;
```

The alternative of granting only SELECT privileges would result in a GRANT statement like this:

```
GRANT SELECT ON some_database.some_table TO some_username;
```

Grants to a user who has two or more access points of origin requires that you append the IDENTIFIED BY clause with a plain text password. Here's the sample syntax:

```
GRANT SELECT ON some_database.some_table
TO some_username IDENTIFIED BY some_password;
```

Sometimes you want to grant restricted privileges on some columns to protect data in other columns of a table. MySQL supports this capability by letting you grant privileges at the column level. You do this by providing a comma-delimited list of authorized columns in parentheses. The following syntax prevents an update to a surrogate key column (typically an automatically numbered ID column), while providing rights to update another column, and the right to select (query), insert, or delete rows from the same table:

```
GRANT SELECT
,    INSERT
,    UPDATE (allowed_column_list)
,    DELETE ON some_database.some_table TO some_username;
```

This grants SELECT, INSERT, and DELETE privileges on the entire table, which is more often the case. The UPDATE privileges are restricted to a designated column.

You don't have the ability to perform this type of restricted grant in the Oracle Database 11*g*. The only way to deploy equivalent functionality would be in a row-level database trigger. Chapter 15 covers database triggers.

The next examples show you how to grant privileges on stored functions and procedures. Stored functions and procedures are the two types of stored programs supported by the MySQL database. This syntax uses the EXECUTE option to grant privileges to run a stored function, which is what you should always do. Some examples on the Internet use the `ALL` option, but that grants a user the ability to run and perform DDL commands on any schema. You don't want to extend the ability to drop a function or procedure beyond the user who is responsible for the code module. More or less, the rule of thumb is never to grant anything that's not absolutely required.

```
GRANT EXECUTE ON FUNCTION some_database.some_function TO some_username;
```

Alternatively, you simply replace the function name with a procedure name to give permissions to run a procedure:

```
GRANT EXECUTE ON PROCEDURE some_database.some_procedure TO some_username;
```

You can also grant privileges with the right to grant them to others. That's done by appending a `WITH GRANT OPTION` clause. The next example gives privileges to select data from a table and the ability to let that user grant the same privilege to select data to others:

```
GRANT SELECT ON some_database.some_table TO some_username
WITH GRANT OPTION;
```

As you can see, there's quite a combination of alternatives when you grant privileges in the MySQL database. The rule with these, as qualified in Chapter 3, is simple: grant privileges only as situations and plans require.

Revoking MySQL Privileges

Revoking privileges works the same way in MySQL as it does in Oracle. You can revoke a selection privilege from a user with the following syntax:

```
REVOKE SELECT ON some_database.some_table FROM some_username;
```

Conveniently, the MySQL database lets you revoke all privileges and the grant option in a single command. The neat thing about the command is you don't have to validate the privileges held by the user first, because it removes all privileges. Here's the syntax for the command:

```
REVOKE ALL PRIVILEGES, GRANT OPTION FROM some_username;
```

This works in all cases where a user has only one access point of origin. You need to qualify the access point of origin when a user exists in the database with two or more different hostname values. This would be the syntax for a company domain hostname:

```
REVOKE ALL PRIVILEGES, GRANT OPTION
FROM 'some_username'@'%.company.com';
```

The user name and hostname must be enclosed in single or double quotes and joined by the `@` symbol. The database uses the two arguments to resolve the ambiguity of the user existing two or more times in the data catalog.

Databases

The implementation of Oracle and MySQL databases differ in some respects, but they serve the same purpose. Databases are synonymous with schemas (or scheme in the Latin plural) and they act as work areas. Most Oracle documentation refers to them as schemas, while most MySQL documentation refers to them as databases. MySQL added *schema* as an alias for the *database* keyword in MySQL 5.0.2.

The significant difference between an Oracle schema and MySQL database is in who owns them. A schema is synonymous with a user in an Oracle database, because it's a private work area for the individual user. This means an Oracle schema is owned by its user. Dependent on the permissions of that Oracle user, he or she can grant privileges to others to use objects in their schema. A database in MySQL isn't owned by anyone in particular but is a private work area. Permissions to work in a MySQL database are granted by the prerogative of the `root` super user. The `root` user may grant limited or unlimited access on a database to one or more users. Grants of permissions can be as narrow as rights to query a single table or column in a table.

The next two segments show you how to define and use databases in Oracle and MySQL. These sections demonstrate the syntax that supports how you grant object privileges. They extend concepts discussed in Chapter 3 on database security.

Oracle Schemas

A brief sidebar in Chapter 2, "Create a Default Oracle User," discussed how you can create a basic database schema. This segment expands on that small example, which allowed you to create a `student` Oracle user/schema with a minimum set of permissions. A user in an Oracle database typically holds permissions to work in a single database schema only. Broader permissions can be granted with syntax covered in Chapter 3, but such grants are discouraged, as mentioned there.

The following syntax (from Chapter 2) lets you create a `student` account:

```
CREATE USER student IDENTIFIED BY student
DEFAULT TABLESPACE users QUOTA 50M ON users
TEMPORARY TABLESPACE temp;
```

It creates a limited account, because a quota limits physical size of the database container. You can add up to 50 megabytes of material in the `student` database, which is physically stored in the `users` tablespace. The `users` tablespace is available in all sample Oracle databases. Note that a *tablespace* is a logical unit that can contain one or more users. One or more physical data files are assigned to a tablespace to make it useful. You would define a `my_tablespace` tablespace of your own like this:

```
CREATE TABLESPACE my_tablespace
DATAFILE 'C:\Oracle\Data\my_tablespace01.dbf' SIZE 5242880
AUTOEXTEND ON NEXT 1310720 MAXSIZE 32767M
LOGGING ONLINE PERMANENT BLOCKSIZE 8192
EXTENT MANAGEMENT LOCAL AUTOALLOCATE DEFAULT NOCOMPRESS
SEGMENT SPACE MANAGEMENT AUTO;
```

This is the syntax Oracle uses to create the sample database's `users` tablespace. This designates the physical data file, assigns it an initial size of 5 MB, the amount to increase file size (an extent), and a maximum size. Then, it enables logging changes, places the tablespace online with a designated blocksize and delegated extent management of an uncompressed file. More on this can be found in the Oracle DBA Handbook (McGraw-Hill). After creating a tablespace, you can add more space to the tablespace by adding physical files. Chapter 7 contains the syntax for adding files to a tablespace.

You can discover the syntax for existing tablespaces by using the following query as the
SYSTEM user:

```
SET LONG 300000
SELECT dbms_metadata.get_ddl('TABLESPACE','USERS') from dual;
```

The SET LONG command expands the display size of output from the built-in function. The
first call parameter designates the object type you want to view, and the second call parameter
provides the object name. The function returns the DDL command that created the target object.

MySQL Databases

Another sidebar in Chapter 2 discussed how to set up a MySQL database. Like Oracle, the
super user holds the privilege for creating databases. This is the root super user in MySQL,
and this user can grant the system privilege to create databases to other administrative users.
The super user can also grant object privileges to users to work in databases.

MySQL users can be granted permissions directly from a super user to work concurrently
in multiple databases. MySQL databases are like schemas in an Oracle database, but they are
unassigned private work areas or containers. They hold tables, views, and stored programs.

A super user creates a database with either of the following syntaxes:

```
CREATE DATABASE studentdb;
```

or

```
CREATE SCHEMA studentdb;
```

By default, MySQL 5.5 and later versions use the InnoDB engine and use the InnoDB
tablespaces defined in the my.ini (Windows) or my.cnf (Linux) file. A default community
edition configuration of those files would look like this:

```
# The home directory for InnoDB
innodb_data_home_dir="C:/MySQL55 InnoDB Datafiles/"
# Memory pool that is used by InnoDB to store metadata information.
innodb_additional_mem_pool_size=3M
# If set to 1, InnoDB will flush (fsync) the transaction logs to the
# disk at each commit, which offers full ACID behavior.
innodb_flush_log_at_trx_commit=1
# The size of the buffer InnoDB uses for buffering log data.
innodb_log_buffer_size=2M
# InnoDB, unlike MyISAM, uses a buffer pool to cache indexes and row data.
innodb_buffer_pool_size=107M
# Size of each log file in a log group.
innodb_log_file_size=54M
# Number of threads allowed inside the InnoDB kernel.
innodb_thread_concurrency=8
```

After creating the database, the super user would create a student user and grant the user
access to a studentdb database with syntax that does the following: specifies from where they

can connect to the database, such as `localhost`, an IP address, or domain, or provides connection from any location. The syntax possibilities are shown in the following examples.

- Connecting only from the `localhost` (or same machine as the database server):

```
CREATE USER 'student'@'localhost' IDENTIFIED BY 'student';
GRANT ALL ON studentdb.* TO 'student'@'localhost';
```

- Connecting only from a designated IP address:

```
CREATE USER 'student'@'172.16.123.129' IDENTIFIED BY 'student';
GRANT ALL ON studentdb.* TO 'student'@'172.16.123.129';
```

- Connecting only from a domain:

```
CREATE USER 'student'@'*.mydomain.com' IDENTIFIED BY 'student';
GRANT ALL ON studentdb.* TO 'student'@'*.mydomain.com';
```

- Connecting from anywhere:

```
CREATE USER 'student'@'%' IDENTIFIED BY 'student';
GRANT ALL ON studentdb.* TO 'student'@'%';
```

Note that the user must be defined for the access route designated in the grant of permissions. If the access route and permissions don't agree, the grant won't work. If you're not sure which databases exist, you can run the following show command:

```
show databases;
```

This lists the databases that an individual may access. The `root` user sees all available database in the MySQL server.

Tables

Database tables are two-dimensional record structures that hold data. Grants of permissions to read and write data are most often made to tables. Sometimes grants restrict access to columns in tables.

Although databases contain tables, tables contain data organized by data types. A data type is the smallest container in this model. It defines what type of values can go into its container. Data values such as numbers, strings, or dates belong respectively in columns defined as numeric, variable length string, and date data types. Data types that hold a single value are scalar data types (or, to borrow some lingo from Java, primitive data types). Tables are seldom defined by a single column. They are typically defined by a set of columns. The set of columns that defines a table is a type of data structure. It is more complex than a single data type because it contains a set of ordered data types. The position of the elements and their data types define the structure of a table. The definition of this type of structure is formally a *record structure*, and the elements are fields of the data structure.

This record structure description can be considered the first dimension of a two-dimensional table. The rows in the table are the second dimension. Rows are organized as an unordered list, because relational operations should perform against all rows regardless of their positional order.

Tables are defined by the DDL `CREATE TABLE` command. The command provides names for columns, data types, default values, and constraints. The column, data type, and default values must always be defined on the same line but constraints can be defined two places. Defining a constraint on the same line as a table column is defining an in-line constraint. This is the typical pattern for *column constraints,* such as a NOT NULL or a single column PRIMARY KEY. You can opt to define column constraints after all columns are defined. When you do so, the constraints are out-of-line constraints. Sometimes constraints involve more than one column. Constraints that apply to two or more columns are *table constraints.*

A NOT NULL constraint is always a column constraint. The ANSI SQL standard requires that all columns in tables be unconstrained by default. An unconstrained or *nullable column* is an optional column when you insert or update a row. A *not null column* is a mandatory column when you insert or update a row. Both the Oracle and MySQL databases adhere to this ANSI standard use. Note that Microsoft SQL Server doesn't adhere to the standard, because it makes all columns mandatory by default.

RDBMS implementations comprise five basic groups of data types: numbers, characters, date-time intervals, large objects, and Boolean data types. The Boolean data type was added in ANSI SQL:1999, and it includes three-valued logic: true, not true, and null. It adopts three-valued logic because the ANSI SQL-89 and later standards accept that any column can be a null allowed—or, simply put, a column can contain no value or be empty.

Although RDBMSs determine which data types they'll support, they also determine how they'll implement them. Some data types are scalar or primitive data types, and others are built on those primitive data types. Only Oracle (and PostgreSQL) supports building composite data types that can be implemented as nested tables.

The Oracle Database 11*g* does not support a Boolean data type. The MySQL database supports an alias Boolean, which maps to a TINYINT data type. The TINYINT data type holds a numeric value of either 0 or 1.

The lack of a Boolean data type does sometimes cause problems, because standard comparison operators don't work with null values. Null values require the IS or IS NOT comparison operator, which is a reference operator rather than a value comparison operator. Table design and management should take into consideration the processing requirements to handle three-valued logic of pseudo-Boolean data types effectively.

Oracle and MySQL also support cloning tables. Rather than repeat an example in both the Oracle and MySQL sections of this chapter, the syntax is better placed here:

```
CREATE TABLE target_table_name AS SELECT * FROM source_table_name;
```

This syntax replicates the structure of an existing table in a new table. It also clones, or copies, all the data from the source table to the target table. When you incorporate a storage

Three-Valued Logic

Three-valued logic means basically that if you find something is true when you look for truth, it is true. By the same token, when you check whether something is false and it is, then it is false. The opposite case isn't proved. That means when something isn't true, you can't assume it is false, and vice versa.

The third case is that if something isn't true, it can be false or null. Likewise, if something isn't false, it can be true or null. Something is null when a Boolean variable is defined but not declared, or when an expression compares something against another variable that is null.

clause in an Oracle database, this process allows you to disable constraints, move the table contents, drop the table, and re-create it with contiguous space. Naturally, you should drop the extra copy after re-creating the table.

The following sections address how you create tables in Oracle and MySQL databases. They individually highlight and compare similarities, differences, and portability.

Oracle Tables

Oracle supports scalar data types, object types, and collections of scalar data types and object types. The collections are also known as object tables. Oracle databases support two uses of object tables. One lets you return a result set through a stored function, which is extremely useful and demonstrated in Chapter 13. The other lets you define a table with columns that use an object table as their data type—basically a table within a table. A table within a table is called a nested table.

This section covers the generalized syntax and how to define the following:

- Sequences
- Scalar data type columns
- Nested table data types
- Column and table constraints
- Externally organized tables
- Partitioned tables

You'll create small, single-column tables in the "Scalar Data Type Columns" sections and explore some database constraints. The nested table data types section shows you how to define a SQL record structure and then deploy it in a table. The column and table constraints section reviews in detail the available approaches to database constraints, some of which are covered in earlier data type sections. The partitioned tables section demonstrates approaches to partitioning the data storage.

Oracle Database 11*g* provides two options when creating tables: You can create ordinary tables that persist from session to session or create temporary tables that exist only during the duration of the session. As a rule, temporary tables are not liked by DBAs because they inherently fragment disks. You should make sure that you work with your DBA when you opt for temporary tables, because the DBA might have created a special tablespace for temporary tables to minimize impacts on other tables.

CAUTION
It's a bad idea to create temporary tables without consulting the DBA about them. This will ensure that you don't inadvertently fragment the production database.

You would create a table like this, where the ellipses represents columns and constraints:

```
CREATE TABLE table_name (...);
```

The general and basic prototype for a relational table with the `CREATE TABLE` statement without storage clause options is:

```
CREATE [GLOBAL] [TEMPORARY] TABLE [schema_name.] table_name
( column_name data_type [{DEFAULT expression | AS (virtual_expression)}]
  [[CONSTRAINT] constraint_name constraint_type]
, [column_name data_type [{DEFAULT expression | AS (virtual_expression)}]
  [[CONSTRAINT] constraint_name constraint_type]
, [...]
, [CONSTRAINT constraint_name constraint_type(column_list)
  [REFERENCES table_name(column_list)]]
, [...]);
```

You create a temporary table by inserting two keywords and one of two clauses. The clauses can be `ON COMMIT PRESERVE ROWS` or `ON COMMIT DELETE ROWS`. The former lets the rows remain during the session, whereas the latter makes the table transactional. You would create a session-based temporary table, like so:

```
CREATE GLOBAL TEMPORARY TABLE table_name
ON COMMIT PRESERVE ROWS
AS
SELECT i.item_title FROM item WHERE i.item_title LIKE 'Star%';
```

Figure 6-1 shows you how the `CREATE TABLE` statement defines a permanent table with different types of column and table constraints. The figure is annotated to help you see available possibilities when you create tables.

In-line constraints are always single column constraints, and they apply to the column defined on the same line. Out-of-line constraints are defined after the last column in a table. When an out-of-line constraint applies to a single column, it is a column constraint. A table constraint is an out-of-line constraint that applies to two or more columns defined in the table. Oracle's `CHECK` constraint and generic `PRIMARY KEY`, `UNIQUE`, and `FOREIGN KEY` constraints can apply to more than a single column, and that makes them possible table constraints.

Sequences

Oracle Database 11*g* doesn't support automatic numbering in tables. It provides a separate `SEQUENCE` data structure for use in surrogate keys. Surrogate keys are artificial numbering sequence values that uniquely define rows. They're typically used in joins, because subsequent redefinition of a natural key doesn't invalidate their ability to support joins across tables. The "Indexes" section later in this chapter qualifies how to use surrogate key columns with the natural key to define row uniqueness and optimize joins.

A typical sequence holds a starting number, an incrementing unit, and a buffer cycling value. Each time you call the sequence with a `sequence_name.NEXTVAL` statement, the value of the sequence increases by one (or whatever else was chosen as the `INCREMENT BY` value). This occurs until the system consumes the last sequence value in the buffer cycle. When the last value has been read from the buffer cache, a new cycle of values is provided to the instance. The default for the cycle or sequence buffer is a set of 20 number values.

You create a `SEQUENCE` structure with the default values, like this:

```
CREATE SEQUENCE sequence_name;
```

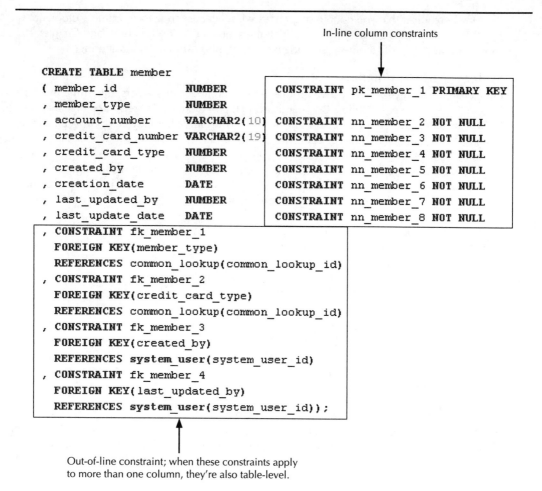

In-line column constraints

```
CREATE TABLE member
( member_id              NUMBER          CONSTRAINT pk_member_1 PRIMARY KEY
, member_type            NUMBER
, account_number         VARCHAR2(10)    CONSTRAINT nn_member_2 NOT NULL
, credit_card_number     VARCHAR2(19)    CONSTRAINT nn_member_3 NOT NULL
, credit_card_type       NUMBER          CONSTRAINT nn_member_4 NOT NULL
, created_by             NUMBER          CONSTRAINT nn_member_5 NOT NULL
, creation_date          DATE            CONSTRAINT nn_member_6 NOT NULL
, last_updated_by        NUMBER          CONSTRAINT nn_member_7 NOT NULL
, last_update_date       DATE            CONSTRAINT nn_member_8 NOT NULL
, CONSTRAINT fk_member_1
  FOREIGN KEY(member_type)
  REFERENCES common_lookup(common_lookup_id)
, CONSTRAINT fk_member_2
  FOREIGN KEY(credit_card_type)
  REFERENCES common_lookup(common_lookup_id)
, CONSTRAINT fk_member_3
  FOREIGN KEY(created_by)
  REFERENCES system_user(system_user_id)
, CONSTRAINT fk_member_4
  FOREIGN KEY(last_updated_by)
  REFERENCES system_user(system_user_id));
```

Out-of-line constraint; when these constraints apply
to more than one column, they're also table-level.

FIGURE 6-1. *Oracle CREATE TABLE statement*

Sometimes application development requires preseeding (inserting before releasing an application to your customer base) rows in tables. Such inserts are done manually without the sequence value or with a sequence starting at the default START WITH value of 1. After preseeding the data, you drop the sequence to modify the START WITH value because Oracle doesn't provide an alternative to modifying it.

Preseeding generally inserts 10 to 100 rows of data, but after preseeding data, the START WITH value is often set at 1001. This leaves developers an additional 900 rows for additional post-implementation seeding of data. You create a sequence starting at that value like this:

```
CREATE SEQUENCE sequence_name START WITH 1001;
```

Oracle requires that you couple sequences with database triggers to mimic automatic numbering. Chapter 8 shows you how to call the sequence to insert values, and Chapter 15 shows you how to write the necessary trigger that supports automatic numbering.

Scalar Data Type Columns

Oracle supports only four of the five groups in SQL: numbers, characters, date-time-intervals, and large objects data types. While a Boolean is available in Oracle's Procedural Language extension, PL/SQL, it isn't provided for as a data type in SQL. Your only alternative to a Boolean data type would be to implement a number data type that mimics a Boolean, as you'll see in the "Boolean" section a bit later.

You also have support for virtual columns, which are created by concatenating or calculating values from other column values in the same row. This became available in Oracle Database11*g*. Virtual columns are typically scalar values, and they're discussed in the last subsection of this section.

Figure 6-2 shows you the data types for SQL. Each standalone box contains a group, and within each group are other boxes that contain subgroups.

NOTE
Remember that a Boolean doesn't exist as a default type.

Oracle also supports ANSI-compliant data types that automatically map to native Oracle data types. Writing scripts in the ANSI standard data types makes your scripts more portable to MySQL databases. Table 6-1 shows you the data type mapping when you use the ANSI standard aliases. Some types don't exist in the Oracle ANSI set, such as `TEXT` for a character large object. Oracle uses `CLOB` for that data type.

Number Data Type   Numbers have four subgroups: three use proprietary Oracle math libraries—binary integers, `PLS_INTEGER`, and `NUMBER` data types. The new IEEE 754 variable data types use the operating system math libraries and are recommended when you want to do more than financial mathematics. For example, a cube root of 27 has mixed results in PL/SQL with the `**` (double asterisks) exponential operator and a `NUMBER` data type, but works perfectly with a `BINARY_DOUBLE` data type.

You can put whole numbers or decimal numbers in any of the numeric data types except the integer types—they only take integers. Number data types allow you to qualify precision and scale. *Precision* is the number of allowed digits that fall before and after a decimal point. *Scale* is the number of allowed digits that follow the decimal point. This same concept applies to the `DEC`, `DECIMAL`, `NUMERIC`, `BINARY_DOUBLE`, and `DOUBLE_PRECISION` data types. For example, the following sets 12 as the maximum number of digits with 2 digits on the right of the decimal point. You define the precision and scale for `DECIMAL` numbers inside parentheses and separated by a comma.

```
SQL> CREATE TABLE sample_number
  2  (column_name   NUMBER(12,2));
```

You can inspect the table by describing it in a SQL*Plus session, or displaying it in SQL*Developer. Here's the SQL*Plus command:

```
DESCRIBE sample_number
```

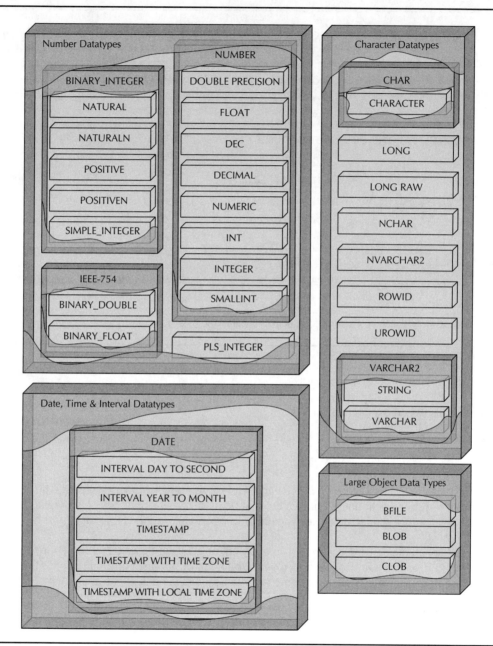

FIGURE 6-2. *SQL scalar types*

ANSI Data Type	Native Data Type	Physical Size
BLOB	BLOB	8 to 32 terabytes
CHAR(n)	CHAR(n)	2000 bytes
DATE	DATE	Date and time to hundredths of a second
DECIMAL(p,s)	NUMBER(p,s)	1×10^{38}
DOUBLE PRECISION	FLOAT(126)	1×10^{26}
FLOAT	FLOAT(126)	1×10^{26}
INT	NUMBER(38)	1×10^{38}
INTEGER	NUMBER(38)	1×10^{38}
NUMERIC(p,s)	NUMBER(p,s)	1×10^{38}
REAL	FLOAT(63)	1×10^{63}
SMALLINT	NUMBER(38)	1×10^{38}
TIMESTAMP	TIMESTAMP(6)	Date and time to hundredths of a second
VARCHAR(n)	VARCHAR2(n)	4000 bytes

See text for explanation of parenthetical numbers/characters

TABLE 6-1. *Oracle ANSI SQL Data Type Map*

It displays the following:

```
Name                     Null?    Type
------------------------ -------- --------------
COLUMN_NAME                       NUMBER(12,2)
```

The preceding syntax creates a one column table with a single numeric column. The column value is optional because it doesn't have a column NOT NULL constraint, which would appear under the Null? title header. That means you could insert a row in the table that consists of only null values.

You can create a table with a mandatory column by adding a NOT NULL constraint on the column. The constraint can be added as an in-line or out-of-line constraint. Here's the in-line constraint syntax for a mandatory column with a system generated constraint name:

```
SQL> CREATE TABLE sample_number
  2  (column_name NUMBER(12,2) NOT NULL);
```

The table with a NOT NULL constrained column looks like this:

```
Name Null? Type
------------------------ -------- --------------
COLULMN_NAME NOT NULL NUMBER(12,2)
```

As a matter of best practice, it is always better to name constraints. You would use a different syntax to create a table with a named NOT NULL constraint. Named constraints are much easier to find when you explore the Oracle 11*g* catalog. An example of the type of error raised without a constraint name appears later in this section for a CHECK constraint. The syntax for a named constraint is as follows:

```
SQL> CREATE TABLE sample_number
  2   (column_name NUMBER(12,2)  CONSTRAINT nn_sample1  NOT NULL);
```

The current table requires a value, which means you can't insert a null value. A 12-digit number with two placeholders to the right of the decimal point follows this pattern:

```
SQL> INSERT INTO sample_number
  2   VALUES ( 1234567890.99 );
```

A different rule applies to the BINARY_FLOAT and FLOAT data types. They have only a precision value and no scale. You can assign scales dynamically, or the values to the right of the decimal point can vary. That's because the nature of a floating decimal point allows for dynamic values to the right of the decimal point.

You would define a floating data type like this:

```
SQL> CREATE TABLE sample_float
  2   (column_name FLOAT(12));
```

Inserting values follows this pattern:

```
SQL> INSERT INTO sample_float
  2   VALUES (12345678.0099);
```

Oracle doesn't natively support an unsigned integer (positive integers), which MySQL supports. By design, Oracle supports both positive and negative numbers in all numeric data types. You can create a numeric data type and then use a CHECK constraint to implement the equivalent of an unsigned integer. The following table design shows that technique with an in-line constraint:

```
SQL> CREATE TABLE unsigned_int
  2   ( column_name NUMBER(38,0) CHECK (column_name >= 0));
```

This column definition allows entry of only a zero or positive integer. The check constraint is entered as an in-line constraint because it affects only a single column. CHECK constraints must be entered as out-of-line constraints when they work with multiple columns. Multiple column constraints are table constraints. An exception is raised if you attempt to insert a negative integer, like this:

```
INSERT INTO unsigned_int VALUES (-1)
*
ERROR at line 1:
ORA-02290: check constraint (SCHEMA_NAME.SYS_C0020070) violated
```

This type of error message isn't as helpful as a named constraint, but you should know how to read it. The SCHEMA_NAME (synonymous with the user name) is the first element of the error, and the system-generated constraint name is the second element.

You can name CHECK constraints in Oracle like this:

```
SQL> CREATE TABLE unsigned_int
  2  ( column_name NUMBER(38,0)
  3    CONSTRAINT ck_unsigned_int_01 CHECK (column_name >= 0));
```

Although the constraint drops down to line 3, there is no comma separating the definition of the column from the constraint. This means the constraint is an in-line constraint. An out-of-line constraint in this example would differ only by having a comma in line 3, like this:

```
SQL> CREATE TABLE unsigned_int
  2  ( column_name NUMBER(38,0)
  3    , CONSTRAINT ck_unsigned_int_01 CHECK (column_name >= 0));
```

Then the same error is raised with this message:

```
INSERT INTO unsigned_int VALUES (-1)
*
ERROR at line 1:
ORA-02290: check constraint (STUDENT.CK_UNSIGNED_INT_01) violated
```

By incorporating the name of the table in the constraint, you can immediately identify the violation without having to read the data catalog to associate it with a table and business rule.

Date Data Type   Dates and timestamps are date types. Their implementation is through complex or real numbers. The integer value represents the date and the decimal value implements time. The range of dates or timestamps is an *epoch*. An epoch is a set of possible dates and date-times that are valid in the database server.

The DATE data type in an Oracle database is a date-time value. As such, you can assign a date-time that is accurate to hundredths of a second. The default date format mask in an Oracle database is dd-mon-rr or dd-mon-yyyy. The rr stands for relative date, and the database server chooses whether the date belongs in the current or last century. The yyyy format mask requires that you explicitly assign the four-digit year to dates.

Here's the syntax to create a DATE column:

```
SQL> CREATE TABLE sample_date
  2  ( column_name DATE DEFUALT SYSDATE);
```

A DATE data type can be assigned a date-time that is equal to midnight by enclosing the date column in a TRUNC function. The TRUNC function shaves off any decimal value from the date-time value. The SYSDATE is a current date-time function available inside an Oracle database.

A more accurate timestamp and timestamps with local or general time zone are also available in Oracle 11g. They're more accurate because they measure time beyond hundredths of a second. You would define a TIMESTAMP like this:

```
SQL> CREATE TABLE sample_timestamp
  2  ( column_name TIMESTAMP DEFUALT SYSTIMESTAMP);
```

You also have INTERVAL DAY TO SECOND and INTERVAL DAY TO MONTH data types. They measure intervening time (like the number of minutes or seconds between two timestamps), which is similar to the TIME data type in MySQL.

Character Data Type   Character data types have several subgroups in an Oracle database. They can be summarized as fixed-length, long, Unicode, row identifiers, and variable-length strings. In all cases, character data types work very much alike. You specify how many characters you plan to store as the maximum number.

This is the syntax for a fixed-length string:

```
SQL> CREATE TABLE variable_string
  2  ( column_name  CHAR(20) CONSTRAINT nn_varstr_01 NOT NULL);
```

You can insert or update a fixed-length string with any number of characters up to the maximum number but the database inserts whitespace after the last character up to the maximum number of characters. That's why you have the RTRIM function to strip trailing characters when they're returned in a query result.

This variable length string is the equivalent:

```
SQL> CREATE TABLE variable_string
  2  ( column_name  VARCHAR2(20) CONSTRAINT nn_varstr_01 NOT NULL);
```

This definition allocates 20 bytes of space. An alternative syntax lets you define space by the number of characters, which supports Unicode strings. That syntax requires including a CHAR flag inside the parentheses. Here's the syntax for a fixed-length string:

```
SQL> CREATE TABLE variable_string
  2  ( column_name  CHAR(20 CHAR) CONSTRAINT nn_varstr_01 NOT NULL);
```

The variable length equivalent is shown here:

```
SQL> CREATE TABLE variable_string
  2  ( column_name  VARCHAR2(20 CHAR) CONSTRAINT nn_varstr_01 NOT NULL);
```

The Oracle database also includes national language character types. They are designed to store Unicode and different character sets in the same database. The syntax for NCHAR or NVARCHAR2 uses the same definition pattern. You specify the maximum size of the string in bytes or characters inside parentheses. CHAR should be used when you define Unicode columns.

The maximum size of a fixed-length CHAR variable is 2000 bytes, and the maximum length of a VARCHAR or VARCHAR2 is 4000 bytes. Beyond that, you can implement a LONG data type, which is 32,767 (the positive portion of 2^{16}), but it's soon to be deprecated. The last choice for a very long string is a Character Large Object (CLOB), which has a maximum size of 8 terabytes when the block size is 8 kilobytes and 32 terabytes when the block size is 32 kilobytes. Oracle makes these large object types available through a built-in API, which you must use to work with these data types.

Large Strings   You can define a table with a CLOB or NCLOB column similar to the following example, but it lacks a physical maximum size and name for the storage clause. The physical size for a CLOB is set by the configuration of the database. As mentioned, the maximum size is set by the block size and is typically 8 terabytes. The Oracle database assigns a system generated name, which can make calculating and maintaining its storage difficult for DBAs. This is true any time you leave something to an implicit behavior, such as naming a constraint or internal storage

```
SQL> CREATE TABLE clob_table
  2  ( column_id   NUMBER
  3  , column_name CLOB DEFAULT '');
```

The DEFAULT keyword assigns an empty string to the column_name column, which is equivalent to an INSERT or UPDATE statement putting a call to EMPTY_CLOB() in the column as its value. The DEFAULT value places the default value in a column only when the INSERT statement uses an overriding signature that excludes the column_name column, like so:

```
SQL> INSERT INTO clob_table (column_id) VALUES (1);
```

You can discover that storage clause by using the DBMS_METADATA package and the GET_DDL function. This does the same thing as a SHOW CREATE TABLE statement in a MySQL database. It reads the data catalog and provides the complete syntax for creating the table. The easiest way to get this information is to run the command from the SQL*Plus prompt. You'll need to expand the default 80 characters of space allotted for displaying a LONG data type before you run the query. Also, you'll need to remember that Oracle stores all metadata strings in uppercase, which means the actual parameters (or arguments) to the GET_DDL function must be in uppercase for it to work.

Here are the SQL*Plus and SQL commands:

```
-- Reset the display value for a large string.
SET LONG 300000
-- Query the data catalog for the full create statement.
SELECT dbms_metadata.get_ddl('TABLE', 'CLOB_TABLE') FROM dual;
```

Some liberty has been taken with reformatting the output to increase readability of it for the book, but this is what would be returned from the query:

```
CREATE TABLE "STUDENT"."CLOB_TABLE"
   ("COLUMN_NAME" CLOB DEFAULT '')
   PCTFREE 10 PCTUSED 40 INITRANS 1 MAXTRANS 255
   NOCOMPRESS NOLOGGING
   STORAGE(INITIAL 65536 NEXT 1048576 MINEXTENTS 1 MAXEXTENTS 2147483645
           PCTINCREASE 0 FREELISTS 1 FREELIST GROUPS 1 BUFFER_POOL DEFAULT)
   TABLESPACE "USERS"
   LOB ("COLUMN_NAME") STORE AS BASICFILE
   (TABLESPACE "USERS"
    ENABLE STORAGE IN ROW CHUNK 8192 RETENTION NOCACHE LOGGING
    STORAGE(INITIAL 65536 NEXT 1048576 MINEXTENTS 1 MAXEXTENTS 2147483645
            PCTINCREASE 0 FREELISTS 1 FREELIST GROUPS 1 BUFFER_POOL DEFAULT))
```

The better way to define a CLOB or BLOB column includes some explicit syntax and a name for the BASICFILE. A BASICFILE means that the CLOB isn't encrypted. The other option in this syntax creates an encrypted file with the SECUREFILE keyword. You should note that a SECUREFILE clause requires that you store the CLOB or BLOB column in a tablespace with automatic segment-space management.

The right way to use a CREATE TABLE statement with a LOB is to name the CLOB or BLOB file. This extra step makes your life easier later, as described in the "XMLTYPE Data Type" section a bit later.

Here's the syntax that assigns a user-defined SEGMENT_NAME at table creation:

```
SQL> CREATE TABLE sample_table
  2  ( column_name CLOB DEFAULT '')
  3  LOB (column_name) STORE AS sample_table_clob
  4    (TABLESPACE users ENABLE STORAGE IN ROW CHUNK 32768
  5     PCTVERSION 10 NOCACHE NOLOGGING
  6     STORAGE (INITIAL 1048576
  7             NEXT 1048576
  8             MINEXTENTS 1
  9             MAXEXTENTS 2147483645));
```

The additional four parameters in the storage clause will be appended by using the default values as noted in the output from the preceding call to the GET_DDL function. The company's DBA should provide guidelines on the STORAGE clause settings.

TIP
The default creates BLOB and CLOB storage with logging enabled. As a rule, these types should have logging turned off.

Boolean   It is possible to mimic a Boolean data type in an Oracle database. To accomplish this, you define a number column and assign a table-level constraint on that column. The constraint would allow only a 0 (for false) or 1 (for true). The syntax to implement a column that performs like a Boolean data type is shown next:

```
SQL> CREATE TABLE sample_boolean
  2  ( column_name NUMBER
  3  , CONSTRAINT boolean_values
  4    CHECK (column_name = 0 OR column_name = 1));
```

This type of column would allow only a null, 0, or 1 to be inserted into the table. Anything else would trigger a constraint violation error, like this:

```
INSERT INTO sample_boolean VALUES (2)
*
ERROR at line 1:
ORA-02290: check constraint (STUDENT.BOOLEAN_VALUES) violated
```

After dropping the original sample_boolean table, you can re-create it with the addition of a NOT NULL constraint. Now it implements two-valued logic, because it disallows the insertion of a null value.

```
SQL> CREATE TABLE sample_boolean
  2  ( column_name NUMBER CONSTRAINT no_null NOT NULL
  3  , CONSTRAINT boolean_values
  4    CHECK (column_name = 0 or column_name = 1));
```

You can also use other comparison operators such as greater than, less than, greater than or equal to, and so forth. It is also possible to use SQL lookup operators such as IN, =ANY, =SOME, or =ALL.

BLOB Data Type   The BLOB data type is very much like the CLOB data type. You can store a binary signature for an image or document inside a BLOB data type. The maximum size is 8 to 32 terabytes and the behaviors and syntax mirror those for the CLOB data type. I won't repeat the syntax here since it is the same BLOB data type already discussed.

XMLTYPE Data Type   The XMLTYPE is a specialized form of a CLOB data type. You use it as the column data type, but then you provide a specialized storage clause that identifies its storage as a CLOB data type. This process follows the pattern that Oracle databases use consistently between subtypes and types.

Here's the syntax to create an XMLTYPE column:

```
SQL> CREATE TABLE item
  2  ( item_id          NUMBER CONSTRAINT pk_item PRIMARY KEY
  3  , item_title       VARCHAR2(30) CONSTRAINT nn_item_01 NOT NULL
  4  , item_description XMLTYPE)
  5  XMLTYPE item_description STORE AS CLOB item_desc_clob
  6  ( TABLESPACE some_tablespace_name
  7    STORAGE (INITIAL 819200 NEXT 819200 )
  8    CHUNK 8192 NOCACHE LOGGING);
```

Notice that line 5 has the storage clause highlighted. That's because a lot of the Oracle documentation simply instructs you to use STORE AS CLOB clause. Unfortunately, that fails to provide a meaningful storage name for matching segments to LOBs in the data catalog. You join the ALL_, DBA_, and USER_LOBS view to the equivalent USER_SEGMENTS view on the SEGMENT_NAME column value. The name of the CLOB in the storage clause facilitates that join. System-generated names can be matched, but that match requires a complex regular expression in the SQL syntax. It's better to provide a name and simplify the DBA's life upfront.

The use of XML inside the Oracle database continues to grow release by release. The XML Developer's Kit (XDK) for Oracle is complex and an awesome resource to delve into when you're going to use XML inside the Oracle database. I'd recommend you start by reading the *Oracle Database Developer's Kit Programmer's Guide*.

Virtual Columns   A virtual column lets you create what are sometimes known as *derived columns*. You need to decide whether virtual or derived best describes them for you, but Oracle has opted for *virtual*, and that's what might crop up on a certification exam. A virtual column lets you store a formula that joins strings from other columns in the same row together or calculate values—the functions are stored in the table, not the values.

The following demonstrates the syntax to create a virtual column that concatenates strings:

```
SQL> CREATE TABLE employee
  2  ( employee_id NUMBER
  3  , first_name  VARCHAR2(20)
  4  , last_name   VARCHAR2(20)
  5  , full_name   VARCHAR2(40) AS (first_name || ' ' || last_name));
```

Line 5 is the virtual column. Instead of a column data type, two columns are joined together with white space in between.

The next example demonstrates a virtual column that uses math operations against values in other columns:

```
SQL> CREATE TABLE salary
  2  ( salary_id    NUMBER        CONSTRAINT pk_salary PRIMARY KEY
  3  , salary       NUMBER(15,2)  CONSTRAINT nn_salary_01 NOT NULL
  4  , bonus        NUMBER(15,2)
  5  , compensation NUMBER(15,2) AS (salary + bonus));
```

Line 5 in this example shows you how to use a math operation in a virtual column. Virtual columns are marked in the database catalog. You can display the VIRTUAL_COLUMN in the ALL_, DBA_, or USER_TAB_COLS view to see if a column is virtual. Any column that has a 'YES' in that column is a virtual column. The formula for the virtual column is in the DATA_DEFAULT column of the same view.

Nested Table Data Types   This section shows you how to create single-level and multiple-level nested tables. Oracle Database 11g supports nested table data types, but MySQL database doesn't. Oracle documentation calls the nesting of tables within nested tables a *multi-level collection*.

Nested tables are tables within a column inside a row of another table. These are object types defined in SQL before they can become data types for columns in a table. The definition can be a one- or two-step process. A one-step process occurs when you create an object type that is a collection of a scalar data type. A two-step process occurs when you create an object type that contains a set of variables. The set of variables in this case becomes a *record structure*. Elements of record structures are *fields*. You create an object type (or record structure) as a schema-level object type, and then you create a collection of the object type.

As an object relational database management system (ORDBMS), Oracle databases let you define object types. Object types have two roles in Oracle databases: One role is as a SQL data type, which you see in this chapter as a nested table. The other acts like a traditional object type inside an object-oriented programming language (OOPL) such as Java, C#, or C++. Instantiable object types are advanced PL/SQL concepts. You can find a full description of how you can define and work with them in Chapter 14 of *Oracle Database 11g PL/SQL Programming*.

Array or List?

An array or list is a collection of the same type of data, which can be a scalar data type or record structure. An array is a structure that has a fixed maximum number of elements that is uniquely indexed by a sequential set of numbers. A sequential set of numbers is also known as a *densely populated index*. Programmers iterate (move across arrays one-by-one) using sequential index values.

A list is like an array but different. A list has no maximum number of elements and can be indexed by a sequential or nonsequential index. A nonsequential set of numbers or strings acts like a sparsely populated index. Programmers must iterate through elements of the list by using an iterator to traverse the links between each element from the first until the last. This behavior is similar to a singly linked list in the C/C++ programming languages.

The elements in arrays or lists can be ordered or unordered. More often than not, arrays are ordered sets. Lists are more frequently unordered sets. The closest corollary to a database table is an unordered list.

Two possible syntaxes can be used for creating a collection of a scalar data type. One creates an array, which has a fixed size; the other creates a list, which has no fixed size. The array is created with this syntax:

```
SQL> CREATE TYPE street_array IS VARRAY(3) OF VARCHAR2(30);
  2  /
```

This creates an array of no more than *three* 30-character variable length strings. The forward slash is required to execute the statement terminated by a semicolon. This is a case where the semicolon acts like a statement terminator, not an execution command.

Alternatively, you can create a list of 30 character variable length strings with this:

```
SQL> CREATE TYPE street_list IS TABLE OF VARCHAR2(30);
  2  /
```

You can then define a table that uses the user-defined type STREET_LIST as a column data type. The following defines an ADDRESS table by using it to capture one to however many street addresses might be required by an address:

```
SQL> CREATE TABLE address
  2  ( address_id      NUMBER
  3  , street_address STREET_LIST
  4  , city            VARCHAR2(30)
  5  , state           VARCHAR2(2)
  6  , postal_code     VARCHAR2(10))
  7  NESTED TABLE street_address STORE AS street_table;
```

The STREET_LIST collection is a column data type on line 3 and requires that you add a NESTED TABLE clause to the CREATE TABLE statement. Line 7 defines the storage name of STREET_TABLE. Chapter 8 shows examples of how you insert into nested tables.

A question some ask is, "How do you create a nested table within a nested table?" Oracle's documentation labels nesting a table within a table as a *multi-level collection*. The most difficult part of nesting a table within a nested table is learning how to write the storage clause. Then, the storage clause syntax is straightforward.

The following extends the original design by changing the ADDRESS table into an object type and then nesting it in an EMPLOYEE table. The first step in this example creates an ADDRESS_TYPE, like this:

```
SQL> CREATE OR REPLACE TYPE address_type AS OBJECT
  2  ( address_id      NUMBER
  3  , street_address STREET_LIST
  4  , city            VARCHAR2(30)
  5  , state           VARCHAR2(2)
  6  , postal_code     VARCHAR2(10));
  7  /
```

You create a list collection of the ADDRESS_TYPE with the following syntax:

```
SQL> CREATE OR REPLACE TYPE address_list AS TABLE OF address_type;
  2  /
```

The EMPLOYEE table holds a nested table of the ADDRESS_TYPE, which in turn holds a nested table of STREET_ADDRESS, as shown next:

```
SQL> CREATE TABLE employee
  2  ( employee_id    NUMBER
  3  , first_name     VARCHAR2(20)
  4  , middle_name    VARCHAR2(20)
  5  , last_name      VARCHAR2(20)
  6  , home_address   ADDRESS_LIST)
  7  NESTED TABLE home_address STORE AS address_table
  8  (NESTED TABLE street_address STORE AS street_table);
```

Line 7 defines the nested table storage for the ADDRESS_TYPE associated with the HOME_ADDRESS column. The parentheses on line 8 indicate that the nested table for STREET_ADDRESS is part of the previous nested table. There's an internally managed link that connects the EMPLOYEE table with the nested HOME_ADDRESS table, and another link that connects the STREET_ADDRESS table to the HOME_ADDRESS column (or nested table).

Although you've seen how to implement nested tables, they're complex and not as flexible to changing business requirements. Use them only when they meet a specific need that can't be met by normal primary-to-foreign key relationships. For more information on nested tables, check the *Oracle Database 11g SQL Language Reference*.

Column and Table Constraints

There are two key differences between column and table constraints. One difference is that a column constraint effects only a single column in the table. The other difference is that a column constraint can be done as an in-line constraint, whereas a table constraint must be done as an out-of-line constraint. That's a natural thing if you pause to think about why that's true. A table constraint applies to multiple columns and in-line constraints only apply to the single column that shares the same line.

The Nested Table Design Pattern

Nested tables are an advanced implementation made possible by the Oracle Object Relational Model (ORM). They provide an internal connection between tables that acts like an inner class in OOPLs.

Like inner classes in OOPL, there's no way to go directly to the inner class. You must first go through the outer (or container) class. This type of relationship between tables in database design is known as an *ID-dependent relationship*. The only way to discover the ID is through the table holding the key to the nested tables.

If subsequent discovery of the business model identifies another use for nested table data, the design must be changed to open up access to the nested data. That means removing the nested table and making it an ordinary table connected by a primary-to-foreign key relationship. That type of change is typically expensive. Ordinary table primary-to-foreign key relationships are more flexible (and for the curious, their official label is *non–ID-dependent relationships*).

As mentioned, the only constraint that is always a column constraint is the NOT NULL constraint. The remaining Oracle constraints, CHECK, UNIQUE, PRIMARY KEY, and FOREIGN KEY constraints can be column or table constraints. You can find coverage of the NOT NULL constraint in the "Number Data Type" section earlier in this chapter. The biggest difference between NOT NULL constraints in an Oracle database versus a MySQL database is that you can name them in Oracle but can't in MySQL. The reason isn't immediately clear, but MySQL treats whether a column is nullable or not null as a property of the column. That's why they're not in the TABLE_CONSTRAINTS view of the INFORMATION_SCHEMA.

Column Constraints   In-line column constraints are most frequently a PRIMARY KEY or NOT NULL constraint. The PRIMARY KEY works in that context when a surrogate key or a single column natural key fills the role of a primary key. Surrogate keys typically follow a naming pattern that takes the name of the table and adds an _ID as a suffix. A PRIMARY KEY constraint on a single column makes the column both not null and unique within the table. NOT NULL constraints apply to single columns only, and they make entry of a column value mandatory when you insert a row or update a row. The only other column constraint is a CHECK constraint in Oracle and the ENUM and SET data types that mimic a CHECK constraint in MySQL.

Oracle supports naming or using a system-generated name for a PRIMARY KEY constraint. The following syntax demonstrates how to define a PRIMARY KEY constraint with a system-generated constraint name:

```
SQL> CREATE TABLE sample
  2  ( sample_id     NUMBER PRIMARY KEY
  3  , sample_text   VARCHAR2(30));
```

You can name the constraint by using this syntax:

```
SQL> CREATE TABLE sample
  2  ( sample_id     NUMBER CONSTRAINT pk_sample PRIMARY KEY
  3  , sample_text   VARCHAR2(30));
```

A FOREIGN KEY constraint works as a column constraint much like the PRIMARY KEY constraint but it has a dependency. You can define only a single column FOREIGN KEY that references (points to) a primary key constrained column. The primary key column can be in the same or a different table. The more common pattern is a different table.

For the following example, assume a SYSTEM_USER table has a SYSTEM_USER_ID primary key constrained column. The example builds on the previous SAMPLE table by adding a CREATED_BY column, which should contain a value from the primary key column of the SYSTEM_USER table. Here's the syntax for an in-line FOREIGN KEY constraint:

```
SQL> CREATE TABLE sample
  2  ( sample_id     NUMBER CONSTRAINT pk_sample PRIMARY KEY
  3  , sample_text   VARCHAR2(30)
  4  , created_by    NUMBER REFERENCES system_user(system_user_id));
```

Line 4 adds a FOREIGN KEY constraint to the SAMPLE table with a system-generated name. Notice that there is no use of the foreign key as a label when creating an in-line FOREIGN KEY constraint. The FOREIGN KEY has two formal parameters: the name of a table followed by the column name in parentheses.

Here's the alternative syntax that names the FOREIGN KEY constraint:

```
SQL> CREATE TABLE sample
  2  ( sample_id     NUMBER CONSTRAINT pk_sample PRIMARY KEY
  3  , sample_text   VARCHAR2(30)
  4  , created_by    NUMBER
  5    CONSTRAINT fk_sample_01 REFERENCES system_user(system_user_id));
```

A CHECK constraint also works as a column constraint. The following syntax shows how to constrain a one-character column to contain a gender value.

```
SQL> CREATE TABLE club_member
  2  ( club_member_id  NUMBER PRIMARY KEY
  3  , first_name        VARCHAR2(30)
  4  , last_name         VARCHAR2(30)
  5  , gender            CHAR(1) DEFAULT 'F' CHECK (gender ('M', 'F')));
```

This syntax creates the CHECK constraint with a system-generated constraint name. It assigns a default value of an 'F' to the gender column when an INSERT statement excludes the column during an insert operation. Excluding the column differs from inserting a null value. A null value in the VALUES clause of an INSERT statement or SET clause of an UPDATE statement overrides the default value and inserts a null value. As an alternative, you could place a NOT NULL constraint on the column to prevent a null value insertion or update, but that removes any value of the DEFAULT phrase.

You can add a constraint name by shifting the constraint from line 5 to a new line 6, as shown here:

```
  5  , gender            CHAR(1) DEFAULT 'F'
  6    CONSTRAINT ck_club_member_01 CHECK (gender IN ('M', 'F')));
```

A UNIQUE constraint typically spans multiple columns but can be applied to a single column. The following example shows how you would define an in-line UNIQUE constraint with a system generated name that includes an automotive VIN (vehicle identification number):

```
SQL> CREATE TABLE vehicle
  2  ( vehicle_id  NUMBER
  3  , vin         VARCHAR2(17) UNIQUE
  4  , make        VARCHAR2(30)
  5  , model       VARCHAR2(30)
  6  , year        VARCHAR2(4));
```

Changing the definition to include a user-defined constraint name, you would modify line 3 to this:

```
  3  , vin         VARCHAR2(17) CONSTRAINT un_vehicle_01 UNIQUE
```

UNIQUE constraints automatically create indexes. This is important only when you're trying to drop an index and can't. Then, you can discover the implicitly created indexes by querying the ALL_, DBA_, or USER_INDEXES and USER_IND_COLUMNS views. Joining the two views gives you all the columns in a unique index. Note that an index created by a UNIQUE constraint can't be dropped independently of the table.

There is also a REF constraint for objects. Although many don't store objects in tables, those that do need the syntax. A REF constraint is more limiting than the nested tables solution, because it disallows nested tables within nested tables—at least, it disallows them when they're collections of scalar data types.

The following example leverages the discussion from the "Nested Table Data Types" section earlier. You create an ADDRESS_TYPES object with a flattened set of columns in place of the list of possible street addresses. Here's the syntax:

```
CREATE OR REPLACE TYPE address_type AS OBJECT
( address_id       NUMBER
, street_address_1 VARCHAR2(20)
, street_address_2 VARCHAR2(20)
, street_address_3 VARCHAR2(20)
, city             VARCHAR2(30)
, state            VARCHAR2(2)
, postal_code      VARCHAR2(10));
```

You then create a table by using the definition of the object type, like this:

```
CREATE TABLE address_list OF address_type;
```

You create a table that uses the collection stored in the ADDRESS_LIST table with the following syntax:

```
SQL> CREATE TABLE employee
  2  ( employee_id     NUMBER
  3  , first_name      VARCHAR2(20)
  4  , middle_name     VARCHAR2(20)
  5  , last_name       VARCHAR2(20)
  6  , home_address    REF address_type SCOPE IS address_list);
```

Line 6 contains the column that uses a reference constraint to find the values for the HOME_ADDRESS column. The SCOPE keyword points to the reference table that uses the object type. The advantage of this approach is that the referenced table can have data inserted and deleted without touching the EMPLOYEE table.

Table Constraints   Table constraints can apply to a single column or multiple columns. That's because table constraints are defined by their position in the CREATE TABLE statement syntax. They occur after the last column definition. However, that really makes them out-of-line constraints. Table constraints apply against multiple columns or impose a unique constraint across rows.

While seldom written as an out-of-line constraint, you can write a single column PRIMARY KEY that way. The reason this is uncommon is that a single PRIMARY KEY constraint imposes both a NOT NULL and UNIQUE column constraint, and they're the only constraints that would displace an in-line PRIMARY KEY. The syntax requires that you provide the column name as an argument to the constraint. You have two options, as with in-line constraints: one uses a system-generated constraint name and the other uses a user-defined constraint name.

Here's an out-of-line PRIMARY KEY constraint with a system-generated constraint name:

```
, PRIMARY KEY(system_user_id)
```

And here's the same constraint with a user-defined name:

```
, CONSTRAINT pk_system_user PRIMARY KEY(system_user_id)
```

A multiple column `PRIMARY KEY` column would look like this:

```
, CONSTRAINT pk_contact PRIMARY KEY(first_name, last_name)
```

Check constraints often occur as out-of-line constraints because the columns involved can hold other in-line constraints, such as a `NOT NULL` constraint. A `CHECK` constraint with a system-generated constraint name looks like this:

```
, CHECK(salary > 0 AND salary < 50000)
```

Adding a user-defined name, the constraint looks like this:

```
, CONSTRAINT ck_employee_01 CHECK(salary > 0 AND salary < 50000)
```

A table constraint on multiple columns would look like the following:

```
, CONSTRAINT ck_employee_02 CHECK
    ((salary BETWEEN      0 AND  49999.99 AND employee_class = 'NON-EXEMPT') OR
(salary BETWEEN  50000 AND 249999.99 AND employee_class = 'EXEMPT')
OR (salary BETWEEN 250000 AND 999999.99 AND employee_class = 'EXECUTIVE'))
```

You create a `UNIQUE` constraint as an out-of-line constraint in two cases. The first case occurs when you've applied a `NOT NULL` in-line constraint and you want to create a `UNIQUE` single-column constraint. The second is when you want to create a multiple-column `UNIQUE` constraint.

Here's the syntax for a single-column `UNIQUE` constraint:

```
, UNIQUE(common_lookup_id)
```

The multiple-column syntax isn't much different for a `UNIQUE` constraint. The only difference is a comma-delimited list of column names in lieu of a single column. This syntax example includes a user-defined constraint name:

```
, CONSTRAINT un_lookup
    UNIQUE(common_lookup_table, common_lookup_column, common_lookup_type)
```

The most popular table-level constraint is a `FOREIGN KEY` constraint. You must provide the `FOREIGN KEY` phrase in an out-of-line constraint, unlike the in-line version that starts with the `REFERENCES` keyword. Here's an example of a `FOREIGN KEY` constraint without a user-defined constraint name:

```
, FOREIGN KEY(system_id) REFERENCES common_lookup(common_lookup_id)
```

The `SYSTEM_ID` column name identifies the column in the table that becomes constrained by the `FOREIGN KEY`. The `REFERENCES` clause identifies the table and column inside the parentheses where the constraint looks to find the list of primary key values.

You would add a `CONSTRAINT` keyword and a user-defined constraint name when you name a `FOREIGN KEY` constraint. The syntax would look like this:

```
, CONSTRAINT fk_system_01 FOREIGN KEY(system_id)
  REFERENCES common_lookup(common_lookup_id)
```

Like a `UNIQUE` constraint, you can provide a single-column reference or a comma-delimited list of columns. Single-column `FOREIGN KEY` constraints generally refer to surrogate keys that are generated values from a sequence. Multiple-column `FOREIGN KEY` values relate to the multiple-column *natural key* of the table.

This concludes how you define constraints in the `CREATE TABLE` statement syntax. You also have the option of adding, dropping, disabling, or enabling constraints with the `ALTER TABLE` statement. Chapter 7 covers how you use the `ALTER TABLE` statement. The next section shows you the syntax to create externally organized tables.

Externally Organized Tables

Oracle lets you define externally organized tables. Externally organized tables appear like ordinary tables in the database but are structures that read-only or read and write files from the operating system. Read-only files can be comma-separated files (CSVs) or position-specific files. Read and write files are stored in an Oracle Data Pump proprietary format. However, only non-proprietary file formats are known as *flat files*.

Oracle SQL*Loader lets you read these flat files with a `SELECT` statement from what appear as standard tables. Oracle Data Pump lets you read with a `SELECT` statement like Oracle SQL*Loader. Oracle Data Pump also lets you write with an `INSERT` statement. The write creates a proprietary formatted file, and the read extracts the data from the file.

Two key preparation steps are required whether you're working with externally organized read-only or read-write files. These steps help you create virtual directories and grant database privileges to read from and write to them. The first subsection shows you those preparation steps, and the next two show you how to work with read-only and read-write files.

Virtual Directories   Virtual directories are structures in the Oracle database, and they're stored in the data catalog. They map virtual directory names to physical operating system directories. Virtual directories make a few assumptions, which can become critical fail points. For the database grants to work successfully, the physical directories must be accessible to the operating system user who installed the Oracle Server. That means the operating system user should have read and write privileges to the related physical directories.

As the `SYS`, `SYSTEM`, or authorized administrator account, you create a virtual directory with the following syntax:

```
SQL> CREATE DIRECTORY upload AS 'C:\Data\Upload';
```

After you create the virtual directory, you must grant permissions to read from and write to the directory. This is true whether you're deploying a read-only file or read-write file because both types of files typically write error, discard, and log files to the same directory.

```
SQL> GRANT READ, WRITE ON DIRECTORY upload TO importer;
```

After creating a virtual directory, you find the mapping of virtual directories to operating system directories in the `DBA_DIRECTORIES`. Only a `SYS` or `SYSTEM` super user can gain access to this conceptual view. Unlike many other administrative views, there is no USER_ DIRECTORIES view.

For reference, virtual directories are also used for BFILE data types. Web developers need to know the list of virtual directories and their associated physical directories. They need that information to ensure their programs place the uploaded files where they belong.

Oracle SQL*Loader Files   After the preparation steps, you can define an externally organized table that uses a read-only file. Line 6 sets the TYPE value as Oracle SQL*Loader and line 7 sets the DEFAULT DIRECTORY as the virtual directory name you created previously:

```
SQL> CREATE TABLE CHARACTER
  2  ( character_id NUMBER
  3  , first_name VARCHAR2(20)
  4  , last_name VARCHAR2(20))
  5    ORGANIZATION EXTERNAL
  6    ( TYPE oracle_loader
  7      DEFAULT DIRECTORY upload
  8      ACCESS PARAMETERS
  9      ( RECORDS DELIMITED BY NEWLINE CHARACTERSET US7ASCII
 10        BADFILE     'UPLOAD':'character.bad'
 11        DISCARDFILE 'UPLOAD':'character.dis'
 12        LOGFILE     'UPLOAD':'character.log'
 13        FIELDS TERMINATED BY ','
 14        OPTIONALLY ENCLOSED BY "'"
 15        MISSING FIELD VALUES ARE NULL )
 16      LOCATION ('character.csv'))
 17  REJECT LIMIT UNLIMITED;
```

Lines 10 through 12 set the virtual directory and log files for any read from the externally organized table. Logs are written with each SELECT statement against the character table when data fails to conform to the definition. After the log file setup, the delimiters define how to read the data in the external file. Line 13 sets the delimiter, FIELD TERMINATED BY, as a comma. Line 14 sets the optional delimiter, OPTIONALLY ENCLOSED BY, as a single quote mark or apostrophe—this is important when you have a comma in a string.

The character file reads a file that follows this format:

```
1,'Indiana','Jones'
2,'Ravenwood','Marion'
3,'Marcus','Brody'
4,'Rene','Belloq'
```

Sometimes, you don't want to use CSV files because you've received position-specific files. That's the case frequently when the information comes from mainframe exports. You can create a position-specific table with the following syntax:

```
SQL> CREATE TABLE grocery
  2  ( grocery_id  NUMBER
  3  , item_name   VARCHAR2(20)
  4  , item_amount NUMBER(4,2))
  5    ORGANIZATION EXTERNAL
  6    ( TYPE oracle_loader
```

```
 7        DEFAULT DIRECTORY upload
 8        ACCESS PARAMETERS
 9        ( RECORDS DELIMITED BY NEWLINE CHARACTERSET US7ASCII
10          BADFILE 'UPLOAD':'grocery.bad'
11          LOGFILE 'UPLOAD':'grocery.log'
12          FIELDS
13          MISSING FIELD VALUES ARE NULL
14          ( grocery_id  CHAR(3)
15          , item_name   CHAR(20)
16          , item_amount CHAR(4)))
17        LOCATION ('grocery.csv'))
18    REJECT LIMIT UNLIMITED;
```

The major difference between the CSV-enabled table and a positionally organized external table is the source signature on lines 14 through 16. The CHAR data type specifies fixed-length strings, which can be implicitly cast to number data types. When a SELECT statement reads the external source, it casts the values from fixed-length strings to their designated numeric and variable-length string data types.

An alternative position-specific syntax replaces lines 14 through 16 with exact positional references, like this:

```
14          ( grocery_id   POSITION(1:3)
15          , item_name    POSITION(4:23)
16          , item_amount  POSITION(24:27)))
```

The casting issue works the same way because POSITION(1:3) expects to find a fixed-length string. The value in the flat file can be cast successfully only when it is a number.

The grocery table reads values from a flat file, like this:

```
1   Apple            1.49
2   Orange           2
```

These are the preferred solutions when importing large amounts of data. Many data imports include values that belong in multiple tables. Import sources that include data for multiple tables are composite import files. Most import source files generally ignore or exclude surrogate key values because they'll change in the new database. Importing the data is important, but taking from the externally managed table into the normalized business model can be tricky. The MERGE statement lets you import data, and based on some logic you can determine whether it's new or existing information. The MERGE statement then lets you insert new information or update rows of existing data, and the MERGE statement is covered in depth in Chapter 12.

Oracle Data Pump Files   Oracle Data Pump lets you read and write data in a proprietary format. It is most often used for backup and recovery. You have import files for reading proprietary formatted files and export tables for saving data in a proprietary format.

The next example requires you to create a new download virtual directory and grant the directory read and write permissions. The following creates a table that exports data to an Oracle Data Pump–formatted file:

```
SQL> CREATE TABLE item_export
  2   ORGANIZATION EXTERNAL
  3   ( TYPE oracle_datapump
```

```
 4    DEFAULT DIRECTORY download
 5    LOCATION ('item_export.dmp')
 6  ) AS
 7  SELECT    item_id
 8  ,         item_barcode
 9  ,         item_type
10  ,         item_title
11  ,         item_subtitle
12  ,         item_rating
13  ,         item_rating_agency
14  ,         item_release_date
15  ,         created_by
16  ,         creation_date
17  ,         last_updated_by
18  ,         last_update_date
19  FROM      item;
```

The exporting process with externally organized tables has only one very noticeable problem: It throws a nasty error when the file already exists, like so:

```
CREATE TABLE item_export
*
ERROR at line 1:
ORA-29913: error IN executing ODCIEXTTABLEOPEN callout
ORA-29400: DATA cartridge error
KUP-11012: file item_export.dmp IN C:\DATA\Download already EXISTS
```

My advice on this type of process is that you create an operating system script, a Java application, or a web solution that checks for the existence of the file before inserting data into the `item_export` table. Alternatively, you can create a set of utilities in Java libraries. You deploy the libraries inside the database, and wrap them with PL/SQL function definitions. They can clean up the file system for you by calling them before you query the table. You can check Chapter 15 of *Oracle Database 11g PL/SQL Programming* for details on writing and deploying Java libraries on the Oracle database.

NOTE
Java libraries work only in the Standard or Enterprise Editions of Oracle Database 11g.

Reversing the process and importing from the external file source isn't as complex. There are a few modifications to the `CREATE TABLE` statement. Here's a sample:

```
SQL> CREATE TABLE item_import
  2  ( item_id             NUMBER
  3  , item_barcode        VARCHAR2(20)
  4  , item_type           NUMBER
  5  , item_title          VARCHAR2(60)
  6  , item_subtitle       VARCHAR2(60)
  7  , item_rating         VARCHAR2(8)
  8  , item_rating_agency  VARCHAR2(4)
```

```
 9  , item_release_date    DATE
10  , created_by           NUMBER
11  , creation_date        DATE
12  , last_updated_by      NUMBER
13  , last_update_date     DATE)
14  ORGANIZATION EXTERNAL
15  ( TYPE oracle_datapump
16    DEFAULT DIRECTORY upload
17    LOCATION ('item_export.dmp'));
```

Notice that the table definition mirrors the source file. This means you must know the source before you can define the external table CREATE TABLE statement.

Partitioned Tables

Partitioning is the process of breaking up a data source into a series of data sources. Partitioned tables are faster to access and transact against. Partitioning data becomes necessary as the amount of data grows in any table. It speeds the search to find rows and insert, update, or delete rows.

Oracle Database 11g supports four types of table partitioning: list, range, hash, and composite partitioning.

List Partitioning   A list partition works by identifying a column that contains a value, such as a STATE column in an ADDRESS table. Partitioning clauses follow the list of columns and constraints.

A list partition could use a STATE column, like the following (the complete example is avoided to conserve space, and the three dots represent the balance of partitions not shown):

```
CREATE TABLE franchise
( franchise_id     NUMBER CONSTRAINT pk_franchise PRIMARY KEY
, franchise_name  VARCHAR(20)
, city            VARCHAR(20)
, state           VARCHAR(20))
PARTITION BY LIST(state)
( PARTITION offshore VALUES('Alaska', 'Hawaii')
, PARTITION west VALUES('California', 'Oregon', 'Washington')
, PARTITION desert VALUES ('Arizona','New Mexico')
, PARTITION rockies VALUES ('Colorado', 'Idaho', 'Montana', 'Wyoming')
, ... );
```

This can be used with other values such as ZIP codes with great effect, but the maintenance of list partitioning can be considered costly. Cost occurs when the list of values changes over time. Infrequent change means low cost, while frequent change means high costs. In the latter case, you should consider other partitioning strategies. Although an Oracle database supports partitioning on a variable-length string, MySQL performs list partitioning only on integer columns.

Range Partitioning   Range partitioning is very helpful on any column that contains a continuous metric, such as dates or time. It works by stating a minimum set that is less than a certain value, and then a group of sets of higher values until you reach the top most set of values. This type of partition helps you improve performance by letting you search ranges rather than complete data sets. Range partitioning is also available in MySQL.

A range example based on dates could look like this:

```
PARTITION BY RANGE(rental_date)
( PARTITION rental_jan2011
  VALUES LESS THAN TO_DATE('31-JAN-11','DD-MON-YY')
, PARTITION rental_feb2011
  VALUES LESS THAN TO_DATE('28-FEB-11','DD-MON-YY')
, PARTITION rental_mar2011
  VALUES LESS THAN TO_DATE('31-MAR-11','DD-MON-YY')
, ... );
```

The problem with this type of partitioning, however, is that the new months require constant management. Many North American businesses simply add partitions for all months in the year as an annual maintenance task during the holidays in November or December. Companies that opt for bigger range increments reap search and access benefits from range partitioning, while minimizing ongoing maintenance expenses.

Hash Partitioning   Hash partitioning is much easier to implement than list or range partitioning. Many DBAs favor it because it avoids the manual maintenance of list and range partitioning. Oracle Database 11*g* documentation recommends that you implement a hash for the following reasons:

- There is no concrete knowledge about how much data maps to a partitioning range.
- The sizes of partitions are unknown at the outset and difficult to balance as data is added to the database.
- A range partition might cluster data in an ineffective way.

This next statement creates eight partitions and stores them respectively in one of the eight tablespaces. The hash partition manages nodes and attempts to balance the distribution of rows across the nodes.

```
PARTITION BY HASH(store)
PARTITIONS 8
STORE IN (tablespace1, tablespace2, tablespace3, tablespace4
        ,tablespace5, tablespace6, tablespace7, tablespace8);
```

As you can imagine the maintenance for this type of partitioning is low. Some DBAs choose this method to get an initial sizing before adopting a list or range partitioning plan. Maximizing the physical resources of the machine ultimately rests with the DBAs who manage the system. Developers need to stand ready to assist DBAs with analysis and syntax support.

Composite Partitioning   Composite partitioning requires a partition and subpartition. The composites are combinations of two types of partitioning—typically, list and range partitioning, or range and hash composite partitioning. Which of these you should choose depends on a few considerations. List and range composite partitioning is done for historical information and is well suited for data warehouses. This method lets you partition on unordered or unrelated column values.

A composite partition like this uses the range as the partition and the list as the subpartition, like the following:

```
PARTITION BY RANGE (rental_date)
  SUBPARTITION BY LIST (state)
  (PARTITION FQ1_1999 VALUES LESS THAN (TO_DATE('1-APR-2011','DD-MON-YYYY'))
    (SUBPARTITION offshore VALUES('Alaska', 'Hawaii')
    , SUBPARTITION west VALUES('California', 'Oregon', 'Washington')
    , SUBPARTITION desert VALUES ('Arizona','New Mexico')
    , SUBPARTITION rockies VALUES ('Colorado', 'Idaho', 'Montana', 'Wyoming')
    , ... )
  ,(PARTITION FQ2_1999 VALUES LESS THAN (TO_DATE('1-APR-2011','DD-MON-YYYY'))
    (SUBPARTITION offshore VALUES('Alaska', 'Hawaii')
    , SUBPARTITION west VALUES('California', 'Oregon', 'Washington')
    , SUBPARTITION desert VALUES ('Arizona','New Mexico')
    , SUBPARTITION rockies VALUES ('Colorado', 'Idaho', 'Montana', 'Wyoming')
    , ... )
  , ... )
```

Range and hash composite partitioning is done for historical information when you also need to stripe data. *Striping* is the process of creating an attribute in a table that acts as a natural subtype or separator of data. Users typically view data sets of one subtype, which means organizing the data by stripes (subtypes) can speed access based on user access patterns.

Range is typically the partition and the hash is the subpartition in this composite partitioning schema. The syntax for this type of partition is shown next:

```
PARTITION BY RANGE (rental_date)
  SUBPARTITION BY HASH(store)
  SUBPARTITIONS 8 STORE IN (tablespace1, tablespace2, tablespace3
                            ,tablespace4, tablespace5, tablespace6
                            ,tablespace7, tablespace8)
  ( PARTITION rental_jan2011
    VALUES LESS THAN TO_DATE('31-JAN-11','DD-MON-YY')
  , PARTITION rental_feb2011
    VALUES LESS THAN TO_DATE('28-FEB-11','DD-MON-YY')
  , PARTITION rental_mar2011
    VALUES LESS THAN TO_DATE('31-MAR-11','DD-MON-YY')
  , ... )
```

NOTE
Developers need to understand techniques, but DBAs often have major decision-making authority in partitioning. Partitioning effectively requires an understanding of the underlying choices made by DBAs in organizing the database.

MySQL Tables

Tables in the MySQL database are slightly different from tables in an Oracle database in three ways. One key difference is that MySQL tables support automatic numbering and the sequence is a property of the table. Another key difference is that MySQL lets you define tables to work with any supported engine, while Oracle has only one engine by default. The last key difference is that MySQL tables don't support nested tables. Other differences are driven by the supported data types. MySQL supports only scalar data types, which include large object types. Large objects are large character or binary arrays and don't require special library handling like the Oracle database counterparts. MySQL supports only two composite data types: ENUM and SET.

Like the Oracle section, this section covers generalized syntax and how to define the following:

- Scalar data type columns
- ENUM and SET data type columns
- Column and table constraints
- Partitioned tables

Matching the organization of the Oracle sections, at least those that are supported by MySQL, this section uses small single tables to show how you can define scalar data types. Column and table constraints work more or less like those in Oracle when you define tables that use the default InnoDB engine (see Chapter 1).

TIP
You should use the default InnoDB engine, because it's the only engine that is fully transactional. Opting to use another database engine, such as MyISAM, would disallow the use of foreign key constraints.

MySQL provides three options for creating tables. One is a temporary table that acts much like the temporary table in Oracle, because it lasts only for the scope of the session. Another pseudo-temporary table exists when you opt to define a table using the ENGINE = MEMORY clause. Tables defined using the Memory engine are available during the runtime instance of the database and discarded when the database is stopped. Memory engine tables aren't transactional and can't be included in an ACID-compliant transaction with InnoDB or MyISAM stored tables. The last option lets you create a table that becomes permanent—at least until you remove it from the database.

The general and basic prototype for the CREATE TABLE statement is:

```
CREATE [TEMPORARY] TABLE [database_name.] table_name
( column_name data_type [NOT NULL]
    [{DEFAULT value | AUTO_INCREMENT | UNIQUE [KEY] | [PRIMARY] KEY}]
    [COMMENT 'comment_text'] | [REFERENCE table_name(column_list)]
    [[CONSTRAINT] constraint_name constraint_type]
, column_name data_type [NOT NULL]
    [{DEFAULT value | AUTO_INCREMENT | UNIQUE [KEY] | [PRIMARY] KEY}]
    [COMMENT 'comment_text'] | [REFERENCE table_name(column_list)]
    [[CONSTRAINT] constraint_name constraint_type]
, [...]
, [CONSTRAINT constraint_name constraint_type(column_list)
    [REFERENCES table_name(column_list)]]
, [...]) AUTO_INCREMENT=start_with_value ENGINE=engine_name;
```

You would create a table like this, where the ellipses represents columns and constraints:

```
CREATE TABLE table_name ( ... );
```

You create a temporary table using this syntax:

```
CREATE TEMPORARY TABLE table_name ( ... );
```

The following syntax lets you create an *in memory* table:

```
CREATE TABLE table_name ( ... ) ENGINE = MEMORY;
```

You would set auto incrementing to start at 1001 with this type of syntax:

```
CREATE TABLE table_name ( ... ) AUTO_INCREMENT=1001 ENGINE = MEMORY;
```

The following SHOW command lets you examine the catalog's definition of a table:

```
SHOW create table table_name;
```

Figure 6-3 shows you how to create a permanent table. It defines multiple columns and implements in-line and out-of-line database constraints. The figure is annotated to help you visualize possibilities. It does exclude DEFAULT values for columns, which are limited to numeric and string literal values in MySQL.

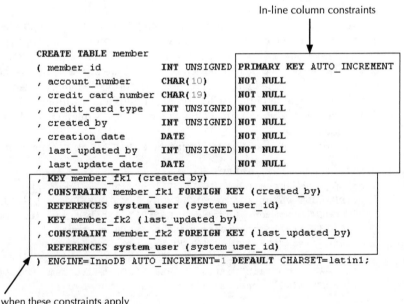

FIGURE 6-3. *MySQL CREATE TABLE statement*

As you see in Figure 6-3, the definition of columns can include in-line constraints, and they precede the definition of out-of-line constraints. The AUTO_INCREMENT clause sets an internal sequence as a property of the table. Unless you set the sequence value with an AUTO_INCREMENT clause to something other than 1, the sequence always starts with 1.

Unsigned integers are used as the data type for the primary and foreign key columns because surrogate primary keys generally start with 1 and increment by 1. These surrogate keys are automatic numbering sequences.

TIP
MySQL trainers frequently recommend in the MySQL DBA course that you start surrogate keys with unsigned integers, because they take less space (4 bytes) than doubles (8 bytes). You can perform table maintenance to change the integer to a double before you reach the 4.2 billion limitation of an integer data type.

Note that the in-line NOT NULL constraints lack user-defined names. That's because MySQL treats NOT NULL constraints as table properties, and you can't assign these constraints names. The lack of constraint names is a weakness in the implementation of NOT NULL constraints. At least, it's a weakness when you're examining constraints from the Oracle DBA's perspective.

The KEY references map to out-of-line CONSTRAINT names. This KEY line is unnecessary when creating FOREIGN KEY constraints. It does, however, find its way into some coding examples on the Internet. They're shown in case you run into them, but I suggest that you leave them out of your code. The best practice is to leave out the KEY line for foreign key columns when creating tables.

The next section discusses data types. You can use any of these when you define columns in MySQL tables.

Scalar Data Type Columns

Scalar data types in MySQL include numeric, date, character, and strings. Character data types are fixed length strings and covered in the "Strings Data Type" section. Several possibilities are available in each of these data type groups, and most are qualified in their respective sections.

The largest variation between MySQL and Oracle is that MySQL stores large character strings as TINYTEXT, TEXT, MEDIUMTEXT, and LONGTEXT data types, and large binary strings as TINYBLOB, BLOB, MEDIUMBLOB, and LONGBLOB data types. Oracle treats these large strings as specialized large objects, which requires separate PL/SQL libraries to manage them. There are no specialized SQL/PSM libraries to manage these large character and binary strings in MySQL.

The following sections cover numeric, Boolean, date, character, and string data types. Boolean data types don't formally exist in SQL for either database. Oracle does support a Boolean data type in their PL/SQL language. This section tells you how to work with integers to support Boolean-like usage in columns as a work around to their absence from SQL. Large character and binary strings are discussed in the "Strings Data Type" section.

Numeric Data Types   MySQL supports numeric data types with two groups: decimal and integer data types. Decimal data types support fixed-point and floating-point numbers. Integers support various sizes of integers.

Defining business data frequently involves numbers with decimal points. These are known as *numeric* data types because they support real numbers. The maximum number of digits allowed for this type of number is 65. The maximum number of digits that can appear to the right of the decimal place is 30.

You can define these types of fixed decimal point numbers with a DEC, DECIMAL, NUMERIC, or FIXED data type label. The labels are synonymous. With any of these data types, you define a 65-digit integer when you exclude the comma and the number of decimal points.

The following CREATE TABLE statement shows examples of defining real number data types:

```
mysql> CREATE TABLE number_table
    -> ( var1  DEC(65,2)
    -> , var2  DECIMAL(65,2)
    -> , var3  NUMERIC(65,2)
    -> , var4  FIXED(65,2));
```

After creating the table, you can describe the table and see that these labels are pseudonyms (aliases) for the DECIMAL data type. I recommend that you use the DECIMAL label, because it's exportable to other databases, and the others are no more than aliases. You would see the following by describing the table:

```
+--------+---------------+------+-----+---------+-------+
| Field  | Type          | Null | Key | Default | Extra |
+--------+---------------+------+-----+---------+-------+
| var1   | decimal(65,2) | YES  |     | NULL    |       |
| var2   | decimal(65,2) | YES  |     | NULL    |       |
| var3   | decimal(65,2) | YES  |     | NULL    |       |
| var4   | decimal(65,2) | YES  |     | NULL    |       |
+--------+---------------+------+-----+---------+-------+
```

The total number of digits in a decimal data type is the *precision* (or more plainly the *width*) and the number of possible digits to the right of the decimal point is the *scale*. The value of the scale can never be greater than the value of the precision. These data types create a fixed decimal point storage type. Any attempt to define a column data type with a scale that is larger than the precision throws an ERROR 1427. This error informs you that FLOAT(M,D), DOUBLE(M,D), or DECIMAL(M,D), where M must be greater than or equal to D.

Sometimes you want to define a data type that accepts numbers with varying decimal sizes. This type of number is a floating-point number. You have two options for floating-point data types: FLOAT and DOUBLE. The alias for DOUBLE is DOUBLE PRECISION. The FLOAT data type is smaller than the DOUBLE data type. According to MySQL documentation, these return approximate numeric data values, and testing finds that the approximation varies depending on the number of digits that appear before and after the decimal point.

You would declare columns of these floating-point numbers like this:

```
CREATE TABLE floating
( var1  FLOAT
, var2  DOUBLE );
```

Alternative syntax would include a precision and scale value. The maximum scale value is 30, but the scale can't be more than the precision value. The following values appear to represent the maximum values for precision and scale:

```
CREATE TABLE floating
( var1  FLOAT(23,23)
, var2  DOUBLE(53,30));
```

Testing on the release found odd results when using a FLOAT data type and a precision above 23. If you opt for these approximate numeric values, please test thoroughly. Sometimes the choice of a floating-point number can be replaced with a DECIMAL data type because you can set more decimal places than you need with the scale parameter and the values are accurate rather than approximate. Choose the DOUBLE when you have a very precise decimal value.

Integers in the MySQL database are signed or unsigned. This is more common in C and C++ programming languages than it is in C# or Java programming. The idea of signed integers is that half the values are negative numbers, half the values minus one are positive numbers, and the last number is a zero. Unsigned integers start with zero and give you twice the number of positive numbers plus one. Table 6-2 qualifies the possible ranges of integer data types.

The TINYINT has two aliases, the BOOL and BOOLEAN data types. When you define a BOOLEAN you get a zero for false and one for true. INT has an INTEGER alias, and BIGINT has a SERIAL alias.

These data types have the same pattern of assignment when you create tables. You provide the integer type and an UNSIGNED keyword when you want zero to be the maximum positive number. A negative to positive number is the default when you only specify the data type of integer, which makes it an unsigned integer.

You would create a table with signed and unsigned integers like this:

```
mysql> CREATE TABLE integer_sample
    -> ( positive_spectrum   INT UNSIGNED PRIMARY KEY AUTO_INCREMENT
    -> , full_spectrum       INT NOT NULL
    -> , fill_full_spectrum INT ZEROFILL
    -> , fill_pos_spectrum   INT UNSIGNED ZEROFILL);
```

Two of the columns use an unsigned integer and the positive_spectrum column uses an in-line PRIMARY KEY constraint. The primary key column designates itself as a surrogate key

Type	Subtype	Storage (Bytes)	Minimum Value	Maximum Value
TINYINT	Signed	1	−128	127
TINYINT	Unsigned	1	0	255
SMALLINT	Signed	2	−32768	32,767
SMALLINT	Unsigned	2	0	65,535
MEDIUMINT	Signed	3	−8,388,608	8,388,607
MEDIUMINT	Unsigned	3	0	16,777,215
INT	Signed	4	−2,147,483,648	2,147,483,647
INT	Unsigned	4	0	4,294,967,295
BIGINT	Signed	8	$−9.2 \times 10^{-18}$	9.2×10^{18}
BIGINT	Unsigned	8	0	1.8×10^{19}

TABLE 6-2.   *MySQL Integer Table*

column by invoking automatic numbering with the AUTO_INCREMENT keyword. The other two columns use a signed integer. The last two columns include an optional ZEROFILL keyword. Columns with ZEROFILL display leading zeros for integers.

Boolean Data Types   There is no Boolean data type in MySQL. Some developers are surprised by the lack of a Boolean data type because MySQL Workbench provides one. Actually, MySQL Workbench uses Boolean as an alias for the TINYINT data type. It's more convenient in MySQL to implement this because two constants are defined in the MySQL Monitor to handle Boolean operations: TRUE and FALSE. You can query these constants like this:

```
SELECT true, false;
```

Here's the return from MySQL Monitor:

```
+------+-------+
| TRUE | FALSE |
+------+-------+
|    1 |     0 |
+------+-------+
```

As mentioned, the range of a TINYINT is 256 values. The range can be either –128 to 127, or zero to 255. The constants don't change the range of the data type.

Date Data Types   Like an Oracle database, dates and timestamps are both date data types. They are typically scalar double-precision numbers linked to an epoch. An *epoch* is a slice of time typically measured in decades. Integer values are mapped to days in the epoch, and the fractions of days, such as hours, minutes, and seconds, are expressed in decimal equivalents.

Table 6-3 shows the available date, date-time, and timestamp data types in MySQL. You should verify what type of data you may need to store for the business rule before choosing one of these data types.

There's only one data type for a date, and it's DATE. The DATE data type takes a date in a four-digit year, hyphen, two-digit month, hyphen, and two-digit day. The format would look like this, yyyy-mm-dd, or like this, yyyymmdd, without the optional hyphens. You can also use a two-digit year, which presents challenges unless you know how and why it works. That format is yy-mm-dd or yymmdd, and it assumes two digit years belong to the last forty or next sixty years. The pattern for inserting values into a data type is known as a *format mask*. This format mask is more like the one in Perl than Oracle's default DATE format masks.

Data Type	Zero Fill Format Mask
DATE	'0000-00-00'
DATETIME	'0000-00-00 00:00:00'
TIMESTAMP	'0000-00-00 00:00:00'
TIME	'00:00:00'
YEAR	'0000'

TABLE 6-3.   *MySQL Date and Time Data Types*

The range of dates in the epoch is 1000-01-01 to 9999-12-31. It's unlikely you'll need to worry about a business date falling outside the range of possibilities.

NOTE
The epoch for dates is much larger than the epoch for timestamps in MySQL.

You can assign a date-time or timestamp value to a DATE column, but the assignment raises a warning message advising you that the assignment loses precision. This warning occurs most frequently when developers assign the date-time result from the NOW() function. This is like assigning a value from a DOUBLE number to a BIGINT, where the decimal portion of the original number is truncated (dropped).

MySQL's NOW() function is very much like the SYSDATE function in Oracle. They both return the current date-time value. Oracle's DATE data type doesn't raise a warning because it's not a DATE but a timestamp. Truncated time-stamps are dates in Oracle, but their storage is as a date-time value.

The following date_sample table demonstrates defining a column with a DATE data type:

```
CREATE TABLE sample_date
( var1   DATE
, var2   DATE DEFAULT '2011-01-01');
```

The default day isn't very helpful, because ideally you want the current day as a default. At present, MySQL doesn't support a call to the UTC_DATE() function as a default value. Default values must be numeric or string literals (ouch).

You cannot assign a current date value, but you can change the DATE data type to a TIMESTAMP data type and assign the current TIMESTAMP value. You can designate only one TIMESTAMP column in any table. A TIMESTAMP column uses a TIMESTAMP data type and has a DEFAULT or ON UPDATE CURRENT_TIMESTAMP event linked to it. That means multiple columns in a table can use a TIMESTAMP data type, provided there is no TIMESTAMP column. You can define other date-time columns using the DATETIME data type.

The syntax for an updated TIMESTAMP column that's always current with the last INSERT or UPDATE to the row would look like this:

```
CREATE TABLE sample
( sample_id  INT UNSIGNED AUTO_INCREMENT PRIMARY KEY
, created    DATETIME
, updated    TIMESTAMP NOT NULL
                    DEFAULT CURRENT_TIMESTAMP
                    ON UPDATE CURRENT_TIMESTAMP);
```

The updated column in the sample table gets the CURRENT_TIMESTAMP with an INSERT statement and gets an updated CURRENT_TIMESTAMP with any UPDATE statement. If you attempted to define a table with two columns that use a TIMESTAMP data type, and one is a TIMESTAMP column, you would raise the following error (reformatted to fit the page):

```
ERROR 1293 (HY000): Incorrect table definition; there can be only
one TIMESTAMP column with CURRENT_TIMESTAMP in DEFAULT or
ON UPDATE clause
```

When You Want It All

Sometimes for a *who-audit* component, you need to know when a row was *created* and *last updated*, and by whom. That is more difficult in MySQL because of the single `TIMESTAMP` column limit. The workaround requires you to implement an *on insert* trigger that assigns the `CURRENT_TIME` to `created` column, while leaving the `updated` column as the single `TIMESTAMP` column in the table.

Assuming the `sample` table definition from the "Date Data Types" section earlier in the chapter, you can write an *on insert* trigger to populate the `created` column with the current timestamp value. The trigger runs only on insertion of the row, while the event handler runs with each `UPDATE` statement. The *on insert* trigger (based on material in Chapters 14 and 15) would look like this in MySQL:

```
-- Replace value from the insert statement.
CREATE TRIGGER sample_t
BEFORE INSERT ON sample
FOR EACH ROW
BEGIN
   SET new.created = current_timestamp();
END;
$$
```

Only one statement is processed in this trigger. It resets the `created` element of the *new* pseudo structure (tied to the table definition in the data catalog). This type of table would let you insert all null values, like this:

```
INSERT INTO sample VALUES (null, null, null);
```

A query against the table would show this:

```
+-----------+---------------------+---------------------+
| sample_id | created             | updated             |
+-----------+---------------------+---------------------+
|         1 | 2011-08-10 12:49:56 | 2011-08-10 12:49:56 |
+-----------+---------------------+---------------------+
```

Contrary to popular opinion, it appears you *can* have it all—well, at least in this one little use case. You implement two set statements with the `CURRENT_DATE` function when the `created` and `updated` *who-audit* columns are `DATE` data types.

Although not supported by MySQL, the Oracle database does support an equivalent call to the `SYSDATE` function, which is a current date-time value. Oracle also supports any of the built-in functions as default values for tables.

Date-times, timestamps, and time data types contain a date and the decimal value that maps to a time. The format for date-times is `yyyy-mm-dd hh:mm:ss`, and the data type is `DATETIME`. In this case, hyphens and colons aren't optional in the format mask for `DATETIME` columns. Although this is a more restrictive format mask than the `DATE` mask, at least there's only one way to do it.

The range of date-times in the epoch is 1000-01-01 00:00:00 to 9999-12-31 00:00:00. This mimics the range of DATE columns, and in many cases the DATE and DATETIME values meet general business requirements.

The TIMESTAMP data type has the same format mask as DATETIME but it works in a completely different epoch. The epoch for a TIMESTAMP is January 1, 1970 to December 31, 2037. That's the end of time for many current computing epochs. The migration effort when the end of epoch approaches 2037 might rival the "Year 2000" conversion from two- to four-year dates.

TIP

Use the DATETIME, *because that way the expiration of the epoch won't cause you a headache, and you can write your own* ON INSERT *or an* ON UPDATE *trigger to capture the current date-time value. Chapter 15 contains examples of triggers.*

TIME is another data type that presents interesting challenges. It measures the interval between 838 hours, 59 minutes, and 59 seconds ago to 838 hours, 59 minutes, and 59 seconds in the future. The format mask for a TIME column is hh:mm:ss or hhmmss, which is similar to the time formatting in the DATETIME and TIMESTAMP data types. The good news here is that the colons are optional, and, better yet, you can insert this as a number or as string when you don't include the colons.

NOTE

The TIMESTAMP *data type is often chosen because it implements an* ON UPDATE *current timestamp trigger.*

Here's a sample table that uses these data types:

```
CREATE TABLE timing
( var1   DATETIME
, var2   TIMESTAMP
, var3   TIME
, var4   YEAR);
```

NOTE

As long as you remember the formatting, masks, date-times, timestamps, and times are fairly straightforward. The best way to keep things simple is to use the DATETIME *not the* TIMESTAMP *data type.*

The YEAR data type is fairly simple. You can define a YEAR column as a two-digit or four-digit year, and when you don't specify which you want, the default is a four-digit year.

Here's an example defining YEAR columns:

```
CREATE TABLE timing
( var1   YEAR
, var2   YEAR(2)
, var3   YEAR(4));
```

If you described the table, you would see the following:

```
+-------+----------+------+-----+---------+-------+
| Field | Type     | Null | Key | Default | Extra |
+-------+----------+------+-----+---------+-------+
| var1  | year(4)  | YES  |     | NULL    |       |
| var2  | year(2)  | YES  |     | NULL    |       |
| var3  | year(4)  | YES  |     | NULL    |       |
+-------+----------+------+-----+---------+-------+
```

Before you deploy these data types, make sure you understand the dates, date-times, times, and years data types. Choose an epoch that is consistent and best for your company, and remember that the TIMESTAMP epoch is short-lived and, where possible, use the DATETIME data type.

Strings Data Types Strings are straightforward because they're one of two things: a bunch of characters grouped together in some meaningful way, or a stream of binary characters that make a picture or document of some sort. The MySQL database stores character and binary strings in a similar way but in different data types.

Character strings are stored in fixed-width or variable-width data types. The CHAR data type stores fixed-width data, and the VARCHAR data type stores variable-width data types. There's also a CHARACTER VARYING alias that maps to the VARCHAR data type, but you should avoid it as legacy syntax. A VARBINARY data type stores binary strings. CHAR can hold only 255 characters of data, and VARCHAR and VARBINARY can have up to 65,535 characters of data.

Beyond 65,535 characters, you have large character and binary strings that are stored as special data types. They can hold large character strings or binary data streams. The families of these data types also start small, which can be misleading. They are the large string data types—one for characters and the other for binary characters. Character data types are TINYTEXT, TEXT, MEDIUMTEXT, and LONGTEXT. Binary character data types are TINYBLOB, BLOB, MEDIUMBLOB, and LONGBLOB.

String data types also support optional settings for the character set and collation. Character sets are important because they designate the available symbols, which may be western European alphabets, Arabic Abjad (a script for Arabic, Persian, and Urdu), or pictograms such as Chinese and Japanese. Collation sets how a language is organized for sorting purposes, such as alphabetizing in English. Unless you override the settings chosen at installation, MySQL uses the defaults for the instance. Character sets and collation are typically matched, but you can override this paring. You can find available character sets by using the following MySQL Monitor command:

```
SHOW CHARACTER SET LIKE 'latin%';
```

This should return the following:

```
+---------+----------------------------+-------------------+--------+
| Charset | Description                | Default collation | Maxlen |
+---------+----------------------------+-------------------+--------+
| latin1  | cp1252 West European       | latin1_swedish_ci |      1 |
| latin2  | ISO 8859-2 Central European| latin2_general_ci |      1 |
| latin5  | ISO 8859-9 Turkish         | latin5_turkish_ci |      1 |
| latin7  | ISO 8859-13 Baltic         | latin7_general_ci |      1 |
+---------+----------------------------+-------------------+--------+
```

National character and variable character types let you use broader character sets, such as Unicode.

The CHAR, CHARACTER, NCHAR, and NATIONAL CHARACTER data types support a *fixed-width* character string of an empty string to a 255 character string. Any of these types allocate space for the entire width of characters, whether they're required or not. The downside to this data type is that you consume space for empty space.

You can store binary, ASCII, or Unicode text in these data types. Optional settings let you override the default character set and collation.

The basic syntax to create columns of these data types is shown here:

```
CREATE TABLE fixed_width
( var1   CHARACTER(10)
, var2   CHAR(10)        BINARY
, var3   CHAR(10)        ASCII
, var4   CHAR(10)        UNICODE
, var5   CHAR(10)        CHARACTER SET utf16 COLLATE utf16_general_ci
, var6   NCHAR(10)
, var7   NATIONAL CHARACTER(10));
```

The BINARY, ASCII, and UNICODE options exist independent of the character set and collate settings. You can't use them on the same column. Also, these don't work with a national character data type, like NCHAR or NATIONAL CHARACTER.

In addition to fixed-width strings, *variable-width* strings provide a maximum length for strings in a column, and they consume space only for the values inserted. They're the preferred solution for most strings, with a maximum length of 65,535 bytes.

Like its fixed-width peers, variable-width strings have multiple keywords that can be used to define these types as columns in a table. VARCHAR and CHARACTER VARYING store strings in the default character set for the database and use the pared default collation. NVARCHAR and NATIONAL VARCHAR data types are available for Unicode strings. You also have a binary option for the VARCHAR and CHARACTER VARYING data types, but you should generally opt for the VARBINARY data type for binary strings.

The following example shows how to define columns of these data types:

```
CREATE TABLE variable_width
( var1   VARCHAR(10)
, var2   VARCHAR(10)              BINARY
, var3   CHARACTER VARYING(10)
, var4   CHARACTER VARYING(10)    BINARY
, var5   NVARCHAR(10)
, var6   NATIONAL VARCHAR(10)
, var7   VARBINARY(10));
```

The VARBINARY does support your setting an override character set and collation. The syntax for a VARBINARY follows the examples provided in the discussion of fixed-width strings for character set and collation.

As a rule, most developers use VARCHAR or NVARCHAR data types. You should consider revising older scripts that use the other types to the more common data types.

Large strings should mean large strings, but TINYTEXT and TINYBLOB have a maximum size of 255 characters. As you can imagine, they're rarely used. TEXT and BLOB data types are equivalent to the VARCHAR and VARBINARY data types with a maximum value of 65,535 bytes. MEDIUMTEXT and MEDIUMBLOB represent what are generally large strings, up to 16,777,215 bytes. LONGTEXT and LONGBLOB data types store up to 4 GB. When you use these types in the database,

---

MySQL Check Constraint Syntax Mystery

At the time of writing, MySQL Server's documentation lists CHECK constraints as valid syntax but doesn't let you use them. You can find the discussion about this valid-but-invalid syntax in MySQL Bug #3464, which was logged in April 2004 and last updated April 2010.

---

they need to be loaded by segments. As a rule of thumb, multiples of the operating system block size (typically 8 KB) are best, such as 8,192 bytes, 32,768 bytes, and so forth.

These data types don't specify size because they're implemented as variable-length character or binary byte streams (a more formal and complex word for strings). As a result, this example defines only two of the types:

```
CREATE TABLE large_strings
( var1   BLOB
, var2   TEXT);
```

The nice thing about BLOB and TEXT data types is that a query with a * for all columns won't raise a display error as it would in an Oracle database. That makes things simpler in one way and more complex in another. All of the strings will roll across your console when you query either of these large stream data types.

ENUM and SET Data Type Columns

The MySQL database supports two complex data types: ENUM and SET. The ENUM stands for enumeration of possible values and SET represents a set of inclusive values. You could make the argument that they're both like nested tables, but they are, in fact, different. You can't use an INSERT or UPDATE statement to change the list of values in either the ENUM or SET data type columns. You can use only the ALTER TABLE statement (see Chapter 7 for that statement syntax) to change the list of values. There's also an occasional opinion that the ENUM and SET data types act like specialized CHECK constraints, because they limit the values in a column to a list of possible values.

The ENUM and SET data types maintain a list of possible values in an array that is densely populated. Densely populated arrays use a sequential numeric index to identify items in the list. MySQL's index for the ENUM and SET data types is a zero-based integer. Both the ENUM and SET data types support overriding the character set and collation for the column. This behavior is consistent with other strings in MySQL and beneficial when supporting a multiple language installation.

The difference between the two data types is that an ENUM data type allows you to pick only one value from the list for each column value. The SET data type lets you pick one to many of the values. The ENUM data type may contain up to 65,535 values, whereas the SET data type can contain only 64 values.

They are defined by a similar rule, a comma-delimited list. The next two subsections provide examples of the ENUM and SET data types.

ENUM Data Type The ENUM type contains a list of values. The column in any row can reference only one of the values from the list.

The CREATE TABLE statement shows how you would define ENUM columns:

```
CREATE TABLE indexed_list
( var1   ENUM('Female','Male')
, var2   ENUM('Female','Male') DEFAULT 'Male'
, var3   ENUM('Female','Male') NOT NULL);
```

These three definitions have very different behaviors. var1 can hold an index value that points to a case-insensitive match to the strings Female or Male, or a null value. It doesn't matter how they're inserted or updated, because MySQL performs a case-insensitive match and then stores the index value from the match found. var2 can hold the same three values, but the DEFAULT value is inserted when you exclude the column from an override INSERT statement (see Chapter 8 for details). The only way to insert a null value in var1 or var2 is to explicitly insert or update the column with a null value. var3 must hold only an index value to a member of the enumeration list. That's because it uses an in-line constraint to prevent a null insertion or update.

NOTE
The worst default case I've ever seen of the misuse of override statements was in a hospital system that assumed a child was available for adoption unless the clerk entered an override character. Needless to say, a lot of parents were upset.

SET Data Type   As discussed, the SET type contains a list of 64 values. The column in any row can reference only zero, one, or all of the values from the list. It can reference zero SET members only when the column is *nullable*. A NOT NULL constrained column must contain at least one value from the list.

You define a column with the SET data type the same way. Only the insert or update syntax differs, because you can enter multiple values. For those who browse the syntax, here's a quick example that should catch your eye:

```
CREATE TABLE inclusive_set
( var1   SET('Ham','Pepperoni','Pineapple','Salami','Sausage'));
```

As mentioned, any insert or update to the column performs a case-insensitive match of the inserted or updated value against the list, and then stores the index values that match in the SET column. This means that queries find the index and return the case-sensitive value from the SET data type.

Column and Table Constraints

Column and table constraints work in MySQL databases more or less the same way they do in an Oracle database. That's because the syntax follows the ANSI SQL standards. You have in-line and out-of-line constraints in the CREATE TABLE statement, and the out-of-line constraints can be column- or table-level constraints.

The biggest difference between the two is that MySQL doesn't allow you to enter constraint names for in-line PRIMARY KEY or NOT NULL constraints. You can name a PRIMARY KEY constraint when you define it as an out-of-line constraint. NOT NULL constraints can't be given a user-defined name because they're treated as column properties inside the table.

MySQL doesn't support a CHECK constraint as the Oracle database does. This means you must use ON INSERT or ON UPDATE database triggers to gain some of the same behaviors. The ENUM and SET data types do constrain the list of possible values, and thereby provide a limited alternative to an Oracle CHECK constraint. It appears that the MySQL team plans to implement a CHECK constraint because it's defined in the documentation.

The following subsections cover column and table constraints. Out-of-line column constraints are included in the table constraints subsection because they're defined after the list of columns in a table.

Column Constraints   Column-level constraints apply only to a single column. Single column primary keys are typically *surrogate* keys (or artificial sequences used to simplify joins and externally identify rows). Foreign keys are single columns when they refer to surrogate primary keys. Unfortunately, you can't define an in-line FOREIGN KEY constraint in MySQL. FOREIGN KEY constraints are InnoDB engine features, not generic features of MySQL. NOT NULL constraints are always column-level constraints, because they make values mandatory in columns.

PRIMARY KEY constraints for surrogate keys also constrain a column to contain unique values in the scope of all rows in a table. Because surrogate keys are supported by sequences, it's important to note that there's a difference between how Oracle and MySQL databases implement sequences. Unlike Oracle, MySQL doesn't support independent sequence structures. MySQL implements sequences as table properties, just as it treats NOT NULL constraints.

The following example shows how to implement in-line PRIMARY KEY and NOT NULL constraints:

```
CREATE TABLE primary_inline
( primary_inline_id  INT UNSIGNED PRIMARY KEY AUTO_INCREMENT
, optional           VARCHAR(10)
, mandatory          VARCHAR(10)  NOT NULL);
```

The important aspect of an unsigned integer is that the maximum value can be twice that of a signed integer. Surrogate primary keys should start with 1 and have the potential to grow as large as necessary, which means their columns should always be unsigned integers or doubles. The rule of thumb creates them as integers until they approach the maximum value, and then you should change them to a double data type.

The PRIMARY KEY clause follows the data type. It imposes two constraints on the column: a NOT NULL and a UNIQUE constraint. The next AUTO_INCREMENT keyword creates a sequence as a table property that starts at 1 and increments by 1. The optional column is unconstrained and the mandatory column is NOT NULL constrained.

You can't define an in-line FOREIGN KEY constraint. They must be defined as table-level constraints even when they refer only to a single column.

UNIQUE constraints that refer to a single column can be defined as in-line constraints. The following demonstrates an in-line UNIQUE constraint:

```
CREATE TABLE unique_table
( unqiue_table_id  INT UNSIGNED PRIMARY KEY AUTO_INCREMENT
, unique_column    VARCHAR(10) UNIQUE);
```

MySQL supports only PRIMARY KEY, NOT NULL, and UNIQUE constraints in-line. As a last word on in-line constraints, remember that FOREIGN KEY constraints are available only when you use the InnoDB engine, and they can't be defined in-line.

Table Constraints   You define table constraints after the last column in a `CREATE TABLE` statement. MySQL lets you define table-level `PRIMARY KEY`, `FOREIGN KEY`, and `UNIQUE` constraints.

The first example shows how to define out-of-line `PRIMARY KEY` and `UNIQUE` constraints:

```
CREATE TABLE outofline
( outofline_id  INT UNSIGNED
, subject_item  VARCHAR(10)
, CONSTRAINT pk_outofline PRIMARY KEY (outofline_id)
, CONSTRAINT un_outofline UNIQUE (subject_item));
```

The examples are out-of-line constraints that work on a single column. Any real table-level constraints would contain a comma-delimited list of column names.

An out-of-line `FOREIGN KEY` constraint is defined like this:

```
CREATE TABLE dependent
( dependent_id  INT UNSIGNED
, outofline_id  INT UNSIGNED
, CONSTRAINT fk_dependent
  FOREIGN KEY (outofline_id) REFERENCES outofline(outofline_id));
```

Table-level `FOREIGN KEY` constraints are slightly more complex than the `PRIMARY KEY` and `UNIQUE` constraints because they have two comma-delimited lists of column names. One column list occurs in the parentheses after the `FOREIGN KEY` phrase, and the other list of columns occurs after the table name in the `REFERENCES` clause. The parentheses after the `FOREIGN KEY` phrase contains columns defined in the current table. The parentheses after the `REFERENCES` phrase contain columns defined in the current table when the current table's name precedes the parentheses; otherwise, it stores a list of columns found in the table that precedes the list of column names. As mentioned, MySQL `FOREIGN KEY` constraints work only when both the primary and foreign key holding tables are defined with the InnoDB engine.

Partitioned Tables

Like the Oracle database, MySQL supports partitioning of tables. It supports range, list, hash, and key partitioning. Range partitioning lets you partition based on column values that fall within given ranges. List partitioning lets you partition based on columns matching one of a set of discrete values. Hash partitioning lets you partition based on the return value from a user-defined expression (the result from a stored SQL/PSM function). Key partitioning performs like hash partitioning, but it lets a user select one or more columns from the set of columns in a table; a hash manages the selection process for you. A hash is a method of organizing keys to types of data, and hashes speed access to read and change data in tables.

Each of the following subsections discusses one of the supported forms of partitioning in MySQL. Naturally, there are differences between Oracle and MySQL implementations.

Range Partitioning   Range partitioning works only with an integer value or an expression that resolves to an integer against the primary key column. The limitation of the integer drives the necessity of choosing an integer column for range partitioning. You can't define a range-partitioned table with a `PRIMARY KEY` constraint unless the primary key becomes your partitioning key, like the one below.

```
CREATE TABLE ordering
( ordering_id      INT UNSIGNED AUTO_INCREMENT
, item_id          INT UNSIGNED
, rental_amount    DECIMAL(15,2)
, rental_date      DATE
, index idx (ordering_id))
PARTITION BY RANGE(item_id)
( PARTITION jan2011 VALUES LESS THAN (10000)
, PARTITION feb2011 VALUES LESS THAN (20000)
, PARTITION mar2011 VALUES LESS THAN (30000));
```

Range partitioning is best suited to large tables that you want to break into smaller pieces based on the integer column. You can also use stored functions that return integers as the partitioning key instead of the numeric literals shown. Few other options are available in MySQL.

List Partitioning   Like an Oracle list partition, a MySQL list partition works by identifying a column that contains an integer value, the `franchise_number` in the following example. Partitioning clauses follow the list of columns and constraints and require a partitioning key to be in the primary key or indexed.

The following list partition works with literal numeric values. MySQL uses the `IN` keyword for list partitions while Oracle doesn't. Note that there's no primary key designated and an index is on the auto-incrementing surrogate key column. A complete example is provided to avoid confusion on how to index the partitioning key:

```
CREATE TABLE franchise
( franchise_id      INT UNSIGNED AUTO_INCREMENT
, franchise_number INT UNSIGNED
, franchise_name    VARCHAR(20)
, city              VARCHAR(20)
, state             VARCHAR(20)
, index idx (franchise_id))
PARTITION BY LIST(franchise_number)
( PARTITION offshore VALUES IN (49,50)
, PARTITION west VALUES IN (34,45,48)
, PARTITION desert VALUES IN (46,47)
, PARTITION rockies VALUES IN (38,41,42,44));
```

The inclusion of a `PRIMARY KEY` constraint on the `franchise_id` column would trigger an ERROR 1503 when the partitioning key isn't the primary key. The reason for the error message is that a primary key implicitly creates a unique index, and that index would conflict with the partitioning by list instruction. The use of a non-unique `idx` index on the `franchise_id` column is required when you want to partition on a non-primary key column.

Columns Partitioning   Columns partitioning is a *new* variant of range and list partitioning. It is included in MySQL 5.5 and forward. Both range and list partitioning work on an integer-based column (using `TINYINT`, `SMALLINT`, `MEDIUMINT`, `INT` [alias `INTEGER`], and `BIGINT`). Columns partitioning extends those models by expanding the possible data types for the partitioning column to include CHAR, VARCHAR, BINARY, and VARBINARY string data types, and DATE, DATETIME, or TIMESTAMP data types. You still can't use other number data types such as DECIMAL and FLOAT. The TIMESTAMP data type is also available only in range partitions with the caveat that you use a UNIX_TIMESTAMP function, according to MySQL Bug 42849.

Hash Partitioning   Hash partitions ensure an even distribution of rows across a predetermined number of partitions. It is probably the easiest way to partition a table quickly to test the result of partitioning on a large table. You should base hash partitions on a surrogate or natural primary key.

The following provides a modified example of the ordering table:

```
CREATE TABLE ordering
( ordering_id      INT UNSIGNED PRIMARY KEY AUTO_INCREMENT
, item_id          INT UNSIGNED
, rental_amount    DECIMAL(15,2)
, rental_date      DATE)
PARTITION BY HASH(ordering_id) PARTITIONS 8;
```

This is the partitioning type that benefits from a PRIMARY KEY constraint because it automatically creates a unique index that can be used by the hash. A non-unique index such as the list partitioning example doesn't work for a hash partition.

Key Partitioning   Key partitioning is valuable because you can partition on columns that aren't integers. It performs along the line of hash partitioning, except the MySQL Server uses its own hashing expression.

```
CREATE TABLE orders_list
( order_list_id      INT UNSIGNED AUTO_INCREMENT
, customer_surname   VARCHAR(30)
, store_id           INT UNSIGNED
, salesperson_id     INT UNSIGNED
, order_date         DATE
, index idx (order_list_id))
PARTITION BY KEY (order_date) PARTITIONS 8;
```

This is the only alternative when you want to partition by date ranges. Like the hash partition, it's easy to deploy. The only consideration is the number of slices that you want to make of the data in the table.

Subpartitioning   The concept of subpartitioning is also known as composite partitioning. You can subpartition range or list partitions with a hash, linear hash, or linear key.

A slight change to the previously created ordering table is required to demonstrate composite partitioning: we'll add a store_id column to the table definition. The following is an example of a range partition subpartitioned by a hash:

```
CREATE TABLE ordering
( ordering_id      INT UNSIGNED AUTO_INCREMENT
, item_id          INT UNSIGNED
, store_id         INT UNSIGNED
, rental_amount    DECIMAL(15,2)
```

```
, rental_date      DATE
, index idx (ordering_id))
PARTITION BY RANGE(item_id)
  SUBPARTITION BY HASH(store_id) SUBPARTITIONS 4
( PARTITION jan2011 VALUES LESS THAN (10000)
, PARTITION feb2011 VALUES LESS THAN (20000)
, PARTITION mar2011 VALUES LESS THAN (30000));
```

Composite partitioning is non-trivial and might require some experimentation to achieve optimal results. Plan on making a few tests of different scenarios before you deploy a solution.

Indexes

Indexes apply against tables. You can index ordinary data, such as scalar columns. Alternatively, you can use a full text index to search a large text column or a spatial index to search specialized spatial columns. These specialized columns support graphics and geometry. Full text indexes use custom parsers that are specific to languages and provide such things as lexical stemming. Both Oracle and MySQL support spatial objects.

Indexes typically resolve by using a B-Tree access path to data, which makes searching data faster. On the downside, indexes need to be refreshed as you insert new data and update existing data. You also have several options for indexes, such as hashes, hash clusters, bitmaps, key-compressed, and function-based indexes.

Unique indexes can work with one or several columns. Naturally, they work with unique data sets. Unique data sets have the highest cardinality possible. Unique indexes work best with multiple columns, because the combination of values increases the effectiveness of B-Tree and bitmap indexes. This is done by reducing the number of levels from the top of the B-Tree to the data, which means the index finds rows quickly. Although it is possible to craft many unique indexes on tables with many columns, you should remember that every unique index places a load on the server for all `INSERT`, `UPDATE`, and `DELETE` statements.

It is also possible to define a non-unique index. These are useful when they have a high cardinality, which means there's a lot of diversity between rows of data. A rule of thumb on non-unique indexes is that the distribution of data should ensure that no single set of column values exceeds 5 percent of the total data set. Following this rule, you shouldn't implement a non-unique index on a gender column that has two possibilities, for example. Likewise, a pair of columns on gender and college class standing wouldn't be a good choice for a non-unique index, because the distribution would approach 12.5 percent. A distribution of 12.5 percent would be a low cardinality value because of the similarity of the data. A non-unique index against low cardinality data would present more overhead than benefit.

Oracle Indexes

You can create a unique or non-unique index in an Oracle database. These are separate structures from the table, and you create them independently of the table in most cases. The exceptions to that creation rule occur when you define a `PRIMARY KEY` or `UNIQUE` constraint on a table, because those constraints implicitly add unique indexes. Unique indexes created by `PRIMARY KEY` and `UNIQUE` constraints can't be dropped from a database unless you alter the table and remove the constraints. You can alter many things about indexes as well as rebuild them with the `ALTER` statement, which is covered in Chapter 8. For reference, all table indexes are dropped from the database when you drop a table.

Indexes work best when they include multiple columns, but you can define an index to work on a single column. An example of a multiple column index that's critical in good design is an index that starts with the surrogate key column and includes all columns in the natural key. The reason for such an index is twofold: The natural key component contains the values that let you search for data based on business aspects of the model. The leading surrogate key lets joins resolve faster with the multiple column index.

Full text indexes work against CLOB data type columns. They let you perform searches using approximate matching and proximity matching. These types of indexes improve performance for advanced text processing such as *stemming*, where you match the root-word stem against actual occurrences of the word in use.

Spatial indexes work with Oracle object types that are specialized PL/SQL program units stored inside the database, such as stored procedures. When you define columns that use these user-defined types, the columns hold a constructor with arguments. These types of objects are known as *collapsed* objects, and you bring them to life with the TREAT function.

You create a unique index with syntax like this:

```
CREATE UNIQUE INDEX index_name
ON table_name (column_name1, column_name2, ...);
```

Oracle indexes use B-Tree by default and also support storage clauses, which are very important on large tables. Like table data, index data should be stored in as much contiguous space as possible. You organize data into contiguous space by ensuring the proper sizing of tablespaces and extents allocated to tables and indexes.

The alternative to a unique index is a *bitmapped* index. Bitmapped indexes work with data that has a low cardinality—in other words, a non-unique set of values, such as a gender column. Some restrictions apply to bitmap indexes. They can't coexist with unique indexes or domain indexes. Likewise, you can't specify bitmap indexes with a global partition index, and you can't create a secondary bitmap index on an index-organized table unless the index-organized table has a mapping table associated with it.

You create a bitmap index with syntax like this:

```
CREATE BITMAP INDEX index_name
ON table_name (column_name1, column_name2, ...);
```

A non-unique index has virtually the same syntax possibilities. All you do is drop the UNIQUE keyword, like so:

```
CREATE INDEX index_name
ON table_name (column_name1, column_name2, ...);
```

Remember that UNIQUE indexes are almost always important, but too many on a single table can slow transaction throughput. Non-unique indexes have less value but present the same demands for updates as UNIQUE indexes. Use non-unique indexes sparingly.

MySQL Indexes

MySQL supports unique and non-unique indexes against single or multiple columns. It also supports full-text searches against large strings (stored in TEXT columns), and spatial indexes against the POINT and GEOMETRY data types. These specialized types and more are supported by the Spatial Extension provided in four engines: MyISAM, InnoDB, NDB, and Archive.

Like Oracle indexes, MySQL indexes work best when they're unique or non-unique against high-cardinality data. They work poorly when placed against low-cardinality data.

You define a unique index with the following syntax:

```
CREATE UNIQUE INDEX index_name
ON table_name(column_name1, column_name2, ...) USING BTREE;
```

In lieu of the `UNIQUE` keyword, you can use `FULLTEXT` and `SPATIAL`. The absence of a qualifier creates a non-unique index. The `USING` subclause is the default, and you can replace `BTREE` with a `HASH` index type. MySQL also supports clauses for storage for the block size of the key and a `WITH PARSER` clause for text-based indexes.

A non-unique index, also known as a *key*, uses this syntax:

```
CREATE INDEX index_name
ON table_name(column_name1, column_name2, ...) USING BTREE;
```

You can also create indexes inside the `CREATE TABLE` statement. The syntax for that type of unique index is shown here:

```
, UNIQUE INDEX (column_name)
```

A non-unique index can be created by using just the `INDEX` keyword or the `KEY` keyword, like so:

```
, KEY (column_name)
```

This concludes the index section, but you might want to review the subpartitioning information earlier in the chapter. There you'll find that a non-unique key is the critical component for creating partitioned tables on non-unique columns.

Summary

This chapter covered how you create data structures, such as databases, users, tables, and indexes. It presented the syntax necessary to create these structures in Oracle and MySQL, and discussed similarities and differences between the databases.

Not all things in Oracle map directly to MySQL, and vice versa. It's important where possible to implement concepts that are more portable than product-specific. Likewise, it's also important that you not overlook opportunities presented by product-specific features.

Mastery Check

The mastery check is a series of true or false and multiple choice questions that let you confirm how well you understand the material in the chapter. You may check the Appendix for answers to these questions.

1. **True** ☐ **False** ☐ A column can be made mandatory by using an in-line `NOT NULL` constraint in Oracle and MySQL databases.

2. **True** ☐ **False** ☐ A `CHECK` constraint can be implemented in a MySQL database.

3. **True** ☐ **False** ☐ A FOREIGN KEY constraint can be implemented against only one
    column.

4. **True** ☐ **False** ☐ You can create tables with nested tables in an Oracle database.

5. **True** ☐ **False** ☐ You can use an UNSIGNED INT data type when creating a table in an
    Oracle database.

6. **True** ☐ **False** ☐ Creating a unique index inside the CREATE TABLE statement is
    possible in MySQL.

7. **True** ☐ **False** ☐ A range partition uses the VALUES IN clause in an Oracle database.

8. **True** ☐ **False** ☐ An ENUM data type allows only one of a list of values to be stored in a
    column.

9. **True** ☐ **False** ☐ MySQL supports composite partitioning.

10. **True** ☐ **False** ☐ A foreign key works whether the data type is a signed or unsigned
    integer.

11. Which of the following data types isn't supported in a MySQL database?

    A. BLOB

    B. MEDIUMCLOB

    C. TEXT

    D. DOUBLE

    E. FLOAT

12. Which of the following data types isn't supported in an Oracle database?

    A. CLOB

    B. BLOB

    C. NCHAR

    D. VARYING CHARACTER

    E. CHAR

13. Which of the following aren't date-time data types (multiple possible answers)?

    A. DATE in Oracle

    B. DATE in MySQL

    C. TIMESTAMP in either database

    D. TIME in MySQL

    E. YEAR in MySQL

14. Which of the following syntax operations are prohibited in MySQL?

    A. Defining an in-line NOT NULL constraint

    B. Defining an in-line FOREIGN KEY constraint

    C. Defining an in-line UNIQUE constraint

    D. Defining an in-line PRIMARY KEY constraint

    E. Defining an out-of-line FOREIGN KEY constraint

15. Which data type is supported by list and range partitioning in MySQL?

    A. FLOAT

    B. CHAR

    C. VARCHAR

    D. DATE

    E. INT

CHAPTER
7

Modifying Users
and Structures

his chapter focuses on how you can change users, databases, tables, and indexes you've created in the database, and it explores how you can change your session to meet your needs in Oracle and MySQL. The chapter is organized by the following topics:

- Users
- Databases
- Sessions
- Tables
- Views
- Indexes

As explained in Chapter 6, users are synonymous with schemas in an Oracle database, and they're distinctly separate in a MySQL database. Databases are private work areas in both cases, and changes to them remain until you remove or change them again. Connections to your database management system are a session, and a session lasts only for the duration of your connection to a database or schema. Any changes to a session are lost when you break the connection by logging out or, in Oracle, by connecting as another user to another database. Tables are permanent structures unless you define them as temporary tables. Changes made to tables, like databases, last until you drop the table, undo the changes, or make new changes. As with tables, indexes exist as long as the table they reference exists, unless you drop or alter the table. Although users can modify index structures, content changes in the index occur only through changes in the referenced tables.

The following sections discuss how you can work with changing and removing users, databases, sessions, tables, and indexes. You'll learn what a developer needs to know to work with these structures in Oracle and MySQL. You won't find an exhaustive listing of all the things you can do with or to databases, because entire books are written on that, such as the *Oracle Database 11g DBA Handbook* (McGraw-Hill, 2008).

Users

The user and schema are inseparable in an Oracle DBMS. They share the same names, and the user generally holds all defined privileges on the schema. That means you must change a user to change a schema or database. Commands that change the database are actually changing accounts on the Oracle server. When you change a database in MySQL, you are changing only a private work area and not the database server.

The following sections cover the Oracle and MySQL commands used to change and remove users. Occasional cross-references exist in the text, so read the Oracle section before the MySQL section.

Oracle Users

Oracle users typically don't have privileges that let them change their user or schema properties unless they've been granted super user privileges. That means commands that change users or schema are run typically by the SYSTEM user. Dropping a user is a rare occasion in most Oracle databases, but changing properties of the user occurs routinely.

Oracle ALTER USER Statement

The prototype for the ALTER USER statement lets you change properties of a user, such as their role, profile, storage, password, and account status. The generic prototype for the ALTER USER statement is shown here:

```
ALTER USER user_name
[IDENTIFIED
{[BY current_password REPLACE new_password] |
 [EXTERNALLY AS 'certificate_name'] |
 [GLOBALLY AS 'directory_name']]}
[DEFAULT TABLESPACE tablespace_name]
[TEMPORARY TABLESPACE {tablespace_name | tablespace_group }]
[QUOTA {size_clause | UNLIMITED} ON tablespace_name]
[PROFILE profile_name]
[DEFAULT ROLE {role_name | ALL EXCEPT role_name | NONE}]
[PASSWORD EXPIRE]
[ACCOUNT {LOCK | UNLOCK}]
[{GRANT | REVOKE} CONNECT THROUGH
 {ENTERPRISE USERS |
  WITH {ROLE {role_name | ALL EXCEPT role_name} |
        NO ROLES} [AUTHENTICATION REQUIRED]}]
```

Using the ALTER USER statement, you can configure one of three different authentication types for a user: password, Secure Sockets Layer (SSL) certificate, and Lightweight Directory Access Protocol (LDAP) certificate. You also have the security options to expire a password (useful when terminating employees) and locking an account.

The other clauses let you change default or temporary tablespaces, or a quota, profile, role, or pass-through authentication, none of which occurs frequently. These changes are also seldom made by developers, because doing so is the DBA's responsibility.

If a user loses a password, you could change the user's password like this:

```
ALTER USER stanley IDENTIFIED stanley;
```

Then you'd need to let the user know the new password and hope somebody doesn't crack it before the user logs in to change it.

Better yet, you can go one more step by expiring the password after changing it. An expired password prompts the user for a new password when he or she logs in. You expire a password like this:

```
ALTER USER stanley PASSWORD EXPIRE;
```

The user would try to connect like this,

```
sqlplus stanley/stanley
```

and would then see the following messages and prompts at the command-line interface to SQL*Plus, where the user would enter a new password:

```
C:\data\oracle>sqlplus stanley/stanley
SQL*Plus: Release 11.1.0.7.0 - Production on Thu Jun 30 21:40:45 2011
Copyright (c) 1982, 2008, Oracle.  All rights reserved.
```

```
ERROR:
ORA-28001: the password has expired

Changing password for stanley
New password:
Retype new password:
Password changed
```

Assuming you've configured the database to use LDAP authentication and provided a wallet, you can also change a login to an LDAP validation, like this:

```
ALTER USER miles IDENTIFIED GLOBALLY AS 'CN=miles,O=apple,C=US'
```

A user can also change his/her password with the `ALTER USER` statement. The following syntax requires that the user know his/her current password:

```
ALTER USER stanley IDENTIFIED BY stanley REPLACE beatles1964;
```

The only problem with the preceding syntax is that it discloses the user's new password in plain text. Unfortunately, there's no way around that syntax limitation. More often than not, individual users remember their passwords and can change it like this:

```
SQL> password
Changing password for STANLEY
Old password:
New password:
Retype new password:
Password changed
```

The reason changes of tablespaces, roles, and profiles aren't done by developers is because they are managed by the super user accounts. These super user accounts are owned by DBAs who administer the physical resources of the database. Developers work closely with the system administrators to ensure that adequate disk space and processing resources are available for the database on any server.

A key DBA activity that you should know how to perform while working in your laptop or desktop development databases is locking and unlocking accounts, such as the oe sample or the legacy scott schemas. You would unlock the oe schema with this syntax:

```
ALTER USER oe ACCOUNT UNLOCK;
```

Alternatively, you can open an account and change the password with a single command like this:

```
ALTER USER scott ACCOUNT UNLOCK IDENTIFIED BY tiger;
```

After you're done with a sample schema like these, you can lock them away by typing this:

```
ALTER USER scott ACCOUNT LOCK;
```

You should never leave user schemas open (unlocked) when you're not actively using them. It's simply a best practice to lock unused schemas that you might need to reopen and likewise to drop obsolete schemas.

Oracle DROP Statement

DROP statements are Data Definition Language (DDL) commands that let you remove structures from the database. The DROP statement uses different prototypes depending on whether you're removing a user, table, object type, function, procedure, or sequence.

The DROP USER statement removes the user and his/her schema. Sometimes other schemas have dependencies on tables or other structures in a schema. You need to specify the CASCADE option when dependencies exist, which will cause the DROP statement to drop them in cascading fashion.

The prototype is small and easy:

```
DROP USER user_name [CASCADE]
```

You could drop the scott sample schema with this command:

```
DROP USER scott;
```

TIP
Try to drop the user without the CASCADE option first, and if it fails, figure out what the dependency is before you append CASCADE to the statement.

MySQL Users

Like Oracle users, MySQL users typically don't have permissions to change or drop other users unless they've been given administrator privileges on the server. This section contains subsections on changing and dropping a user.

MySQL SET PASSWORD Statement

There is no ALTER USER statement in MySQL. If you're asking how you or an administrator can change a user's password without an ALTER USER statement, there is a way. This section shows you the syntax.

A root super user can add a password or change a password with the following syntax:

```
SET PASSWORD FOR user_name = PASSWORD('password_string');
```

If the user name existed in the database with more than one hostname value, the syntax changes to this:

```
SET PASSWORD FOR 'user_name'@'host_string' = PASSWORD('new_password');
```

The host_string can have several possible values. It can be localhost for server-only connections, a '%' for anywhere, an IP address, or a DNS recorded machine name, domain, or subdomain address. You can find more on user connections in the "MySQL Databases" section of Chapter 6.

Individual users can also change their own password with the following variation on the SET PASSWORD command syntax:

```
mysql> SET PASSWORD = PASSWORD('new_password');
```

No other aspects of MySQL users are subject to change other than grants of privileges. That's because a MySQL user is distinct from a database, and a user is really only a name, encrypted password, and a host linked to a group of privileges. Some DBAs and developers update user information in the data catalog, which is fine when you're running the Community Edition. You should not alter the data dictionary without the guidance of Oracle Support for commercially licensed versions of MySQL.

MySQL DROP USER Statement

A `root` super user or other authorized administrative user can drop a user with the following syntax:

```
DROP USER user_name;
```

Users create tables, views, and routines in databases, so you can drop a user without any impact on the structures they've created. Although this approach differs from that of Oracle, you should find it easy to use and leverage.

Database

Changes to the database are typically the responsibility of the DBA. They involve allocation of space to support what resides in the database. Oracle uses the `ALTER DATABASE` statement to change the definition of the user's private work area. You can find more on setting these parameters in the *Oracle Database Administrator's Guide 11g*.

MySQL treats databases quite differently from Oracle, and although you can use the `ALTER DATABASE` statement in MySQL, its uses are relatively small—all you can do is change the collation or character set. Both of these settings belong to the DBA role.

Sessions

Changes to the session or connection are supported by the `ALTER SESSION` statement in an Oracle database, but the MySQL database has no equivalent. Two key `ALTER SESSION` statement commands should be at every developer's finger tips: one that enables tracing and another that accesses conditional compilation statements in PL/SQL.

Enable SQL Tracing

You need the `ALTER SESSION` privilege to work with SQL tracing commands. Without the `ALTER SESSION` privilege, you'd raise this type of error when you try to enable or disable SQL tracing with the `DBMS_SESSION` package:

```
BEGIN DBMS_SESSION.SESSION_TRACE_ENABLE(); END;
*
ERROR at line 1:
ORA-01031: insufficient privileges
ORA-06512: at "SYS.DBMS_SESSION", line 269
ORA-06512: at line 1
```

The `ALTER SESSION` privilege can be granted by the `SYS` or `SYSTEM` user with this command:

```
GRANT ALTER SESSION TO user_name;
```

The newer and Oracle-recommended way to enable SQL tracing is to use the `DBMS_SESSION` or `DBMS_SYSTEM` packages. The `DBMS_SESSION` package is generally available to developers, while `DBMS_SYSTEM` is reserved for super users and those with DBA privileges.

DBA Insight

DBAs have much wider permissions than average users, and they have great knowledge about the internal workings of the database. DBAs can identify the security ID (SID) and serial number values for any active session.

With this information, DBAs can enable and disable tracing with the `DBMS_SYSTEM` package. To use it, they need to know how to identify your session's unique identifier and serial number.

A DBA would call the following to enable a user's session for tracing:

```
EXECUTE DBMS_SYSTEM.SET_SQL_TRACE_IN_SESSION(sid, serial#);
```

The reason that DBAs assume this role is because they're unwilling or prevented by policy to provide access to individual users. For example, a DBA may enable tracing on a session running the Oracle e-Business Suite in a schema where the developer lacks privileges. After confirming that the user has generated the trace file, the DBA will disable tracing because it consumes physical resources.

The `DBMS_SESSION` package lets you enable tracing, like this:

```
SQL> EXECUTE DBMS_SESSION.SESSION_TRACE_ENABLE();
```

After you've run the code for tracing purposes, you should disable SQL tracing with another call to the `DBMS_SESSION` package:

```
SQL> EXECUTE DBMS_SESSION.SESSION_TRACE_DISABLE();
```

There's also an older (legacy) way to enable and disable tracing that still works, notwithstanding Oracle's announcement that it has been deprecated. It requires that you hold the `ALTER SESSION` privilege. You enable tracing within your session with this command:

```
ALTER SESSION SET sql_trace = true;
```

You can disable it by setting `sql_trace` to `false`, like so:

```
ALTER SESSION SET sql_trace = false;
```

You've got the old and then the new techniques. The new technique creates a published method that lets Oracle hide, abstract, or encapsulate logic so that they can change keywords without changing command structures. My recommendation is that you go with Oracle's recommended syntax and move to the `DBMS_SESSION` package. Table 7-1 lists the tracing levels available in the Oracle database.

The default tracing level for the Oracle database is level 4, which means SQL parsing, executing, fetching, and bind variables are traced. Sometimes you need to get both waits and bind variables, and you can change your session to provide that level of tracing (as qualified in Table 7-1).

The following example changes the tracing level to the maximum setting (level 12):

```
ALTER SESSION
SET EVENTS = '10046 trace name context forever, level 12';
```

Level Flag	Tracing Level
0	No generated statistics
1	Standard trace output includes SQL parsing, executing, and fetching
2	Same as level 1
4	Same as level 1 plus information on bind variables
8	Same as level 1 plus information on waits
12	Same as level 1 plus information on bind variables and waits

TABLE 7-1. *SQL Tracing Levels*

After you've complete the tracing process, don't forget to return your session to the default. That's because the higher level of information incurs a performance cost when you re-enable tracing in the session. You can reset the session to the default with this command:

```
ALTER SYSTEM
SET EVENTS = '10046 trace name context forever, level 4'
```

This should be all you need on the database side, but you'll also need to understand how to use Oracle's `tkprof` command-line utility. `tkprof` formats the trace statistics into a readable (with practice) report. Please check Chapter 21 of the *Oracle Database Performance Tuning Guide* for more on the `tkprof` utility.

Enable Conditional Compilation

Oracle introduced *conditional compilation* in Oracle Database 10*g* Release 2. It allows you to embed debugging logic in your production programs that runs only when you want it to run. This is convenient, because a particular error might show up only when a specific customer is using your code, and there's no inexpensive way to track down the problem without performing a test at the customer's site. Traditionally, somebody would have to write a customer version of the stored program, ship it to the customer, and teach the customer how to test it. Conditional compilation eliminates that need.

A quick sample of how you embed a debugging message with conditional compilation is the following anonymous block PL/SQL program with a conditional `IF` block (you can find more on PL/SQL in Chapter 13):

```
SQL> SET SERVEROUTPUT ON SIZE UNLIMITED
SQL> BEGIN
  2    NULL; -- At least one statement without debug enabled.
  3    $IF $$DEBUG = 1 $THEN
  4      dbms_output.put_line('Debug Level 1 Enabled.');
  5    $END
  6  END;
  7  /
```

The first line sets a SQL*Plus environment variable that allows you to display output from PL/SQL block programs (check Chapter 2 for more details). Line 2 has a single `NULL;` statement, because there must be at least one statement in any block for it to parse (compile) and run. Lines 3 to 5 contain a block that runs only when you've enabled conditional compilation.

Naturally, this requires that you have the `ALTER SESSION` privilege, as discussed in the preceding section. You enable conditional compilation with this statement:

```
SQL> ALTER SESSION SET PLSQL_CCFLAGS = 'debug:1';
```

Now it will print the following message from inside the `IF` block:

```
Debug Level 1 Enabled.
```

As you might have guessed, there would be no recompilation of a stored program required to run the code in debug mode. Likewise, you can disable it by resetting the `PLSQL_CCFLAGS` value.

You've now learned the most critical things available for development through the `ALTER SESSION` statement. You can do many more things at the session level, and I suggest that you explore these.

Tables

Table definitions and constraints change over time for many reasons. These changes occur because developers discover more information about the business model, which requires changes to table definitions. This section examines how you can add, modify, and remove columns or constraints; rename tables, columns, or constraints; and drop tables.

First, however, you need to understand how table definitions are stored in the data catalogs. When you understand the rules of these structures and how they're stored, you can appreciate why SQL is able to let you change so much, so easily.

Data Catalog Table Definitions

The data catalog stores everything by the numbers, which happens to be through surrogate primary keys. The database also maintains a unique index on object names, which means that you can use a name only once per schema in an Oracle or MySQL database. This list of unique values is known as the schema's namespace.

Oracle Data Catalog

As discussed, Oracle maintains the data catalog in the `SYS` schema and provides access to administrative views, which are prefaced by `ALL_`, `DBA_`, and `USER_`. The `USER_` preface is available to every schema for objects that a user owns. The `ALL_` and `DBA_` prefixes give you access to objects owned by others, and only super or administrative users have access privileges to these views.

Many developer tools, such as the Oracle SQL Developer, Quest's Toad for Oracle, or Oracle CASE tools, can easily display information from the data catalog views. Sometimes you need to explore a database for specific information, and the fastest way would be to launch a few quick queries against the data catalog. The catalog view that lets you explore column definitions is the `USER_TAB_COLUMNS` view (short for table's columns).

The following query leverages some SQL*Plus formatting to let you find the definition of a specific table and display it in a single page format:

```
SQL> COLUMN column_id FORMAT 999 HEADING "Column|ID #"
SQL> COLUMN table_name FORMAT A12 HEADING "Table Name"
SQL> COLUMN column_name FORMAT A18 HEADING "Column Name"
SQL> COLUMN data_type FORMAT A10 HEADING "Data Type"
SQL> COLUMN csize FORMAT 999 HEADING "Column|Size"
SQL> SELECT    utc.column_id
  2  ,          utc.table_name
  3  ,          utc.column_name
  4  ,          utc.data_type
  5  ,          NVL(utc.data_length,utc.data_precision) AS csize
  6  FROM      user_tab_columns utc
  7  WHERE     utc.table_name = 'CONTACT';
```

The table name is in uppercase because Oracle maintains metadata text in an uppercase string. You could replace line 7 with the following line that uses the UPPER function to promote the text case before comparison, if you prefer to type table names and other metadata values in lowercase or mixed case:

```
  7  WHERE     utc.table_name = UPPER('contact');
```

The query displays the following:

Column ID #	Table Name	Column Name	Data Type	Column Size
1	CONTACT	CONTACT_ID	NUMBER	22
2	CONTACT	MEMBER_ID	NUMBER	22
3	CONTACT	CONTACT_TYPE	NUMBER	22
4	CONTACT	FIRST_NAME	VARCHAR2	20
5	CONTACT	MIDDLE_NAME	VARCHAR2	20
6	CONTACT	LAST_NAME	VARCHAR2	20
7	CONTACT	CREATED_BY	NUMBER	22
8	CONTACT	CREATION_DATE	DATE	7
9	CONTACT	LAST_UPDATED_BY	NUMBER	22
10	CONTACT	LAST_UPDATE_DATE	DATE	7

The column_id value identifies the position of columns for INSERT statements. The ordered list is set when you define a table with the CREATE TABLE statement or is reset when you modify it with an ALTER TABLE statement. Columns keep the position location when you change the columns' name or data type. Columns lose their position when you remove them from a table's definition, and when you add them back, they appear at the end of the positional list of values. There's no way to shift their position in an Oracle database without dropping and re-creating the table, which differs from how it's done in MySQL, where you can shift the position of columns with an ALTER TABLE statement.

Each column has a data type that defines its physical size. The foregoing example shows that number data types take up to 22 characters, the strings take 20 characters, and the dates take 7 characters. As you learned in Chapter 6, numbers can also have a specification (the values to the right of the decimal point) that fits within the maximum length (or precision) of the data type.

The USER_CONSTRAINTS and USER_CONS_COLUMNS views hold information about constraints. The USER_CONSTRAINTS view holds the descriptive information about the type of constraint, and the USER_CONS_COLUMNS view holds the list of columns participating in the constraint.

You would use a query like this to discover constraints and columns (formatting provided by the SQL*Plus commands):

```
SQL> COLUMN table_name FORMAT A12 HEADING "Table Name"
SQL> COLUMN constraint_name FORMAT A16 HEADING "Constraint|Name"
SQL> COLUMN position FORMAT A8 HEADING "Position"
SQL> COLUMN column_name FORMAT A18 HEADING "Column Name"
SQL> SELECT    ucc.table_name
  2  ,          ucc.constraint_name
  3  ,          uc.constraint_type ||':'|| ucc.position AS position
  4  ,          ucc.column_name
  5  FROM       user_constraints uc JOIN user_cons_columns ucc
  6  ON         uc.table_name = ucc.table_name
  7  AND        uc.constraint_name = ucc.constraint_name
  8  WHERE      ucc.table_name = 'CONTACT'
  9  ORDER BY   ucc.constraint_name
 10  ,          ucc.position;
```

which would produce the following output:

```
                     Constraint
Table Name           Name                Position Column Name
-------------        ------------------   -------- ------------------
CONTACT              PK_CONTACT_1         P:1      CONTACT_ID
CONTACT              UNIQUE_NAME          U:1      MEMBER_ID
CONTACT              UNIQUE_NAME          U:2      FIRST_NAME
CONTACT              UNIQUE_NAME          U:3      MIDDLE_NAME
CONTACT              UNIQUE_NAME          U:4      LAST_NAME
```

The first line of output reports a single column primary key, which is most often a surrogate primary key. You can tell that because a constraint_type column value represents the code (P) for a PRIMARY KEY constraint, as qualified in Table 7-2. In the query, the position column is the

Constraint Code	Constraint Meaning
C	Represents a CHECK or NOT NULL constraint
P	Represents a PRIMARY KEY constraint
R	Represents a FOREIGN KEY, which is really referential integrity between tables and why an R is the code value
U	Represents a UNIQUE constraint

TABLE 7-2. *Constraint Codes and Types*

concatenated result of the constraint type code and position number related to the column name. The remaining lines report a UNIQUE constraint that spans four columns, which is the natural key for the table. It's an imperfect third-normal form (3NF) key for the subject of the table, but it's an adequate natural key for our demonstration purposes.

The material in this section has described how you find definitions for tables and constraints. You'll find this information helpful when you need to change definitions or remove them from tables.

MySQL Data Catalog

MySQL has two data catalogs: an updatable catalog in the mysql database and the read-only catalog in the information_schema database. The read-only view is the user view of the database catalog.

The columns table contains information about columns in tables and is equivalent to the user_tab_columns view in Oracle. You can examine the data catalog by using a CASE tool, such as MySQL Workbench, Quest's Toad for MySQL, or other vendor products, or you can write quick queries.

You can inspect a table (contact in this case) with the following query:

```
SELECT    c.ordinal_position
,         c.table_name
,         c.column_name
,         c.data_type
,         IFNULL(c.character_maximum_length,c.numeric_precision) AS size
FROM      columns c
WHERE     c.table_name = 'CONTACT';
```

which would display the following:

```
+------------------+------------+------------------+-----------+------+
| ordinal_position | table_name | column_name      | data_type | SIZE |
+------------------+------------+------------------+-----------+------+
|                1 | contact    | contact_id       | int       |   10 |
|                2 | contact    | member_id        | int       |   10 |
|                3 | contact    | contact_type     | int       |   10 |
|                4 | contact    | first_name       | char      |   20 |
|                5 | contact    | middle_name      | char      |   20 |
|                6 | contact    | last_name        | char      |   20 |
|                7 | contact    | created_by       | int       |   10 |
|                8 | contact    | creation_date    | date      | NULL |
|                9 | contact    | last_updated_by  | int       |   10 |
|               10 | contact    | last_update_date | date      | NULL |
+------------------+------------+------------------+-----------+------+
```

The ordinal_position column records the order of the column set by the CREATE TABLE statement. Like Oracle, these positions remain the same when you change column names or data types, and a column gets the last ordinal_position number when a column is dropped and then re-added to the table. Unlike Oracle, MySQL lets you shift the position of columns with the ALTER TABLE statement.

The physical size of numeric and string columns are reported, but the size of dates isn't. You can check the data catalog of a table to monitor the impact of changes made by the ALTER TABLE statement.

Table-level constraints are in the `table_constraints` and `key_column_usage` views. Table-level constraints should have a name, but no syntax exists to name the `UNIQUE [KEY]` or `PRIMARY KEY` values. MySQL actually has rules for how these are stored in the data catalog.

Dynamic queries require that you set a session variable that matches the one in the query, because, unlike in Oracle, in MySQL, there are no substitution variables that prompt for inputs when you call scripts. The following script uses `@sv_table_name` as a session variable, and you'd set it this way before calling the script from a file:

```
mysql> SET @sv_table_name = 'rental_item';
```

The following query lets you find keys and constraints on MySQL tables, provided you're using the `information_schema` database:

```
SELECT     tc.constraint_name
,          tc.constraint_type
,          kcu.ordinal_position
,          kcu.column_name
FROM       table_constraints tc JOIN key_column_usage kcu
ON         tc.table_name = kcu.table_name
AND        tc.constraint_name = kcu.constraint_name
AND        tc.table_name LIKE @sv_table_name
ORDER BY   tc.constraint_name
,          tc.constraint_type
,          kcu.ordinal_position;
```

This query only works "as is" if you're connected to the `information_schema` database. You could enable it to run without using the database by modifying the table declarations in the `FROM` clause, like this:

```
FROM       information_schema.table_constraints tc INNER JOIN
               information_schema.key_column_usage kcu
```

When you've previously set the `@sv_table_name` session variable with a value of `rental_item` (the `table_name`), you would see the following results in the sample database:

constraint_name	constraint_type	ordinal_position	column_name
natural_key	UNIQUE	1	rental_item_id
natural_key	UNIQUE	2	rental_id
natural_key	UNIQUE	3	item_id
natural_key	UNIQUE	4	rental_item_type
natural_key	UNIQUE	5	rental_item_price
PRIMARY	PRIMARY KEY	1	rental_item_id
rental_item	UNIQUE	1	rental_item_id
rental_item	UNIQUE	2	rental_id
rental_item	UNIQUE	3	item_id
rental_item	UNIQUE	4	rental_item_type
rental_item	UNIQUE	5	rental_item_price

The result set appears to have three possible candidate keys: two unique constraints on the same set of columns and a primary key on what appears to be a surrogate key (a column based on a sequence value). It's likely that a mistake was made in this situation that led to deployment of two unique constraints.

There's also a hidden rule in this result set (that is, I couldn't find it in the documentation): the unique key in MySQL takes the table name as a constraint name. The `natural_key` constraint belongs to a unique index that was added to the table. You should have only one of these per table across all five columns, either a `UNIQUE KEY` or a `UNIQUE INDEX`. My suggestions would be the `UNIQUE KEY`, which should span the five columns.

A `UNIQUE INDEX` on only the four columns that make up the natural key is critical when you run the `LOAD DATA` statement, use `INSERT` statements with the `ON DUPLICATE KEY` clause, or when you run the `REPLACE INTO` statement. The `UNIQUE INDEX` should enclose a natural key and should guarantee that only one row contains those values. The presence of two matching unique constraints doesn't improve your searching speed, but it does slow down the inserting, updating, and deleting of data. You should delete one of these unique indexes, because it would speed your transaction and updates: any `INSERT`, `UPDATE`, or `DELETE` statement results in maintenance that changes the values in the index.

The output also shows a primary key based on a surrogate key. Notice that the constraint name is `PRIMARY` by default. The `PRIMARY` constraint is on the surrogate key column only, but the `UNIQUE rental_item` key includes the surrogate key column, and the surrogate key column leads the `UNIQUE KEY` to speed joins. This technique leverages five columns to speed the B-Tree resolution to any given row.

The following sections explore how you make changes to tables. Part of the following discussion refers to how those changes impact the ordering of columns in the data catalog.

Adding, Modifying, and Dropping Columns

Database tables help you normalize information that supports businesses, research, or engineering processes. In the real world, requirements change, and eventually modifying a table becomes necessary. Some of these changes are relatively trivial, such as changing a column name or data type. Some changes are less trivial, such as when some descriptive item (column) is overlooked, a column isn't large enough to hold a large number or string, or a column of data needs to be renamed or moved to another column. You can make any of these changes using the `ALTER TABLE` statement.

More involved changes occur in three situations:

- When you must change a column's data type when it already contains rows of data
- When you rename a column when existing SQL statements already use the older column
- When you shift the position of adjoining columns that share the same data type

When you need to change a column's data type and the column contains data, you need to develop a data migration plan. Small data migration might entail adding a new column, moving the contents from one column to the other, and then dropping the original column. Unless the database supports an implicit casting operation from the current to future data type, you will need a SQL statement to change the data type explicitly and put it into the new column.

Changing the name of a column in a table seems a trifling thing, but it's not insignificant when application software uses that column name in SQL statements. Any change to the column name will break the application software. You need to identify all dependent code artifacts and ensure that they're changed at the same time you make the changes to the column in the table. A full regression testing plan needs to occur when columns are renamed in tables that support working application software. You can start by querying the `ALL_`, `DBA_`, or `USER_DEPENDENCIES` views that preserve dependencies about tables and stored program units.

Shifting the position of columns can have two different types of impacts. One potential impact is that you break `INSERT` statements that don't use a column list before the `VALUES` clause or subquery. This happens when the columns have different data types, because the `INSERT` statements will fail and raise errors. The other potential impact is much worse, because it produces corrupt data. This happens when you change the position of two columns that share the same data type. This change doesn't break `INSERT` statements in an easily detectable way, as did the other scenario, because it simply inserts the data into the wrong columns. The fix is the same as when you change the positions of columns that have different data types, but the extent of the fix depends on when you notice the problem and how much corrupt data you need to sanitize (fix).

MySQL supports a `SET` clause in `INSERT` statements. This variation on traditional `INSERT` statements provides the closest thing to named notation that exists in SQL. Named notation using the `SET` clause pairs the column name directly with the value.

These risks should be managed by your company's release engineering team and should be subject to careful software configuration management of your code repository. You can leverage the `ALL_`, `DBA_`, and `USER_DEPENDENCIES` views in Oracle to check on dependencies in your software. Unfortunately, there is no equivalent view in MySQL.

Release Engineering

Release engineering is a component of software engineering, and it focuses on how you plan and control the creation and evolution of software—in other words, how you set, enforce, evaluate, and manage software standards. The more time you take to avoid problems, the less time you'll take fixing them.

During the course of normal product release cycles, release engineers manage multiple code branches and dependency trees. Good release engineers invest proactively in software configuration management, because they know it helps identify where problems exist. In a proactive model, you examine process and software dependencies to identify and manage risk exposure. You take corrective action before the event occurs in this approach, which requires you to set and enforce standards that prevent errors.

For example, in a database-centric application, you would check the impact of table definition changes before making them. That's because those types of changes can destabilize your application software. You flag all code modules that depend on existing table and view definitions so you can have them changed concurrently as part of the project. Identifying errors before regression testing by quality and assurance teams is less expensive than fixing these errors after deployment.

This type of good release engineering requires a code repository that tracks dependencies and prevents check-ins that would break other code modules. You need to understand the dependencies in your software process to create an effective process, and you need process automation to manage it. Like any good application that prevents a user from entering garbage data, release management should prevent dependency invalidation. Sometimes this means disallowing changes until you understand their full impact.

The SQL prototypes and mechanics of column maintenance differ between Oracle and MySQL. The next two sections qualify how you make these types of changes in the two databases.

Oracle Column and Constraint Maintenance

The `ALTER TABLE` statement allows you to add columns or constraints, to modify properties of columns and constraints, and to drop columns or constraints. A number of DBA type properties are excluded from the `ATLER TABLE` prototype, and the focus here is on those features that support relational tables.

Here's the basic prototype for the `ALTER TABLE` statement:

```
ALTER TABLE [schema_name.]table_name
[RENAME TO new_table_name]
[READ ONLY]
[READ WRITE]
[{NO PARALLEL | PARALLEL n}]
[ADD
  ({column_name data_type [SORT][DEFAULT value][ENCRYPT key] |
    virtual_column_name} data_type [GENERATED][ALWAYS] AS (expression)}
  ,{column_name data_type [SORT][DEFAULT value][ENCRYPT key] |
    virtual_column_name} data_type [GENERATED][ALWAYS] AS (expression)}
  [, ...])]
[MODIFY
  ({column_name data_type [SORT][DEFAULT value][ENCRYPT key] |
    virtual_column_name} data_type [GENERATED][ALWAYS] AS (expression)}
  ,{column_name data_type [SORT][DEFAULT value][ENCRYPT key] |
    virtual_column_name} data_type [GENERATED][ALWAYS] AS (expression)}
  [, ...])]
[DROP
  (column_name {CASCADE CONSTRAINTS | INVALIDATE} [CHECKPOINT n]
  ,column_name {CASCADE CONSTRAINTS | INVALIDATE} [CHECKPOINT n]
  [, ...])]
[ADD [CONSTRAINT constraint_name]
  {PRIMARY KEY (column_name [,column_name [, ...]) |
   UNIQUE (column_name [,column_name [, ...]) |
   CHECK (check_condition) |
   FOREIGN KEY (column_name [,column_name [, ...])
   REFERENCES table_name (column_name [,column_name [, ...])}]
[MODIFY data_type [SORT][DEFAULT value][ENCRYPT key] |
    virtual_column_name} data_type [GENERATED][ALWAYS] AS (expression)}
  [, ...])]
[RENAME COLUMN old_column_name TO new_column_name]
[RENAME CONSTRAINT old_constraint_name TO new_constraint_name]
```

The following sections provide working examples that add, modify, rename, and drop columns and constraints. Notice that you don't add a `NOT NULL` constraint to a column, but you modify the property of an existing column.

Adding Oracle Columns and Constraints   This section shows you how to add columns and constraints. It also provides some guidance on when you can constrain a column as `NOT NULL`.

Here's how you add a new column to a table:

```
SQL> ALTER TABLE rental_item
  2    ADD (rental_item_price  NUMBER);
```

If the table contains no data, you could also add the column with a NOT NULL constraint, like this:

```
SQL> ALTER TABLE rental_item ADD
  2    (rental_item_price  NUMBER CONSTRAINT nn8_rental_item NOT NULL);
```

Adding a column with a NOT NULL constraint fails when rows are included in the table, because when you add the column, its values are empty in all the table rows. The attempt would raise the following error message:

```
ALTER TABLE rental_item
            *
ERROR at line 1:
ORA-01758: table must be empty to add mandatory (NOT NULL) column
```

You can disable the constraint until you've entered any missing values, and then you can re-enable the constraint. After you've added values to all rows of a nullable column, you can constrain the column to disallow null values. The syntax requires you to modify the column, like so:

```
SQL> ALTER TABLE rental_item MODIFY
  2    (rental_item_price  NUMBER CONSTRAINT nn8_rental_item NOT NULL)
  3  DISABLE CONSTRAINT nn8_rental_item;
```

You can also add more than one column at a time with the ALTER TABLE statement. The following would add two columns:

```
SQL> ALTER TABLE rental_item
  2    ADD (rental_item_price  NUMBER)
  3    ADD (rental_item_type   NUMBER);
```

Notice that no comma appears between the two ADD clauses; a comma *is* included when you perform the same statement in MySQL. There's no cute mnemonic to keep this straight, so you'll just have to remember it (probably after you've looked it up a dozen times or so).

That's it for columns. Now you'll see how to add the other four constraints that work with the ADD clause: PRIMARY KEY, CHECK, UNIQUE, and FOREIGN KEY. Note that, as demonstrated in the case of NOT NULL, you can raise errors with these statements when you already have data in a table and it fails to meet the rule of the constraint.

All the following examples work when tables are empty or conform to the constraint rules. After all, what would be the point of a database constraint that didn't constrain behaviors?

This example adds a PRIMARY KEY constraint to a surrogate key column. A primary key in this case restricts a single column's behavior. Here's the syntax:

```
SQL> ALTER TABLE calendar
  2    ADD PRIMARY KEY (calendar_id);
```

The alternative would be to add a PRIMARY KEY constraint on the natural key columns, like this:

```
SQL> ALTER TABLE calendar
  2    ADD PRIMARY KEY (month_name, start_date, end_date);
```

The CHECK constraint is very powerful in Oracle, because it lets you enforce a single rule or a complex set of rules. In the following example, you add the column and then an out-of-line constraint on the new column:

```
SQL> ALTER TABLE calendar
  2    ADD (month_type VARCHAR2(1))
  3    ADD CONSTRAINT ck_month_type
  4    CHECK(month_type = 'S' AND month_shortname = 'FEB'
  5      OR  month_type = 'M' AND month_shortname IN ('APR','JUN','SEP', 'NOV')
  6      OR  month_type = 'L')
```

The CHECK constraint verifies that a month_type value must correspond to a combination of its value and the value of the month_shortname column. Any month with less than 30 days holds an S (short), with 30 days holds an M (medium), and with 31 days holds an L (long).

The following UNIQUE constraint guarantees that no start_date and end_date combination can exist twice in a calendar table:

```
SQL> ALTER TABLE calendar
  2    ADD CONSTRAINT un_california UNIQUE (start_date, end_date);
```

A FOREIGN KEY constraint works with surrogate or natural keys by referencing the table and column or columns that are in its primary key. The next example sets the two foreign keys in a translation table between the rental and item tables:

```
SQL> ALTER TABLE rental_item
  2    ADD CONSTRAINT fk_rental_id_1
  3      FOREIGN KEY (rental_id) REFERENCES rentals (rental_id)
  4    ADD CONSTRAINT fk_rental_id_2
  5      FOREIGN KEY (item_id) REFERENCES items (item_id);
```

The next example sets a FOREIGN KEY on the natural key of the contact table, as shown earlier in this chapter. This references three natural columns and one foreign key column:

```
SQL> ALTER TABLE delegate
  2    ADD CONSTRAINT fk_natural_contact
  3      FOREIGN KEY ( member_id, first_name, middle_name, last_name )
  4      REFERENCES contact (member_id, first_name, middle_name, last_name);
```

The key concept is that you can add both column- and table-level (that is, multiple column) constraints with the ALTER TABLE statement. As shown, you can also add the column and then the constraint that goes with it.

Modifying Oracle Columns and Constraints   Oracle lets you change column names, data types, and constraints with the ALTER TABLE statement. Although column names and data types change routinely during major software upgrades, as discussed, these changes can and do cause problems, because existing code can depend on the type or names of columns and encounter failures when they change unexpectedly.

The following examples demonstrate what you're likely to encounter when working with modifying tables. The first example lets you change the name of a column:

```
SQL> ALTER TABLE calendar
  2    RENAME COLUMN calendar_name TO full_month_name;
```

If you want to change the names of two or more columns in one ALTER STATEMENT, you would try something like this:

```
SQL> ALTER TABLE calendar
  2    RENAME COLUMN calendar_name TO full_month_name
  3    RENAME COLUMN calendar_short_name TO short_month_name;
```

But this would fail and raise an ORA-23290 error:

```
ALTER TABLE calendar
*
ERROR at line 1:
ORA-23290: This operation may not be combined with any other operation
```

The failure occurs because you can't combine a RENAME clause with any other clause in an ALTER TABLE statement. It's simply disallowed with no more elaboration than that, as you can see in the *Oracle Database Administrator's Guide 11*g.

Data type changes are straightforward when the table contains no data, but you can't change the type when data exists in the column. A quick example attempts to change a start_date column using a DATE data type to using a VARCHAR2 data type. The following syntax would work when no data is included in the column but fails when data exists:

```
SQL> ALTER TABLE calendar
  2    MODIFY (start_date VARCHAR2(9));
```

With data in the column, it raises this error message:

```
   MODIFY (start_date VARCHAR2(9))
          *
ERROR at line 2:
ORA-01439: column to be modified must be empty to change datatype
```

You would add a NOT NULL constraint to the start_date column with the following DML statement:

```
SQL> ALTER TABLE calendar
  2  MODIFY (start_date DATE NOT NULL );
```

The only problem with the foregoing statement is that it creates a NOT NULL constraint with a system-generated name. The best practice would assign the constraint a name like so:

```
SQL> ALTER TABLE calendar
  2  MODIFY (start_date DATE CONSTRAINT nn_calendar_1 NOT NULL);
```

Now you know how to rename columns and change column data types. The next section shows you how to drop columns and constraints.

Dropping Oracle Columns and Constraints   You drop columns from tables rarely, but the syntax is easy. You would drop the following `short_month_name` column from the `calendar` table with this:

```
SQL> ALTER TABLE calendar
  2  DROP COLUMN short_month_name;
```

You would encounter a problem dropping a column when the column is involved in a table constraint (a constraint across two or more columns). For example, attempting to drop a `middle_name` column from the `contact` table fails when the column is referenced by a multiple column `UNIQUE` constraint (see example in the "Oracle Data Catalog" section earlier in this chapter). The statement would look like this:

```
SQL> ALTER TABLE contact
  2  DROP COLUMN middle_name;
```

and it would raise the following error message:

```
DROP COLUMN middle_name
            *
ERROR at line 2:
ORA-12991: column is referenced in a multi-column constraint
```

This is quite different from MySQL, where you can drop a column that's a member of a multiple-column `UNIQUE` constraint. My preference is Oracle's approach, in which the table can't be dropped until you decide what you're going to do about the `UNIQUE` constraint.

NOTE
Dropping columns when the table contains data can fragment the storage in physical files.

Dropping constraints is easy, because all you need to know is a constraint's name. A query to find the name is available in the "Oracle Data Catalog" section earlier in this chapter. The following drops the `unique_name` constraint from the `contact` table:

```
SQL> ALTER TABLE contact
  2  DROP CONSTRAINT unique_name;
```

This concludes the discussion about adding, modifying, and dropping columns and constraints in an Oracle database. The next section focuses on the same tasks for a MySQL database.

MySQL Column and Constraint Maintenance

This section shows you how to add, modify, and drop columns and constraints from MySQL tables. MySQL provides the same functionality for relational tables, and it also lets you reorder the position of columns in tables.

As with the Oracle prototype, some of the DBA-related options have been excluded here. The abbreviated prototype for the ALTER TABLE statement is shown here:

```
ALTER [{ONLINE | OFFLINE}] [IGNORE] TABLE table_name
ADD {[COLUMN] column_name data_type
      { NOT NULL |
        [CONSTRAINT [constraint_name]] PRIMARY KEY (column_list) |
        [CONSTRAINT [constraint_name]] FOREIGN KEY (column_list)
         REFERENCES table_name (column_list) |
        [CONSTRAINT [constraint_name]] UNIQUE (column_list)}
        [{FIRST | AFTER column_name }] |
      [COLUMN] column_name data_type
      { NOT NULL |
        [CONSTRAINT [constraint_name]] PRIMARY KEY (column_list) |
        [CONSTRAINT [constraint_name]] FOREIGN KEY (column_list)
         REFERENCES table_name (column_list) |
        [CONSTRAINT [constraint_name]] UNIQUE (column_list)} |
      {INDEX | KEY} index_name index_type (index_column_list)
      {KEY_BLOCK_SIZE [=] value |
       USING {BTREE | HASH} |
       WITH PARSER parser_name} |
      { [CONSTRAINT [constraint_name]] PRIMARY KEY (column_list) |
        [CONSTRAINT [constraint_name]] FOREIGN KEY (column_list)
         REFERENCES table_name (column_list) |
        [CONSTRAINT [constraint_name]] UNIQUE (column_list)} |
      ALTER [COLUMN] column_name {SET DEFAULT literal | DROP DEFAULT} |
      CHANGE [COLUMN] old_name new_name data_type
      { NOT NULL |
        [CONSTRAINT [constraint_name]] PRIMARY KEY (column_list) |
        [CONSTRAINT [constraint_name]] FOREIGN KEY (column_list)
         REFERENCES table_name (column_list) |
        [CONSTRAINT [constraint_name]] UNIQUE (column_list)}
        [{FIRST | AFTER column_name}] |
      MODIFY [COLUMN] column_name data_type
      { NOT NULL |
        [CONSTRAINT [constraint_name]] PRIMARY KEY (column_list) |
        [CONSTRAINT [constraint_name]] FOREIGN KEY (column_list)
         REFERENCES table_name (column_list) |
        [CONSTRAINT [constraint_name]] UNIQUE (column_list)}
        [{FIRST | AFTER column_name}] |
      DROP [COLUMN] column_name |
      DROP PRIMARY KEY |
      DROP {INDEX | KEY} index_name |
      DROP FOREIGN KEY foreign_key_name |
      DISABLE KEYS |
      ENABLE KEYS |
      RENAME [TO] new_table_name |
      ORDER BY column_name [, column_name], [...]
```

Adding MySQL Columns and Constraints   Like the equivalent Oracle section, this section
shows you how to add columns and constraints. It highlights differences between creating
columns and constraints in the two databases.

You can add a column with the `ALTER TABLE` statement, like this:

```
mysql> ALTER TABLE rental_item
    ->   ADD (rental_item_price INT UNSIGNED);
```

Other than the change in data type, the statement is a virtual mirror to the Oracle syntax to add
a column. In MySQL, the parentheses surrounding the column name are optional. That means
you could also run the statement without parentheses, like this:

```
mysql> ALTER TABLE rental_item
    ->   ADD rental_item_price INT UNSIGNED;
```

You can also add columns with inline constraints, as you can with Oracle. The differences
between column- and table-level constraints are the same as the differences between using inline
versus out-of-line constraints in the `CREATE TABLE` statement. For example, you can create the
`rental_item_price` column with a `NOT NULL` constraint with this syntax:

```
mysql> ALTER TABLE rental_item
    ->   ADD (rental_item_price INT UNSIGNED NOT NULL);
```

As Chapter 6 explains, you can't name `NOT NULL` constraints in MySQL, because they're
properties of tables, not separate constraints. Although Oracle disallows the creation of a `NOT
NULL` constraint on a column with existing rows, MySQL allows this. MySQL prevents the error
from occurring, because it automatically populates numeric columns with a zero, text columns
with an empty string, and dates with a zero value (formatted as 0000-00-00).

TIP
Unlike Oracle, an empty string is not the same as a null value in
MySQL.

The `ALTER TABLE` statement in MySQL also lets you add multiple columns. Unlike Oracle,
MySQL requires commas between the `ADD` clauses, like so:

```
mysql> ALTER TABLE rental_item
    ->   ADD (rental_item_price DECIMAL(10,2))
    -> , ADD (rental_item_type INT UNSIGNED);
```

MySQL's process for adding columns differs from Oracle's in only two ways. You place a
comma between `ADD` clauses, and you can assign a `NOT NULL` constraint to columns that have

existing rows. MySQL supports PRIMARY KEY, NOT NULL, UNIQUE, and FOREIGN KEY constraints, but it doesn't support the CHECK constraint. Chapter 6 covers the ENUM and SET data types, which provide limited behaviors such as CHECK constraints. Foreign keys are not provided by the MySQL Server because they are a feature of database engines, such as the InnoDB engine.

Oracle requires you to modify a column to add a NOT NULL constraint, and MySQL is no different. However, MySQL provides two different syntax styles for performing the same task, and they're in the "Modifying MySQL Columns and Constraints" section, up next. Here's an example of a NOT NULL constraint:

```
mysql> ALTER TABLE calendar
    ->   MODIFY start_date DATE NOT NULL;
```

Primary keys can be assigned to surrogate (auto-incrementing columns) or to natural keys. You add a PRIMARY KEY constraint to a surrogate key column with the default constraint name like this:

```
mysql> ALTER TABLE calendar
    ->   ADD PRIMARY KEY (calendar_id);
```

Alternatively, you can name the PRIMARY KEY constraint, and add it this way:

```
mysql> ALTER TABLE calendar
    ->   ADD CONSTRAINT pk_calendar PRIMARY KEY (calendar_id);
```

A primary key can also be assigned to multiple columns with the following syntax:

```
mysql> ALTER TABLE rental_item
    ->   ADD CONSTRAINT pk_rental_item
    ->     PRIMARY KEY ( rental_item_id
    ->                 , rental_id
    ->                 , item_id
    ->                 , rental_item_price
    ->                 , rental_item_type );
```

You can use two syntax approaches to assign FOREIGN KEY constraints. One doesn't include a user-assigned name and the other does. You would create a FOREIGN KEY without naming it like this:

```
mysql> ALTER TABLE rental_item
    ->   ADD FOREIGN KEY (rental_id)
    ->     REFERENCES rental (rental_id);
```

Adding a user-assigned name is easy: you place it between the CONSTRAINT and FOREIGN KEY, as shown:

```
mysql> ALTER TABLE rental_item
    ->   ADD CONSTRAINT fk_rental_item_2 FOREIGN KEY (item_id)
    ->     REFERENCES item (item_id);
```

Finally, you can use the ALTER TABLE statement to add a UNIQUE constraint with the following syntax:

```
mysql> ALTER TABLE calendar
    ->    ADD CONSTRAINT unique_month
    ->        UNIQUE ( month_name
    ->              , month_shortname
    ->              , start_date
    ->              , end_date );
```

Naturally, like all the constraint examples, you can exclude the constraint name when you add a UNIQUE constraint with the ALTER TABLE statement. Here's the syntax:

```
mysql> ALTER TABLE calendar
    ->    ADD UNIQUE ( month_name
    ->              , month_shortname
    ->              , start_date
    ->              , end_date );
```

As a rule, naming constraints is the best practice. It makes finding your constraints much easier when you need to remove them in MySQL.

Modifying MySQL Columns and Constraints   MySQL lets you change column names, data types, nullability, and positions in the list of columns. Changing any of these column properties poses a risk to existing code bases, as discussed earlier in the chapter. That being said, code evolves when the data model evolves to improve software products.

This section shows you how to evolve your table by changing its properties. The first thing to examine is changing the data type of a column. Changing a data type is easy when the table contains no data, but it's tricky when data is present. You can change types with data in the column only when the database can implicitly convert the data from the old to the new data type. Notice that Oracle handles the data type conversions the same way, but the set of data types that qualify for implicit conversion differ.

The following calendar table supports these examples on changing data type:

```
+-----------------+-------------------+------+-----+---------+-------+
| Field           | Type              | Null | Key | Default | Extra |
+-----------------+-------------------+------+-----+---------+-------+
| calendar_id     | int(10) unsigned  | NO   | PRI | NULL    |       |
| month_name      | varchar(10)       | YES  | MUL | NULL    |       |
| month_shortname | varchar(3)        | YES  |     | NULL    |       |
| start_date      | date              | YES  |     | NULL    |       |
| end_date        | date              | YES  |     | NULL    |       |
+-----------------+-------------------+------+-----+---------+-------+
```

Assuming there's no data in this table, the following changes the data type of the start_date column to a string:

```
mysql> ALTER TABLE calendar
    ->    MODIFY start_date VARCHAR(10) NULL;
```

Here's another syntax possibility to perform the same conversion of data types:

```
mysql> ALTER TABLE calendar
    ->   CHANGE start_date start_date VARCHAR(10) NULL;
```

Having changed the data type successfully, let's insert the following data:

```
+-------------+------------+------------------+------------+------------+
| calendar_id | month_name | month_shortname  | start_date | end_date   |
+-------------+------------+------------------+------------+------------+
|           1 | January    | Jan              | 01-01-2011 | 2011-01-31 |
+-------------+------------+------------------+------------+------------+
```

The string in the `start_date` column is a noncompliant date format for MySQL. The database has no implicit method for changing the string into a date. The syntax to attempt a change from the `VARCHAR(10)` to a `DATE` data type is shown next:

```
mysql> ALTER TABLE calendar
    ->   MODIFY start_date DATE NOT NULL;
```

It would raise the following error:

```
ERROR 1292 (22007): Incorrect date value: '01-01-2011' for column
```

After updating the value in the `start_date` column to a 4-digit year, 2-digit month, and 2-digit day, the same `ALTER TABLE` statement changes the data type. This same syntax lets you change constraints by treating them like table properties.

You can also rename columns, like so:

```
mysql> ALTER TABLE calendar
    ->   CHANGE month_shortname short_month_name VARCHAR(3);
```

You can rename tables as well as columns with this syntax:

```
mysql> ALTER TABLE calendar
    ->   RENAME TO vcalendar;
```

Changing the nullability of a column is straightforward. You have two options. Here's the first:

```
mysql> ALTER TABLE calendar
    ->   CHANGE start_date start_date DATE NOT NULL
    -> , CHANGE end_date end_date DATE NOT NULL;
```

Or, with the `MODIFY` clause (an Oracle extension to the original MySQL `CHANGE` clause), you can make the `end_date` column null allowed:

```
mysql> ALTER TABLE calendar
    ->   MODIFY end_date DATE NULL;
```

Any column can have a `DEFAULT` value, and the `ALTER TABLE` statement lets you set it when unset, change it when set to another value, and remove it. This syntax sets or resets an integer column's `DEFAULT` value:

```
mysql> ALTER TABLE rental_item
    ->   ALTER COLUMN rental_item_price SET DEFAULT 1;
```

The ALTER COLUMN clause in an ALTER TABLE statement can confuse some, because they expect a MODIFY COLUMN clause. You can remove a DEFAULT column value with this syntax, which sets it to a null value:

```
mysql> ALTER TABLE rental_item
    ->    ALTER COLUMN rental_item_price DROP DEFAULT;
```

The ability to shift column positions is powerful and not available without dropping and re-creating a table in Oracle. You can do this when you want to position columns in a certain order. Consider, for example, the following table. Two new columns have been added as members of a natural primary key. They appear after the who-audit columns (the created by, creation date, last updated by, and last update date columns).

```
+------------------+-------------------+------+-----+---------+
| Field            | Type              | Null | Key | Default |
+------------------+-------------------+------+-----+---------+
| rental_item_id   | int(10) unsigned  | NO   | PRI | NULL    |
| rental_id        | int(10) unsigned  | NO   | PRI | NULL    |
| item_id          | int(10) unsigned  | NO   | PRI | NULL    |
| created_by       | int(10) unsigned  | NO   | MUL | NULL    |
| creation_date    | date              | NO   |     | NULL    |
| last_updated_by  | int(10) unsigned  | NO   | MUL | NULL    |
| last_update_date | date              | NO   |     | NULL    |
| rental_item_price| int(10) unsigned  | NO   | PRI | NULL    |
| rental_item_type | int(10) unsigned  | NO   | PRI | NULL    |
+------------------+-------------------+------+-----+---------+
```

Because the columns are part of the primary key, it makes more sense to position them with the rest of the primary key. The following command puts them in a better position:

```
mysql> ALTER TABLE rental_item
    ->    MODIFY rental_item_price int unsigned AFTER item_id
    -> , MODIFY rental_item_type int unsigned AFTER rental_item_price;
```

and changes the table definition to this:

```
+------------------+-------------------+------+-----+---------+
| Field            | Type              | Null | Key | Default |
+------------------+-------------------+------+-----+---------+
| rental_item_id   | int(10) unsigned  | NO   | PRI | NULL    |
| rental_id        | int(10) unsigned  | NO   | PRI | NULL    |
| item_id          | int(10) unsigned  | NO   | PRI | NULL    |
| rental_item_price| int(10) unsigned  | NO   | PRI | 0       |
| rental_item_type | int(10) unsigned  | NO   | PRI | 0       |
| created_by       | int(10) unsigned  | NO   | MUL | NULL    |
| creation_date    | date              | NO   |     | NULL    |
| last_updated_by  | int(10) unsigned  | NO   | MUL | NULL    |
| last_update_date | date              | NO   |     | NULL    |
+------------------+-------------------+------+-----+---------+
```

Notice that the five primary key columns are now shifted into positions 1 to 5. The preceding command also changed the new columns' DEFAULT values to 0. This occurs with many of the clauses in the `ALTER TABLE` statement. You can't reset the `DEFAULT` value in the same `ALTER TABLE` statement, but you can issue this follow-up statement to reset the `DEFAULT` values:

```
mysql> ALTER TABLE rental_item
    ->   ALTER rental_item_price DROP DEFAULT
    -> , ALTER rental_item_type DROP DEFAULT;
```

In this section, you've seen how to change column names, data types, nullability, and position in the list of columns. The `ALTER TABLE` statement lets you change one column at a time or a series of columns or constraints by delimiting statements with a comma.

Dropping MySQL Columns and Constraints   MySQL lets you remove columns or constraints from tables. There's no recovery point when you drop a column, because it's a DDL statement, and no logging of the deleted data is performed. On the other hand, Oracle does support flashback technology, which provides a recovery point.

MySQL, actually the InnoDB engine, disallows dropping a primary or foreign key column unless you've first removed the constraint. MySQL lets you drop any unconstrained column and any column that's part of a non-unique or unique constraint.

In the "Adding MySQL Columns and Constraints" section earlier in the chapter, an `ALTER TABLE` statement added a `unique_month` constraint to the `calendar` table. Using the query logic from the "MySQL Data Catalog" section, you can see the definition of the unique constraint in the data catalog. It would look like this:

```
+-----------------+-----------------+------------------+-----------------+
| constraint_name | constraint_type | ordinal_position | column_name     |
+-----------------+-----------------+------------------+-----------------+
| unique_month    | UNIQUE          |                1 | month_full_name |
| unique_month    | UNIQUE          |                2 | short_name      |
| unique_month    | UNIQUE          |                3 | start_date      |
| unique_month    | UNIQUE          |                4 | end_date        |
+-----------------+-----------------+------------------+-----------------+
```

The following syntax lets you drop a `short_name` column from the `calendar` table, which is also part of the unique constraint:

```
ALTER TABLE calendar
  DROP COLUMN short_name;
```

If you `DESCRIBE` the table, the column is gone; requerying the data catalog shows you that the unique index has changed from a four-column to a three-column index. Here's the output from the new data catalog query:

```
+-----------------+-----------------+------------------+-----------------+
| constraint_name | constraint_type | ordinal_position | column_name     |
+-----------------+-----------------+------------------+-----------------+
| unique_month    | UNIQUE          |                1 | month_full_name |
| unique_month    | UNIQUE          |                2 | start_date      |
| unique_month    | UNIQUE          |                3 | end_date        |
+-----------------+-----------------+------------------+-----------------+
```

The `short_name` column is no longer a member of the `unique_month` index, and likewise the column is no longer part of the `calendar` table.

The following lets you remove the unique index from the `calendar` table:

```
mysql> ALTER TABLE calendar
    ->    DROP INDEX unique_month;
```

Although dropping a constraint doesn't remove the data, it deletes a business rule. Some business rules have small impacts on data integrity, but others have potentially large impacts. In general, don't drop anything until you're sure you don't need it.

Dropping Tables

You use the `DROP TABLE` statement to remove tables from the database. The `DROP TABLE` statement can fail when other tables or views have referential integrity (foreign key) dependencies on the table or view. The prototypes are shown in the Oracle and MySQL subsections.

Dropping Oracle Tables

Oracle lets you drop only a single table with a `DROP TABLE` statement. You can drop tables when they contain data or when they're empty. This statement also drops global temporary tables. You can set aside referential integrity by using the `CASCADE CONSTRAINTS` clause.

The prototype for the `DROP TABLE` statement is shown here:

```
DROP TABLE [schema_name.]table_name [CASCADE CONSTRAINTS] [PURGE];
```

A `DROP TABLE` statement against a table that has foreign keys referencing it raises an exception:

```
DROP TABLE parent
          *
ERROR at line 1:
ORA-02449: unique/primary keys in table referenced by foreign keys
```

The `CASCADE CONSTRAINTS` clause removes dependencies from other tables, such as `FOREIGN KEY` constraints that reference the table. It does not remove the data from the other table's previous foreign key column, which is important if you plan on re-creating the table and re-importing data. Any re-import of data would need to ensure that primary key values would map to existing foreign key values.

The `PURGE` keyword is required when you're dropping a partitioned table. The `PURGE` keyword starts a series of subtransactions that drop the all partitions of the tables. The first successful subtransaction marks the table as `UNUSABLE` in the data catalog. This flag in the data catalog ensures that only a `DROP TABLE` statement works against the remnants of the table. If you encounter a problem trying to access a table, you can query the `status` column value to see if it's unusable. The `UNUSABLE` column is in the `ALL_`, `DBA_`, or `USER_TABLES`, `USER_PART_TABLES`, `USER_ALL_TABLES`, `USER_OBJECT_TABLES`, or `USER_OBJECTS` administrative views.

Dropping MySQL Tables

In MySQL, unlike Oracle, the `DROP TABLE` statement doesn't manage referential integrity issues with a `CASCADE` clause. MySQL does let you check whether a table exists before you attempt to drop it (`IF EXISTS` clause), and it lets you use a single `DROP TABLE` statement to remove multiple tables. It would be great to see these two features in Oracle.

NOTE
A quick reminder on foreign key features: Foreign keys aren't native components in the MySQL Server; they're implementation elements of MySQL engines. Users deploying referential integrity use the InnoDB engine.

Here's the prototype for the MySQL DROP statement:

```
DROP [TEMPORARY] TABLE [IF EXISTS] table_name [, table_name [, ...]]
[{RESTRICT | CASCADE}];
```

NOTE
The CASCADE keyword does not change the behavior in MySQL but is permitted to make porting easier.

While working with the InnoDB engine and referential integrity, you can disable dependencies by setting the following session variable:

```
SET FOREIGN_KEY_CHECKS = 0;
```

This command disables referential integrity checking for the InnoDB engine. It's handy in a re-runnable script that drops and creates tables. Just make sure you re-enable that checking at the end of your script, like this:

```
SET FOREIGN_KEY_CHECKS = 1;
```

The TEMPORARY keyword in the DROP statement doesn't stop any transactions currently working with TEMPORARY tables, because it simply waits on their completion. Because temporary tables are visible only within the scope of a session, the TEMPORARY keyword doesn't check access rights to the table.

Indexes

As mentioned in Chapter 6, *indexes* are structures that hold search trees that help SQL statements find rows of interest faster. These search trees can be Balanced Trees (B-Trees), hash maps, and other mapping data structures.

There are many reasons for fixing indexes in Oracle and MySQL, and the following is a list of some of the major reasons for altering an index:

- Rebuilding or coalescing an existing index
- Deallocating unused space or allocating new space
- Enabling and specifying the degree of parallelism for storing the index
- Changing storage parameters to improve index performance
- Enabling or disabling logging
- Enabling or disabling key compression
- Marking the index as unusable

- Making the index invisible
- Renaming the index
- Starting or stopping index usage monitoring

The next two sections review some basics of using indexes from a developer's perspective. Clearly, storage and parallel optimization belong to the DBAs, because they know the critical resources of CPUs, memory, and disk space.

Oracle Index Maintenance

The Oracle ALTER INDEX statement lets you manage indexes, and DROP INDEX lets you remove indexes. You can also use the ALTER TABLE statement to enable primary key column(s) to use indexes.

The prototype for the ALTER INDEX statement, minus the DBA options, is shown here:

```
ALTER INDEX [schema_name.]index_name [COMPILE] |
[{ENABLE | DISABLE}] |
[UNUSABLE] |
[REBUILD [{PARTITION partition_clause |
           SUBPARTITION subpartition_clause |
           [{REVERSE | NOREVERSE}]}] |
[{VISIBLE | INVISIBLE}] |
[RENAME TO new_index_name] |
[COALESCE] |
[{MONITORING | NOMONITORING} USAGE] |
```

The first thing developers want to do when they've discovered poor throughput in a query is disable the index to see what impact it has on their code. I'll show you how to do that, but it's generally better done by modifying the query so that it doesn't run the index by concatenating an empty string to a string or by adding a 0 to a number or date.

You can enable an index when it's necessary:

```
ALTER INDEX nk_rental_item ENABLE;
```

Or you can disable it:

```
ALTER INDEX nk_rental_item DISABLE;
```

Sometimes you want to mark an index to rebuild it. You do that with the UNUSABLE keyword:

```
ALTER INDEX nk_rental_item UNUSABLE;
```

You can rebuild an index, provided it isn't partitioned, with this:

```
ALTER INDEX nk_rental_item REBUILD;
```

If you don't have the space to rebuild an index online, you can try offline rebuilding, or *coalescing* the index. Coalescing is like defragmenting a disk. When you coalesce an index it reorganizes the data and maintains fully free blocks, which eliminate the cost of releasing and reallocating blocks. Many DBAs choose to coalesce indexes because of the speed, absence of locking, and minimal incremental disk space requirements.

This syntax coalesces an index:

```
ALTER INDEX nk_rental_item COALESCE;
```

The idea of visibility or invisibility might seem odd, but the VISIBLE and INVISIBLE keywords make an index visible or invisible to the Oracle cost-based optimizer for queries. DML statement, such as INSERT, UPDATE, and DELETE statements, maintain an invisible index, but queries don't use it. As a rule, from Oracle 11g forward, you want the optimizer to see indexes. You can discover whether an index is invisible by checking the visibility column in the ALL_, DBA_, or USER_INDEXES view.

TIP
Setting an index to INVISIBLE is without merit when the DBA has set the OPTIMIZER_USE_INVISIBLE_INDEXES parameter to true, because it makes all invisible indexes visible.

You make an index visible with this:

```
ALTER INDEX nk_rental_item VISIBLE;
```

Renaming an index is something to consider if you originally chose a poorly descriptive index name. Here's the syntax:

```
ALTER INDEX nk_rental_item RENAME TO naturalkey_rental_item;
```

You can use the ALTER TABLE statement to let a table's primary key column use an existing index, like so:

```
ALTER TABLE rental_item ENABLE PRIMARY KEY USING nk_rental_item;
```

Don't forget that some views in the data catalog let you see the indexes you've already created.

MySQL Index Maintenance

Although index maintenance isn't as diverse in MySQL as it is in Oracle, you still have some options. MySQL uses the ALTER TABLE statement to perform index maintenance, such as adding or dropping an index.

Here's the syntax to add a non-unique index:

```
mysql> ALTER TABLE calendar
    ->    ADD INDEX unique_month ( calendar_month_name
    ->                           , start_date
    ->                           , end_date ) USING BTREE;
```

A unique index requires only one additional word, as shown here:

```
mysql> ALTER TABLE calendar
    ->    ADD UNIQUE INDEX unique_month ( calendar_month_name
    ->                                  , start_date
    ->                                  , end_date ) USING BTREE;
```

You can remove the index with the `DROP INDEX` clause, like so:

```
mysql> ALTER TABLE calendar
    ->    DROP INDEX unique_month;
```

You cannot disable a unique index, but you can turn off a non-unique index while you perform some updates to a table. This lets you fix data and regenerate indexes. Here's the syntax:

```
mysql> ALTER TABLE calendar DISABLE KEYS;
```

Don't forget to re-enable the non-unique index after you're done performing the table maintenance:

```
mysql> ALTER TABLE calendar ENABLE KEYS;
```

Views

View creation is covered in Chapter 11. Views are stored queries and Chapter 11 shows you how they work. The syntax for removing a view from Oracle or MySQL is very similar and is shown in the following sections.

Oracle Drop Views

Oracle doesn't provide syntax for conditionally dropping tables or views as does MySQL. You can write a PL/SQL block that verifies whether the view exists, by querying the `USER_OBJECTS` or `USER_VIEWS` administrative view.

Here's the prototype for dropping a view:

```
DROP VIEW [schema_name.]view_name CASCADE CONSTRAINTS;
```

The `CASCADE CONSTRAINTS` is required when other tables have foreign key dependencies on the view. Without the clause, an error is raised and dropping the view is disallowed. Oracle supports dropping only a single object with the `DROP VIEW` statement.

MySQL Drop Views

MySQL lets you remove views. The `IF EXISTS` clause lets you check whether the view exists before you try to remove it and allows you to write conditional `DROP` statements.

Here's the prototype for a removing a view:

```
DROP VIEW view_name [, view_name2 [, ...]]  IF EXISTS;
```

Notes are generated as warning messages when views are present, but when the view doesn't exist, an error is suppressed and not raised. The statement also lets you remove a comma-separated list of views, which isn't possible with the Oracle syntax.

Summary

The chapter explored how you can maintain structures in the database. It explored the various syntax combinations that support modifying, such as users, databases, sessions, tables, views, and indexes. The chapter compared maintenance methods between the Oracle and MySQL database.

Mastery Check

The mastery check is a series of true or false and multiple choice questions that let you confirm how well you understand the material in the chapter. You may check the Appendix for answers to these questions.

1. **True** ☐ **False** ☐ A *user* in Oracle is synonymous with a *schema*.
2. **True** ☐ **False** ☐ In an Oracle database, a user can change his or her password with an `ALTER USER` statement.
3. **True** ☐ **False** ☐ You must know a user's password to change their password as a super user, such as `SYSTEM`, in an Oracle database.
4. **True** ☐ **False** ☐ In a MySQL database, a user can change his or her password with an `ALTER USER` statement.
5. **True** ☐ **False** ☐ You can add a `NOT NULL` constraint to an existing column when it contains null values.
6. **True** ☐ **False** ☐ You can lock and unlock accounts in MySQL.
7. **True** ☐ **False** ☐ Oracle has deprecated tracing using the `DBMS_SYSTEM` package and replaced it with the `ALTER SESSION` statement.
8. **True** ☐ **False** ☐ Oracle lets you embed logic in your stored functions and procedures that is run only when you enable specialized session variables.
9. **True** ☐ **False** ☐ It's always best to define a `UNIQUE KEY` and `INDEX` when they work with the same columns in a MySQL database.
10. **True** ☐ **False** ☐ You can modify a column's data type when it contains data in an Oracle database, but not a MySQL database.
11. Which of the following is not a valid constraint flag in Oracle?
    A. A P
    B. A N
    C. A C
    D. A R
    E. A U
12. Which rule applies in an Oracle database to changing the data type of a column?
    A. Any column can be changed when the table is empty.
    B. All columns can be changed except those that are members of a primary key, whether the table contains data or not.
    C. All variable length string columns (`VARCHAR2`) can be changed to a `DATE` data type column regardless of the format mask involved when the table is full.
    D. All non-key columns can be changed when the table is full.
    E. None of the above

13. Which of the following isn't a keyword in an Oracle ALTER TABLE statement?

    A. An ALTER clause

    B. A CHANGE clause

    C. A MODIFY clause

    D. A DROP clause

    E. An ADD clause

14. Which of the following isn't a keyword in a MySQL ALTER TABLE statement?

    A. A CHANGE clause

    B. A MODIFY clause

    C. A DROP clause

    D. A DISABLE clause

    E. A READ ONLY clause

15. Which of the following constraints can't be added to a table in MySQL?

    A. The PRIMARY KEY constraint

    B. The FOREIGN KEY constraint

    C. The CHECK constraint

    D. The UNIQUE constraint

    E. The NOT NULL constraint

CHAPTER
8

Inserting Data

he INSERT statement lets you enter data into tables and views in two ways: via an INSERT statement with a VALUES (and in MySQL with a VALUES or SET) clause and via an INSERT statement with a query. The VALUES clause takes a list of literal (strings, numbers, and dates represented as strings), expressions (return values from functions), or variable values.

Query values are results from SELECT statements that are subqueries (covered in Chapter 11). INSERT statements work with scalar, single-row, and multiple-row subqueries. The list of columns in the VALUES clause or SELECT clause of a query (a SELECT list) must map to the positional list of columns that defines the table. That list is found in the data dictionary or catalog. Alternatively to the list of columns from the data catalog, you can provide a named list of those columns. The named list *overrides* the positional (or *default*) order from the data catalog and must provide at least all mandatory columns in the table definition. Mandatory columns are those that are not null constrained.

MySQL and Oracle databases differ in how they implement the INSERT statement. MySQL supports multiple row inserts with a VALUES clause; Oracle does not support this. Oracle and MySQL both support default and override signatures as qualified in the ANSI SQL standards. Oracle also provides a multiple-table INSERT statement, which MySQL does not provide. This chapter covers how you enter data with an INSERT statement that is based on a VALUES clause or a subquery result statement, as well as multiple-table INSERT statements.

The INSERT statement has one significant limitation: its *default signature*. The default signature is the list of columns that define the table in the data catalog. The list is defined by the position and data type of columns. The CREATE statement defines the initial default signature, and the ALTER statement can change the number, data types, or ordering of columns in the default signature.

The default prototype for an INSERT statement allows for an optional column list that overrides the default list of columns. Like methods in object-oriented programming languages (OOPLs), an INSERT statement without the optional column list constructs an instance (or row) of the table using the default constructor. The override constructor for a row is defined by any INSERT statement when you provide an optional column list. That's because it overrides the default constructor.

The generic prototype for an INSERT statement is confusing when it tries to capture both the VALUES clause and the result set from a query. Therefore, I've opted to provide two generic prototypes. The first uses the VALUES clause:

```
INSERT
INTO [{LOW_PRIORITY | DELAYED | HIGH_PRIORITY}] [IGNORE] table_name
[( column1, column2, column3, ...)]
VALUES
( value1, value2, value3, ...)
[ON DUPLICATE KEY
 UPDATE column_name1 = expression1
 [,     column_name2 = expression2
 [, ...]]];
```

MySQL also supports multiple rows in the VALUES clause, which supports this modification to the VALUES clause:

```
VALUES
  ( value1A, value2A, value3A, ...)
, ( value1B, value2B, value3B, ...);
```

Overriding vs. Overloading

OOPLs have special vocabularies. You define a class in OOPLs by writing a program that outlines the rules for how to create an instance of a class and the methods available for any instance of that class.

Objects have special methods known as constructors that let you create instances. The default constructor generally has no formal parameters. When writing the code for a class, you can define constructors that override the default constructor's behavior. These user-defined constructors are known as *overriding* constructors. Objects also have methods that perform actions against the instance, and some of these methods are overloaded, which means a given method name supports different lists of formal parameters. This is known as *method overloading*.

The list of parameters in an overriding constructor is also known as the *overriding signature*, defined as something that serves to set apart or identify. The same logic makes the formal parameter list of any method a signature of that method.

The class is also known as an object *type*, which is a data type. A table in a database is an object type, because it contains a definition of what it can include. Every row is an instance of that object type.

As qualified in Chapter 1, SQL is a set-based declarative language. Declarative languages hide the implementation details while providing a means for the developer to state what should happen. The default signature to enter a row of data is read from the data catalog and compared against the list of values in a VALUES clause or query. The INSERT statement's optional column list lets you override the default signature to enter a row of data, but the database checks to ensure that you conform to any not null column-level constraints.

MySQL supports another less frequently used syntax that resembles the UPDATE statement. It's a named assignment prototype with a SET clause:

```
INSERT
INTO [{LOW_PRIORITY | DELAYED | HIGH_PRIORITY}] [IGNORE] table_name
SET column_name1 = expression1
[,  column_name2 = expression2
[, ...]]
[ON DUPLICATE KEY
 UPDATE column_name1 = expression2
 [,     column_name2 = expression2
 [, ...]]];
```

The prototype of an INSERT statement based on a result set from a query is shown next:

```
INSERT
INTO [{LOW_PRIORITY | DELAYED | HIGH_PRIORITY}] [IGNORE] table_name
[( column1, column2, column3, ...)]
( SELECT value1, value2, value3, ...
  FROM    some_table
  WHERE   some_column = some_value )
[ON DUPLICATE KEY
```

```
UPDATE column_name1 = expression1
[,      column_name2 = expression2
[, ...]]];
```

Notice that the prototype for an INSERT statement with the result set from a query doesn't use the VALUES clause at all. A parsing error occurs when the VALUES clause and query both occur in an INSERT statement.

Default signatures present a risk of data corruption through insertion anomalies, which occur when you enter bad data in tables. Mistakes transposing or misplacing values can occur more frequently with a default signature, because the underlying table structure can change. As a best practice, always use named notation by providing the optional list of values; this should help you avoid putting the right data in the wrong place.

TIP
Inserts should always rely on named notation to help you avoid adding data in the wrong columns.

This chapter provides examples that use the default and override syntax for INSERT statements in both Oracle and MySQL. The Oracle sections also support multiple-table INSERT statements and a RETURING INTO clause, which is an extension of the ANSI SQL standard. Oracle uses the RETURNING INTO clause to manage large objects and some of the features of Oracle's dynamic SQL. Note that Oracle also supports a bulk INSERT statement, which is covered in Chapter 13 because it requires knowledge of PL/SQL.

Insert by Values

Inserting by the VALUES clause is the most common type of INSERT statement. It's most useful when interacting with single row inserts. You typically use this type of INSERT statement when working with data entered through end user web forms. In some cases, users can enter more than one row of data using a form, which occurs, for example, when a user places a meal order in a restaurant and the meal and drink are treated as order items. The restaurant order entry system would enter a single row in the order table and two rows in the order_item table (one for the meal and the other for the drink). How the code enters the multiple order items can differ between an Oracle and MySQL database, because MySQL supports multiple items in the VALUES clause, while Oracle doesn't. For example, an Oracle implementation might open a loop and process two dynamic INSERT statements (see Chapter 13), while a MySQL implementation might create, prepare, execute, and de-allocate a prepared statement that inserts two rows in a single INSERT statement (see Chapter 14).

The next two subsections explain how to use INSERT statements with the VALUES clause in an Oracle or MySQL database.

Oracle Insert by Values

Oracle supports only a single row insert through the VALUES clause. Multiple row inserts require an INSERT statement from a query. This section covers single row INSERT statements and the "Oracle Insert by Query" section covers multiple row inserts.

The VALUES clause of an INSERT statement accepts scalar values, such as strings, numbers, and dates. It also accepts calls to arrays, lists, or user-defined object types, which are called *flattened objects*. Oracle supports VARRAY as arrays and nested tables as lists. They can both contain elements of a scalar data type or user-defined object type. Chapter 6 shows you how to create these data types.

The following sections discuss how you use the VALUES clause with scalar data types, how you convert various data types, and how you use the VALUES clause with nested tables and user-defined object data types.

Inserting Scalar Data Types

The basic syntax for an INSERT statement with a VALUES clause can include an optional *override signature* between the table name and VALUES keyword. With an override signature, you designate the column names and the order of entry for the VALUES clause elements. Without an override signature, the INSERT signature checks the definition of the table in the database catalog. The positional order of the column in the data catalog defines the positional, or default, signature for the INSERT statement. You can discover the structure of a table in Oracle or MySQL with the DESCRIBE command issued at the SQL*Plus or MySQL Monitor command line:

```
DESCRIBE table_name;
```

The semicolon is unnecessary in Oracle but required by the MySQL Monitor. Semicolons are execution commands and are covered in Chapter 2.

You'll see the following after describing the rental table in SQL*Plus:

```
Name                                     Null?    Type
---------------------------------------- -------- --------
RENTAL_ID                                NOT NULL NUMBER
CUSTOMER_ID                              NOT NULL NUMBER
CHECK_OUT_DATE                           NOT NULL DATE
RETURN_DATE                                       DATE
CREATED_BY                               NOT NULL NUMBER
CREATION_DATE                            NOT NULL DATE
LAST_UPDATED_BY                          NOT NULL NUMBER
LAST_UPDATE_DATE                         NOT NULL DATE
```

The rental_id column is a *surrogate key,* or an artificial numbering sequence. The combination of the customer_id and check_out_date serves as a *natural key,* because a DATE data type is a date-time value. If it were only a date, the customer would be limited to a single entry for each day, and limiting customer rentals to one per day isn't a good business model.

The basic INSERT statement would require that you look up the next sequence value before using it. You should also look up the surrogate key column value that maps to the row where your unique customer is stored in the contact table. For this example, assume the following facts:

- Next sequence value is 1086
- Customer's surrogate key value is 1009
- Current date-time is represented by the value from the SYSDATE function
- Return date is the fifth date from today
- User adding and updating the row has a primary (surrogate) key value of 1
- Creation and last update date are the value returned from the SYSDATE function.

An INSERT statement must include a list of values that match the positional data types of the database catalog, or it must use an override signature for all mandatory columns.

You can now write the following INSERT statement, which relies on the default signature:

```
SQL> INSERT INTO rental
  2  VALUES
  3  ( 1086
  4  , 1009
  5  , SYSDATE
  6  , TRUNC(SYSDATE + 5)
  7  , 1
  8  , SYSDATE
  9  , 1
 10  , SYSDATE);
```

If you weren't using SYSDATE for the date-time value on line 5, you could manually enter a date-time with the following Oracle proprietary syntax:

```
  5  , TO_DATE('15-APR-2011 12:53:01','DD-MON-YYYY HH24:MI:SS')
```

The TO_DATE function is an Oracle-specific function. The generic conversion function would be the CAST function. The problem with a CAST function by itself is that it can't handle a format mask other than the database defaults ('DD-MON-RR' or 'DD-MON-YYYY')—for example, consider this syntax:

```
  5  , CAST('15-APR-2011 12:53:02' AS DATE)
```

It raises the following error:

```
  5  , CAST('15-APR-2011 12:53:02' AS DATE) FROM dual
         *
ERROR at line 1:
ORA-01830: date format picture ends before converting entire input string
```

You actually need to double cast this type of format mask when you want to store it as a DATE data type. The working syntax casts the date-time string as a TIMESTAMP data type before recasting the TIMESTAMP to a DATE, like so:

```
  5  , CAST(CAST('15-APR-2011 12:53:02' AS TIMESTAMP) AS DATE)
```

Before you could have written the preceding INSERT statement, you would need to run some queries to find the values. You would secure the next value from a rental_s1 sequence in an Oracle database with the following command:

```
SQL> SELECT  rental_s1.NEXTVAL FROM dual;
```

This assumes two things, because sequences are separate objects from tables. First, code from which the values in a table's surrogate key column come must appear in the correct sequence. Second, a sequence value is inserted only once into a table as a primary key value.

In place of a query that finds the next sequence value, you would simply use a call against the .NEXTVAL pseudo column in the VALUES clause. You would replace line 3 with this:

```
  3  ( rental_s1.NEXTVAL
```

The .NEXTVAL is a pseudo column, and it instantiates an instance of a sequence in the current session. After a call to a sequence with the .NEXTVAL pseudo column, you can also call back the prior sequence value with the .CURRVAL pseudo column.

NOTE
Sequences are separate objects from tables, and your code ensures that only the appropriate sequence maps to the correct table.

Assuming the following query would return a single row, you can use the contact_id value as the customer_id value in the rental table:

```
SQL> SELECT    contact_id
  2  FROM       contact
  3  WHERE      last_name = 'Potter'
  4  AND        first_name = 'Harry';
```

Taking three steps like this is unnecessary, however, because you can call the next sequence value and find the valid customer_id value inside the VALUES clause of the INSERT statement. The following INSERT statement uses an override signature and calls for the next sequence value on line 11. It also uses a scalar subquery to look up the correct customer_id value with a scalar subquery on lines 12 through 15.

```
SQL> INSERT INTO rental
  2  ( rental_id
  3  , customer_id
  4  , check_out_date
  5  , return_date
  6  , created_by
  7  , creation_date
  8  , last_updated_by
  9  , last_update_date )
 10  VALUES
 11  ( rental_s1.nextval
 12  ,(SELECT    contact_id
 13    FROM       contact
 14    WHERE      last_name = 'Potter'
 15    AND        first_name = 'Harry')
 16  , SYSDATE
 17  , TRUNC(SYSDATE + 5)
 18  , 1
 19  , SYSDATE
 20  , 3
 21  , SYSDATE);
```

When a subquery returns two or more rows because the conditions in the WHERE clause failed to find and return a unique row, the INSERT statement would fail with the following message:

```
,(SELECT    contact_id
    *
ERROR at line 3:
ORA-01427: single-row subquery returns more than one row
```

In fact, the statement could fail when two or more "Harry Potter" names exist in the data set, because three columns make up the natural key of the contact table. The third column is the member_id, and all three should be qualified inside a scalar subquery to guarantee that it returns only one row of data.

Handling Oracle's Large Objects   Oracle's large objects present a small problem when they're not null constrained in the table definition. In this case, you must insert empty object containers or references when you perform an INSERT statement.

Assume, for example, that you have the following three large object columns in a table:

```
Name                             Null?    Type
-------------------------------  -------- -----------------------
ITEM_DESC                        NOT NULL CLOB
ITEM_ICON                        NOT NULL BLOB
ITEM_PHOTO                                BINARY FILE LOB
```

The item_desc column uses a CLOB (Character Large Object) data type, and it is a required column; it could hold a lengthy description of a movie, for example. The item_icon column uses a BLOB (Binary Large Object) data type, and it is also a required column. It could hold a graphic image. The item_photo column uses a binary file (an externally managed file). It could hold a null or a reference to an external graphic image; fortunately, the item_photo column isn't a required column.

Oracle provides two functions that let you enter an empty large object:

```
empty_blob()
empty_clob()
```

Although you could insert a null value in the item_photo column, you can also enter a reference to an Oracle database virtual directory file. Here's the syntax to enter a valid BFILE name with the BFILENAME function call:

```
10   , BFILENAME('VIRTUAL_DIRECTORY_NAME', 'file_name.png')
```

You can insert a large character or binary stream into BLOB and CLOB data types by using the stored procedures and functions available in the DBMS_LOB package. These operations require a working knowledge of PL/SQL programming, which isn't covered until Chapter 13, where you'll see an example that inserts a large CLOB column.

You can use an EMPTY_CLOB function or a string literal up to 32,767 bytes long in a VALUES clause. You must use the DBMS_LOB package when you insert a string that is longer than 32,767 bytes. That also changes the nature of the INSERT statement and requires that you append the RETURNING INTO clause. Here's the prototype for this Oracle proprietary syntax:

```
INSERT INTO some_table
[( column1, column2, column3, ...)]
VALUES
( value1, value2, value3, ...)
RETURNING column1 INTO local_variable;
```

The local_variable is a reference to a procedural programming language. It lets you insert a character stream into a target CLOB column or a binary stream into a BLOB column.

DBA Heads-up on Large Object Storage

CLOB and BLOB columns are stored with the rest of a row when they're smaller than 4000 bytes. Larger versions are stored out-of-line, which means they're placed in a contiguous space that is away from the rest of the related row.

DBAs often designate a special tablespace for the storage clauses of BLOB and CLOB columns. This extra step is beneficial, because large objects change less frequently and consume a lot of storage. They're also generally on different backup schedules than other transactional columns in a table.

Capturing the Last Sequence Value   Sometimes you insert into a series of tables in the scope of a transaction, like those described in Chapter 4. In this scenario, one table gets the new sequence value (with a call to sequence_name.NEXTVAL) and enters it as the surrogate primary key, and another table needs a copy of that primary key to enter into a foreign key column. While scalar subqueries can solve this problem, Oracle provides the .CURRVAL pseudo column for this purpose.

The steps to demonstrate this behavior require a parent and child table. The parent table is defined as follows:

```
Name                                   Null?    Type
-----------------------------------    -------- --------------
PARENT_ID                              NOT NULL NUMBER
PARENT_NAME                                     VARCHAR2(10)
```

The parent_id column is the primary key for the parent table. You include the parent_id column in the child table. In the child table, the parent_id column holds a copy of a valid primary key column value as a foreign key to the parent table.

```
Name                                   Null?    Type
-----------------------------------    -------- --------------
CHILD_ID                               NOT NULL NUMBER
PARENT_ID                                       NUMBER
PARENT_NAME                                     VARCHAR2(10)
```

After creating the two tables, you can manage inserts into them with the .NEXTVAL and .CURRVAL pseudo columns. The sequence calls with the .NEXTVAL insert primary key values, and the sequence calls with the .CURRVAL insert foreign key values.

You would perform these two INSERT statements as a group:

```
SQL> INSERT INTO parent
  2  VALUES
  3  ( parent_s1.NEXTVAL
  4  ,'One Parent');

SQL> INSERT INTO child
  2  VALUES
  3  ( child_s1.NEXTVAL
  4  , parent_s1.CURRVAL
  5  ,'One Child');
```

The .CURRVAL pseudo column for any sequence fetches the value placed in memory by call to the .NEXTVAL pseudo column. Any attempt to call the .CURRVAL pseudo column before the .NEXTVAL pseudo column raises an ORA-02289 exception. The text message for that error says the sequence doesn't exist, which actually means that it doesn't exist in the scope of the current session. Line 4 in the insert into the child table depends on line 3 in the insert into the parent table.

You can use comments in INSERT statements to map to columns in the table. For example, the following shows the technique for the child table from the preceding example:

```
SQL> INSERT INTO child
  2  VALUES
  3  ( child_s1.NEXTVAL     -- CHILD_ID
  4  , parent_s1.CURRVAL    -- PARENT_ID
  5  ,'One Child')          -- CHILD_NAME
  6  /
```

Comments on the lines of the VALUES clause identify the columns where the values are inserted. A semicolon doesn't execute this statement, because a trailing comment would trigger a runtime exception. You must use the semicolon or forward slash on the line below the last VALUES element to include the last comment.

TIP
A comment on the last line of any statement requires that you exclude the semicolon and place it or a forward slash on the next line.

Data Type Conversions

Oracle supports a series of conversion functions that let you convert data types from one type to another. The generic SQL conversion function is CAST, which lets you convert the following data types.

Convert from BINARY_FLOAT or BINARY_DOUBLE Data Type to BINARY_FLOAT, BINARY_DOUBLE, CHAR, VARCHAR2, NUMBER, DATE, TIMESTAMP, NCHAR, NVARCHAR

Convert from CHAR or VARCHAR2 Data Type to BINARY_FLOAT, BINARY_DOUBLE, CHAR, VARCHAR2, NUMBER, DATE, TIMESTAMP, DATE, TIMESTAMP, INTERVAL, RAW, ROWID, UROWID, NCHAR, NVARCHAR

Here's an example of converting a string literal date into a timestamp:

```
CAST('14-FEB-2011' AS TIMESTAMP WITH LOCAL TIME ZONE)
```

This example works because the date literal conforms to the default format mask for a date in an Oracle database. A nonconforming date literal would raise a conversion error. Many possibilities are available because you can organize the valid elements of dates many ways. A nonconforming date literal should be converted by using the TO_DATE or TO_TIMESTAMP function, because each of these lets you specify an overriding date format mask value, such as this conversion to a DATE data type:

```
TO_DATE('2011-02-14', 'YYYY-MM-DD')
```

Or this conversion to a TIMESTAMP data type:

```
TO_TIMESTAMP('2011-02-14 18:11:28.1500', 'YYYY-MM-DD HH24:MI:SS.FF')
```

Converting to an INTERVAL data type is covered in the next section, because you first must extract a time property as a number. It's also possible that implicit casting of a numeric string can change the base data type to an integer for you. The method of implicit or explicit conversion depends on how you get the initial data value.

Convert from NUMBER Data Type to BINARY_FLOAT, BINARY_DOUBLE, CHAR, VARCHAR2, NUMBER, DATE, TIMESTAMP, NCHAR, NVARCHAR

Interval conversions are a bit more complex, because you need more than one function to convert them. Typically, you pull the value from a DATE or TIMESTAMP data type and EXTRACT the element of time by identifying its type before converting that value to an INTERVAL type. The following provides an example:

```
NUMTODSINTERVAL(EXTRACT(MINUTE FROM some_date), 'MINUTE')
```

You will use this type of built-in function layering frequently in some situations. It's always a better approach to understand and use the built-in functions before you write your own stored functions.

Convert from DATETIME or INTERVAL Data Type to CHAR, VARCHAR2, DATE, TIMESTAMP, DATE, TIMESTAMP, INTERVAL, NCHAR, NVARCHAR

Convert from RAW Data Type to CHAR, VARCHAR2, RAW, NCHAR, NVARCHAR

Convert from ROWID or UROWID Data Type to CHAR, VARCHAR2, ROWID, UROWID, NCHAR, NVARCHAR

NOTE
You cannot cast a UROWID to a ROWID in the UROWID of an index organized table.

Convert from NCHAR or NVARCHAR2 Data Type to BINARY_FLOAT, BINARY_DOUBLE, NUMBER, NCHAR, NVARCHAR

Inserting Arrays and Nested Tables

The ability to insert arrays and nested tables in an Oracle database is an important feature made possible by the *object-relational* technology of the database. You can access these embedded structures only through the containing table, which makes them much like inner classes in object-oriented programming. From a database modeling perspective, they're ID-dependent data sets, because the only relationship is through the row of the containing table.

You can walk through a simple design and development exercise by creating a collection of a scalar data type, a table that contains the data type, and then an INSERT statement to populate the table with data. You create the user-defined collection data type by using this syntax:

```
CREATE TYPE number_array IS VARRAY(10) OF NUMBER;
```

After you have the user-defined collection type, create a table that uses it and a sequence for an automatic numbering column, like so:

```
SQL> CREATE TABLE sample_nester
  2  ( nester_id    NUMBER
  3  , array_column NUMBER_ARRAY);
SQL> CREATE SEQUENCE sample_nester_s1;
```

You enter values into the table by calling a collection constructor. Calls are made to the data type name, not the column name, like so:

```
SQL> INSERT INTO sample_nester
  2  VALUES
  3  ( sample_nester_s1.NEXTVAL
  4  , NUMBER_ARRAY(0,1,2,3,4,5,6,7,8,9));
```

Here are formatting instructions and an ordinary query against this table:

```
SQL> COLUMN ARRAY_COLUMN FORMAT A44
SQL> SELECT * from sample_nester;
```

which returns the following:

```
NESTER_ID ARRAY_COLUMN
---------- --------------------------------------------
        1 NUMBER_ARRAY(0, 1, 2, 3, 4, 5, 6, 7, 8, 9)
```

The value in the `ARRAY_COLUMN` is a call to the user-defined collection data type's constructor. This collection is a simple array of ten numbers. You can join the `nester_id` column against all ten elements in the collection with the following syntax:

```
SQL> SELECT nester_id
  2  ,       collection.column_value
  3  FROM    sample_nester CROSS JOIN TABLE(array_column) collection;
```

The `TABLE` function extracts the element of the collection into a SQL result set, which can then be treated like a normal set of rows from any table. Oracle always returns collections of base scalar data types into a `COLUMN_VALUE` column. The results from the sample query follow:

```
NESTER_ID COLUMN_VALUE
---------- ------------
        1            0
        1            1
        1            2
 ...
        1            8
        1            9
```

Here's a multilevel `INSERT` statement based on the employee table from Chapter 6. The following inserts a single row that contains an `address_list` collection of two instances of the `address_type` user-defined object type, which in turn holds a collection of a `street_list` nested table of variable-length strings:

```
SQL> INSERT INTO employee
  2  ( employee_id
  3  , first_name
  4  , last_name
  5  , home_address )
  6  VALUES
  7  ( employee_s1.NEXTVAL
  8  ,'Sam'
  9  ,'Yosemite'
 10  , address_list(
 11     address_type( 1
 12                 , street_list('1111 Broadway','Suite 322')
 13                 ,'Oakland'
 14                 ,'CA'
 15                 ,'94612')
 16     , address_type( 2
 17                 , street_list('1111 Broadway','Suite 525')
 18                 ,'Oakland'
 19                 ,'CA'
 20                 ,'94612')));
```

Lines 10 through 20 insert a nested table (list) of two `address_type` instances. The sequence numbers are manually entered because this type of design would always start elements of a nested table with a sequence value of 1. This is an implementation of an ID-dependent relationship. The nested table is accessible only through the row of a table, and as such, it acts only when connected with the containing row.

NOTE
Nested tables are complex to access and model. As mentioned in Chapter 6, they also create type chaining, which presents maintenance headaches during major software releases. If you opt to use them, you should have a good reason for adding the complexity.

Multiple-Table Insert Statements

As mentioned, Oracle SQL syntax lets you perform multiple-table inserts with the `INSERT` statement. A multiple-table `INSERT` statement can be useful when you receive an import source file that belongs in more than one table. You should be aware of some caveats with this type of multiple-table insert. For example, a one-to-one mapping must exist between all the data in the same row. When you have a one-to-many relationship between columns in the single import source table, the `MERGE` statement is a better solution, as discussed in Chapter 12.

Here's the prototype for the multiple table `INSERT` statement:

```
INSERT {ALL | FIRST}
  [WHEN comparison_clause THEN ]
   INSERT INTO table_name_one
   ( column_list )
```

```
    VALUES
    ( value_list )
[[WHEN comparison_clause THEN ]
    INSERT INTO table_name_two
    ( column_list )
    VALUES
    ( value_list ) ]
    [ ... ]
    [ELSE
    INSERT INTO table_name_else
    ( column_list )
    VALUES
    ( value_list ) ]
  query_statement;
```

A multiple-table insert can be performed in three ways: One uses the ALL keyword but excludes the WHEN clauses. The second uses the ALL keyword while including the WHEN clauses. The last uses a FIRST keyword instead of the ALL keyword and inserts to the first table before moving to the second, and so forth.

The multiple-table INSERT statement variations are discussed in the following subsections, but they're all supported by the following three tables and sequences.

The rank_index is the first table, and it contains a string for the military service, such as Army, Navy, Marines, and Air Force, with their accompanying abbreviated and full-titled ranks.

```
-- Create the rank_index table and sequence.
CREATE TABLE rank_index
( rank_id          NUMBER
, rank_service     VARCHAR2(10)
, rank_short_name  VARCHAR2(4)
, rank_full_name   VARCHAR2(30));
CREATE SEQUENCE rank_index_s;
```

The soldier and sailor tables are target tables for the inserts from the multiple-table INSERT statement. They contain the rank and name of soldiers and sailors, respectively:

```
-- Create the soldier table and sequence.
CREATE TABLE soldier
( soldier_id    NUMBER
, soldier_rank  VARCHAR2(4)
, soldier_name  VARCHAR2(20));
CREATE SEQUENCE soldier_s;

-- Create the sailor table and sequence.
CREATE TABLE sailor
( sailor_id    NUMBER
, sailor_rank  VARCHAR2(4)
, sailor_name  VARCHAR2(20));
CREATE SEQUENCE sailor_s;
```

All the examples get their data from a SELECT statement that uses the dual pseudo table and a fabricated result set. The INSERT ALL or INSERT FIRST statement inserts the data into one or both of the target tables. The tables are unconstrained because constraints aren't required for the examples.

Multiple-Table INSERT ALL Without WHEN Clauses Our first example shows you how to insert data into multiple tables without any qualifications. Values from each row returned by the query are inserted into the `soldier` and `sailor` tables. Unfiltered multiple-table `INSERT` statements put rows into all tables referenced by an `INTO` clause. In this regard, the `INSERT ALL` statement works like a *switch* statement with fall through in C#, C++, or Java. (*Fall through* means that after meeting the condition of one case statement, all subsequent case statements are valid and their code blocks also run.)

```
SQL> INSERT ALL
  2  INTO soldier
  3  VALUES
  4  (soldier_s.NEXTVAL,service_rank,service_member_name)
  5  INTO sailor VALUES
  6  (sailor_s.NEXTVAL,service_rank,service_member_name)
  7  SELECT 'MSG' AS service_rank
  8  ,       'Ernest G. Bilko' AS service_member_name FROM dual
  9  UNION ALL
 10  SELECT 'CPO' AS service_rank
 11  ,       'David Vaught' AS service_member_name FROM dual;
```

No `ELSE` block is used in the example. This type of statement would also run the `ELSE` block and perform any insert found in it.

Queries against the target tables show you that both rows are inserted into both tables:

```
SQL> SELECT * FROM soldier;

SOLDIER_ID SOLD SOLDIER_NAME
---------- ---- --------------------
         1 MSG  Ernest G. Bilko
         2 CPO  David Vaught

SQL> SELECT * FROM sailor;

 SAILOR_ID SAIL SAILOR_NAME
---------- ---- --------------------
         1 MSG  Ernest G. Bilko
         2 CPO  David Vaught
```

This type of statement is useful when you want to put data from one row of a table or view into multiple tables. Unfiltered `INSERT ALL` statements don't let you choose among a set of tables (like a filtered `INSERT ALL` statement), and they're used less than filtered statements.

Multiple-Table INSERT ALL with WHEN Clauses The multiple-table `INSERT ALL` statement also works with `WHEN` clauses that determine into which table they'll insert. The logic can include subqueries, as shown in the following example:

```
SQL> INSERT ALL
  2  WHEN service_rank IN (SELECT rank_short_name
  3                        FROM   rank_index
  4                        WHERE  rank_service = 'ARMY') THEN
```

```
 5  INTO soldier
 6  VALUES
 7  (soldier_s.NEXTVAL,service_rank,service_member_name)
 8  WHEN service_rank IN (SELECT rank_short_name
 9                          FROM   rank_index
10                          WHERE  rank_service = 'NAVY') THEN
11  INTO sailor
12  VALUES
13  (sailor_s.NEXTVAL,service_rank,service_member_name)
14  SELECT 'MSG' AS service_rank
15  ,        'Ernest G. Bilko' AS service_member_name FROM dual
16  UNION ALL
17  SELECT 'CPO' AS service_rank
18  ,        'David Vaught' AS service_member_name FROM dual;
```

The WHEN clause on line 2 checks whether the service rank belongs in the Army. It inserts into the soldier table any row in which the query's service_rank value matches the subquery's rank_short_name value. The second WHEN clause does the same kind of evaluation against Navy ranks. Any rows that don't match one of the two criteria are discarded because there is no ELSE clause.

Queries against the target tables yield the following results:

```
SQL> SELECT * FROM soldier;

SOLDIER_ID SOLD SOLDIER_NAME
---------- ---- --------------------
         1 MSG  Ernest G. Bilko

SQL> SELECT * FROM sailor;

 SAILOR_ID SAIL SAILOR_NAME
---------- ---- --------------------
         2 CPO  David Vaught
```

The filtered INSERT ALL places rows from one source query into one or only the correct tables. This is the best practice—or at least the most frequently used version of the statement.

Multiple-Table INSERT FIRST with WHEN Clauses   The INSERT FIRST works differently from the INSERT ALL statement. The INSERT FIRST inserts data into the first table only when it meets a WHEN clause condition. This means it performs like a switch statement in C#, C++, or Java where fall through is disabled. For your reference (in case you don't write programs in those languages), you disable fall through by adding a break statement in each case statement's code bock. The break statement signals completion and forces an exit from the switch statement. The FIRST keyword effectively does that for all WHEN clause statement blocks.

Here's an example using the concept of conscripts (draftees). The first one goes to the Army (line 2), the next four go to the Navy (line 6), and any others get to go home without serving in the military:

```
SQL> INSERT FIRST
  2  WHEN id < 2 THEN
  3  INTO soldier
```

```
 4   VALUES
 5   (soldier_s.NEXTVAL,'PVT',draftee)
 6   WHEN id BETWEEN 2 AND 5 THEN
 7   INTO sailor
 8   VALUES
 9   (sailor_s.NEXTVAL,'SR',draftee)
10   SELECT 1 AS ID,'John Sanchez' AS draftee FROM dual
11   UNION ALL
12   SELECT 2 AS ID,'Michael Deegan' AS draftee
13   FROM dual
14   UNION ALL
15   SELECT 3 AS ID,'Jon Voight' AS draftee FROM dual;
```

You'll see in the result set that only two draftees went in the Navy, so there weren't enough conscripts drafted today. The statement will need to be rewritten tomorrow for the new batch of draftees unless the rules change every day. The queries and results are shown next:

```
SQL> SELECT * FROM soldier;

SOLDIER_ID SOLD SOLDIER_NAME
---------- ---- --------------------
         1 PVT  John Sanchez

SQL> SELECT * FROM sailor;

 SAILOR_ID SAIL SAILOR_NAME
---------- ---- --------------------
         2 SR   Michael Deegan
         3 SR   Jon Voight
```

My suggestion is that INSERT FIRST statement is probably suited to dynamic creation inside Native Dynamic SQL (NDS). You can see examples of NDS in Chapter 13.

MySQL Insert by Values

INSERT statements in the MySQL database are used similarly to how they're used in the Oracle database. MySQL does let you insert multiple rows with a single VALUES clause, which isn't supported by the Oracle database. On the other hand, MySQL is a relational database and doesn't support object types or nested tables, as does Oracle 11*g*.

The following sections cover inserting scalar data types and performing data type conversions. MySQL treats all data types, including large character and binary strings, as scalar data types.

Inserting Scalar Data Types

MySQL lets you insert one or more rows through a VALUES clause. You don't have to call a sequence to use the clause during inserts, because sequences are a table property in MySQL. The INSERT statement mirrors more or less that of an Oracle database, because INSERT statements adhere to the ANSI SQL standard.

You can include an overriding signature in a MySQL INSERT statement just as you can in Oracle. You can exclude the single column designed with the AUTO_INCREMENT phrase, as well as any optional columns. The column created with an AUTO_INCREMENT phrase is a *surrogate primary key column.* Like Oracle, the INSERT statement checks the definition of the table in the data catalog. It checks the catalog when you exclude a column list and verifies constraints when you attempt to insert data.

Mirroring the steps from the Oracle discussion, you can use the DESCRIBE command to view the table definition from the catalog. The semicolon is required when describing a table in the MySQL Monitor, like so:

```
DESCRIBE table_name;
```

Using our rental table in My SQL requires a couple data type changes. That's because MySQL's DATE is a date, not a date-time data type. The DATETIME data type in MySQL is a date-time type equivalent to the DATE data type in an Oracle database. Here's the definition of the rental table (without the default value column) in MySQL:

```
+-----------------+-------------------+------+-----+----------------+
| Field           | Type              | Null | Key | Extra          |
+-----------------+-------------------+------+-----+----------------+
| rental_id       | int(10) unsigned  | NO   | PRI | auto_increment |
| customer_id     | int(10) unsigned  | NO   | MUL |                |
| check_out_date  | time              | NO   |     |                |
| return_date     | datetime          | NO   |     |                |
| created_by      | int(10) unsigned  | NO   | MUL |                |
| creation_date   | time              | NO   |     |                |
| last_updated_by | int(10) unsigned  | NO   | MUL |                |
| last_update_date| time              | NO   |     |                |
+-----------------+-------------------+------+-----+----------------+
```

Like the Oracle table, the rental_id column is a surrogate primary key. The extra column description tells you that it's an automatically generated sequence value. Sequences are positive integers or doubles, which means they're defined as unsigned integers or unsigned doubles. It's a convention, and a recommendation, that surrogate primary keys use integers until they approach the 4 billion limit of the data type.

The syntax for this INSERT statement with literal values doesn't differ much from the Oracle equivalent, except for the MySQL proprietary NOW(), ADDDATE(), and UTC_DATE() function calls.

```
INSERT INTO rental
VALUES
( 1
, 2
, NOW()
, ADDDATE(UTC_DATE(),INTERVAL 5 DAY)
, 1
, NOW()
, 1
, NOW());
```

You can discover the next sequence value by using this syntax in MySQL Monitor:

```
show table status like 'rental'\G
```

The \G displays output vertically with the column names on the left and values on the right, as covered in Chapter 2. The show command displays this after one insert into the table:

```
****************** 1. row ******************
           Name: rental
         Engine: InnoDB
        Version: 10
     Row_format: Compact
           Rows: 1
 Avg_row_length: 16384
    Data_length: 16384
Max_data_length: 0
   Index_length: 49152
      Data_free: 8388608
 Auto_increment: 2
    Create_time: 2011-01-14 22:18:59
    Update_time: NULL
     Check_time: NULL
      Collation: latin1_swedish_ci
       Checksum: NULL
  Create_options:
        Comment:
```

The important difference between the surrogate primary key column in Oracle and the same in MySQL deals with the auto-incrementing columns in MySQL. Although you do need to provide the column placeholder in the VALUES clause in MySQL, you can simply enter NULL and the correct sequence will be entered. This isn't true in Oracle, unless you've deployed an ON INSERT trigger to capture the sequence value and mapped it to the rental_id column.

In short, here is the preferred way to write an INSERT statement that uses the default signature and literal values or expression results (such as the dates from the NOW function or the date from the ADDDATE function). The INSERT statement uses a VALUES clause in MySQL:

```
INSERT INTO rental
VALUES
( null
, 2
, NOW()
, ADDDATE(UTC_DATE(),INTERVAL 5 DAY)
, 1
, NOW()
, 1
, NOW());
```

At this point, you know how to perform an INSERT statement with a null value and the default signature. It is preferred that you use a list of columns to designate what you're inserting in the VALUES clause. An INSERT statement that uses an overriding signature that excludes the auto-incrementing column follows:

```
INSERT INTO rental
( customer_id
, check_out_date
```

```
, return_date
, created_by
, creation_date
, last_updated_by
, last_update_date )
VALUES
( SELECT    c.contact_id
  FROM      contact c JOIN member m
  ON        c.member_id = m.member_id
  WHERE     c.first_name = 'Harry'
  AND       IFNULL(c.middle_name,'x') = IFNULL(null,'x')
  AND       c.last_name = 'Potter'
  AND       m.account_number = 'SLC-000006' )
, NOW()
, ADDDATE(UTC_DATE(),INTERVAL 5 DAY)
, 1
, NOW()
, 1
, NOW());
```

NOTE
*Remember that you can use scalar subqueries in MySQL, but they do
not exist in Oracle. Subqueries in the VALUES clause can return only
a single row when matched with literal values.*

You can also rewrite this in MySQL to work with the SET clause. The only problem with the
SET clause, however, is that it's not portable to other databases. Here's an example of the syntax
to INSERT with the SET clause:

```
INSERT INTO rental
SET customer_id = ( SELECT c.contact_id
                    FROM   contact c JOIN member m
                    ON     c.member_id = m.member_id
                    WHERE  c.first_name = 'Harry'
                    AND    IFNULL(c.middle_name,'x') = IFNULL(null,'x')
                    AND    c.last_name = 'Potter'
                    AND    m.account_number = 'SLC-000006' )
, check_out_date = NOW()
, return_date = ADDDATE(UTC_DATE(),INTERVAL 5 DAY)
, created_by = 1
, creation_date = NOW()
, last_updated_by = 1
, last_update_date = NOW();
```

The customer_id value comes from a scalar subquery (see Chapter 11) against the
contact and member tables. The WHERE clause contains the business elements that help
identify the surrogate primary key (the contact_id column) for the contact table.

Data Type Conversions

Like the Oracle database, MySQL supports the CAST and CONVERT functions and the BINARY operator. The CAST function works with the following data types: BINARY, CHAR, DATE, DATETIME, SIGNED or UNSIGNED INTEGER, and TIME. The CONVERT function lets you modify a strings character set, and the BINARY operator is shorthand for a CAST function that changes a character to a binary string.

CAST Function   The CAST function also lets you specify a character set that you want to apply through the casting operation. Here's the prototype for the CAST function:

```
CAST(expression_or_variable AS data_type [CHARACTER SET character_set])
```

You would convert a double precision number to a string like so:

```
CAST(111.4586 AS CHAR(30))
```

Alternatively, you can change the character set when you cast a double to a character, like this:

```
CAST(111.4586. AS CHAR(30) CHARACTER SET utf8)
```

NOTE
Casting a string to a DATE, DATETIME, or TIME data type has some added restrictions. The string must conform to the default string literal for a date, which is YYYY-MM-DD (a four-digit year, two-digit month, and two-digit day). Any attempt to convert a different format mask fails and returns a null value.

CONVERT Function   The CONVERT function is slightly different from the CAST function. Here's the prototype:

```
CONVERT([character_set] string_value USING character_set)
```

To convert a string from the default character set to a Unicode character set, use the following syntax:

```
CONVERT('Hello mate!' USING utf8)
```

BINARY Operator   The difference between a function and operator in this case is parentheses: there aren't any in the operator. Here's the syntax to convert a string to a binary string:

```
BINARY 'Hello Mate!'
```

Insert by Queries

Inserting data from queries eliminates the VALUES clause—doing so actually replaces the clause with the query. The default and override signatures remain the same. Matching the columns returned by the SELECT statement replaces matching VALUES clause columns against the override column list or table definition.

The prototype changes slightly for the INSERT statement when the source becomes the results from a query rather than a list of values. The VALUES keyword must be dropped when you use a query or the INSERT statement fails.

The following prototype works for Oracle and MySQL databases and includes options for joining more than one table on various conditions and uses ANSI SQL-92 syntax:

```
INSERT INTO table_name
[( column_name1, column_name2, ...)]
 ( SELECT    column_value1, column_value2, ...
   FROM      table1
[[ JOIN table2 ON table1.column_name1 = table2.column_name2] ... ]
 [ WHERE    some_logical_conditions ]);
```

The prototype provides an optional list of column names for an override signature. Then it provides a single table query, optional join with potentially more joins, and ultimately a WHERE clause to filter rows. The column names of the query do not need to match the column names of the table to which the values are being added. Only the data types of the query's columns must match the data types of the table's columns. Fixed- and variable-length strings in queries must contain no more than the number of bytes or characters allowed by the table's definition.

INSERT statements from queries generally collect information from a series of tables. The number of rows returned for all columns must match. A problem occurs when literal values must map to a multiple row data set. The solution to this problem is to multiply the single row of the literal values against the multiple rows of the data set using a CROSS JOIN, which produces a Cartesian Product (every row in one table matched to every row in the other).

For example, let's say you need to enter an active price flag of *Y* with an amount of *$5* and an inactive price flag of *N* with an amount of *$3* for all merchandise in your item table. You need to multiply the single row of numeric and string literals by the number of rows in the table before inserting them into the price table. The solution would be an INSERT statement from a query that fabricates (or produces) a data set not found in your raw data, like this:

```
SQL>  INSERT INTO price
  2   (SELECT    price_s1.NEXTVAL
  3   ,          i.item_id
  4   ,          dt.active_flag
  5   ,          dt.amount
  6    FROM      (SELECT   'Y' AS active_flag
  7              ,          5  AS amount
  8               FROM     dual
  9               UNION ALL
 10               SELECT   'N' AS active_flag
 11              ,          3  AS amount
 12               FROM     dual) dt CROSS JOIN item i);
```

The in-line view creates a two-column by two-row table with the values 'Y' and 5 in one row and the values 'N' and 3 in the other row. The number of rows in the item table will be multiplied by the two rows in the fabricated table and the combined and balanced row set joined by a sequence value for each row in the outer SELECT clause. The only change required to implement this sample in a MySQL database switches the price_s1.NEXTVAL pseudo column with a null value.

NOTE
The CROSS JOIN is a forward reference to Chapter 11. If you're new to SQL and want to understand the full nature of the Oracle and MySQL examples, you should check out the basics of join mechanics in Chapter 11.

The next two sections demonstrate the syntax for INSERT statements with queries, with two approaches shown: the first shows a query that contains all the mandatory columns, and the other shows a query that contains only some of the mandatory columns with additional values that come from string literals. The only differences between Oracle and MySQL are the functions that can convert a query return column to match the definition of a table column and the handling of automatic numbering through sequences.

Oracle Insert by Queries

Here we'll show a query that contains all the columns necessary to insert a row in a table and a query that doesn't contain all the columns necessary for the INSERT statement. The latter mixes string literals with query results through a CROSS JOIN operation, which fabricates data sets.

The INSERT statement will put the data into a table defined as follows:

```
Name                            Null?    Type
------------------------------- -------- ---------------------------
KNIGHT_ID                       NOT NULL NUMBER
KNIGHT_NAME                     NOT NULL VARCHAR2(20)
KINGDOM_ALLEGIANCE_ID           NOT NULL NUMBER
```

The knight table has three columns. The knight_id column is first and holds a surrogate key column that would store a sequence value. The knight_name and kingdom_allegiance_id columns hold a natural key, which is unique. That means there can be only one *Peter the Magnificent* with allegiance to a given kingdom stored in the kingdom table, because the kingdom_allegiance_id column holds a foreign key that points to the kingdom_id column in the kingdom table. The following conventions are used in this model: Primary key columns are surrogate key columns, and they use the name of the table plus an _id suffix; foreign key columns can have names that differ from their related primary key column names.

The query finds knights in the available_knight table. The following INSERT statement puts the data into the table:

```
SQL> INSERT INTO knight
  2  ( knight_id
  3  , knight_name
  4  , kingdom_allegiance_id )
  5  ( SELECT   knight_s1.NEXTVAL
  6  ,          knight_name
  7  ,          (SELECT   kingdom_id
  8             FROM      kingdom
  9             WHERE     kingdom_name = 'Narnia')
 10    FROM     available_knight);
```

The query gets the values from the `available_knight` table, and a subquery on lines 5 through 10 gets the correct foreign key value from the `kingdom` table. Inside the query, a call to the `knight_s1` sequence value ensures the surrogate key is automatically populated.

An alternative syntax would exclude the surrogate key column, because an `ON INSERT` database trigger populates the column. Database triggers support this activity effectively, and many developers use them for this purpose.

The use of an override signature means you can reshuffle the order of columns to fit particular business needs. Be sure to make the same changes in the override signature that you make in the query. The number of possibilities varies with the complexity of queries required to solve the business problems.

MySQL Insert by Queries

Leveraging the same example from the "Oracle Insert by Queries" section, you need only change the first column value returned by the query. The `.NEXTVAL` pseudo column is an Oracle-only solution. In MySQL, you would perform the query with a `null` value as the first column of the query, like so:

```
mysql> INSERT INTO knight
    -> ( knight_id
    -> , knight_name
    -> , kingdom_allegiance_id )
    -> ( SELECT    null
    -> ,           knight_name
    -> ,           (SELECT   kingdom_id
    ->             FROM      kingdom
    ->             WHERE     kingdom_name = 'Narnia')
    ->     FROM    available_knight);
```

An alternative example would implement an override signature that excludes the surrogate key (or auto-incrementing) column. The syntax would then be as follows:

```
mysql> INSERT INTO knight
    -> (  knight_name
    -> , kingdom_allegiance_id )
    -> ( SELECT   knight_name
    -> ,          (SELECT   kingdom_id
    ->            FROM      kingdom
    ->            WHERE     kingdom_name = 'Narnia')
    ->     FROM   available_knight);
```

The power of inserting from queries is substantial. It lets you collect data from many sources and then insert rows of data in a single statement.

Summary

In this chapter, you learned about inserting data. You can insert a row at a time with a `VALUES` clause and many rows at a time with a subquery. The syntax for these statements differs little between the Oracle and MySQL databases. The most significant issue is handling sequence values.

Mastery Check

The mastery check is a series of true or false and multiple choice questions that let you confirm how well you understand the material in the chapter. You may check the Appendix for answers to these questions.

1. **True** ☐ **False** ☐ An INSERT statement supports multiple row inserts through the VALUES clause in Oracle.

2. **True** ☐ **False** ☐ An INSERT statement supports multiple row inserts through the VALUES clause in MySQL.

3. **True** ☐ **False** ☐ The list of columns in an override signature must match the number and data types of the list of values in the VALUES clause.

4. **True** ☐ **False** ☐ You can insert data into nested tables with an INSERT statement in an Oracle database.

5. **True** ☐ **False** ☐ In an Oracle database, you can use a .CURRVAL pseudo column in a VALUES clause provided the sequence has been placed in scope through an earlier .NEXTVAL pseudo column call.

6. **True** ☐ **False** ☐ A null value that maps to an auto-incrementing column in a MySQL database inserts the next number in the table's sequence.

7. **True** ☐ **False** ☐ In MySQL, you can use an override signature only when you want to insert sequence values.

8. **True** ☐ **False** ☐ An INSERT statement that uses a query can insert one to many rows of data in both Oracle and MySQL databases.

9. **True** ☐ **False** ☐ MySQL supports the .NEXTVAL pseudo column.

10. **True** ☐ **False** ☐ Both Oracle and MySQL databases let you use subqueries in the VALUES clause of an INSERT statement.

11. Which of the following data types requires a built-in function call to put a long variable length character string in a VALUES clause of an INSERT statement?

   A. BLOB

   B. MEDIUMCLOB

   C. TEXT

   D. CLOB

   E. VARCHAR

12. In an Oracle database, how many rows can you insert through a VALUES clause?

   A. 1

   B. 2

   C. 3

   D. 4

   E. Many

13. In an MySQL database, how many rows can you insert through a VALUES clause?

  A. 1

  B. 2

  C. 3

  D. 4

  E. Many

14. When you use a query instead of a VALUES clause, which of the following is true about the query?

  A. The query can contain scalar subqueries.

  B. The query can return only one row at a time.

  C. The query must return a unique data set.

  D. The query can't be the product of a join between two or more tables.

  E. The query is independent of the table structure, which means you can return more columns than the table will accept.

15. Which of the following can't be put in a VALUES clause?

  A. 1

  B. 2

  C. 3

  D. Unlimited

  E. None of the above

CHAPTER
9

Updating Data

he UPDATE statement lets you change data in tables and views by resetting values in one or more columns. A single UPDATE statement can change one, many, or all rows in a table. The new values can come from literal values, variables, or correlated query results. *Correlation* is the matching of one set of data with another through join operations. This chapter discusses equijoin (equality value joins); Chapter 11 examines join options in detail.

Oracle and MySQL implement basic UPDATE statement syntax in a similar way, but Oracle supports a record update and large object interface that aren't available in MySQL. The large object interface appends the RETURINING INTO clause to UPDATE statements. MySQL supports a multiple table UPDATE statement, a priority flag, and a LIMIT phrase, which are not supported in Oracle.

This chapter covers how you do the following:

■ Update by values and queries

■ Update by correlated queries

An UPDATE statement's most important behavior is that it works against all rows in a table unless a WHERE clause or correlated join limits the number of rows. This means you should always limit which rows should be changed by providing a WHERE clause or correlated join. The list of columns in the SET clause of an UPDATE statement is the expression list.

Changes by the UPDATE statement are hidden until committed in an Oracle database, but are immediately visible in nontransactional databases such as MySQL. Therefore, you must start a transaction scope in MySQL and work with tables that use the InnoDB engine when you want to use ACID-compliant UPDATE statements.

Update by Values and Queries

Some UPDATE statements use date, numeric, or string literals in the SET subclause. The SET subclause can work with one to all columns in a table, but you should never update a primary surrogate key column. Any update of the externally known identifier column risks compromising the referential integrity of primary and foreign keys.

The generic UPDATE statement prototype with values resetting column values looks like this:

```
UPDATE some_table
SET     column_name = 'expression'
[,      column_name = 'expression' [, ...]
WHERE [NOT] column_name {{= | <> | > | >= | < | <=} |
                        [NOT] {{IN | EXISTS} | IS NULL}} 'expression'
[{AND | OR} [NOT] comparison_operation] [...];
```

The target table of an UPDATE statement can be a table or updateable view. An expression can be a numeric or string literal or the return value from a function or subquery. The function or subquery must return only a single row of data that matches the data type of the assignment target. The right operand of the assignment can contain a different data type when its type can be implicitly cast to the column's data type, or explicitly cast to it with the CAST or proprietary built-in function. In the generic example, a subquery needs to return a single column and row (this type of subquery is a *scalar subquery* or SQL *expression*). Ellipses replace multiple listing in the SET and WHERE clauses.

The `WHERE` clause lets you evaluate truth or non-truth, which is the purpose of each comparison operation. The comparison operators in the prototype are divided into sets of related operators by using curly braces—first the math comparisons, then the set and correlation comparisons, and finally the null comparison. The `{AND | OR}` `[NOT]` are logical operators. The `AND` operator evaluates the truth of two comparisons, or, with enclosing parentheses, the truth of sets of comparison operations. The `OR` operator evaluates the truth of one or the other comparison operator, and it employs short-circuit evaluation (the statement is true when the first comparison is true). The negation operator (`NOT`) checks whether a statement is false.

An actual `UPDATE` statement against an `item` table would look like this when you enter the actual movie name in lieu of a placeholder value:

```
SQL> UDPATE item
  2  SET    item_title = 'Pirates of the Caribbean: On Stranger Tides'
  3  ,      item_rating = 'PG-13'
  4  WHERE  item_title = 'Pirates of the Caribbean 4';
```

Variations to this syntax exist in Oracle, but this is the basic form for `UPDATE` statements in both databases. Specifics for Oracle and MySQL are covered in the following sections.

Oracle Update by Values and Queries

The biggest difference between Oracle and other databases is that Oracle allows you to reset record structures, not just columns. Recall from Chapter 6 that the definition of a table is equivalent to the definition of a record structure, and a record structure is a combination of two or more columns (or fields).

The prototype of an `UPDATE` statement for Oracle differs from the generic profile, as you can see:

```
UPDATE {some_table | TABLE(query_statement)}
  SET    {column_name = 'expression' | DEFAULT |
         (column_list) = (expression_list)} [, ...]]
  WHERE [NOT] {column_name | (column_list)}
               {{= | <> | > | >= | < | <=} |
                [NOT] {IN | =ANY | =SOME | =ALL } |
                [NOT] {IS NULL | IS SET} | [NOT] EXISTS} {'expression' | (expression_
list)}
  [{AND | OR } [NOT] comparison_operation] [...]
  [RETURNING {column_name | (column_list)}
   INTO {local_variable | (variable_list)}];
```

Oracle extends the target of the `UPDATE` statement from a table or view (traditionally a named query inside the data catalog) to a result set. In Oracle's lexicon, the result set is formally an aggregate result set—that is, the result set acts like a normal query's return set in processing memory (inside the SGA, or System Global Area). The `TABLE` function makes this possible. (The `TABLE` function was previously known as the `THE` function—that's no joke, but ancient history from Oracle 8*i*, along with some error messages that have never been updated.)

Oracle also extends the behavior of assignment in the `SET` operator by allowing you to assign a record structure to another record structure. A (data) record structure in the `SET` operator is any list of two or more columns from the table definition, which is less than the complete data structure of the table or its definition in the data catalog. Ellipses replace the continuing list of possible elements in the `SET` and `WHERE` clauses.

The WHERE clause comparison operators are also expanded in an Oracle database. They are separated by curly braces, like the generic prototype, with math comparisons, set comparisons, null comparisons, and correlations. Set comparisons act as lookup operators and are covered in the "Multiple Row Subqueries" section of Chapter 11, and correlation is explained in the "Correlated Queries" section of the same chapter.

The RETURNING INTO clause allows you to shift a reference to columns that you've updated but not committed into variables. Those variables are critical to how you update large objects in the database.

Here's an example of how you would use Oracle's record structure assignment operation in a SET clause:

```
SQL> UDPATE item
  2  SET   (item_title, item_rating) =
  3          (SELECT 'Pirates of the Caribbean: On Stranger Tides'
  4          ,        'PG-13'
  5          FROM   dual)
  6  WHERE  item_title = 'Pirates of the Caribbean 4';
```

The values reset the columns item_title and item_rating on all lines where item_title is "Pirates of the Caribbean 4." The subquery uses string literals inside a query against the dual table. This is straightforward and not much different from the comma-delimited SET clauses for each column. You might wonder why you should bother with implementing this twist on the other syntax. That's a great question! There's not much added value with date, numeric, or string literals from the pseudo table dual, but the value occurs when the source is a row returned from a query. The record structure syntax allows you to assign a row's return values directly from a single-row subquery with multiple columns to a row of the target table.

Here's an example of an assignment from a subquery to record structure:

```
SQL> UDPATE item
  2  SET   (item_title, item_rating) =
  3          (SELECT item_title, item_rating
  4          FROM   import_item
  5          WHERE  item_barcode = 'B004A8ZWUG')
  6  WHERE  item_title = 'Pirates of the Caribbean 4';
```

The item_title and item_rating values from the subquery are assigned to the equivalent columns in the item table when the item_title column holds the string literal value. The power of this type of assignment increases when you add correlation, because you can process sets of data in a single UPDATE statement. (That's covered in the "Update by Correlated Queries" section later in this chapter.)

Two specialized forms of UPDATE statements are included in the Oracle 11g database. One works with collections of object types, and the other works with scalar and large object types. The ability to use the result of the TABLE function inside an UPDATE statement lets you update nested tables (collections of object types). A RETURNING INTO clause supports scalar and large objects by returning the values or references from the UPDATE statement to the calling scope. The calling scope is the SQL*Plus session in the examples but could be an external program written in PL/SQL or C, C++, C#, or Java. This technique gives you access to recently updated values without your having to requery the table, and in the case of large objects, it allows you to read and write to large objects through a web application.

RETURNING INTO Clause

You can append the `RETURNING INTO` clause to any `UPDATE` statement. The `RETURNING INTO` clause lets you retrieve updated column values into locally scoped variables so that you can avoid requerying the columns after the `UPDATE` statement.

To demonstrate this concept, even the smallest example uses session-level bind variables. The bind variables eliminate the need for a procedural programming language such as Java or PHP to demonstrate the concept.

Recall from Chapter 2 that SQL*Plus commands declare session-level bind variables. This example requires a pair of session-level variables to act as target of the `RETURNING INTO` clause. You can declare these two bind variables with this syntax:

```
SQL> VARIABLE bv_title  VARCHAR2(60)
SQL> VARIABLE bv_rating VARCHAR2(60)
```

The following demonstrates an `UPDATE` statement that uses the `RETURNING INTO` phrase:

```
SQL> UPDATE item
  2  SET    (item_title,item_rating) =
  3            (SELECT 'Pirates of the Caribbean: On Stranger Tides'
  4            ,        'PG-13'
  5            FROM dual)
  6  WHERE   item_title = 'Pirates of the Caribbean 4'
  7  RETURNING item_title, item_rating INTO :bv_title, :bv_rating;
```

The values updated into the table are returned in the local variables. They can be displayed by using SQL*Plus formatting and a query:

```
COLUMN bv_title  FORMAT A44 HEADING ":bv_title"
COLUMN bv_rating FORMAT A12 HEADING ":bv_rating"
SELECT :bv_title AS bv_title, :bv_rating AS bv_rating FROM dual;
```

The `HEADING` value is enclosed in double quotes so that a colon can be used in the column titles. This returns the literal values from the query against the `dual` table:

```
:bv_title                                     :bv_rating
--------------------------------------------- ------------
Pirates of the Caribbean: On Stranger Tides   PG-13
```

Note that the `RETURNING INTO` phrase has several restrictions:

- It fails when updating more than a single row.
- It fails when the expression list includes a primary key or other `NOT NULL` column when a `BEFORE UPDATE` trigger is defined on the table.
- It fails when the expression list includes a `LONG` data type.
- It fails when the `UPDATE` statement is parallel processing or working against a remote object.
- It is disallowed when updating a view that has an `INSTEAD OF` trigger.

Returning scalar, `BLOB`, or `CLOB` data types is the most effective way to leverage the `RETURNING INTO` phrase. The `RETURNING INTO` phrase is very advantageous in web applications. A web application would implement a stored procedure (see Chapter 13) to start a transaction context and pass a reference for updating a CLOB column. The following (explained in more detail later) provides an example of such a procedure:

```
SQL> CREATE OR REPLACE PROCEDURE web_load_clob_from_file
  2  ( pv_item_id     IN      NUMBER
  3  , pv_descriptor IN OUT CLOB ) IS
  4  BEGIN
  5    -- A FOR UPDATE makes this a DML transaction.
  6    UPDATE     item
  7    SET        item_desc = empty_clob()
  8    WHERE      item_id = pv_item_id
  9    RETURNING item_desc INTO pv_descriptor;
 10  END web_load_clob_from_file;
 11  /
```

The pv_descriptor parameter in the procedure's signature on line 3 uses an IN OUT mode of operation, which is a *pass-by-reference* mechanism. It effectively enables the sending of a reference to the CLOB column out to the calling program. The RETURNING INTO clause assigns the reference to the parameter on line 9. With the reference, the external program can then update the CLOB column.

> **NOTE**
> *Check Chapter 8 in* Oracle Database 11*g* PL/SQL Programming *(McGraw-Hill, 2008) for the details on how to write this type of programming logic.*

Nested Tables

Nested tables are lists, which are like arrays but without a maximum number of rows. As such, lists mimic database tables when they're defined by object types. Object types act like record data structures in an Oracle database. This is possible because Oracle is an object relational database.

The original SQL design didn't consider the concept of object types or collections of object types. This leaves Oracle with the responsibility to fit calls to these object types within SQL extensions. The interface is rather straightforward but has limitations as to what you can perform on nested tables and arrays through INSERT and UPDATE statements. You can insert or update complete nested tables, but you can replace only certain elements of the nested tables. PL/SQL lets you access and manipulate the elements of nested tables and arrays.

This example revisits the employee table from Chapters 6 and 8. Here's the definition of the table:

Name	Null?	Type
EMPLOYEE_ID		NUMBER
FIRST_NAME		VARCHAR2(20)
MIDDLE_NAME		VARCHAR2(20)
LAST_NAME		VARCHAR2(20)
HOME_ADDRESS		ADDRESS_LIST

How to Write to a CLOB Column from PHP

Here's an example that might help you better understand this feature. Although this book isn't about how to write PHP to work with an Oracle or MySQL database, PHP can show you how to capture the handle from the web_load_clob_from_file procedure.

Here's part of a PHP function to write a large file to a CLOB column:

```
if ($c = @oci_connect(SCHEMA,PASSWD,TNS_ID)) {
  // Declare input variables.
  (isset($_POST['id']))    ? $id = (int) $_POST['id'] : $id = 1021;
  (isset($_POST['title'])) ? $title = $_POST['title'] : $title = "Harry #1";

  // Declare a PL/SQL statement and parse it.
  $stmt = "BEGIN web_load_clob_from_file(:id,:item_desc); END;";
  $s = oci_parse($c,$stmt);

  // Define a descriptor for a CLOB and variable for CLOB descriptor.
  $rlob = oci_new_descriptor($c,OCI_D_LOB);
  oci_define_by_name($s,':item_desc',$rlob,SQLT_CLOB);

  // Bind PHP variables to the OCI types.
  oci_bind_by_name($s,':id',$id);
  oci_bind_by_name($s,':item_desc',$rlob,-1,SQLT_CLOB);

  // Execute the PL/SQL statement.
  if (oci_execute($s,OCI_DEFAULT)) {
    $rlob->save($item_desc);
    oci_commit($c); }

  // Release statement resources and disconnect from database.
  oci_free_statement($s);
  oci_close($c); }

else {
    // Assign the OCI error and manage error.
    $errorMessage = oci_error();
    print htmlentities($errorMessage['message'])."<br />";
    die(); }
```

The four boldfaced lines make reading and writing to the CLOB column possible. The lines, respectively, define an anonymous PL/SQL block as a statement, create a socket, map the placeholder and the statement to the socket, and write the CLOB through the socket to the file.

If you're interested in learning more about PHP and the Oracle database, you can check *Oracle Database 10g Express Edition PHP Web Programming* (McGraw-Hill, 2006). The first 12 chapters cover PHP and the last 3 cover Oracle's OCI library.

The `home_address` column is a user-defined type (UDT) collection named `address_list`. To avoid your having to flip back to Chapter 7, I'll explain here: The `address_list` UDT holds an `address_type` UDT (object type that acts like a record data structure), and the `address_type` UDT holds another nested table of a scalar variable. This means the table holds multiple nested tables.

You can also describe the `address_list` UDTs with the `DESCRIBE` command in SQL*Plus:

```
address_list TABLE OF ADDRESS_TYPE
 Name                                      Null?     Type
 ---------------------------------------- -------- ------------------
 ADDRESS_ID                                         NUMBER
 STREET_ADDRESS                                     STREET_LIST
 CITY                                               VARCHAR2(30)
 STATE                                              VARCHAR2(2)
 POSTAL_CODE                                        VARCHAR2(10)
```

This collection is a nested table. You can tell that because it says `TABLE OF`. A UDT array would print a `VARRAY(n) OF` phrase before the UDT name. This example includes a nested `street_list` collection. You can describe it the same way and it shows the following:

```
street_list TABLE OF VARCHAR2(30)
```

As mentioned, this type of table structure is called *multiple table nesting*. It is inherently complex. This type of design also presents migration issues when you want to modify the UDTs. You must put the data some place, drop the table, and then add the UDTs in the reverse order of how you created them—at least until you arrive at the UDT that you want to change. After making the change, you'll need to re-create all data types and tables and migrate the data back into the new table.

When you perform an update, you need to replace the entire nested table element. You can read out what's there and identify where the change goes through PL/SQL or some other procedural language that leverages the Oracle Call Interface (OCI), Open Database Connectivity (ODBC), or Java Database Connectivity (JDBC). This assumes you've written the code logic to capture all existing data and dynamically construct an `UPDATE` statement. Native Dynamic SQL (NDS) lets you dynamically create these types of SQL statements, which are like prepared statements in MySQL. You can read about NDS in Chapter 13 and prepared statements in Chapter 14.

In Chapter 8, we inserted a row into the `EMPLOYEE` table. With a forward reference to material in Chapter 11, here's how you would extract the information from the nested tables into an ordinary result set of scalar columns:

```
-- These SQL*Plus commands format the columns for display.
COLUMN employee_id FORMAT 999 HEADING "ID|EMP"
COLUMN full_name   FORMAT A16 HEADING "Full Name"
COLUMN address_id  FORMAT 999 HEADING "ID|UDT"
COLUMN st_address  FORMAT A16 HEADING "Street Address"
COLUMN city        FORMAT A8  HEADING "City"
COLUMN state       FORMAT A5  HEADING "State"
COLUMN postal_code FORMAT A5  HEADING "Zip|Code"

SQL> SELECT    e.employee_id
  2  ,          e.first_name || ' ' || e.last_name AS full_name
```

```
 3   ,           st.address_id
 4   ,           sa.column_value AS st_address
 5   ,           st.city
 6   ,           st.state
 7   ,           st.postal_code
 8   FROM        employee e CROSS JOIN
 9               TABLE(e.home_address) st CROSS JOIN
10               TABLE(street_address) sa
11   ORDER BY 2, 3;
```

This SELECT statement uses the cross join to extract nested table material to the single containing row that holds it. In this process, the cross join makes copies of the content of the single row for each row of the nested table. This example first unwinds street_address within home_address, and then home_address within the container employee table. It returns four rows, because there are two rows in each of the nested tables and only one row in the sample table. Cross joins yield Cartesian products, which are the number of rows in one set times the other set, or in this case the multiplied product of rows in three sets ($1 \times 2 \times 2 = 4$). The statement above renders the following output:

ID EMP	Full Name	ID UDT	Street Address	City	State	Zip Code
1	Sam Yosemite	1	1111 Broadway	Oakland	CA	94612
1	Sam Yosemite	1	Suite 322	Oakland	CA	94612
1	Sam Yosemite	2	1111 Broadway	Oakland	CA	94612
1	Sam Yosemite	2	Suite 525	Oakland	CA	94612

Let's assume you want to change the Suite 322 in the second row to Suite 521. The UPDATE statement would look like this when you replace the entire structure:

```
SQL> UPDATE employee e
  2  SET    e.home_address =
  3         address_list(
  4           address_type( 1
  5                       , street_list('1111 Broadway','Suite 322')
  6                       ,'Oakland'
  7                       ,'CA'
  8                       ,'94612')
  9         , address_type( 2
 10                       , street_list('1111 Broadway','Suite 521')
 11                       ,'Oakland'
 12                       ,'CA'
 13                       ,'94612'))
 14  WHERE  e.first_name = 'Sam'
 15  AND    e.last_name = 'Yosemite';
```

The syntax to replace the content of a UDT uses the name of the data type as an object constructor and then provide a list. Lines 4 to 8 are highlighted to demonstrate the constructor for an address_type UDT. Line 10 is separately highlighted to show the constructor for a street_list UDT. In the preceding statement, a comma-delimited list lets you construct nested tables. Needless to say, you probably want to nest only data that changes infrequently and that fails to merit its own table.

You can also replace only an element of the nested `address_type` by using some complex `UPDATE` syntax. The `UPDATE` statement is complex because it uses a query to find a nested table in one row of the employee table. The `TABLE` function then casts the object collection into a SQL result set (formally, an aggregate result set). This type of result set can also be called an inline view, runtime table, derived table, or common table expression. The `UPDATE` statement lets you change the city value for the first element of the `address_type` UDT in the `address_list` collection:

```
SQL> UPDATE TABLE (SELECT  e.home_address
  2                        FROM    employee e
  3                        WHERE   e.employee_id = 1) e
  4    SET    e.city = 'Fremont'
  5    WHERE e.address_id = 1;
```

Unfortunately, the city was correct for the address but *Suite 521* is wrong. It should be *Suite 522*. There is no way to replace only one element of a varray or nested table of a scalar data type. An attempt would use the same cross joining logic shown earlier in the query that unfolds nested tables, like so:

```
SQL> UPDATE TABLE(SELECT  addr.street_address
  2                       FROM    employee e CROSS JOIN TABLE(e.home_address) addr
  3                       WHERE   e.employee_id = 1
  4                       AND     addr.address_id = 1)
  5    SET column_value = 'Suite 522'
  6    WHERE column_value = 'Suite 521';
```

Although the query returns the expected result set, the assignment in the `SET` clause fails. You can't make an assignment to the default `column_value` column returned by an unwound nested table of a scalar data type. It raises an ORA-25015 error:

```
SET column_value = 'Suite 522'
      *
ERROR at line 5:
ORA-25015: cannot perform DML ON this nested TABLE VIEW COLUMN
```

The error documentation does not seem to explain why it doesn't work. Hazarding a guess, I think that collections of scalar data types are handled differently than collections of UDTs. At least, there's a difference between them because scalar collections work in the result cache PL/SQL functions while collections of UDTs don't.

The following lets you reset the city and replaces the nested address element:

```
SQL> UPDATE TABLE (SELECT  e.home_address
  2                        FROM    employee e
  3                        WHERE   e.employee_id = 1) e
  4    SET    e.street_address = street_list('1111 Broadway','Suite 522')
  5    ,      e.city = 'Oakland'
  6    WHERE e.address_id = 1;
```

Line 4 stores a complete constructor of the scalar collection. It's not terribly difficult when only a few elements exist, but it becomes tedious with long lists. The alternative to an `UPDATE` statement like these is PL/SQL, which allows you to navigate the collections element-by-element and then process the individual list elements.

In general, with collections, you store nested tables, varrays, and object types the same way—with a call to their object type, which serves as a constructor method. You pass values inside the parentheses as actual parameters (also called arguments). The TREAT function lets you instantiate these in memory.

NOTE
Chapter 13 shows you how to implement a basic object type, and it and the SQL statements that support it are discussed there. Chapter 10 in Oracle Database 11g PL/SQL Programming Workbook *or Chapter 14 in* Oracle Database 11g PL/SQL Programming *(McGraw-Hill, 2008) cover the details of object types.*

Large Objects

Large objects present complexity in Oracle, because you need to load them by segments. After all, they can grow to 32 terabytes in size. BLOB and CLOB are the only two data types stored physically inside the database. The other large object type, BFILE, is a locator that points to an external directory location (see Chapter 12) and filename. The first argument is a call to a virtual directory that you've created in the database, and the second argument is the relative filename.

An ordinary UPDATE statement handles changes to BFILE locators like this:

```
SET = bfilename('virtual_directory_name', 'relative_file_name')
```

The BLOB and CLOB data types require special handling. The most common need is to overwrite the column value. That's because these are binary or character streams and they're seldom simply edited.

The following illustration shows you how to update a BLOB column. BLOB columns larger than 4 kilobytes are stored out-of-line from the transactional table, because they're infrequently changed and less frequently backed-up. It is also common practice to change these columns by themselves after any updates to the scalar columns of a table.

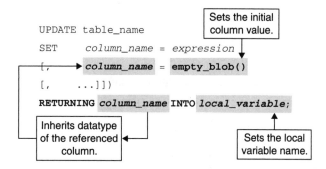

This prototype statement demonstrates the syntax if you were to update a single row, and the WHERE clause is excluded to simplify the illustration. The first step of an update to a BLOB column is re-initialization, which occurs with an EMPTY_BLOB() function call. The second phase maps the column name in a row to an external stream (receiving end), which uses the column name as an identifier. The third step assigns the stream (originating end) to a local program variable.

Basically, this is a socket communication between a program and the database, and it lasts until all segments have been loaded into the column.

The local variable in this example can be a PL/SQL variable or any external OCI, ODBC, or JDBC programming language variable. The local variable data type must support a mapped relationship to the native Oracle data type.

The CLOB data type works the same way, and as you can see in the next illustration, there's no SQL statement difference. Only the call to the EMPTY_CLOB() differs, but it's an important difference that you shouldn't overlook.

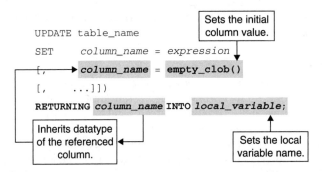

The XML_TYPE data types use the EMPTY_CLOB() function to clear the columns' contents. After all, XML_TYPE columns are specializations of the CLOB data type.

MySQL Update by Values

MySQL updates by value just as Oracle UPDATE statements do—at least, they do this the same way when assigning values to single columns in the SET subclause. The interesting thing about MySQL is that you don't require specialized handling for large binary or character strings. This simplifies things considerably.

MySQL does give you some added options that aren't available in Oracle UPDATE statements. The options let you do the following:

- Set the runtime priority for an UPDATE statement.

- Ignore errors in an UPDATE statement.

- Add an ORDER BY clause to an UPDATE statement.

- Set a LIMIT on rows processed by an UPDATE statement.

Given the number of additional options, here's a MySQL-specific prototype:

```
UPDATE [LOW_PRIORITY] [IGNORE] table_name
SET     column_name = expression [, ...]
WHERE   [NOT]      {column_name | expression} = {expression | DEFAULT}
[{AND | OR} [NOT] {column_name | expression} = {expression | DEFAULT} [...]]
[ORDER BY {select_list_element | position_id} [ASC|DESC] [, ... ]]
[LIMIT number_of_rows];
```

The `IGNORE` keyword lets the `UPDATE` statement complete when it encounters errors. The `LOW_PRIORITY` keyword lets you defer `UPDATE` statement processing behind other priority tasks. Note that it's not a good idea to use the `LOW_PRIORITY` keyword unless you're performing maintenance and interactive users are disconnected from the system, because deferred processing can lead to transactional inconsistencies. Ellipses indicate that you can add elements to the `SET` and `WHERE` clauses.

A new small table seems appropriate to show some of the features of the MySQL `UPDATE` statement with a value clause. The following creation statement defines the table:

```
mysql> CREATE TABLE teeshirt
    -> ( teeshirt_id   INT UNSIGNED PRIMARY KEY AUTO_INCREMENT
    -> , teeshirt_slogan  VARCHAR(60)
    -> , teeshirt_size    VARCHAR(10) DEFAULT 'Medium');
```

A `DEFAULT` value is assigned to the third column. An `INSERT` statement uses the `DEFAULT` value whenever an override signature excludes the column name. An `UPDATE` statement uses the default value whenever it is explicitly assigned to a column in a `SET` clause. Here's a data set with five rows:

```
+-------------+------------------+---------------+
| teeshirt_id | teeshirt_slogan | teeshirt_size |
+-------------+------------------+---------------+
|           1 | Spartans        | Large         |
|           2 | Cardinals       | X-Large       |
|           3 | Cal Bears       | X-Large       |
|           4 | Bruins          | 2X-Large      |
|           5 | Trojans         | Large         |
+-------------+------------------+---------------+
```

The following update statement changes the *Cal Bears* slogan string to *Bears* and uses the default to set the tee shirt size to *Medium*:

```
mysql> UPDATE teeshirt
    -> SET     teeshirt_slogan = 'Bears'
    -> ,       teeshirt_size = DEFAULT
    -> WHERE   teeshirt_slogan = 'Cal Bears';
```

A query of the modified data set returns the following changes for the row identified by a 3 in the `teeshirt_id` column:

```
+-------------+------------------+---------------+
| teeshirt_id | teeshirt_slogan | teeshirt_size |
+-------------+------------------+---------------+
|           3 | Cal Bears        | Medium        |
+-------------+------------------+---------------+
```

The `LIMIT` clause restricts how many rows are impacted by the `UPDATE` statement. This is useful when you want to update only a certain number of rows, but it's most useful when you combine it with the `ORDER BY` clause, which allows you to pre-sort the records before applying the `LIMIT` clause. This way, the `LIMIT` clause is targeted based on the ordering of rows.

The following update will set the tee shirt size to *Medium* for the two highest surrogate key ID values because the ORDER BY clause performs a descending sort:

```
mysql> UPDATE   teeshirt
    -> SET      teeshirt_size = DEFAULT
    -> ORDER BY teeshirt_id DESC
    -> LIMIT 2;
```

The ORDER BY and LIMIT clauses were the only restrictions on which columns were changed by the UPDATE statement. Here are the modified results:

```
+-------------+------------------+---------------+
| teeshirt_id | teeshirt_slogan  | teeshirt_size |
+-------------+------------------+---------------+
|           1 | Spartans         | Large         |
|           2 | Cardinals        | X-Large       |
|           3 | Bears            | Medium        |
|           4 | Bruins           | Medium        |
|           5 | Trojans          | Medium        |
+-------------+------------------+---------------+
```

Although this technique is possible, it's generally a good idea to use it only when you're working with changes to a small data set. The WHERE clause should generally filter the rows changed by the UPDATE statement.

Update by Correlated Queries

Correlated queries let you change data in columns based on the join to other tables. The join statement is the point of correlation—comparison of two or more objects. The join statement is always in the WHERE clause of the correlated subquery, because it has scope access to the containing DML statement. Basically, you can think of the UPDATE statement as calling a correlated subquery, like a function. A UPDATE statement calls any correlated subquery once for every row it processes.

Oracle and MySQL databases support correlated UPDATE statements. MySQL also supports multiple-table UPDATE statements that act like correlated queries. The section on MySQL correlated queries covers a multiple-table UPDATE statement. Although correlated UPDATE statements work almost exactly alike in both Oracle and MySQL, SQL functions differ between the two databases.

Oracle Correlated Queries

A subquery that matches a value directly works as the right operand in a SET clause assignment. Sometimes, finding the value requires matching column values from other tables against the rows of the table you're updating. For example, when you need to identify a rental item's price on a rental agreement and an inventory item, you would need to cross join the rental and item tables before filtering the results through joins to the rental_item table. At least, that's what you need to do in the book's sample application, because the rental_item table is an association table. It resolves a logical many-to-many relationship between the rental and item tables. In the rental_item association table, some columns belong to the relationship between the rental and item tables, such as prices associated with specific rental item and rental agreements.

A correlated `UPDATE` statement lets SQL find all potential matches and update all affected prices in the `rental_item` table. Basically, the computer sorts out all the relationships shared through the `rental_item` association table.

The following example illustrates the correlated `UPDATE` statement that accomplishes this:

```
UPDATE     rental_item ri
SET        ri.rental_item_price =
           (SELECT    p.amount
            FROM      price p CROSS JOIN rental r
            WHERE     p.item_id      = ri.item_id
            AND       p.price_type = ri.rental_item_type
            AND       r.rental_id   = ri.rental_id
            AND       r.check_out_date
                        BETWEEN p.start_date
                        AND NVL(p.end_date,TRUNC(SYSDATE)));
```

> Corellation between subquery and UPDATE statement.

The `CROSS JOIN` result set for the `price` and `rental` tables is every row in one table matched against every row in the other table. A date range filter finds all rows between a `start_date` and `end_date`, or the current date. The remaining rows in the result set are then matched through an inner join to the table being updated. The range join operation (technically a range non-equijoin) works because a current date value is substituted for a possible null `end_date` value.

NOTE
Most data models that use time-events to bracket unique sets leave the current value with an open end date. The implementation of null as the open end date is the more common modeling solution.

TIP
The `TRUNC` function shaves the fractional time component off a date-time data type and coverts the value to a date-time of midnight. There is no pure date data type in an Oracle database.

A correlated `UPDATE` statement such as this changes the values of multiple rows. No `WHERE` clause is required in this type of update, because the inner join finds only the rows that should be changed. Inner joins are equijoin—a join based on the equality of values from two columns or two sets of columns (see Chapter 11 for more on joins).

MySQL Correlated Queries

MySQL supports correlated `UPDATE` statements similar to Oracle, except you can update a single column only through the `SET` clause with a specific correlated `UPDATE` statement. MySQL also supports multiple-table `UPDATE` statements that act like correlated queries.

Building on the example from the Oracle section, only one change is required for this to work in MySQL. The Oracle proprietary `NVL` function must be replaced by the MySQL proprietary

IFNULL function. Both perform the same task: they replace a null value with a default value. Since TRUNC and SYSDATE are also proprietary to an Oracle database, you use the UTC_DATE function in MySQL. The NOW function would also work but raises a warning message when it's implicitly cast to a date, which is a loss of precision from the MySQL Server's perspective.

An example of the correlated UPDATE statement for MySQL is shown in the following illustration:

```
UPDATE    rental_item ri                      ┌────────────────────────┐
SET       ri.rental_item_price =              │ Corellation between    │
          (SELECT    p.amount                 │ subquery and           │
          FROM       price p CROSS JOIN rental r │ UPDATE statement.   │
          WHERE      p.item_id    = ri.item_id └────────────────────────┘
          AND        p.price_type = ri.rental_item_type
          AND        r.rental_id  = ri.rental_id
          AND        r.check_out_date
                         BETWEEN p.start_date
                         AND IFNULL(p.end_date,UTC_DATE()));
```

Similar to the explanation in the Oracle discussion, this query resolves through the three column joins between the updated rental_item table and columns from the cross joined product of the price and rental tables. This join updates only the rental_item table rows that match the criteria in the subquery, which is filtered by *rentals* that fall within a certain *price date range*.

The next section shows the multiple-table UPDATE statement available in MySQL. Multiple-table UPDATE statements are not portable to other database servers.

Multiple-Table Update Statement

The multiple-table UPDATE statement uses ANSI SQL-92 syntax for joins, which uses keywords such as JOIN and CROSS JOIN. A JOIN is shorthand notation for an INNER JOIN. Inner joins add the rows from one table to another table where one or a set of columns hold values that match. Chapter 11 covers join syntax in more detail.

Here's the prototype for a multiple-table UPDATE statement:

```
UPDATE [LOW_PRIORITY] [IGNORE] target_table_name table_alias
[{INNER | LEFT | RIGHT} JOIN table_name table_alias
  {ON      table_alias.column_name = table_alias.column_name
    [AND {table_alias.column_name = table_alias.column_name |
          table_alias.column_name BETWEEN table_alias.column_name
                              AND table_alias.column_name} |
  USING(column_name [, column_name [, ...]])} [...]
SET    column_name = expression [, ...]
WHERE  [NOT]      {column_name | expression} = {expression | DEFAULT}
[{AND | OR} [NOT] {column_name | expression} = {expression | DEFAULT} [...]];
```

The multiple-table UPDATE statement prototype supports LOW PRIORITY and IGNORE like the other UPDATE statements. Table aliases should be used for clarity, and they're supported. When you opt not to use table aliases, be sure to use table names to qualify columns or you'll raise an ambiguous column error.

You can perform INNER, LEFT, or RIGHT JOIN operations in multiple-table UPDATE statements, and you can check Chapter 11 for more on join mechanics. It is possible to have joins to multiple tables, and you can also use the BETWEEN operator to filter cross join result sets. The SET and WHERE clauses work the same as in other UPDATE statements.

Refactoring the preceding correlated subquery, it can be written as the following multiple-table UPDATE statement:

```
UPDATE     rental_item ri
JOIN       rental r ON  ri.rental_id = r.rental_id
JOIN       price p  ON  ri.item_id = p.item_id
                    AND ri.rental_item_type = p.price_type
                    AND r.check_out_date BETWEEN
                            p.start_date AND IFNULL(p.end_date,UTC_DATE())
SET        ri.rental_item_price = p.amount;
```

UPDATE statements typically work with tables. This changes with multiple-table UPDATE statements, because a series of tables are joined together to create a temporary result set. This is done by a *partial* inner join between the rental_item table and both the rental and price tables. The completion of the join between the rental_item and price table includes a range filter that finds rows based on the occurrence of a checkout date between a start and end date for a row in the price table. The IFNULL function guarantees that the upward range element isn't a null value, which would cause the statement to fail.

The join syntax for a multiple-table UPDATE statement is what you would see in a SELECT statement when querying data. For this reason alone, it is probably more widely used than a correlated statement. As mentioned, multiple-table UPDATE statements aren't portable to other databases. I'd recommend that you use it to sort out what should go into a correlated UPDATE statement and then write the correlated UPDATE statement for portability's sake.

Summary

This chapter covered methods for updating data. The UPDATE statement lets you change column values by direct assignment of literal values for one to many rows of a table. If you exclude a filtering WHERE clause from an UPDATE statement, all rows in the table are updated. The UPDATE statement also lets you correlate against rows in other tables. MySQL lets you perform multiple-table UPDATE statements, which mirror correlated update statements but have syntax more similar to that found in SELECT statements.

Mastery Check

The mastery check is a series of true or false and multiple choice questions that let you confirm how well you understand the material in the chapter. You may check the Appendix for answers to these questions.

1. **True** ☐ **False** ☐ An UPDATE statement supports multiple row changes with only one set of date, numeric, or string literals.

2. **True** ☐ **False** ☐ An UPDATE statement supports DEFAULT values in Oracle databases only.

3. **True** ☐ **False** ☐ The SET clause must contain a list of all mandatory columns.

4. **True** ☐ **False** ☐ A multiple-table UPDATE statement in MySQL performs as a correlated UPDATE statement.

5. **True** ☐ **False** ☐ MySQL supports a nested table UPDATE statement.

6. **True** ☐ **False** ☐ A BLOB or CLOB requires the RETURNING INTO phrase to work with procedural programming modules.

7. **True** ☐ **False** ☐ The IGNORE keyword lets an Oracle or MySQL UPDATE statement run successfully even when it encounters errors.

8. **True** ☐ **False** ☐ A LOW_PRIORITY assignment lets an UPDATE statement run behind other DML statements in the database.

9. **True** ☐ **False** ☐ MySQL supports the RETURNING INTO phrase in UPDATE statements.

10. **True** ☐ **False** ☐ A multiple column and row UPDATE is possible in either Oracle or MySQL databases.

11. Which of the following data types requires a RETURNING INTO phrase to interact with procedural programs (multiple answers possible)?

    A. BLOB

    B. MEDIUMCLOB

    C. TEXT

    D. CLOB

    E. VARCHAR

12. In an Oracle database, what are the maximum number of rows that you can update through a SET clause when values are assigned by literals?

    A. 1

    B. 2

    C. 3

    D. 4

    E. Many

13. In a MySQL database, what are the maximum number of rows that you can update through a SET clause when values are assigned by literals?

    A. 1

    B. 2

    C. 3

    D. 4

    E. Many

14. When you use a correlated query instead of a SET clause in Oracle or MySQL, what filters the rows updated?

   A. The WHERE clause

   B. The SET clause

   C. The joins between the updated table and correlated subquery

   D. The ORDER BY clause

   E. The LIMIT clause

15. What can't you change with an UPDATE statement in an Oracle database?

   A. A collection of a UDT

   B. An element of a UDT

   C. A collection of a scalar data type

   D. An element of a scalar data type

   E. None of the above

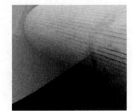

CHAPTER
10

Deleting Data

he DELETE FROM statement lets you remove data from tables and views. There are two types of DELETE FROM statements: One uses literal values or subquery comparisons in a WHERE clause; the other uses correlated results from a subquery. It is also possible to combine values or subquery results with correlated results in the WHERE clause. MySQL offers a variation on correlated statements with a multiple-table DELETE FROM statement. This chapter covers how you use both statements.

Like the UPDATE statement, a DELETE FROM statement removes all rows found in a table unless you filter what you want to remove in a WHERE clause. A DELETE FROM statement also writes redo logs, similar to INSERT and UPDATE statements, and supports bulk processing options inside Oracle's PL/SQL blocks.

The DELETE FROM statement has a closely related cousin, the DDL TRUNCATE statement. DBAs often disable constraints, copy a table's contents to a temporary table, TRUNCATE or DROP the table, re-create the table with a new storage clause, and then INSERT the old records from the temporary table. The TRUNCATE statement doesn't log deletions; it simply removes the allocated storage space in a tablespace, which makes it much faster for routine DBA maintenance tasks.

NOTE
Chapter 6 covers how to use the CREATE TABLE statement to clone a table.

The DELETE FROM statement also works on nested tables in the Oracle database. Deleting nested tables without removing the row from the table is the exception rather than the rule for a DELETE FROM statement, as you'll see in the next section.

The following two sections demonstrate the syntax for deleting rows by value matches and by correlation between two or more tables. Value matches can be literal values or ordinary subqueries. Correlation between two or more tables requires joins between tables, and MySQL includes a multiple-table DELETE FROM statement that illustrates it.

Delete by Value Matches

This DELETE FROM statement uses a table name and a WHERE clause that allows you to filter which rows you want to remove from a table. The WHERE clause works with date, numeric, and string literal values.

Here's the basic prototype for a DELETE FROM statement:

```
DELETE FROM table_name
WHERE [NOT] column_name {{= | <> | > | >= | < | <=} |
                         [NOT] {{IN | EXISTS} | IS NULL}} 'expression'
[{AND | OR } [NOT] comparison_operation] [...];
```

An actual DELETE FROM statement would look like this:

```
SQL> DELETE FROM item
  2  WHERE  item_title = 'Pirates of the Caribbean: On Stranger Tides'
  3  AND    item_rating = 'PG-13';
```

The first line sets the target table for the deletion operation. Lines 2 and 3 filter the rows to find those that will be deleted. All rows meeting those two criteria are removed from the table and immediately become invisible to the current user in transaction mode. As explained in Chapter 4, in the two-phase commit (2PC) model, the first phase removes rows from the current user's view, and the second phase removes them from the system. Between the first and second phases, other users see the deleted rows and can make decisions based on their existence—unless you've locked them in the context of a transaction.

You should lock rows that are possibly subject to deletion before running DELETE FROM statements. This is straightforward in a transactional database, such as Oracle. In a MySQL database, locks require more precautions because they exist only when you're working within the scope of a transaction using InnoDB-managed tables. You can use SQL cursors to lock rows when deletions run inside PL/SQL or SQL/PSM stored program units. You lock the rows in a SQL cursor by appending a FOR UPDATE clause. Regardless of your method of operation, failure to lock rows before deleting them can lead to insertion, update, or deletion anomalies. The anomalies can occur because other DML statements can make decisions on the unaltered rows, which are visible to other sessions before a COMMIT statement.

TIP
MySQL can perform this type of locking only when tables are defined using the InnoDB engine and in the scope of an explicit transaction scope.

In addition to using literal values in the WHERE clause, you can use ordinary subqueries. Ordinary subqueries act independently of the parent DML statement and return a SELECT list for comparision against values in the DELETE FROM statement.. These subqueries do have a restriction: they can return only a single row when you use an equality comparison operator, such as the equal (=) operator. You can also use multiple-row subqueries, but they require a lookup operator. As mentioned in Chapter 6, four lookup operators can be used: IN, =ANY, =SOME, and =ALL. The IN, =ANY, and =SOME operators behave similarly. They allow you to compare a column value in a row against a list of column values, and they return true if one value matches—this is like an OR logical operator in a procedural IF statement. The =ALL also allows you to compare a column value in a row against a list of column values, and it returns true when all values in the list match the single column value. The =ALL performs like an AND logical operator in a procedural IF statement. For reference, there is no standard *exclusive OR* operator in SQL.

Inside the WHERE clause, you can use AND or OR logical operators. The order of precedence requires that a group of logical comparisons connected by the AND logical operator are processed as a block before anything connected later by an OR logical operator.

Modifying the preceding example, let's add an OR logical comparison based on the release date. The following statement uses the default order of operation in the WHERE clause:

```
SQL> DELETE FROM item
  2  WHERE   item_title = 'Pirates of the Caribbean: On Stranger Tides'
  3  AND     item_rating = 'PG-13'
  4  OR      TRUNC(item_release_date) < TRUNC(SYSDATE,'YY');
```

This removes all rows where the literal values match the item_title and item_rating or all rows where the item_release_date precedes the first day of the year. You must use parentheses to change the order of operation.

Transaction Management

The basis for a transaction doesn't require specialized steps in an Oracle database, because Oracle statements are natively transactional and use a 2PC process to insert, update, or delete rows from tables. MySQL isn't transactional natively, so you must start and end a transaction scope.

The simplest example in MySQL is an insert between a `parent` and `child` table, where the `parent` table holds the primary key column and the `child` table holds a copy in a foreign key column. Here's the example:

```
START TRANSACTION;
INSERT INTO parent VALUES (NULL, 'One');
INSERT INTO child VALUES (NULL, last_insert_id(),'Two');
COMMIT;
```

The `START TRANSACTION;` statement starts a transaction scope. The first column in the `VALUES` clause for both tables is a null, which lets the automatic sequence provide the number. You can enter descriptive text in the second column in the `parent` table and third column in the `child` table. The second column in the `child` table holds a foreign key, which is a copy of a primary key column from the `parent` table. The `last_insert_id()` function in MySQL captures the sequence value used in the preceding `INSERT` statement to the `parent` table—it's similar to the `.CURRVAL` in an Oracle database. The last element is the `COMMIT` statement, which ends the transaction scope.

An alternative to the `START TRANSACTION;` statement is the `BEGIN WORK;` statement. It works the same way, as you can see:

```
BEGIN WORK;
INSERT INTO parent VALUES (NULL, 'One');
INSERT INTO child VALUES (NULL, last_insert_id(),'Two');
COMMIT;
```

In the scope of the transaction, no other session can see the inserted values until the `COMMIT` statement ends the transaction and makes changes permanent. You could substitute `DELETE FROM` statements for the `INSERT` statements, and no one would be able to see the deleted row until you committed the changes.

Let's say the business rule changes and now requires that the `item_title` matches the literal value, and either the `item_rating` matches the literal value or the `item_release_date` is less than the first day of the current year. A modified statement would look like this:

```
SQL> DELETE FROM item
  2  WHERE   item_title = 'Pirates of the Caribbean: On Stranger Tides'
  3  AND    (item_rating = 'PG-13'
  4  OR      TRUNC(item_release_date) < TRUNC(SYSDATE,'YY'));
```

The parentheses on lines 3 and 4 change the order of operation and remove only rows with matching `item_title` values and matches in other criteria.

Alternatives to values in the WHERE clause can be subqueries that return one or more column values. You can write a DELETE FROM statement when the query returns only one row, like this:

```
SQL> DELETE FROM item
  2  WHERE (item_title,item_rating) =
  3         (SELECT 'Pirates of the Caribbean: On Stranger Tides'
  4         ,       'PG-13'
  5         FROM    dual);
```

Line 2 contains an equal (=) comparison operator that works only when a single row is returned by the subquery. All queries from the dual pseudo table return one row unless a UNION or UNION ALL set operator fabricates a multiple row set. See Chapter 11 for details on the use of set operators to fabricate data sets.

The IN, =ANY, and =SOME lookup operators work when the subquery returns one or more rows. It's always best to use a lookup operator unless you want to raise an exception when the subquery returns more than one row. This type of exception signals when a prior business rule has been violated—the rule that the subquery supports.

The following demonstrates a DELETE FROM statement with a multiple column lookup operator:

```
SQL> DELETE FROM item
  2  WHERE (item_title,item_rating) IN
  3         (SELECT 'Pirates of the Caribbean: On Stranger Tides'
  4         ,       'PG-13'
  5         FROM    error_item);
```

Oracle and MySQL both support the demonstrated DELETE FROM syntax variations, which eliminates the need for a specialized MySQL section in this chapter. A separate section is required, however, to cover the use of a DELETE FROM statement when you're working with nested table elements in rows of a table in Oracle.

Delete Nested Table Row Elements

As mentioned, nested tables are object relational database management system (ORDBMS) structures. MySQL doesn't support nested tables, but Oracle does. Chapters 6 and 7 showed you how to create and alter tables with nested tables. Chapter 8 showed you how to insert nested tables, and Chapter 9 showed you how to update nested tables.

The following example builds on the employee table introduced in Chapters 6, 7, 8, and 9. The following data should be included in the table by the conclusion of Chapter 9, but it won't be formatted like the following (which was reformatted to fit on the printed page):

```
  ID Full Name     Street Address Nested Table
---- ------------- ----------------------------------------------------
   1 Yosemite Sam  ADDRESS_LIST
                   ( ADDRESS_TYPE
                     (1,STREET_LIST(...),'Oakland','CA','94612')
                   , ADDRESS_TYPE
                     (2,STREET_LIST(...),'Oakland','CA','94612')
                   )
   2 Bugs Bunny    ADDRESS_LIST
                   ( ADDRESS_TYPE
```

```
        (1,STREET_LIST(...),'Beverly Hills','CA','90210')
    , ADDRESS_TYPE
        (2,STREET_LIST(...),'Beverly Hills','CA','90210')
      )
```

Previous DELETE FROM statements would let you remove the row with *Yosemite Sam* or *Bugs Bunny* but not an element of the nested employee table. The DELETE FROM statement applied against a view of the nested table would let you remove a row element.

The following statement lets you remove a row element from the nested table:

```
DELETE FROM TABLE (SELECT e.home_address
                   FROM   employee e
                   WHERE  e.employee_id = 1) ha
WHERE  ha.address_id = 1;
```

This DELETE FROM statement removes row elements from the view created inside the call to the TABLE function. The SELECT list inside the runtime view returns row elements for deletion. The WHERE clause for the DELETE FROM statement identifies the row to process.

This works only on collection of user-defined object types. It doesn't work for nested tables built as collections of a scalar data type, such as a date, number, or string. You must replace the collection of a scalar data type with a new collection that doesn't include the undesired element. PL/SQL lets you read through and eliminate undesired elements from any nested table structure. While reading the records, you can capture all the records you want to keep and then update the table's collection with the locally stored collection values.

After the preceding DELETE FROM statement, you would hold the following in the employee table:

```
 ID Full Name     Street Address Nested Table
 ---- ------------- -----------------------------------------------------
    1 Yosemite Sam  ADDRESS_LIST
                    ( ADDRESS_TYPE
                      (2,STREET_LIST(...),'Oakland','CA','94612')
                    )
    2 Bugs Bunny    ADDRESS_LIST
                    ( ADDRESS_TYPE
                      (1,STREET_LIST(...),'Beverly Hills','CA','90210')
                    , ADDRESS_TYPE
                      (2,STREET_LIST(...),'Beverly Hills','CA','90210')
                    )
```

Notice that the first nested row has been removed from the nested table in the Yosemite Sam row. Maintenance on nested tables is possible when they are collections of object types, but it's not possible when they are collections of scalar variables.

Delete by Correlated Queries

Although deletions can remove one to many rows when the conditions of the WHERE clause are met, they can also work with joins between tables. Like the UPDATE statement, the DELETE FROM statement supports correlated joins that allow you to work with multiple tables when deleting rows. A separate multiple-table syntax exists for MySQL, which uses standard join syntax covered in more depth in Chapter 11.

Correlated joins use the `EXISTS` keyword in the `WHERE` clause. The actual equality or inequality of the join is in the `WHERE` clause of the subquery. The subquery has scope access to the target table of the `DELETE FROM` statement, shown in the following illustration, which makes referencing it in the subquery possible.

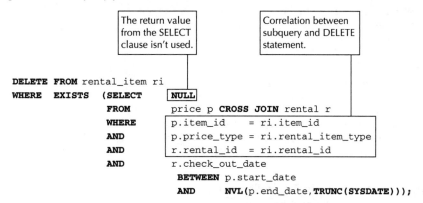

There is one difference between Oracle and MySQL databases in this statement. The `NVL` function is an Oracle built-in function, and the equivalent for a MySQL database is the `IFNULL` function. The last line would look like this in MySQL:

```
BETWEEN p.start_date AND IFNULL(p.end_date, UTC_DATE()));
```

Correlated subqueries in the `WHERE` clause don't return a value, because the match occurs in the subquery's `WHERE` clause. That's why a `NULL` is frequently returned from correlated subqueries, but you can return anything you'd like. In the preceding example, two columns from the price table and one column from the rental table match three columns in the target `rental_item` table of the `DELETE FROM` statement. The three columns from the `rental_item` table are the natural key. Together they uniquely identify rows as the natural key. A match between the three columns and a range filter against a start and end date guarantees unique row deletions.

MySQL Delete by Multiple-Table Statement

The multiple-table `DELETE FROM` statement uses interesting syntax, but it is not necessary, because correlation works well. It also isn't portable, whereas correlated subuqeries are portable to other databases. Unlike the multiple-table `UPDATE` statement, the multiple-table `DELETE FROM` statement uses both ANSI SQL-89 comma-delimited tables in the `FROM` clause and ANSI SQL-92 with join syntax.

The two subsections cover the ANSI SQL-89 and ANSI SQL-92 syntax. They offer different approaches, but the advantage of ANSI SQL-92 is its support of outer joins.

ANSI SQL-89 Multiple-Table Statement

Here's the generic ANSI SQL-89 prototype:

```
DELETE target_table
FROM target_table, join_table alias [, join_table alias [, …]]
WHERE [NOT] column_name {{= | <> | > | >= | < | <=} |
                          [NOT] {{IN | EXISTS} | IS NULL}} 'expression'
[{AND | OR } [NOT] comparison_operation] [...];
```

In the ANSI SQL-89 approach, the multiple-table DELETE FROM statement doesn't support the use of table aliases for the target table but does for join tables. Join conditions are placed in the WHERE clause and qualified by the target table name or the join table name or alias.

In the following example, the rental_item table is the target table. You also must repeat the rental_item table in the FROM clause.

The following converts the previous DELETE FROM correlated subquery into a multiple-table DELETE statement:

```
DELETE rental_item
FROM   rental_item, price p, rental r
WHERE  p.item_id    = rental_item.item_id
AND    p.price_type = rental_item.rental_item_type
AND    r.rental_id  = rental_item.rental_id
AND    r.check_out_date BETWEEN p.start_date
                       AND     IFNULL(p.end_date,UTC_DATE());
```

ANSI SQL-92 Multiple-Table Statement

Here's the generic ANSI SQL-92 prototype:

```
DELETE table_alias, table_alias [, table_alias [, ...]]
FROM   table [[AS] alias] {LEFT | RIGHT | INNER | FULL} JOIN
       table [[AS] alias]
{ USING ( column [, column [, ... ]]) |
    ON {table | alias}.column = {table | alias}.column
  [ AND {table | alias}.column = {table | alias}.column
  [ AND ... ]}
[ another_join [ ...]]
WHERE [NOT] column_name {{= | <> | > | >= | < | <=} |
                         [NOT] {{IN | EXISTS} | IS NULL}} 'expression'
[{AND | OR } [NOT] comparison_operation] [...];
```

In the ANSI SQL-92 approach, the multiple-table DELETE FROM statement does support the use of table aliases for all tables. Join conditions are placed in the USING or ON subclauses of the FROM clause.

The following converts the previous multiple-table DELETE statement into the newer syntax and demonstrates INNER JOIN syntax. A INNER JOIN in this case deletes rows from the primary table whether or not matches are found in the other tables.

```
DELETE ri, p, r
FROM   rental_item AS ri INNER JOIN price AS p
ON ri.item_id = p.item_id AND ri.rental_item_type = p.price_type
INNER JOIN rental AS r ON ri.rental_id = r.rental_id
WHERE r.check_out_date BETWEEN p.start_date AND IFNULL(p.end_date,UTC_DATE());
```

The choice of whether you delete by correlation or multiple-table syntax is yours, but correlation is the best practice and uses the most portable syntax. The multiple-table syntax is more like the syntax of joins in queries, and that's probably why developers like to use it.

Summary

This chapter covered how you delete data. As with the INSERT and UPDATE statements, you can delete based on literal values or on subqueries. Correlated subqueries let you validate related tables for matching values and generally ensure greater control and smaller procedural code segments.

Mastery Check

The mastery check is a series of true or false and multiple choice questions that let you confirm how well you understand the material in the chapter. You may check the Appendix for answers to these questions.

1. True ☐ False ☐ A DELETE FROM statement supports multiple-row deletes when more than one row matches the conditions of the WHERE clause.

2. True ☐ False ☐ A DELETE FROM statement has the same syntax in Oracle as MySQL when the WHERE clause uses values, subqueries, or correlated subqueries.

3. True ☐ False ☐ The deletion of rows is immediate in all cases.

4. True ☐ False ☐ A TRUNCATE statement deletes rows similar to a DELETE FROM statement and writes pending changes to a redo log file.

5. True ☐ False ☐ In the scope of a transaction, the DELETE FROM statement has two phases when the table uses a MyISAM engine.

6. True ☐ False ☐ In the scope of a transaction, the DELETE FROM statement has two phases when the table uses an InnoDB engine.

7. True ☐ False ☐ Oracle databases support a multiple-table DELETE FROM statement that uses ANSI SQL-92 syntax with JOIN keywords.

8. True ☐ False ☐ MySQL databases support a multiple-table DELETE FROM statement that uses ANSI SQL-89 syntax with JOIN keywords.

9. True ☐ False ☐ Oracle and MySQL support multiple-column matches from subqueries.

10. True ☐ False ☐ A non-correlated subquery always returns a null value.

11. Which of the following comparison operators work with a subquery that returns a single row with a single column?

    A. =

    B. =ANY

    C. =ALL

    D. IN

    E. All of the above

12. Which of the following comparison operators work with a subquery that returns a single row with multiple columns?

   A. =

   B. =ANY

   C. =ALL

   D. IN

   E. All of the above

13. Which of the following comparison operators work with a subquery that returns multiple different rows with multiple columns?

   A. =

   B. =ANY

   C. =NONE

   D. =ALL

   E. All of the above

14. A multiple-table DELETE FROM statement requires how many references to the target table?

   A. 0

   B. 1

   C. 2

   D. 3

   E. None of the above

15. Which type of DELETE FROM statement doesn't support table aliases for the target table?

   A. A DELETE FROM statement that only performs value comparisons in the WHERE clause

   B. A DELETE FROM statement that uses value and expression (subquery) comparisons in the WHERE clause

   C. A DELETE FROM statement that uses correlated subqueries in the WHERE clause

   D. A multiple-table DELETE FROM statement that uses joins in the FROM clause

   E. None of the above

CHAPTER
11

Querying

he SQL SELECT statement lets you query data from the database. In many of the previous chapters, you've seen examples of queries. Queries support several different types of subqueries, such as nested queries that run independently or correlated nested queries. Correlated nested queries run with a dependency on the outer or containing query.

This chapter shows you how to work with column returns from queries and how to join tables into multiple table result sets. Result sets are like tables because they're two-dimensional data sets. The data sets can be a subset of one table or a set of values from two or more tables. The SELECT list determines what's returned from a query into a result set. The SELECT list is the set of columns and expressions returned by a SELECT statement. The SELECT list defines the record structure of the result set, which is the result set's first dimension. The number of rows returned from the query defines the elements of a record structure list, which is the result set's second dimension.

You filter single tables to get subsets of a table, and you join tables into a larger result set to get a superset of any one table by returning a result set of the join between two or more tables. Joins expand the SELECT list by adding columns or expressions, and set operations expand the number of rows returned.

This chapter covers three topics:

- Query results
- Join results
- Views: stored queries

The query results section shows you how to manage column values; perform concatenation or parsing, math, and date calculations; and execute data type casting operations. It also shows you how to perform conditional logic and aggregation operations.

The join results section shows you how to perform cross, inner, natural, left outer, right outer, and full outer joins between tables. It demonstrates both the ANSI SQL-89 and ANSI SQL-92 syntax for joins. This section also covers how to expand Oracle's nested tables into two-dimensional result sets and how to use the INTERSECT, UNION, UNION ALL, and MINUS set operators.

You'll examine the basic flow of operation for SELECT statements, which applies to both databases. The biggest difference between SELECT statements in Oracle and MySQL databases involve their built-in functions. Built-in functions let you perform specialized behaviors such as casting from one type to another, date mathematics, and null replacements. You'll also understand how to create views, which are stored queries.

Query Results

A SELECT statement (query) reads differently from how it acts. In English, a *query* selects something from a table, or a set of tables, where certain conditions are true or untrue. Translating that English sentence into programming instructions is the beauty and complexity of SQL. Although English seems straightforward, queries work in a different event order. The event order also changes with different types of queries.

Queries can be divided into three basic types:

- Queries that return columns or results from columns
- Queries that aggregate, or queries that return columns or results from columns by adding, averaging, or counting between rows

■   Queries that return columns or results selectively (filtered by conditional expressions such as *if statements*), and these types of queries may or may not aggregate result sets

You can return column values or expressions in the SELECT list. Column values are straightforward, because they're the values in a column. Expressions aren't quite that simple. Expressions are the results from calculations. Some calculations involve columns and string literal values, such as concatenated results (strings joined together to make a big string), parsed results (substrings), or the mathematical result of the columns, literal values, and function returns. Mathematical results can be calculated on numeric or date data types and returned as function results from several built-in functions in both databases.

You can also be selective in your SELECT list, which means you can perform if-then-else logic in any column. The selectivity determines the resulting value in the final result set. Result sets are also formally called *aggregate results* because they've been assembled by SELECT statements.

Here's the basic prototype for a SELECT list:

```
SELECT {column_name | literal_value | expression } AS alias [,     {...}]]
WHERE [NOT] column_name {{= | <> | > | >= | < | <=} |
                          [NOT] {{IN | EXISTS} | IS NULL}} 'expression'
[{AND | OR } [NOT] comparison_operation] [...];
```

You can return three things as an element in the *SELECT* list: a column value from a table or view, a literal value, and an expression. The *column value* is easy to understand, because it's the value from the column—but what is its data type? A column returns the value in its native data type when you call the query from a procedural programming language, such as C, C#, C++, Java, PL/SQL, or SQL/PSM, or as a subquery. Subqueries are queries within queries and are covered in the "Subqueries" section later in this chapter. A column returns a string when you call the query from SQL*Plus or MySQL Monitor, and it is written to a console or a file. *Literal values* must have a column alias when you want to reuse the value in a procedural program or as a subquery result, and in those cases the values must be a string or number. *Expressions* are more difficult because they're the result of processing operations, such as concatenation or calculation, or they return results from built-in or user-defined functions.

The next three examples show you how the types of queries work. All examples use queries from a single table to let you focus on the differences between types.

Queries that Return Columns or Results from Columns

Figure 11-1 shows how a query returns a result set of column values in the SELECT list. You can see how the elements are labeled and processed and the figure helps you visualize table aliases, column aliases, basic comparison operations, and the basic order of clauses within the SELECT statement.

The following list qualifies the ANSI SQL pattern for processing a single table query:

■   It finds a table in the FROM clause.

■   It *optionally* assigns a table alias as a runtime placeholder for the table name.

■   It gets the table definition from the data catalog to determine the valid column names (not shown in the figure because it's a hidden behavior).

■   If a table alias is present (and it is), it optionally maps the alias to the table's data catalog definition.

■   It filters rows into the result set based on the value of columns in the WHERE clause.

- The list of columns in the SELECT clause filters the desired columns from the complete set of columns in a row.
- If an ORDER BY clause occurs in the query, rows are sorted by the designated columns.

Figure 11-1 also demonstrates table and column aliases. The table alias is generally unnecessary when writing a query against a single table. It is useful and necessary when you want to avoid typing complete table names to disambiguate column names that are the same in two or more tables. Because the FROM clause is read first, all references to the item table are mapped to i in the rest of the query. This means that a reference to item.item_title would not be found.

TIP
The AS keyword is optional when setting column aliases but ensures clarity that an alias follows it. Consistent use increases typing but decreases support costs.

Column aliases shorten the item_title and item_rating column names to *title* and *rating*, respectively. Aliases let you use shorter or more descriptive words for columns in a specific use case. Sometimes the shorter words aren't appropriate as column names because they're too general, such as *title*. The AS keyword is optional in both Oracle and MySQL databases, but I recommend that you use it, because the clarity can simplify maintenance of queries. Just note that AS works only with column aliases and would create a statement parsing error if you tried to use it before a table alias.

NOTE
The AS keyword cannot precede a table alias in Oracle; it can precede only a column alias. MySQL supports an AS keyword for a table alias.

In our example, we can modify the SELECT list to return an expression by concatenating a string literal of "MPAA:" (Motion Picture Association of America) to the item_rating column.

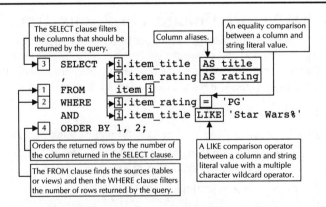

FIGURE 11-1. *Queries that return columns or results from columns*

Concatenating strings is like gluing them together to form a big string. It would look like this in Oracle using a *piped concatenation*:

```
SELECT    i.item_title AS title
,         'MPAA: ' || i.item_rating AS rating
```

The two vertical bars (||) are *pipes,* and when you use them to glue strings together, it's known as *piped concatenation.* MySQL doesn't support piped concatenation, so you use a built-in function to glue strings together, like so:

```
SELECT    i.item_title AS title
,         CONCAT('MPAA: ',i.item_rating) AS rating
```

The CONCAT built-in function returns a string by concatenating the call parameters sequentially. Notice that literals and column values are equal call parameters to the function. Both of these would return results like these:

```
TITLE                         RATING
-------------------------     ----------
Star Wars I                   MPAA: PG
Star Wars II                  MPAA: PG
Star Wars III                 MPAA: PG
```

In another context, you can perform mathematical operations and string formatting. The following SELECT list retrieves a transaction_date and a transaction_amount column from the transaction table:

```
SQL> SELECT    t.transaction_date
  2  ,          TO_CHAR(t.transaction_amount,'90.00') AS price
  3  ,          TO_CHAR(t.transaction_amount * .0875,'90.00') AS tax
  4  ,          TO_CHAR(t.transaction_amount * 1.0875,'90.00') AS total
  5  FROM       transaction t
  6  WHERE      t.transaction_date = '10-JAN-2009';
```

The TO_CHAR function formats the final number as a string. The 90.00 format mask instructs the display as follows: a 9 means display a number when present and ignore the number when it is not present; 0 means display a number when it is present and display a 0 when no number is present. Inside the TO_CHAR function on lines 3 and 4, the column value is multiplied by numeric literals that represent sales tax and price plus sales tax. The query would produce output like so:

```
Date        Price   Tax     Total
---------   ------  ------  ------
10-JAN-09   9.00    0.79    9.79
10-JAN-09   3.00    0.26    3.26
10-JAN-09   6.00    0.53    6.53
```

The output is left-aligned, which means it's formatted as a number, because strings are displayed as right-aligned.

The equivalent formatting function in MySQL is the FORMAT function, which performs like this:

```
,         FORMAT(t.transaction_amount * .0875,2) AS tax
```

The FROM clause takes a single table or a comma-separated list of tables when writing queries in ANSI SQL-89 format. The FROM clause takes tables separated by join keywords and their join criterion or criteria in ANSI SQL-92 syntax.

The `WHERE` clause performs two types of comparisons. One is an equality comparison of two values, which can come from columns, literals, or expressions. The other is an inequality comparison, which can check when one value is found in another (such as a substring of a larger string); when one value is greater than, greater than or equal to, less than, or less than or equal to another; when one value isn't equal to another value; when one value is in a set of values; or when one value is between two other values. You can also state a negative comparison, such as `WHERE NOT`. The `WHERE NOT` comparison acts like a *not equal to* operation.

Two specialized operators let you limit the number of rows returned by a query. Oracle supports a `ROWNUM` pseudo column and MySQL supports the `LIMIT` function. You use `ROWNUM` in Oracle to retrieve only the top five rows, like this:

```
WHERE rownum <= 6;
```

Here's the `LIMIT` function in MySQL:

```
WHERE LIMIT 5;
```

These are handy tools when you've presorted the data and know where to cut off the return set. When you forget to sort, the results generally don't fit what you're looking for.

The data set in the table determines whether the query returns unique or non-unique data—that is, there could be multiple rows with an `item_title` of "Star Wars: A New Hope," and they would be returned because they match the criteria in the `WHERE` clause. You can use the `DISTINCT` operator to suppress duplicates without altering the logic of the `WHERE` clause (see Figure 11-2).

Regular Expression Alternatives

Both Oracle and MySQL databases provide regular expression alternatives to the `LIKE` comparison operator. They aren't cross-portable, which makes the `LIKE` comparison operator the more generic or application-neutral approach.

Oracle Regular Expression Alternative   Oracle provides a variation on the generic SQL `LIKE` comparison with the `REGEXP_LIKE` function. The last line of the query in Figure 11-1 could use the following in an Oracle database:

```
AND      REGEXP_LIKE(i.item_title,'^Star Wars.+');
```

More information on the regular expression functions provided by the Oracle Database is in Appendix E of *Oracle Database 11g PL/SQL Programming*.

MySQL Regular Expression Alternative   MySQL also provides a variation on the generic SQL `LIKE` comparison operator. It uses the `REGEXP` operator. The last line of the query in Figure 11-1 could use the following in a MySQL database:

```
AND      i.item_title REGEXP '^Star Wars.+';
```

The regular expression match in both cases uses the carat (^) symbol (above the 6 on most keyboards) at the beginning to indicate the beginning of the string. They both likewise use the dot-plus (.+), which says look for any number of other trailing characters.

```
                       ┌──────────────────────────────┐
                       │ Guarantees a unique set of rows. │
                       └──────────────────────────────┘
                                    │
                                    ▼
        SELECT       ┌────────┐
                     │DISTINCT│
                     └────────┘
                     i.item_title  AS title
             ,       i.item_rating AS rating
        FROM         item i
        WHERE        i.item_rating = 'PG'
        AND          i.item_title LIKE 'Star Wars%'
        ORDER BY 1, 2;
```

FIGURE 11-2. *Query that returns distinct columns or results from columns*

There is no difference between Oracle and MySQL when using the DISTINCT operator, which sorts the set to return a unique set—one copy of every row. Other than an incremental sort and disposal of duplicate rows, the query in Figure 11-2 performs more or less the same steps as the query shown in Figure 11-1. The next two subsections discuss subqueries and *in-line views*, also known as *runtime* or *derived tables*.

Subqueries

Subqueries are any SELECT statement nested within another DML statement, such as INSERT, UPDATE, DELETE, and SELECT statements. Subqueries have been demonstrated in earlier chapters because they're very useful.

Four types of basic subqueries can be used:

- **Scalar subqueries**   Return only one column and one row of data
- **Single-row subqueries**   Return one or more columns in one row of data
- **Multiple-row subqueries, ordinary subqueries, or subqueries**   Return one or more columns in one or more rows of data
- **Correlated subqueries**   Return nothing, but they effect a join between the outer DML statement and correlated subquery

Another subquery can be used inside the FROM clause of a SELECT statement. This type of subquery is actually a *runtime view*, or *derived table*. It isn't technically a subquery. The following sections describe the uses and occurrences of subqueries in DML statements.

Scalar Subqueries   Scalar subqueries return only one thing: one column from one row. They return a single value from a query. That's because scalar variables are numbers, dates, strings, and timestamps. Scalar data types are like primitive data types in the Java programming language.

Scalar subqueries are much like functions. You put comparative statements in the WHERE clause to find a single row, similar to defining formal parameters in a function. Then you return a single column in the SELECT clause, which inherits its data type from the data catalog. The SELECT clause designates the return data type of a function just like the return keyword in procedural programming languages.

You can use scalar subqueries in the following places in DML statements:

- The VALUES clause of an INSERT statement
- The SELECT clause of a SELECT statement

- The SET clause of an UPDATE statement
- The WHERE clause of a SELECT, UPDATE, or DELETE statement

NOTE
Chapter 8 shows you how to use scalar subqueries in the VALUES clause. Chapter 9 shows you how to use scalar subqueries in the SET and WHERE clauses of an UPDATE statement, and Chapter 10 shows you how to use them in the WHERE clause of a DELETE statement.

Single-Row Subqueries Single-row subqueries return one or more columns from a single row. This is more or less like returning a record data type. You can apply the same analogy of comparative statements in the WHERE clause mapping to formal parameter definitions and the return type mapping to the list of columns in the SELECT clause. When you exclude the scalar behaviors of a single-row subquery, the following uses remain:

- The SET clause of an UPDATE statement
- The WHERE clause of a SELECT, UPDATE, or DELETE statement

NOTE
Chapter 9 shows the use of single-row subqueries in the SET clause of UPDATE statements. Chapters 9 and 10 show the respective use of single-row subqueries in the WHERE clauses of UPDATE and DELETE statements.

Multiple-Row Subqueries Multiple-row subqueries are frequently called ordinary subqueries or just subqueries. These subqueries return one to many columns and rows of data. That means they return result sets that mimic two-dimensional tables.

You can use multiple-row subqueries only in the WHERE clause of SELECT, UPDATE, or DELETE statements. You also must use a valid lookup comparison operator, such as the IN, =ANY, =SOME, or =ALL operators. These operators act like a chain of logical OR comparisons in a WHERE clause, because they look to see if the leftmost operand in the comparison is found in the list of possible values. The leftmost operand can be a single column or a record data type comprising two or more columns.

A couple of quick examples to qualify these behaviors might help. These examples use the pseudo dual table to keep them bare bones. The list of values inside a set of parentheses is the same as the value set returned by a multiple-row subquery. Here's a standard use of a logical or lookup comparison that deals with a single column:

```
SELECT 'True Statement' FROM dual
WHERE  'Lancelot' IN ('Arthur','Galahad','Lancelot');
```

This is equivalent to the chaining of logical or statements in the WHERE clause, like this:

```
SELECT 'True Statement' FROM dual
WHERE 'Lancelot' = 'Arthur'
OR    'Lancelot' = 'Galahad'
OR    'Lancelot' = 'Lancelot';
```

The syntax doesn't change much when you make the comparison of a record type to a list of record types. The only other change is the substitution of the =ANY lookup operator for the IN operator. As you can see, the lookup operators work the same way in this example:

```
SELECT 'True Statement' FROM dual
WHERE ('Harry Potter and the Chamber of Secrets','PG') =ANY
      (('Harry Potter and the Sorcerer's Stone','PG')
      ,('Harry Potter and the Chamber of Secrets','PG')
      ,('Harry Potter and the Prisoner of Azkaban','PG'));
```

which would work like this with a set of logical OR comparisons:

```
SELECT 'True Statement' FROM dual
WHERE (('Harry Potter and the Order of the Phoenix','PG-13') =
          ('Harry Potter and the Sorcerer's Stone','PG')
OR        ('Harry Potter and the Order of the Phoenix','PG-13') =
          ('Harry Potter and the Chamber of Secrets','PG')
OR        ('Harry Potter and the Order of the Phoenix','PG-13') =
          ('Harry Potter and the Prisoner of Azkaban','PG'));
```

The =ALL lookup operator is different, because it checks whether a scalar or record data type is found in all instances of a list. This means it works on a logical and comparison basis. This statement

```
SELECT 'True Statement' FROM dual
WHERE 'Lancelot' =ALL ('Lancelot','Lancelot','Lancelot');
```

is roughly equivalent to this:

```
SELECT 'True Statement' FROM dual
WHERE 'Lancelot' = 'Lancelot'
AND   'Lancelot' = 'Lancelot'
AND   'Lancelot' = 'Lancelot';
```

Although these examples use lists of literal values, you could substitute multiple-row subqueries. In many cases, this type of comparison is unnecessary because the same logic can be resolved through ordinary join statements.

The only problem with lookup comparison operators is that they don't easily extend the behavior of the LIKE comparison operator. Figure 11-2 introduced a LIKE operator against a string literal with a wildcard operator. When the literal value is replaced by a subquery, the comparison no longer works when the query returns more than one row. It would fail with an ORA-01427 error in Oracle, which tells you a "single-row subquery returns more than a one row."

You can fix this behavior by doing two things. Substitute an IN, =ANY, or =SOME lookup comparison operator for the LIKE comparison operator, and use the SUBSTR function to make the comparison against exact matches. This allows you to match the substrings that should be the same. This particular match (shown in Figure 11-3) starts at the first character, which is position 1, because characters in strings are 1-based, not 0-based, in databases, and use the first nine characters.

Oracle and MySQL both support the SUBSTR function. MySQL implements the SUBSTR function as an alias for the SUBSTRING built-in, which works exactly like the equivalent function in Oracle.

```
SELECT    DISTINCT
          i.item_title  AS title
,         i.item_rating AS rating
FROM      item i
WHERE     i.item_rating =  'PG'
AND       SUBSTR(i.item_title,1,9) =SOME
          (SELECT    SUBSTR(ti.item_title,1,9)
           FROM      temp_item ti)
ORDER BY 1, 2;
```

A match using a combination of the SUBSTR function and a lookup comparison operator.

FIGURE 11-3. *Wildcard comparison against multiple row subquery*

Correlated Subqueries   Correlated subqueries join the inside query to a value returned by each row in the outer query. As such, correlated subqueries act as function calls made for each row returned by the outer query. The rule of thumb on correlated subqueries requires that you join on uniquely indexed columns for optimal results. Ordinary subqueries typically outperform correlated subqueries when you can't join on uniquely indexed columns.

Correlated subqueries appear to return something when they're inside the SET clause of an UPDATE statement. If you flip back to Chapter 9, you'll see that a multiple-row subquery actually returns the value based on a match between the row being updated and a nested correlated subquery. The actual update is performed by a multiple-row subquery, not a correlated subquery. Correlated subqueries can't return values through the SELECT list; they can only match results in their WHERE clause.

You can use correlated subqueries in the following:

- The SELECT list
- The SET clause of an UPDATE statement
- The WHERE clause of a SELECT, UPDATE, or DELETE statement

The multiple-row subquery example extends the behavior of Figure 11-2. The multiple-row subquery runs once for the outer query and returns a list of values. The IN, =ANY, or =SOME lookup operator lets you perform a lookup to determine whether a variable is found in the list of returned values.

Although less efficient, a correlated subquery can be used to solve this type of comparison problem with a regular expression. Oracle lets you perform it with the REGEXP_LIKE function, like this:

```
AND       EXISTS
  (SELECT NULL
   FROM    temp_item ti
   WHERE   REGEXP_LIKE(i.item_title,'^'||SUBSTR(ti.item_title,1,9)||'.+'));
```

Or you can do it like this with MySQL's REGEXP operator:

```
AND       EXISTS
  (SELECT NULL
   FROM    temp_item ti
   WHERE   i.item_title REGEXP CONCAT('^',SUBSTR(ti.item_title,1,9),'.+'));
```

In these correlated query examples, you see Oracle's piped concatenation model and MySQL's CONCAT function. Oracle's resolution is case sensitive while MySQL's is case insensitive.

In-line Views

An in-line view is a query inside the FROM clause of a query or inside a WITH clause. The WITH clause is newer and was introduced in the ANSI SQL-1999 standard. There's no implementation of the WITH clause in MySQL at the time of writing. In-line views are also labeled as runtime or derived tables, and Microsoft calls them Common Table Expressions (CTE).

The query in a FROM or WITH clause dynamically creates a view at runtime. It's possible that the same in-line view can be used in multiple places within a large query. When an in-line view appears in multiple places within a query, it is run multiple times. This is inefficient and unnecessary when the WITH clause is supported in the database. The WITH clause provides an in-line view with a named reference, runs it only once, and lets you use the name reference in more than one place in the query.

Here's a sample of an in-line view in the FROM clause:

```
SQL> SELECT   c.first_name||' '||c.last_name AS person
  2  ,         inline.street_address
  3  ,         inline.city
  4  ,         inline.state_province
  5  FROM      contact c INNER JOIN
  6            (SELECT    a.contact_id
  7            ,          sa.street_address
  8            ,          a.city
  9            ,          a.state_province
 10            FROM       address a INNER JOIN street_address sa
 11            ON         a.address_id = sa.address_id) inline
 12  ON        inline.contact_id = c.contact_id;
```

The in-line view is on lines 6 through 11 and the join between the inline view and contact table is on line 12. The in-line view must return the foreign key column in the SELECT list for it to be used later in the join on line 12. Failure to return the key column in the SELECT list of the in-line view would leave nothing to use in a JOIN statement.

The only change required to run the preceding example in a MySQL database can be made on line 1. MySQL doesn't support piped concatenation as Oracle does, so you need to replace the concatenating line with the following in MySQL:

```
mysql> SELECT   CONCAT(c.first_name,' ',c.last_name) AS person
```

Although it's possible to enable piped concatenation in MySQL, don't bother. Even when you enable it, you can't perform piped concatenation inside call parameters to other functions. That more or less means it works only some of the time. It's better just to recognize that the CONCAT function in MySQL is your friend and use it. It's recursive and takes however many arguments you require, as opposed to Oracle's implementation that takes only two arguments, like this:

```
SELECT CONCAT('Not ',CONCAT('a recursive ','function.')) AS result
FROM dual;
```

This prints the following:

```
RESULT
-------------------------
Not a recursive function.
```

The preceding in-line view can be refactored to work with a `WITH` clause, like this:

```
SQL> WITH inline AS
  2  (SELECT    a.contact_id
  3      ,         sa.street_address
  4      ,         a.city
  5      ,         a.state_province
  6   FROM      address a INNER JOIN street_address sa
  7   ON        a.address_id = sa.address_id)
  8  SELECT   c.first_name||' '||c.last_name AS person
  9      ,         inline.street_address
 10      ,         inline.city
 11      ,         inline.state_province
 12  FROM     contact c INNER JOIN inline inline
 13  ON       inline.contact_id = c.contact_id;
```

Line 12 references the inline name of the in-line view, which is on lines 1 to 7. Line 12 identifies an `INNER JOIN` between the contact table and in-line view, and line 13 provides the criteria to match values between the table and view. Large queries have a tendency to reuse in-line views in multiple places, which isn't a good thing. In-line views must be run each time they're encountered in the query. The `WITH` clause fixes this performance nightmare, because the query is run once, given a name, and then the result sets are usable anywhere else in the query. The `WITH` clause should always be used unless your code must be portable to MySQL, which doesn't support it.

It's also possible to have multiple in-line views. You list them with a designated name in a comma-delimited list. Figure 11-4 shows a small example of a `WITH` clause that promotes the ordinary query to a view. The lines and arrows help you see the use of the names for the in-line views in the query.

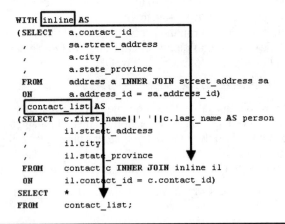

FIGURE 11-4. *With clause*

The benefit of the WITH clause is that it runs once and can be used multiple times in the scope of the query. The only downside with the syntax is that it's not portable between Oracle and MySQL, but that might change someday.

Queries that Aggregate

Aggregation is one of those buzz words in databases. Aggregation means counting, adding, and grouping results of COUNT, SUM, AVERAGE, MIN, and MAX functions. Aggregation queries add one or two more clauses than those presented in Figure 11-1. Figure 11-5 shows the GROUP BY and HAVING clauses.

The GROUP BY clause must refer to all non-aggregated columns in the SELECT list, because they're not unique and there's no sense in returning all the rows when you need only one row with the non-unique columns and the aggregated result. The GROUP BY instructs the database to do exactly that: return only distinct versions of non-unique columns with the aggregated result columns. As you can see in Figure 11-5, the GROUP BY clause runs after the query has identified all rows and columns. The COUNT function takes an asterisk (*) as its single argument. The * represents an indirection operator that points to rows returned by the query. The * is equivalent to the ROWID pseudo column in Oracle. It counts rows whether a row contain any values or not.

NOTE
The ROWID is one of the places where the concept of indirection and a pointer shows itself in databases.

After the database returns the aggregated result set, the HAVING clause filters the result set. In the example, it returns only those aggregated results that have two or more non-unique item_title and item_rating rows in the table. The ORDER BY then sorts the return set.

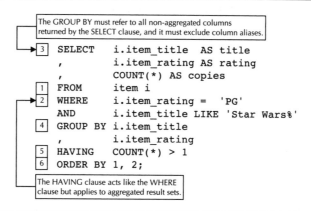

The GROUP BY must refer to all non-aggregated columns returned by the SELECT clause, and it must exclude column aliases.

```
3  SELECT    i.item_title  AS title
   ,          i.item_rating AS rating
   ,          COUNT(*) AS copies
1  FROM      item i
2  WHERE     i.item_rating =  'PG'
   AND       i.item_title LIKE 'Star Wars%'
4  GROUP BY  i.item_title
   ,          i.item_rating
5  HAVING    COUNT(*) > 1
6  ORDER BY 1, 2;
```

The HAVING clause acts like the WHERE clause but applies to aggregated result sets.

FIGURE 11-5. *Order of operation on aggregate queries*

Oracle's ROWID Pseudo Column
Oracle also supports a ROWID pseudo column that is the physical address for the row. If you want, you can substitute the ROWID pseudo column for the asterisk(*) in the COUNT function.

The following list qualifies the ANSI SQL pattern for processing a single table query with aggregation and a GROUP BY and HAVING clause:

- It finds a table in the FROM clause.

- It *optionally* assigns a table alias as a runtime placeholder for the table name.

- It gets the table definition from the data catalog to determine the valid column names.

- If a table alias is present (and it is), it optionally maps the alias to the table's data catalog definition.

- It filters rows into the result set based on the value of columns in the WHERE clause.

- The list of columns in the SELECT clause filters the desired columns from the complete set of columns in a row.

- The aggregation function triggers a check for a GROUP BY clause when non-aggregated columns are returned in the SELECT list, and then aggregates results.

- The HAVING operator filters the result set from the aggregation or the GROUP BY aggregation.

- If an ORDER BY clause occurs in the query, rows are sorted by the designated columns.

We'll work through the basic aggregation steps most developers use frequently. They cover the COUNT, SUM, AVERAGE, MAX, and MIN functions. The following discussions use two sets of ordinal and cardinal numbers (some values not displayed to save space) that are stored in the ordinal table, like so:

```
    ID LIST_SET              LIST_NAME   LIST_VALUE
---------- -------------------- ---------- ----------
     1 Value Set A           Zero                 0
     2 Value Set A           One                  1
     3 Value Set A           Two                  2
     4 Value Set A           Three                3
     5 Value Set A           Four                 4
     6 Value Set A           Five                 5
     7 Value Set A           Six                  6
     8 Value Set A           Seven                7
     9 Value Set A           Eight                8
    10 Value Set A           Nine                 9
    11 Value Set A
    12 Value Set B           Zero                 0
    13 Value Set B           One                  1
   ...
    21 Value Set B           Nine                 9
    22 Value Set B
```

You've been exposed to the data set to help you understand how the aggregation functions work in the following subsections.

Aggregate Columns Only

The COUNT function has two behaviors: counting by reference and counting by value. They differ on how they treat null values. You count the number of physical rows when you count by reference, and you count the physical values when you count by value.

The count by reference example counts the number of rows in the ordinal table, like this:

```
SQL> SELECT COUNT(*) AS number_of_rows FROM ordinal;
```

It returns the following:

```
NUMBER_OF_ROWS
--------------
            22
```

The count by value example counts the values in the list_value column. The list_value column contains two null values. The column name is substituted for the asterisk, like this:

```
SQL> SELECT COUNT(list_value) AS number_of_values FROM ordinal;
```

It returns the following:

```
NUMBER_OF_VALUES
----------------
              20
```

The return set is 2 less than the number of rows. That's because the COUNT function doesn't count null values. You can also count all values (which is the default performed in the preceding example) or distinct values only. Both approaches exclude null values.

The following query demonstrates counting using the default, an explicit ALL, and DISTINCT number of values found in the list_name and list_value columns:

```
SQL> SELECT COUNT(list_name) AS default_number
  2  ,       COUNT(ALL list_name) AS explicit_number
  3  ,       COUNT(DISTINCT list_value) AS distinct_number
  4  FROM    ordinal;
```

Here are the results:

```
DEFAULT_NUMBER EXPLICIT_NUMBER DISTINCT_NUMBER
-------------- --------------- ---------------
            20              20              10
```

Notice that the COUNT function returns the same number with or without the ALL keyword. That's because the default is ALL, which is provided when you don't use it. It also counts the occurrences of strings or numbers. You count each individual element when the ALL is specified, not just the unique set of elements. The DISTINCT keyword forces a unique sort of the data set before counting the results.

The SUM, AVG, MAX, and MIN functions work only with numbers. The following demonstrates the SUM and AVG functions against the list_value column:

```
SQL> SELECT SUM(ALL list_value) AS sum_all
  2  ,       SUM(DISTINCT list_value) AS sum_distinct
  3  ,       AVG(ALL list_value) AS avg_all
  4  ,       AVG(DISTINCT list_value) AS avg_distinct
  5  FROM    ordinal;
```

Here's the result set:

```
   SUM_ALL SUM_DISTINCT    AVG_ALL AVG_DISTINCT
---------- ------------ ---------- ------------
        90           45        4.5          4.5
```

The sum of two sets of the ordinal numbers is 90, and one set is 45. The average of ALL or the DISTINCT set is naturally the same.

The next example runs the MAX and MIN functions:

```
SQL> SELECT MIN(ALL list_value) AS min_all
  2  ,       MIN(DISTINCT list_value) AS min_distinct
  3  ,       MAX(ALL list_value) AS max_all
  4  ,       MAX(DISTINCT list_value) AS max_distinct
  5  FROM    ordinal;
```

It produces these results:

```
   MIN_ALL MIN_DISTINCT    MAX_ALL MAX_DISTINCT
---------- ------------ ---------- ------------
         0            0          9            9
```

The minimum or maximum of two sets of the same group of numbers is always the same. The minimum is 0 and the maximum is 9 for ordinal numbers.

Aggregate and Non-aggregate Columns

The principal of returning aggregate and non-aggregate columns starts with understanding that you get only one row when you add a column of numbers. By extension, you get one row for every type of thing you count. A real-world example of that would be counting a bag of fruit. You separate the fruit into groups, such as apples, oranges, pears, and apricots. Then you count the number of each type of fruit.

The following counts the number of rows and values for each unique value in the list_set column:

```
SQL> SELECT    list_set AS grouping_by_column
  2  ,          COUNT(*)
  3  ,          COUNT(list_value)
  4  FROM      ordinal
  5  GROUP BY list_set;
```

And here are the results of this query:

```
GROUPING_BY_COLUMN        COUNT(*)  COUNT(LIST_VALUE)
--------------------      --------  -----------------
Value Set A                   11                   10
Value Set B                   11                   10
```

The results tells us that we have 11 rows in each group and only 10 values, which means each group has one row that contains a null value. You change the SELECT list and GROUP BY clause when you want to identify the rows with the null values.

The following query returns a 0 when the list_value column is null and a 1 otherwise:

```
SQL> SELECT   list_set AS grouping_by_not_null
  2  ,         list_name AS group_by_null_too
  3  ,         COUNT(*)
  4  ,         COUNT(list_value)
  5  FROM      ordinal
  6  WHERE     list_set = 'Value Set A'
  7  GROUP BY list_set
  8  ,         list_name;
```

And here are the results from the query:

```
GROUPING_BY_NOT_NULL GROUP   COUNT(*)  COUNT(LIST_VALUE)
-------------------- -----   --------  -----------------
Value Set A          Zero         1                    1
Value Set A          Five         1                    1
Value Set A          Three        1                    1
Value Set A          Four         1                    1
Value Set A          One          1                    1
Value Set A          Two          1                    1
Value Set A          Eight        1                    1
Value Set A          Nine         1                    1
Value Set A          Seven        1                    1
Value Set A          Six          1                    1
Value Set A                       1                    0
```

The only problem with the return set is that the cardinal numbers aren't in numeric order. That requires a special ORDER BY clause with a CASE statement. You could add the following to the last query to get them sorted into numeric order:

```
  9  ORDER BY CASE
 10             WHEN list_name = 'Zero'  THEN 0
 11             WHEN list_name = 'One'   THEN 1
 12             WHEN list_name = 'Two'   THEN 2
 13             WHEN list_name = 'Three' THEN 3
 14             WHEN list_name = 'Four'  THEN 4
 15             WHEN list_name = 'Five'  THEN 5
 16             WHEN list_name = 'Six'   THEN 6
 17             WHEN list_name = 'Seven' THEN 7
 18             WHEN list_name = 'Eight' THEN 8
 19             WHEN list_name = 'Nine'  THEN 9
 20           END;
```

This type of ORDER BY clause lets you achieve numeric ordering without changing any of the data. Note that null values are always sorted last in an ascending sort and first in a descending sort.

NOTE
Ascending sorts put nulls last while descending sorts put nulls first.

The following query demonstrates the GROUP BY for the SUM, AVG, MAX, and MIN functions:

```
SQL> SELECT    list_set AS grouping_by_not_null
  2  ,          SUM(list_value) AS ordinal_sum
  3  ,          AVG(list_value) AS ordinal_avg
  4  ,          MIN(list_value) AS ordinal_min
  5  ,          MAX(list_value) AS ordinal_max
  6  FROM      ordinal
  7  GROUP BY list_set;
```

It displays the following:

GROUPING_BY_NOT_NULL	ORDINAL_SUM	ORDINAL_AVG	ORDINAL_MIN	ORDINAL_MAX
Value Set A	45	4.5	0	9
Value Set B	45	4.5	0	9

This returns the expected result set from the functions. They naturally match for each set of ordinal numbers. If you were to alter the data set, you could get different results.

Queries that Return Columns or Results Selectively

Queries that return columns or results selectively depend on conditional logic. Originally, SQL wasn't designed to contain any conditional logic. Oracle introduced conditional logic as an extension to the definition in the 1980s. It implemented the DECODE function. Other vendors followed Oracle's lead, and MySQL implements the IF function. Finally, the ANSI SQL definition added the CASE operator, which you saw illustrated in an ORDER BY clause in the preceding section.

You need to understand the different proprietary solutions and the CASE operator before you see an exhibit of selective aggregation. The following sections discuss the Oracle proprietary DECODE function, the MySQL IF function, and the CASE statement before discussing selective aggregation.

Oracle Proprietary DECODE Statement

The DECODE function allows you to perform if-then-else logic on equality matches. It doesn't support inequalities except as the else condition of an equality comparison. You can nest DECODE functions as call parameters to a DECODE function. The DECODE function is not portable. As a best practice, avoid the DECODE function. As a reality check, millions of lines of code use the DECODE function, which makes its coverage essential and learning it unavoidable.

Here's the prototype for the DECODE function:

```
DECODE(expression, search, result
              [, search, result [, ... ]]
              [, default])
```

The function requires at least an expression or column return value, a search value, and a result before an optional default value. You can also add any number of pairs of search values and results before the optional default value.

Some SQL*Plus formatting is necessary to get a clean test in Oracle. You can check back to Chapter 2 for instructions on these formatting commands:

```
-- Set null to a visible string.
SET NULL "<Null>"
-- Set column formatting for an alphanumeric string.
COLUMN "Test 1" FORMAT A9
COLUMN "Test 2" FORMAT A9
COLUMN "Test 3" FORMAT A9
COLUMN "Test 4" FORMAT A9
COLUMN "Test 5" FORMAT A9
COLUMN "Test 6" FORMAT A9
COLUMN "Test 7" FORMAT A9
```

The following single test case covers the outcome possibilities of a DECODE function:

```
SQL> SELECT    DECODE('One','One','Equal') AS "Test 1"
  2  ,         DECODE('One','Two','Equal') AS "Test 2"
  3  ,         DECODE('One','One','Equal','Not Equal') AS "Test 3"
  4  ,         DECODE('One','Two','Equal','Not Equal') AS "Test 4"
  5  ,         DECODE('One','Two','Equal'
  6                          ,'Three','Equal') AS "Test 5"
  7  ,         DECODE('One','Two','Equal'
  8                          ,'Three','Equal','Not Equal') AS "Test 6"
  9  ,         DECODE('One','Two','Equal'
 10                          ,'Three','Equal'
 11                          ,'One','Equal','Not Equal') AS "Test 7"
 12  FROM      dual;
```

The query returns the following results:

Test 1	Test 2	Test 3	Test 4	Test 5	Test 6	Test 7
Equal	<Null>	Equal	Not Equal	<Null>	Not Equal	Equal

Tests I and 2   These tests use the DECODE function as an if-then block of code. The first call parameter to the DECODE function is what you're trying to match with the second call parameter. When they match, the third call parameter is returned. When they fail to match, the null value is returned.

TIP
The mnemonic for an if-then block is three call parameters to the DECODE function.

This behavior is handy when you're counting success in a selective aggregation model, because the following would count only individuals who are single:

```
SQL> WITH inline AS
  2  (SELECT 'Single' AS marital_status FROM dual
  3   UNION ALL
  4   SELECT 'Single' AS marital_status FROM dual
  5   UNION ALL
  6   SELECT 'Married' AS marital_status FROM dual)
  7  SELECT COUNT(DECODE(inline.marital_status,'Single',1)) AS Single
  8  FROM   inline;
```

It returns the number of single rows:

```
    SINGLE
----------
         2
```

This demonstrates that it selectively counts results based on matches and nonmatches in the fabricated table of three rows. What it can't do is provide the count of nonmatches.

Tests 3 and 4   These tests use the DECODE function as an if-then-else block of code. The first, second, and third call parameters work like tests 1 and 2. The thing that's different with an else condition is that something meaningful is returned when the first call argument fails to match the second call argument.

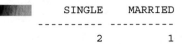

NOTE
The mnemonic for an if-then-else block is four call parameters to the DECODE function.

This behavior is even better than the results from tests 1 and 2 for selective aggregation. It lets you count matches and nonmatches by using two columns instead of one in the SELECT list. You can count the single and married rows, like so:

```
SQL> WITH inline AS
  2  (SELECT 'Single' AS marital_status FROM dual
  3   UNION ALL
  4   SELECT 'Single' AS marital_status FROM dual
  5   UNION ALL
  6   SELECT 'Married' AS marital_status FROM dual)
  7  SELECT COUNT(DECODE(inline.marital_status,'Single',1)) AS Single
  8  ,      COUNT(DECODE(inline.marital_status,'Married',1)) AS Married
  9  FROM   inline;
```

The two columns now give us this more meaningful result:

```
    SINGLE    MARRIED
---------- ----------
         2          1
```

This demonstrates that you can ask two sides of the same question by putting the results in separate columns. This is a form of SQL transformation.

Tests 5, 6, and 7   These tests use the DECODE function as if-then-elseif and if-then-elseif-else blocks of code. They act more or less like traditional switch statements, except Oracle doesn't support fall-through behavior. Fall-through behavior would return a result for the first and every subsequent case statement where the conditions were met.

The first, second, and third call parameters work like tests 1 through 4, but call parameters 4 and 5, 6 and 7, 8 and 9, and so forth would be cases. The lack of an even number of parameters means there's no default case. That means an odd number of parameters 5 and above make a DECODE function into a switch without a default condition. Likewise, an even number of parameters 6 and above make a DECODE function into a switch with a default condition.

NOTE
The mnemonic for an if-then-elseif block is five or any greater odd number of call parameters, and the mnemonic for an if-then-elseif-else block is six or any greater even number of call parameters to the DECODE function.

This behavior allows us to test more than just two cases. The downside is that quickly it becomes verbose. You can now count the single, divorced, and married rows, like so:

```
SQL> WITH inline AS
  2  (SELECT 'Single' AS marital_status FROM dual
  3   UNION ALL
  4   SELECT 'Single' AS marital_status FROM dual
  5   UNION ALL
  6   SELECT 'Divorced' AS marital_status FROM dual
  7   UNION ALL
  8   SELECT 'Annulled' AS marital_status FROM dual
  9   UNION ALL
 10   SELECT 'Married' AS marital_status FROM dual)
 11  SELECT COUNT(DECODE(inline.marital_status,'Single',1)) AS Single
 12  ,       COUNT(DECODE(inline.marital_status,'Divorced',1)) AS Divorced
 13  ,       COUNT(DECODE(inline.marital_status,'Married',1)) AS Married
 14  FROM    inline;
```

The data set now has four classifications in the in-line view but only three evaluations in the SELECT list. Any person whose marital status is annulled is excluded from your SQL report. The results would be the following:

```
    SINGLE   DIVORCED    MARRIED
---------- ---------- ----------
         2          1          1
```

You could capture the annulled marriages by some math operation, such as the following, with the DECODE function:

```
 11  SELECT COUNT(DECODE(inline.marital_status,'Single',1)) AS Single
 12  ,       COUNT(DECODE(inline.marital_status,'Divorced',1)) AS Divorced
 13  ,       COUNT(DECODE(inline.marital_status,'Married',1)) AS Married
 14  ,       COUNT(inline.marital_status) -
 15         (COUNT(DECODE(inline.marital_status,'Single',1)) +
```

```
16              COUNT(DECODE(inline.marital_status,'Divorced',1)) +
17              COUNT(DECODE(inline.marital_status,'Married',1))) AS Other
18  FROM   inline
```

It would now give you this:

```
    SINGLE   DIVORCED   MARRIED    OTHER
---------- ---------- ---------- ----------
         2          1          1          1
```

This is the limit of what you can do with the DECODE function. Next, you'll examine the MySQL IF function, which doesn't include a case element.

MySQL Proprietary IF Function

The IF function allows you to perform an if-then-else logic based on equality, inequality, range, and element in set comparisons. As conditional functions go, the MySQL IF function is superior to the Oracle DECODE function, because the IF function isn't limited to equality comparisons only.

Here's the prototype for the IF function:

```
IF(comparison_expression, expression_when_true, expression_when_false)
```

The IF function evaluates whether a comparison expression is true or false. The IF function processes and returns the second expression when the comparison expression is true and the third expression when it isn't true. You can nest IF functions in all IF function expressions. The expressions returned for true and false must be returned as strings, floating point, or integer numbers.

The following subsections qualify the most frequent type of use cases with the IF function.

Numeric Comparisons   Numeric comparisons are the easiest place to start. Here's a query that tests the most likely numeric comparisons you would use:

```
SELECT IF((1 = 1),"E: (1 = 1)","NE:(1 = 1)") AS comparison
UNION ALL
SELECT IF((1 = 1.0),"E: (1 = 1.0)","NE:(1 = 1.0)") AS comparison
UNION ALL
SELECT IF((1 = 1.1),"E: (1 = 1.1)","NE:(1 = 1.1)") AS comparison
UNION ALL
SELECT IF((1 > 1),"E: (1 > 1)","NE:(1 > 1)") AS comparison
UNION ALL
SELECT IF((1 <> 2),"E: (1 <> 2)","NE:(1 <> 2)") AS comparison;
```

The output of these comparisons is in the following result set, where *E* means equal and *NE* means not equal:

```
+--------------+
| comparison   |
+--------------+
| E: (1 = 1)   |
| E: (1 = 1.0) |
| NE:(1 = 1.1) |
| NE:(1 > 1)   |
| E: (1 <> 2)  |
+--------------+
```

The comparison of two integers of equal values is a true scenario. The comparison of an integer and decimal is true when the decimal casts as an integer of equal value. The comparison of an integer to a decimal is false when the decimal integer isn't equal to the decimal value. The inequality comparison is false because the integers hold the same values. The not equal comparison confirms that 1 is not equal to 2.

String Comparisons String comparisons are straightforward if you come from a MySQL background, but they can be a bit confusing when you come from an Oracle background. That's because MySQL uses case-insensitive comparisons by default, while Oracle uses a case-sensitive comparison.

The following SELECT statement illustrates how you can perform case-insensitive and case-sensitive comparisons:

```
SELECT   IF(('One' = 'one')
           ,"E: ('One' = 'one')"
           ,"NE:('One' = 'one')") AS string_comparison
       , IF((BINARY 'One' = 'one')
           ,"E: (BINARY 'One' = 'one')"
           ,"NE:(BINARY 'One' = 'one')") AS binary_comparison; comparisons:
```

The first column performs a case-insensitive comparison while the second column performs a binary comparison. Binary comparisons are case-sensitive. Here are the results of the query:

```
+--------------------+----------------------------+
| string_comparison  | binary_comparison          |
+--------------------+----------------------------+
| E: ('One' = 'one') | NE:(BINARY 'One' = 'one')  |
+--------------------+----------------------------+
```

NOTE
A string of "One" is less than a string of "one," because uppercase letters have a lower ASCII binary value than their lowercase equivalents—the opposite of what you might expect.

Range Comparisons Range comparisons work with the BETWEEN operator. You can perform range comparisons against dates, numbers, or strings. The first column of the range comparison example compares whether the UTC_DATE function value is between two literal values (true at the time of writing). The second column uses a NOT BETWEEN operator to demonstrate a false result.

```
SELECT
  IF((UTC_DATE() BETWEEN '2011-05-05' AND '2011-07-04')
    ,"T:(UTC_DATE() BETWEEN date1 AND date2)"
    ,"F:(UTC_DATE() NOT BETWEEN date1 AND date2)") AS in_range
,IF((UTC_DATE() NOT BETWEEN '2011-05-05' AND '2011-07-04')
    ,"T:(UTC_DATE() NOT BETWEEN date1 AND date2)"
    ,"F:(UTC_DATE() BETWEEN date1 AND date2)") AS out_of_range\G
```

Notice the odd formatting? It's been changed here to fit on the page. The \G execution puts column labels to the left and results to the right. Here are the results of this query:

```
*********************** 1. row ***********************
    in_range: T: (UTC_DATE() BETWEEN date1 AND date2)
out_of_range: F: (UTC_DATE() BETWEEN date1 AND date2)
```

The UTC_DATE function returned must either be inside or outside the range. You always evaluate true first and false second. The first column returns true because the value is found within the range and the second column returns false because the value is not outside of the range. More or less, the first column's truth is whether the value is between the others and the second column's truth is whether it isn't.

In-set Comparisons   Determining whether a value is within a set is also possible with the IF function. The following demonstrates an in-set and not in-set comparison operation by performing one against strings and the other against binary strings:

```
SELECT
  IF(('bat' IN ('BAT','BALL'))
    ,"T: ('bat' IN ('BAT','BALL'))"
    ,"F: ('bat' NOT IN ('BAT','BALL'))") AS in_set
, IF((BINARY 'bat' NOT IN ('BAT','BALL'))
    ,"T: (BINARY 'bat' NOT IN ('BAT','BALL'))"
    ,"F: (BINARY 'bat' IN ('BAT','BALL'))") AS not_in_set\G
```

The results confirm what we would suspect—the case-insensitive string is found in the set while the case-sensitive (binary) string isn't:

```
*********************** 1. row ***********************
    in_set: T: ('bat' IN ('BAT','BALL'))
not_in_set: T: (BINARY 'bat' NOT IN ('BAT','BALL'))
```

The only problem with this type of comparison is that you can make it only against literal values or other columns returned in the same row. MySQL offers another possibility. The following query returns In stock if the subquery finds a match, and Out of stock when it doesn't:

```
SELECT
  IF('Star Wars VII' IN (SELECT item_title FROM item)
    ,'In stock','Out of stock') AS data_inlieu_no_row_found;
```

returns the following:

```
+--------------------------+
| data_inlieu_no_row_found |
+--------------------------+
| Out of stock             |
+--------------------------+
```

You would get an empty set if you rewrote the query using a WHERE clause that checks whether the literal value equals any value in the item_title column. The foregoing query gives you a descriptive result whether or not it's found.

ANSI SQL CASE Operator

The CASE operator is the most portable, and it allows for equality and inequality evaluation, range comparisons, and in-set comparisons. It also supports multiple CASE statements, such as a switch statement without fall-through characteristics. You can likewise use comparisons against subqueries and correlated subqueries.

In an Oracle database, the following query matches case-insensitive strings from the in-line view against string literals for the primary colors on the color wheel:

```
SQL> SELECT    inline.color_name
  2  ,          CASE
  3                WHEN UPPER(inline.color_name) = 'BLUE' THEN
  4                   'Primary Color'
  5                WHEN UPPER(inline.color_name) = 'RED' THEN
  6                   'Primary Color'
  7                WHEN UPPER(inline.color_name) = 'YELLOW' THEN
  8                   'Primary Color'
  9                ELSE
 10                   'Not Primary Color'
 11             END AS color_type
 12  FROM      (SELECT 'Red' AS color_name FROM dual
 13             UNION ALL
 14             SELECT 'Blue' AS color_name FROM dual
 15             UNION ALL
 16             SELECT 'Purple' AS color_name FROM dual
 17             UNION ALL
 18             SELECT 'Green' AS color_name FROM dual
 19             UNION ALL
 20             SELECT 'Yellow' AS color_name FROM dual) inline
 21  ORDER BY 2 DESC, 1 ASC
```

This query works in MySQL whether you leave it as is or modify it by removing the UPPER function around the inline.color_name column. The CASE operator includes several WHEN clauses that evaluate conditions and an ELSE clause that acts as the default catchall for the CASE operator. Note that END by itself terminates a CASE operator. If you were to put END CASE, the word *CASE* would become the column alias.

Although the sample evaluates only a single logical condition, each WHEN clause supports any number of AND or OR logical operators. Any comparison phrase can use the standard equality and inequality comparison operators; the IN, =ANY, =SOME, and =ALL lookup operators; and scalar, single-row, multiple-row, and correlated subqueries.

You would get the following results from the preceding query in Oracle—at least you would when you format the color_name column to an alphanumeric 10 character string in SQL*Plus (check Chapter 2 for syntax):

```
COLOR_NAME COLOR_TYPE
---------- -----------------
Blue       Primary Color
Red        Primary Color
Yellow     Primary Color
Green      Not Primary Color
Purple     Not Primary Color
```

There's a lot of power in using the CASE operator, but you need to understand the basics and experiment. For example, you saw how to get an in-stock or out-of-stock answer with the IF function in MySQL. You can rewrite that query with a CASE operator that runs in an Oracle or MySQL database, and it would look like this:

```
SELECT CASE
          WHEN 'Star Wars VII' IN (SELECT item_title FROM item)
          THEN 'In-stock'
          ELSE 'Out-of-stock'
       END AS yes_no_answer
FROM   dual;
```

The foregoing query is limited, but it mirrors the MySQL query that used the IF function. A more useful approach that works in Oracle or MySQL databases is the following query with the CASE operator. It uses an in-line view to fabricate a data set that's used as the decision-making parameter to the WHEN clause in the CASE operator.

```
SELECT inline.query_string
,      CASE
          WHEN inline.query_string IN (SELECT item_title FROM item)
          THEN 'In-stock'
          ELSE 'Out-of-stock'
       END AS yes_no_answer
FROM   (SELECT 'Star Wars II' AS query_string FROM dual
        UNION ALL
        SELECT 'Star Wars VII' AS query_string FROM dual) inline;
```

It returns the following output from a MySQL database:

```
+---------------+---------------+
| query_string  | yes_no_answer |
+---------------+---------------+
| Star Wars II  | In-stock      |
| Star Wars VII | Out-of-stock  |
+---------------+---------------+
```

The CASE operator also allows you to validate complex math or date math. Date math isn't very transferable between an Oracle and MySQL database, because of the differences between their implementations. The following subsections explain Oracle and MySQL date math and provide a CASE statement that leverages date math in each database.

Oracle Date Math   Oracle's date math is very straightforward. You simply add or subtract numbers from a date to get a date in the future or past, respectively. The only twist in the model is that the DATE data type is a date-time not a date. You can shave off the hours and minutes of any day with the TRUNC function and make the date-time equivalent to midnight the morning of a date. This is the closest you have to a true DATE data type in an Oracle database.

The following example looks at yesterday, today, and tomorrow:

```
SQL> SELECT    SYSDATE - 1 AS yesterday
  2  ,          SYSDATE     AS today
  3  ,          SYSDATE + 1 AS tomorrow
  4  FROM       dual;
```

The results are deceiving, because Oracle automatically prints them as dates, like so:

```
YESTERDAY TODAY     TOMORROW
--------- --------- ---------
19-JUN-11 20-JUN-11 21-JUN-11
```

If we convert the date-time values to strings with formatting instructions down to the second, you would see the full date-time stamp. This query uses the Oracle proprietary TO_CHAR function to do that:

```
SQL> SELECT   TO_CHAR(SYSDATE - 1,'DD-MON-YYYY HH24:MI:SS') AS Yesterday
  2  ,         TO_CHAR(SYSDATE    ,'DD-MON-YYYY HH24:MI:SS') AS Today
  3  ,         TO_CHAR(SYSDATE + 1,'DD-MON-YYYY HH24:MI:SS') AS Tomorrow
  4  FROM     dual;
```

It yields the following:

```
YESTERDAY            TODAY                TOMORROW
-------------------- -------------------- --------------------
19-JUN-2011 22:59:45 20-JUN-2011 22:59:45 21-JUN-2011 22:59:45
```

You could use the TRUNC function to shave the decimal portion of time, which would give you 12 midnight in the morning of each day. The following query truncates the time from the SYSDATE value:

```
SQL> SELECT   TO_CHAR(TRUNC(SYSDATE)-1,'DD-MON-YYYY HH24:MI') AS Yesterday
  2  ,         TO_CHAR(TRUNC(SYSDATE)  ,'DD-MON-YYYY HH24:MI:SS') AS Today
  3  ,         TO_CHAR(TRUNC(SYSDATE)+1,'DD-MON-YYYY HH24:MI:SS') AS Tomorrow
  4  FROM     dual;
```

The results show that everything is now 12 midnight the morning of each day:

```
YESTERDAY        TODAY                TOMORROW
---------------- -------------------- --------------------
19-JUN-2011 00:00 20-JUN-2011 00:00:00 21-JUN-2011 00:00:00
```

This means any date plus an integer of 1 yields a day that is 24 hours in the future and any date minus an integer of 1 yields a day that is 24 hours behind the current date-time value. The TRUNC function also lets you get the first day of a month or the first day of a year. It works like this:

```
SQL> SELECT   TRUNC(SYSDATE,'MM') AS first_day_of_month
  2  ,         TRUNC(SYSDATE,'YY') AS first_day_of_year
  3  FROM     dual;
```

Here are the results for any day in June:

```
FIRST_DAY_OF_MONTH FIRST_DAY_OF_YEAR
------------------ -----------------
01-JUN-11          01-JAN-11
```

If you subtract two days, you get the number of days between them, like so:

```
SQL> SELECT TO_DATE('30-MAY-2011') - TO_DATE('14-FEB-2011') AS days
  2  FROM dual;
```

This query would tell us the number of days between Valentine's Day and Memorial Day, as shown here:

```
     DAYS
----------
      105
```

Although you can subtract days, you can't add them. If you tried to add dates, the following error would be raised:

```
SELECT TO_DATE('30-MAY-2011') + TO_DATE('14-FEB-2011')
                              *
ERROR at line 1:
ORA-00975: date + date not allowed
```

Table 11-1 provides additional built-in functions that can help when you're performing date math on an Oracle database. Although the table's not inclusive of timestamp functions, it covers those functions that work with dates. You can check the *Oracle Database SQL Reference* for more information on the timestamp built-ins.

Date Function	Description

ADD_MONTHS	Lets you add or subtract months, like so:
	`SELECT ADD_MONTHS(SYSDATE, 3)`
	`FROM dual;`

CAST	Lets you convert a string that uses the Oracle default date format masks of `DD-MON-RR` or `DD-MON-YYYY` to a DATE data type. The example uses an INSERT statement to show the conversion:
	`INSERT INTO some_table`
	`VALUES`
	`(CAST('15-APR-11' AS DATE));`

CURRENT_DATE	Finds the current system date: `SELECT CURRENT_DATE FROM dual;`

GREATEST	Finds the most forward date in a set of dates. It works like this to find tomorrow:
	`SELECT GREATEST(SYSDATE,SYSDATE + 1)`
	`FROM dual;`

EXTRACT	Lets you extract the integer that represents a year, month, day, hour, minute, or second from a DATE data type. The following prototypes show you how to grab the day, month, or year from a DATE data type:
	`SELECT EXTRACT(DAY FROM SYSDATE) AS dd`
	`,      EXTRACT(MONTH FROM SYSDATE) AS mm`
	`,      EXTRACT(YEAR FROM SYSDATE) AS yy`
	`FROM dual;`

LEAST	Finds the most forward date in a set of dates. It works like this to find yesterday:
	`SELECT LEAST(SYSDATE -1,SYSDATE)`
	`FROM dual;`

TABLE 11-1. *Oracle Built-in Date Functions*

Date Function	Description

LAST_DAY	Lets you find the last date of the month for any date, like so:
	`SELECT last_day(SYSDATE)`
	`FROM dual;`

LEAST	Finds the most forward date in a set of dates. It works like this to find yesterday:
	`SELECT LEAST(SYSDATE -1,SYSDATE)`
	`FROM dual;`

MONTHS_BETWEEN	Lets you find the decimal value between two dates. The function returns a positive number when the greater date is the first call parameter and a negative number when it's the second call parameter. Here's an example:
	`SELECT MONTHS_BETWEEN('25-DEC-11',SYSDATE)`
	`FROM dual;`

NEXT_DAY	Lets you find the date of the next day of the week, like so:
	`SELECT next_day(SYSDATE,'FRIDAY')`
	`FROM dual;`

ROUND	Shaves off the decimal portion of a DATE when the current date-time is before noon. Alternatively, it adds the complement of the decimal to make the day midnight of the next day. Use it like this: `SELECT ROUND(SYSDATE) FROM dual;`
SYSDATE	Finds the current system date: `SELECT SYSDATE FROM dual;`

TO_CHAR	Lets you apply a format to a date, like so:
	`SELECT`
	`  TO_CHAR(SYSDATE,'DD-MON-YYYY HH24:MI:SS')`
	`FROM dual;`
	Supports the following format syntax:
	DD – Two-digit day
	MM – Two-digit month
	MON – Three-character month, based on NLS_LANG value
	YY – Two-digit year
	YYYY – Two-digit absolute year
	RR – Two-digit relative year
	HH – Two-digit hour, values 1 to 12
	HH24 – Two-digit hour, values 0 to 23
	MI – Two-digit minutes, values 0 to 59
	SS – Two-digit seconds, values 0 to 59

TO_DATE	Converts a string to a DATE data type. Lets you to convert nonstandard DATE format masks, which come from external import sources. The default format masks of DD-MON-RR and DD-MON-YYYY also work with the TO_DATE function but can be cast to a DATE with the CAST function. The TO_DATE function would convert a MySQL default format date string to a DATE with this syntax: `SELECT TO_DATE('2011-07-14','YYYY-MM-DD') FROM dual;`

TABLE 11-1. *Oracle Built-in Date Functions* (continued)

The EXTRACT function works in both Oracle and MySQL databases. Blending the conditional CASE operator with the EXTRACT date function, you can write a statement that finds transaction_amount values for a given month. The following is such a statement:

```
SQL> SELECT   CASE
  2                WHEN EXTRACT(MONTH FROM transaction_date) = 1 AND
  3                    EXTRACT(YEAR FROM transaction_date) = 2011 THEN
  4                  transaction_amount
  5                END AS "January"
  6     FROM    transaction;
```

Lines 2 and 3 identify transaction amounts from a month and year, and only transaction_amount values for January 2011 would be returned by the query. However, it would also return null value rows for every other month and year present in the table. You need to filter the query with a WHERE clause to restrict it to the data of interest. The CASE operator in a SELECT list works in tandem with the WHERE clause of a query.

Another approach could have you return a Y as an active_flag value when the item_release_date values are less than or equal to 30 days before today, and an N when they're greater than 30 days. You would write that CASE operator like this:

```
SQL> SELECT CASE
  2                WHEN (SYSDATE - i.release_date) <= 30 THEN 'Y'
  3                WHEN (SYSDATE - i.release_date) >  30 THEN 'N'
  4              END AS active_flag
  5     FROM   item i;
```

In conclusion, the CASE operator is more flexible than the DECODE or IF function. The best practice is to write portable code with the CASE operator.

MySQL Date Math   MySQL's date math is very different from Oracle's approach. You can't add or subtract numbers from dates. You must use designated functions. The fact that some functions have aliases makes the list of functions longer. My recommendation is that you choose the function or its alias and use it consistently, such as the DATE_ADD function or its synonym ADDDATE.

The DATE_ADD function has the following prototype:

```
DATE_ADD(date, INTERVAL number date_interval)
```

The UTC_DATE function returns the current date in MySQL, and you can add 6 days to it like this:

```
SELECT DATE_ADD(UTC_DATE(), INTERVAL 6 DAY);
```

Alternatively, you can add a week by using a different interval data type, like so:

```
SELECT DATE_ADD(UTC_DATE(), INTERVAL 1 WEEK);
```

Subtracting units from dates works the same way as adding them. For example, you would subtract 6 days like this:

```
SELECT DATE_SUB(UTC_DATE(), INTERVAL 6 DAY);
```

And you could subtract a week like this:

```
SELECT DATE_SUB(UTC_DATE(), INTERVAL 1 WEEK);
```

Table 11-2 shows the available intervals and formats for adding to or subtracting from dates. Some intervals in the table are integers and others are strings. The strings are enclosed in single quotes. For clarity, a data type column qualifies which are integers or strings. The format masks support the function's internal parser.

The difference between two dates is numeric, as in Oracle. You use the DATEDIFF function to calculate it. Here's an example that returns the number of days between Memorial Day and Valentine's Day:

```
SELECT DATEDIFF('2011-05-30','2011-02-14');
```

It returns 105, which is the same as would be returned by Oracle's calculation. Date math functions work solidly in both implementations. Table 11-3 qualifies the date functions you will most likely use, and you can find the date-time function in the *MySQL 5.5 Reference Manual* in Chapter 11.7, "Date and Time Functions."

Interval	Data Type	Format Mask
DAY	Integer	Dd
DAY_HOUR	String	'dd hh'
DAY_MICROSECOND	String	'dd.nn'
DAY_MINUTE	String	'dd hh:mm'
DAY_SECOND	String	'dd hh:mm:ss.nn'
HOUR	Integer	Hh
HOUR_MICROSECOND	String	'dd hh'
HOUR_MINUTE	String	'dd nn'
HOUR_SECOND	String	'dd hh:mm'
MICROSECOND	Integer	Nn
MINUTE	Integer	Mm
MINUTE_MICROSECOND	String	'mm.nn'
MINUTE_SECOND	String	'mm:ss'
MONTH	Integer	Mm
QUARTER	Integer	Qq
SECOND	Integer	Ss
SECOND_MICROSECOND	String	'ss.nn'
WEEK	Integer	Ww
YEAR	Integer	Yy
YEAR_MONTH	String	'yy-mm'

TABLE 11-2. *DATE_ADD and DATE_SUB Interval Values*

Date Function	Description
ADDDATE	An alias for the DATE_ADD function that lets you add an interval to a date and returns a new date, like so: `SELECT ADDDATE(UTC_DATE(), INTERVAL 1 DAY);`

CAST	Lets you convert a string that uses the Oracle default date format masks of YYYY-MM-DD to a DATE data type. This example uses an INSERT statement to show the conversion:
	`INSERT INTO some_table`
	`VALUES`
	`(CAST('2011-04-15' AS DATE));`

CURDATE	Finds the current system date and is synonymous with the CURRENT_DATE function: `SELECT CURDATE();`
CURRENT_DATE	Finds the current system date and is synonymous with the CURDATE function: `SELECT CURRENT_DATE();`

DATE	Creates a DATE from a default date or date-time string. The defaults are YYYY-MM-DD for a date and YYYY-MM-DD HH:MI:SS for a date-time. It works like this with a date format:
	`SELECT DATE('2011-07-04');`
	It works like this with a date-time format:
	`SELECT DATE('2011-07-04 06:00:01');`

DATE_ADD	The function called when you use the ADDDATE synonym, which lets you add an interval to a date and returns a new date. It uses the intervals qualified in Table 11-2, like this: `SELECT DATE_ADD(UTC_DATE(), INTERVAL 1 DAY);`

DATE_FORMAT	Lets you apply a format to a date, like so:
	`SELECT DATE_FORMAT(UTC_DATE(),'%D %M %Y');`
	It would return
	
	`+------------------------------------+`
	`| DATE_FORMAT(UTC_DATE(),'%D %M %Y') |`
	`+------------------------------------+`
	`| 21st June 2011                     |`
	`+------------------------------------+`
	This function supports the following format syntax:
	%b – Abbreviated month name
	%c – Two-digit month
	%d – Two-digit day, where a zero precedes a single-digit day
	%D – One- or two-digit day with English suffix: 1st, 2nd
	%e – One- or two-digit day
	%h – Two-digit hour, values 1 to 12
	%H – Two-digit hour, values 0 to 23
	%i – Two-digit minutes, values 0 to 59
	%I – Two-digit hour, values 1 to 12
	%j – Three-digit day of the year, values 001 to 366
	%k – Two-digit hour, values 0 to 23
	%l – Two-digit hour, values 1 to 12
	%m – Two-digit month, values 1 to 12
	%M – Full month name
	%p – A.M. or P.M. designation
	%s – Two-digit seconds, values 0 to 59
	%S – Two-digit seconds, values 0 to 59
	%y – Two-digit year
	%Y – Four-digit year

TABLE 11-3. *MySQL Built-in Date Functions*

Date Function	Description
DATE_SUB	Lets you subtract an interval from a date and returns a new date. It uses the intervals qualified in Table 11-2, like so: `SELECT DATE_SUB(UTC_DATE(), INTERVAL 1 DAY);`
DATEDIFF	Lets you subtract one date from another. When the first date is greater than the second date, it returns a positive number. When the first date is less than the second date, it returns a negative number. `SELECT DATEDIFF(date1, date2);`
DAY	Synonymous with the DAYOFMONTH function and returns the two-digit value for the current day: `SELECT DAY(UTC_DATE());`
DAYNAME	Returns the language representation for the day of the week, such as Monday, Tuesday, and so on: `SELECT DAYNAME(UTC_DATE());`
DAYOFMONTH	Synonymous with the DAY function and returns the two-digit value for the current day: `SELECT DAY(UTC_DATE());`
DAYOFWEEK	The DAYOFWEEK function returns the one digit value for the current day of the week, values are 1 to 7. `SELECT DAYOFWEEK(UTC_DATE());`
DAYOFYEAR	Returns the one- to three-digit value for the current day of the year; values are 1 to 366. `SELECT DAYOFYEAR(UTC_DATE());`

EXTRACT	Lets you extract the integer that represents a year, month, day, hour, minute, or second from a DATE data type. The following prototypes show how to grab the day, month, or year from a DATE data type:
	`SELECT EXTRACT(DAY FROM UTC_DATE()) AS dd`
	`,      EXTRACT(MONTH FROM UTC_DATE()) AS mm`
	`,      EXTRACT(YEAR FROM UTC_DATE()) AS yy`
	`FROM dual;`

LAST_DAY	Lets you find the last date of the month for any date, like so: `SELECT last_day(UTC_DATE());`
MONTHNAME	Returns the name of the month: `SELECT MONTHNAME(UTC_DATE());`
NOW	Lets you find the current date-time stamp and is equivalent to the Oracle SYSDATE function. `SELECT NOW();`

STR_TO_DATE	Lets you apply a format to a date string, like so:
	`SELECT DATE_FORMAT('11-07-04','%D %M %Y');`
	Returns this:
	<pre>+----------------------------------+
	| DATE_FORMAT('11-07-04','%D %M %Y') |
	+----------------------------------+
	| 4th July 2011 |
	+----------------------------------+</pre>The function uses the same formatting commands as the DATE_FORMAT function.

SUBDATE	Lets you subtract an interval from a date and returns a new date. It uses the intervals qualified in Table 11-2, like so: `SELECT SUBDATE(UTC_DATE(), INTERVAL 1 DAY);`
SYSDATE	Finds the current system date: `SELECT SYSDATE FROM dual;`

TABLE 11-3. *MySQL Built-in Date Functions* (continued)

As mentioned, the EXTRACT function is portable and works the same way in MySQL and Oracle. Other date math must change to reflect the product-specific date math function. For example, in the Oracle section, you saw a CASE operator that calculated when to select an active or inactive flag value. That example compared the number of days between two dates, where the one date was subtracted from the other.

In MySQL, that would require the DATEDIFF function, like this:

```
SQL> SELECT CASE
  2            WHEN DATEDIFF(UTC_DATE(),i.release_date) <= 30 THEN 'Y'
  3            WHEN DATEDIFF(UTC_DATE(),i.release_date) >  30 THEN 'N'
  4          END AS active_flag
  5  FROM   item i;
```

The Oracle and MySQL date math sections prepare you to see how selective aggregation works. They also provide you with some immediate capabilities in your queries.

Selective Aggregation

Selective aggregation uses conditional logic, similar to the DECODE function, IF function, or CASE operator inside aggregation functions. The conditional decision-making of these if-then-else functions lets you filter what you count, sum, average, or take the maximum or minimum value of. Understanding this is the first step toward transforming data into useful data sets for accountants and other professional data analysts. The second step lets you transform aggregated rows into column values, which you accomplish through column aliases.

The next example demonstrates transforming rows of data into a financial report where the columns represents months, quarters, and year-to-date values and the rows represent account numbers charged for various expenses.

Although the example uses the EXTRACT function, which works the same way both in Oracle and MySQL, the formatting for a report differs. For convenience, they're covered in separate subsections.

Oracle Selective Aggregation   The following query returns a column of data for the month of January 2011. Since all numbers are stored as positive values, a nested CASE operator evaluates the transaction_type column in the same row to determine whether to add or subtract the value. Debits are added and credits are subtracted, because this works with an asset account.

```
SQL> SELECT    t.transaction_account AS "Transaction"
  2             LPAD(TO_CHAR
  3             (SUM
  4               (CASE
  5                  WHEN EXTRACT(MONTH FROM transaction_date) = 1 AND
  6                       EXTRACT(YEAR FROM transaction_date) = 2011 THEN
  7                    CASE
  8                      WHEN t.transaction_type = 'DEBIT' THEN
  9                        t.transaction_amount
 10                      ELSE
 11                        t.transaction_amount * -1
 12                    END
 13                END),'99,999.00'),10,' ') AS "JAN"
 14  FROM    transaction t
 15  GROUP BY t.transaction_account;
```

You would see something like this when you expand beyond a single column, which has been limited to the first three months of the year and two rows of data:

```
Transaction      Jan         Feb         Mar
---------------  ----------  ----------  ----------
10-12-551234       2,671.20    4,270.74    5,371.02
10-14-551234        -690.06   -1,055.76   -1,405.56
```

The value passed to the SUM function is all rows that meet the selectivity criteria. The criteria are the result of a CASE and nested CASE operator. The business result is the total expense grouped by the transaction account number. The LPAD function right-aligns the string returned by the TO_CHAR function, which formats the number always to have two decimal places, even when it's zero cents.

Line 5 could be replaced by the following to capture a first quarter result:

```
5   WHEN EXTRACT(MONTH FROM transaction_date) IN (1,2,3) AND
```

Moreover, you could generate a year-to-date or year-end report for a completed year by eliminating the validation criterion for the month.

MySQL Selective Aggregation   The following query returns the same data as the preceding Oracle equivalent. The differences are in how the values are converted to strings and formatted for output.

```
mysql> SELECT    t.transaction_account AS "Transaction"
    2 ->          LPAD(FORMAT
    3 ->          (SUM
    4 ->            (CASE
    5 ->              WHEN EXTRACT(MONTH FROM transaction_date) = 1 AND
    6 ->                    EXTRACT(YEAR FROM transaction_date) = 2011 THEN
    7 ->               CASE
    8 ->                 WHEN t.transaction_type = 'DEBIT' THEN
    9 ->                   t.transaction_amount
   10 ->                 ELSE
   11 ->                   t.transaction_amount * -1
   12 ->               END
   13 ->            END),2),10,' ') AS "JAN"
   14 -> FROM      transaction t
   15 -> GROUP BY t.transaction_account;
```

The output for the first three months would look like this:

```
+---------------+------------+------------+------------+
| Transaction   | Jan        | Feb        | Mar        |
+---------------+------------+------------+------------+
| 10-12-551234  |   2,957.40 |   4,022.70 |   5,654.04 |
| 10-14-551234  |    -750.48 |    -992.16 |  -1,437.36 |
+---------------+------------+------------+------------+
```

Like the Oracle example, the selectivity occurs in the value returned to the SUM function. While the LPAD function works the same way in MySQL, the FORMAT function replaces the TO_CHAR function. The balance of the FORMAT and LPAD functions are displayed in ordinary text after the boldface text on line 13.

Join Results

You can join tables, logical structures that store physical data, or views, logical structures that store directions on how to find data stored in other views or tables, into larger result sets. Views can be subsets of tables, filtered to show only some columns and rows, as covered in the "Query Results" section at the beginning of the chapter. Views can also be the result sets combined from two or more tables or views. You combine tables through join operations.

Although joins in procedural programming languages would involve an outer and inner loop to read two sets into memory, SQL doesn't have loops. As a set-based declarative language, SQL operates like an automatic transmission that hides the clutch and gear-changing process. Imperative languages, on the other hand, are like standard transmissions. Imperative languages require the developer to master the nature of manually switching gears. Managing the clutch and gears would be equivalent to writing outer and inner loops and conditional logic to join the results from two sets into one. SQL joins hide the complexity by letting the developer state what he or she wants without specifying the implementation details.

You can perform several types of joins in SQL. They can be organized into an abstract Unified Modeling Language (UML) inheritance diagram, which is a hierarchy, as shown in Figure 11-6.

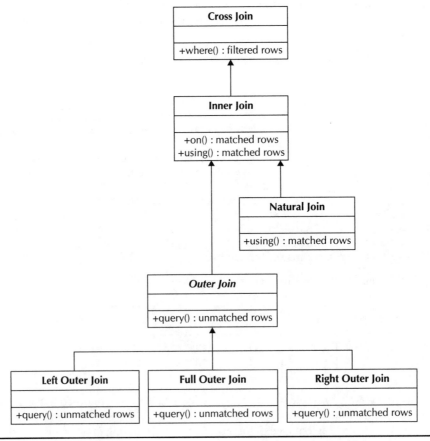

FIGURE 11-6. *Join inheritance tree*

This type of hierarchy is also known as an inverted tree. The top of the hierarchy is the root node and the bottom nodes are the leaf nodes. The root node is the parent node and is not derivative of any other node. Nodes below the root (or parent) node are its child nodes. Leaf nodes aren't parents yet but may become so later; they are child nodes. Nodes between the root and leaf nodes are both parent and child nodes.

Inheritance trees indicate that the most generalized behaviors are in the root node, and most specialized behaviors are in leaf nodes. The inheritance tree tells us the following:

- A *cross join* is the most generalized behavior in joins, and it inherits nothing but implements the base behaviors for join operations in a set-based declarative language.

- An *inner join* is the *only* child of a cross join, and it inherits the behaviors of a cross join and provides some additional features (specialized behaviors) by extending the parent class's behaviors.

- A *natural join* is a child of an inner join, and it inherits and extends the parent class's behaviors. The natural join is also a leaf node, which means no other class extends its behaviors.

- An *outer join* is an abstract class, which means its implementations are available only to subclasses, but it does extend the behavior of the parent class. Through the parent class, it also extends the behavior of the root node or grandparent class.

- A *left join* is a concrete class that extends its abstract parent class and all other classes preceding its parent in the tree. It implements a left outer join behavior beyond the inherited inner join operations.

- A *full join* is a concrete class that extends its abstract parent class and all other classes preceding its parent in the tree. It implements a full outer join behavior beyond the inherited inner join operations.

- A *right join* is a concrete class that extends its abstract parent class and all other classes preceding its parent in the tree. It implements a right outer join behavior beyond the inherited inner join operations.

The subsections qualify what the various join types do. Each section uses Venn diagrams to depict the relationship of sets. Unlike basic sets with a list of elements, the rows in tables are vectors, or record structures. A vector is often visualized as a line, and the line is made up of points. A record structure is like a line when it's labeled as a vector but isn't composed of points. The points in a record data structure are the elements, and each element of a row belongs to a column in a table or view.

There are two types of joins between tables: one splices rows from one table together with rows from another table, and the other splices like collections together. The spliced rows become larger record structures. Splicing together two collections requires that both original collections have the same record structure or table definition. The cross, inner, natural, and outer joins work with splicing rows together. You use set operators to splice together collections of the same record structure.

The next two subsections cover joins that splice rows together and joins that splice collections together. They should be read sequentially because there are some dependencies between the two sections.

Joins that Splice Together Rows

Tables should contain all the information that defines a single subject when the tables are properly normalized. This section assumes you're working with normalized tables. You'll see the differences between ANSI SQL-89 and ANSI SQL-92 joins throughout the subsequent sections.

TIP
You should learn both ANSI SQL-89 and ANSI SQL-92 join semantics.

As a refresher, normalized tables typically contain a set of columns that uniquely defines every row in the table, and collectively these columns are the natural key of the table. Although possible but rare, a single column can define the natural key. The best example of that use case is a `vehicle` table with a `vin` (vehicle identification number) column. Tables also contain surrogate key columns, which are artificial numbers generated through sequences. Surrogate key columns don't define anything about the data, but they uniquely define rows of a table and should have a one-to-one relationship to the natural key of a table. Although the surrogate and natural keys are both candidates to become the primary key of a table, you should always select the surrogate key.

The primary key represents rows of the table externally, and you can copy it to another table as a foreign key. Matches between the primary and foreign key columns let you join tables into multiple-subject record structures. Joins between primary and foreign key values are known as *equijoins* or joins based on an equality match between columns. Joins that don't match based on the equality of columns are *non-equijoins*, and they're filtered searches of a Cartesian product. The "Cross Join" section that follows explains these types of joins.

The natural key differs from a surrogate key because it represents the columns that you use to find a unique row in a table, and it contains descriptive values that define the unique subject of a normalized table. When you write a query against a single table, you use the natural key columns in the `WHERE` clause to find unique rows.

Cross joins are the most generalized form; outer joins are the most specialized.

Cross Join

A cross join in SQL produces a Cartesian product, which is the rows of one table matched against all the rows of another table. It is equivalent to a for loop reading one row from one collection and then a nested for loop appending all rows from another collection to copies of that one row. The operation is repeated for every row in the outer for loop.

A Venn diagram for a cross join is shown in Figure 11-7. The discrete math represents that one set is multiplied by the other. For example, a cross join between a `customer` and `address` table would return 32 rows when the `customer` table holds 4 rows and the `address` table holds 8 rows.

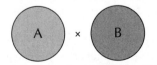

$$\forall A,B \mid A \times B = \{(x,y) \mid x \in A \wedge y \in B\}$$

FIGURE 11-7. *Cross join Venn diagram*

Cross joins are useful when you want to perform a non-equijoin match, such as looking up transaction amounts based on their transaction dates within a calendar month. In this case, you'd be filtering a Cartesian product to see when one column in a table holds a value between two columns in the other table. This is also known as a "filtered cross join" statement.

The difference between ANSI SQL-89 and ANSI SQL-92 syntax for a cross join is that the tables are comma-delimited in the FROM clause for ANSI SQL-89, whereas, they're bridged by a CROSS JOIN operator in ANSI SQL-92.

ANSI SQL-89 Cross Join   The following shows a filtered cross join between the transaction and calendar tables:

```
SQL> SELECT    c.month_short_name
  2  ,          t.transaction_amount
  3  FROM       calendar c, transaction t
  4  WHERE      t.transaction_date BETWEEN c.start_date AND c.end_date
  5  ORDER BY EXTRACT(MONTH FROM t.transaction_date);
```

Notice that the FROM clause on line 3 lists comma-delimited tables, and the WHERE clause on line 4 doesn't have an equality based join between the primary and foreign key columns.

The query would display the following type of result set:

```
Month
Name   Amount
-----  ------
JAN     32.87
JAN     38.99
MAR      9.99
APR     43.19
```

A GROUP BY clause on a line 5 combined with a SUM aggregation formula on line 2 would return three rows of aggregated data, one row for each distinct month:

```
SQL> SELECT    c.month_short_name
  2  ,          SUM(t.transaction_amount)
  3  FROM       calendar c, transaction t
  4  WHERE      t.transaction_date BETWEEN c.start_date AND c.end_date
  5  GROUP BY c.month_short_name
  6  ORDER BY EXTRACT(MONTH FROM t.transaction_date);
```

This type of cross join logic is extremely useful when you're creating financial statements with SQL queries. It filters results based on whether the value of one table's column is between the values of two columns of another table.

ANSI SQL-92 Cross Join   Like the prior syntax example, this example shows a filtered cross join between the transaction and calendar tables:

```
SQL> SELECT    c.month_short_name
  2  ,          t.transaction_amount
  3  FROM       calendar c CROSS JOIN transaction t
  4  WHERE      t.transaction_date BETWEEN c.start_date AND c.end_date
  5  ORDER BY EXTRACT(MONTH FROM t.transaction_date);
```

Cartesian Product

A Cartesian product is the result of a cross join in SQL. The Cartesian product is named after René Descartes, who is known for penning the phrase, *"Cogito ergo sum."* Translated, it means, "I think therefore I am." He was also a 17th century mathematician who developed the theory of analytical geometry, which lays the foundation for calculus and many aspects of set theory. Set theory is a major foundational element for relational calculus and databases.

This query would return the same result set from the sample data set found in the video store database (see Introduction for details). Notice that in lieu of the comma-delimited tables on line 3, two tables are separated by the CROSS JOIN operator.

You also can refactor this query to use the following syntax:

```
SELECT     c.month_short_name
,          t.transaction_amount
FROM       calendar c INNER JOIN transaction t
ON         (t.transaction_date BETWEEN c.start_date AND c.end_date)
ORDER BY EXTRACT(MONTH FROM t.transaction_date);
```

Although this appears to be an inner join operation, it actually runs as a filtered cross join. The ON subclause performs a range comparison that determines whether the transaction_date column value is found between the dates of two columns from the calendar table. Why is the last syntax important if it's misleading and does the same thing? Because Oracle has recently included this on the certification test.

Inner Join

An inner join in SQL produces an intersection between two tables. It lets you splice rows into one large row. It is equivalent to a for loop reading one row from one collection, then a nested for loop reading another row, and finally a conditional if statement checking whether they match. When they match, you have an intersection, and only those rows are returned by an INNER JOIN operator.

The Venn diagram for an inner join is shown in Figure 11-8. The discrete math represents that one set intersects the other. For example, when you match a table with a primary and foreign key value, you get only those rows that match both the primary and foreign key values.

There are two key differences between ANSI SQL-89 and ANSI SQL-92 syntax for an inner join. One is that tables are comma-delimited in the FROM clause for ANSI SQL-89, and they're

$$\forall A,B \mid A \cap B = \{x \in A \cap B \mid x \in A \vee x \in B\}$$

FIGURE 11-8. *Inner join Venn diagram*

separated by the INNER JOIN operator in ANSI SQL-92. The other is that the join condition is in the WHERE clause in ANSI SQL-89 and the FROM clause in ANSI SQL-92. You use a USING clause when the primary and foreign key column(s) share the same column name and the ON clause when they don't. However, you can use the ON clause when the column names are the same.

ANSI SQL-89 Inner Join The following shows you how to join the member and contact tables on their respective primary and foreign key columns. Notice that the tables are comma-delimited and that the join is performed in the WHERE clause.

```
SQL> SELECT    COUNT(*)
  2  FROM      member m, contact c
  3  WHERE     m.member_id = c.member_id;
```

The query returns the number of rows where the values in the two *member_id* columns match exactly. This is an equijoin (or equality value match) relationship.

For outer join subsections, the parent table will always be on the left side of the operator and the child table will be on the right side. If you swap their locations, the results would likewise invert, because the left join of parent to child is the same as the right join of child to parent.

ANSI SQL-92 Inner Join Like the preceding example, this example shows you how to join the member and contact tables on their respective primary and foreign key columns. The INNER JOIN operator replaces the comma-delimited notation of the older syntax pattern.

Two subclause notations are available for joins: the USING subclause and the ON subclause. The USING subclause works when the column or columns have the same name. These operators are required in inner and outer joins but not with the NATURAL JOIN operator.

Here's the USING prototype:

```
FROM    table [alias] {LEFT | INNER | RIGHT | FULL} JOIN table [alias]
USING ( column [, column [, … ]])
```

You can provide as many columns as you need in the USING subclause. You should enter them as a comma-separated list. They are processed as though they were connected through a series of logical AND statements.

The ON prototype works when the columns have the same or different names. Here's its prototype:

```
FROM    table [alias] {LEFT | INNER | RIGHT | FULL} JOIN table [alias]
   ON {table | alias}.column = {table | alias}.column
[ AND {table | alias}.column = {table | alias}.column
[ AND ... ]
```

Notice that the following tables aren't comma-delimited. The INNER JOIN operator replaces the comma between tables. This join uses the USING subclause to match primary and foreign key columns that share the same name.

```
SQL> SELECT    m.account_number
  2  ,         c.last_name || ', ' || c.first_name AS customer_name
  3  FROM      member m INNER JOIN contact c USING(member_id);
```

You must use the ON subclause when the column name or column names aren't the same, but you can also use them when they're the same. Here is an example of the ON subclause syntax:

```
SQL> SELECT   m.account_number
  2  ,         c.last_name || ', ' || c.first_name AS customer_name
  3  FROM      member m INNER JOIN contact c ON m.member_id = c.member_id;
```

Both of these queries return the number of rows where the values in the two member_id columns match exactly. Like the older syntax, that means they return the intersection between the two tables and a result set that potentially includes data from both tables.

Natural Join   A natural join doesn't exist in the ANSI SQL-89 standard. It exists only in the ANSI SQL-92 standard. The intent of a natural join is to provide the intersection between two sets. It's called a natural join because you don't have to provide the names of the primary or foreign key columns. The natural join checks the data catalog for matching column names with the same data type, and then it creates the join condition implicitly for you.

```
SQL> SELECT   m.account_number
  2  ,         c.last_name || ', ' || c.first_name AS customer_name
  3  FROM      member m NATURAL JOIN contact c;
```

The only problem with a natural join occurs when columns share the same column name and data type but aren't the primary or foreign keys. A natural join will include them in the join condition. Attempting to match non-key columns that make up the who-audit columns excludes rows that should be returned. The who-audit is composed of the created_by, creation_ date, last_updated_by, and last_update_date columns (or like column names).

Outer Joins

Outer joins allow you to return result sets that are found both in the intersection and outside the intersection. Applying the paradigm of a parent table that holds a primary key and child table that holds a foreign key, three relationships are possible when foreign key integrity is enforced by the API rather than database constraints:

- **Scenario 1**   A row in the parent table matches one or more rows in the child table.
- **Scenario 2**   A row in the parent table doesn't match any row in the child table.
- **Scenario 3**   A row in the child table doesn't match any row in the parent table, which makes the row in the child table an orphan.

Any or all of the three scenarios can occur. Inner joins help us find the results for scenario 2, but outer joins help us find rows that meet the criteria of scenarios 1 and 3.

NOTE
The ANSI SQL-89 syntax has no provision for outer joins.

Oracle provided outer join syntax before it was defined by the ANSI SQL-92 definition. Oracle's syntax works with joins in the WHERE clause. You append a (+) on the column of a table in the join, and it indicates that you want the relative complement of that table. A relative complement contains everything not found in the original set.

For example, the following SELECT statement uses an Oracle proprietary outer join, and you would get all account_number values from the member table that had a contact or didn't have a contact. That's because any member_id values found in the member table that aren't found in the contact table are returned with the inner join result set.

```
SQL> SELECT   m.account_number
  2  FROM      member m, contact c
  3  WHERE     m.member_id = c.member_id(+);
```

If you change the SELECT list and switch the (+) from the contact table's column to the member table's member_id column, you would get any orphaned rows from the contact table. Here's the syntax to get orphaned contacts' names:

```
SQL> SELECT   c.last_name || ', ' || c.first_name AS customer_name
  2  FROM      member m, contact c
  3  WHERE     m.member_id(+) = c.member_id;
```

Line 3 has the change of the (+) from one side of the join to the other. As mentioned, the (+) symbol is included on a column of one table in a join and effectively points to its relative complement in the other table. Having positioned the member table on the left and contact table on the right in the previous examples, when the (+) is pointing from a contact table's column, you get the equivalent of a left join. Switch the (+) to point from a column in the member table and you get the equivalent of a right join.

Oracle's proprietary syntax isn't portable to any other platform. It also doesn't support full outer join behavior unless you combine results with a UNION ALL set operator, which is covered in the "Union" subsection later in this chapter.

Left Outer Join   A left join in SQL extends an inner join because it returns the intersection between two tables plus the right relative complement of the join. The right relative complement is everything in the table to the left of the join operation that's not found in the table on the right. The Venn diagram for a left join is shown in Figure 11-9.

A left join splices several rows into one large row, and it puts null values in the columns from the table on the right when nothing is found in those columns. Left joins use join conditions like those in the inner join section. The ANSI SQL-92 syntax supports a left join operation. That means JOIN statements are in the FROM clause not the WHERE clause, and you use either the ON or USING subclauses to qualify the joining columns.

The following lets you find any account_number values in the member table, whether or not they have valid customer information in the contact table:

```
SQL> SELECT   m.account_number
  2  FROM      member m LEFT OUTER JOIN contact c
  3  ON        m.member_id = c.member_id;
```

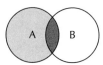

$$\forall A,B \mid A \cap B + A \setminus B = \{x \in A \wedge x \in B\} + \{y \in A \wedge y \neg\in B\}$$

FIGURE 11-9.   *Left join Venn diagram*

The LEFT OUTER JOIN phrase is the fully qualified syntax, but the OUTER keyword is optional in Oracle and MySQL databases. If you were to reverse the relative positions of the member and contact tables, only the account_number values that meet the conditions of an INNER JOIN operator are returned. That's because you would get the right relative complement of the member table, not the contact table. The right relative complement of the member table returns the data rows in the contact table that have foreign key values that don't resolve to primary key values in the member table. Naturally, this type of data set is possible only when you're not maintaining database-level foreign key constraints.

The more frequent use of a LEFT JOIN would be to look for orphaned customers, in order to delete them from the database. In that use case, you'd write the statement like this:

```
SQL> SELECT    c.last_name || ', ' || c.first_name AS customer_name
  2  FROM      contact c LEFT JOIN member m
  3  ON        m.member_id = c.member_id;
```

Notice that the values in the SELECT list should come from the table that holds data not from the table that may not contain data. Otherwise, you get a bunch of null values. The preceding query returns rows from the contact table that don't point back to a row in the member table, and such rows would be orphans. They are referred to as orphans because their foreign key column values aren't found in the list of primary key column values. This can occur when there aren't foreign key constraints in the database.

Right Outer Join   Like a left join, a right join in SQL extends an inner join. A right join returns the intersection between two tables, plus the left relative complement of the join. The left relative complement is everything in the table to the right of the join operation that's not found in the table on the left. This makes the right join a mirror image of the left join, as shown in Figure 11-10.

A right join splices rows into one large row like the inner and left join. It puts null values in the columns from the table on the left when they don't match columns that exist in the table on the right. Right joins use join conditions like those in the inner and left join operations. That means they adhere to the ANSI SQL-92 syntax rules, and JOIN statements are in the FROM clause not the WHERE clause. You can choose to use the ON or USING subclauses to qualify joining columns.

The first example, shown next, lets you find all customer names in the contact table—those tables that have a valid foreign key value that matches a valid primary key value, and those that have an invalid foreign key value. Invalid foreign key values can exist only when you opt not to enforce database-level foreign key constraints. Rows holding invalid foreign key values are known as *orphaned* rows because the row with a valid primary key doesn't exist. This follows the paradigm that the parent holds the primary key and the child holds the foreign key (copy of the primary key).

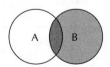

$$\forall A, B \mid A \cap B + B \setminus A = \{x \in A \land x \in B\} + \{y \in B \land y \neg \in A\}$$

FIGURE 11-10.   *Right join Venn diagram*

This example returns all customer names from the `contact` table and really doesn't require a join operation at all:

```
SQL> SELECT    c.last_name || ', ' || c.first_name AS customer_name
  2  FROM      member m RIGHT JOIN contact c
  3  ON        m.member_id = c.member_id;
```

A more meaningful result would exclude all rows where the primary key value is missing. That's easy to do by adding a single filtering `WHERE` clause statement that says "return rows only where there's no valid primary key in the `member` table." Here's the example:

```
SQL> SELECT    c.last_name || ', ' || c.first_name AS customer_name
  2  FROM      member m RIGHT JOIN contact c
  3  ON        m.member_id = c.member_id
  4  WHERE     m.member_id IS NULL;
```

Line 4 filters the return set so that it returns only the orphaned customer names. You would use that type of statement to delete orphan records, typically as a subquery in a `DELETE FROM` statement. Here's an example of such a statement:

```
SQL> DELETE FROM contact
  2  WHERE   contact_id IN (SELECT   c.contact_id
  3                         FROM     member m RIGHT JOIN contact c
  4                         ON       m.member_id = c.member_id
  5                         WHERE    m.member_id IS NULL);
```

The right and left join semantics are very useful for cleaning up data when foreign key values have lost their matching primary key values. They help you find the relative complements of outer joins when you subtract the inner join rows.

Full Outer Join   A full outer join provides the inner join results with the right and left relative complements of left and right joins, respectively. The combination of the two relative complements without the intersection is known as the *symmetric difference*. The Venn diagram for a full outer join is shown in Figure 11-11.

Like the left and right joins, a full outer join splices rows into one large row, like the inner and left join. It puts null values in the columns from the table on the left and right. Assume the following `FULL JOIN` syntax (by the way, `OUTER` is an optional keyword and seldom used):

```
SQL> SELECT    m.account_number
  2  ,         c.last_name || ', ' || c.first_name AS customer_name
  3  FROM      member m FULL JOIN contact c
  4  ON        m.member_id = c.member_id;
```

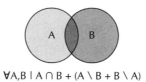

$$\forall A,B \mid A \cap B + (A \setminus B + B \setminus A)$$

FIGURE 11-11.   *Full join Venn diagram*

This query's result set would return null values for the `account_number` when there isn't a foreign key using a primary key in the member table, and the `customer_name` when a foreign key value isn't found in the primary key list. This type of analysis is done when database-level foreign key constraints aren't maintained and the API fails to synchronize primary and foreign key values properly. You need to figure out which customers should be associated with a member, because a member row would never be written unless a contact row was also written. This kind of problem occurs more often than you might expect.

You would filter out the inner join by using the following syntax or the `MINUS` set operator (shown later):

```
SQL> SELECT    m.account_number
  2  ,          c.last_name || ', ' || c.first_name AS customer_name
  3  FROM      member m FULL JOIN contact c
  4  ON        m.member_id = c.member_id
  5  WHERE     m.member_id IS NOT NULL
  6  AND       c.member_id IS NOT NULL;
```

This wraps up joins. Next you'll see how to work with set operators. The next section builds on the examples in this section.

Joins that Splice Collections

Set operations often combine or filter row sets. That means they act as the glue that binds together two queries. The queries must return the same `SELECT` list, which means the column names and data types must match.

The basic prototype glues the top query to the bottom query. Both top and bottom queries can have their own `GROUP BY` or `HAVING` clauses, but only one `ORDER BY` clause can appear at the end. You can splice more than two queries by using other set operators in sequence. The value operations are performed top-down unless you use parentheses to group set operations. The default order of precedence splices the first query result set with the second, and they become a master set that in turn is spliced by another set operator with a subsequent query. Here's a prototype with only a single table in the `FROM` clause:

```
SELECT column_list
FROM some_table
[WHERE some_condition [{AND | OR } some_condition [ ...]]]
[GROUP BY column_list]
[HAVING aggregation_function]
{INTERSECT | UNION | UNION ALL | MINUS}
SELECT column_list
FROM some_table
[WHERE some_condition [{AND | OR } some_condition [ ...]]]
[GROUP BY column_list]
[HAVING aggregation_function]
[ORDER BY column_list];
```

As qualified in the prototype, there are four set operators in SQL: `INTERSECT`, `UNION`, `UNION ALL`, and `MINUS`. The `INTERSECT` operator finds the intersection of two sets and returns a set of unique rows. The `UNION` set operator finds the unique set of rows, and returns them. The `UNION ALL` set operator finds and returns an unsorted merge of all rows from both queries, which results in two copies of any like rows. The MINUS set operator removes the rows in the second query from the rows of the first query where they match.

The following sections discuss the set operators in more depth and provide examples and use cases for them. They're organized in what is the general frequency of use.

Union

The UNION set operator acts like a union in set math and returns the unique things from two sets. This is a two step process: first it gathers the rows into one set and then it sorts them and returns the unique set. Figure 11-12 shows the Venn diagram for a UNION set operation, which looks exactly like a full outer join Venn diagram. The difference between the two is that a full outer join returns all the columns from two tables into one new and larger row, while the UNION merges one set of rows with another (matching set) uniquely.

The UNION set operator lets Oracle achieve a full outer join with its proprietary syntax. One query (A) gets the left join and the other query (B) gets the right join, and the UNION set operator sorts the non-unique row set and returns a unique set.

The code for an Oracle proprietary full outer join would look like this:

```
SQL> SELECT    m.account_number
  2  ,          c.last_name || ', ' || c.first_name AS customer_name
  3  FROM      member m, contact c
  4  WHERE     m.member_id = c.member_id(+)
  5  UNION
  6  SELECT    m.account_number
  7  ,          c.last_name || ', ' || c.first_name AS customer_name
  8  FROM      member m, contact c
  9  WHERE     m.member_id(+) = c.member_id;
```

The first query returns a left join, which is the inner join between the columns and the right relative complement (those things in the left table not found in the right table). The second query returns the right join. The right join holds a copy of the left relative complement and a second copy of the inner join result set. The UNION set operator sorts the non-unique set and discards the second copy of the inner join.

This is more or less the use case for the UNION set operator. You use it when you can't guarantee that the queries return exclusive sets of rows.

Union All

The UNION ALL set operator differs from the UNION set operator in one key way: it doesn't sort and eliminate duplicate rows. That's a benefit when you can guarantee that two queries return exclusive row sets, because a sorting operation requires more computing resources. The Venn

$$\forall A,B \mid A \cap B + (A \setminus B + B \setminus A)$$

FIGURE 11-12.   *Venn diagram for a UNION set operator*

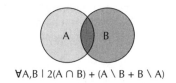

$$\forall A,B \mid 2(A \cap B) + (A \setminus B + B \setminus A)$$

FIGURE 11-13. *Venn diagram for* UNION ALL *operator*

diagram for a UNION ALL shown in Figure 11-13 looks remarkably like the one for a UNION. The difference is seen in the discrete math below the figure that indicates that it holds two copies of the intersection between the row sets.

The UNION ALL set operator is the preferred solution when you can guarantee that queries one and two return unique rows, which means there's no intersection. A symmetrical difference between two sets is the easiest way to demonstrate this set operator, because it is the combined results of the left and right relative complements. This means it doesn't include the intersection between two row sets.

```
SQL> SELECT    m.account_number
  2  ,         c.last_name || ', ' || c.first_name AS customer_name
  3  FROM      member m LEFT JOIN contact c
  4  ON        m.member_id = c.member_id
  5  WHERE     m.member_id IS NOT NULL
  6  UNION ALL
  7  SELECT    m.account_number
  8  ,         c.last_name || ', ' || c.first_name AS customer_name
  9  FROM      member m RIGHT JOIN contact c
 10  ON        m.member_id = c.member_id
 11  WHERE     c.member_id IS NOT NULL;
```

The first query (A) is a left join that excludes the inner join set, and the second query (B) is a right join that excludes the inner join set. It returns only the symmetric difference between the two row sets.

Intersect

The INTERSECT set operator returns only the unique rows found in two queries. It's useful when you want to find rows that meet the criteria of two different queries. The Venn diagram for the INTERSECT set operator shown in Figure 11-14 is exactly like that for the inner join. The only difference is one joins row sets and the other joins column sets.

$$\forall A,B \mid A \cap B = \{x \in A \cap B \mid x \in A \lor x \in B\}$$

FIGURE 11-14. *Venn diagram for* INTERSECT *operator*

While it might look like a lot of work to get the unique set of rows with an INTERSECT set operator, you can verify that the inner join between the member and contact table is the unique intersection of rows. The INTERSECT operator returns the rows that match between query one (A) and query two (B), which is the INNER JOIN between the two tables.

```
SQL> SELECT    m.account_number
  2  ,          c.last_name || ', ' || c.first_name AS customer_name
  3  FROM      member m LEFT JOIN contact c
  4  ON        m.member_id = c.member_id
  5  INTERSECT
  6  SELECT    m.account_number
  7  ,          c.last_name || ', ' || c.first_name AS customer_name
  8  FROM      member m RIGHT JOIN contact c
  9  ON        m.member_id = c.member_id;
```

This query returns the same set of information as an INNER JOIN between the *member* and *contact* table using the member_id column. The two relative complements are discarded because the collective values of all columns in the matching rows differ.

Minus

The MINUS set operator lets you subtract the matching rows of the second query from the first query. It allows you to find the symmetric difference between two sets, or the relative complement of two sets. Although you can accomplish both of these tasks without set operators by checking whether the joining columns aren't null, sometimes it's a better fit to use set operators to solve this type of problem.

The Venn diagram for the MINUS set operator shown in Figure 11-15 is different from those for JOIN statements because it excludes the intersection area. I was tempted to provide two examples in this section: one that subtracts the inner join from a full join and another that subtracts the cross join from the same full join. The result would be the same row set, because the only row matches between a full and inner join are the intersection rows, which is the same for a full and cross join. That's because the possible nonjoins in a Cartesian product aren't found in a full join result set.

Here's the full join minus the cross join:

```
SQL> SELECT    m.account_number
  2  ,          c.last_name || ', ' || c.first_name AS customer_name
  3  FROM      member m FULL JOIN contact c
  4  ON        m.member_id = c.member_id
  5  WHERE     m.member_id IS NOT NULL
  6  MINUS
  7  SELECT    m.account_number
  8  ,          c.last_name || ', ' || c.first_name AS customer_name
  9  FROM      member m CROSS JOIN contact c;
```

You always subtract a cross join from a full join when you want the symmetrical difference because it is less expensive than subtracting an inner join.

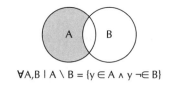

$$\forall A,B \mid A \setminus B = \{y \in A \wedge y \neg \in B\}$$

FIGURE 11-15. *Venn diagram for* MINUS *operator*

Views: Stored Queries

Views are stored queries. They can return a subset of one table or a superset of several tables.
They can include columns from tables or columns that are the result of expressions, such as string
operations, numeric or date math results, or calls to built-in or user-defined functions. Some
views are view only (read only) and others are updateable (read-write).

You create views much as you do other things in the database. The next two sections qualify
how you create views in Oracle and MySQL. As you'll see, there are some syntax differences.

Creating Oracle Views

Oracle supports ordinary views that are read-only or read-writeable. Here's the basic prototype
for creating a view in Oracle:

```
CREATE [OR REPLACE] [[NO] FORCE] VIEW view_name
[( column_name [inline_constraint] [, ...]
[,CONSTRAINT constraint_name
  UNIQUE (column_name) RELY DISABLE NONVALIDATE]
[,CONSTRAINT constraint_name
  PRIMARY KEY (column_list) RELY DISABLE NONVALIDATE]
AS select_statement
[WITH {READ ONLY | CHECK OPTION}]
```

The OR REPLACE clause is very helpful because you don't have to drop the previous view before
re-creating it with a new definition. Although NO FORCE is the default, FORCE tells the DBMS to
create the view even when the query references things that aren't in the database. This is handy
when you're doing a major upgrade, because you can run views concurrently with scripts that
change the definition of tables.

You can query the data catalog to find invalid views. This query returns a list of all invalid
views in a user's schema:

```
SQL> SELECT   object_name
  2  ,         object_type
  3  ,         status
  4  FROM      user_objects
  5  WHERE     status = 'INVALID';
```

A read-only view occurs when the query (SELECT statement) contains a subquery, collection
expression, selectivity operator (DECODE function or CASE operator), or DISTINCT operator in
the SELECT list; or when the query uses a join, set operator, aggregate function, or GROUP BY,

ORDER BY, MODEL, CONNECT BY, or START WITH clause. The last two clauses are hybrid Oracle clauses that support recursive queries. You can't write to base rows when views perform these types of operations. However, you can deploy INSTEAD OF triggers in Oracle that unwind the logic of the query and let you write to the base rows. Chapter 15 shows a simple example of an INSTEAD OF trigger.

The following is an example of a read-only view:

```
SQL> CREATE OR REPLACE VIEW employee_view
  2  ( employee_id
  3  , employee_name
  4  , employee_status
  5  , CONSTRAINT pk_employee
  6    PRIMARY KEY (employee_id) RELY DISABLE NOVALIDATE)
  7  AS
  8  SELECT    c.contact_id AS employee_id
  9  ,         c.last_name || ', ' || c.first_name ||
 10            CASE
 11              WHEN c.middle_name IS NULL
 12              THEN ' '
 13              ELSE ' '||c.middle_name
 14            END AS employee_name
 15  ,         CASE
 16              WHEN c.contact_type = common_lookup_id
 17              THEN 'Active'
 18              ELSE 'Inactive'
 19            END AS employee_status
 20  FROM      contact c INNER JOIN common_lookup cl
 21  ON        common_lookup_table = 'CONTACT'
 22  AND       common_lookup_column = 'CONTACT_TYPE'
 23  AND       common_lookup_type = 'EMPLOYEE';
```

Line 6 has a primary key constraint on employee_id, which maps inside the subquery to the primary key contact_id column for the contact table. The employee_name column is selectively concatenated from other columns in the contact table, and the employee_status column is fabricated through the combination of a JOIN and CASE operator. Since this is a read-only view, there would be no entry in the user_updatable_columns conceptual view.

A read-write trigger can contain derived columns or expressions, but you cannot write to those specific columns. The following creates a view with two derived columns:

```
SQL> CREATE OR REPLACE VIEW transaction_view AS
  2  SELECT    t.transaction_id AS id
  3  ,         t.transaction_account AS account
  4  ,         t.transaction_type AS purchase_type
  5  ,         t.transaction_date AS purchase_date
  6  ,         t.transaction_amount AS retail_amount
  7  ,         t.transaction_amount * .0875 AS sales_tax
  8  ,         t.transaction_amount * 1.0875 AS total
  9  ,         t.rental_id AS rental_id
 10  ,         t.payment_method_type AS payment_type
 11  ,         t.payment_account_number AS account_number
```

```
 12  ,              t.created_by
 13  ,              t.creation_date
 14  ,              t.last_updated_by
 15  ,              t.last_update_date
 16  FROM           transaction t;
```

Lines 7 and 8 contain results from a calculation based on column values multiplied by numeric constants. You can write to the base table through this view by providing an override signature that excludes the two derived columns. Chapter 8 discusses the mechanics of using override signatures in INSERT statements.

You can see which columns are updatable with the following query (formatted with SQL*Plus commands):

```
COLUMN column_name FORMAT A20
COLUMN updatable   FORMAT A9
SQL> SELECT    column_name
  2  ,          updatable
  3  FROM       user_updatable_columns
  4  WHERE      table_name = 'TRANSACTION_VIEW'
  5  AND        updatable = 'NO';
```

It would return the two derived columns, where the column names are the aliases assigned in the query:

```
COLUMN_NAME          UPDATABLE
-------------------- ---------
SALES_TAX            NO
TOTAL                NO
```

The WITH CHECK OPTION clause limits the rows that you can change with an UPDATE statement or DELETE FROM the table, by applying a rule that you can touch only those rows that you can see in the view. For example, login protocols often set the CLIENT_INFO value when they validate a user's privileges in a web application. Adding a WHERE clause on line 17 could limit the visible rows to those that match the value of the session's CLIENT_INFO value, like this:

```
 17  WHERE TO_NUMBER(NVL(SYS_CONTEXT('userenv','client_info'),-1)) = 0;
```

If a view becomes invalid, you can query the USER_DEPENDENCIES concept view. It shows you which dependencies are missing. Replacing the dependencies allows the next DML against the view to work.

The following query finds dependencies for a view:

```
SQL> SELECT    name
  2  ,          referenced_owner||'.'||referenced_name AS reference
  3  ,          referenced_type
  4  FROM       user_dependencies
  5  WHERE      type = 'VIEW'
  6  AND        name = 'view_name';
```

Views are powerful and complex. Although the views you've seen only store queries and rules, Oracle also supports materialized views, which are query results stored in the database.

The results in materialized views are often not current with the moment and can be hours or a day or more old. Materialized views are created when the cost of returning a result set is very high and places an inordinate load on the server during normal operational windows. Materialized views are often used in data marts and warehouses.

Creating MySQL Views

MySQL, like Oracle, supports ordinary views that are read-only or read-writeable. Here's the basic prototype for creating a view:

```
CREATE [OR REPLACE]
[ALGORITHM = {UNDEFINED | MERGE | TEMPTABLE}]
[DEFINER = { user | CURRENT_USER }]
[SQL SECURITY { DEFINER | INVOKER }]
 VIEW view_name
 [(column_list)]
 AS select_statement
 [WITH [{CASCADED | LOCAL}] CHECK OPTION]
```

Again, the OR REPLACE clause is helpful because you don't have to drop the previous view before re-creating it with a new definition. The OR REPLACE clause was added in MySQL 5.0.1. Several algorithm and security features are available with views. The ALGORITHM clause instructs the MySQL engine how to process the view; it's a SQL extension and UNDEFINED is the default option. The MERGE algorithm can't be used when a subquery exists in the SELECT list, an aggregate function is in the query, or a DISTINCT, GROUP BY, HAVING, LIMIT clause, or a UNION or UNION ALL set operator exists.

You can set the definer value of the view as a named user or as the current user, at least if you have super user privileges. CURRENT_USER is the default value for the CREATE VIEW statement. You can also define a view in a DEFINER or INVOKER mode of operations. The DEFINER mode means that the view runs with the privileges of the user who defined the view, and the INVOKER mode means that the view runs with the privileges of the user who calls the view. The WITH CHECK OPTION works as it does in Oracle, restricting updatable views only to those rows a user can see.

MySQL imposes several restrictions on views:

- There can be no subqueries in the SELECT list.
- The SELECT statement cannot refer to system or user variables—session variables.
- The SELECT statement cannot refer to prepared statement variables. (Prepared statements are covered in Chapter 14 and they are dynamic SQL statements.)
- The SELECT statement cannot refer to temporary tables or tables that haven't been created yet.
- You cannot associate a trigger with a view, which means there is no equivalent to an Oracle INSTEAD OF trigger.
- As of MySQL 5.0.52, column aliases have a maximum length of 64, not 256 like tables.

TIP
The ORDER BY inside a view is overridden when you put an ORDER BY clause in a query that calls an ordered view. As a rule, avoid ordering inside views.

A view can become obsolete when it refers to a table that was removed. The tables referenced in the FROM clause of a SELECT statement are dependencies for the view. When a DML statement against a view fails, you can use the CHECK TABLE statement to find out what dependency is missing. Here's the syntax:

```
CHECK TABLE current_rental;
```

A dependency table was dropped from the database to populate failure messages. Since the screen dump doesn't fit nicely on a page, the following list summarizes the three messages that appear when the studentdb database is missing the rental_item table:

- 'studentdb.rental_item' doesn't exist
- 'studentdb.current_rental' references invalid table(s) or column(s) or function(s) or definer/invoker of view lack rights to use them
- Corrupt

The first two explain that the table is missing, and because it's missing, the columns cannot be found. The last message says the view is corrupt; Oracle would report it as invalid.

The read-only view requires some modifications to run in MySQL, because it doesn't support constraints in a view and uses piped concatenation. Here's the modified view statement:

```
CREATE OR REPLACE VIEW employee_view
( employee_id
, employee_name
, employee_status )
AS
SELECT    c.contact_id AS employee_id
,         CONCAT(c.last_name,', ',c.first_name,
            CASE
              WHEN c.middle_name IS NULL
                THEN ' '
                ELSE CONCAT(' ',c.middle_name)
            END) AS employee_name
,         CASE
            WHEN c.contact_type = common_lookup_id
            THEN 'Active'
            ELSE 'Inactive'
          END AS employee_status
FROM      contact c INNER JOIN common_lookup cl
ON        common_lookup_table = 'CONTACT'
AND       common_lookup_column = 'CONTACT_TYPE'
AND       common_lookup_type = 'EMPLOYEE';
```

The read-write view works without any changes.

NOTE
Be careful when you incorporate user-defined functions in views, because they can invalidate views when the functions have different privileges than the views.

Summary

This chapter covered how you query results from tables and examined string concatenation, numeric, and date mathematics. It explored the various clauses of SELECT statements and the ways to filter result sets in the WHERE clause. The chapter also explored built-in Oracle and MySQL date functions; subqueries were also covered.

The chapter also covered how you perform joins between tables by splicing columns together into new record structures, and how you perform set operations between sets of rows. You should have learned the difference between cross, inner, left outer, right outer, and full outer joins, as well as the difference between the UNION, UNION ALL, INTERSECT, and MINUS set operators.

Mastery Check

The mastery check is a series of true or false and multiple choice questions that let you confirm how well you understand the material in the chapter. You may check the Appendix for answers to these questions.

1. **True** ☐ **False** ☐ A SELECT statement can concatenate strings.
2. **True** ☐ **False** ☐ A SELECT statement can add, subtract, multiply, and divide numbers to return derived results in the SELECT list.
3. **True** ☐ **False** ☐ Date mathematics work the same way in both Oracle and MySQL databases, because you can get yesterday's date by subtracting one from the current date.
4. **True** ☐ **False** ☐ A scalar subquery returns one to many columns and only one row of data.
5. **True** ☐ **False** ☐ An INNER JOIN can splice a set of columns from one table with a set of columns from another table based on a column that shares the same value.
6. **True** ☐ **False** ☐ A LEFT JOIN returns the INNER JOIN results plus everything in the left table of the join not found in the right table.
7. **True** ☐ **False** ☐ In MySQL, you can use the IF function to perform conditional operations.
8. **True** ☐ **False** ☐ In Oracle, you can use the DECODE function to perform conditional operations.
9. **True** ☐ **False** ☐ You use the UNION ALL set operator performs the exact same thing as a UNION set operator.
10. **True** ☐ **False** ☐ You can't filter results in the WHERE clause on negation of a comparison.
11. Which of the following returns a null and works as a subquery?
    A. A scalar subquery
    B. A single-row subquery
    C. A multiple-row subquery
    D. A correlated subquery
    E. None of the above

12. How many columns does a scalar subquery return?

   A. 1

   B. 2

   C. 3

   D. 4

   E. Many

13. What is the maximum number of rows you can update with a correlated subquery?

   A. 1

   B. 2

   C. 3

   D. 4

   E. Many

14. The MINUS set operator yields the symmetric difference in which of the following examples?

   A. The left join minus the right join

   B. The left join minus the inner join

   C. The right join minus the inner join

   D. The full join minus the cross join

   E. The full join minus the right join

15. Which clause holds the join between tables in ANSI SQL-92?

   A. The WHERE clause

   B. The GROUP BY clause

   C. The FROM clause

   D. The ORDER BY clause

   E. None, because the natural join principal always manages the process

CHAPTER
12

Merging Data

ometimes you need to insert new data and update existing data to relational tables during a bulk import of a physical file. You can accomplish this type of insert or update activity using a MERGE statement in Oracle and a REPLACE INTO statement in MySQL. MySQL also supports a merge operation with the ON DUPLICATE KEY clause of the INSERT statement (introduced in Chapter 7). This chapter covers these statements as methods for merging data in Oracle and MySQL.

Data import files often present interesting challenges, because they frequently contain rows of data that belongs in multiple tables (*denormalized data sets*). Import processes have to deal with this reality and discover the rules in order to break them up into normalized data sets. Only normalized data sets fit into the merge processes, because they work with single tables.

You need to understand why these files contain data from multiple tables. Although data modelers normalize information into single subject tables to avoid insertion, deletion, and update anomalies, analysts seldom use information in isolation. That's because the data is useful to them only when it's been assembled into information. Analysts typically apply business rules against data from a set of related tables. This means that they get these denormalized record sets from a query. As qualified in Chapter 11, queries let you assemble data into meaningful and actionable information, which makes the information as a whole greater than the sum of its data parts.

As developers of database-centric applications, we seldom have control over the origin of these files. Although it's not critical that we know where the files come from and why they're important, it can be helpful. Typically called *flat*, *loader*, or *batch import* files, these files are *import sources* that feed corrections and additions into our data repositories.

Import sources come from many places, such as business staff that sanitize data (analyzing data against business rules and fixing it) or other business partners. Business partners can be organizations within the corporation or company, or other companies with whom your company does business. The business staff sanitizing or exchanging data within the company are intra-company import sources. Intra-company imports can come from other IT organizations or from finance departments without professional IT staff. Those coming from other IT organizations are considered *business-to-business (B2B)* exchanges, and they package their outgoing files as export files. These export files support order management systems or financial systems. Professionally packaged export files are typically organized in an agreed upon XML (eXtensible Markup Language) or EDI (Electronic Data Interchange) formats.

Files coming from your company's internal finance, accounting, or operations departments are considered *consumer-to-business (C2B)* exchanges. That label works because the import files are typically comma-separated value (CSV) files from Microsoft Excel, which is what you would expect from a consumer (internal information consumer). These CSV files are typically managed by procedural programming interfaces.

This chapter demonstrates importing and merging data based on CSV and XML files on an *ad hoc* basis. The first section shows you how to use the MERGE statement and Oracle external tables as source files for the import source. You can flip back to Chapter 7 if you'd like to refresh your knowledge about external tables. The second section on MySQL shows you how to use the LOAD DATA and LOAD XML statements to get the values into a table, and then explains how to merge values with the REPLACE INTO statement and INSERT statement with the ON DUPLICATE KEY clause. You can flip back to Chapter 8 to read more about the INSERT statement than just its application demonstrated here.

Merging Data in Oracle

The MERGE statement in Oracle works similarly to the INSERT ALL statement presented in Chapter 8. It merges data from a query into a *target table* based on criteria evaluated in the ON subclause. The query in the subclause can be described as the *source result set*. The result set is like a virtual table, and virtual tables can be composed of data from multiple tables or a subset of data from one table. The results from a query can be thought of as the *source table*. The MERGE differs from the INSERT ALL statements because the WHEN clause only supports two logical conditions, MATCHED and NOT MATCHED, and the MERGE statement works with only one target table.

The MERGE statement has the following prototype:

```
MERGE INTO table_name
USING (select_statement) query_alias
ON ( condition_match [ {AND | OR } condition_match [...]] )
WHEN MATCHED THEN
update_statement
WHEN NOT MATCHED THEN
insert_statement;
```

Merging data from a source table to a target table requires that you know the columns that define the natural key of the target table, and in some cases the natural keys of all tables collapsed into the import source file. It also requires an outer join based on the natural key to ensure you always return the relative complement of the target table. The relative complement would be all the rows found in the source table that aren't found in the target table. The set of rows in the relative complement exists only when you're adding new rows from an import source file.

External data sets seldom have a copy of surrogate keys, because those columns aren't useful to analysts working with the data. The absence of surrogate keys means that you need to use the natural keys to determine how to get parts of the import source into their respective normalized tables. An outer join based on the natural key in the source query always returns a null value as the surrogate key. This is helpful for two reasons: the lack of a surrogate key identifies new rows, and surrogate keys can be auto-generated by available sequences.

You attempt a surrogate key match in the ON clause of a MERGE statement, and the ON DUPLICATE KEY clause of the INSERT statement assumes the same match when the surrogate key column is the table's primary key value. MySQL's REPLACE INTO statement performs a unique row match to find duplicates and inserts only new rows. New rows have a natural key that doesn't already exist in the table, and those are the only rows inserted by the REPLACE INTO statement.

Although not all import source files contain new rows, most do. The following sections contain the steps necessary for importing or modifying data through bulk uploads. Bulk imports are frequently accomplished through the use of externally organized tables, which were introduced in Chapter 6. An externally organized table is a table that points to a flat file (often a CSV file) deployed on the operating system. External tables in Oracle require that a DBA set up virtual directories and grants.

MySQL doesn't support externally organized tables, but it does support LOAD DATA and LOAD XML statements to reach out to the operating system and read a flat file into a table. Both databases require the system administrator to prepare and secure a directory in the operating system to support these flat files.

Step 1: Create a Virtual Directory

You must create at least one virtual directory to use external tables. Creating virtual directories and granting privileges to read and write to them are tasks reserved to the SYS or SYSTEM super user. The following lets a super user create an upload virtual directory and grant privileges to the student user to read and write to the directory:

```
CREATE DIRECTORY upload AS 'C:\import\upload';
GRANT READ, WRITE ON DIRECTORY upload TO student;
```

For this example, both read and write privileges are granted to the student user because the file needs to read the import source file and write log files from and to the same directory. Reading and writing files from the same virtual directory isn't recommended as a best practice, however. You should create badfile, discard, and log virtual directories to hold their respective output files, and then grant only read privilege to the upload directory. You should grant read and write privileges to the badfile, discard, and log virtual directories, especially if you're writing modules to let your business users confirm the upload of data.

Step 2: Position Your Physical CSV File

After you create the upload virtual directory in the import database, you need to create the physical directory in the file system of the server's operating system. Creating the physical directory after the virtual directory should help show you that a virtual directory's definition is independent of its physical directory. Virtual directories only store data that maps the virtual directory name to a physical directory, and they do not validate the existence of that location until you try to use it.

This example uses a kingdom_import.csv file that holds data for the kingdom and knight tables. The data in the file describe two epochs of the mythical kingdom of Narnia:

```
'Narnia',77600,'Peter the Magnificent','20-MAR-1272','19-JUN-1292',
'Narnia',77600,'Edmund the Just','20-MAR-1272','19-JUN-1292',
'Narnia',77600,'Susan the Gentle','20-MAR-1272','19-JUN-1292',
'Narnia',77600,'Lucy the Valiant','20-MAR-1272','19-JUN-1292',
'Narnia',42100,'Peter the Magnificent','12-APR-1531','31-MAY-1531',
'Narnia',42100,'Edmund the Just','12-APR-1531','31-MAY-1531',
'Narnia',42100,'Susan the Gentle','12-APR-1531','31-MAY-1531',
'Narnia',42100,'Lucy the Valiant','12-APR-1531','31-MAY-1531',
```

Notice that there are no surrogate key values in the data set. This means that the MERGE statement needs to provide them.

Step 3: Create Example Tables

You should now connect to the student schema in the database. As the student user, create two internally defined tables, the kingdom and knight tables; then create one externally defined table, the kingdom_knight_import table. The kingdom table is the parent and the knight table is the child in this relationship. This means a column in the knight table holds a foreign key that references (points back to) a column in the kingdom table. The kingdom_id column is the primary key in the kingdom table, and the kingdom_allegiance_id column holds the copy of the primary key value as a foreign key in the knight table.

Here's the CREATE TABLE statement for the kingdom table:

```
SQL> CREATE TABLE kingdom
  2  ( kingdom_id      NUMBER
  3  , kingdom_name    VARCHAR2(20)
  4  , population      NUMBER);
```

And here is its sequence:

```
CREATE SEQUENCE kingdom_s1;
```

Here's the CREATE TABLE statement for the knight table:

```
SQL> CREATE TABLE knight
  2  ( knight_id               NUMBER
  3  , knight_name             VARCHAR2(24)
  4  , kingdom_allegiance_id   NUMBER
  5  , allegiance_start_date   DATE
  6  , allegiance_end_date     DATE);
```

Here is its sequence:

```
CREATE SEQUENCE knight_s1;
```

Here is the CREATE TABLE statement for the kingdom_knight_import table:

```
SQL> CREATE TABLE kingdom_knight_import
  2  ( kingdom_name            VARCHAR2(8)
  3  , population              NUMBER
  4  , knight_name             VARCHAR2(24)
  5  , allegiance_start_date   DATE
  6  , allegiance_end_date     DATE)
  7    ORGANIZATION EXTERNAL
  8    ( TYPE oracle_loader
  9      DEFAULT DIRECTORY upload
 10      ACCESS PARAMETERS
 11      ( RECORDS DELIMITED BY NEWLINE CHARACTERSET US7ASCII
 12        BADFILE      'UPLOAD':'kingdom_import.bad'
 13        DISCARDFILE  'UPLOAD':'kingdom_import.dis'
 14        LOGFILE      'UPLOAD':'kingdom_import.log'
 15        FIELDS TERMINATED BY ','
 16        OPTIONALLY ENCLOSED BY '"'
 17        MISSING FIELD VALUES ARE NULL )
 18      LOCATION ('kingdom_import.csv'))
 19    REJECT LIMIT UNLIMITED;
```

There is no sequence for an external table. Recall that there is also no surrogate key in the data set or the definition of this externally managed table. (You can find more about externally managed tables in Chapter 6.)

Step 4: Test Configuration

You should be able to query from the externally managed table after the first three steps have completed successfully. This query should return eight rows:

```sql
SQL> SELECT    kingdom_name AS kingdom
  2  ,          population
  3  ,          knight_name
  4  ,          TO_CHAR(allegiance_start_date,'DD-MON-YYYY') AS start_date
  5  ,          TO_CHAR(allegiance_end_date,'DD-MON-YYYY') AS end_date
  6  FROM       kingdom_knight_import;
```

You should get the following data set if it works:

```
KINGDOM   POPULATION KNIGHT_NAME             START_DATE  END_DATE
--------  ---------- ---------------------- ----------- -----------
Narnia         77600 Peter the Magnificent  20-MAR-1272 19-JUN-1292
Narnia         77600 Edmund the Just        20-MAR-1272 19-JUN-1292
Narnia         77600 Susan the Gentle       20-MAR-1272 19-JUN-1292
Narnia         77600 Lucy the Valiant       20-MAR-1272 19-JUN-1292
Narnia         42100 Peter the Magnificent  12-APR-1531 31-MAY-1531
Narnia         42100 Edmund the Just        12-APR-1531 31-MAY-1531
Narnia         42100 Susan the Gentle       12-APR-1531 31-MAY-1531
Narnia         42100 Lucy the Valiant       12-APR-1531 31-MAY-1531
```

An error like the following occurs when you failed in setting up the physical directory or file, the virtual directory, or the grant of permissions:

```
SELECT    kingdom_name
*
ERROR at line 1:
ORA-29913: error in executing ODCIEXTTABLEOPEN callout
ORA-29400: data cartridge error
KUP-04040: file kingdom_import.csv in UPLOAD not found
```

You need to fix whatever piece is broken before continuing.

CAUTION
Oracle assumes that any physical directory is on the local system disks. It is possible that you could run into the error shown in the example if the physical directory is a virtual directory itself.

Step 5: Merge the Import Source

Merges work with one table at a time, and they must start with the least dependent table. The `kingdom` table is the one without dependencies and should be the first table where you merge data. In a real situation, the `MERGE` statements would be bundled into a stored procedure and wrapped in Transaction Control Language (TCL) commands to make sure both statements worked or failed. TCL would require a `SAVEPOINT` before the first `MERGE` statement and a `COMMIT` after the last `MERGE` statement, and the following should appear in an exception handler in the event one `MERGE` statement failed:

```sql
ROLLBACK TO savepoint_name;
```

The following MERGE statement reads data from the externally managed kingdom_knight_ import table and performs a LEFT JOIN operation between a copy of the target and source tables:

```
SQL>   MERGE INTO kingdom target
  2    USING
  3     (SELECT DISTINCT
  4            k.kingdom_id
  5     ,      kki.kingdom_name
  6     ,      kki.population
  7      FROM  kingdom_knight_import kki LEFT JOIN kingdom k
  8      ON    kki.kingdom_name = k.kingdom_name
  9      AND   kki.population = k.population) SOURCE
 10    ON (target.kingdom_id = SOURCE.kingdom_id)
 11    WHEN MATCHED THEN
 12    UPDATE SET kingdom_name = SOURCE.kingdom_name
 13    WHEN NOT MATCHED THEN
 14    INSERT VALUES
 15    ( kingdom_s1.NEXTVAL
 16    , SOURCE.kingdom_name
 17    , SOURCE.population);
```

The only time line 4 returns a kingdom_id value from the kingdom table is when the row already exists. The row can exist only when the natural key values match, which means the surrogate keys on line 10 also match. The UPDATE statement on line 12 doesn't change anything, because when line 10 matches, the kingdom_name column values also match on line 8. The INSERT statement on lines 14–17 runs when there is no match between the natural keys. Notice that the INSERT statement excludes a target table name, because it works with the target table of the MERGE statement. The source values in the INSERT statement come from the relative complement of the kingdom table (non-matching natural keys or new data). These are new rows from the import source file. Check Chapters 6 and 11 if you have any questions on how outer joins work.

The merge should report the number of rows merged, which might exceed the number of new rows inserted into the table. You confirm the number of rows inserted with the following query:

```
SQL> SELECT * FROM kingdom;
```

It returns the following:

```
KINGDOM_ID KINGDOM_NAME          POPULATION
---------- -------------------- ----------
         1 Narnia                    42100
         2 Narnia                    77600
```

Note that the ON subclause should use the natural key, and the nested UPDATE statement must SET a column not found in the ON clause. Changing line 12 from kingdom_name to kingdom_id raises this error message:

```
ON (target.kingdom_id = SOURCE.kingdom_id)
    *
```

```
ERROR at line 9:
ORA-38104: Columns referenced in the ON Clause cannot be updated:
"TARGET"."KINGDOM_ID"
```

The second MERGE statement can work only when there are matching rows in the kingdom table for new rows in the import source file. That's why it performs an INNER JOIN operation between the kingdom and kingdom_knight_import tables before it performs an outer join against the knight table.

Here is the second MERGE statement:

```
SQL> MERGE INTO knight target
  2  USING
  3   (SELECT kn.knight_id
  4   ,       k.kingdom_id
  5   ,       kki.knight_name
  6   ,       kki.allegiance_start_date
  7   ,       kki.allegiance_end_date
  8    FROM   kingdom_knight_import kki INNER JOIN kingdom k
  9    ON     kki.kingdom_name = k.kingdom_name
 10    AND    kki.population = k.population LEFT JOIN knight kn
 11    ON     k.kingdom_id = kn.kingdom_allegiance_id
 12    AND    kki.knight_name = kn.knight_name
 13    AND    kki.allegiance_start_date = kn.allegiance_start_date
 14    AND    kki.allegiance_end_date = kn.allegiance_end_date) source
 15  ON (target.knight_id = source.knight_id)
 16  WHEN MATCHED THEN
 17  UPDATE SET target.knight_name = source.knight_name
 18  WHEN NOT MATCHED THEN
 19  INSERT
 20  ( knight_id
 21  , knight_name
 22  , kingdom_allegiance_id
 23  , allegiance_start_date
 24  , allegiance_end_date)
 25  VALUES
 26  ( knight_s1.NEXTVAL
 27  , source.knight_name
 28  , source.kingdom_id
 29  , source.allegiance_start_date
 30  , source.allegiance_end_date);
```

Although it works like the last MERGE statement, the query that provides the source uses an INNER JOIN operator to confirm that a matching kingdom exists. It checks whether a new knight exists in the import source only when a valid kingdom for that knight exists. The matching criterion on line 15 is the surrogate key value of the knight table. This is the same rule as for the prior MERGE statement.

Lines 20–24 show an overriding signature for the INSERT statement. Other than the absence of a target table name, the INSERT statement works as it does on its own. (For more on overriding signatures for INSERT statements, see Chapter 8.) A query for this data set requires a couple of SQL*Plus formatting commands to make it fit nicely here in the book, like so:

```
COLUMN knight_id      FORMAT 999 HEADING "Knight|ID #"
COLUMN knight_name FORMAT A22 HEADING "Knight Name"
COLUMN kingdom_allegiance_id FORMAT 999 HEADING "Allegiance|ID #"
COLUMN allegiance_start_date FORMAT A9 HEADING "Start|Date"
COLUMN allegiance_end_date FORMAT A9 HEADING "End|Date"
```

The query would be as follows:

```
SQL> SELECT * FROM knight;
```

and the knight table should yield the following rows:

```
Knight                           Allegiance Start     End
   ID # Knight Name                   ID # Date      Date
------ --------------------- ---------- --------- ---------
     1 Peter the Magnificent          2 20-MAR-72 19-JUN-92
     2 Edmund the Just                2 20-MAR-72 19-JUN-92
     3 Susan the Gentle               2 20-MAR-72 19-JUN-92
     4 Lucy the Valiant               2 20-MAR-72 19-JUN-92
     5 Peter the Magnificent          1 12-APR-31 31-MAY-31
     6 Edmund the Just                1 12-APR-31 31-MAY-31
     7 Susan the Gentle               1 12-APR-31 31-MAY-31
     8 Lucy the Valiant               1 12-APR-31 31-MAY-31
```

At the end of this step, you see the results from the kingdom and knight tables. There should be two rows in the kingdom table for two epochs of Narnia and eight rows in the knight table for the two visits by the four Pevensie children, who become kings and queens in this mythical land (at least in the first two books).

A verification of the ability to merge data can be achieved by adding a single row to the kingdom_import.csv file, which would give it this extra line for Caspian X:

```
'Narnia',40100,'Caspian X','31-MAY-1531','30-SEP-1601',
```

Rerunning the MERGE statements, you would see one row added to previous two rows in the kingdom table, and one row added to the previous eight rows in the knight table. The UPDATE clause of the statement assigns the existing knight_id surrogate key value back to the same column, which results in no net change.

Merging Data in MySQL

You merge data in MySQL with an INSERT statement that uses the ON DUPLICATE KEY clause or a REPLACE INTO statement. The MySQL INSERT statement with the ON DUPLICATE KEY clause is the closest to the MERGE statement in Oracle because it can validate on a natural key. While the REPLACE INTO statement also accomplishes a merge, it doesn't use a natural key comparison. The REPLACE INTO statement performs an elimination of duplicate rows based on a unique key.

Unlike Oracle, MySQL doesn't support externally managed tables. In lieu of external tables, MySQL lets you import sources through the LOAD DATA statement or export data with a SELECT statement and an INTO OUTFILE clause. Both import and export data processes are covered in the first of the following three subsections. The subsequent sections cover examples of using both merge approaches: the INSERT statement with the ON DUPLICATE KEY clause and the REPLACE INTO statement.

Import and Export Data Processes

MySQL lets you input data from plain text files with the LOAD DATA statement and export data to plain text files with a SELECT statement with the INTO OUTFILE clause. The SELECT statement also supports the output of XML tagged data, and when combined with the INTO OUTFILE clause, the SELECT statement can export table data into XML files. Import sources can now also be XML files because of the LOAD XML statement added in MySQL 5.5.

Importing Data in MySQL

Some of the LOAD DATA statement options can be confusing until you understand the rules governing how you should use this statement. These options work differently based on whether you create a constrained or an unconstrained import table. The import table takes the place of the externally managed table in the Oracle technology example—you grab the data from the import table to move it into the normalized tables.

An unconstrained table is the default for externally managed tables in Oracle. Although that approach might seem fine in MySQL because it works with Oracle's external tables and MERGE statement, it's not workable in MySQL—at least, it's not workable unless you always clean up the previously imported data by truncating the table or deleting all rows from the last merge. That's because the LOAD DATA statement adds everything in the import source to the target table unless you've specified a unique or primary key for the target table.

When you've specified a unique or primary key, the LOAD DATA statement replaces the row where the key columns match with a new row or ignores the new row in the import source. Ignoring the row is safe when non-key columns won't change between imports, but it is unsafe when non-key columns might change. Fortunately, the default is the REPLACE option in the LOAD DATA statement, which means changes in import source rows replace existing rows when the key matches.

Here is the prototype for the LOAD DATA statement:

```
LOAD DATA [{LOW_PRIORITY | CONCURRENT}] [LOCAL] INFILE 'file_name'
[{REPLACE | IGNORE}] INTO TABLE [database_name.]table_name
[PARTITION (partition_name [,...])]
[CHARACTER SET characterset_name]
[{FIELDS | COLUMNS}
 [TERMINATED BY 'character']
 [[OPTIONALLY] ENCLOSED BY 'character']
 [ESCAPED BY 'character']]
[LINES
 [STARTING BY 'character']
 [TERMINATED BY 'character']]
[IGNORE number LINES]
[({table_column_name | session_variable} [, {...}])]
[SET table_column_name = expression [,...]]
```

Only super users, or those users to whom a super user grants a global privilege such as FILE, can run the LOAD DATA statement. The minimum privileges required for a user to run the LOAD DATA statement are the global FILE privilege and the INSERT privilege on the target table.

You would grant the global `FILE` privilege with the following syntax:

```
GRANT FILE ON *.* TO user_name;
```

Users without the global `FILE` privilege can include the `LOCAL` keyword to run a file from the computer where they're running MySQL Monitor. MySQL Monitor is the client software for the database and can be run on a remote client or on the server where the database is running. Sometimes `LOCAL` behavior is disallowed by the DBA because of its security implications, and when it is disallowed you get the following error:

```
ERROR 1148 (42000): The used command is not allowed with this MySQL version
```

This error means that you'll find the following setting in your `my.ini` (Windows) or `my.cnf` (Linux) file in the `[mysqld]` section:

```
local-infile=0
```

You can reset the `local-infile` parameter to 1 or remove it from the configuration file. Then, you'll need to stop and start the MySQL server for the new setting to take effect. The `LOCAL` parameter doesn't present security restrictions, but does allow you to import data from a client machine where you're running MySQL Monitor. This provides tremendous control to developers over flat files that might contain company-sensitive information. As a rule, you don't want to craft a process in which you load bulk data from remote machines, because this is insecure and can place an inordinate load on your network bandwidth. The best practice is to run imports through specialized users that can access MySQL only from the (`localhost`) server.

Like many DML statements in MySQL, the `LOAD DATA` statement lets you specify *low priority* or *concurrent* threaded operations. A low priority operation means that the `INSERT` statement waits until no queries are pending against the table; concurrent operations work with MyISAM files by dividing the insert into threads, which can perform concurrent insert operations. Concurrency works provided there are no free disk blocks between the two concurrent insertion loci (points of inserts). You can also override the default character set by providing one of your own choosing.

The `REPLACE` and `IGNORE` options provide instructions to the `LOAD DATA` statement that govern behavior when the import target table has a unique or primary key. The default raises an exception when a duplicate key is encountered, stops processing, and raises the following error:

```
ERROR 1062 (23000): Duplicate entry 'duplicate_row' for key 'key_name'
```

The `REPLACE` option replaces the row when the key values match a row in the target table, and it inserts a new row when they don't match. The `IGNORE` disables the replacing behavior and simply ignores import source rows when the key values match a row in the target table.

As mentioned, you should ensure that all import target tables have a unique or primary key. Without such a key, the `LOAD DATA` command simply adds values to the target table without avoiding duplication. You should place that unique or primary key on the natural key columns of the table, because flat files don't typically store surrogate key values.

The `PARTITION` clause is new in MySQL 5.6.2. It lets you specify a list of partitions for the data load. If a failure in loading one partition occurs, it causes the entire statement to fail.

`FIELDS` represent literal values or variables, and `COLUMNS` represent columns in the `SELECT` list of a query. Note another syntax nuance when you use a query inside an `INSERT` statement with the `ON DUPLICATE KEY` clause: You can't assign an alias to the result set as you would with an inline view, and you must refer to the column name using a fully qualified reference to

`SELECT` list columns. A fully qualified reference includes a table name or alias from the query, a dot, and the column name.

The `FIELDS TERMINATED BY` clause refers to the character that separates field or column values. Typically, this is a comma (,) in CSV files, but sometimes it's a tab (represented by a backslash and lowercase letter t [\t]) when the source file is a tab-separated value (TSV) file. The tab is the default value for the `TERMINATED BY` clause when you don't provide an override value. Table 12-1 shows a list of special metacharacters and their escape sequence values.

The `ENCLOSED BY` clause is optional, and using the `OPTIONAL` keyword before the `ENCLOSED BY` phrase is rarely done. The default for `ENCLOSED BY` is an empty string, and excluding the clause is equivalent to entering this:

```
ENCLOSED BY ''
```

Double quotes (") is the most common overriding value for the `ENCLOSED BY` clause and would be entered like so:

```
ENCLOSED BY '"'
```

The backslash (\) character is the default value for the `ESCAPED BY` clause. You would assign a backslash like this:

```
ESCAPED BY '\\'
```

By default, the `STARTING BY` clause is an empty string, and the `LINES TERMINATED BY` clause is a newline (metacharacter \n) character. You should use these defaults in a Linux system. In Windows, using a combination of a newline and carriage return (metacharacters \n\r) is required, because that's how the platform's software writes line returns. The exception to that rule is the Microsoft WordPad application that writes only a newline character.

NOTE
The default LINES TERMINATED BY value is \n because it is designed to run on a Linux system.

Metacharacter	Escape Sequence
\0	An ASCII NUL (0x00) character
\b	A backspace character
\n	A newline (linefeed) character
\r	A carriage return character
\t	A tab character
\z	An ASCII 26 (CTRL-Z) file close character
\N	A NULL

TABLE 12-1. *Escape Characters*

The second `IGNORE` option in the `LOAD DATA` statement has to do with skipping header lines at the top of an import source file. You would use this to skip two header lines in the import source file:

```
IGNORE 2 LINES
```

TIP
Use \n\r to terminate lines on the Windows platform because that's how Microsoft's operating system writes line returns.

The column list at the end of the statement allows you to override the definition of the table and import only mandatory columns. You can also override an import source field with a local session variable. The last choice is the `SET` option, which lets you assign a value to a column from an expression. A key restriction on the `SET` option is that you can't use values from the import source file.

It seems best to provide a quick example here (others are provided in the "Merging with the INSERT Statement" and "Merging with the REPLACE INTO Statement" sections). This example uses the `IGNORE n LINES` option for a header in the source file, an overriding column list, and the `SET` option.

The first step is to define the `employee` table, like this:

```
CREATE TABLE employee
( name           VARCHAR(20) PRIMARY KEY
, salary         DECIMAL(8,2)
, bonus          DECIMAL(8,2)
, upload_date    DATETIME);
```

Stage a file on the server with a two-row header. For this example, the file is placed in the `C:\Data\Upload` directory:

```
Employee Name,Salary
-------------,--------
"Harry James",52121.82,
"Sally Fields",54234.22,
```

To use the `SET` option with a calculation, you need to define a session variable:

```
SET @rate = .05;
```

The last step is to import the source file into the table with this statement:

```
LOAD DATA INFILE 'c:/Data/mysql/employee.csv'
REPLACE INTO TABLE employee
FIELDS TERMINATED BY ','
ENCLOSED BY '"'
ESCAPED BY '\\'
LINES TERMINATED BY '\r\n'
IGNORE 2 LINES
( name, salary )
SET bonus = 1000 * @rate
,    upload_date = NOW();
```

A query against the employee table shows two rows:

```
+--------------+----------+-------+---------------------+
| name         | salary   | bonus | upload_date         |
+--------------+----------+-------+---------------------+
| Harry James  | 52121.82 | 50.00 | 2011-06-26 22:01:42 |
| Sally Fields | 54234.22 | 50.00 | 2011-06-26 22:01:42 |
+--------------+----------+-------+---------------------+
```

As you can tell, the import process offers you some nice options for text-based files. The LOAD XML statement extends those behaviors for XML files.

Here is the LOAD XML statement prototype, which is available starting in MySQL 5.5:

```
LOAD XML [{LOW_PRIORITY | CONCURRENT}] [LOCAL] INFILE 'file_name'
[{REPLACE | IGNORE}] INTO TABLE [database_name.]table_name
[PARTITION (partition_name [,...])]
[CHARACTER SET characterset_name]
[ROWS IDENTIFIED BY '<xml_tag_name>']
[IGNORE number [LINES | ROWS]]
[({table_column_name | session_variable} [, {...}])]
[SET table_column_name = expression [,...]]
```

The clauses of the LOAD XML statement are a subset of those found in the LOAD DATA statement. The single exception is the ROWS IDENTIFIED BY clause, which maps the root node of an XML structure. If no value is specified in this clause, ROW is the assumed XML tag name for root nodes.

Leveraging the employee table from the prior example, the following example shows you how to load an XML file. The import source file must be changed from a CSV to an XML file, like this:

```
<?xml version="1.0"?>
<list>
  <name>Harry James</name>
  <salary>52121.82</salary>
</list>
<list>
  <name>Sally Fields</name>
  <salary>54234.22</salary>
</list>
```

This example uses an overriding column list and the SET option, which means you need to set the session variable:

```
SET @rate = .05;
```

Here's the LOAD XML statement that works with these:

```
LOAD XML INFILE 'c:/Data/mysql/employee.xml'
INTO TABLE employee
ROWS IDENTIFIED BY '<list>'
( name, salary )
```

```
SET bonus = 1000 * @rate
,   upload_date = NOW();
```

A query of the table yields these rows:

```
+--------------+----------+-------+---------------------+
| name         | salary   | bonus | upload_date         |
+--------------+----------+-------+---------------------+
| Harry James  | 52121.82 | 50.00 | 2011-06-26 22:50:50 |
| Sally Fields | 54234.22 | 50.00 | 2011-06-26 22:50:50 |
+--------------+----------+-------+---------------------+
```

You've now seen how to load flat files (CSVs) and XML files. The next section shows you how to extract data from a MySQL database into an external file.

Exporting Data from MySQL

Unlike Oracle's spooling feature, MySQL lets you configure and format files in a specialized SELECT statement. It takes the column values from the SELECT list and puts them into the external file. The statement uses the same formatting clauses as the LOAD DATA statement, but instead of striping delimiters it puts them into the data set.

Here's the prototype for the SELECT INTO OUTFILE statement:

```
SELECT [column_name1 [,column_name2 [,...]]] INTO OUTFILE file_name
[CHARACTER SET characterset_name]
[TERMINATED BY 'character']
[[OPTIONALLY] ENCLOSED BY 'character']
[ESCAPED BY 'character']
[TERMINATED BY 'character']
FROM file_name
WHERE [condition1 {AND | OR} condition2 [{AND | OR} ...]];
```

Applying the syntax to the employee table that was populated by the LOAD DATA statement earlier, you can query the data and put it in an employee.txt file. The following statement returns all columns from the employee table (provided the user has the global FILE privilege and operating system write privileges to the directory):

```
SELECT * INTO OUTFILE 'c:/Data/mysql/employee.txt'
FIELDS TERMINATED BY ','
ENCLOSED BY '"'
ESCAPED BY '\\'
LINES TERMINATED BY '\r\n'
FROM employee;
```

And here is the contents of the employee.txt file that was generated by the SELECT INTO OUTFILE statement:

```
"Harry James","52121.82","50.00","2011-06-26 23:18:02"
"Sally Fields","54234.22","50.00","2011-06-26 23:18:02"
```

Merging with the INSERT statement

The `INSERT INTO` statement in MySQL works very much like the `MERGE` statement in Oracle. You can override the default signature of the table by providing a list of at least all mandatory columns. This list is the override signature for the `INSERT` statement, as discussed in Chapter 8.

The prototype for the `INSERT INTO` statement with an `ON DUPLICATE KEY` clause is:

```
INSERT INTO table_name
[(column_name_list)]
{VALUES (value_list) [,(value_list) [,(...)]] | (select_statement)}
ON DUPLICATE KEY UPDATE update_list;
```

After the optional column list, you must choose whether you use a `VALUES` clause with a list of values or a subquery. Recall that you don't include the `VALUES` clause when you provide a subquery to an `INSERT` statement. The `INSERT` statement supports multiple value lists, as it does without the `ON DUPLICATE KEY` clause. The `UPDATE` should include those things that might change, such as non-key column values.

The following subsections show you how to merge values in the `kingdom` and `knight` tables using the `INSERT INTO` statement with the `ON DUPLICATE KEY` in a MySQL database. It takes one fewer step in MySQL than in the Oracle process, because MySQL doesn't support virtual directories. MySQL also doesn't support externally managed tables, and you'll see how to use the `LOAD DATA` statement to grab an external CSV file.

Step 1: Position Your Physical CSV File

As with the preceding examples, you should put the `kingdom_mysql_import.csv` file in the `C:\Data\MySQL` directory. You'll need to modify the coding examples if you use a different directory. The file differs from the Oracle example file in only one way: the dates use the MySQL default date format mask. This makes the upload work smoothly.

Here's the content of the file:

```
Narnia, 77600,'Peter the Magnificent',12720320,12920609
Narnia, 77600,'Edmund the Just',12720320,12920609
Narnia, 77600,'Susan the Gentle',12720320,12920609
Narnia, 77600,'Lucy the Valiant',12720320,12920609
Narnia, 42100,'Peter the Magnificent',15310412,15310531
Narnia, 42100,'Edmund the Just',15310412,15310531
Narnia, 42100,'Susan the Gentle',15310412,15310531
Narnia, 42100,'Lucy the Valiant',15310412,15310531
```

Step 2: Create Example Tables

Connect to the MySQL server and choose a database in which you will work. Then create the three tables for this example. The first table is a temporary table using the Memory database engine, because it should exist only during the import session. Here's the `CREATE TEMPORARY TABLE` statement:

```
CREATE TEMPORARY TABLE kingdom_knight_import
( kingdom_name          VARCHAR(20)
, population            INT UNSIGNED
, knight_name           VARCHAR(24)
, allegiance_start_date DATE
```

```
, allegiance_end_date    DATE
, CONSTRAINT import
  UNIQUE ( kingdom_name
         , population
         , knight_name
         , allegiance_start_date
         , allegiance_end_date )) ENGINE=MEMORY;
```

Notice that the table is created with a unique key, which ensures that duplicate records won't be loaded twice. It's clearly not a perfect natural key, but it works to support the data set for the problem. The unique key qualifies the natural key of the two subjects in the import table: the kingdom and knight subjects. The kingdom_name and population columns are the natural key of the kingdom table, while the other three columns in the unique key qualify the natural key of the knight table.

The target tables are normal tables, assuming this is a real model. You would use CREATE TABLE statements to build them (shown a bit later). They both use surrogate keys that are populated by auto-incrementing sequence values, and they specify being built using the InnoDB engine (a precaution for anybody testing in an MyISAM database).

As stated, MySQL doesn't support external tables. This means you need to load the import source into the import table. The following LOAD DATA statement loads the source file into the kingdom_knight_import table, which is a mirror to the external file's structure.

```
LOAD DATA INFILE 'c:/Data/mysql/kingdom_mysql_import.csv'
REPLACE INTO TABLE kingdom_knight_import
FIELDS TERMINATED BY ','
ENCLOSED BY '"'
ESCAPED BY '\\'
LINES TERMINATED BY '\r\n';
```

The REPLACE clause ensures that duplicate rows are never inserted into the import table. Any duplicate row would raise an exception when the REPLACE or IGNORE option is excluded from the LOAD DATA statement.

After staging the import data into a database table, you need to create the two normalized tables where you're going to put the final data sets. This CREATE TABLE statement creates the kingdom table, which is the parent table in the relationship between the two tables. Here's the syntax:

```
CREATE TABLE kingdom
( kingdom_id     INT UNSIGNED PRIMARY KEY AUTO_INCREMENT
, kingdom_name   VARCHAR(20)
, population     INT UNSIGNED
, CONSTRAINT unique_kingdom
  UNIQUE ( kingdom_name, population )) ENGINE=INNODB;
```

The next statement creates the knight table. As the child table in the relationship, it also includes a foreign key constraint to the kingdom table. The foreign key maps the link between the kingdom_id and kingdom_allegiance_id columns. Here's the syntax:

```
CREATE TABLE knight
( knight_id            INT UNSIGNED PRIMARY KEY AUTO_INCREMENT
, knight_name          VARCHAR(24)
```

```
, kingdom_allegiance_id INT UNSIGNED
, allegiance_start_date DATE
, allegiance_end_date   DATE
, CONSTRAINT import
  UNIQUE ( knight_name
         , population
         , kingdom_allegiance_id
         , allegiance_start_date
         , allegiance_end_date )
, CONSTRAINT fk_kingdom FOREIGN KEY (kingdom_allegiance_id)
  REFERENCES kingdom (kingdom_id)) ENGINE=INNODB;
```

You don't need sequences, because they're properties of tables where one column holds the AUTO_INCREMENT keyword. The unique keys in these tables prevent the INSERT INTO statement with an ON DUPLICATE KEY clause from adding the same row more than once.

Step 3: Test Configuration
At this point, you can query the results from the kingdom_knight_import table. It should contain the eight rows from the external file. This query formats the output into a single page:

```
mysql> SELECT   kingdom_name AS "Kingdom"
    -> ,        population AS "Citizens"
    -> ,        knight_name AS "Knight's Name"
    -> ,        allegiance_start_date AS "Start Date"
    -> ,        allegiance_end_date AS "End Date"
    -> FROM     kingdom_knight_import;
```

It should return the following:

```
+---------+----------+-------------------------+------------+------------+
| Kingdom | Citizens | Knight's Name           | Start Date | End Date   |
+---------+----------+-------------------------+------------+------------+
| Narnia  |    77600 | 'Peter the Magnificent' | 1272-03-20 | 1292-06-09 |
| Narnia  |    77600 | 'Edmund the Just'       | 1272-03-20 | 1292-06-09 |
| Narnia  |    77600 | 'Susan the Gentle'      | 1272-03-20 | 1292-06-09 |
| Narnia  |    77600 | 'Lucy the Valiant'      | 1272-03-20 | 1292-06-09 |
| Narnia  |    42100 | 'Peter the Magnificent' | 1531-04-12 | 1531-05-31 |
| Narnia  |    42100 | 'Edmund the Just'       | 1531-04-12 | 1531-05-31 |
| Narnia  |    42100 | 'Susan the Gentle'      | 1531-04-12 | 1531-05-31 |
| Narnia  |    42100 | 'Lucy the Valiant'      | 1531-04-12 | 1531-05-31 |
+---------+----------+-------------------------+------------+------------+
```

If you didn't get the right results, revisit the steps and fix what's missing. Make sure that you didn't try to reuse the Oracle import source, because the default date formats differ between the two files.

Step 4: Merge from the Import Source
The import source in MySQL is an internally managed table that mirrors the import source file's structure. You loaded the data from the external file into the table with the LOAD DATA statement in Step 2.

Before examining how a query can load all the relevant data from the `kingdom_knight_` `import` table, you will see how a `VALUES` clause works in this `INSERT` statement. This example uses string and numeric literal values inside the `VALUES` clause and loads one of the two Narnia rows into the `kingdom` table:

```
INSERT INTO kingdom
(kingdom_name, population)
VALUES
('Narnia',77600)
ON DUPLICATE KEY
UPDATE kingdom_id = kingdom_id;
```

The statement uses an overriding signature and inserts only the second and third columns of the table. The `INSERT` statement updates the `kingdom_id` column with the current row's column value when a duplicate row is found, and it inserts a row when no other row is found that shares the unique key values.

You could query the table after the `INSERT` statement, and you should see this:

```
+------------+---------------+------------+
| kingdom_id | kingdom_name | population |
+------------+---------------+------------+
|          1 | Narnia       |      77600 |
+------------+---------------+------------+
```

The next `INSERT` statement works with two rows of literal values in the `VALUES` clause. The statement inserts only one new row, because the first row is already inserted by the previous statement.

The syntax for a list of rows in the `VALUES` clause is shown here:

```
INSERT INTO kingdom
(kingdom_name, population)
VALUES
('Narnia',77600),('Narnia',42100)
ON DUPLICATE KEY
UPDATE kingdom_id = kingdom_id;
```

The results now contain these two rows:

```
+------------+---------------+------------+
| kingdom_id | kingdom_name | population |
+------------+---------------+------------+
|          1 | Narnia       |      77600 |
|          2 | Narnia       |      42100 |
+------------+---------------+------------+
```

The `ON DUPLICATE KEY` clause combined with unique key (index) on the `kingdom` table prevented a reload of the first row of data. Both rows could have been loaded with a query from the internal import source table, like this:

```
INSERT INTO kingdom
( kingdom_id, kingdom_name, population )
```

```
( SELECT    DISTINCT
            k.kingdom_id
  ,         kki.kingdom_name
  ,         kki.population
  FROM      kingdom_knight_import kki LEFT JOIN kingdom k
  ON        kki.kingdom_name = k.kingdom_name
  AND       kki.population = k.population )
  ON DUPLICATE KEY
  UPDATE kingdom_id = k.kingdom_id;
```

Although not necessary, because the query provides values for all columns defined in the kingdom table, the column list qualifies the column names of the target table of the INSERT statement. The LEFT JOIN operator returns the right relative complement or every row from the table on the left of the operator and matching rows from the table on the right or null values. That means you get all rows from kingdom_knight_import and all rows from the kingdom table, or null values. In this scenario, the null values map to the kingdom_id column for those rows returned as the right relative complement (or new rows not found in the kingdom table). Since the kingdom_id column is an auto-incrementing column, MySQL automatically assigns the next sequence value to the table when it receives a null value in an auto-incrementing column.

If you had deleted all rows from the table before running the preceding INSERT statement, it would insert two rows: one row for each unique combination of the kingdom_name and population columns not found in the kingdom table. It wouldn't insert any new rows if both columns matched the result sets previously returned by the query.

The k.kingdom_id provided in the UPDATE clause is required, because the subquery can't have an alias, and the column definition must match exactly with a column returned by the SELECT list of the query. The match requires that you use any alias provided inside the subquery and dot notation that precedes the column name (like kn.knight_id).

After you've inserted values in the kingdom table, you can insert values in the knight table. Any row returned from the query that fails to match the kingdom_id primary key value with the kingdom_allegiance_id foreign key values is excluded from the result set. This behavior enforces referential integrity between the two tables.

The query in the following statement secures the (surrogate) foreign key from the parent table through the aforementioned join and returns null values for the knight_id column when inserting new knights:

```
INSERT INTO knight
( SELECT    kn.knight_id
  ,         kki.knight_name
  ,         k.kingdom_id
  ,         kki.allegiance_start_date AS start_date
  ,         kki.allegiance_end_date AS end_date
  FROM      kingdom_knight_import kki INNER JOIN kingdom k
  ON        kki.kingdom_name = k.kingdom_name
  AND       kki.population = k.population LEFT JOIN knight kn
  ON        k.kingdom_id = kn.kingdom_allegiance_id
  AND       kki.knight_name = kn.knight_name
  AND       kki.allegiance_start_date = kn.allegiance_start_date
  AND       kki.allegiance_end_date = kn.allegiance_end_date )
  ON DUPLICATE KEY
  UPDATE knight_id = kn.knight_id;
```

You should see that the column list isn't necessary and isn't provided. That means the list of column values returned by the query must match against the data catalog definition of the `knight` table, and it does. As mentioned in the preceding `INSERT` statement, the `kn.knight_id` value in the `UPDATE` clause must match exactly with a column returned by the `SELECT` list of the subquery.

Merging with the REPLACE INTO Statement

The `REPLACE INTO` statement in MySQL works like the `MERGE` statement in Oracle with a key difference: there's no `ON` subclause. The `REPLACE INTO` statement sorts the target data set, determines whether a matching row exists, and inserts source rows when they're new. More or less, it performs similar to a `UNION ALL` operation on the two sets followed by a `MINUS` operation. The `MINUS` operation subtracts the existing rows in the target table from the new source result set. See Chapter 11 for more on how set operators work.

Here's the prototype of the `REPLACE INTO` statement:

```
REPLACE INTO table_name
( select_statement );
```

Like the Oracle `MERGE` statement, you need to know the columns that define the natural key of the target table for the `REPLACE INTO` statement. The natural key is the basis of the join between the target and source tables in the nested `SELECT` statement. Also, the final join to the target table in the nested query must be an outer join, because that's the only way to find the new rows and return a sequence generated surrogate key value. The new rows are the relative complement of the existing rows.

Step 1: Position Your Physical CSV File

Because you should have provisioned the `kingdom_mysql_import.csv` file in the `C:\Data\MySQL` directory earlier, there's no need to repeat the instructions here.

Step 2: Create Example Tables

These tables should already exist in the database (if you followed the steps earlier in the chapter). You should also have run the `LOAD DATA` statement to move the import source file contents into an internally managed table. If you skipped these steps, do them now.

You should delete the rows from the `knight` and `kingdom` tables, like this:

```
TRUNCATE TABLE knight;
TRUNCATE TABLE kingdom;
```

Removing the data from the tables should avoid confusion as to whether something worked using this or the prior section's syntax. Next, you'll test your configuration.

Step 3: Test Configuration

Rather than flip back at this point, you can query the results from the `kingdom_knight_import` table and determine whether they're correct. This is the same query used earlier, and it formats the output into a single page:

```
mysql> SELECT    kingdom_name AS "Kingdom"
    ->  ,        population AS "Citizens"
    ->  ,        knight_name AS "Knight's Name"
    ->  ,        allegiance_start_date AS "Start Date"
    ->  ,        allegiance_end_date AS "End Date"
    -> FROM      kingdom_knight_import;
```

It should return the following:

```
+---------+----------+-------------------------+------------+------------+
| Kingdom | Citizens | Knight's Name           | Start Date | End Date   |
+---------+----------+-------------------------+------------+------------+
| Narnia  |    77600 | 'Peter the Magnificent' | 1272-03-20 | 1292-06-09 |
| Narnia  |    77600 | 'Edmund the Just'       | 1272-03-20 | 1292-06-09 |
| Narnia  |    77600 | 'Susan the Gentle'      | 1272-03-20 | 1292-06-09 |
| Narnia  |    77600 | 'Lucy the Valiant'      | 1272-03-20 | 1292-06-09 |
| Narnia  |    42100 | 'Peter the Magnificent' | 1531-04-12 | 1531-05-31 |
| Narnia  |    42100 | 'Edmund the Just'       | 1531-04-12 | 1531-05-31 |
| Narnia  |    42100 | 'Susan the Gentle'      | 1531-04-12 | 1531-05-31 |
| Narnia  |    42100 | 'Lucy the Valiant'      | 1531-04-12 | 1531-05-31 |
+---------+----------+-------------------------+------------+------------+
```

As with the prior section's instructions, revisit the setup steps and fix what's missing if you don't see this data. Is it possible that you truncated this table when you removed the data from the target tables?

Step 4: Merge from the Import Source

Like the example of the INSERT statement with the ON DUPLICATE KEY clause, this example works with an internally managed table that mirrors the import source file's structure. The first example uses a REPLACE INTO statement with a distinct subquery (one returning a unique row set); the subquery performs an outer join between the import and target tables:

```
REPLACE INTO kingdom
( kingdom_id, kingdom_name, population )
(SELECT   DISTINCT
          k.kingdom_id
,         kki.kingdom_name
,         kki.population
FROM      kingdom_knight_import kki LEFT JOIN kingdom k
ON        kki.kingdom_name = k.kingdom_name
AND       kki.population = k.population);
```

Notice that this is the same LEFT JOIN that is used in the INSERT statement of the preceding example. It also uses a fully qualified target list, although one isn't required because the query's columns align themselves with the definition of the kingdom table.

The next REPLACE INTO statement performs a match between the kingdom and knight tables before an outer join against the kingdom_knight_import table. It is also the same query shown in the equivalent INSERT ON DUPLICATE KEY statement.

```
REPLACE INTO knight
(SELECT   kn.knight_id
,         kki.knight_name
,         k.kingdom_id
,         kki.allegiance_start_date AS start_date
,         kki.allegiance_end_date AS end_date
FROM      kingdom_knight_import kki INNER JOIN kingdom k
ON        kki.kingdom_name = k.kingdom_name
AND       kki.population = k.population LEFT JOIN knight kn
ON        k.kingdom_id = kn.kingdom_allegiance_id
```

```
AND        kki.knight_name = kn.knight_name
AND        kki.allegiance_start_date = kn.allegiance_start_date
AND        kki.allegiance_end_date = kn.allegiance_end_date);
```

Many developers prefer the `REPLACE INTO` statement over the `INSERT ON DUPLICATE KEY` statement for imports. They work more or less the same way, but the `INSERT ON DUPLICATE KEY` statement is more similar to the Oracle `MERGE` statement, and it makes the logic more portable between databases.

Summary

This chapter discussed how you import data in Oracle and MySQL databases. It showed you the process of leveraging external import sources through external files in Oracle and through the `LOAD DATA` and `LOAD XML` statements in MySQL.

Sample programs showed you how to take denormalized import source files and merge them into relational tables. You also learned how you can use the Oracle `MERGE` statement and the `INSERT ON DUPLICATE KEY` and `REPLACE INTO` statements in conjunction with outer joins to merge data with existing tables.

Mastery Check

The mastery check is a series of true or false and multiple choice questions that let you confirm how well you understand the material in the chapter. You may check the Appendix for answers to these questions.

1. **True** ☐ **False** ☐ In Oracle, you use external tables to import data from CSV files.

2. **True** ☐ **False** ☐ MySQL supports external files with the `LOAD LOCAL DATA INFILE` statement.

3. **True** ☐ **False** ☐ The definition of an external table relies on the ability to create virtual directories.

4. **True** ☐ **False** ☐ You need to grant only `READ ON DIRECTORY` privileges to read external data and write error log files.

5. **True** ☐ **False** ☐ The `ON` clause in an external table definition sets the criteria for whether or not you should insert or update records.

6. **True** ☐ **False** ☐ You can update columns used to evaluate joins in the `ON` clause of a subquery.

7. **True** ☐ **False** ☐ You can load XML files with the `LOAD DATA` statement.

8. **True** ☐ **False** ☐ You can load XML files with the `LOAD XML` statement.

9. **True** ☐ **False** ☐ The `INSERT ON DUPLICATE KEY` statement supports a multiple row `VALUES` clause.

10. **True** ☐ **False** ☐ The `REPLACE INTO` statement works only with a subquery.

11. Which of the following isn't a valid option of the `MERGE` statement in Oracle?

    A. The `OPTIONALLY ENCLOSED BY` option

    B. The `ACCESS PARAMETERS` option

    C. The `FIELDS TERMINATED BY` option

    D. The `ROWS IDENTIFIED BY` option

    E. The `DEFAULT DIRECTORY` option

12. Which of the following isn't a valid option of the `LOAD DATA` statement in MySQL?

    A. The `LINES TERMINATED BY` option

    B. The `ENCLOSED BY` option

    C. The `FIELDS TERMINATED BY` option

    D. The `ROWS IDENTIFIED BY` option

    E. The `ESCAPED BY` option

13. Which of the following isn't a valid option of the `LOAD XML` statement in MySQL?

    A. The `LINES TERMINATED BY` option

    B. The `ENCLOSED BY` option

    C. The `FIELDS TERMINATED BY` option

    D. The `ROWS IDENTIFIED BY` option

    E. The `ESCAPED BY` option

14. Which of the following options or clauses enables a `LOAD DATA` statement to replace the values of non-key columns?

    A. A `REPLACE` option

    B. An `IGNORE` option

    C. An `IGNORE` *n* `LINES` option

    D. An `IGNORE` *n* `ROWS` option

    E. An `ESCAPED BY` clause

15. The target table of an `INSERT ON DUPLICATE KEY` statement requires which of the following?

    A. A primary key constraint

    B. A foreign key constraint

    C. An index

    D. A non-unique key

    E. None of the above

CHAPTER
13

PL/SQL Programming Language

racle introduced the PL/SQL programming language more than 20 years ago in the Oracle 6 database. PL/SQL provides a procedural extension to SQL and lets you call SQL from a PL/SQL program, or vice versa. This chapter introduces you to the basics of writing stored programs in Oracle 11*g* and provides a summary overview of PL/SQL. You can find more complete treatment in *Oracle Database 11g PL/SQL Programming*.

Chapter 4 showed you the concept of transactional units built with combinations of INSERT, UPDATE, and DELETE statements. It also introduced Transactional Control Language (TCL). With PL/SQL, you bring the two together to write powerful database-centric programs.

In this chapter you'll learn the basics of writing PL/SQL programs. The chapter covers the following topics:

- PL/SQL blocks and stored programs
- PL/SQL variables
- PL/SQL control structures
- Bulk operations
- Native Dynamic SQL (NDS)
- Exception handling

As you read through these sections, remember that PL/SQL is a strongly typed language. Strongly typed languages constrain how you assign or compare values of different data types. PL/SQL borrows its block syntax from the Ada and Pascal programming languages. It's a natural fit with SQL, which is probably why MySQL stored procedures look so much like PL/SQL.

The PL/SQL assignment operator (:=) makes writing PL/SQL assignments straightforward. It also eliminates any confusion between the assignment operator and comparison operator (=) in PL/SQL. This differs from the mixed model of assignment operators in SQL/PSM, as you'll see in Chapter 14.

PL/SQL Blocks

PL/SQL blocks come in two types: *anonymous* (or unnamed) and *named* blocks. Anonymous block programs have a fixed scope, while named blocks are more extensible resources. Named blocks are stored programs in an Oracle database.

You can use anonymous block programs in scripts or nested inside other program units. They have scope only in the context of the program unit or script where you put them. You can't call anonymous blocks from other blocks by name, because they haven't got a name. All variables are passed to these local blocks by reference, which is the default in PL/SQL's scope model. This means an anonymous block program unit can reference any variables in the external or calling scope. The single exception to this rule occurs when you declare a local variable that replaces a calling scope variable.

You can store named block programs directly as functions or procedures in a schema. These functions and procedures are schema-level named programs. Their scope is the most flexible for three reasons: You can call them from the schema where they're defined. Alternatively, you can call them from another schema that's been granted the *execute* privilege on the named program unit. Lastly, you can call schema-level programs across a DB_LINK. DB_LINKs support calls between two database instances across the network. Schema-level named programs present an interesting comparative paradigm, because they act as public access methods in the scope of the schema but protected access methods in the scope of the database.

Beyond schema level functions and procedures, you can create packages, which consist of a package specification and a body. These are containers for groups of related functions and procedures. You can store named block programs inside packages in two ways: One way requires that you publish the package function or procedure. You do this by defining the function or procedure specification inside the package specification. This makes package functions and procedures callable from other programs in the same schema or from other programs in schema where other users have the *execute* privilege on the package. These are package functions and procedures. They're closest to static methods with a protected access scope. You can also store functions and procedures exclusively in package bodies. This limits them to internal package access only, and you call these package-level programs *units*. They're most like private access methods in object-oriented languages such as Java.

You can store named block programs inside user-defined types (UDTs). Like named block programs inside packages, you can deploy these as published or unpublished methods. You can also make these static or instance methods. Static methods are available without an existing instance, while instance methods require that you first create an instance of the UDT in memory. Static methods act like package functions and procedures, while instance methods act like object type functions and procedures.

Finally, you can store named block programs inside the declaration block of anonymous or named block programs. These named block programs are known as *local* named block programs. You can call them only from within the scope of their host program. They can't see other locally named programs unless these other programs are declared before the local programs in the same runtime scope. You can fix this by adopting forward references before declaring local functions. A *forward reference* is a stub for a named block. The stub includes the subroutine name, parameter list, and any return type. Local named blocks are like package-level program units or private access methods in object-oriented languages such as Java.

Table 13-1 qualifies all the delimiters, including the operators, you will see in PL/SQL. Short examples are provided where possible.

Anonymous Blocks

Here is the basic prototype for an anonymous block PL/SQL program:

```
[DECLARE]
  declaration_statements
BEGIN
  execution_statements
[EXCEPTION
  exception_statements]
END;
/
```

Symbol	Type	Description
:=	Assignment	The *only assignment operator* used in PL/SQL. You assign a right operand to a left operand, like so: `a := b + c;` This adds the numbers in variables b and c, and then assigns the result to variable a. The addition occurs before the assignment due to operator precedence.

:	Association	The *host variable indicator* precedes a valid identifier name and designates that identifier as a session-level variable, also known as a *bind variable*, that can be defined with SQL*Plus. Only the CHAR, CLOB, NCHAR, NCLOB, NUMBER, NVARCHAR2, REFCURSOR, and VARCHAR2 data types are available for session variables. Here's the prototype:
		`VARIABLE variable_name datatype_name`
		This example implements the prototype by creating a session-level variable length string:
		`SQL> VARIABLE my_string VARCHAR2(30)`
		You can then assign a value using an anonymous block PL/SQL program:
		`BEGIN`
		`   :my_string := 'A string literal.';`
		`END;`
		`/`
		You can then query the result from the `dual` pseudo table:
		`SELECT :my_string FROM dual;`
		or reuse the variable in another PL/SQL block program, because the variable enjoys a session-level scope. A subsequent anonymous block program in a script could then print the value in the session variable:
		`BEGIN`
		`   dbms_output.put_line(:my_string);`
		`END;`
		`/`
		This is a flexible way to exchange variables between multiple statements and PL/SQL blocks in a single script file.

&	Association	The *substitution indicator* lets you pass actual parameters into anonymous block PL/SQL programs. Never assign substitution variables inside declaration blocks, because assignment errors don't raise an error that you can catch in your exception block. Make substitution variable assignments in the execution block. This example demonstrates the assignment of a string substitution variable to a local variable in an execution block: `A := '&string_in';`

TABLE 13-1. *PL/SQL Delimiters*

Symbol	Type	Description
%	Association	The *attribute indicator* lets you link a database catalog column, row, or cursor attributes. You anchor a variable data type when you link a variable to a catalog object such as a table or column. The "Composite Variable Types" section later in the chapter examines how to anchor variables to database catalog items with this operator.
=>	Association	Use the *association operator* in name notation function and procedure calls.

.	Association	The *component selector* glues references together—such as a schema and table, package and function, or object and member method. It is also used to link cursors and cursor attributes (columns). Here are some prototype examples:
		`schema_name.table_name`
		`package_name.function_name`
		`object_name.member_method_name`
		`cursor_name.cursor_attribute`
		These are referenced throughout this chapter.

@	Association	Use the *remote access indicator* to access a remote database through database links.
||	Concatenation	Use the *concatenation operator* to glue strings together: `a := 'Glued'||' '||'together.';`
=	Comparison	The *comparison operator* tests for equality of value and implicitly does type conversion where possible. There is no identity comparison operator, because PL/SQL is a strongly typed language. PL/SQL comparison operations are equivalent to identity comparisons, because you can compare only like-typed values.
–	Comparison	The *negation operator* changes a number from its positive to negative value.
<> != ^=	Comparison	Three *not-equal comparison operators* perform exactly like behaviors. You can use whichever suits your organizational needs.
>	Comparison	This *inequality comparison operator* indicates that the left operand is greater than the right operand.
<	Comparison	This *inequality comparison operator* indicates that the left operand is less than the right operand.
>=	Comparison	This *inequality comparison operator* indicates that the left operand is greater than or equal to the right operand.

TABLE 13-1.   *PL/SQL Delimiters* (continued)

Symbol	Type	Description
<=	Comparison	This *inequality comparison operator* indicates that the left operand is less than or equal to the right operand.
'	Delimiter	Use the *character string delimiter* to define a string literal value. You can assign a string literal to a variable a, `a := 'A string literal.';` to create a string literal from the set of characters between the character string delimiters.
(	Delimiter	Use the *opening expression* or *list delimiter* to place a list of comma-delimited numeric or string literals or identifiers inside parentheses. Use parentheses to enclose formal and actual parameters to subroutines, or to produce lists for comparative evaluations.
)	Delimiter	The *closing expression* or *list delimiter*. See the opening expression or list delimiter entry for more information.
,	Delimiter	The *item separator* delimits items in lists.
<<	Delimiter	Use the *opening delimiter* for labels in PL/SQL. Labels are any valid identifiers in the programming language.
>>	Delimiter	Use the *closing delimiter* for labels in PL/SQL.
--	Delimiter	With the *single comment operator*, everything to the right is treated as text and not parsed as part of a PL/SQL program. Here's an example: `-- This is a single line comment.`

/*	Delimiter	Use the *opening multiple-line comment delimiter* for comments; it instructs the parser to ignore everything until it reaches the closing multiple-line comment delimiter. Here's an example:
		`/* This is line one.`
		`   This is line two. */`
		You can format multiple line comments in many ways; choose one way that suits your organization's purposes and stick with it.

*/	Delimiter	The *closing multiple-line comment delimiter* instructs the parser that the text comment is complete, and everything after it should be parsed as part of the program unit.

TABLE 13-1. *PL/SQL Delimiters* (continued)

Symbol	Type	Description

"	Delimiter	Use the *quoted identifier delimiter* to access tables created in case-sensitive fashion from the database catalog. This is required with database catalog objects created in a case-sensitive way and is applicable from Oracle 10*g* forward. This example creates a case-sensitive table or column by using quoted identifier delimiters:
		`CREATE TABLE "Demo"`
		`("Demo_ID"   NUMBER`
		`, demo_value VARCHAR2(10));`
		Insert a row by using this quote-delimited syntax:
		`INSERT INTO "Demo1" VALUES`
		`(1,'One Line ONLY.');`
		Like the SQL syntax, PL/SQL requires the quoted identifier delimiter to find the database catalog object:
		`BEGIN`
		`  FOR i IN (SELECT   "Demo_ID", demo_id`
		`            FROM     "Demo") LOOP`
		`    dbms_output.put_line(i."Demo_ID");`
		`    dbms_output.put_line(i.demo_id);`
		`  END LOOP;`
		`END;`
		`/`
		You must refer to any column names by using quote delimited syntax in the first output line, where the loop index (`i`) is followed by the component selector (`.`), and then a quote delimited identifier (`"Demo_ID"`). No quotes are required to access the case-insensitive column. If you forget to enclose a case-sensitive column name (identifier), your program returns a PLS-00302 error that says the identifier is not declared.
		You can also use this delimiter to build identifiers that include reserved symbols, such as an `"X+Y"` identifier.

+	Math	Use the *addition operator* to add a left and right operand and return a result.
/	Math	Use the *division operator* to divide a left operand by a right operand and return a result.

TABLE 13-1. *PL/SQL Delimiters* (continued)

Symbol	Type	Description
**	Math	The *exponential operator* raises a left operand to the power designated by a right operand. This operator is given the highest precedence for math operators in the language. As a result, a fractional exponent must be enclosed in parentheses (also known as expression or list delimiters) to designate order of operation. Without parentheses, the left operand is raised to the power of the numerator and the result divided by the denominator of a fractional exponent. You raise 3 to the third power and assign the result of 27 to variable a by using the following syntax: `a := 3**3;` You raise 8 to the fractional power of 1/3 and assign the result of 2 to variable a by using the following syntax: `a := 8**(1/3);` The parentheses ensure that the division operation occurs first. Exponential operations take precedence over other mathematical operations without parenthetical grouping.
*	Math	Use the *multiplication operator* to multiply a left operand by a right operand and return a result.
-	Math	Use the *subtraction operator* to subtract the right operand from the left operand and return a result.
;	Statement	The *statement terminator* must be included to close any statement or block unit.

TABLE 13-1. *PL/SQL Delimiters* (continued)

The DECLARE statement starts the optional declaration block. The BEGIN statement ends any declaration block and begins the execution block. The optional EXCEPTION statement may end the execution block; the END statement ends either the execution or optional exception block.

Prototypes are great, but they don't show you how to implement the code. You'll now see how to write a simple *Hello World* anonymous block program in PL/SQL. You can run the command from a file, the SQL*Plus command line, SQL*Developer, or a commercial tool developed for Oracle 11*g*, such as Quest's Toad.

CAUTION
Tools are great when you understand what they do and dangerous when you don't. Make sure you know how to use a tool and understand what it does before you employ it.

As mentioned in Chapter 2, most programmers use tools, but the command line is the closest environment to what you'll embed in C#, C++, Java, or PHP programs. Anonymous PL/SQL blocks can be embedded in your application code just like SQL statements. Throughout this book, we use display code and code interactions at the command line.

Static Anonymous Block

Two small details can cause you grief in PL/SQL. The first is that as a strongly blocked language, it requires you to include at least a single statement in each and every block. The second detail is that you'll need to manage output from your PL/SQL programs by enabling a SQL*Plus formatting environment variable SERVEROUTPUT.

For example, the following might look like a complete program, but it isn't. It doesn't have at least one statement in the block to make it work:

```
SQL> BEGIN
  2   END;
  3   /
```

You might wonder why a forward slash (/) is included on the line below the program unit since there's a semicolon after the END. The semicolon terminates the anonymous block and a forward slash executes the program by sending it to the PL/SQL runtime engine. This program fails with the following error, which basically says it got to the end of the block without finding a single statement:

```
END;
*
ERROR at line 2:
ORA-06550: line 2, column 1:
PLS-00103: Encountered the symbol "END" when expecting one of the following:
begin case declare exit for goto if loop mod null pragma
raise return select update while with <an identifier>
<a double-quoted delimited-identifier> <a bind variable> <<
close current delete fetch lock insert open rollback
savepoint set sql execute commit forall merge pipe
```

The minimal programming unit for an anonymous block includes one statement in the execution block. Conveniently, PL/SQL provides a null statement. You can use null statements in blocks to make sure you have basic block control logic correct before you write detailed block logic. Here's the smallest working anonymous block program.

```
SQL> BEGIN
  2      NULL;
  3   END;
  4   /
```

You'll want to remember this, because if you don't, it can cost you many fruitless hours of debugging.

You didn't need the SQL*Plus environment variable SERVEROUTPUT in this basic block test, because nothing was being output from the program. The *Hello World* program requires that you output a line of text, and that means you must enable SERVEROUTPUT before running your PL/SQL block.

TIP
The effective use of the null statement can help you organize and develop code faster by creating the blocks first and logic second.

As mentioned in Chapter 2, if you "fat finger" something while typing a SQL or PL/SQL statement, you can start over by pressing three keys: ENTER for a line return, a period, and then ENTER again to add another line return to abort your active statement.

The *Hello World* program prints text by calling a stored procedure from a standard package in the Oracle database. The DBMS_OUTPUT.PUT_LINE call is more or less similar to echo in scripting languages or the System.out.println() static method call in Java. Moreover, this is PL/SQL's way of sending messages to standard out (STDOUT). Standard out is the output stream of a programming envirnonment and it typically prints text to the console (monitor). You can also redirect standard out to send text to a file. This standard out treatment in PL/SQL is substantially different from MySQL, where you can simply select something and display it from a stored procedure. As discussed in Chapter 14, that technique isn't possible in MySQL functions, and debugging them is much more complex than it should be. Oracle supports the same standard out management in all blocks.

The process of running a *Hello World* program looks like this:

```
SQL> SET SERVEROUTPUT ON SIZE UNLIMITED
SQL> BEGIN
  2    dbms_output.put_line('Hello World.');
  3  END;
  4  /
```

It prints this:

```
Hello World.
```

Reserved words and keywords in Oracle are case-insensitive. We've chosen to follow the most common use case for capitalization. This should more-or-less mimic what you'd find in any Generic Syntax Highlighter (GeSHi) editor. String literals in PL/SQL are enclosed by single quotes (apostrophes), as they are in SQL. String literals between the quotes are case-sensitive, and you back-quote a single quote with another single quote. Unlike MySQL, where single and double quotes are interchangeable, Oracle uses only single quotes to delimit strings.

This section demonstrates how to handle output, but that's it. The *Hello Somebody* program in the next section shows you how to handle both input and output from an anonymous program.

Dynamic Anonymous Block

The *Hello Somebody* program prints text by calling the same stored procedure from the *Hello World* program. This section focuses on how input parameters work in PL/SQL anonymous block program units. Input parameters are unknowns before they arrive at any program. This is a crucial fact.

You need to plan for both good and bad input parameters. This can be tricky, because a declaration block acts like a header file does in a C or C++ program. Your exception block can't capture runtime errors in the declaration block. The program simply fails with an unhandled exception. In this section, you'll learn how to avoid this forever by always making assignments in the execution block. The trick revolves around your understanding what it means to *define* a variable versus *declare* a variable.

You define a variable by assigning it a name and data type. You declare a variable by defining it and assigning it a value. In some programming languages, assignment is called *initialization*. The rule of thumb on whether you call it one or the other depends on the data type. You typically assign

The Assignment Model and Language

All programming languages assign values to variables. They typically assign a value from the right to a variable on the left. The following pattern assigns the right operand to the left operand in PL/SQL:

```
left_operand := right_operand;
```

The left operand must always be a variable. The right operand can be a value, variable, or function. Functions must return a variable value when they're right operands and are often called *expressions*. This makes functions return values synonymous with expressions. Notice that no SET statement is required to make an assignment, as is required in MySQL stored programs.

The trick here is that only functions returning a SQL data type can be called in SQL statements. Functions returning PL/SQL data types work only inside PL/SQL blocks, and then only in PL/SQL scope (that's exclusively within the PL/SQL engine).

values to scalar variables. Scalar variables hold the value of only one thing and are primitives in Java. On the other hand, you initialize object types. The key object types in Oracle are collections and user-defined object types. Object types are also known as *composite* data types because they can contain multiple things. You'll find more on initializing these composite data types in the "Composite Variable Types" section later in this chapter.

You assign input parameters to anonymous block programs by using substitution variables. SQL*Plus supports the use of substitution variables, which are prefaced by an ampersand (&), in the interactive and batch console. Substitution variables are variable-length strings or numbers. You should never assign dynamic values in the declaration block.

The following program defines a variable, assigns it a value, and prints it:

```
SQL> DECLARE
  2    lv_whom VARCHAR2(30);
  3  BEGIN
  4    lv_whom := '&input';
  5    dbms_output.put_line('Hello '|| lv_whom ||'.');
  6  END;
  7  /
```

You might not notice the single quotes around the substitution variable, but they're critical. When the program is run without a valid string value and no quotes, the engine parses over the null value and excludes the right operand in an assignment. The program would throw a PLS-00103 exception because there is no right operand, whereas the engine interprets two single quotes without anything between them as a null string (at least in Oracle this is an implicit assignment of a null value to a string data type).

Notice that no example here includes the assignment being made in the declaration block. That would be bad coding practice. By extension, you should avoid assigning actual parameters to local variables in their declaration blocks. Otherwise, your code might fail at runtime because in functions and procedures formal parameters have no size constraints in PL/SQL.

Although constants aren't really too useful in anonymous block programs, this is a great place to show you the syntax. The CONSTANT reserved word is placed between the variable name and the data type. You must declare a constant in your declaration block, which means it is both defined and assigned an *immutable* value.

The preceding anonymous block is recycled to include a constant on line 2, as follows:

```
SQL> DECLARE
  2    lv_hello CONSTANT VARCHAR2(5) := 'Hello';
  3    lv_whom VARCHAR2(30);
  4  BEGIN
  5    lv_whom := '&input';
  6    dbms_output.put_line(lv_hello ||' '|| lv_whom ||'.');
  7  END;
  8  /
```

An alternative method for processing interactive session-level variables involves what Oracle calls *bind* variables. You preface bind variables with a colon (:) inside a PL/SQL block. You can define bind variables in the scope of a SQL*Plus session. In that scope, only the CHAR, CLOB, NCHAR, NCLOB, NUMBER, NVARCHAR2, REFCURSOR, and VARCHAR2 data types are available. The term "bind variable" also applies to the handling of placeholders in Native Dynamic SQL (NDS) and for read-write hooks into the database Private Global Area (PGA). You also use read-write hooks to manage large objects (LOBs) and read hooks to read reference cursors.

You can create SQL*Plus session variables by using the VARIABLE keyword. Like the example with substitution variables, you should never assign values to bind variables in the declaration block.

The following program defines a session-level bind variable, similar to the example in Chapter 2. The colon doesn't precede the definition of the variable in the session. You use the colon only inside the PL/SQL program scope. This allows the PL/SQL runtime engine to reach out and access the variable in the SQL*Plus session scope. You use a PL/SQL block to assign a value

Reserved Words and Keywords

You can't really find a perfect source for reserved words and keywords. A careful review of the documentation in Oracle Database 11*g* sources reveals it is imperfect. You can type the following at a SQL*Plus prompt for a fairly accurate list of PL/SQL reserved words:

```
SQL> HELP RESERVED WORDS (PL/SQL)
```

There's no equivalent `help` command for keywords. You can query the V$RESERVED_WORDS view, which appears out-of-date for a partial list. If you leave the parenthetical (PL/SQL) off the `help` command, SQL*Plus will return both SQL and PL/SQL reserved words. Perhaps we'll get clarity on these in a subsequent release of the database. Chapter 2 introduced these concepts.

to the bind variable. Then you can access the bind variable from any subsequent program for the duration of the connected session.

```
SQL> VARIABLE bv VARCHAR2(30)
SQL> BEGIN
  2    :bv := 'Sam';
  3  END;
  4  /
```

After assigning a value to the session-level bind variable, you can use it as a right operand:

```
SQL> DECLARE
  2    lv_whom VARCHAR2(30);
  3  BEGIN
  4    lv_whom := :bv;
  5    dbms_output.put_line('Hello '|| lv_whom ||'.');
  6  END;
  7  /
```

This prints the following:

```
Hello Sam.
```

You could put any of these anonymous block programs in a file and run them from the SQL*Plus command line. As discussed in Chapter 2, SQL*Plus is both an interactive and batch programming environment. Flip back to Chapter 2 for assistance running any of these programs.

Nested Blocks

You can put unnamed blocks inside other blocks. These nested blocks can't have names, as they can in MySQL. You could rewrite the preceding example with a nested block like this:

```
SQL> DECLARE
  2    -- Declare local variables.
  3    lv_salutation VARCHAR2(5) := 'Hello';
  4    lv_whom VARCHAR2(30);
  5  BEGIN
  6    -- Assign the external bind variable value.
  7    lv_whom := :bv;
  8    -- Nested anonymous block.
  9    DECLARE
 10      /* Declare nested local variable, overwriting external
 11         local variable in the process. */
 12      lv_salutation VARCHAR2(7) := 'Goodbye';
 13    BEGIN
 14      -- Print message to standard out.
 15      dbms_output.put_line(lv_salutation ||' '|| lv_whom ||'.');
 16    END;
 17    -- Print message to standard out.
 18    dbms_output.put_line(lv_salutation ||' '|| lv_whom ||'.');
 19  END;
 20  /
```

Notice that `lv_salutation` is declared in both the outer and inner anonymous blocks. The physical size of the outer block `lv_salutation` variable is five characters long, and the value is "Hello", whereas the inner block uses a physical size of seven characters and a value of "Goodbye". The second declaration replaces both the size and value, which lasts for the duration of the nested block. You can see this because both messages are printed to standard out with the `dbms_output.put_line` procedure.

Here's the output:

```
Goodbye Sam.
Hello Sam.
```

Although the two local variables share the same name, they share different physical sizes and values. This example demonstrates scope and the ability of subordinate blocks to override existing variable data types and contents.

You can also nest named blocks inside other named blocks or anonymous blocks. I've included this later in the formal discussion of functions and procedures to illustrate the nesting of local functions and procedures in anonymous blocks. The forward reference to `hector` in the `jack` procedure lets you see the concept of forward-referencing stubs.

The problem with nested named blocks, however, is they're not published blocks. This means that one might call another before the one being called is defined. This type of design problem is known as a *scope error*. The scope of the called program is unknown until after the call is made. It raises a PLS-00313 exception and results in a compile-time error.

```
SQL> DECLARE
  2    PROCEDURE jack IS
  3    BEGIN
  4      dbms_output.put_line(hector||' World!');
  5    END jack;
  6    FUNCTION hector RETURN VARCHAR2 IS
  7    BEGIN
  8      RETURN 'Hello';
  9    END hector;
 10  BEGIN
 11    jack;
 12  END;
 13  /
```

Lines 2 through 5 define a local procedure, `jack`. Inside procedure `jack` is a call on line 4 to the function `hector`. The function isn't defined at this point in the anonymous block, and it raises an out-of-scope error:

```
    dbms_output.put_line(hector||' World!');
                         *
ERROR at line 4:
ORA-06550: line 4, column 26:
PLS-00313: 'B' not declared in this scope
ORA-06550: line 4, column 5:
PL/SQL: Statement ignored
```

This is a compile-time error, because all anonymous block programs are parsed before they're executed. Parsing is a compile-time process. Parsing recognizes identifiers, which are reserved words, predefined identifiers, quoted identifiers, user-defined variables, subroutines, or UDTs. Named blocks are identifiers. Function `hector` isn't recognized as an identifier, because PL/SQL reads identifiers into memory from top to bottom. This is a single-pass parsing process. Under a single-pass parser, function `hector` isn't defined before it's called in procedure `jack`.

You can fix this by using *forward references*. A forward reference to a function or procedure requires only the signature of the function or procedure rather than the signature and implementation. Forward references are equivalent to the concept of an *interface* in Java. These prototypes are *stubs* in PL/SQL. The stub lets the compilation accept the identifier name of a named block before you implement the block.

The following provides forward references for all local functions and procedures. I recommend that you always provide these stubs in your programs when you implement local scope named blocks.

```
SQL> DECLARE
  2    PROCEDURE jack;
  3    FUNCTION hector RETURN VARCHAR2;
  4    PROCEDURE jack IS
  5    BEGIN
  6      dbms_output.put_line(b||' World!');
  7    END jack;
  8    FUNCTION hector RETURN VARCHAR2 IS
  9    BEGIN
 10      RETURN 'Hello';
 11    END hector;
 12  BEGIN
 13    jack;
 14  END;
 15  /
```

Lines 2 and 3 provide the stubs to procedure `jack` and function `hector`. This program passes the compile time validation because it's able to resolve all symbols from top to bottom of the anonymous block. Nested blocks are very useful, but you need to use them correctly.

The biggest risk of locally named PL/SQL blocks is that they replace schema-level named functions and procedures. To avoid this, you should consider a naming convention (like an `lv_` preface) for locally named blocks that ensures they won't replace schema-level names in your stored programs.

Named Blocks

Functions and procedures are the named blocks in PL/SQL. They can be deployed inside anonymous or other named block programs, inside UDTs, or in packages. Functions return a value and can be called from SQL DML statements, consumed as call parameters to other functions and procedures, and used to produce values as right operands in assignments (see "The Assignment Model and Language" sidebar earlier in the chapter).

Functions and procedures can accept parameters of scalar, composite, and collection data types. Scalar data types are SQL-based data types, and you can use them in SQL and PL/SQL contexts.

Collection Data Type	Scope	AQL Call Parameter	PL/SQL Call Parameter	SQL Function Return	PL/SQL Function Return
Varray	SQL	Yes	Yes	Yes	Yes
Nested Table	SQL	Yes	Yes	Yes	Yes
Aggregate Table	SQL			Yes	
Varray	PL/SQL		Yes		Yes
Nested Table	PL/SQL		Yes		Yes
Associative Array	PL/SQL		Yes		Yes

TABLE 13-2. *Collection Access and Return Type Scopes*

Composite data types can be defined as PL/SQL record types or as SQL object types, and varray and nested table collections can use either. Associative arrays can use only SQL scalar data types and PL/SQL record data types.

Table 13-2 shows you how you can use these composite data types as parameters in functions or procedures, and when and where you can use them as return data types in functions. The most notable issue raised by this distinction is that PL/SQL has two different deployment strategies: One involves writing programs to support other PL/SQL programs, and the other involves writing programs to support SQL.

The following sections address function and procedure architecture and development. You'll find collections explained in the "PL/SQL Variables: Types, Assignments, and Operators" section later in this chapter, which provides small examples of PL/SQL functions and procedures.

Function Architecture

Before you see the details of how you implement and use functions, you should first understand what a function is and how it works. Functions are *black boxes*, production facilities in which you add raw things and take processed things out.

The two major function architectures, *pass-by-value* and *pass-by-reference* models, are used in different ways. You choose the former when you want a standalone behavior and the latter when functions act as subroutines inside the transaction scope of another program unit.

Pass-by-Value Functions   A *pass-by-value* function receives values when they're called. The functions returns a single thing upon completion. The tricky parts with this type of function are the data types of the inputs and outputs. Inputs are formal parameters and have only one mode in pass-by-value programs, and that's an IN-only mode. An IN-only mode means that you send a copy of either a variable value or a literal value into the function as a raw input. These copies are actual parameters or call parameters. All raw materials (call parameters) are consumed during the production of the finished goods—or the return value of this type of function. The return type value of the function must be assigned to a variable in a PL/SQL block, but it can also be returned as an expression in a SQL query.

The Black Box

The *black box* (the term comes from the engineering lexicon) is part of verification and validation. *Verification* is a process that examines whether you built something right. *Validation* checks whether you built the right thing. For example, you validate that the manufacturing line is producing iPod nanos, and then you verify that they're being made according to the new specification.

Integration testing validates whether components work as a part. You can't see how the product works. You only know what it should do when you provide input, such as a function that should add two numbers. If 1 plus 1 equals 2, then the function appears to work based on expectations. This is black box testing.

While black box testing is the process of validation, verification requires peering into the black box to inspect how it behaves. This type of testing is called *white box testing* because you can see how things actually work—step-by-step. Unit testing verifies that your function or procedure builds the thing right. An example would be verifying that you're using the right formula to calculate the future value of money using compounding interest.

The following illustration depicts how a pass-by-value function works. What's hidden in this context? The hidden element of a stored program in an Oracle database is the back door that lets a function transact against the database. This means a function's black box can contain an INSERT, UPDATE, or DELETE statement. Actually, it can contain a set of statements. The collection of statements can collectively be a transaction. This back door to a transactional database is available only when you use the function in an *exclusively* PL/SQL scope.

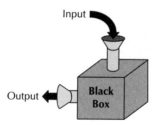

Pass-by-Reference Function   When you call a *pass-by-reference* function, you send one or more references to local variables as actual parameters. Formal parameters, therefore, can have any one of three possible modes: IN, OUT, and IN OUT.

The following list (from *Oracle Database 11g PL/SQL Programming Workbook*) describes subroutine parameter modes:

- **IN**   The IN mode, the default mode, means you send a copy as the actual parameter. Any formal parameter defined without an explicit mode of operation is implicitly an IN-only mode parameter. It means a formal parameter is read-only. When you set a formal parameter as read-only, you can't alter it during the execution of the subroutine. You *can* assign a default value to a parameter, making the parameter optional. You use the IN mode for all formal parameters when you want to define a pass-by-value subroutine.

- **OUT** The OUT mode means you send a reference, but a *null* as an initial value. An OUT mode formal parameter is write-only. When you set a formal parameter as write-only, no initial physical size is allocated to the variable. You allocate the physical size and value inside your subroutine. You can't assign a default value, which would make an OUT mode formal parameter optional. If you attempt that, you raise a PLS-00230 error. The error says that an OUT or IN OUT mode variable cannot have a default value. Likewise, you cannot pass a literal as an actual parameter to an OUT mode variable, because that would block writing the output variable. If you attempt to send a literal, you'll raise an ORA-06577 error with a call from SQL*Plus, and a PLS-00363 error inside a PL/SQL block. The SQL*Plus error message states the output parameter is not a bind variable, which is a SQL*Plus session variable. The PL/SQL error tells you that the expression (or, more clearly, literal) cannot be an assignment target. You use an OUT mode with one or more formal parameters when you want a write-only pass-by-reference subroutine.

- **IN OUT** The IN OUT mode means you send a reference and starting value. A formal parameter is read-write. When you set a formal parameter as read-write, the physical size of the actual parameter is provided. While you can change the contents of the variable inside the subroutine, you can't change or exceed the actual parameter's allocated size. The IN OUT mode restrictions on default values and literal values mirror those of the OUT mode.

TIP
As you move between Oracle and MySQL, remember that the
IN OUT parameter mode in PL/SQL is two words, and the INOUT
parameter mode of SQL/PSM is a single word.

Although you can call a pass-by-reference function by using session-level variables, that's really not the functions' role. Pass-by-reference functions belong as components in the scope of either pass-by-value functions or stored procedures. The next illustration shows the generalized format of pass-by-reference functions.

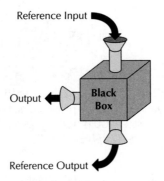

Interestingly, raw materials (call parameters) aren't fully consumed in pass-by-reference functions, as they are in pass-by-value functions. While IN-only mode parameters are fully consumed, IN OUT mode variables are returned generally in an altered state. OUT mode variables are the result of some processing inside the black box that you opt not to return through the function's formal return type.

Function Model Choices

What are the rules of thumb with regard to choosing a pass-by-value or pass-by-reference function? They're quite simple, as you'll see.

You should implement a pass-by-value function when you want to produce a result by consuming the input. You also should implement a pass-by-value function when you want to use the function in a SQL statement. A pass-by-value function is ideal when its transaction scope is autonomous. In object-oriented programming terms, you want to use a pass-by-value function when you want the lowest possible coupling—*message coupling*.

When programs are loosely coupled, they're more flexible and reusable in applications. Tightly coupled programs are intrinsically linked to form a processing unit—like root beer and vanilla ice cream are used make a traditional root beer float, so are these programs blended to form a processing unit.

You implement a pass-by-reference function when you need to couple behavior of the calling and called program units (known as *data coupling*). This happens when the function is called in a single threaded execution scope, which is the default in most transactional database applications. Tightly coupled programs such as these let you opt to return values through the IN OUT or OUT mode formal parameters. When the parameters receive raw and return processed data, the formal return value of the function becomes a signal of success or failure.

PL/SQL functions that use the return type to signal success or failure typically implement either a Boolean or number data type. They use the Boolean when you design them to work exclusively inside PL/SQL blocks and a number when they might need to work in either a SQL or PL/SQL scope.

A pass-by-value function is ideal when you want to couple client-side interaction with server-side modules. In this context, you should define the function as autonomous. Autonomous functions run in their own transaction scope and are thereby independent of the calling transaction scope. The only way you know whether they succeeded or failed is to capture their return state through the function return type.

A pass-by-reference function is generally a bad idea when you simply want to couple two server-side programs. When the programs are on the same tier and might be called in the same serial transaction scope, you should implement the behavior as a pass-by-reference procedure. A pass-by-reference procedure is a specialized form of a function that returns no value. Procedures are most similar to C, C++, C#, or Java methods that return a *void* rather than a tangible data type.

Function Development

It took a few pages to get here, but the foundation material presented so far should help you in using these functions without guessing at their purpose. Here is the prototype for a function in PL/SQL:

```
FUNCTION function_name
( parameter [IN][OUT] [NOCOPY]
    {sql_datatype | plsql_datatype} [{DEFAULT | :=} value]
[, parameter [IN][OUT] [NOCOPY]
    {sql_datatype | plsql_datatype} [{DEFAULT | :=} value]
[, ...])
RETURN {sql_data_type | plsql_data_type}
[ AUTHID {DEFINER | CURRENT_USER}]
[ DETERMINISTIC | PARALLEL_ENABLED ]
[ PIPELINED ]
```

```
[ RESULT_CACHE [ RELIES ON table_name (column [, column])]] IS
  declaration_statements;
BEGIN
  execution_statements;
  RETURN variable;
[EXCEPTION
  exception_handling_statements;]
END [function_name];
/
```

One of the more important aspects of PL/SQL functions is how you can call them in SELECT, INSERT, UPDATE, and DELETE statements. You should know some key restrictions before you begin the design phase. A PL/SQL function cannot contain a DML statement or call another PL/SQL unit that contains a DML statement without raising an ORA-14551 exception. That error means you cannot perform a DML operation inside a query in the same transaction scope. You can perform a DML operation inside a query when the function runs autonomously or calls an autonomous stored program that runs the DML statement. That works because an autonomous stored program runs in an external scope from the query or SQL statement.

A key difference between parameters in PL/SQL versus SQL/PSM stored programs is that you can assign default values in PL/SQL, which makes certain parameters optional. You can exclude optional parameters when they're at the end of a list of parameters or when you use named notation (shown in the "Deterministic Clause" section a bit later). When you have two optional parameters of the same data type, you risk entering the right values in the wrong parameter field. That's why named notation is preferred.

PL/SQL functions also can return only a subset of their native data types. Officially, you can return only a BLOB, BFILE, BINARY_DOUBLE, BINARY_FLOAT, BYTE, CHAR, CLOB, NCHAR, NCLOB, NVARCHAR2, REFCURSOR, or VARCHAR2 data type. You can also return collections of scalar variables of those aforementioned data types in a SQL or PL/SQL context. You can return collections of composite variables (often known as object tables) in a SQL context. Although you can return aggregate tables defined in PL/SQL in a PL/SQL context, they can also be returned in a SQL context through pipelined functions. You can also return collections of user-defined object types.

Several types of functions work well when called from SQL. The next sections review seven of them: deterministic, parallel enabled, pipelined table, result cache, system reference cursor, recursive, and pass-by-value functions. All but one of these examples use the pass-by-value model, because that's generally the best practice for functions called by SQL statements. This means that the parameter mode will always be IN-only for all but the last example.

The following sections demonstrate how to implement deterministic, parallel enabled, pipelined table, and result cache functions.

Deterministic Clause A deterministic function guarantees that it always works the same way with any inputs. It also guarantees that the function doesn't read or write data from external sources, such as other stored programs or database tables.

The pv function shows you how to create a simple deterministic function. These are great tools when you need to apply a formula to a set of values.

```
SQL> CREATE OR REPLACE FUNCTION pv
  2  ( future_value    NUMBER
  3  , periods         NUMBER
```

```
4   , interest          NUMBER )
5   RETURN NUMBER DETERMINISTIC IS
6   BEGIN
7     RETURN future_value / ((1 + interest/100)**periods);
8   END pv;
9   /
```

You can call this program with the CALL method, like this:

```
SQL> VARIABLE result NUMBER
SQL> CALL pv(10000,5,6) INTO :result;
SQL> COLUMN money_today FORMAT 99,999.90
SQL> SELECT :result AS money_today FROM dual;
```

This would print today's value of $10,000, five years in the future at 6 percent annual interest, barring another financial meltdown, like this:

```
MONEY_TODAY
-----------
   7,472.58
```

Alternatively, you can query data as input values and return values like this:

```
SQL> WITH data_set AS
  2  ( SELECT  235000 AS principal
  3  ,             30 AS years
  4  ,          5.875 AS interest
  5    FROM       dual )
  6  SELECT pv(principal,years,interest) AS money_today
  7  FROM   data_set;
```

which returns this result:

```
MONEY_TODAY
-----------
  42,390.17
```

The foregoing syntax on line 6 in the SQL statement that calls the pv function uses positional notation. Starting in Oracle 11*g*, you can use *named notation* in SQL or PL/SQL statements, like this:

```
SQL> WITH data_set AS
  2  ( SELECT  235000 AS principal
  3  ,             30 AS years
  4  ,          5.875 AS interest
  5    FROM       dual )
  6  SELECT pv(future_value => principal
  7            ,periods => years
  8            ,interest => interest) AS money_today
  9  FROM   data_set;
```

Lines 6 through 8 show you how to deploy named notation. Named notation uses the names of the formal parameters for a function, and they allow you to pass variables that share the same name—at least, they do when you put them on the right side of the equal and greater than symbol set (=>) as values.

NOTE
Deterministic clauses are acceptable functions that you can put in materialized views. They're also what Oracle recommends for user-defined functions that you use in SQL statement clauses.

PARALLEL_ENABLE Clause The `merge` function shows you how to create a simple function that can be called from either the SQL or PL/SQL context. It takes three strings and concatenates them into one. This type of function removes concatenation from your queries by placing it into a function. It has the benefit of ensuring that format masks are always maintained in a single location.

```
SQL> CREATE OR REPLACE FUNCTION merge
  2  ( last_name     VARCHAR2
  3  , first_name    VARCHAR2
  4  , middle_name VARCHAR2 )
  5  RETURN VARCHAR2 PARALLEL_ENABLE IS
  6  BEGIN
  7    RETURN last_name ||', '||first_name||' '||middle_name;
  8  END;
  9  /
```

The `PARALLEL_ENABLE` clause on line 5 lets you designate that the function is safe to parallelize during query optimization. Although the SQL engine can make these decisions, designating the function as safe does save a few milliseconds. Function-based indexes are often built on functions that are both deterministic and parallel-enabled.

TIP
Deterministic functions should be parallel-enabled when they return more than one row and their result set is dynamic based on queries from the database.

You can call this program like this:

```
SQL> SELECT merge(c.last_name, c.first_name, c.middle_name) AS customer
  2  FROM    contact c;
```

You should parallel-enable PL/SQL wrappers to Java program libraries, because the Oracle 11*g* optimizer never deems that a Java library is thread-safe. Unfortunately, there's no guarantee that the cost optimizer will act on your suggestion.

Pipelined Table Clause A pipelined table function lets you translate collections of SQL or PL/SQL record data types into SQL-compatible aggregate tables. You access aggregate tables through SQL statements by using the `TABLE` function.

NOTE
The pipelined table clause is very powerful, but we've not yet covered variables in PL/SQL and you've not been shown how to work with collections. Nevertheless, the subject fits best here—you might want to skip it now and/or come back to reread this section after you understand collection data types and cursors.

You create a record structure as the first step in creating a traditional pipelined table function. Record structures are exclusively PL/SQL structures; however, when you create a pipelined table function, Oracle creates implicit catalog entries that let you translate the PL/SQL record to an aggregate table. An *aggregate table* is another name for query results—it's good vocabulary to know when you're reading other Oracle documentation.

The only way to create a reusable record structure is to put it inside a package specification. (You can read more on packages in the "Package Architecture" and "Package Development" sections later in this chapter.) The same rule holds true for an exclusively PL/SQL collection type. The package wraps it and defines it where we can't readily see the structure's data type unless we view the package source.

This example creates our record structure inside a library package specification:

```
SQL> CREATE OR REPLACE PACKAGE pipelining_library IS
  2    TYPE common_lookup_record IS RECORD
  3    ( common_lookup_id        NUMBER
  4    , common_lookup_type      VARCHAR2(30)
  5    , common_lookup_meaning   VARCHAR2(255));
  6    TYPE common_lookup_table IS TABLE OF common_lookup_record;
  7  END pipelining_library;
  8  /
```

Lines 2 through 5 hold the definition for a record structure, which resembles the definition of a table. Line 6 creates a collection of the record structure. These use a common convention in PL/SQL programming, appending _RECORD and _TABLE to user-defined data types of a *record* and *nested table* collection, respectively. As you will see in the "PL/SQL Variables: Types, Assignments, and Operators" section later in this chapter, a *nested table* acts like a *list* in C#, C++, and Java programming languages.

Having created the structure, we can now define a pipelined table function in one of two ways: We can create one inside a package body or as a schema-level function. The only difference is that we don't need to reference the package name when we define the function inside the same `pipelining_library` package body. We need to reference the package name when we define the function in another package body or as a schema-level function, so that the base record structure or collection type can be found.

Here's our sample standalone (schema-level) pipelined table function:

```
SQL> CREATE OR REPLACE FUNCTION get_common_lookup_record_table
  2  ( pv_table_name  VARCHAR2, pv_column_name VARCHAR2 )
  3  RETURN pipelining_library.common_lookup_table
  4  PIPELINED IS
  5
  6    -- Declare a local variables.
  7    lv_counter INTEGER := 1;
```

```
 8    lv_table    PIPELINING_LIBRARY.COMMON_LOOKUP_TABLE :=
 9                    pipelining_library.common_lookup_table();
10
11    -- Define a dynamic cursor that takes two formal parameters.
12    CURSOR c (table_name_in VARCHAR2, table_column_name_in VARCHAR2) IS
13      SELECT    common_lookup_id
14      ,         common_lookup_type
15      ,         common_lookup_meaning
16      FROM      common_lookup
17      WHERE     common_lookup_table = UPPER(table_name_in)
18      AND       common_lookup_column = UPPER(table_column_name_in);
19
20  BEGIN
21    FOR i IN c (pv_table_name, pv_column_name) LOOP
22      lv_table.EXTEND;
23      lv_table(lv_counter) := i;
24      PIPE ROW(lv_table(lv_counter));
25      lv_counter := lv_counter + 1;
26    END LOOP;
27  END;
28  /
```

Line 3 defines the function's dependence on a collection defined in the `pipelining_library` package, which must be in the specification to be available for our definition. (See Chapter 9 in *Oracle Database 11g PL/SQL Programming* for more on packages.) Line 4 defines the function as a pipelined table function—or pipelined for the compiler. We declare an empty collection inside the function's declaration block on lines 8 and 9.

The guts of how this function converts a PL/SQL data type into something usable in SQL is shown on lines 22 through 24. Line 22 allocates space to a collection, line 23 assigns the values retrieved by the cursor (the dynamic `SELECT` statement on lines 13 through 18), and line 24 converts the row through a pipe from a PL/SQL data type to a SQL data type. The actual SQL data type is an aggregate result set, which is more or less what any `SELECT` statement returns.

You can test the function, but a bit of formatting makes the output cleaner. These SQL*Plus commands set the display column sizes before you query the collection:

```
SQL> COLUMN common_lookup_id      FORMAT 9999 HEADING "ID"
SQL> COLUMN common_lookup_type    FORMAT A16  HEADING "Lookup Type"
SQL> COLUMN common_lookup_meaning FORMAT A30  HEADING "Lookup Meaning"
SQL> SELECT   *
  2  FROM     TABLE(get_common_lookup_record_table('ITEM','ITEM_TYPE'));
```

The `TABLE` function lets you translate an aggregate table or nested table (as discussed in Chapters 8 and 9 with nested tables). A pipelined function inherits the record structure element names from an implicit data type, which is created in the catalog when you compile the pipelined function. It is also removed from the catalog when you drop the pipelined function.

The query returns this:

```
   ID Lookup Type      Lookup Meaning
----- ---------------- ------------------
 1013 DVD_FULL_SCREEN  DVD: Full Screen
 1014 DVD_WIDE_SCREEN  DVD: Wide Screen
```

```
1015 GAMECUBE          Nintendo GameCube
1016 PLAYSTATION2      PlayStation2
1019 VHS_DOUBLE_TAPE   VHS: Double Tape
1018 VHS_SINGLE_TAPE   VHS: Single Tape
1017 XBOX              XBOX
```

A pipelined table function call works only in a SQL context, as in the foregoing example. You can consume the results in a PL/SQL block, provided you do so in a SQL statement; but that begs the question of why you would have converted it in the first place.

RESULT_CACHE Clause   The result cache function has the same problem as the pipelined table function: it requires that composite variables and loops appear in the body of the program. Both are covered in the "PL/SQL Variables: Types, Assignments, and Operators" and "PL/SQL Control Structures" sections later in the chapter. (Glance over [or skip] this section now if you want, and return after you've gathered more knowledge of Oracle data types and PL/SQL structures.)

The result cache is a new feature of Oracle 11g. It allows you to define a function and hold the result sets in a cache for reuse. This is quite an improvement over simply pinning packages in memory to speed execution. You query the result cache rather than the source table or view with the second, third, and so on, queries of the function. This reduces computation cycles and improves throughput.

Result cache functions do have some limitations, however. They can return only scalar variables or collections of scalar variables. The get_common_lookup function returns a list of variable-length strings.

You can also link the result cache to the source table or tables. When you link a result cache to a table, you ensure that any underlying change to the table flushes the previous result cache. This prevents a dirty read from the cache and compels the function to seek a read-consistent result set.

You define a result cache function that uses the RELIES_ON clause, which ensures that any change to the underlying data will clear the cache. This lets you use a result cache to store primary key values that can be used as foreign key values.

The first thing required for this example is a SQL collection. This syntax creates a user-defined nested table (acts like a traditional list) collection data type:

```
SQL> CREATE OR REPLACE TYPE lookup_types IS TABLE OF VARCHAR2(30);
  2  /
```

You define the function with the following syntax:

```
SQL> CREATE OR REPLACE FUNCTION get_common_lookup
  2  ( pv_table_name VARCHAR2
  3  , pv_column_name VARCHAR2 ) RETURN LOOKUP_TYPES
  4  RESULT_CACHE RELIES_ON(common_lookup) IS
  5
  6    -- A counter variable to manage insertion to the collection.
  7    lv_counter    INTEGER := 1;
  8
  9    -- A local string variable for each row return.
 10    lv_lookup_type VARCHAR2(30);
 11
```

```
12      -- A local variable of a user-defined scalar collection type.
13      lookups LOOKUP_TYPES := lookup_types();
14
15      -- A cursor to find the lookup id values.
16      CURSOR c
17      ( cv_table_name VARCHAR2
18      , cv_column_name VARCHAR2) IS
19        SELECT   common_lookup_type
20        FROM     common_lookup
21        WHERE    common_lookup_table = UPPER(cv_table_name)
22        AND      common_lookup_column = UPPER(cv_column_name);
23
24   BEGIN
25     -- Open the cursor and start a loop.
26     OPEN c(pv_table_name, pv_column_name);
27     LOOP
28       FETCH c INTO lv_lookup_type;
29
30       -- Exit when no more records found.
31       EXIT WHEN c%NOTFOUND;
32
33       -- Allocate space and assign value to the collection.
34       lookups.EXTEND;
35       lookups(lv_counter) := lv_lookup_type;
36
37       -- Increment the counter for the collection.
38       lv_counter := lv_counter + 1;
39     END LOOP;
40     RETURN lookups;
41   END get_common_lookup;
42   /
```

Line 4 contains the definition of a result cache that relies on the current contents of the common_lookup table. Any change to the table will cause the cached results to be discarded, and the next call to the function will retrieve new values and store them in the result cache. The body of the function deals with material covered in the "PL/SQL Variables: Types, Assignments, and Operators" and "PL/SQL Control Structures" sections later in this chapter. Line 40 contains the return of a SQL collection data type.

You call the function with SQL*Plus formatting, like this:

```
SQL> COLUMN common_lookup_type    FORMAT A16   HEADING "Lookup Type"
SQL> SELECT column_value AS ITEM_TYPE
  2   FROM   TABLE(get_common_lookup('ITEM','ITEM_TYPE'));
```

This query returns the same result set as the one displayed for the pipelined table, and it isn't displayed here because you can flip back a couple pages to the original.

System Reference Cursor Functions   Systems reference cursors are PL/SQL-only structures. They're very powerful when coupled with external programming languages that support the OCI8 libraries, such as PHP. You can define a strongly or weakly typed system reference cursor.

Strongly typed reference cursors are anchored to a table or view, while weakly typed reference cursors can accept any record structure assigned by a query. The SYS_REFCURSOR is the default weakly typed system reference cursor.

You define a strongly typed reference cursor anchored to the item table like this:

```
TYPE some_cursor_name IS REF CURSOR RETURN item%ROWTYPE;
```

You define a weakly typed reference cursor like this:

```
TYPE some_cursor_name IS REF CURSOR;
```

Although you can define a weakly typed reference cursor, it doesn't make sense to do so. You should always use the SYS_REFCURSOR when you require a weakly typed reference cursor, because it's predefined and universally available.

The following shows you how to write a function that returns a weakly typed, default, system reference cursor:

```
SQL> CREATE OR REPLACE FUNCTION get_full_titles
  2    RETURN SYS_REFCURSOR IS
  3      lv_titles SYS_REFCURSOR;
  4    BEGIN
  5      OPEN lv_titles FOR
  6      SELECT   item_title
  7      ,            item_subtitle
  8      FROM     item;
  9      RETURN lv_titles;
 10    END;
 11    /
```

Line 2 defines the return type as the generic weakly typed system reference cursor, and line 3 defines a variable using the generic system reference cursor. Line 5 shows you how to open the reference cursor.

You have two ways to call this function from the command line. The first approach is how you'd embed a query in a C#, Java, or PHP program, where it would be treated as a normal query result set. The example includes the SQL*Plus formatting commands:

```
SQL> COLUMN item_title FORMAT A30
SQL> COLUMN item_subtitle FORMAT A40
SQL> SELECT get_full_titles FROM dual;
```

This version uses the CALL statement to put the function in a SQL*Plus session variable:

```
SQL> VARIABLE output REFCURSOR
SQL> CALL get_full_titles() INTO :output;
SQL> SELECT :output FROM dual;
```

It's a bit more complex to manage the output of a weakly typed system reference cursor in a PL/SQL program. First you must know the structure that it will return, or you can't process it. The upside is that it's manageable, like an ordinary query inside C#, Java, and PHP program units.

Recursive Functions   You can define recursive functions in PL/SQL. They're neat devices when they fit a problem, but they can have a high cost in terms of computational cycles when they don't. Recursive functions call themselves until they reach a base case, which is similar to a leaf node in a search tree.

You can use two varieties of recursion: One is called *linear* recursion, because it calls only one copy of itself inside each recursion. The other is called *nonlinear* recursion, because it calls itself two or more times inside each function when the base case isn't met.

Here is the standard Fibonacci problem, which is a nonlinear recursion example:

```
CREATE OR REPLACE FUNCTION Fibonacci
( n BINARY_DOUBLE ) RETURN BINARY_DOUBLE IS
BEGIN
  IF n <= 2 THEN
    RETURN 1;
  ELSE
    RETURN fibonacci(n - 2) + fibonacci(n - 1);
  END IF;
END fibonacci;
/
```

My advice on recursion is simple: use it only when you know how it works.

Pass-by-Reference Functions   Pass-by-reference functions can exhibit many of the behaviors we've worked through earlier in the chapter. As discussed, they can have IN, IN OUT, or OUT mode parameters. An IN mode parameter passes in a value that can change but is consumed wholly. An IN OUT mode parameter passes in a reference and value, and the value can change before it is returned to the calling program. An OUT mode parameter passes in nothing but can return something.

A simple example of this concept is a program with only one input parameter and one input and output parameter. The input and output parameter increments each time you call the program.

```
SQL> CREATE OR REPLACE FUNCTION adding
  2  ( a IN      NUMBER
  3  , b IN OUT NUMBER ) RETURN NUMBER IS
  4  BEGIN
  5    b := b + 1;
  6    RETURN a + b;
  7  END;
  8  /
```

We'll use bind variables to keep this as simple as possible to illustrate the approach. You have to define them in the session, and then assign values to bind variables inside a PL/SQL block, like this:

```
SQL> VARIABLE one NUMBER
SQL> VARIABLE two NUMBER
SQL> BEGIN
  2    :one := 1;
  3    :two := 0;
  4  END;
  5  /
```

We'll also need an output variable, like this one:

```
SQL> VARIABLE output NUMBER
```

Now we can call the pass-by-reference function with the bind variables:

```
SQL> VARIABLE output NUMBER
SQL> CALL adding(:one,:two) INTO :output;
SQL> CALL adding(:one,:two) INTO :output;
```

We can then query the two bind variables, like this:

```
SQL> SELECT :one, :two FROM dual;
```

The query prints this:

```
     :ONE       :TWO
---------- ----------
         1          2
```

After two calls, the input-only variable is the same, but the input and output variable has grown by two. That would continue as long as we call it. The most useful way to use pass-by-reference functions is when you want to ensure that something happens and returns the changed values.

Procedure Architecture

A *procedure* is essentially a function with a void return type. As such, you can't use it as a right operand because it doesn't have a return value. Procedures, like functions, are black boxes.

Procedures provide a named subroutine that you call within the scope of a PL/SQL block. Although the behavior differs slightly whether you pass call parameters by *value* or *reference*, the inputs and outcomes are the only way to exchange values between the calling block and the procedure.

The nature of the call parameters provides you with two procedure architectures. They are a *pass-by-value* or *pass-by-reference* model. A pass-by-value model accepts values to perform a task, while a pass-by-value model accepts values or references to perform a task. Reference variable values can change inside a procedure like this, and can return altered values to the external variable references. You chose a pass-by-value model when you want a delegation behavior, and a pass-by-reference model when you want a shared or cooperative processing behavior.

In a delegation behavior, the inputs are consumed by the subroutine and nothing is returned to the calling scope. Shared or cooperative processing means that a subroutine performs an operation on one or more calling scope variables. Cooperative processing doesn't consume all inputs but refines some of them. It acts like an oil refinery that processes crude oil, additives, and chemicals into fuel.

Pass-by-Value Procedures   A *pass-by-value* procedure receives values when they're called. They return nothing tangible to the calling scope block, but they can interact with the database. Pass-by-value procedures implement a delegation model. Procedures are often used to group and control a series of DML statements in the scope of a single transaction.

The mode of all formal parameters is IN-only for pass-by-value procedures. This means they receive a copy of an external variable or a numeric or string literal when you call the procedure. Call parameters can't be changed during the execution of a subroutine. You can transfer the contents from a call parameter to a local variable inside the procedure and then update that the local variable.

The following illustration depicts how a pass-by-value procedure works. What's hidden in this context? The hidden element of any stored program is that it can change data in the database. This means a procedure's black box can contain an INSERT, UPDATE, or DELETE statement. As mentioned,
a procedure often contains one or more DML statements. These procedures frequently define a single transaction, which means all or nothing occurs.

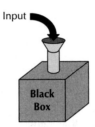

Pass-by-Reference Procedures   You send one or more references to local variables as actual parameters when you call a *pass-by-reference* function. Therefore, formal parameters can have an IN (the default), IN OUT, or OUT mode. These modes were described earlier in the chapter.

Although you can call a pass-by-reference function by using session-level variables, that's really not their role. Pass-by-reference functions belong as components inside other anonymous or named blocks. The next illustration shows you the generalized format of pass-by-reference functions.

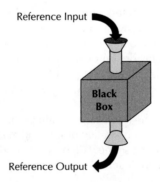

IN OUT call parameters aren't fully consumed by *pass-by-reference* procedures. Although IN-only mode parameters are fully consumed, OUT mode variables don't have a value to consume. IN OUT mode variables are designed to submit a reference with a value and receive a replacement value at the conclusion of a subroutine, like a procedure.

OUT mode variables are the result of some processing inside the *black box*. They are generally derived by some algorithm that uses other call parameters and constant values inside the procedure. Sometimes OUT mode variables perform similar roles to a function's formal return type.

Procedure Development

Procedures are more straightforward than functions because you have fewer options to define them. You can define them as pass-by-value or pass-by-reference models.

Like functions, you can call procedures interactively at the SQL*Plus command line. Examples in the next two sections show you how to create and call pass-by-value and pass-by-reference procedures.

Here's the prototype for a PL/SQL procedure:

```
PROCEDURE procedure_name
( parameter [IN] [OUT] [NOCOPY]
    {sql_datatype | plsql_datatype} [{DEFAULT | :=} value]
[, parameter [IN] [OUT] [NOCOPY]
    {sql_datatype | plsql_datatype} [{DEFAULT | :=} value]
[, ...])
  [AUTHID {DEFINER | CURRENT_USER}] IS
  declaration_statements;
BEGIN
  execution_statements;
[EXCEPTION
  exception_handling_statements]
END [procedure_name];
/
```

At least one of the sample programs uses a local bind variable as a call parameter. This is a demonstration case and unlikely to be something you'll do in production, however. Note that procedures can only manage bind variables as call parameters. Any attempt to use a bind variable inside a stored procedure definition raises a PLS-00049 exception.

Pass-by-Value Procedures A basic pass-by-value procedure simply takes a call parameter and performs some action with it. That action consumes the copy, because at the conclusion of the procedure the values no longer exist. It is possible that they were printed or that they were inserted or updated into database tables. They might also have simply filtered INSERT, UPDATE, or DELETE statements.

Here's a small example pass-by-value program that works in the same transaction scope as the calling program. It takes only one parameter, which uses the default IN-only mode.

```
SQL> CREATE OR REPLACE PROCEDURE print_hello
  2  ( pv_whom VARCHAR2 ) IS
  3  BEGIN
  4      dbms_output.put_line('Hello '||pv_whom||'!');
  5  END;
  8  /
```

We can see the output by setting a SQL*Plus environment variable and printing it:

```
SQL> SET SERVEROUTPUT ON SIZE 1000000
SQL> EXECUTE print_hello('there');
Hello there!
```

We can modify this program slightly and demonstrate the calling scope of variables in a nested block within a named block:

```
SQL> CREATE OR REPLACE PROCEDURE print_hello
  2  ( pv_whom VARCHAR2 ) IS
  3    lv_default CONSTANT VARCHAR2(30) := 'world';
  4    lv_whom            VARCHAR2(30);
  5  BEGIN
  6    BEGIN
  7      IF pv_whom IS NULL THEN
  8        lv_whom := lv_default;
  9      ELSE
 10        lv_whom := pv_whom;
 11      END IF;
 12    END;
 13    dbms_output.put_line('Hello '||lv_whom||'!');
 14  END;
 15  /
```

This little example teaches a number of principles. Notice that the only values available to print are either a runtime call variable or a local constant. The nested block is the only place where the lv_whom variable is assigned a value. While the lv_whom variable is defined in the external scope, it is available in any nested block regardless of how many levels might separate it from the container's scope. The container in this case is the procedure.

If you call the program without a parameter value it prints the following:

```
SQL> EXECUTE print_hello(null);
Hello world!
```

Alternatively, you can call the program with a valid string, like:

```
SQL> EXECUTE print_hello('Hagrid');
Hello Hagrid!
```

You must call the procedure with a null or string value because the formal parameter is required or mandatory. Interestingly, passing a null is the way to send nothing. This is consistent with the generalized principle in programming that you signal a loss of precision by explicit casting. You signal your knowledge of sending nothing when you call the procedure with a null value.

An attempt to call the procedure without a value would trigger the following exception:

```
SQL> EXECUTE print_hello;
BEGIN print_hello; END;
      *
ERROR at line 1:
ORA-06550: line 1, column 7:
PLS-00306: wrong number or types of arguments in call to 'PRINT_HELLO'
ORA-06550: line 1, column 7:
PL/SQL: Statement ignored
```

These programs have illustrated the idea of what pass-by-value programs do and how they work. A more practical example is a procedure that controls a set of DML statements.

Pass-by-Reference Procedures   A basic pass-by-reference procedure takes one or more call parameters by reference. Inside the procedure, the values of the reference variables can change. Their scope is defined by the calling program unit, and to some extent pass-by-reference procedures treat variables much like nested anonymous blocks. The following demonstrates the ability of a nested anonymous block to access a calling scope variable:

```
SQL> DECLARE
  2    lv_outside VARCHAR2(50) := 'Declared in outer block.';
  3  BEGIN
  4    BEGIN
  5      lv_outside := 'Re-assigned a value in the anonymous block.';
  6    END;
  7    dbms_output.put_line('Variable Value ['||lv_outside||']');
  8  END;
  9  /
```

This prints the value assigned inside the nested block, as shown:

```
Variable Value [Re-assigned a value in the anonymous block.]
```

Although the preceding example demonstrates that anonymous inner blocks have access to calling block variables, procedures work a bit differently. A procedure has access only to variables or values it receives at call time, and those variables or values are actual parameters. You can pass either a value or variable to an IN mode parameter, but must pass a variable to an IN OUT or OUT mode parameter. That's because a procedure can't assign a value to a call parameter unless it's a variable in memory.

The following demonstrates a pass-by-reference procedure that mimics the behavior of the preceding nested anonymous block program:

```
SQL> CREATE OR REPLACE PROCEDURE change_string
  2  ( pv_string IN OUT VARCHAR2 ) IS
  3  BEGIN
  4    pv_string := 'We''re inside the procedure.';
  5  END;
  6  /
```

The procedure has only one formal parameter and its mode is IN OUT, which means it is passed by reference. Line 4 in the stored procedure performs the same feature as line 5 in the nested anonymous block.

After you declare a local SQL*Plus bind variable, you can call the stored procedure as follows:

```
SQL> VARIABLE no_real_value VARCHAR2(50)
SQL> EXECUTE change_string(:no_real_value);
```

You can see the local results by calling the SQL*Plus PRINT command:

```
SQL> PRINT no_real_value
```

Here are the results:

```
NO_REAL_VALUE
-------------------------------------------
We're inside the procedure.
```

A similar PL/SQL block program calls a pass-by-reference procedure like the following:

```
SQL> DECLARE
  2    lv_outside VARCHAR2(50) := 'Declared in outer block.';
  3  BEGIN
  4    change_string(lv_outside);
  5    dbms_output.put_line('Variable Value ['||lv_outside||']');
  6  END;
  7  /
```

This program prints the same value as the previous one. Line 4 shows you how to call a pass-by-reference variable. It also shows you that the value was changed inside the named block program. This is more or less the same type of behavior that you find on Line 5 of the preceding nested anonymous block.

The uses of pass-by-value procedures like these should be limited in scope, or more precisely inside a single transaction scope. That's the default setting, but you can define them to run in their own transaction scope. You declare that type of function with the anonymous precompiler instruction, PRAGMA AUTONOMOUS_TRANSACTION.

The following shows you how to create an *autonomous* pass-by-reference procedure:

```
SQL> CREATE OR REPLACE PROCEDURE change_string
  2  ( pv_string IN OUT VARCHAR2 ) IS
  3    PRAGMA AUTONOMOUS_TRANSACTION;
  4  BEGIN
  5    pv_string := 'We''re inside the procedure.';
  6  END;
  7  /
```

Line 3 shows the syntax to declare a procedure as independent of the calling program's transaction scope. You should avoid this unless you've got a compelling business problem that requires such a design.

Package Architecture

Packages are stored libraries in the database. They are owned by the user schema where they're created, such as tables or views. This ownership means that packages are schema-level objects in the database catalog, like standalone functions and procedures.

Package specifications declare variables, data types, functions, and procedures, which publish them to the local schema. You use package variables and data types in other PL/SQL blocks, and call published functions and procedures from PL/SQL blocks inside or outside of the package where they're declared. Packages let you overload functions and procedures. You implement overloading by defining functions or procedures with different parameter lists. A parameter list is determined by the sequential data types, not the parameter names, so simply changing names on two parameters of the same data type doesn't create a different parameter list.

All users, other than the owner, must be granted the EXECUTE privilege on a package to call its published components. This mimics the same rules for tables, views, SQL data types, or standalone modules (such as standalone functions and procedures). Published components have context inside the package, just as a standalone component has context inside a user's schema.

The Oracle 11g security model lets you grant the EXECUTE privilege on any package to all users (through a *grant to public*). This effectively makes it possible to grant public access to packages. Alternatively, you can restrict access to packages. These security tools let you narrow privileges to targeted audiences.

You define (*declare* and *implement*) package-only scope functions and procedures in package bodies. Package-only scope functions and procedures can access anything in the package specification. They can also access anything declared before them in the package body. However, they cannot access anything declared after them in the package body, because PL/SQL uses a single-pass parser. Parsers place identifiers into a temporary namespace as they read through the source code. A parser fails when identifiers are referenced before they are declared. This is why identifiers are declared in a certain order in PL/SQL declaration sections.

Typically, you declare identifiers in the following order: data types, variables, cursors, exceptions, functions, and procedures. You can define variables after cursors, which is handy when the variable anchors its data type to the cursor structure. That particular behavior is shown in the "Simple Loop Statements" section later in this chapter.

Package Development

Package development starts with planning what shared data types and cursors should be bundled with which functions and procedures. Shared data types let you exchange information using the specifications of scalar, record structures, and collection data types that a package can require. Shared cursors, on the other hand, present the possibility that a query might be reused many times and would be more effectively designed and deployed in one location—in the package specification.

When you deploy packages with shared cursors, you must guarantee their integrity by using the following precompiler instruction:

```
PRAGMA SERIALLY_REUSABLE;
```

If you fail to remember this fact, a shared cursor might be read by one program starting at the beginning and another somewhere between the first and last row. That means they run the risk of being read inconsistently, which is the *worst* type of error you can introduce to PL/SQL. The simple rule is this: When you deploy shared cursors, the package must be serially reusable (always fresh to anyone that calls it).

NOTE
Packages that contain shared cursors must be defined as serially reusable code artifacts in the database.

Variables and cursors are declared exactly as they are in other PL/SQL blocks. Functions and procedures are like schema-level objects with one exception: you no longer can use Data Definition Language (DDL) commands to work with them individually. All DDL commands apply to the package specification or body. Likewise, all function and procedure definitions in the package specification must be implemented in the package body the same way. That means names, parameter lists (including default values) for procedures and names, and return types for functions.

Here's the prototype for a package specification:

```
CREATE [OR REPLACE] package_name {IS | AS}
[TYPE type_name IS
 {RECORD (column_list) | VARRAY(n) | TABLE [INDEX BY data_type]}]
[variable_name data_type {DEFAULT | :=} value; [ ...]]
[CURSOR cursor_name
 (parameter data_type [, parameter data_type [, ...]) IS
  SELECT statement; [ ...]]
[TYPE reference_cursor IS REF CURSOR
 [ RETURN {catalog_row | cursor_row | record_structure}] [ ...]]
[user_exception EXCEPTION; [ ...]]
[PRAGMA SERIALLY_REUSABLE;]
[FUNCTION prototype;] [ ...]
[PROCEURE prototype;] [ ...]
[FUNCTION body;] [ ...]
[PROCEDURE body;] [ ...]
END [package_name];
/
```

You can implement a package specification with only data types, variables, cursors, and exceptions, or you can also add functions and procedures. You don't need to define a package body when a package specification has no functions or procedures, because there's nothing to implement in the package body. Packages without implementations are called *bodiless packages*. You must provide an implementation of any function or procedure definition from a package specification in the package body.

The data types supported in packages are scalar and PL/SQL composite data types; that means you can't define an object type. You would raise the following compile-time error when you attempt to put an object type in a package specification or body:

```
PLS-00540: object not supported in this context.
```

TIP
You cannot implement a user-defined object type in a package.

The sample `overloading` package shows you how to define a serially reusable package. It's done by including a `SERIALLY_REUSABLE` precompiler instruction in both the package specification and body. A serially reusable package guarantees all callers of a package function a fresh copy of any shared cursors. The downside of a serially reusable function is that it isn't callable from `SELECT` statements.

The overloading package also shows you how to define an overloaded function. It creates a package-level salutation function that takes two or three parameters. Notice that in the package specification, only the function definitions exist, as shown:

```
SQL> CREATE OR REPLACE PACKAGE overloading IS
  2
  3    -- Force fresh copy of shared cursor.
  4    PRAGMA SERIALLY_REUSABLE;
  5
  6    -- Define a default salutation.
```

```
 7    FUNCTION salutation
 8    ( pv_long_phrase   VARCHAR2 DEFAULT 'Hello'
 9    , pv_name          VARCHAR2 ) RETURN VARCHAR2;
10
11    -- Define an overloaded salutation.
12    FUNCTION salutation
13    ( pv_long_phrase   VARCHAR2 DEFAULT 'Hello'
14    , pv_name          VARCHAR2
15    , pv_language       VARCHAR2 ) RETURN VARCHAR2;
16
17  END;
18  /
```

Line 4 contains the precompiler instruction that makes this package serially reusable. Lines 8 and 13 contain a parameter with a default value; that same default value must occur for the parameters in the package body. The only difference that can exist between the definition in the package specification and body is that the DEFAULT keyword is interchangeable with a colon equal symbol set (:=).

After creating the package specification with functions or procedures, you need to create a package body. The following example creates a package body that has a shared cursor and two overloaded functions. The functions both use the shared cursor, and these functions are the only ones that can use the shared cursor. That's because the cursor is declared in the package body rather than the specification.

The example depends on this table:

```
CREATE TABLE salutation_translation
( short_salutation   VARCHAR2(4)
, long_salutation    VARCHAR2(12)
, phrase_language    VARCHAR2(12));
```

You would seed it with the following values:

```
INSERT INTO salutation_translation VALUES ('Hi','HELLO','ENGLISH');
INSERT INTO salutation_translation VALUES ('Bye','GOODBYE','ENGLISH');
INSERT INTO salutation_translation VALUES ('Ciao','SALUTE','ITALIAN');
INSERT INTO salutation_translation VALUES ('Ciao','ADDIO','ITALIAN');
```

Here's the implementation of the package body:

```
SQL> CREATE OR REPLACE PACKAGE BODY overloading IS
  2
  3      -- Force fresh copy of shared cursor.
  4      PRAGMA SERIALLY_REUSABLE;
  5
  6      CURSOR c
  7      ( cv_long_phrase VARCHAR2
  8      , cv_language VARCHAR2 ) IS
  9        SELECT   short_salutation
 10        ,        long_salutation
 11        FROM     salutation_translation
 12        WHERE    long_salutation = UPPER(cv_long_phrase)
```

```
13       AND       phrase_language = UPPER(cv_language);
14
15    -- Define a default salutation.
16    FUNCTION salutation
17    ( pv_long_phrase  VARCHAR2 DEFAULT 'Hello'
18    , pv_name          VARCHAR2 ) RETURN VARCHAR2 IS
19
20       -- Local variables.
21       lv_short_salutation  VARCHAR2(4) := '';
22       lv_language          VARCHAR2(10) DEFAULT 'ENGLISH';
23
24    BEGIN
25       -- Read shared cursor and return concatenated result.
26       FOR i IN c(pv_long_phrase, lv_language) LOOP
27         lv_short_salutation := i.short_salutation;
28       END LOOP;
29       RETURN lv_short_salutation || ' ' || pv_name || '!';
30    END;
31
32    -- Define an overloaded salutation.
33    FUNCTION salutation
34    ( pv_long_phrase  VARCHAR2 DEFAULT 'Hello'
35    , pv_name          VARCHAR2
36    , pv_language      VARCHAR2) RETURN VARCHAR2 IS
37
38       -- Local variable.
39       lv_short_salutation  VARCHAR2(4) := '';
40
41    BEGIN
42       -- Read shared cursor and return concatenated result.
43       FOR i IN c(pv_long_phrase, pv_language) LOOP
44           lv_short_salutation := i.short_salutation;
45       END LOOP;
46       RETURN lv_short_salutation || ' ' || pv_name || '!';
47    END;
48
49  END;
50  /
```

You can test either of these overloaded functions inside a PL/SQL block or by calling them with the CALL statement at the SQL*Plus prompt. A SQL*Plus scope variable is required to use the CALL statement, as covered in Chapter 2. The following declares the variable and calls the function result into the :message bind variable (using the DEFAULT language value set on line 22):

```
VARIABLE message VARCHAR2(30)
CALL overloading.salutation('Hello','Ringo') INTO :message;
```

You can query the result now and see "Hello Ringo!" or call the overloaded function with three parameters like this:

```
CALL overloading.salutation('Addio','Lennon','Italian') INTO :message;
```

A query like this,

```
SELECT :message AS "Goodbye Message" FROM dual;
```

yields this:

```
Message
---------------
Ciao Lennon!
```

When you make a package serially reusable, it becomes unavailable in the context of a SELECT statement. By way of example, this query,

```
SQL> SELECT overloading.salutation('Addio','Lennon','Italian') AS "Message"
  2  FROM dual;
```

raises this error:

```
SELECT overloading.salutation('Addio','Lennon','Italian') AS "Message"
       *
ERROR at line 1:
ORA-06534: Cannot access Serially Reusable package "STUDENT.OVERLOADING"
ORA-06512: at line 1
```

It is possible to query functions from packages when they're not serially reusable, and the general rule for most commercial packages is that they're not serially reusable. The only time you need to define a package as serially reusable is when it has a shared cursor. Moving the shared cursor into each of the functions would eliminate the need to make this package serially reusable.

Packages are extremely effective for bundling your code into related modules, and this is something you should generally opt for in application design. Now you know how to implement packages.

PL/SQL Variables: Types, Assignments, and Operators

PL/SQL supports many more data types than Oracle's SQL dialect does. These variables can be classified into two main groups: scalar and composite.

A scalar variable contains one and only one thing. In Java, primitives are scalar variables. Characters, integers, and various number data types are scalar variables in most programming languages. Strings are also scalar variables in the context of relational databases.

A composite variable contains more than one scalar or other composite variable in some type of data structure. Structures can be arrays, reference cursors, and user-defined types such as arrays, records, or objects.

Some data types are unconstrained, but others are constrained. Constrained data types derive specialized behavior from their generalized or unconstrained data type. For example, a user-defined data type of positive integers is a specialization of an integer data type. An unconstrained data type doesn't place artificial limits on the range of a data type.

The program examples presented here demonstrate the assignment of string or numeric literal values to three base data types. Date, timestamp, or interval data types use the TO_CHAR or CAST built-in function to convert string literal values into valid dates or timestamps. Likewise, you'll need to convert them back to strings to print them with the `print_line` procedure of the `dbms_output` package. After we show you how to work with the base data types, we'll show you how to work with composite data types.

PL/SQL lets you explicitly or implicitly define data types. Implicit definitions rely on anchoring them to a table or column definition. You anchor data types to catalog objects with pseudo columns or a table. A `%TYPE` is a pseudo column that lets you anchor a data type to the definition of a column in a table. Alternatively, a `%ROWTYPE` lets you anchor a record type to the definition of a table or view in the database catalog, or to a `CURSOR` structure in your PL/SQL block.

Text Data Types

As you learned in Chapter 6, several text data types exist. You probably use variable-length strings more frequently than the others, because they meet most needs. You can put 4000-byte text into the `VARCHAR`, `VARCHAR2`, and `NVARCHAR2` data types in SQL, but you can put 32,767 bytes in the same data types PL/SQL. That's typically enough space for most text entries. You should put larger text entries in the `CLOB` data type.

You have an alternative to variable-length data types in the `CHAR`, `NCHAR`, and `CHARACTER` data types. You use them when you want to allocate a fixed-size string. In most cases, you forfeit space for little if any tangible benefit. A perfect use case for a `CHAR` data type is a column that contains the two-character codes for U.S. states, because it won't allocate space unnecessarily.

You assign literal values to variable or fixed-length data types the same way. In fact, you make assignments to a `CLOB` the same way when the string could really fit in an ordinary text data type. Entries longer than 32,767 bytes are covered in Chapter 8 of *Oracle Database 11*g *PL/SQL Programming*, because they involve external programming languages or the `DBMS_LOB` package.

This sample program shows you the assignment and subsequent space allocation for both variable and fixed-length data types:

```
SQL> DECLARE
  2    lv_fixed     CHAR(40)     := 'Something not quite long.';
  3    lv_variable  VARCHAR(40)  := 'Something not quite long.';
  4    lv_clob      CLOB         := 'Something not quite long.';
  5  BEGIN
  6    dbms_output.put_line('Fixed Length   ['||LENGTH(lv_fixed)||']');
  7    dbms_output.put_line('Varying Length ['||LENGTH(lv_variable)||']');
  8    dbms_output.put_line('CLOB Length    ['||LENGTH(lv_clob)||']');
  9  END;
 10  /
```

This program prints the space allocation sizes:

```
Fixed Length   [40]
Varying Length [25]
CLOB Length    [25]
```

The `LONG` and `LONG RAW` data types are provided *only for backward compatibility*. You should not use them. `CLOB` data types are the replacements for the *soon to be deprecated* `LONG` and `LONG RAW` data types. You can read more about `CLOB`, `BLOB`, and `BFILE` data types in Chapter 8 in *Oracle Database 11*g *PL/SQL Programming*. The `ROWID` is provided only for backward compatibility, and its replacement is the *universal row ID—*UROWID. You'll generally use these only during DBA work, and you'll usually rely on their implicit conversion to variable-length strings.

Date Types

Dates are always complex in programming languages. The DATE data type is the base type for dates, times, and intervals. The following discussion shows you how to use dates. As previously discussed, Oracle has two default date masks, and they support implicit casting to DATE data types. They are a two-digit day, three-character month, two-digit year (DD-MON-RR); and a two-digit day, three-character month, four-digit year (DD-MON-YYYY). Any other string literal requires an overriding format mask with the TO_DATE built-in SQL function.

The next example shows you how to assign variables with implicit and explicit casting from conforming and nonconforming strings. Nonconforming strings rely on formatting masks, which you can find in Chapter 5 of the *Oracle Database SQL Language Reference 11g*.

```
SQL> DECLARE
  2    lv_date_1  DATE  := '28-APR-75';
  3    lv_date_2  DATE  := '29-APR-1975';
  4    lv_date_3  DATE  := TO_DATE('19750430','YYYYMMDD');
  5  BEGIN
  6    dbms_output.put_line('Implicit ['||lv_date_1||']');
  7    dbms_output.put_line('Implicit ['||lv_date_2||']');
  8    dbms_output.put_line('Explicit ['||lv_date_3||']');
  9  END;
 10  /
```

This program prints the following:

```
Implicit [28-APR-75]
Implicit [29-APR-75]
Explicit [30-APR-75]
```

When you want to see the four-digit year, you use the TO_CHAR built-in function with the appropriate format mask. Dates work differently in Oracle than they do in MySQL, but they work in PL/SQL as they do in SQL. Check back to the full discussion in Chapter 11. You can add a day simply by adding an integer to a date variable, as shown in the following program:

```
SQL> DECLARE
  2    lv_date  DATE  := '12-MAY-1975';
  3  BEGIN
  4    lv_date := lv_date + 3;
  5    dbms_output.put_line('Date ['||lv_date||']');
  6  END;
  7  /
```

This prints a date three days after the original date:

```
15-May-75
```

You can also work with parts of a day, because dates are really scalar numbers. The integer value sets the date and any fractional value sets the hours, minutes, and seconds. You use the

TRUNC built-in function to round down a date to the base date or integer value. This is important when you want to perform interval calculations about the number of elapsed days.

```
SQL> DECLARE
  2    lv_date_1  DATE  := SYSDATE;
  3    lv_date_2  DATE  := lv_date_1;
  4  BEGIN
  5    dbms_output.put_line(TO_CHAR(lv_date_1,'DD-MON-YY HH24:MI:SS'));
  6    dbms_output.put_line(TO_CHAR(TRUNC(lv_date_2),'DD-MON-YY HH24:MI:SS'));
  7  END;
  8  /
```

This example prints this:

```
30-APR-09 00:04:13
30-APR-09 00:00:00
```

As you can see from the results, the TRUNC built-in function reduces the scalar date to a whole integer. With the TRUNC command, you are able to calculate the number of days between two dates.

Number Types

Numbers are straightforward in PL/SQL. You assign integer and complex numbers the same way to all but the new IEEE 754-format data types.

The basic number data type is NUMBER. You can define a variable as an unconstrained or constrained NUMBER data type by qualifying the *precision* or *scale*. Precision constraints prevent the assignment of larger precision numbers to target variables. Scale limitations shave off part of the decimal value but allow assignment with a loss of value.

The following example demonstrates what happens when you assign a larger precision NUMBER data type value to a variable with a smaller precision. The first number between the opening parenthesis and comma defines the precision, or total number of digits, to the left and right of the decimal point. The second number between the comma and the closing parenthesis defines the scale, or total number of digits, to the right of the decimal point.

```
SQL> DECLARE
  2    lv_number1  NUMBER(6,2);
  3    lv_number2  NUMBER(15,2) := 21533.22;
  4  BEGIN
  5    lv_number1 := lv_number2;
  6    dbms_output.put_line(lv_number1);
  7  END;
  8  /
```

The assignment on line 5 throws the following exception:

```
DECLARE
*
ERROR at line 1:
ORA-06502: PL/SQL: numeric or value error: number precision too large
ORA-06512: at line 5
```

The error is thrown because the physical digits of the NUMBER(6,2) data type can't hold all the digits from the source variable. To eliminate the error, you need to change the precision value from 6 to 7. That allows the entire number to fit in the data type.

The next example leaves the precision at 6 but changes the decimal scale to 1. As mentioned, this change lets the assignment work. Unfortunately, you lose the precision of the hundredth decimal value by shaving it off.

```
SQL> DECLARE
  2     lv_number1  NUMBER(6,1);
  3     lv_number2  NUMBER(15,2)  := 21533.22;
  4  BEGIN
  5     lv_number1  := lv_number2;
  6     dbms_output.put_line(lv_number1);
  7  END;
  8  /
```

Here's how the value in lv_number1 after the assignment prints:

```
21533.2
```

You lose the entire decimal value when you assign a NUMBER data type with a decimal to any of the integer data types. Unlike Java and most other procedural programming languages, PL/SQL doesn't require you to acknowledge this loss of precision by making the assignment explicit.

You can see the implicit casting of a NUMBER data type to an INTEGER data type in the following code:

```
SQL> DECLARE
  2     lv_number1  INTEGER;
  3     lv_number2  NUMBER(15,2)  := 21533.22;
  4  BEGIN
  5     lv_number1 := lv_number2;
  6     dbms_output.put_line(lv_number1);
  7  END;
  8  /
```

The program would print this:

```
21533
```

Likewise, you could perform the same task on line 5 by using the FLOOR function before making the assignment between two variables (that use the NUMBER data type), like so:

```
  5     lv_number1 := FLOOR(lv_number2);
```

The FLOOR function effectively rounds down to the nearest integer value. It shows you explicitly how to *shave off a decimal value*.

You should avoid mixing and matching numeric data types to avoid the loss of mathematical value in your data. When you must mix numeric data types, you can prevent the loss of mathematical value during assignments by disallowing such assignments or qualifying in comments that you don't care about the loss of information. The latter is a valid approach when you're reporting in hundreds, thousands, and millions, provided you do the sum first before discarding the sum's decimal value.

The new IEEE 754-format data types are single-precision and double-precision numbers. Their design supports scientific computing. The `BINARY_FLOAT` is a *32-bit* floating point number, and the `BINARY_DOUBLE` is a *64-bit* floating point number.

```
SQL> DECLARE
  2    lv_number1  BINARY_FLOAT;
  3    lv_number2  BINARY_DOUBLE := 89015698736543.4028234663852886E+038d;
  4  BEGIN
  5    dbms_output.put_line(lv_number2);
  6    lv_number1 := lv_number2;
  7    dbms_output.put_line(lv_number1);
  8  END;
  9  /
```

prints the following:

```
8.9015698736543403E+051
Inf
```

The output from this program shows you what happens when you assign a value from a `BINARY_DOUBLE` to a `BINARY_FLOAT` variable. The outcome might result in an error, but it most certainly won't manifest itself during the assignment. Your program will probably throw an exception when you attempt to use the new variable. The `Inf` represents infinity or a value outside the range of values for the `BINARY_FLOAT` data type.

In this case, the `BINARY_DOUBLE` value is simply too large for a `BINARY_FLOAT` data type. The value assigned to the `BINARY_FLOAT` is infinity because the 64-bit value represents infinity within the scope of a 32-bit data type. Note that no error is raised during the assignment, and the implicit casting could break your program's downstream logic.

Composite Variable Types

Composite variables differ from scalar variables because they hold copies of more than one thing. Composite variables can hold a structure of data, which is more or less like a row of data. Alternatively, composite variables can hold collections of data. Beginning with Oracle Database 9*i*, Release 2, the following variable types can be used:

- **A SQL UDT** This can hold a structure of data. Two implementations are possible with a UDT: an ordinary structure and an instantiable object type. The latter returns a copy of a class instance and the former returns a set of related data.

- **A PL/SQL record type** This can hold a structure of data, like its SQL cousin. You can implement it by anchoring the data type of elements to columns in tables, views, and cursors, or you can explicitly define it. You should consider explicit declarations, because nesting these types doesn't work well in some cases that are hard to identify.

- **A SQL collection** This can hold a list of any scalar SQL data type. You have two possibilities with SQL collections: A *varray* behaves virtually like a standard array in any procedure or object-oriented programming language. It has a fixed number of elements in the list when you define it as a UDT. The other, a *nested table*, behaves like a list in standard programming languages. It doesn't have a fixed number of elements at definition and can scale to meet your runtime needs within your PGA memory constraints.

■ **A PL/SQL collection** This can hold a list of any scalar SQL data type or record type, and it can also hold a list of any PL/SQL record type. Unlike with the other collections, you're not limited to a numeric index value. You can also use a string as the index value. This is aptly named for that duality of character as an *associative* array. Many experienced programmers still call this a PL/SQL table, as established in the Oracle Database 8 documentation.

You see how to implement a PL/SQL-only solution before the more flexible and extensible solution. The best solution returns a SQL collection with a record structure, because you don't have to wrap it in a pipelined table function to use it in SQL. You should note what works and doesn't work when making assignments to these data types.

One of the major downsides of pipelined table functions is that they create system-generated name types in the data catalog. These become tedious to tie back to your application and more expensive to maintain in your code tree.

You can implement a PL/SQL record structure and collection in a simple anonymous block program. The sample program does forward-reference cursors and loops, which you find in the "PL/SQL Control Structures" section a bit later.

Here's the code for an anonymous block:

```
SQL> DECLARE
  2      -- Declare a local user-defined record structure.
  3      TYPE title_structure IS RECORD
  4      ( title VARCHAR2(60), subtitle VARCHAR2(60));
  5
  6      -- Declare a variable that uses the record structure.
  7      TYPE title_table IS TABLE OF title_structure;
  8
  9      -- Define search string variable.
 10      lv_search_title    VARCHAR2(60);
 11      lv_search_type     VARCHAR2(30);
 12
 13      -- Declare counter variable for assignment to the collection
 14      lv_counter         PLS_INTEGER := 1;
 15
 16      -- Declare a variable of the collection type.
 17      lv_title_table     TITLE_TABLE := title_table();
 18
 19      -- Declare dynamic cursor structure.
 20      CURSOR c
 21      ( cv_search_title   VARCHAR2
 22      , cv_search_type    VARCHAR2 ) IS
 23        SELECT   item_title, item_subtitle
 24        FROM     item
 25        WHERE    REGEXP_LIKE(item_title,'^'||cv_search_title||'*+')
 26        AND      item_type =
 27                   (SELECT common_lookup_id
 28                    FROM   common_lookup
 29                    WHERE  common_lookup_type = 'DVD_WIDE_SCREEN')
 30        ORDER BY release_date;
 31
```

```
32  BEGIN
33
34    -- Assign substitution variable to search string.
35    lv_search_title := '&search_title';
36    lv_search_type := '&search_type';
37
38    -- Open the cursor and map results to collection.
39    FOR i IN c (lv_search_title, lv_search_type) LOOP
40      lv_title_table.EXTEND;              -- Extends memory space.
41      lv_title_table(lv_counter) := i;   -- Assigns values.
42      lv_counter := lv_counter + 1;      -- Increments counter.
43    END LOOP;
44
45    -- Read through the collection to show it contains values.
46    FOR i IN 1..lv_title_table.COUNT LOOP
47      dbms_output.put_line(lv_title_table(i).title);
48    END LOOP;
49  END;
50  /
```

This program defines the PL/SQL record structure on lines 3 and 4, and the collection of the record structure on line 7. Two substitution placeholder variables are defined on lines 10 and 11. Line 17 creates a variable of the collection and instantiates a null collection. If you fail to instantiate the collection on line 17, you would raise a compile time error because of line 40, which would look like this:

```
DECLARE
*
ERROR at line 1:
ORA-06531: Reference to uninitialized collection
ORA-06512: at line 40
```

To avoid the error, you should always instantiate collections when they're declared. Line 40, the trigger for an uninitialized collection, is actually where the program attempts to allocate memory to the structure. It can't allocate memory to an uninitialized structure. Line 47 shows you the syntax to capture the numeric index and element value of a record type collection. Notice the use of parentheses instead of square brackets: most developers learn to reference an array's index within square brackets.

Lines 20 through 22 define cursor parameters, which are substituted on lines 25 and 29. The substitution variables are assigned on lines 35 and 36, and then passed as calling parameters to the dynamic cursor on line 39. An EXCEPTION block is excluded to let you see any error during compile or runtime. Check Chapter 2 for how to test the program with substitution variables.

TIP
*Line 25 of the first composite variable type uses ' *+ ' in the regular expression, but you should generally use ' .+ ', which does the same thing.*

The more elegant and effective solution is to define SQL data types for a record structure and collection of record structures. This is tricky, because you would use the same object definitions to create instantiatable object types, but these aren't instantiatable object types where you gain access to methods to operate against instances. They are reusable SQL record structures or UDTs. You can find their type definitions in the database catalog.

Creating these models is a three-step process: You define the record structure as an object type, then the collection, and finally a function to show how to return the collection from a PL/SQL-to-SQL context. Ultimately, you can simply query the models inside a SQL statement. This makes lists and arrays of SQL object types reusable in the context of external programming languages such as C#, C++, Java, and Hypertext Preprocessor (PHP).

You create the base SQL UDT like this:

```
SQL> CREATE OR REPLACE TYPE title_structure IS OBJECT
  2  ( title varchar2(60), subtitle varchar2(60));
  3  /
```

You can create the collection by using a varray or nested table. The nested table is always the more flexible and least subject to change because it doesn't have a fixed maximum size. You create a SQL collection of the object type like this:

```
SQL> CREATE OR REPLACE TYPE title_table IS TABLE OF title_structure;
  2  /
```

The function is a rather trivial example but is effective by its readability and small size (it has one less input parameter than the earlier anonymous block). Naturally, when you write real logic, it will be a bit more complex, because this could easily be solved as an ordinary query:

```
SQL> CREATE OR REPLACE FUNCTION get_full_titles
  2  ( title_in VARCHAR2 ) RETURN TITLE_TABLE IS
  3
  4    -- Declare a variable that uses the record structure.
  5    lv_counter         PLS_INTEGER := 1;
  6
  7    -- Declare a variable that uses the record structure.
  8    lv_title_table     TITLE_TABLE := title_table();
  9
 10    -- Declare dynamic cursor structure.
 11    CURSOR c ( cv_search VARCHAR2 ) IS
 12      SELECT   item_title, item_subtitle
 13      FROM     item
 14      WHERE    REGEXP_LIKE(item_title,'^.+'||cv_search||'.+','i')
 15      AND      item_type =
 16                 (SELECT common_lookup_id
 17                  FROM   common_lookup
 18                  WHERE  common_lookup_type = 'DVD_WIDE_SCREEN')
 19      ORDER BY release_date;
 20
 21  BEGIN
 22    -- Open the cursor and map results to collection.
```

```
23    FOR i IN c (title_in) LOOP
24      lv_title_table.EXTEND;              -- Extends memory.
25
26      /* The assignment pattern for a SQL Collection is
27         incompatible with the cursor return type, and you must
28         construct an instance of the object type before
29         assigning it to collection. */
30      lv_title_table(lv_counter) := title_structure(i.item_title
31                                                    ,i.item_subtitle);
32      lv_counter := lv_counter + 1;    -- Increment counter.
33    END LOOP;
34    RETURN lv_title_table;
35  END;
36  /
```

Line 8 declares the collection variable by instantiating it as a null value collection. Inside the *for* loop, line 24 extends memory space for a new element in the collection. Lines 30 and 31 assign an instance of the title structure to an indexed element of the collection. It is critical that you note that the assignment requires that you explicitly construct an instance of the structure by passing actual parameters of equal type.

You can then query the result as follows:

```
SQL> SELECT title FROM TABLE(get_full_titles('Harry'));
```

The column name is no longer that of the table but is that of the element in the SQL record structure. It returns the set of Harry Potter movies available in the video store as of Christmas 2011 (aren't we glad it's over):

```
TITLE
-------------------------------------------
Harry Potter and the Sorcerer's Stone
Harry Potter and the Chamber of Secrets
Harry Potter and the Prisoner of Azkaban
Harry Potter and the Goblet of Fire
Harry Potter and the Order of the Phoenix
Harry Potter and the Deathly Hallows, Part 1
Harry Potter and the Deathly Hallows, Part 2
```

Composite variables are tremendously valuable assets in the PL/SQL and SQL programming environment. They let you define complex logic in named blocks that you can then simple query in C#, Java, or PHP programs. You should take advantage of them wherever possible.

PL/SQL Control Structures

Control structures do two things: They check logical conditions and branch program execution, and they repeat (iterate) over a condition until it is met or they're instructed to exit. The *if*, *elsif*, *else*, and CASE statements are *conditional* structures, while loops allow you to repeat behaviors and are known as *iterative* structures.

If Statement

The *if* or *elsif* statements work on a concept of Boolean logic. A Boolean variable or an expression, like a comparison of values, is the only criterion for an *if* or *elsif* statement. While this seems simple, it really isn't, because truth or untruth has a third case in an Oracle database. A Boolean variable or expression can be true, false, or null. This is called *three-valued logic*, and it was explained in Chapter 6.

You can manage three-valued logic by using the NVL built-in function. It allows you to impose an embedded check for a null and return the opposite of the logical condition you attempted to validate on lines 5 and 7 in the next program sample.

The following illustrates checking for truth of a Boolean and truth of an expression, ultimately printing the message that neither condition is true:

```
SQL> DECLARE
  2    lv_boolean BOOLEAN;
  3    lv_number  NUMBER;
  4  BEGIN
  5    IF NVL(lv_boolean,FALSE) THEN
  6      dbms_output.put_line('Prints when the variable is true.');
  7    ELSIF NVL((lv_number < 10),FALSE) THEN
  8      dbms_output.put_line('Prints when the expression is true.');
  9    ELSE
 10      dbms_output.put_line('Prints when both variables are null values.');
 11    END IF;
 12  END;
 13  /
```

This prints

```
Prints when variables are null values.
```

This always prints the *else* statement, because the variables are only defined, not declared. PL/SQL undeclared variables are always null values.

The NVL built-in function lets you create programs that guarantee behavior, which is most likely one of the critical things you should do as a developer. The guarantee becomes possible because you're changing the rules and making natural three-valued logic behave as two-valued logic. Sometimes, that's not possible, but oddly enough, when it isn't possible, there's a use case that will compel you to provide code for the null condition.

CASE Statement

The CASE statement appears very similar to a switch structure in many programming languages, but it doesn't perform in the same way, because it doesn't support fall through. Fall through is the behavior of finding the first true case and then performing all remaining cases. The CASE statement in PL/SQL performs like an *if-elsif-else* statement.

There are two types of CASE statements: the *simple* case and the *searched* case. You can use a CHAR, NCHAR, or VARCHAR2 data type in simple CASE statements and any Boolean expression in searched *case* statements.

The following program shows how to write a simple CASE statement. The selector variable is a VARCHAR2 variable assigned a value through a substitution variable.

```
SQL> DECLARE
  2    lv_selector VARCHAR2(20);
  3  BEGIN
  4    lv_selector := '&input';
  5    CASE lv_selector
  6      WHEN 'Apple' THEN
  7        dbms_output.put_line('Is it a red delicious apple?');
  8      WHEN 'Orange' THEN
  9        dbms_output.put_line('Is it a navel orange?');
 10      ELSE
 11        dbms_output.put_line('It''s a ['||lv_selector||']?');
 12    END CASE;
 13  END;
 14  /
```

The WHEN clauses validate their values against the CASE selector on line 5. When one WHEN clause matches the selector, the program runs the instructions in that WHEN clause and exits the CASE block. The *break* statement found in languages such as C, C++, C#, and Java is implicitly present.

TIP
The CASE statement in PL/SQL differs from the CASE statement in SQL, because the former ends with END CASE, not simply END. Don't try the SQL syntax in PL/SQL, because it will raise an exception.

A searched CASE statement works different from a simple CASE because it doesn't limit itself to an equality match of values. You can use a searched CASE to validate whether a number is in a range or in a set. The selector for a searched CASE is implicitly true and can be excluded unless you want to check for untruth. You provide a false selector value on line 2 if the WHEN clauses validate against a false condition, like this:

```
  2    CASE FALSE
```

The following program validates against truth:

```
SQL> BEGIN
  2    CASE
  3      WHEN (1 <> 1) THEN
  4        dbms_output.put_line('Impossible!');
  5      WHEN (3 > 2) THEN
  6        dbms_output.put_line('A valid range comparison.');
  7      ELSE
  8        dbms_output.put_line('Never reached.');
  9    END CASE;
 10  END;
 11  /
```

The range validation on line 5 is met, and it prints this:

```
A valid range comparison.
```

Unlike the *if* and *elsif* statements, you don't need to reduce the natural three-valued logic to two-valued logic. If a searched CASE statement's WHEN clause isn't met, it continues until one is met or the *else* statement is reached.

Iterative Structures

Iterative statements are blocks that let you repeat a statement or a set of statements. These statements come in two varieties: a guard-on-entry and guard-on-exit loop. Figure 13-1 shows the execution logic for these two types of loops.

Three loop structures in PL/SQL let you implement iteration: the *for*, *while*, and simple loop structures. You can use them either with or without a cursor. A *cursor* is a PL/SQL structure that lets you access the result of a query row-by-row or as a bulk operation.

For Loop Statements

You can implement the *for* loop as a *range* or *cursor* loop. A *range* loop moves through a set of sequential numbers, but you need to know the beginning and ending values. It is a guard-on-exit looping structure. You can navigate through a *for* loop forward or backward by using an ascending integer range. Here's an example:

```
SQL> BEGIN
  2    FOR i IN 0..9 LOOP
  3      dbms_output.put_line('['||i||'] ['||TO_CHAR(i+1)||']');
  4    END LOOP;
  5  END;
  6  /
```

The value of the *iterator*, i, is equal to the numbers in the inclusive range values. The iterator has a PLS_INTEGER data type. This program prints this:

```
[0] [1]
[1] [2]
[2] [3]
 ...
[7] [8]
[8] [9]
[9] [10]
```

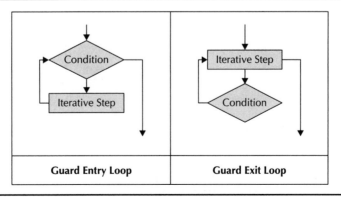

| Guard Entry Loop | Guard Exit Loop |

FIGURE 13-1. *Iterative statement logic flows*

Range *for* loops typically start with *1* and move to a higher number, but you can use a *0* (zero) as the low value in the range. A *0* is rarely used as a starting point, because arrays and cursors use 1-based numbering. The example shows you how to do it, but I want you to know that you *shouldn't* do it.

The next range loop moves through the sequence from the highest to the lowest number, and it uses a 1-based number model. Notice that the only evidence of decrementing behavior is the REVERSE reserved word.

```
SQL> BEGIN
  2     FOR i IN REVERSE 1..9 LOOP
  3        dbms_output.put_line('['||i||'] ['||TO_CHAR(i+1)||']');
  4     END LOOP;
  5  END;
  6  /
```

Cursor *for* loops work with data sets returned by queries. Two static patterns are possible, in addition to an implicit dynamic cursor and a parameterized dynamic cursor. The first example shows you how to write a static cursor without a declaration block. You should write this type of code only when you're doing a quick test program or standalone script.

```
SQL> BEGIN
  2     FOR i IN (SELECT item_title FROM item) LOOP
  3        dbms_output.put_line(i.item_title);
  4     END LOOP;
  5  END;
  6  /
```

Line 2 contains the static cursor inside parentheses. At runtime, the query becomes an implicit cursor. Implicit cursors like these should *always be static queries*. You should put queries into formal cursors, and then call them in the execution block, like this:

```
SQL> DECLARE
  2     CURSOR c IS
  3        SELECT item_title FROM item;
  4  BEGIN
  5     FOR i IN c LOOP
  6        dbms_output.put_line(i.item_title);
  7     END LOOP;
  8  END;
  9  /
```

The program declares a formal static cursor on lines 2 and 3. The *for* loop implicitly opens and fetches records from the cursor on line 5. This type of program is more readable than the preceding example. It is also adaptable if your requirements evolve from a static to dynamic cursor. Whether or not you define cursors with formal parameters, you can include variables in a formal cursor declaration.

The following shows you how to implement a cursor with a formal parameter. The formal parameter creates a dynamic cursor.

```
SQL> DECLARE
  2     lv_search_string VARCHAR2(60);
  3     CURSOR c (cv_search VARCHAR2) IS
```

```
 4        SELECT    item_title
 5        FROM      item
 6        WHERE     REGEXP_LIKE(item_title,'^'||cv_search||'*+');
 7   BEGIN
 8     FOR i IN c ('&input') LOOP
 9       dbms_output.put_line(i.item_title);
10     END LOOP;
11   END;
12   /
```

The lines of interest are 3, 6, and 8. Line 3 declares the formal parameter for a dynamic cursor. Line 6 shows the use of the formal parameter in the cursor. Line 8 shows the actual parameter calling the cursor. The call parameter is a substitution variable because the anonymous block then becomes dynamic. You can eliminate the formal parameter from the cursor on line 3 and replace the formal cursor parameter on line 6 with a substitution variable, but that's a very poor coding practice. As a rule, you should always define formal parameters for dynamic cursors.

This concludes the basics of a *for* loop. A twist on the *for* loop involves the WHERE CURRENT OF clause, which is discussed in the next section.

WHERE CURRENT OF Clause   A big to do about nothing would be the WHERE CURRENT OF clause. In my opinion, bulk operations are generally the better solution. It's important, however, to show an example in a workbook like this, so I've included two.

The first example shows you how to lock a row with the cursor and then update the same table in a *for* loop, as follows:

```
SQL> DECLARE
  2     CURSOR c IS
  3       SELECT * FROM item
  4       WHERE  item_id BETWEEN 1031 AND 1040
  5       FOR UPDATE;
  6   BEGIN
  7     FOR I IN c LOOP
  8       UPDATE item SET last_updated_by = 3
  9       WHERE CURRENT OF c;
 10     END LOOP;
 11   END;
 12   /
```

Line 5 locks the rows with the FOR UPDATE clause. Line 9 correlates the update to a row returned by the cursor.

The next example demonstrates how to use the WHERE CURRENT OF in a bulk operation. It's an unavoidable forward reference to material covered later in this chapter.

```
SQL> DECLARE
  2     TYPE update_record IS RECORD
  3     ( last_updated_by  NUMBER
  4     , last_update_date DATE );
  5     TYPE update_table IS TABLE OF UPDATE_RECORD;
  6     updates UPDATE_TABLE;
  7     CURSOR c IS
```

```
 8        SELECT last_updated_by, last_update_date
 9        FROM item
10        WHERE  item_id BETWEEN 1031 AND 1040
11        FOR UPDATE;
12  BEGIN
13    OPEN c;
14    LOOP
15      FETCH c BULK COLLECT INTO updates LIMIT 5;
16      EXIT WHEN updates.COUNT = 0;
17      FORALL i IN updates.FIRST..updates.LAST
18        UPDATE item
19        SET    last_updated_by = updates(i).last_updated_by
20        ,      last_update_date = updates(i).last_update_date
21        WHERE CURRENT OF c;
22  END;
23  /
```

Like the row-by-row example, the FOR UPDATE clause on line 9 locks the rows. The WHERE CURRENT OF clause on line 21 correlates the update to the rows returned by the bulk collected cursor.

Now that I've shown you how to do it, you might wonder why would you want to? The same thing can be accomplished by a correlated UPDATE statement, like this:

```
SQL> UPDATE item i1
  2  SET    last_updated_by = 3
  3  ,      last_update_date = TRUNC(SYSDATE)
  4  WHERE  EXISTS (SELECT NULL FROM item i2
  5                 WHERE  item_id BETWEEN 1031 AND 1040
  6                 AND    i1.ROWID = i2.ROWID);
```

In fact, Oracle's documentation indicates that it recommends correlated UDPATE and DELETE statements over the use of the WHERE CURRENT OF clause. *I must also recommend native SQL solutions when they're available.*

The range and cursor *for* loops are powerful iterative structures. Their beauty lies in their simplicity, and their curse lies in their implicit opening and closing of cursor resources. You should use these structures when access to the data is straightforward and row-by-row auditing isn't required. When you need to perform row-by-row auditing, you should use a *while* or simple loop because they give you more control.

While Loop Statements

A *while* loop is a guard-on-entry loop: You need to manage both the entry and exit criteria of a *while* loop. Unlike the *for* loop, with the *while* loop you don't need an index value because you can use other criteria to meet the control entrance and exit. If you use an index, the Oracle 11*g* CONTINUE statement can make control more complex, because it allows you to abort an iteration and return to the top of the loop:

```
SQL> DECLARE
  2    lv_counter NUMBER := 1;
  3  BEGIN
  4    WHILE (lv_counter < 5) LOOP
```

```
  5         dbms_output.put('Index at top ['||lv_counter||']');
  6         IF lv_counter >= 1 THEN
  7           IF MOD(lv_counter,2) = 0 THEN
  8             dbms_output.new_line();
  9             lv_counter := lv_counter + 1;
 10             CONTINUE;
 11           END IF;
 12           dbms_output.put_line('['||lv_counter||']');
 13         END IF;
 14         lv_counter := lv_counter + 1;
 15       END LOOP;
 16     END;
 17     /
```

This prints the following:

```
Index at top [1][1]
Index at top [2]
Index at top [3][3]
Index at top [4]
```

Only odd number counter values make it to the bottom of the loop, as illustrated by the second printing of the counter value. That's because the CONTINUE statement prints a line return and returns control to the top of the loop. You could also do the same thing with the GOTO statement and label. You enclose labels inside *guillemets*, also known as angle brackets. They're available in releases prior to Oracle 11*g*, and although it pains me to tell you about them, here's an example:

```
SQL> DECLARE
  2       lv_counter NUMBER := 1;
  3   BEGIN
  4     WHILE (lv_counter < 5) LOOP
  5       dbms_output.put('Index at top ['||lv_counter||']');
  6       IF lv_counter >= 1 THEN
  7         IF MOD(lv_counter,2) = 0 THEN
  8           dbms_output.new_line();
  9           GOTO skippy;
 10         END IF;
 11         dbms_output.put_line('['||lv_counter||']');
 12       END IF;
 13       << skippy >>
 14       lv_counter := lv_counter + 1;
 15     END LOOP;
 16   END;
 17   /
```

The GOTO statement on line 9 skips to the incrementing instruction for the control variable on line 13. It is actually a bit easier to read than the CONTINUE statement shown earlier.

The GOTO statement should be avoided whenever possible, however. The CONTINUE should be used minimally and carefully. The *while* loop is powerful but can be tricky if you're not careful when using a CONTINUE statement. A poorly coded *while* loop that contains a CONTINUE statement can cause an infinite loop.

Simple Loop Statements

The simple loop statement is anything but simple. You use it when you want to control everything that surrounds access to an explicit cursor. Some of these controls are provided through four built-in cursor attributes:

- **%FOUND**   Returns TRUE only when a DML statement has changed or returned one or more rows
- **%ISOPEN**   Returns TRUE when an explicit cursor is open and FALSE when an explicit cursor isn't open or for any implicit cursor (Implicit cursors close immediately after running.)
- **%NOTFOUND**   Returns TRUE when a DML statement fails to change or cursor fails to return at least one row
- **%ROWCOUNT**   Returns the number of rows changed by a DML statement or the number of rows returned by a cursor or SELECT INTO statement

These attributes work with cursors or ordinary SQL statements. You access ordinary SQL statements by referring to SQL instead of a cursor name. A SELECT-INTO, INSERT, UPDATE, or DELETE statement is *found* when it processes rows and *not found* when it doesn't. For example, the following anonymous block uses cursor attributes to manage printing log statements to the console:

```
SQL> BEGIN
  2     UPDATE   system_user
  3     SET      last_update_date = SYSDATE;
  4     IF SQL%FOUND THEN
  5        dbms_output.put_line('Updated ['||SQL%ROWCOUNT||']');
  6     ELSE
  7        dbms_output.put_line('Nothing updated!');
  8     END IF;
  9   END;
 10   /
```

The SQL%FOUND on line 4 checks whether a SQL statement was processed. As you may have surmised, SQL isn't just an acronym in Oracle PL/SQL, it is a reserved word that links to an anonymous cursor. If SQL%FOUND returns TRUE, then line 5 prints the number of rows updated in the table.

A typical simple loop opens a cursor, fetches rows from a cursor, processes rows from a cursor, and closes a cursor. The following program demonstrates those steps and illustrates an anchored data type:

```
SQL> DECLARE
  2     lv_id    item.item_id%TYPE;    -- This is an anchored type.
  3     lv_title VARCHAR2(60);
  4     CURSOR c IS
  5       SELECT   item_id, item_title
  6       FROM     item;
  7   BEGIN
  8     OPEN c;
```

```
 9    LOOP
10      FETCH c INTO lv_id, lv_title;
11      EXIT WHEN c%NOTFOUND;
12      dbms_output.put_line('Title ['||lv_title||']');
13    END LOOP;
14    CLOSE c;
15  END;
16  /
```

This program defines one variable by anchoring the data type to the definition of the ITEM_ID column in the item table. When the definition of the table changes, you don't have to change your program because it will adjust automatically. Automatic adjustments of data type work best when changes are limited to size within a type and they collapse when changes of a column's data type isn't supported by implicit type casting. The second variable is explicitly assigned a data type, and any change to the table would require a change to the assigned data type. The first statement after you start a simple loop fetches a row of data, and the second, line 11, checks to make sure a row was fetched. Line 11 also exits the loop when no record is found, which is typically after all rows have been read or no rows were found.

You can extend the preceding model by creating a user-defined record structure and returning the row into a single record structure. Record structures are composite variables. The following example uses a %ROWTYPE pseudo attribute to anchor a catalog table definition to a local variable:

```
SQL> DECLARE
 2    lv_item_record item%ROWTYPE;    -- This is an anchored type.
 3    CURSOR c IS
 4      SELECT    *
 5      FROM      item;
 6  BEGIN
 7    OPEN c;
 8    LOOP
 9      FETCH c INTO lv_item_record;
10      EXIT WHEN c%NOTFOUND;
11      dbms_output.put_line('Title ['||lv_item_record.item_title||']');
12    END LOOP;
13    CLOSE c;
14  END;
15  /
```

On line 11, the LV_ITEM_RECORD.ITEM_TITLE statement returns the value of a field in the row of data. The dot between the local variable and column name is the *component selector*. You actually read this reference from right to left. It means the ITEM_TITLE is selected from the LV_ITEM_RECORD component, which is a local record structure variable.

You could also create a record type explicitly. This is often done when you want only a subset of the columns in a table and you don't want to create a view or anchor the variable to a cursor. A local record set variable would be like the following:

```
TYPE item_record IS RECORD
( id     NUMBER
, title VARCHAR2(60));
```

The best approach simply lets you anchor a local variable to the SELECT list returned by a CURSOR, which is a natural record structure. You could rewrite the program like this:

```
SQL> DECLARE
  2    CURSOR c IS
  3      SELECT   *
  4      FROM     item;
  5    lv_item_record c%ROWTYPE;
  6  BEGIN
  7    OPEN c;
  8    LOOP
  9      FETCH c INTO lv_item_record;
 10      EXIT WHEN c%NOTFOUND;
 11      dbms_output.put_line('Title ['||lv_item_record.item_title||']');
 12    END LOOP;
 13    CLOSE c;
 14  END;
 15  /
```

Line 5 declares a variable that anchors itself to the definition of a CURSOR. If you change the cursor, the variable automatically adjusts. This is the most flexible and least-coupled way to anchor a variable in PL/SQL. It's also worth mentioning that declaring a variable after a cursor is supported in Oracle but not MySQL.

You'll encounter some glitches down the road with local types like these, because they're limited exclusively to a PL/SQL context. The "Composite Variable Types" section earlier in this chapter shows the better alternative.

Bulk Operations

Oracle 10*g* and 11*g* (supported releases at the time of writing) provide bulk processing capabilities. They differ somewhat from the structures we've presented, but they follow the general look and feel. Where possible, bulk processing should be the default in your batch and high-volume processing of data.

The following program shows you how to select groups of rows into array structures. You do this with the BULK COLLECT clause. I've chosen a limit of 20 simply to make it simple with the sample data. Real-world solutions can be hundreds or thousands of records at a time, but I'd recommend limiting this to a range of 250 to 500.

```
SQL> DECLARE
  2    TYPE title_record IS RECORD
  3    ( title    VARCHAR2(60)
  4    , subtitle VARCHAR2(60));
  5    TYPE title_collection IS TABLE OF TITLE_RECORD;
  6    lv_title_collection TITLE_COLLECTION;
  7    CURSOR c IS
  8      SELECT   item_title, item_subtitle
  9      FROM     item;
 10  BEGIN
 11    OPEN c;
 12    LOOP
 13      FETCH c BULK COLLECT INTO lv_title_collection LIMIT 20;
```

```
14       EXIT WHEN lv_title_collection.COUNT = 0;
15       FOR i IN 1..lv_title_collection.COUNT LOOP
16         dbms_output.put_line('['||lv_title_collection(i).title||']');
17       END LOOP;
18     END LOOP;
19     CLOSE c;
20   END;
21   /
```

This program is more complex than earlier examples and forward references the concept of collections. After creating a record structure, you create another local collection data type. You then create a variable of the collection type. Line 13 bulk collects the collection of a record structure into a single variable. The range FOR loop on lines 15 through 17 reads the collection and prints only one column value from the each record.

After you've selected the data, you should be able to insert or update target tables in the same bulk-processing units. You can do so with the FORALL statement. The following lets you perform a bulk update:

```
SQL> DECLARE
  2     TYPE title_record IS RECORD
  3     ( id         NUMBER
  4     , title      VARCHAR2(60)
  5     , subtitle VARCHAR2(60));
  6     TYPE title_collection IS TABLE OF TITLE_RECORD;
  7     lv_title_collection TITLE_COLLECTION;
  8     CURSOR c IS
  9       SELECT   item_id, item_title, item_subtitle
 10       FROM     item;
 11   BEGIN
 12     OPEN c;
 13     LOOP
 14       FETCH c BULK COLLECT INTO lv_title_collection LIMIT 20;
 15       EXIT WHEN lv_title_collection.COUNT = 0;
 16         FORALL i IN lv_title_collection.FIRST..lv_title_collection.LAST
 17           UPDATE   item_temp
 18           SET      item_title = lv_title_collection(i).title
 19           ,        item_subtitle = lv_title_collection(i).subtitle
 20           WHERE    item_id = lv_title_collection(i).id;
 21     END LOOP;
 22   END;
 23   /
```

The FORALL statement on lines 16 through 20 updates 20 rows at a time, but it could easily update more. Bulk processing reduces the context switches in the database and improves online transaction processing application throughput.

Native Dynamic SQL

NDS is equivalent to prepared statements in MySQL. Dynamic SQL allows you to make your programs flexible and lets you create templates for DDL and DML commands. The templates can act like *lambda-style functions* with an unknown number of input and output parameters, but generally they have a fixed number of inputs. These parameters aren't quite as tidy as functions or procedures, or, for that matter, object types, because they act as *placeholders* in a statement. Oracle jargon and documentation more frequently call these placeholders *bind variables*, but the terms are interchangeable.

As you can imagine, there needs to be a clear process to make something this flexible practical. The process involves two to four steps, depending on which type of dynamic statement you're using:

1. All statements are parsed at runtime.

2. Statements have local variables bound into them when they contain placeholders; this works much the same for external programming languages with prepared statements, too.

3. Statements are executed.

4. Values are returned to the calling statement. These values can be returned in several contexts, as we discuss in this section.

Dynamic statements happen one of two ways. You can glue them together, which is the plain way of saying concatenating strings. Concatenation is a risky behavior; we might say that it is practicing unsafe computing, because it's subject to SQL injection attacks. Oracle 11*g* provides the DBMS_ASSERT package to help mitigate risks, but binding variables, the second way, is much safer.

You should use bind variables because SQL injection strings can't be assigned to string data types unless they're prequalified as strings. This lets you sanitize your input values before using them. Likewise, DBMS_ASSERT does the same thing. Use it when you feel compelled to concatenate fragments into dynamic statements or when you require a dynamic table name.

The sidebar "SQL Injection Attacks" comes from *Oracle Database 11g PL/SQL Programming*. I think it qualifies the problem and also explains DBMS_ASSERT.

NDS Statements Without Bind Variables

NDS statements without bind variables are straightforward when they're static strings, because you can safely embed them in program logic ahead of their execution. They're not quite so safe when you're gluing statements together unless you can guarantee their source, vetting them by using the DMBS_ASSERT package.

Here's the prototype for an NDS statement without bind variables:

```
EXECUTE IMMEDIATE statement;
```

The statement is a VARCHAR2 variable of typically 4,000 characters. It can't include a terminating semicolon when it contains a string but must end with a semicolon when it contains a PL/SQL anonymous block.

Two approaches start with static NDS statements and data catalog-driven NDS statements. It seems reasonable that the data catalog merits some trust and user privileges can govern these statements' effective use. The other approach shows concatenated NDS statements.

Static or Data Catalog-Driven NDS Statements

The easiest example of a static NDS statement is provided by DDL statements. For example, MySQL supports an IF EXISTS clause that checks whether or not a table, index, function, or procedure exists before dropping it. Oracle doesn't have that syntax, and developers have to devise a mechanism of their own to avoid runtime errors when they write scripts that drop indexes, tables, sequences, and object types.

SQL Injection Attacks

SQL injection attacks are attempts to fake entry by using unbalanced quotes in SQL statements. Dynamic SQL is a place where hackers try to exploit your code.

Oracle now has the DBMS_ASSERT package to help you prevent SQL injection attacks. DBMS_ASSERT has the following functions:

- The ENQUOTE_LITERAL function takes a string input and adds a leading and trailing single quote to the output string.

- The ENQUOTE_NAME function takes a string input and promotes it to uppercase before adding a leading and trailing double quote to the output string. There's an optional Boolean parameter that lets you disable capitalization when you set it to false.

- The NOOP function takes a string input and returns the same value as an output without any validation. The NOOP function is overloaded and can manage a VARCHAR2 or CLOB data type.

- The QUALIFIED_SQL_NAME function validates the input string as a valid schema-object name. This function lets you validate your functions, procedure, packages, and user-defined objects. The actual parameter evaluates in lowercase, mixed case, or uppercase.

- The SCHEMA_NAME function takes a string input and validates whether it is a valid schema name. The actual parameter needs to be uppercase for this to work properly. So, you should pass the actual parameter inside a call to the UPPER function.

- The SIMPLE_SQL_NAME function validates the input string as a valid schema-object name. This function lets you validate your functions, procedure, packages, and user-defined objects.

- The SQL_OBJECT_NAME function validates the input string as a valid schema-object name. This function lets you validate your functions, procedures, and packages. At the time of writing it raised an ORA-44002 error when checking a user-defined object type.

You can find more about the DBMS_ASSERT package in the *Oracle Database PL/SQL Packages and Types Reference*. Oracle NDS is immune to SQL injection attacks when you use bind variables as opposed to gluing things together.

The following anonymous block checks the database catalog to see if a TRANSACTION table exists before attempting to drop it. It uses a static shell string for the command but executes it only if the cursor returns a row.

```
SQL> BEGIN
  2    FOR i IN (SELECT null
  3              FROM   user_objects
  4              WHERE  object_name = 'TRANSACTION') LOOP
  5      EXECUTE IMMEDIATE 'DROP TABLE transaction CASCADE CONSTRAINTS';
```

```
6     END LOOP;
7   END;
8   /
```

Line 5 contains an NDS call to a static command. The problem with this type of statement is maintenance. We'd need to replace the transaction table name in both the query and NDS statement.

NOTE
These techniques let us perform DDL inside NDS statements, but as a rule they should be used only in upgrade scripts.

A better alternative would be to leverage the cursor to return the name of the table to drop. Since we also have a sequence named `TRANSACTION_S1`, the statement could handle both with slight modification and dynamic substitution.

The following shows how you can do this:

```
SQL> BEGIN
  2     FOR i IN (SELECT object_name
  3                    ,      object_type
  4               FROM   user_objects
  5               WHERE  REGEXP_LIKE(object_name,'TRANSACTION.+')) LOOP
  6       IF i.object_type = 'SEQUENCE' THEN
  7         EXECUTE IMMEDIATE 'DROP SEQUENCE '||i.object_name;
  8       ELSIF i.object_type = 'TABLE' THEN
  9         EXECUTE IMMEDIATE
 10           'DROP TABLE '||i.object_name||' CASCADE CONSTRAINTS';
 11       END IF;
 12     END LOOP;
 13   END;
 14   /
```

Lines 6 and 8 evaluate the return value for `OBJECT_TYPE`, and lines 7 through 10 dynamically glue the values from the `OBJECT_NAME` into statements. We could also rewrite the statement to use the object type dynamically from the cursor, but we'd still have to manage appending the `CASCADE CONSTRAINTS` clause. That's why we didn't bother.

A more permanent solution would let you write this type of code for any objects in the database once, and deploy it as a stored program. The `drop_ifexists` procedure does just that by leveraging NDS statements, as shown:

```
SQL> CREATE OR REPLACE PROCEDURE drop_ifexists
  2   ( pv_type    VARCHAR2
  3   , pv_object VARCHAR2 ) AUTHID CURRENT_USER IS
  4
  5     -- String for DDL command.
  6     sql_text   VARCHAR2(2000);
  7
  8     -- Declare a parameterized cursor.
```

```
 9     CURSOR find_object
10     ( cv_type    VARCHAR2
11     , cv_object VARCHAR2 ) IS
12       SELECT    uo.object_name
13       ,         uo.object_type
14       FROM      user_objects uo
15       WHERE     uo.object_name = UPPER(cv_object)
16       AND       uo.object_type = UPPER(cv_type);
17
18   BEGIN
19
20     -- Open the cursor with the input variables.
21     FOR i IN find_object(pv_type, pv_object) LOOP
22
23       -- Check for a table and append cascade constraints.
24       IF i.object_type = 'TABLE' THEN
25         sql_text := 'DROP '||i.object_type||' '
26                     || i.object_name||' CASCADE CONSTRAINTS';
27       ELSE
28         sql_text := 'DROP '||i.object_type||' '||i.object_name;
29       END IF;
30
31       -- Run dynamic command.
32       EXECUTE IMMEDIATE sql_text;
33     END LOOP;
34   END drop_ifexists;
35   /
```

There's no regular expression to capture table and sequence names in one pass, because the procedure takes an object type as a second parameter, as shown on lines 2 and 3. Line 3 also has an AUTHID CURRENT_USER, which makes this an invoker rights program. It means you could implement it as a system-wide program unit because the system user can grant the EXECUTE privilege on the procedure to PUBLIC, and create a PUBLIC synonym for the procedure. If you made that change, you'd change user_objects to dba_objects, and you'd add a filtering statement in the WHERE clause against the owner column of the dba_objects view. Alternatively, you can implement it safely in your schema. Lines 24 to 29 qualify how you create these NDS statements based on the values from the data catalog.

Concatenated NDS Statements

The preceding examples used concatenation, too, but they did it with values returned from the data catalog. For example, they returned the table name instead of binding it into the statement, and they glued it into the string before running the statement. You might ask, why not also bind the table name? We didn't do this because it's not supported. It raises an ORA-00903 error if you attempt to bind a table name in an NDS DDL. Naturally, without the WHERE clause in the cursor, the anonymous block would remove all tables and sequences found in a schema. It's an important note, because dynamic processing can have big consequences if it's done incorrectly.

The DBMS_ASSERT isn't useful when we're querying the data dictionary, but it becomes useful when we write a procedure that takes inputs from an external source. The next example creates a stored procedure that uses the DBMS_ASSERT package to sanitize inputs:

```
SQL> CREATE OR REPLACE PROCEDURE insert_lookup
  2  ( table_name      VARCHAR2
  3  , lookup_table    VARCHAR2
  4  , lookup_column   VARCHAR2
  5  , lookup_type     VARCHAR2
  6  , lookup_code     VARCHAR2 := ''
  7  , lookup_meaning VARCHAR2 ) IS
  8
  9    stmt VARCHAR2(2000);
 10
 11  BEGIN
 12    stmt := 'INSERT INTO '||dbms_assert.simple_sql_name(table_name)
 13           || ' VALUES '
 14           || '( common_lookup_s1.nextval '
 15           || ','||dbms_assert.enquote_literal(lookup_table)
 16           || ','||dbms_assert.enquote_literal(lookup_column)
 17           || ','||dbms_assert.enquote_literal(lookup_type)
 18           || ','||dbms_assert.enquote_literal(lookup_code)
 19           || ','||dbms_assert.enquote_literal(lookup_meaning)
 20           || ', 3, SYSDATE, 3, SYSDATE)';
 21
 22    EXECUTE IMMEDIATE stmt;
 23
 24  END insert_lookup;
 25  /
```

Line 12 still uses concatenation—and, no, it isn't an error. The one thing you can't bind into a statement is a table name, which must be glued into the statement. The SIMPLE_SQL_NAME function validates that the runtime table name is a valid schema-object name. Lines 15 through 19 use the ENQUOTE_LITERAL function, which puts leading and trailing quotes around any input parameter.

You could call the INSERT_LOOKUP procedure with named notation like this:

```
SQL> BEGIN
  2    insert_lookup(table_name => 'COMMON_LOOKUP'
  3                 ,lookup_table => 'CATALOG'
  4                 ,lookup_column => 'CATALOG_TYPE'
  5                 ,lookup_type => 'CROSS_REFERENCE'
  6                 ,lookup_meaning => 'Cross Reference');
  7  END;
  8  /
```

Note that the call to the INSERT_LOOKUP procedure excludes the LOOKUP_CODE parameter found on line 6 of the procedure. We can do that because the parameter has a default value and is an *optional* parameter. Named notation allows us to work exclusively with the mandatory columns in the procedure's signature.

This is about all you can do without bind variables. The next section shows you how to use bind variables in a number of ways.

NDS Statements with Bind Variables

As mentioned earlier in the chapter, bind variables are placeholders in strings that become dynamic statements. Although they're interspersed inside the statement, they occur in positional order. NDS statements require that bind variables be called in positional order, which starts from the beginning of the statement and continues as if it were a single stream until the end of statement.

Here's the prototype for an NDS statement with bind variables:

```
EXECUTE IMMEDIATE statement
[USING [ {IN | IN OUT | OUT} variable_name
       [,{IN | IN OUT | OUT} variable_name [, ...]]]]
[RETURNING INTO [ {IN OUT | OUT} variable_name
                [,{IN OUT | OUT} variable_name [, ...]]]];
```

You place your call parameters in the USING subclause. Call parameters can be local variables or literals—either strings or numbers. At least that's true when you're using IN mode parameters. IN OUT or OUT mode variables must be local variables. A compile-time error would be thrown if you used a literal value with anything other than an IN-only mode.

NOTE
Date literals aren't really dates. They're strings that meet a default format mask for implicit casting to a DATE data type.

Following are some key recommendations from the Oracle 11g documentation governing the use of placeholder variables:

- If a dynamic SQL SELECT statement returns at most one row, you should return the value through an INTO clause. This requires that you either open the statement as a reference cursor or enclose the SQL statement inside an anonymous block. The former does not use an IN OUT or OUT mode parameter in the USING clause, while the latter requires it.

- If a dynamic SQL SELECT statement returns more than one row, you should return the value through a BULK COLLECT INTO clause. Like the INTO clause, the bulk collection requires that you either open the statement as a reference cursor or enclose the SQL statement inside an anonymous block. The former does not use an IN OUT or OUT mode parameter in the USING clause, while the latter requires it.

- If a dynamic SQL statement is a DML with input-only placeholders, you should put them in the USING clause.

- If a dynamic SQL statement is a DML and uses a RETURNING INTO clause, you should put the input values in the USING clause and the output values in the NDS RETURNING INTO clause.

- If the dynamic SQL statement is a PL/SQL anonymous block or CALL statement, you should put both input and output parameters in the USING clause. All parameters listed in the USING clause are IN mode only. You must override the default and designate them as IN OUT or OUT.

TIP
Don't enclose dynamic statements in PL/SQL anonymous blocks. *You should use the* RETURNING INTO *subclause, because that's what the design calls for. If you opt for the enclosing block, remember that this behavior could get deprecated.*

The following example rewrites lines 12 through 22 of the INSERT_LOOKUP procedure from the preceding section. This one uses placeholders (or bind variables). Notice two things about the placeholder call parameters: they're locally scoped variables and they are IN-only mode parameters.

```
12      stmt := 'INSERT INTO '||dbms_assert.simple_sql_name(table_name)
13           || ' VALUES '
14           || '( common_lookup_s1.nextval '
15           || ',:lookup_table '
16           || ',:lookup_column '
17           || ',:lookup_type '
18           || ',:lookup_code '
19           || ',:lookup_meaning '
20           || ', 3, SYSDATE, 3, SYSDATE)';
21
22      EXECUTE IMMEDIATE stmt
23      USING lookup_table, lookup_column, lookup_type,
24            lookup_code, lookup_meaning;
```

Line 12 still glues the table in, because that's unavoidable. Lines 15 to 19 contain placeholder variables. You can always spot placeholders because they're preceded by a colon. The formal parameter list contains local variables on lines 23 and 24 as part of the USING subclause.

TIP
You must glue a CHR(58) *into the statement when you want to add a colon as an ordinary string component.*

It is only for convenience that the :LOOKUP_TYPE placeholder and LOOKUP_TYPE local variable are the same string. They don't have to be the same, but it makes your code much more readable and supportable.

The preceding dynamic statements have used only placeholders as inputs. The next program demonstrates an input placeholder while returning the result set as a weakly typed reference cursor. Unlike the collection examples used previously, the next example uses a PL/SQL record type. This is, unfortunately, a requirement when you return a reference cursor. There is no way to assign the row contents of a reference cursor to an object type. It's probably the only remaining place where pipelined table functions serve a purpose.

TIP
You can get a function to compile by doing a BULK COLLECT *into a table of an object type, but it'll fail at runtime with an ORA-00932 error.*

The anonymous block shows you how to return a dynamic result set. As you'll probably notice, you must know the internals of the record structure to work with this approach.

```
SQL> DECLARE
  2    TYPE lookup_record IS RECORD            -- Record structure
  3    ( lookup_type      VARCHAR2(30)
  4    , lookup_code      VARCHAR2(5)
  5    , lookup_meaning   VARCHAR2(255));
  6
  7    lookup_cursor      SYS_REFCURSOR;
  8    lookup_row         LOOKUP_RECORD;
  9    stmt               VARCHAR2(2000);
 10  BEGIN
 11    stmt := 'SELECT   common_lookup_type '
 12           || ','     common_lookup_code '
 13           || ','     common_lookup_meaning '
 14           || 'FROM   common_lookup '
 15           || 'WHERE  REGEXP_LIKE(common_lookup_type,:input)';
 16
 17    OPEN lookup_cursor FOR stmt USING '(CR|D)E(D|B)IT';
 18    LOOP
 19      FETCH lookup_cursor INTO lookup_row;
 20      EXIT WHEN lookup_cursor%NOTFOUND;
 21      dbms_output.put_line(
 22        '['||lookup_row.lookup_type||'] ['||lookup_row.lookup_code||']');
 23    END LOOP;
 24    CLOSE lookup_cursor;
 25  END;
 26  /
```

Lines 2 through 5 contain the definition of a local PL/SQL record type. Line 17 shows passing in a regular expression, which is then resolved inside the dynamic statement. Line 19 demonstrates that you call the system reference cursor into a variable of the record type.

NOTE
You can't assign a cursor variable to an object type, because there's no syntax to support its constructor. An attempt raises an ORA-00308 error. This means you must assign the variable to a PL/SQL record type.

It's important to note that NDS doesn't limit you to row-by-row processing. You can alter this anonymous block to perform a bulk operation. Bulk operations require that you define some package components first (covered earlier in the "Pipelined Table Clause" section).

This concludes the review of dynamic NDS statements, but there's more that you can do; take this as a challenge to explore.

Exception Handling

PL/SQL provides an optional block for exception handling. It manages any exceptions that occur while running the execution block. Errors raised in the declaration block are thrown to and managed by the calling scope program. Oracle provides two built-in exception management functions. They are:

- **SQLCODE** Returns a negative number that maps to the Oracle predefined exceptions, but one special case, the NO_DATA_FOUND exception, returns 100.

- **SQLERRM** Is overloaded and provides the following behaviors: Returns the actual error as a negative integer; returns a user-defined exception when the number is positive or not found in the predefined Oracle exception list; and returns the actual number parameter as a negative integer with the Oracle-defined message.

The simplest exception handler uses the Oracle keyword OTHERS, and it catches all raised exceptions from the execution block:

```
SQL> DECLARE
  2    lv_letter   VARCHAR2(1);
  3    lv_phrase   VARCHAR2(2) := 'AB';
  4  BEGIN
  5    lv_letter := lv_phrase;
  6  EXCEPTION
  7    WHEN OTHERS THEN
  8      dbms_output.put_line('Error:'||CHR(10)||SQLERRM);
  9  END;
 10  /
```

The assignment of a two-character string to a single-character string on line 5 raises (throws) an exception, which is caught by the exception handler and printed to console, like:

```
Error:
ORA-06502: PL/SQL: numeric or value error: character string
buffer too small
```

Oracle also provides a set of predefined exceptions in the STANDARD package. Table 13-2 lists and describes these exceptions. Standard error names can replace the OTHERS keyword. The VALUE_ERROR keyword could do so on line 7, as shown:

```
  7    WHEN VALUE_ERROR THEN
```

This would catch the ORA-06502 error but not any other exception, which means we would now need two error handlers. We'll need one error handler for the specific *"numeric or value error"* and another for everything else, more or less a *"catch all"* handler. The new exception block would look like this:

```
  6  EXCEPTION
  7    WHEN VALUE_ERROR THEN    -- Specific error handler.
  8      dbms_output.put_line('Error:'||CHR(10)||SQLERRM);
  9    WHEN OTHERS THEN         -- General error handler.
 10      dbms_output.put_line('Error:'||CHR(10)||SQLERRM);
 11  END;
 12  /
```

Many developers use only the OTHERS as a *"catch all,"* but good coding practices recommend specific exception handlers. You should always place the specific exception handler before the OTHERS handler.

We also have the ability to define user-defined exceptions and write dynamic exceptions. The next two subsections discuss how.

EXCEPTION NAME	ERROR	EXCEPTION RAISED WHEN
ACCESS_INTO_NULL	ORA-06530	You encounter this when attempting to access an uninitialized object.
CASE_NOT_FOUND	ORA-06592	You encounter this when you have defined a CASE statement without an ELSE clause and none of the CASE statements meet the runtime condition.
COLLECTION_IS_NULL	ORA-06531	You encounter this when attempting to access an uninitialized NESTED TABLE or VARRAY.
CURSOR_ALREADY_OPEN	ORA-06511	You encounter this when attempting to open a cursor that is already open.
DUP_VAL_ON_INDEX	ORA-00001	You encounter this when attempting to insert a duplicate value to a table's column when there is a unique index on it.
INVALID_CURSOR	ORA-01001	You encounter this when attempting a disallowed operation on a cursor, like closing a closed cursor.
INVALID_NUMBER	ORA-01722	You encounter this when attempting to assign something other than a number to a number or when the LIMIT clause of a bulk fetch returns a non-positive number.
LOGIN_DENIED	ORA-01017	You encounter this when attempting to log in to a program with an invalid username or password.
NO_DATA_FOUND	ORA-01403	You encounter this when attempting to use the SELECT-INTO structure and the statement returns a null value, when you attempt to access a deleted element in a nested table, or when you attempt to access an uninitialized element in an index-by table (called an associative array since Oracle 10g).
NO_DATA_NEEDED	ORA-06548	You raise this error when a call to a PIPELINED table function signals no need for further rows.

TABLE 13-2. *Predefined Exceptions in the Standard Package* (continued)

EXCEPTION NAME	ERROR	EXCEPTION RAISED WHEN
NOT_LOGGED_ON	ORA-01012	You encounter this when a program issues a database call and is not connected, which is typically after the instance has disconnected your session.
PROGRAM_ERROR	ORA-06501	You encounter this all too often when an error occurs that Oracle has not yet formally trapped. This happens with a number of the Object features of the database.
ROWTYPE_MISMATCH	ORA-06504	You encounter this when your cursor structure fails to agree with your PL/SQL cursor variable, or an actual cursor parameter differs from a formal cursor parameter.
SELF_IS_NULL	ORA-30625	You encounter this error when you try to call an object type non-static member method in which an instance of the object type has not been initialized.
STORAGE_ERROR	ORA-06500	You encounter this error when the SGA has run out of memory or been corrupted.
SUBSCRIPT_BEYOND_COUNT	ORA-06533	You encounter this error when the space allocated to a NESTED TABLE or VARRAY is smaller than the subscript value used.
SUBSCRIPT_OUTSIDE_LIMIT	ORA-06532	You encounter this error when you use an illegal index value to access a NESTED TABLE or VARRAY, which means a non-positive integer.
SYS_INVALID_ROWID	ORA-01410	You encounter this error when you try to convert a string into an invalid ROWID value.
TIMEOUT_ON_RESOURCE	ORA-00051	You encounter this error when the database is unable to secure a lock to a resource.
TOO_MANY_ROWS	ORA-01422	You encounter this when using the SELECT-INTO and the query returns more than one row.
USERENV_COMMITSCN_ERROR	ORA-01725	You can only use the function USERENV('COMMMITSCN') as a top-level expression in a VALUES clause of an INSERT statement or as a right operand in the SET clause of an UPDATE statement.
VALUE_ERROR	ORA-06502	You encounter this when you try to assign a variable into another variable that is too small to hold it.
ZERO_DIVIDE	ORA-01476	You encounter this when you try to divide a number by zero.

TABLE 13-2. *Predefined Exceptions in the Standard Package* (continued)

User-Defined Exceptions

You can declare user-defined exceptions two ways. One way lets you declare an EXCEPTION variable and catch it by a user-defined exception number (oddly enough 1 is that number), and the other lets you map an exception name to a known Oracle error code.

```
SQL> DECLARE
  2     lv_error EXCEPTION;
  3  BEGIN
  4    RAISE lv_error;
  5    dbms_output.put_line('Can''t get here.');
  6  EXCEPTION
  7    WHEN OTHERS THEN
  8      IF SQLCODE = 1 THEN
  9        dbms_output.put_line('This is a ['||SQLERRM||'].');
 10      END IF;
 11  END;
 12  /
```

The example declares a user-defined exception of lv_error on line 2 and raises it as an exception on line 4. The generic OTHERS exception traps the error on line 7, and the IF statement checks for a user-defined exception on line 8.

This program raises the exception and prints:

```
This is a [User-Defined Exception].
```

By default all user-defined exceptions have a SQLCODE value of 1. You could also replace the user-defined exception on line 4 with a call to a standard error from Table 13-2.

```
  4     RAISE program_error;
```

A two-step declaration process lets you declare an exception and map it to a number. The first step declares the variable and the second step maps the variable to an EXCEPTION_INIT precompiler instruction.

```
SQL> DECLARE
  2     lv_sys_context VARCHAR2(20);
  3     lv_error EXCEPTION;
  4     PRAGMA EXCEPTION_INIT(lv_error,-2003);
  5  BEGIN
  6     lv_sys_context := SYS_CONTEXT('USERENV','PROXY_PUSHER');
  7  EXCEPTION
  8    WHEN lv_error THEN
  9      dbms_output.put_line('This is a ['||SQLERRM||'].');
 10  END;
 11  /
```

Line 3 declares the local exception variable and line 4 maps the Oracle error code to the user-defined exception. Line 6 throws an error because it provides an invalid PROXY_PUSHER string as a call parameter to the SYS_CONTEXT function.

The preceding test program raises an exception and prints:

```
This is a [ORA-02003: invalid USERENV parameter].
```

The ORA-02003 is a real error code found in the `SYS.STANDARD` package. You can read the specification of that package to find a complete list of standard errors.

Dynamic User-Defined Exceptions

Dynamic user-defined exceptions let you raise a customized exception by assigning a number in the range of -20,000 to -20,999. The `RAISE_APPLICATION_ERROR` function provides this ability in Oracle. The prototype is:

```
RAISE_APPLICATION_ERROR(error_number, error_message [, keep_errors])
```

The following program shows how to raise a dynamic user-defined exception:

```
SQL> DECLARE
  2    lv_error  EXCEPTION;
  3    PRAGMA EXCEPTION_INIT(lv_error,-20001);
  4  BEGIN
  5    RAISE_APPLICATION_ERROR(-20001,'A less original message.');
  6  EXCEPTION
  7    WHEN lv_error THEN
  8      dbms_output.put_line(SQLERRM);
  9  END;
 10  /
```

Line 2 declares the exception variable and line 3 maps the error to a value in the range of available values. Line 5 throws the exception and line 7 catches the error.

TIP
There are critical and non-critical errors in any database-centric application. Critical errors should raise a failure message to the application and customer, while non-critical errors should be recorded and addressed later by support staff. Database triggers are the best place to put programming logic for non-critical errors.

Oracle 11*g* also provides a stack trace management function in the `DBMS_UTILITY` package. It's the `FORMAT_ERROR_BACKTRACE` function. Handling errors is important and much more can be said about managing them in an `EXCEPTION` block. You should check Chapter 5 in the *Oracle Database 11g PL/SQL Programming* book for more information on PL/SQL exception handling.

Summary

This chapter covered the basics of the PL/SQL programming language. It has introduced you to data types, blocks, conditional and iterative structures, bulk processing, NDS statements, and exception handling. You've learned how to write functions and procedures, and about the mode of operation of parameters in pass-by-value and pass-by-reference subroutines.

Mastery Check

The mastery check is a series of true or false and multiple choice questions that let you confirm how well you understand the material in the chapter. You may check the Appendix for answers to these questions.

1. **True** ☐ **False** ☐ A basic block in PL/SQL must have at least a NULL; statement to compile.

2. **True** ☐ **False** ☐ The ELSEIF lets you branch execution in an *if* statement.

3. **True** ☐ **False** ☐ The DECLARE block is where you put all variable, cursor, and local functions and procedure implementations.

4. **True** ☐ **False** ☐ An EXCEPTION block is where you put handling for errors raised in the declaration block of the same anonymous or named program unit.

5. **True** ☐ **False** ☐ The colon equal symbol set (:=) is the only assignment operator in PL/SQL.

6. **True** ☐ **False** ☐ You need to provide forward referencing stubs for local functions or procedures to avoid a "procedure or function not declared in this scope" error.

7. **True** ☐ **False** ☐ Oracle supports both simple and searched CASE statements.

8. **True** ☐ **False** ☐ Oracle supports SQL and PL/SQL collections as parameter and return value data types.

9. **True** ☐ **False** ☐ Packages let you define overloaded functions and procedures.

10. **True** ☐ **False** ☐ Native Dynamic SQL (NDS) statements work with bind variables for table names in any type of DML statement.

11. Which parameter modes are supported in Oracle PL/SQL (multiple answers possible)?

    A. IN

    B. INOUT

    C. OUT

    D. IN OUT

    E. All of the above

12. Which of the following are valid loop structures in PL/SQL (multiple answers possible)?

    A. A simple loop

    B. A *for* loop

    C. A *while* loop

    D. An *until* loop

    E. All of the above

13. A simple CASE statement works with which of the following data types (multiple answers possible)?

    A. A TEXT data type

    B. A VARCHAR2 data type

    C. An NCHAR data type

    D. A CHAR data type

    E. A DATE data type

14. Which of the following isn't a keyword in PL/SQL?

    A. RECORD

    B. REVERSE

    C. CURSOR

    D. LIMIT

    E. STRUCTURE

15. Which of the following isn't a cursor attribute?

    A. %FOUND

    B. %ISOPEN

    C. %TYPE

    D. %NOTFOUND

    E. %ROWCOUNT

CHAPTER
14

SQL/PSM Basics

his chapter introduces you to the basics of writing stored programs in MySQL. MySQL 5.0 and forward provide stored programs in the SQL/PSM (SQL/Persistent Stored Module) engine. SQL/PSM is a procedural language (or imperative language as qualified in Chapter 1). SQL/PSM allows you to write blocks of code that contain transactional units.

Chapter 4 introduced transactional units, which are a set of `INSERT`, `UPDATE`, and `DELETE` statements bundled within Transaction Control Language (TCL) statements. The TCL statements let you bookmark where your transaction starts, undo partial results when any statement fails, and then commit your work when all statements are complete. MySQL lets you implement transactional units in SQL/PSM stored programs.

The chapter organizes the material as follows:

- SQL/PSM stored programs
- SQL/PSM variables
- Control structures
- Prepared statements

Chapter 13 covers PL/SQL basics, and rather than repeat general content about stored programs in this chapter, I will refer you to Chapter 13 for information. This chapter qualifies the differences between PL/SQL and SQL/PSM programming.

SQL/PSM Stored Programs

Chapter 13 introduced the concept of unnamed (anonymous) and named blocks. It also described how PL/SQL supports both types of blocks and lets you call anonymous blocks inside SQL*Plus. MySQL's version of stored programs adheres to ANSI SQL-2003 (or more accurately ISO/IEC 9075-4:2003) and supports named blocks only in SQL/PSM. You can call functions in SQL statements and run procedures with the `CALL` statement from the MySQL Monitor.

You create stored programs with the `CREATE FUNCTION` or `CREATE PROCEDURE` statement. A user must hold the `CREATE ROUTINE` privileges to create functions and procedures in a database. Other users must have at least `EXECUTE` privilege on the stored functions or procedures to run them.

The behaviors of functions and procedures differ in how you define and run them. A function returns a value and is known as an expression. You can use function calls inside SQL statements, as right operands in assignments, and as call parameters to other functions and procedures. Function results can be assigned in MySQL Monitor sessions or inside stored functions or procedures. The only difference between the syntax is the type of target variable (or left operand) you use: you must use a session variable when working outside of a function or procedure. The following three examples show you how to work with a user-defined `unary` function (the `unary` function adds one to the call parameter value).

Inside a SQL statement, this query returns *1*:

```
SELECT unary(0);
```

As a right operand, the following assigns *1* to an `@holding` variable (see Chapter 2 for more detail on session variables):

```
SET @holding = unary(0);
```

As a call parameter to itself combined with a query, this returns *2*:

```
SELECT unary(unary(0));
```

You can't use procedures the same way, because they don't officially return anything, and they act like a C#, C++, or Java method that returns a void data type. As mentioned, you call procedures from the MySQL Monitor command line and functions from within SQL statements.

Chapter 2 explains the MySQL Monitor requirement concerning how you create a stored program. The key to creating these programs is resetting the DELIMITER value from the default semicolon (;) to something else, such as a double dollar symbol set ($$) before trying to compile a stored program. That change of the DELIMITER's value is necessary because you need to use a semicolon to terminate statements in stored programs. After you reset the DELIMITER, in this case to a double dollar symbol set, the $$ acts as the statement execution operator, which allows you to run a CREATE FUNCTION or CREATE PROCEDURE statement. You don't have to use the $$ if you would prefer to use the \g or \G to compile the program, but it seems some published materials exclude these options.

You should reset the DELIMITER's value to the default semicolon value after compiling your stored programs. That change typically helps you while working with SQL in MySQL Monitor because you're familiar with using semicolons to terminate SQL statements.

Although all the moving parts haven't been qualified, a quick example of how you create a stored procedure should help you visualize the written explanation and learn how to compile stored programs in the database. Compile means to check for syntax errors before putting the code in the database.

Here's how you would write a small script file to compile a procedure in the database:

```
-- Set delimiter to create a stored program.
DELIMITER $$

-- Drop any older copy of the procedure.
DROP PROCEDURE IF EXISTS hello_world$$

-- Create the new procedure.
CREATE PROCEDURE hello_world()
BEGIN
  SELECT "Hello World!";
END;
$$

-- Reset the delimiter to the default semicolon value.
DELIMITER ;
```

Notice that no CREATE OR REPLACE syntax is in the example file like that found in Oracle. You must drop a procedure when it exists before you can modify it. At the end of the DROP PROCEDURE and CREATE PROCEDURE statements, there's a double dollar symbol, because that's the DELIMITER value at that point in the script. At the end of the script, the DELIMITER value is reset to the default semicolon.

Another difference between MySQL and Oracle is that SQL/PSM stored programs have only a single block, and everything fits between the BEGIN and END keywords. Everything is composed of declarations, executions, and exception sections and any nested anonymous (or unnamed) or named nested blocks. For example, you could replace the prior example's single block with an outer and inner block, like this:

```
CREATE PROCEDURE hello_world()
BEGIN
  SELECT "Hello Named Block World!";
  -- A nested anonymous block.
  BEGIN
    SELECT "Hello Anonymous Inner Block World!";
  END;
END;
$$
```

The highlighted block is an unnamed block, which is like nested anonymous blocks in PL/SQL. Unnamed blocks can exists only inside the execution segment of a named block or nested within another unnamed block that's inside a named block.

Although MySQL lets you write an unnamed block, the recommended way to write a nested block is to name it. That's why the nested block prototype is this:

```
[label:] BEGIN
  variable_declarations;
  cursor_declarations;
  handler_declarations;
  statements;
END [label];
```

Rewriting the hello_world procedure, it would look like this with a nested named block:

```
CREATE PROCEDURE hello_world()
BEGIN
  SELECT "Hello Named Block World!";
  -- A nested named block.
  nested:BEGIN
    SELECT "Hello Anonymous Inner Block World!";
  END nested;
END;
$$
```

The rules for organizing coding components are included in the "Function and Procedure Coding Rules" section later in this chapter. Did you notice the single line comments qualifying unnamed or named blocks? The double dash symbol set (--) is really a double dash and a white space symbol set (--). If you forget and start the comment without an intervening space, you raise an ERROR 1064. The error message isn't very meaningful, but the error indicates you have a syntax failure on the preceding line.

You can create a multiple-line comment with a forward slash and asterisk symbol set (/*), the single or multiple-line comment, and the asterisk and forward slash symbol set (*/). Here's a multiple-line comment:

```
/* This is a multiple line comment example but it also works
   for single line comments. */
```

You can test this stored procedure like this:

```
mysql> CALL hello_world();
```

It prints the "Hello World!" string to the console, which is only possible inside a stored procedure. A SELECT statement of a string literal is your only way to echo out messages from a stored procedure. It is disallowed inside a function, and trying it raises this compilation error:

```
ERROR 1415 (0A000): Not allowed to return a result set from a function
```

The only way you can access a procedure is to call it. The CALL statement works from the interactive MySQL Monitor prompt or inside another function or procedure. You can't call a function from the MySQL Monitor prompt. You can put function calls only inside SQL statements, as right operands in assignments, and as call parameters to other functions and procedures.

Debugging Stored Programs

Once you compile a stored program successfully, you need to test its runtime behavior. That's easy to do inside stored procedures, because you can use a SELECT statement to display the contents of local variables, such as this debugging procedure:

```
CREATE PROCEDURE debugging(IN pv_more INT)
BEGIN
  DECLARE lv_base INT DEFAULT 6;
  SET lv_base = lv_base + pv_more;
  SELECT CONCAT("Debugging [",lv_base,"]") AS "Debugging(n)";
END;
$$
```

You call the program like this:

```
CALL debugging(2);
```

It returns this:

```
+----------------+
| Debugging(n)   |
+----------------+
| Debugging [8]  |
+----------------+
```

It isn't that easy in a stored function, because you can't use a SELECT statement that acts as query, as you can in a procedure. You must use a SELECT-INTO statement inside a function and assign the output to a variable. That means seeing an interactive debug message from a function is a three step process.

First you need to declare relevant session-level variables in the MySQL Monitor session, like this:

```
SET @sv_counter = 0;
SET @sv_message = '';
```

The @sv_counter session variable holds a zero initially, and the @sv_message an empty string (not a null). Next, define your function with testing embedded, like so:

```
CREATE FUNCTION debugging() RETURNS INT
BEGIN
  SELECT @sv_counter + 1 INTO @sv_counter;
  SELECT CONCAT('[Debug #',@sv_counter,']') INTO @sv_message;
  RETURN 1;
END;
$$
```

The first SELECT-INTO increments the @sv_counter, and the second SELECT-INTO statement puts the @sv_counter value into a debug message that is assigned to @sv_message. You can now test the debugging technique by querying the debugging function and then the @sv_message variable. Here are the queries:

```
SELECT debugging();
SELECT @sv_message AS "Internal Content";
```

The return value from the @sv_message variable is shown here:

```
+------------------+
| Internal Content |
+------------------+
| [Debug #1]       |
+------------------+
```

This is the cleanest way to test what's happening in the runtime context of your stored function. You also have the option of writing the behaviors to tables, but that takes much more coding.

As named blocks, functions and procedures have parameter lists. Parameter lists are comma-separated variable names (parameters) with data types. They're called *formal* parameters when you define a function or procedure, and they're *actual* parameters when you call that stored program (and actual parameters are often called arguments). You define a stored program when you write and compile it, and you call a stored program when you run it.

Any function or procedure that is defined with parameters requires you to provide the parameters when you call it, and SQL/PSM doesn't support default parameter values. This means that, unlike Oracle where you have mandatory and optional parameter values, MySQL only has mandatory (or required) parameters. When you define parameters, they have three parts in a procedure: a variable name, a data type, and a mode of operation. Parameters in functions have only a variable name and a data type because function parameters have an IN-only mode of operation, which means pass-by-value. Pass-by-value functions are like making a cake: ingredients go in, they get mixed up, and, voilá, you have a cake. All the ingredients are fully consumed by the process of making the cake, just like all the input parameters are fully consumed to return the function value.

NOTE
Functions are like a black box (see Chapter 13): you put something in, and out comes something else that was manufactured by the logic of the function.

The mode of operation comes first in SQL/PSM parameter lists, and this differs from PL/SQL, where the mode of operation is between the variable name and data type. The possible values are listed in Table 14-1, but remember that the INOUT and OUT work only in stored procedures, not functions.

You can use any variable name that meets the SQL/PSM convention as a parameter name when you define a function or procedure. In this book, all parameter values start with pv_. We'll cover the standard for handling variables in the "SQL/PSM Variables" section later in this chapter.

Hacking the Lack of Default Parameters

Although there's no direct and complete workaround to deal with the absence of default parameters in SQL/PSM, you do have a way to mimic that behavior. This example contains forward-references from several future sections of this chapter. However, you can declare a local variable and then vet incoming parameter values to ensure that they're not null or empty strings, as shown here (line numbers added to show substitution possibility):

```
mysql> CREATE PROCEDURE hello(pv_name VARCHAR(10))
    2 -> DETERMINISTIC CONTAINS SQL
    3 -> BEGIN
    4 ->    -- Declare a local variable with default value.
    5 ->    DECLARE lv_name  VARCHAR(20) DEFAULT 'World';
    6 ->
    7 ->    /* Only assign when call parameter is not null or not a
    8 ->       zero length string. */
    9 ->    IF NOT (ISNULL(pv_name) OR LENGTH(pv_name) = 0) THEN
   10 ->      SET lv_name = pv_name;
   11 ->    END IF;
   12 ->
   13 ->    -- Return greeting to console.
   14 ->    SELECT CONCAT("Hello ",lv_name,"!") AS "Greeting";
   15 -> END;
   16 -> $$
```

Line 9 rejects assigning the input when it's null or an empty string. You also have the alternative of using a regular expression to accomplish the same task. The syntax (divided across two lines to fit the book formatting) for that is shown here:

```
    9 ->    IF NOT lv_name REGEXP
   10 ->            CONCAT('(^|^.+)',pv_name,'(.+$|$)') THEN
```

The operative word here is *mimic*, because this type of coding doesn't replace the concept of default parameter values. Although this is a hack, it's one that you might need to use until MySQL adds default parameter values at some future date.

Mode Value	Mode Definition
IN	The IN mode is the default, and it means a copy of a value is passed when you call the stored program. A stored program is known as a *pass-by-value* module when all parameters use the IN mode of operation.
OUT	The OUT mode is a reference to a variable defined outside of the stored program's scope. You pass the reference to a stored program when you call it; the stored program can assign a value to that parameter during runtime (external reference variable). This is one of two modes that support a pass-by-reference operation. A stored program is known as a pass-by-reference module when at least one parameter uses this mode of operation.
INOUT	The INOUT mode is a reference to a variable defined outside of the stored program's scope. An INOUT mode parameter can, but doesn't have to, include a value, and it works like an OUT mode parameter otherwise. This means a stored program that contains one variable with this mode of operation is a *pass-by-reference* module.

TABLE 14-1. *Parameter Modes of Operation*

You can use any of the supported data types, and those are the same as SQL data types qualified in Chapter 6.

NOTE
The syntax of the INOUT mode differs from the PL/SQL programming language where it is IN OUT (with a space between the two mode indicators). As noted, the parameter name and mode are juxtaposed in the parameter list, too. Please take care not to confuse the two approaches.

As discussed, SQL/PSM stored programs work only in named blocks that are stored in the data catalog. Nested blocks should have names but can be nameless (anonymous) inside a stored function or procedure. The lack of anonymous blocks in SQL/PSM means that to demonstrate features of the programming language, such as *if*, CASE, and loop statements, you need to learn how to write basic stored functions and procedures.

The next sections discuss the general coding rules for stored programs, including functions and procedures. Since you're learning how to create these named blocks while learning the basic semantics of the language, the programming logic is kept very simple.

Function and Procedure Coding Rules

MySQL stored functions and procedures have only a single block between the BEGIN and END keywords. You must add your declarations, execution instructions, and exception handling inside this block, which is substantially different from the three-block model in Oracle's PL/SQL.

How you sequence these components in MySQL stored programs is important. Unlike, PL/SQL, there's no declaration block or exception block. The components (declarations, execution instructions, and exceptions) simply appear in order from the start to the end of a single MySQL block. If you put them out of sequence, you'll raise compile time exceptions.

Before we delve into the organization of code elements in the statement block, let's discuss the restrictions that govern stored programs and the declaration, execution, and exception components.

Stored Program Restrictions

Several restrictions govern what you can put in stored programs. The following lists summarize procedure and function restrictions. They're found online in Appendix E of the MySQL Reference. Although the restrictions differ between functions and procedures, procedures are the least restrictive. Functions inherit all the procedure restrictions plus others.

Procedure Restrictions   Stored procedures have the following restrictions:

- They can't use LOCK TABLES or UNLOCK TABLES statements.

- They can't use the ALTER VIEW statement.

- They can't use the LOAD DATA or LOAD TABLE statement.

- They can't delay INSERT statements, but a compilation error is not raised when a developer uses the INSERT DELAYED syntax.

- They can't use the phrase BEGIN WORK because it can be mistaken for starting an anonymous block unit of work. Instead, the START TRANSACTION statement is used.

Function Restrictions   All the restrictions on stored procedures apply to functions. Stored functions also have more restrictions, as noted here:

- They can't use SELECT statements to return results; however, they can use the SELECT-INTO statement. This means you place results from the query into local or session variables.

- They can't use the SHOW, EXPLAIN, FLUSH, and CHECK TABLE statements.

- They can't use the PREPARE, EXECUTE, and DEALLOCATE statements, which are used for prepared statements.

- They can't use Transaction Control Language (TCL) SAVEPOINT, COMMIT, or ROLLBACK statements.

- They can't access a table that has been changed by a stored program that called it.

- They can't reuse temporary tables with multiple aliases or they run the risk of raising a *"Can't re-open table"* error.

- They can't call themselves, which means they can't be recursive functions, contrary to PL/SQL functions. Stored procedures can support recursive calls, but they're disabled by default. You enable stored procedures to work recursively by changing the value of the max_sp_recursion_depth to a positive number. Moreover, you should also change the thread_stack parameter when you enable recursive procedures. You should make those changes only after consulting with your DBA.

Declaration Components

Declaration elements must be at the top of any block in MySQL stored programs, and they must also precede anything that would belong in an execution block. The order for the declaration group is variables, CONDITION variables, cursors, and then handlers.

Variables   Variable declarations must go first; here's the prototype for variables:

```
DECLARE variable_name data_type [DEFAULT value];
```

Variable names should be meaningful, and you should consider using some naming convention for local variables, such as lv_ (check the book's introduction for guidelines adopted). Also, you should consider grouping local variables by their utility in your program. A suggestion would be control, data, and handler variables. Although not required, you can assign local variables initial values with the DEFAULT keyword.

Please note that you can declare signed or unsigned integer and double data types in stored programs. When you want to assign default values, you append the DEFAULT clause with a valid value within the data type's range of values. DEFAULT values must be string or numeric literals, and a DATE data type requires a string that conforms to the default date format mask. A two- or four-digit year, one- or two-digit month, and one- or two-digit day works with delimiting hyphens, but without hyphens you need to use a four-digit year, two-digit month, and two-digit day.

Following are declarations of DATE data types with hyphenated and nonhyphenated string literals:

```
DECLARE my_hyphen_date      DATE DEFAULT '11-7-4';
DECLARE my_no_hyphen_date   DATE DEFAULT '20110704';
```

As a rule of thumb, you want to assign default values only to variables that act like constants or counters. That way, you can use the IFNULL to verify variables that should receive a value by assignment of a call parameter.

You would declare variables with null values like this:

```
DECLARE my_signed_integer    INT;
DECLARE my_unsigned_integer  INT UNSIGNED;
DECLARE my_signed_double     DOUBLE;
DECLARE my_unsigned_double   DOUBLE UNSIGNED;
DECLARE my_fixed_string      CHAR(2);
DECLARE my_variable_string   VARCHAR(10);
DECLARE my_date              DATE;
```

CONDITION Variables   After variables, you declare CONDITION variables. A CONDITION variable maps a variable name to an error code. Using CONDITION variables is like using the EXCEPTION_INIT *pragma* (pre-compiler instruction) in PL/SQL.

Here's the prototype for CONDITION variables:

```
DECLARE condition_name CONDITION
FOR {SQLSTATE [VALUE] value | error_code};
```

The optional keyword VALUE isn't a typo or terribly useful in writing the statement of the value description, so the required value is a valid five-character SQLSTATE value, such as 42S02. The SQLSTATE value appears inside parentheses after the error code from a raised exception.

When you map a CONDITION, the condition name replaces the SQLSTATE value or error code. CONDITION variables are useful because they make your code more readable. For example, a common SQL error occurs when you attempt to insert a row that violates a unique key or constraint:

```
ERROR 1062 (23000): Duplicate entry 'table' for key 'constraint'
```

The error code is 1062 and the SQLSTATE is the five-digit code 23000 in parentheses, which in this instance is all numbers. You have two ways to declare a CONDITION variable. One uses the numeric error code:

```
DECLARE duplicate CONDITION FOR 1062;
```

The other uses the SQLSTATE string value, like so:

```
DECLARE duplicate CONDITION FOR SQLSTATE '23000';
```

In both examples, the CONDITION variable fails to follow the recommended lv_ prefacing rule. The reason is that the name of the variable spells out the meaning and the local variable designation would detract from the variable name explaining its use to maintenance programmers.

You'll see how to use these CONDITION variables in the handler examples later in this section. They should make your error handling more readable.

Cursors   Cursors are a structure built on a SELECT statement that is stored in the program unit. Stored programs read and process cursors row-by-row. Cursors come after CONDITION variables in the declaration portion of the block.

Here's the CURSOR prototype:

```
DECLARE cursor_name CURSOR FOR
    SELECT {alias.column_name | literal | placeholder} AS column_alias
    [,        ...]
    FROM     table_name alias
             [{CROSS | INNER | LEFT | RIGHT | FULL} JOIN table_name alias
     {ON      alias.column_name = alias.column_name |
       USING(alias.column_name [, ...])} [...]]
    WHERE [NOT] column_name {{= | <> | > | >= | < | <=} |
                        [NOT] {{IN | EXISTS} | IS NULL}}
                 {'expression' | column_name | placeholder}
[{AND | OR } [NOT] comparison_operation] [...];
```

Note that cursors don't take parameters, unlike Oracle PL/SQL cursors. Although you can make cursors dynamic, you do that by placing either parameter, local, or session variables in the SELECT statements. That's possible because the cursor's SELECT statements have runtime access to all parameter, local, and session variables.

A static CURSOR structure doesn't include any placeholders and simply queries the table(s) the same way each time. The results change as the data in the tables changes. Here's an example of a static CURSOR structure:

```
DECLARE get_titles CURSOR FOR
    SELECT i.item_title
    FROM   item i
    WHERE  i.item_rating LIKE 'PG%'
```

While a static CURSOR structure can contain a wildcard operator, it still searches each time for PG type movies. That's considered a static query and CURSOR structure.

A dynamic CURSOR structure includes placeholders in the statement. Placeholders change anytime you run the CURSOR structure, and placeholders are typically call parameter values. This book adopts a pv_ preface to all parameter variables. Here's an example of a dynamic CURSOR:

```
DECLARE get_titles CURSOR FOR
   SELECT i.item_title
   FROM   item i
   WHERE  i.item_rating LIKE CONCAT(pv_mpaa_rating,'%');
```

Dynamic cursors are the more frequently occurring of the two because they're the most useful. Static cursors do exist, however, and they meet routine application needs.

Handlers   After the declaration of CURSOR structures come the HANDLER declarations. Handlers are event listeners, and they listen for different types of errors. You have the option of creating two types of handlers: the CONTINUE and EXIT handlers. A third, the UNDO type, exists in the syntax but isn't implemented yet.

Here's the prototype for handlers:

```
DECLARE {CONTINUE | EXIT | UNDO} HANDLER FOR
{SQLSTATE [VALUE] value | SQLEXCEPTION | SQLWARNING | NOT FOUND |
 error_code | CONDITION } [, ...]
 statement_block;
```

A CONTINUE HANDLER hears an event, takes the prescribed action, and continues the program execution with the next execution instruction. An EXIT HANDLER hears an event, takes the prescribed action, and exits the block.

There are two generalized types of events: specific events and range events. Specific events are a SQLSTATE value, an error code, or a CONDITION variable that maps to either a SQLSTATE value or an error code.

A HANDLER that belongs to a specific event only fires when that event occurs. After being triggered, a HANDLER either continues or exits the block. When you want to take action after two or more events, use a CONTINUE HANDLER, because you can set different local variables with each and then use an IF block to manage the combined event.

Range events are SQLWARNING, NOT FOUND, or SQLEXECEPTION. They listen for the following events:

- SQLWARNING listens for SQLSTATE values starting with 1.
- NOT FOUND listens for SQLSTATE values starting with 2.
- SQLEXCEPTION listens for SQLSTATE values starting with 3.

Here are a few examples of defining handlers. The first one works with the duplicate CONDITION defined in the "Condition Variable" section earlier in this chapter, and a SAVEPOINT of all_or_none set at the beginning of a transaction. It is an EXIT HANDLER for a duplicate key violation:

```
DECLARE EXIT HANDLER FOR duplicate
   BEGIN
     ROLLBACK TO all_or_none;
   END;
```

The preceding EXIT HANDLER defines an anonymous block that will be executed if a duplicate key is violated on an INSERT or UPDATE statement. The duplicate CONDITION is the triggering event for the EXIT HANDLER. It's handy because at the moment the event is raised, some part of the transaction has failed, and this lets you abort the complete transaction. If and when the UNDO HANDLER works, it will follow this pattern.

If you hadn't previously set a CONDITION variable (such as duplicate) that maps to an event, you would rewrite the EXIT HANDLER to target the error code or SQLSTATE value. This EXIT HANDLER takes action on the error code:

```
DECLARE EXIT HANDLER FOR 1062
  BEGIN
    ROLLBACK TO all_or_none;
  END;
```

You would use the EXIT HANDLER for a SQLSTATE value, which replaces the error code value of the earlier example with a SQLSTATE string (notice the SQLSTATE value is a string not a number, and not all SQLSTATE strings are completely numeric values):

```
DECLARE EXIT HANDLER FOR SQLSTATE '23000'
  BEGIN
    ROLLBACK TO all_or_none;
  END;
```

The CONTINUE HANDLER example resets a local variable from 0 to 1, which is the traditional way of using integers such as Boolean variables. In this model, 0 is false and 1 is true. Like the CONDITION variable, this variable doesn't use the lv_ preface because its name connotes meaning.

You declare the local fetched variable like this:

```
DECLARE fetched INT DEFAULT 0;
```

The CONTINUE HANDLER resets the value when triggered, as shown:

```
DECLARE CONTINUE HANDLER FOR NOT FOUND SET fetched = 1;
```

You use this type of CONTINUE HANDLER inside a simple loop to signal that all rows have been fetched from a cursor. You can see the full example in the "Cursor Simple Loops" section later in this chapter.

The declaration of CONTINUE HANDLERs is the last element that belongs in your program declaration, and it must always come after the cursor definition. CONTINUE HANDLERs define the rules when they're invoked and the action that should be taken.

Execution Components

The execution elements should be grouped together in a cohesive framework. You put assignment operations anywhere inside the execution component.

Here's the prototype for assignments in SQL/PSM:

```
SET variable_name1 = expression [, variable_name2 = expression [, …]];
```

Notice that the *equal* symbol (=) assignment operator in SQL/PSM differs from the *colon equal* symbol set (:=) in PL/SQL. However, the colon equal symbol set also works as an assignment operator in MySQL.

The following statements show the *right operand* being assigned to the *left operand*, or the value of pv_name assigned to the lv_name variable. This one uses the equal symbol:

```
SET lv_name = pv_name;
```

And this one uses the colon equal symbol set:

```
SET lv_name := pv_name;
```

Beyond the variable-to-variable assignment, you also can assign a value to a session variable or from one variable to another variable through the SELECT-INTO statement. The syntax to SET a session variable is shown here:

```
SET @myvar := pv_name;
```

Or you can switch SELECT for the SET and assign a value to a session variable (not a local variable):

```
SELECT @myvar := 'Hello There';
```

You also can make an assignment through a SELECT-INTO statement, like this:

```
SELECT pv_name INTO @myvar;
```

The content of the @myvar variable outlives scope of variables declared and defined inside functions or procedures. You can assign values from stored programs into session variables anywhere inside the execution component. Don't forget that there are risks when you use session variables, because they maintain their state between program units. It's too easy to forget to reinitialize a session variable and inadvertently corrupt runtime performance in some combination missed by your unit testing.

CAUTION
Don't overuse session variables because their state value carries from one program unit to another.

NOTE
The SELECT-INTO statement works inside or outside stored programs in the MySQL Monitor.

Although you can set and reset variables anywhere in the statement block, you should try to assign values before you begin conditional and iterative statements. Inside IF blocks you *set conditional logic*—in other words, "you want to set a variable value when one or more variables have specified values." More is found on IF blocks in the "*If* Statements" section later in the chapter.

In the execution section, you open, execute, and fetch cursors. This activity can be outside a loop when you want to read only one row. When you want to read more than one variable, you open the cursor before the loop, fetch inside the loop, and close the cursor after the loop. Loops give you the opportunity to transact against sets of data returned from cursors.

After you've worked out the logic flow of your transaction across one or more tables, you should add your TCL. The first thing to add is a START TRANSACTION statement. Don't use the BEGIN WORK statement because it has problems in stored programs. After starting the transaction, set a SAVEPOINT. The SAVEPOINT should precede any DML (that's INSERT, UPDATE, or DELETE) statements.

Exception Components

After all the DML statements, you should evaluate any control variables set by handlers and ROLLBACK the transaction when a failure occurs. Finally, you should add a COMMIT statement to make the transaction permanent when the program hasn't encountered any errors.

The exception section should check for changes in the default values of handlers and ROLLBACK transactions when they occur. The exception section is also where you should put any COMMIT statement (in the ELSE block checking for changes to handlers).

SQL/PSM Functions

You can define stored functions two ways in MySQL. One creates SQL/PSM functions stored in the database, and the other creates user-defined functions (UDFs) that are stored in external C, C#, or C++ library files. We focus on the former, written in the SQL/PSM block structure. The difference is noted here because you can't create *aggregate functions* unless you create them as UDFs with a C-language callable library.

NOTE
The C language is beyond the scope of this book, but if you're interested in writing an aggregate function, you'll find instructions in Chapter 20.2.2. "Adding a New User-Defined Function" in the MySQL online reference.

Here's the prototype for creating a stored function:

```
CREATE [AGGREGATE] FUNCTION function_name
([  parameter_name data_type
 [, parameter_name data_type
 [, ...]]] RETURNS {string | integer | decimal}
[{LANGUAGE SQL | SONAME shared_object_library}]
[[NOT] DETERMINISTIC]
[{CONTAINS SQL | NO SQL | MODIFIES SQL DATA | READS SQL DATA}]
[SQL SECURITY {DEFINER | INVOKER}]
[COMMENT comment_string]
BEGIN
  function_body_statements;
  RETURN expression;
END;
```

It was tempting to list parameter in the prototype, but it would remove visibility to the structure of parameters in MySQL. Every parameter must have a name and data type. The parameter name becomes a variable in the scope of the function. A CREATE FUNCTION statement will fail when you put a mode of operation in the parameter list.

CAUTION
Parameters in MySQL functions are a parameter name and a data type, which differs from Oracle's pattern that allows modes of operation.

You can create aggregate functions only when you develop UDFs. Any attempt to use the `AGGREGATE` keyword in a SQL/PSM stored program raises a compilation error. (If you'd like to know more about what aggregate functions do, you can read about them in Chapter 11.)

Stored functions return a value that can be a string, an integer, or a decimal data type. Notice the plurality of `RETURNS`—it's `RETURN` in PL/SQL. Take care when typing this to make sure you're entering a plural, because MySQL doesn't provide a meaningful error message when you type `RETURN`.

`LANGUAGE SQL` is the default, and it means you're writing the function body natively in SQL/PSM. The `SONAME` option applies only to UDFs, and the shared object file would be a C-callable library (without a `main()` function) program.

All functions are *nondeterministic* by default. Nondeterministic functions return different results with the same data, because they typically depend on volatile (changing) data in tables. *Deterministic functions* always return the same result from the same inputs, such as adding, subtracting, multiplying, or dividing numbers. Signaling that a function is deterministic lets the server maximize memory usage when running the function.

The next optional clause lets you specify whether a function excludes SQL, includes SQL, reads SQL, or modifies data through SQL. See the "SQL/PSM Procedures" section later in the chapter for information on when these apply. You don't generally have to provide these SQL mode values when the function is deterministic. Unfortunately, nondeterministic functions can throw exceptions when you haven't included a SQL mode value and the binary log is enabled.

TIP
The absence of a SQL mode in a function definition can raise an error when the function is nondeterministic and the binary log is enabled.

`SQL SECURITY` is set to `DEFINER` by default. The definer of any function is the user account that creates the function. Functions belong to databases, and any user who has the `EXECUTE` privilege on a definer rights function can run it as if they were the creator. The `INVOKER` option means that a user runs with their privileges and not the same privileges as the one who defined the function.

`COMMENT` is the last option and is occasionally overlooked. It's recommended that you include a description of the function in the comment field. It's recoverable when you query the `routines` table in the `information_schema` database, and when you describe the function with the `SHOW` command. That said, you can see the content of the function body with this `SHOW` command:

```
SHOW CREATE FUNCTION function_name;
```

The following demonstrates a `DETERMINISTIC` function that adds two floating point numbers and returns a sum as a floating point number. Don't forget to preset the `DELIMITER` value to $$ before creating the function, and reset the `DELIMITER` to a semicolon afterward.

```
mysql> CREATE FUNCTION add_numbers
    -> ( a DOUBLE
    -> , b DOUBLE ) RETURNS DOUBLE
```

```
-> DETERMINISTIC
-> BEGIN
->    RETURN a + b;
-> END;
-> $$
```

This function is a pass-by-value function, because all SQL/PSM functions in MySQL are pass-by-value or use IN-only parameter modes of operation. You can't put an explicit IN mode of operation in a parameter list because MySQL stored functions don't support any user-defined mode of operation in the parameter list. Likewise, MySQL doesn't support default parameter values in stored functions. These are all substantial differences from the Oracle PL/SQL model, which supports pass-by-reference functions and default values for parameters.

After creating the function, you have three options that let you return or consume results from it. You can query the results, assign the results to a local session variable, or pass the results as a call parameter to the same or different function or procedure.

As with unary() function example earlier, this queries the results in MySQL Monitor:

```
SELECT add_numbers(4.342,7.896) AS "Result";
```

It would return this:

```
+---------+
| Result  |
+---------+
| 12.238  |
+---------+
```

This assigns the result to a local session variable:

```
mysql> SET @myvar = add_numbers(4.342,7.896);
```

Or you can use the SELECT-INTO statement to assign the value, like so:

```
mysql> SELECT add_numbers(4.342,7.896) INTO @myvar;
```

In either case, you can query the result from the session variable:

```
mysql> SELECT @myvar AS "Result";
```

You would get the same result set for an ordinary query.

This last example submits the result of the function (also known as an expression) as a call parameter to a second copy of the function:

```
mysql> SELECT add_numbers(add_numbers(4.342,7.896),2) AS "Result";
```

The result is two greater than it was before:

```
+---------+
| Result  |
+---------+
| 14.238  |
+---------+
```

You'll see more complex examples of functions in the "SQL/PSM Variables," "SQL/PSM Control Structures," and "Prepared Statements" sections later in this chapter. For now, you've learned the basic block structure for MySQL stored functions.

SQL/PSM Procedures

Procedures differ from functions in a couple ways. Unlike functions, procedures don't return a value, can't be used as a right operand in an assignment, and can't be call parameters to other functions or procedures. Procedure parameters can have IN, INOUT, and OUT modes of operation, whereas functions are limited to IN-mode operation only. Procedures can echo out content, such as debugging statements or results from queries, while functions cannot.

MySQL provides two basic types of stored procedures: pass-by-value and pass-by-reference procedures. A procedure is a pass-by-value routine when all parameters have an IN mode of operation, and it is a pass-by-reference routine when any parameter has an INOUT or OUT mode of operation.

Here's the prototype for creating a stored procedure:

```
CREATE PROCEDURE procedure_name
( [ [{IN | OUT | INOUT }] parameter_name data_type
  [, [{IN | OUT | INOUT }] parameter_name data_type
  [, ...]]])

[LANGUAGE SQL]
[[NOT] DETERMINISTIC]
[{CONTAINS SQL | NO SQL | MODIFIES SQL DATA | READS SQL DATA}]
[SQL SECURITY {DEFINER | INVOKER}]
[COMMENT comment_string]
BEGIN
  procedure_body;
END;
```

LANGUAGE SQL is the only choice when writing procedures in SQL/PSM. Like deterministic functions, deterministic procedures return the same result every time when the parameters are unchanged. Nondeterministic procedures don't return the same results when they process the same call (input) parameters, because they frequently alter their behavior based on changing values in database tables.

You should provide a SQL mode of operation that matches what the procedure does. For example, here are some scenarios for the different SQL modes:

- NO SQL applies when no SQL statement appears in the procedure.

- CONTAINS SQL applies when a SQL statement selects a string or numeric literal for display or assignment to a session variable in a procedure.

- MODIFIES SQL DATA applies when an INSERT, UPDATE, or DELETE statement appears with or without SELECT statements in a procedure.

- READS SQL DATA applies when only a SELECT statement is used to retrieve data in a procedure.

Like functions, all procedures are *nondeterministic* by default. Nondeterministic procedures return different results with the same data because they typically depend on volatile (changing) data in tables. *Deterministic procedures* always return the same result from the same inputs when they don't interact with the data in the database.

SQL SECURITY is set to DEFINER by default. As mentioned in the preceding "SQL/PSM Functions" section, the original definer is the user who created the procedure in a database. Any user with the EXECUTE privilege on that procedure can run it with the same permissions as the original creator. The INVOKER model runs the procedure with their user privileges.

The last option for creating procedures is the same as creating a function: the COMMENT clause. Although it's not highlighted in the "SQL/PSM Function" section, you should put a description in the COMMENT clause of both functions and procedures.

The following procedure samples examine the behaviors of SQL mode and, where appropriate, the behaviors of pass-by-value and pass-by-reference procedures.

NO SQL Mode of Operation

A NO SQL mode of operation works well in a deterministic procedure because it doesn't interact with changeable data through SQL statements. In this section, you'll see the behaviors of parameters with the IN, INOUT, and OUT modes of operation.

The following examples rely on a @sv_name *session variable* (that's why the name includes sv_ in it). You define a session variable in MySQL like this:

```
SET @sv_name = 'Bilbo';
```

Once set, you can use session variables as sources of data or targets. You read the data from sources and write data to targets. In these examples, @sv_name is both a source and target, which means the program reads from it and writes to it. This is a substantial difference between MySQL and Oracle, because a named block in PL/SQL can't reference a bind variable.

Note that the examples don't include the DELIMITER syntax (setting to a $$ and resetting to a ;), because it's assumed you've mastered it by this point in the chapter.

Pass-by-value NO SQL Procedures   There are three steps each to testing and explaining programs in this section: Defining a session variable, re-assigning a value to the session variable, and querying the session variable.

The first example is a *parameterless* procedure, which means it has an empty parameter list. It's in the pass-by-value section because it uses a session variable inside it, which couples it to an environment dependency.

This example relies on the earlier example, repeated here:

```
SET @sv_name = 'Bilbo';
```

Define a no_sql procedure as follows:

```
CREATE PROCEDURE no_sql()
DETERMINISTIC NO SQL
BEGIN
  -- Reset the session variable.
  SET @sv_name = 'Frodo';
END;
$$
```

The no_sql procedure takes no call parameter (because it's defined as a parameterless procedure), is deterministic, and uses a NO SQL mode of operation. Inside the procedure, a string literal is assigned to the session variable. You call the procedure with this syntax:

```
CALL no_sql;
```

Or, with parentheses, like this:

```
CALL no_sql();
```

After calling the procedure, you query the result of the session variable:

```
SELECT @sv_name AS "Current Baggins";
```

You'll see that the session variable's value is "Frodo" not "Bilbo," because the session variable was assigned a new value inside the procedure. Although the no_sql procedure works, demonstrates a concept, and is short, it doesn't look like code most developers would need to write. A more reasonable approach to the procedure includes rewriting the no_sql procedure to take a single pv_name input parameter, like this:

```
CREATE PROCEDURE no_sql(IN pv_name VARCHAR(10))
DETERMINISTIC NO SQL
BEGIN
  -- Reset the session variable.
  SET @sv_name = pv_name;
END;
$$
```

Notice a few things with this no_sql procedure: The IN mode of operation designates this as a pass-by-value procedure. Unlike Oracle's approach where the mode follows the parameter name, the mode operator precedes the parameter name in MySQL procedures. The parameter's data type is assigned a fixed size, which means any calling scope variable must fit inside the data type's allocated space. This is different from PL/SQL, where function and procedure parameters inherit the size of the call parameter for IN, IN OUT, and OUT mode parameters.

You would call this more natural pass-by-value procedure like this:

```
CALL no_sql('Frodo');
```

After calling the procedure, you query the result of the session variable:

```
SELECT @sv_name AS "Current Baggins";
```

Like the previous version of the no_sql procedure, you'll see that the session variable's value is "Frodo" not "Bilbo," because that's the call parameter's value. The @sv_name session variable is assigned the pv_name (parameter) value inside the procedure.

Pass-by-Reference NO SQL Procedures The same three steps are required in this test that were required in the preceding section's tests: Defining a session variable, reassigning a value to the session variable, and querying the session variable.

The first test of a pass-by-reference no_sql procedure simply changes the parameter's mode of operation from IN to INOUT. Here's the new CREATE PROCEDURE statement:

```
CREATE PROCEDURE no_sql(INOUT pv_name VARCHAR(10))
DETERMINISTIC NO SQL
BEGIN
  -- Reset the session variable.
  SET @sv_name = pv_name;
  -- Reset the parameter variable.
  SET pv_name := CONCAT(pv_name," ",'Baggins');
END;
$$
```

The new procedure definition assigns the single call parameter value to the @sv_name session variable and then assigns the call parameter, a white space, and string literal ("Baggins") to the call parameter. This is what you would expect, because the call parameter is a reference and not a value. Actually, the parameter's mode of operation doesn't change your ability to assign values inside the procedure to a parameter. This is different from what would happen in an Oracle database, because it disallows assignments inside a named block to an IN mode parameter.

If you call the new no_sql procedure with a string literal,

```
CALL no_sql('Frodo');
```

you would get the following error message (the output has been manually wrapped to fit on the page) because you can't call a pass-by-reference procedure with a literal value. You must call the procedure with a variable. Only variables have references that can receive the return value at completion of the procedure.

```
ERROR 1414 (42000): OUT or INOUT argument 1 for routine
studentdb.no_sql is not a variable or NEW pseudo-variable
in BEFORE trigger
```

Now that the string literal has been ruled out, here are the rules for this example:

- You must call a pass-by-reference procedure with a variable.
- You must call a procedure with a variable no larger than the formal parameter's data type.
- You can't return a value through the parameter that is larger than the formal parameter's data type.

Assuming that the @sv_name hasn't been defined in the session, and the @sv_new_name session variable holds a "Frodo" string, you would assign the default value to the @sv_name variable by calling the no_sql procedure like this:

```
SET @sv_new_name = 'Frodo';
CALL no_sql(@sv_new_name);
```

The procedure triggers the following error, because the "Frodo Baggins" string is larger than ten characters (the width of the formal parameter):

```
ERROR 1406 (22001): Data too long for column 'pv_name' at row 1
```

You run this query to check results:

```
SELECT @sv_name, @sv_new_name;
```

It returns these results:

```
+-----------+---------------+
| @sv_name  | @sv_new_name  |
+-----------+---------------+
| Frodo     | Frodo         |
+-----------+---------------+
```

Although the procedure successfully assigns the "Frodo" string to the `@sv_name` session variable, the second assignment fails. The original value of `@sv_new_name` is returned by the query.

You can fix the problem by redefining the `no_sql` procedure with a `pv_name` parameter sized at 20 characters, like this (don't forget to set the `DELIMITER` to `$$`):

```
CREATE PROCEDURE no_sql(INOUT pv_name VARCHAR(20))
DETERMINISTIC NO SQL
BEGIN
   -- Reset the session variable.
   SET @sv_name = pv_name;
   -- Reset the parameter variable.
   SET pv_name := CONCAT(pv_name," ",'Baggins');
END;
$$
```

After resetting the `DELIMTER` value to a semicolon, you can test the new `no_sql` procedure with these statements:

```
SET @sv_new_name = 'Frodo';
CALL no_sql(@sv_new_name);
SELECT @sv_name, @sv_new_name;
```

The query results would be the following:

```
+-----------+---------------+
| @sv_name  | @sv_new_name  |
+-----------+---------------+
| Frodo     | Frodo Baggins |
+-----------+---------------+
```

Having mastered the `INOUT` mode of operation, let's see the impacts of the `OUT` mode of operation. An `OUT` mode parameter doesn't accept any input value with a variable reference, but it does return a value at the completion of the procedure.

Based on the knowledge of what an `OUT` mode parameter does, let's change the procedure's logic. Here's the new `CREATE PROCEDURE` statement:

```
CREATE PROCEDURE no_sql(OUT pv_name VARCHAR(20))
DETERMINISTIC NO SQL
BEGIN
   -- Reset the session variable.
```

```
  SET @sv_name = IFNULL(pv_name,'Frodo');
  -- Reset the parameter variable.
  SET pv_name := CONCAT(@sv_name," ",'Baggins');
END;
$$
```

You can test how the OUT mode parameter works by assigning a "Bilbo" string to the @sv_new_name session variable before calling the procedure as shown (don't forget to reset the DELIMITER value):

```
SET @sv_new_name = 'Bilbo';
CALL no_sql(@sv_new_name);
SELECT @sv_name, @sv_new_name;
```

The query returns the following results:

```
+----------+---------------+
| @sv_name | @sv_new_name  |
+----------+---------------+
| Frodo    | Frodo Baggins |
+----------+---------------+
```

@sv_name will always be "Frodo," because even though we pass a value to the procedure, it will always ignore it, because it's an OUT mode parameter. OUT mode parameters have no value at the start of the module but generally have one on completion of the module.

CONTAINS SQL Mode of Operation

A CONTAINS SQL mode of operation also works well in a deterministic procedure for the same reason the NO SQL mode of operation works: neither interacts with changeable data through SQL statements.

Next, you'll learn how to write procedures without any parameters and pass-by-value parameters, and how to write procedures with pass-by-reference parameters.

Pass-by-Value CONTAINS SQL Procedures   This section covers procedures without any parameters and pass-by-value parameters. Like the NO SQL mode of operation procedures, it uses session variables to demonstrate pass-by-value parameters.

The first version of the contains_sql procedure simply returns a string literal. Here's the CREATE PROCEDURE statement:

```
CREATE PROCEDURE contains_sql()
DETERMINISTIC CONTAINS SQL
BEGIN
  SELECT "Hello World!" AS "Hello There";
END;
$$
```

You call the procedure with this syntax:

```
CALL contains_sql;
```

Here is it with parentheses, which are optional in the call syntax:

```
CALL contains_sql();
```

It would return this output:

```
+---------------+
| Hello There   |
+---------------+
| Hello World!  |
+---------------+
```

The query results come from a SELECT statement against the pseudo table dual, which MySQL lets you omit in a query. This type of query uses SQL but doesn't interact with the database, which makes it a CONTAINS SQL procedure.

The next example accepts a single IN mode parameter of pv_whom. It uses the value of pv_whom to return a "Hello Somebody" result. Here's the CREATE PROCEDURE statement for this:

```
CREATE PROCEDURE contains_sql(IN pv_whom VARCHAR(10))
DETERMINISTIC CONTAINS SQL
BEGIN
  SELECT CONCAT("Hello ",pv_whom,"!") AS "Hello There";
END;
$$
```

You would call the procedure like this to use it successfully:

```
CALL contains_sql('Geoffrey');
```

It would return the following:

```
+-----------------+
| Hello There     |
+-----------------+
| Hello Geoffrey! |
+-----------------+
```

Alternative calls could be made by passing an empty string with two single or double quotes together without any intervening white space, or with a NULL value. The result would be a hello and an exclamation mark and null, respectively. Neither is much use, and that's why they're not shown. However, mentioning them provides the opportunity to remind you that no optional parameters are available in SQL/PSM functions or procedures.

Pass-by-Reference CONTAINS SQL Procedures You can create a pass-by-reference procedure that contains SQL by using the SELECT-INTO statement. The following CREATE PROCEDURE statement shows you how to do this with a deterministic procedure:

```
CREATE PROCEDURE contains_sql(INOUT pv_whom VARCHAR(20))
DETERMINISTIC CONTAINS SQL
BEGIN
  SELECT CONCAT("Hello ",pv_whom,"!")
```

```
    INTO pv_whom;
END;
$$
```

Before calling a pass-by-reference procedure, you need to declare a session variable. This creates a @sv_whom session variable:

```
SET @sv_whom = 'Rubeus';
```

You can call this `contains_sql` procedure with this syntax:

```
CALL contains_sql(@sv_whom);
```

You can query the value of the @sv_whom session variable after running the procedure:

```
SELECT @sv_whom AS "Hagrid Who?";
```

You will see this result:

```
+---------------+
| Hagrid Who?   |
+---------------+
| Hello Rubeus! |
+---------------+
```

We won't illustrate the OUT parameter, because it was covered in the earlier "Pass-by-Reference NO SQL Procedures" section. Just remember that you would need to replace this

```
SELECT CONCAT("Hello ",pv_whom,"!")
INTO pv_whom;
```

with a SELECT-INTO statement that includes an IFNULL function call:

```
SELECT CONCAT("Hello ",IFNULL(pv_whom,'Rubeus'),"!")
INTO pv_whom;
```

MODIFIES SQL DATA Mode of Operation

The simplest MODIFIES SQL example is a wrapper to an INSERT, UPDATE, or DELETE statement. The `modifies_sql` procedure wraps an INSERT statement to the contact table.

Here's the CREATE PROCEDURE statement that defines the wrapper:

```
CREATE PROCEDURE modifies_sql
( pv_member_id          INT UNSIGNED
, pv_first_name         CHAR(20)
, pv_middle_name        CHAR(20)
, pv_last_name          CHAR(20)
, pv_contact_type       CHAR(12)
, pv_created_by         INT
, pv_creation_date      DATE
, pv_last_updated_by    INT
, pv_last_update_date   DATE) MODIFIES SQL DATA
BEGIN
```

```
-- Insert statement in contact table.
INSERT INTO contact
VALUES
( null
, pv_member_id
, (SELECT   common_lookup_id
   FROM      common_lookup
   WHERE     common_lookup_table = 'CONTACT'
   AND       common_lookup_column = 'CONTACT_TYPE'
   AND       common_lookup_type = pv_contact_type)
, pv_first_name
, pv_middle_name
, pv_last_name
, pv_created_by
, pv_creation_date
, pv_last_updated_by
, pv_last_update_date );
END;
$$
```

You call this type of procedure with the required parameters that support the internal INSERT statement:

```
CALL modifies_sql(10,'Rubeus',NULL,'Hagrid','CUSTOMER'
                  ,1,UTC_DATE(),1,UTC_DATE());
```

The statement inserts the record into the contact table and demonstrates a MODIFIES SQL DATA procedure. There's no transactional control in this model, because we haven't covered control structures. The next example demonstrates a transaction against two tables, where transaction controls guarantee that both inserts work or both fail. This example was too large to display without providing line numbers (even though they're not part of MySQL Monitor):

```
mysql> CREATE PROCEDURE member_contact
    2 -> ( pv_member_type          CHAR(12)
    3 -> , pv_account_number       CHAR(19)
    4 -> , pv_credit_card_number   CHAR(19)
    5 -> , pv_credit_card_type     CHAR(12)
    6 -> , pv_first_name           CHAR(20)
    7 -> , pv_middle_name          CHAR(20)
    8 -> , pv_last_name            CHAR(20)
    9 -> , pv_contact_type         CHAR(12)) MODIFIES SQL DATA
   10 ->
   12 -> BEGIN
   12 ->
   13 ->    /* Declare variables to manipulate auto generated
   14 ->       sequence values. */
   15 ->    DECLARE lv_member_id          int unsigned;
   16 ->
   17 ->    /* Declare local constants for who-audit columns. */
   18 ->    DECLARE lv_created_by         int unsigned DEFAULT 1;
   19 ->    DECLARE lv_creation_date      date DEFAULT UTC_DATE();
```

```
20 ->    DECLARE lv_last_updated_by   int unsigned DEFAULT 1;
21 ->    DECLARE lv_last_update_date  date DEFAULT UTC_DATE();
22 ->    /* Declare a locally scoped variable. */
23 ->    DECLARE duplicate_key INT DEFAULT 0;
24 ->
25 ->    /* Declare a duplicate key handler */
26 ->    DECLARE CONTINUE HANDLER FOR 1062 SET duplicate_key = 1;
27 ->
28 ->    /* Start the transaction context. */
29 ->    START TRANSACTION;
30 ->
31 ->    /* Create a SAVEPOINT as a recovery point. */
32 ->    SAVEPOINT all_or_none;
33 ->
34 ->    /* Insert into the first table in sequence based on
35 ->       inheritance of primary keys by foreign keys. */
36 ->    INSERT INTO member
37 ->    ( member_type
38 ->    , account_number
39 ->    , credit_card_number
40 ->    , credit_card_type
41 ->    , created_by
42 ->    , creation_date
43 ->    , last_updated_by
44 ->    , last_update_date )
45 ->    VALUES
46 ->    ((SELECT   common_lookup_id
47 ->      FROM     common_lookup
48 ->      WHERE    common_lookup_table = 'MEMBER'
49 ->      AND      common_lookup_column = 'MEMBER_TYPE'
50 ->      AND      common_lookup_type = pv_member_type)
51 ->    , pv_account_number
52 ->    , pv_credit_card_number
53 ->    ,(SELECT   common_lookup_id
54 ->      FROM     common_lookup
55 ->      WHERE    common_lookup_table = 'MEMBER'
56 ->      AND      common_lookup_column = 'CREDIT_CARD_TYPE'
57 ->      AND      common_lookup_type = pv_credit_card_type)
58 ->    , lv_created_by
59 ->    , lv_creation_date
60 ->    , lv_last_updated_by
61 ->    , lv_last_update_date );
62 ->
63 ->    /* Preserve the sequence by assigning it to a
64 ->       variable name. */
65 ->    SET lv_member_id = last_insert_id();
66 ->
67 ->    /* Insert into the first table in sequence based on
68 ->       inheritance of primary keys by foreign keys. */
69 ->    INSERT INTO contact
```

```
70 ->    VALUES
71 ->    ( null
72 ->    , lv_member_id
73 ->    ,(SELECT    common_lookup_id
74 ->      FROM      common_lookup
75 ->      WHERE     common_lookup_table = 'CONTACT'
76 ->      AND       common_lookup_column = 'CONTACT_TYPE'
77 ->      AND       common_lookup_type = pv_contact_type)
78 ->    , pv_first_name
79 ->    , pv_middle_name
80 ->    , pv_last_name
81 ->    , lv_created_by
82 ->    , lv_creation_date
83 ->    , lv_last_updated_by
84 ->    , lv_last_update_date );
85 ->
86 ->    /* This acts as an exception handling block. */
87 ->    IF duplicate_key = 1 THEN
88 ->      /* This undoes all DML statements to this point in
89 ->         the procedure. */
90 ->      ROLLBACK TO SAVEPOINT all_or_none;
91 ->    END IF;
92 ->
93 ->    /* This commits the write when successful and is
94 ->       harmless otherwise. */
95 ->    COMMIT;
96 -> END;
$$
```

Line 29 starts a transaction, which means nothing is visible to others until everything in the procedure is committed or rolled back. The statement at line 32 sets a SAVEPOINT, which is like a bookmark in the transaction scope. If any part of the transaction fails, it lets the program undo any changes made after the bookmark. The INSERT statement to the member table uses an override signature that excludes the member_id column, which is set to auto-increment (as a surrogate key column). The INSERT statement triggers the sequence and inserts the next sequence value when you exclude the auto-incrementing column or provide it with a null value.

MySQL doesn't have a .NEXTVAL or .CURRVAL set of pseudo columns for sequence values, but it does have a specialized function that captures the last sequence value provided in a session. Line 65 shows how you use the LAST_INSERT_ID function to capture the last sequence value from the INSERT statement to the member table. It also assigns the last sequence value to a local lv_member_id variable. Assuming the auto-incrementing column is also the primary key (which it is), the captured sequence value can now become a foreign key value for another column. That's what happens on line 72 in the INSERT statement to the contact table.

Line 87 manages only a single exception, which is a duplicate key violation. The error is triggered when a call to the member_contact procedure attempts to duplicate a unique key in either the member or contact table. When that occurs, anything after the SAVEPOINT is rolled back as if it never happened on line 90. Both inserts are successful when there's no error and they are committed by line 95.

You would call the procedure with the following statement:

```
mysql> CALL member_contact('INDIVIDUAL','R11-514-35'
    ->                     ,'1111-1111-1111-1111','VISA_CARD'
    ->                     ,'Snape','','Severus','CUSTOMER');
```

This example shows you how to link INSERT statements with transaction controls. Although it shows you only two tables, these types of procedure generally process work over several tables.

READS SQL DATA Mode of Operation

A procedure that reads data is very much like the CONTAINS SQL procedure, with one exception: it actually queries data from a table or view. You can call procedures that return data from SELECT statements using external programming languages such as C, C#, C++, Java, or PHP. Everything except the syntax of the SQL is the same as a query called from one of these procedural programming languages.

Here's a CREATE PROCEDURE statement that shows you how to read SQL data:

```
CREATE PROCEDURE reads_sql_data(IN pv_item_title VARCHAR(60))
NOT DETERMINISTIC READS SQL DATA
BEGIN
  SELECT i.item_title
  FROM   item i
  WHERE  i.item_title LIKE CONCAT(pv_item_title,'%');
END;
$$
```

In the reads_sql_data procedure, the parameter filters the result set of the query. You can make a call to the reads_sql_data procedure like this:

```
CALL reads_sql_data('Star');
```

The procedure returns the following data set:

```
+---------------+
| item_title    |
+---------------+
| Star Wars I   |
| Star Wars II  |
| Star Wars II  |
| Star Wars III |
+---------------+
```

You've learned how to work with procedures that use all four modes of operation. These concepts support the majority of operations with stored programs in MySQL other than pass-by-value functions.

SQL/PSM Variables

In MySQL, consider variables as local program structures. You declare them at the start of your execution block. The three types of variable structures in SQL/PSM programs are listed in the order that you must declare them:

■ Variables that hold a value, such as integers, strings, and dates

■ Cursors that hold a reference to a query

■ Handlers that are event listeners

You can use any variable name that meets the SQL/PSM convention, which is rather broad compared to Oracle's PL/SQL definition. Variable names can be larger than 255 characters, can include special characters, and can start with a number, character, or special character. There aren't too many reasons for using variable names longer than 40 characters or so, but you might run into a business case for an extremely long variable name.

The following sections cover variables, cursors, and handlers. Although there's no magic to coding standards, they are useful, and you should consider labeling local variables with an `lv_` preface, and session and handler variables with `sv_` and `hv_`, respectively. As mentioned earlier, sometimes control variable names convey meaning, and in those cases, the prefacing element can be discarded. That's the convention used throughout the book.

SQL/PSM Local Variables

All the MySQL data types introduced in Chapter 6 are available for your use in stored programs except one. The missing one is `CONDITION`, which is used to map a meaningful string to MySQL Error Numbers (qualified in Chapter 20.3.4.7 of the online MySQL Reference). You need to put variable declarations as the first thing in your executable blocks of code.

Here's the prototype for declaring local variables:

```
DECLARE variable_name1 [, variable_name2 [, ...] data_type [DEFAULT value];
```

You should consider program clarity when you opt to declare multiple variables in a single `DECLARE` statement. Although it's permitted, ask yourself these questions: Is it useful and does it make the code more supportable? If you answer yes to both questions, then declaring multiple variables on a single line is fine.

A specialized type of variable is a `CONDITION` variable, which was covered earlier in the "Condition Variables" section. Condition variables are critical when you want to add descriptive labels to MySQL error numbers.

Here's the prototype to declare a `CONDITION`:

```
DECLARE condition_name CONDITION FOR mysql_error_number;
```

Although `CONDITION` variables are used only by `HANDLER` variables, they must be implemented before `CURSOR` structures, such as other variables. The following defines a `CONDITION` variable for a MySQL Error 1062, which is thrown when you try to insert or update a column value that violates a `UNIQUE` constraint:

```
DECLARE duplicate_entry CONDITION FOR 1062;
```

Math Operators	Operator Descriptions
+	The addition operator.
-	The subtraction operator, subtracts the right operand from the left operand.
*	The multiplication operator.
/	The division operator.
DIV	The integer division operator.
%	The modulo math operator, which is an integer math operation that returns the remainder of an integer division. For example, all odd numbers divided by 2 return a modulus of 1.

TABLE 14-2. *SQL/PSM Math Operators*

It's a good practice to create a master list of CONDITION variables and use them throughout your implementation. Failure to set a standard for CONDITION variable names typically results in the evolution of too many variations.

Table 14-2 shows the valid math operators.

The following procedure declares three integers. It initializes two of the numbers through the optional DEFAULT phrase, assigns one local a parameter value, and divides the quantity by a second parameter value. Then it returns the result as a DECIMAL number. Here's the CREATE FUNCTION statement:

```
CREATE FUNCTION declare_numbers
( pv_argument DECIMAL(15,2)
, pv_divisor  DECIMAL(15,2)) RETURNS DECIMAL
DETERMINISTIC NO SQL
BEGIN
  /* Declare local numbers. */
  DECLARE lv_one, lv_two DECIMAL(15,2) DEFAULT 76;
  DECLARE lv_three       DECIMAL(15,2);

  /* Assign parameter value to local variable. */
  SET lv_three = pv_argument;

  /* Return the result of the math function. */
  RETURN (lv_one + lv_two + lv_three) / pv_divisor;
END;
$$
```

Two of the local variables were declared by using the DEFAULT keyword, which is one of three ways to assign parameter values or local variables to other local variables. Notice that the assignment of the parameter value (pv_argument) to the local variable (lv_three) is made with the SET operator. That's the second way to assign a value. The third way would be to walk the assignment through a SELECT-INTO statement, like this:

```
SELECT pv_argument INTO lv_three;
```

A fourth assignment alternative works only for values returned from a cursor. You assign those values to local variables through a FETCH-INTO statement, which you'll see in the "SQL/PSM Cursors" section shortly.

You would call the function like this:

```
SELECT declare_numbers(73,15) AS "Square Root of 225";
```

Here's the result:

```
+--------------------+
| Square Root of 225 |
+--------------------+
|                 15 |
+--------------------+
```

The function definition is similar when you're working with a string, with some differences. You must specify the physical length of a fixed or variable length string in the parameter list and in the return data type specification, as shown in the following declare_string function:

```
CREATE FUNCTION declare_string
  (pv_argument VARCHAR(10)) RETURNS VARCHAR(20)
DETERMINISTIC NO SQL
BEGIN
  /* Declare local variables. */
  DECLARE lv_one VARCHAR(10) DEFAULT "One";
  DECLARE lv_two VARCHAR(10);

  /* Assign parameter value to local variable. */
  SET lv_two = pv_argument;

  /* Return the result of gluing strings together - concatenation. */
  RETURN CONCAT("[",lv_one,"], [",lv_two,"]...");
END;
$$
```

The pv_argument parameter accepts strings up to ten characters in length, while the function returns strings up to twenty characters in length. The following calls the result through a query:

```
mysql> SELECT declare_string('Two') AS "Marching ...";
```

It returns the following:

```
+-----------------+
| Marching ...    |
+-----------------+
| [One], [Two]... |
+-----------------+
```

The next function takes an input argument as a DATE data type and returns the internal set date and dynamic date in a formatted string:

```
CREATE FUNCTION assign_date
(pv_argument DATE) RETURNS VARCHAR(30)
DETERMINISTIC NO SQL
BEGIN
  /* Declare local variables. */
  DECLARE lv_one DATE DEFAULT "2011-07-04";
  DECLARE lv_two DATE;

  /* Assign parameter value to local variable. */
  SELECT pv_argument INTO lv_two;

  /* Return the result of the math function. */
  RETURN CONCAT("[",DATE_FORMAT(lv_one,'%d-%b-%Y'),"]"
               ,"[",DATE_FORMAT(lv_two,'%d-%b-%Y'),"]");
END;
$$
```

The function accepts a string, provided it's in the default date format, which is covered in Chapter 6. The parameter value is assigned to the local variable through the SELECT-INTO statement, rather than with the SET statement syntax. Inside the function, the DATE_FORMAT function alters the display to a non-default date format.

You call the assign_date function like this:

```
SELECT assign_date('2011-07-14') AS "Date Values";
```

It returns this:

```
+---------------------------+
| Date Values               |
+---------------------------+
| [04-Jul-2011][14-Jul-2011] |
+---------------------------+
```

CAUTION
Be careful with date values when you change their format mask to anything other than the default, because they can generate runtime errors. A best practice would be to stay with the default format mask.

SQL/PSM Cursors

Cursors are local structures that reference a SELECT statement. A cursor returns one row at a time from a SELECT statement. The SELECT statement can contain a static string or a dynamic string. A dynamic string means the SELECT statement includes a local or parameter variable. In MySQL, cursors can't be defined like functions with a parameter list, which differs from Oracle. Oracle's approach is the preferred solution for dynamic cursors, because they've got formal definitions governing the input parameters, whereas MySQL uses scope access to variables inside the SELECT statement.

NOTE
You must declare cursors after variables that hold values and before handlers. If you forget the rule, your stored programs won't compile.

Cursors hold SELECT statements like a variable holds a string. The difference is that you can open, fetch, and close cursors. The OPEN statement parses and executes a query. The FETCH statement reads a single row from the result set. The CLOSE statement deallocates the cursor resources. This works the same way in an Oracle database, discounting bulk collects.

SQL/PSM Static Cursors

The easiest way to demonstrate a cursor without forward referencing control structures, such as *if-then-else* and loop statements, is to define a cursor, open it, fetch only one row from it, and close it. The static_cursor procedure does exactly that for you, as you can see:

```
CREATE PROCEDURE static_cursor()
NOT DETERMINISTIC
READS SQL DATA
BEGIN
  /* Declare a local variable. */
  DECLARE lv_item_title VARCHAR(60);

  /* Declare a cursor. */
  DECLARE cursor_name CURSOR FOR
    SELECT    i.item_title
    FROM      item i
    WHERE     i.item_title LIKE 'C%';

  /* Open, fetch one row, and close cursor. */
  OPEN cursor_name;
  FETCH cursor_name INTO lv_item_title;
  CLOSE cursor_name;

  /* Display local variable contents. */
  SELECT lv_item_title;
END;
$$
```

The OPEN, FETCH-INTO, and CLOSE operations in this procedure ensure that only one row is returned. The logic of these three statements alone would make it work as if you'd appended a LIMIT n clause, where n equals 1.

The OPEN and CLOSE operations take only a cursor name, but the FETCH-INTO statement takes the results of a query and puts them into local variables. That means the FETCH-INTO must have a list of local variables that matches the SELECT list columns, and the match is based on columns' respective data types.

Here's the prototype of the FETCH-INTO statement:

```
FETCH cursor_name INTO local_variable1 [, local_variable2 [, ...];
```

You can call the procedure like this:

```
CALL static_cursor();
```

which returns the first row when any rows are found, and the cursor raises the following error message when none are found:

```
ERROR 1329 (02000): No data - zero rows fetched, selected, or processed
```

Static cursors have limited use, because most business problems require dynamic cursors. The next section demonstrates how to implement dynamic cursors.

SQL/PSM Dynamic Cursors

Staying with the open, fetch, and close model, we can illustrate how a dynamic cursor works. A dynamic cursor is a string that includes local variable names that act like placeholders. In lieu of a function or procedure list of parameters, a cursor lets you intersperse parameters inside the string. At runtime, the placeholders are replaced with the values of local variables.

The dynamic_cursor procedure shows how to implement a dynamic cursor:

```
CREATE PROCEDURE dynamic_cursor(IN pv_item_title VARCHAR(60))
NOT DETERMINISTIC
READS SQL DATA
BEGIN
  /* Declare a local variable. */
  DECLARE lv_item_title VARCHAR(60);

  /* Declare a cursor. */
  DECLARE cursor_name CURSOR FOR
    SELECT   i.item_title
    FROM     item i
    WHERE    i.item_title LIKE pv_item_title;

  /* Open, fetch one row, and close cursor. */
  OPEN cursor_name;
  FETCH cursor_name INTO lv_item_title;
  CLOSE cursor_name;

  /* Display local variable contents. */
  SELECT lv_item_title;
END;
$$
```

The key is the pv_item_title placeholder inside the cursor_name cursor. The value sent through the call parameter is assigned to the placeholder and opens the cursor with the call-time value.

You can test the program with a call like this:

```
CALL dynamic_cursor('Star%');
```

It returns the first item_title value that starts with the four-character "Star" string. It could be replaced with a REGEXP comparison over the LIKE operand.

SQL/PSM Handlers

Handlers are event managers. They create asynchronous mini programs that listen for events, such as an error message. When they hear the message, they take action. The action typically means that they reset their default value.

While presented earlier, the HANDLER prototype is shown here again so you don't have to flip back to it:

```
DECLARE {CONTINUE | EXIT | UNDO} HANDLER FOR
{SQLSTATE [VALUE] value | SQLEXCEPTION | SQLWARNING | NOT FOUND |
 error_code | condition } [, ...]
statement_block;
```

You've learned about CONDITION variables. Now you can see where they fit in the context of a HANDLER in a full sample program.

The event_handler procedure shows you the benefit of handlers. The handler in this case checks whether all rows are found. The LIMIT clause guarantees that only one row is returned, which allows us to avoid a loop. Unfortunately, the example did require a forward reference to *if-then-else* control structure to demonstrate how handlers act as exception processing blocks. Here's the code:

```
CREATE PROCEDURE event_handler(IN pv_item_title VARCHAR(60))
NOT DETERMINISTIC
READS SQL DATA
BEGIN
  /* Declare a local variable. */
  DECLARE lv_item_title VARCHAR(60);

  /* Declare variables that hold handler's current state. */
  DECLARE fetched INT DEFAULT 0;

  /* Declare a cursor. */
  DECLARE cursor_name CURSOR FOR
    SELECT   i.item_title
    FROM     item i
    WHERE    i.item_title LIKE CONCAT(pv_item_title,'%') LIMIT 1;

  /* Declare a not found record handler to close a cursor loop. */
  DECLARE CONTINUE HANDLER FOR NOT FOUND SET fetched = 1;

  /* Open, fetch one row, and close cursor. */
  OPEN cursor_name;
  FETCH cursor_name INTO lv_item_title;

  /* Close the cursor when last record read. */
  IF fetched = 1 THEN
    CLOSE cursor_name;
  END IF;
```

```
  /* Display local variable contents. */
  SELECT lv_item_title;
END;
$$
```

The `fetched` variable departs from the naming convention because it's tied to a generic behavior of fetching rows from cursors. Its default value is 0, because it's false until all rows are fetched. The `CONTINUE HANDLER` for a `NOT FOUND` event (which means all rows are processed) sets the `fetched` variable to 1. The `IF` block checks the value of the fetched variable and closes the cursor. The `IF` block acts as an exception block, since one doesn't exist in MySQL.

You would call it like this:

```
CALL event_handler('Star');
```

It returns only the first row found:

```
+---------------+
| lv_item_title |
+---------------+
| Star Wars I   |
+---------------+
```

`CONTINUE` or `EXIT HANDLER` variables help you manage your program, and `CONDITION` variables help you make your code more readable and supportable. If you changed the handler from a `CONTINUE HANDLER` to an `EXIT HANDLER`, the program would terminate.

SQL/PSM Control Structures

As mentioned, control structures do one of two things: They check logical conditions and branch program execution, or they repeat (iterate) over a condition unit it is met or they're instructed to exit. In MySQL, the *if, elseif, else*, and `CASE` statements are conditional structures, while loops let you repeat instructions or iterate (move over rows in a cursor one-by-one) across data.

If and `CASE` statements work on comparing values. Table 14-3 lists the valid comparison operators available in SQL/PSM stored programs.

Table 14-3 shows a couple of comparison operators that might raise an eyebrow and a bit of curiosity: the *not equal* (<>) and the null safe operator (<=>). They're very different things, because the <> only works when both values contain a value and the values are different. The <> returns false when one of the values *contains* a null, whereas the <=> returns true when both variables *are* nulls.

If Statements

The *if* or *else-if* statements work on a concept of Boolean logic. Boolean logic requires the comparison of two values, or sets of such comparisons. You use logical `AND` or `OR` operators to form logical statements.

An `AND` (inclusive) operator checks whether *this and that* comparisons are both true, or if one is false. The fact that an inclusive logical operator checks only one side of an `AND` operator is short-circuit analysis, because if one is false, it doesn't matter whether the other is true. Collectively, they're false, while all that is truly known is that both aren't true. An `OR` (exclusive) operator checks

Operator	Operator Description
=	The equal operator returns true when the left and right operands are equal and false when they're not.
>	The greater than operator returns true when the left operand is greater than the right operand and false when it is not.
>=	The greater than or equal operator returns true when the left operand is greater than or equal to the right operand and false when it is not.
<	The less than operator returns true when the left operand is less than the right operand and false when it is not.
<=	The less than or equal operator returns true when the left operand is less than or equal to the right operand.
<> or !=	The not equal operator returns true when the left operand isn't equal to the right operand and false when they're equal.
<=>	The null safe operator returns true when either the left and right operand hold matching values or the left and right operand are null values, and false when the values differ or only one of the values is null.
NOT	The NOT or negation operator works with other comparison operators, and returns true when the other operator returns false and vice versa.
BETWEEN	The BETWEEN operator returns true when a value is between two other boundary values and false when it's not.
EXISTS	The EXISTS operator returns true when it finds that an IF EXISTS statement verifies a comparison or row return, and false when it doesn't.
IN	The IN , =ANY, and =SOME operators look to see if a left operand is found in a sequence of values in the right operand, and returns true when found in the sequence and false when it is not found.
=ALL	The =ALL operator looks to see if a left operand is found in all of the sequence values in the right operand and returns true when found and false when not found in the sequence.
IS NULL	The IS NULL operator checks whether a left operand is a null value, and it returns true when the value is null or false when it is not.
LIKE	The LIKE operator checks whether a left operand is like (more or less a substring of) the right operand and returns true when that's the case or false when it's not.
REGEXP	The REGEXP operator uses regular expressions to find similar patterns of strings or numbers in a left operand and returns true when found and false when not.

TABLE 14-3. *Comparison Operators*

AND	TRUE	FALSE
TRUE	TRUE	FALSE
FALSE	FALSE	FALSE

TABLE 14-4. *Inclusive Two-Valued Logic*

whether *this or that* other comparison is true. Like an inclusive logical operator, the exclusive operator needs to know only if one is true to evaluate the statement as true. These concepts can be shown in *two-valued logic* truth tables. Table 14-4 shows inclusive logic and 14-5 shows exclusive logic.

Unfortunately, databases don't allow us to work in two-valued logic, because it's possible that a variable might contain a null value. When you compare anything against a null, it's null, not the Boolean true or false. This makes two true comparisons true, and anything else false, or two false comparisons true, and anything else false. (More on this logical marvel can be found in the "Three-valued Logic" sidebar in Chapter 6.) Three-valued logic has two possible outcomes: two things evaluate as true or they don't, and we don't care if one or both of the comparison results was null because null is treated as false.

OR	TRUE	FALSE
TRUE	TRUE	TRUE
FALSE	TRUE	FALSE

TABLE 14-5. *Exclusive Two-Valued Logic*

Tables 14-6 shows the inclusive (AND) three-valued logic truth table, and Table 14-7 shows the exclusive (OR) three-valued logic truth table.

AND	TRUE	FALSE	NULL
TRUE	TRUE	FALSE	FALSE
FALSE	FALSE	FALSE	FALSE
NULL	FALSE	FALSE	FALSE

TABLE 14-6. *Inclusive Three-Valued Logic*

OR	TRUE	FALSE	NULL
TRUE	TRUE	TRUE	TRUE
FALSE	TRUE	FALSE	FALSE
NULL	TRUE	FALSE	FALSE

TABLE 14-7. *Exclusive Three-Valued Logic*

Two prototypes are possible with *if* statements: the first checks whether something is true or not, and the second checks whether a series of things are true or not.

Here's the *if-then* and *if-then-else-if-then* prototype:

```
IF expression THEN
   statement;
[ELSEIF expression THEN
   statement; ]
[...]
[ELSE
   statement; ]
END IF;
```

Notice that MySQL SQL/PSM uses `ELSEIF` while Oracle PL/SQL uses `ELSIF`, dropping the second "e" from else. MySQL isn't forgiving when you leave the second "e" out of the `ELSEIF` operator.

The following examples show you two-valued logic resolutions for comparing numbers. The first example shows you the comparison of two numbers with values guaranteed by the `IFNULL` function prior to the assignment of parameter values to the local variables:

```
CREATE PROCEDURE check_match
( IN pv_one INT
, IN pv_two INT)
DETERMINISTIC NO SQL
BEGIN
  /* Declare two numbers without values, null by default. */
  DECLARE lv_one INT;
  DECLARE lv_two INT;

  /* Assign call parameters to local variables. */
  SET lv_one = IFNULL(pv_one,1);
  SET lv_two = IFNULL(pv_two,1);

  /* Compare their equality of value. */
  IF lv_one = lv_two THEN
    SELECT "They do match!";
  ELSE
    SELECT "They don't match!";
  END IF;
END;
$$
```

The preceding comparison works, and the message "They do match!" prints to console when the call parameters match or one is a null and the other is a 1. It works because the values match, or the IFNULL function substitutes a 1 for a null value. If the call parameters differ, the values would no longer match and the "They don't match!" string would print.

If you remove the DEFAULT value assignment from lv_two, the comparison would also fail, because something compared against a null is null, and null isn't true. You can resolve that type of three-valued logic problem by using the IFNULL function in MySQL. It works like the NVL function demonstrated in Chapter 13.

The following example uses the IFNULL to print a new message (numbers added for clarity):

```
mysql> CREATE PROCEDURE check_match
    2 -> ( IN pv_one INT
    3 -> , IN pv_two INT)
    4 -> DETERMINISTIC NO SQL
    5 -> BEGIN
    6 ->    /* Declare two numbers without values, null by default. */
    7 ->    DECLARE lv_one INT DEFAULT 1;
    8 ->    DECLARE lv_two INT;
    9 ->
   10 ->    /* Assign call parameters to local variables. */
   11 ->    SET lv_one = pv_one;
   12 ->    SET lv_two = pv_two;
   13 ->
   14 ->    /* Compare their equality of value. */
   15 ->    IF lv_one = lv_two THEN
   16 ->      SELECT "They do match!" AS "Matched";
   17 ->    ELSEIF IFNULL(lv_one,'x') = 'x' OR IFNULL(lv_two,'x') = 'x' THEN
   18 ->      SELECT "They don't match because at one is null!" AS "One Null";
   19 ->    ELSE
   20 ->      SELECT "They don't match!" AS "Not Matched";
   21 ->    END IF;
   22 -> END;
   23 -> $$
```

lv_two is null when the pv_two call parameter is null, and the IF statement on line 15 would be skipped because a null can't be equal to anything. This means the ELSEIF statement on line 17 is true, and line 18 prints a message. That's because any number value in the lv_one variable won't equal the substitute x value from the IFNULL statement when lv_two is null.

The IFNULL works differently from the NVL in Oracle, because it allows the two call parameters to have different data types. The NVL would require that the second call parameter, known as the substitution value, hold a number, not a string.

You can rewrite the ELSEIF comparisons with the ISNULL function, which is simpler and provides you with what you really want to know. The ELSEIF statement would look like this:

```
   17 ->    ELSEIF ISNULL(lv_one) OR ISNULL(lv_two) THEN
```

One of the variables must be a null for this exclusive statement to return a true value. It's also possible that both can be null values with the preceding comparison.

The following calls the procedure with matching values:

```
CALL check_match(3,3);
```

This yields the following results:

```
+----------------+
| Matched        |
+----------------+
| They do match! |
+----------------+
```

You get the ELSEIF block answer when you change the first call parameter to a null value, like this:

```
CALL check_match(null,3);
```

which returns this:

```
+------------------------------------------------+
| One Null                                       |
+------------------------------------------------+
| They don't match because at least one is null! |
+------------------------------------------------+
```

The last call provides two non-matching integers:

```
CALL check_match(1,3);
```

It returns this:

```
+------------------+
| Not Matched      |
+------------------+
| They don't match! |
+------------------+
```

The logic isn't difficult to resolve matches, non-matches, and within non-matches any value mismatches. The next example demonstrates that with one null variable and two null variables. You can do it with this check_match procedure:

```
CREATE PROCEDURE check_match
( IN pv_one INT
, IN pv_two INT)
DETERMINISTIC NO SQL
BEGIN
  /* Declare two numbers without values, null by default. */
  DECLARE lv_one INT;
  DECLARE lv_two INT;

  /* Assign call parameters to local variables. */
  SET lv_one = pv_one;
  SET lv_two = pv_two;
```

```
   /* Compare their equality of value. */
   IF lv_one = lv_two THEN
     SELECT "They do match!" AS "Matched";
   ELSEIF pv_one <=> pv_two THEN
     SELECT "They match because both are null!" AS "Both Null";
   ELSEIF IFNULL(lv_one,'x') = 'x' OR IFNULL(lv_two,'x') = 'x' THEN
     SELECT "They don't match because at least one is null!" AS "One Null";
   ELSE
     SELECT "They don't match!" AS "Not Matched";
   END IF;
END;
$$
```

A new call to the `check_match` procedure lets you compare two null values with the *null safe equal* operator:

```
CALL check_match(null,null);
```

It returns this:

```
+-----------------------------------+
| Both Null                         |
+-----------------------------------+
| They match because both are null! |
+-----------------------------------+
```

The null safe equal operator lets you check whether both the left and right operands are null values (described in Table 14-3), and when they're both null, the comparison returns true. The null safe equal operator is powerful, convenient, and unfortunately not available in Oracle.

TIP
The null safe equal operator lets you evaluate two null values as equal instead of as null.

The trick in the logic that resolves three-value logic into two-value logic depends on two techniques: the comparisons and the order of the comparisons. First, the `IF` statement examines value matches, the first `ELSEIF` examines when both are null values, the second `ELSEIF` examines when one is null (the program can't get to that evaluation if both are null), and the `ELSE` captures value mismatches. You should be careful when you have to pare the logic to the simpler two-value model.

You can also perform set lookups inside an `IF` block, such as the one demonstrated in the following `in_set` procedure:

```
CREATE PROCEDURE in_set
(IN pv_one INT)
DETERMINISTIC NO SQL
BEGIN
   /* Lookup a value in a sequence (list of numbers or strings). */
   IF pv_one IN (1,2,3) THEN
     SELECT "They do match!";
```

```
      ELSE
        SELECT "They don't match!";
      END IF;
   END;
   $$
```

Calling the `in_set` procedure with a 1, 2, or 3 prints "They do match!" while calling it with any other integer prints "They don't match!" You can also replace the literal numeric list with the results from a query and perform a match.

The following rewritten `in_set` procedure shows you the syntax (numbers added to correlate possible substitutions code lines):

```
mysql> CREATE PROCEDURE in_set(IN pv_string VARCHAR(60))
    2 -> DETERMINISTIC NO SQL
    3 -> BEGIN
    4 ->   /* Lookup a value in a result set. */
    5 ->   IF pv_string IN (SELECT item_title FROM item) THEN
    6 ->     SELECT "It's found in the query!";
    7 ->   ELSE
    8 ->     SELECT "It's not found in the query!";
    9 ->   END IF;
   10 -> END;
   11 -> $$
```

A call to the rewritten `in_set` procedure looks like this:

```
call in_set('Cars');
```

It returns "It's found in the query!"

The `=ANY`, `=SOME`, and `=ALL` comparison operators currently work only inside stored programs in MySQL 5.6. They do work in queries outside of stored programs in earlier releases but raise a compile-time error inside stored programs. In MySQL 5.6, you can change line 5 to work with either the `=ANY` or `=SOME` comparison operator in place of the `IN` operator, like this with the `=ANY` operator:

```
    5 ->   IF pv_string =ANY (SELECT item_title FROM item) THEN
```

Or like this with the `=SOME` operator:

```
    5 ->   IF pv_string =SOME (SELECT item_title FROM item) THEN
```

The `IF EXISTS` also works with query return results. An example of that behavior is included in the "DDL Prepared Statements" section later in this chapter.

CASE Statements

MySQL supports two types of `CASE` statements. One is a simple `CASE` statement and the other is a searched `CASE` statement. Both types of `CASE` statements work like an *if-then-elseif-then-else* block. The simple `CASE` checks for a value that matches an expression, and the searched `CASE` checks the truth of the `WHEN` clause statement.

Simple CASE Statement

As mentioned, the simple CASE statement work by comparing the result of an expression against literal values in the WHEN clause. The expression can be a variable or a function call returning a variable.

This is the prototype for a simple CASE statement:

```
CASE expression
   WHEN value THEN
     statement_block;
  [WHEN value THEN
     statement_block;
  [ ...]]
  [ELSE
     statement_block;]
END CASE;
```

Unlike the CASE operator in SQL, where END closes the operation, the CASE statement in SQL/PSM stored programs requires the following:

```
END CASE;
```

A sample procedure illustrates how to implement a simple CASE statement. The procedure takes a primary color as a string and then prints a message about that primary color. Any other color or a null value prints a message about *The Color Purple* movie.

```
CREATE PROCEDURE simple_case(IN pv_color VARCHAR(10))
DETERMINISTIC NO SQL
BEGIN
  CASE IFNULL(pv_color,"Purple")
    WHEN 'Blue' THEN
      SELECT 'The color blue.';
    WHEN 'Red' THEN
      SELECT 'The color red.';
    WHEN 'Yellow' THEN
      SELECT 'The color yellow.';
    ELSE
      SELECT 'The Color Purple won the Oscar.';
  END CASE;
END;
$$
```

You would call it like this:

```
CALL simple_case(null);
```

The procedure with a null value returns the "The Color Purple won the Oscar." The simple CASE statement has limited uses, because it must exactly match the expression to the value of the WHEN clause. The searched CASE provides more flexibility and is described in the next section.

Searched CASE Statement

A searched CASE statement works by evaluating whether WHEN clause comparisons are true. When they are true, they match, and result is processed in that statement block. The comparisons in the WHEN clauses must be exclusive by design, but when they overlap, it performs the statement block of the first match.

Here's the searched CASE prototype:

```
CASE
  WHEN condition THEN
    statement_block;
 [WHEN condition THEN
    statement_block;
 [ ...]]
 [ELSE
    statement_block;]
END CASE;
```

Here's a quick example of a searched CASE statement that uses a bidding process (numbers added for clarity):

```
mysql> CREATE PROCEDURE searched_case(IN pv_bid DECIMAL(15,2))
    2 -> DETERMINISTIC NO SQL
    3 -> BEGIN
    4 ->   /* Set a reserve amount on a bid. */
    5 ->   DECLARE lv_reserve_amount DECIMAL(15,2) DEFAULT 10000;
    6 ->   DECLARE lv_buy_it_now     DECIMAL(15,2) DEFAULT 15000;
    7 ->
    8 ->   /* Use a searched case to check bid reasonableness. */
    9 ->   CASE
   10 ->     WHEN pv_bid < lv_reserve_amount THEN
   11 ->       SELECT 'Unacceptable bid, reject it.';
   12 ->     WHEN pv_bid BETWEEN  lv_reserve_amount
   13 ->                        AND (lv_buy_it_now - .01) THEN
   14 ->       SELECT 'Acceptable bid, register it.';
   15 ->     WHEN pv_bid >= lv_buy_it_now THEN
   16 ->       SELECT 'Sold!';
   17 ->     ELSE /* Handle a null bid. */
   18 ->       SELECT 'Bids must be numbers!';
   19 ->   END CASE;
   20 -> END;
   21 -> $$
```

The second WHEN clause subtracts a penny from the lv_buy_it_now variable to ensure that the second and third WHEN clause condition don't overlap. Although this hack of subtracting a penny

Problems with DECIMAL Comparisons

The DECIMAL data type doesn't work like the NUMBER data type in Oracle. You get an approximate number if you don't set the precision and scale of a DECIMAL data type in MySQL. In Oracle, you get an exact number if you exclude the precision and scale from a NUMBER data type.

Just remember DECIMAL data types in MySQL don't work like NUMBER data types in Oracle, and *always* provide the precision and scale to DECIMAL numbers. Otherwise, you'll get unexpected results.

works by preventing a `pv_bid` value equal to the `lv_buy_it_now` to skip the `WHEN` clause comparison on lines 12 and 13, it doesn't fix the real problem. It does let an exact `lv_buy_it_now` value make it to line 15, where it meets the comparison condition.

The program also handles the possibility that the web form allows a null bid into the procedure. The `ELSE` clause handles a null call parameter. It is always a good practice when writing `CASE` statements to include an `ELSE` clause.

CAUTION
Subtracting a penny to make the cases work is a hack! *Something like that should* never *happen in good code!*

The following call to the procedure shows the hack would let you "buy it now" at the auction:

```
CALL searched_case(15000);
```

The `BETWEEN` comparison operator is an inclusive range operator, which doesn't meet the need for an exclusive comparison on lines 12 and 13. A better solution is to replace the `BETWEEN` comparison operator with its natural inclusiveness with a logical comparison that is exclusive of the terminating range values:

```
12 ->     WHEN pv_bid > lv_reserve_amount AND pv_bid < lv_buy_it_now THEN
13 ->         SELECT 'Accpetable bid, register it.';
```

Loop Statements

MySQL supports three loop structures: simple, `REPEAT UNTIL`, and `WHILE`. The simple loop doesn't evaluate any condition on entry or exit. A `REPEAT UNTIL` loop evaluates a condition on exit, and a `WHILE` loop evaluates a condition on entry.

NOTE
The following subsections build on materials progressively, so you should read them in the order in which they are presented.

Simple Loop

A simple loop has no entrance or exit requirements. Left by itself, a simple loop could run forever as an infinite loop. Here's the prototype:

```
label: LOOP
   statement_block;
END LOOP label;
```

You must put a `LEAVE` statement inside the loop to instruct it to stop execution. For those converting from Oracle PL/SQL, this differs from the `EXIT` statement in Oracle PL/SQL. Here's the `LEAVE` statement prototype:

```
LEAVE label;
```

The label is required component of the LEAVE statement, and it needs to be synchronized with the label of the simple loop. Here's a sample simple loop:

```
CREATE PROCEDURE simple_loop()
BEGIN
  /* Declare a control variable. */
  DECLARE i INT DEFAULT 0;

  /* A simple loop. */
  small_loop:LOOP

    /* Create an exit criteria. */
    IF i = 10 THEN
      LEAVE small_loop;
    END IF;

    /* Print to the console for each iteration in the loop. */
    SELECT CONCAT('Loop value [',i,']');

    /* Increment the counter. */
    SET i = i + 1;
  END LOOP;
END;
$$
```

You would call this procedure like this:

```
CALL simple_loop;
```

This would print ten values—one value for each trip (iteration) through the loop. (These are not shown because they don't add much to the concept.)

Before entering a simple loop, you need to set a control variable that will trigger an exit from the loop. This control variable can be a cursor or a counter variable. After entering a simple loop, the first criterion needs to check the exit criteria, and when met, exit the loop. In the sample loop, the criterion is the value of the control variable. When the exit criteria isn't met, the loop processes statements, and then at the end of the loop increments the control variable. Eventually, the control criterion is met and you exit the loop.

Cursor Simple Loops   The next example shows you how to implement a simple loop with a cursor as the control variable. It has different syntax and requires that you set a handler to determine when no more rows are found in the cursor, which is the criterion for exiting the loop.

```
CREATE PROCEDURE cursor_loop()
BEGIN
  /* Declare a local variable for cursor retrieved data. */
  DECLARE lv_movie_title VARCHAR(60);

  /* Declare a handler variable. */
  DECLARE fetched      INT DEFAULT 0;

  /* Cursors must come after variables and before event handlers. */
```

```
DECLARE movie_cursor CURSOR FOR
  SELECT    i.item_title
  FROM      item i;

/* Declare a not found record handler to close a cursor loop. */
DECLARE CONTINUE HANDLER FOR NOT FOUND SET fetched = 1;

/* Open cursor and start simple loop. */
OPEN movie_cursor;
cursor_loop:LOOP

  /* Fetch a record from the cursor. */
  FETCH movie_cursor
  INTO  lv_movie_title;

  /* Place the catch handler for no more rows found
     immediately after the fetch operation.          */
  IF fetched = 1 THEN LEAVE cursor_loop; END IF;

  /* Print to the console for each iteration in the loop. */
  SELECT CONCAT('Movie Title [',lv_movie_title,']') AS "Movie Title";

END LOOP cursor_loop;
CLOSE movie_cursor;
END;
$$
```

The cursor loop isn't really much different from the control variable simple loop. Control is delegated to a variable and handler. The `fetched` variable is declared with a default value and then used as a target in a CONTINUE HANDLER. When the CONTINUE HANDLER encounters a NOT FOUND event, it resets the value of the `fetched` variable. The reset value then meets the condition of the *if* statement and leaves (exits) the loop. A cursor loop like this reads the lack of a next row from the SELECT statement and sets the exit criterion.

You could call the `cursor_loop` procedure like so:

```
CALL cursor_loop;
```

If you change the CONTINUE HANDLER to an EXIT HANDLER, you can remove the IF block checking the fetched variable. Here's the syntax for the new EXIT HANDLER:

```
/* Declare a not found record handler to close the procedure. */
DECLARE EXIT HANDLER FOR NOT FOUND SET fetched = 1;
```

Beyond the LEAVE statement, you can also use the ITERATE statement. The ITERATE statement is like the CONTINUE statement in Oracle 11*g*. The ITERATE allows you to skip over processing a cycle (or iteration) of the loop. Here's the prototype for the ITERATE statement:

```
ITERATE label;
```

The following can be inserted into the preceding example and skips all `item_title` values that don't start with the letter *C*:

```
IF lv_movie_title NOT LIKE 'C%' THEN
  ITERATE cursor_loop;
END IF;
```

ITERATE stops processing the loop at its location and returns control locus to the top of the loop statement. The ITERATE statement is powerful and risky; make sure you use it wisely.

REPEAT UNTIL Loop

The REPEAT UNTIL loop always runs once because it doesn't guard entry to the loop, which makes it a lot like the simple loop. Using ITERATE inside a REPEAT UNTIL loop is risky, because it returns control to the top of the loop and bypasses any validation checking at the end of the loop.

Here's the prototype for a REPEAT UNTIL loop:

```
label: LOOP
  statement_block;
  IF expression THEN LEAVE loop_label; END IF;
END LOOP;
```

Here's an example of how you implement the REPEAT UNTIL loop:

```
CREATE PROCEDURE repeat_until()
BEGIN
  /* Declare a control variable. */
  DECLARE i INT DEFAULT 0;

  /* A simple loop. */
  small_loop:REPEAT

    /* Increment the counter. */
    SET i = i + 1;

    /* Print to the console for each iteration in the loop. */
    SELECT CONCAT('Loop value [',i,']');

    /* Set the exit criterion. */
    UNTIL i = 10
  END REPEAT;
END;
$$
```

The REPEAT UNTIL loop changes the LOOP keywords to REPEAT keywords. The exit criterion isn't a statement by itself; it's part of the loop block and as such requires no semicolon.

Cursor REPEAT UNTIL Loop The REPEAT UNTIL loop can also support cursors but isn't the best solution for cursors, because you have to manage an extra trip through the loop. It also forces you to enclose your DML action inside an IF block to prevent it running when no new rows are found. The most common practice uses cursor simple loops, because the exit can immediately follow the FETCH-INTO statement.

The exit check for a REPEAT UNTIL loop is at the bottom of the iteration cycle. The position of the exit check (UNTIL clause) can present problems when the iteration statement block contains certain DML statements, such as an INSERT or SELECT statement.

The problem is caused by putting the statement blocks between the FETCH-INTO and UNTIL clause. The NOT FOUND handler isn't triggered until there aren't any more rows, which means the balance of the loop could process the last values fetched from a cursor twice, and reinsert or requery that same data.

Here's a procedure that manages a query inside a REPEAT UNTIL loop:

```
CREATE PROCEDURE cursor_loop()
BEGIN
  /* Declare a local variable for cursor retrieved data. */
  DECLARE lv_movie_title VARCHAR(60);

  /* Declare a handler variables. */
  DECLARE fetched       INT DEFAULT 0;

  /* Cursors must come after variables and before event handlers. */
  DECLARE movie_cursor CURSOR FOR
    SELECT  i.item_title
    FROM    item i;

  /* Declare a not found record handler to close a cursor loop. */
  DECLARE CONTINUE HANDLER FOR NOT FOUND SET fetched = 1;

  /* Open cursor and start simple loop. */
  OPEN movie_cursor;
  cursor_loop:REPEAT

    /* Fetch a record from the cursor. */
    FETCH movie_cursor
    INTO  lv_movie_title;

    /* Only run when a fresh row was found. */
    IF fetched = 0 THEN
      /* Print to the console for each iteration in the loop. */
      SELECT CONCAT('Movie Title [',lv_movie_title,']')
             AS "Movie Title", "Hi";
    END IF;

    /* Set the catch handler. */
    UNTIL fetched = 1
  END REPEAT;
  CLOSE movie_cursor;
END;
$$
```

The trick to managing DML statements inside a REPEAT UNTIL loop requires that you enclose the iteration's statement block inside an IF block. The IF block checks that the NOT FOUND handler hasn't reset its fetched control variable. The UNTIL clause checks whether the NOT FOUND handler has reset the control variable and exits the loop when that condition is met.

Another alternative would be to place a LEAVE statement inside the IF block but that would create two points of exit, and it's a bad idea to have two points of exit from a loop. Moreover, a REPEAT UNTIL block isn't well suited to work with a cursor.

WHILE Loop

The WHILE loop guards entry to the loop by stating a criterion or criteria. Here's the basic prototype for the WHILE loop:

```
label: WHILE expression DO
   statement_block;
END WHILE label;
```

The following procedure demonstrates how to use a WHILE loop:

```
CREATE PROCEDURE while_loop()
BEGIN
   /* Declare a control variable. */
   DECLARE i INT DEFAULT 0;

   /* Start a while loop. */
   while_loop:WHILE i <= 10 DO

      /* Print to the console for each iteration in the loop. */
      SELECT CONCAT('Loop value [',i,']');

      /* Increment the counter. */
      SET i = i + 1;
   END WHILE while_loop;
END;
$$
```

The WHILE loop checks whether the counter variable is less than the exit limit. After the validation of the condition, the DO keyword leads into the loop, and like the simple loop the label both precedes and closes the loop structure.

Cursor WHILE Loop   Like the REPEAT UNTIL loop, the WHILE loop exits after the statement block. In fact, a WHILE loop validates and exits at the top of the iteration after a CONTINUE HANDLER would report no records found. It's a better solution than a REPEAT UNTIL loop because the ITERATE statement lets you jump to the top of the loop.

Here's a cursor WHILE loop example:

```
CREATE PROCEDURE while_loop()
BEGIN
   /* Declare a local variable for cursor retrieved data. */
   DECLARE lv_movie_title VARCHAR(60);

   /* Declare a handler variables. */
   DECLARE fetched        INT DEFAULT 0;

   /* Cursors must come after variables and before event handlers. */
   DECLARE movie_cursor CURSOR FOR
```

```
    SELECT    i.item_title
    FROM      item i;

/* Declare a not found record handler to close a cursor loop. */
DECLARE CONTINUE HANDLER FOR NOT FOUND SET fetched = 1;

/* Start a while loop. */
OPEN movie_cursor;
while_loop:WHILE fetched = 0 DO

  /* Fetch a record from the cursor. */
  FETCH movie_cursor
  INTO  lv_movie_title;

  /* Force exit when no more rows found. */
  IF fetched = 1 THEN ITERATE while_loop; END IF;

  /* Print the console for each iteration in the loop. */
  SELECT CONCAT('Movie Title [',lv_movie_title,']')
         AS "Movie Title";
  END WHILE while_loop;
  CLOSE movie_cursor;
END;
$$
```

You would call this with the following syntax:

```
CALL while_loop;
```

The highlighted IF block lets you jump to the top of the next iteration of the loop, where the criteria evaluation stops the program execution. You can use a WHILE loop to manage cursors because it works very much like a simple loop.

Prepared Statements

Prepared statements let you create dynamic SQL statements in the MySQL Monitor or stored procedures. Oracle supports substitution variables in SQL*Plus for interactive dynamic SQL statements, and Native Dynamic SQL (NDS) for PL/SQL program units. NDS is the closest corollary to MySQL prepared statements.

Note that prepared statements work with session variables, not local program variables. Use session variables in all situations.

The following sections show you how to use prepared statements at the interactive MySQL Monitor command line and within stored program units.

Prepared Statements at the Command Line

Sometimes you have a complex query that you want to run repeatedly with different values. That's an ideal use case for prepared statements. You can configure prepared statements in five steps, which follow.

Step 1: Set the DML Statement
Write a DML statement shell as a prepared statement, and add question marks (?) in as placeholders for substitution variables. Think of the placeholders as formal parameters to a function or procedure. The following SELECT statement shell is the example we'll use for testing purposes:

```
SET @SQL := 'SELECT i.item_title
           ,        i.item_rating
           FROM    item i
           WHERE   i.item_title REGEXP ?';
```

After you assign the DML statement to a session variable, you can query the session variable, like this:

```
SELECT @SQL AS "Result Set";
```

You would see the SQL statement shell that you entered as the result set.

Step 2: Prepare the DML Statement
Prepare the statement like this:

```
PREPARE stmt FROM @SQL;
```

Notice that you don't need to use a session variable for the statement name. Likewise, you don't have to declare the variable outside of the PREPARE statement syntax.

Step 3: Set a Session Variable for Substitution
You can assign a literal or numeric value, the result from a function, or a regular expression. The following implements a substitution session variable and assigns it a regular expression that looks for a string starting with anything before the literal "war" and ending with anything:

```
SET @sv_item_title := '(^|^.+)war(.+$|$)';
```

Step 4: Execute the Prepared Statement
The EXECUTE statement runs the prepared statement by using a session variable as a substitution variable. Here's the prototype:

```
EXECUTE statement_variable
USING @session_variable [, @session_variable [, ...];
```

The following shows how you would EXECUTE a statement in this problem set:

```
EXECUTE stmt USING @sv_item_title;
```

It returns the following data set:

```
+---------------+-------------+
| item_title    | item_rating |
+---------------+-------------+
| Star Wars I   | PG          |
| Star Wars II  | PG          |
| Star Wars II  | PG          |
| Star Wars III | PG13        |
+---------------+-------------+
```

Step 5: Deallocate the Prepared Statement

You deallocate space with the following command:

```
DEALLOCATE PREPARE stmt;
```

Prepared Statements in Stored Programs

It's often more useful to package prepared statements inside stored procedures. Likewise, it's important to note that MySQL supports DDL and DML prepared statements differently. The difference allows DML statements to substitute values through the ? (question mark) placeholder. DDL statements require that you manually substitute values through concatenation.

Beyond writing definer rights stored programs that leverage prepared statements, you have the option of writing invoker rights stored programs. You write invoker rights stored programs when you want to create library modules for your API. The next three sections show you how to write definer rights stored procedures for DML and DDL statements, and an invoker rights stored procedure that leverages a MySQL built-in session DATABASE discovery function.

DML Prepared Statements

The same five steps are required here, but they're bundled into the stored procedure. The following shows you how to implement a DML prepared statement in a procedure:

```
CREATE PROCEDURE prepared_dml
( pv_item_title VARCHAR(60))
BEGIN
   /* Declare a local variable for the SQL statement. */
   DECLARE stmt VARCHAR(1024);

   /* Set a session variable with two parameter markers. */
   SET @SQL := 'SELECT item_title
                FROM item i
                WHERE item_title REGEXP ?';

   /* Assign the formal parameters to session variables
      because prepared statements require them. */
   SET @sv_item_title := pv_item_title;

   /* Dynamically allocated and run statement. */
   PREPARE stmt FROM @SQL;
   EXECUTE stmt USING @sv_item_title;
   DEALLOCATE PREPARE stmt;
END;
$$
```

The only additional step required to put this in a procedure was the declaration of the stmt variable. You would call this with the following regular expression, which looks for a "war" string or anything string with "war" in it:

```
CALL prepared_dml('(^|^.+)war(.+$|$)');
```

You would see the following output from the sample database:

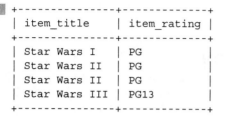

```
+---------------+-------------+
| item_title    | item_rating |
+---------------+-------------+
| Star Wars I   | PG          |
| Star Wars II  | PG          |
| Star Wars II  | PG          |
| Star Wars III | PG13        |
+---------------+-------------+
```

DDL Prepared Statements

The biggest difference here is that you can't use placeholders when you want to include DDL prepared statements. You must concatenate literals and variables into one large string before preparing the DDL statements.

This DDL example shows you how to discover and remove foreign key constraints from a table. The procedure also includes an IF EXISTS statement to verify the presence of the foreign key before trying to remove it.

```
CREATE PROCEDURE dropForeignKey
( pv_database   VARCHAR(64)
, pv_table      VARCHAR(64)
, pv_constraint VARCHAR(64))
BEGIN
  /* Declare a local variable for the SQL statement. */
  DECLARE stmt VARCHAR(1024);

  /* Set a session variable with two parameter markers. */
  SET @SQL := CONCAT('ALTER TABLE '
                    ,pv_table
                    ,' DROP FOREIGN KEY '
                    ,pv_constraint);

  /* Check if the constraint exists. */
  IF EXISTS (SELECT NULL
             FROM   information_schema.referential_constraints
             WHERE  constraint_schema = pv_database
             AND    TABLE_NAME = pv_table
             AND    constraint_name = pv_constraint)
  THEN
    /* Dynamically allocated and run statement. */
    PREPARE stmt FROM @SQL;
    EXECUTE stmt;
    DEALLOCATE PREPARE stmt;
  END IF;
END;
$$
```

Like the other calls, you would use this syntax:

```
CALL dropForeignKey(database(),'RENTAL_ITEM','U_RENTAL_ITEM');
```

The call leverages the built-in DATABASE function that returns the current database name, the table name, and a constraint name. The IF EXISTS statement is very powerful and simple to use. By using it, the program avoids raising an error when the foreign key isn't there.

Invoker Rights Prepared Statements

The previous DDL prepared statement example showed you how to use the DATABASE() function as a call parameter. The MySQL built-in DATABASE() function lets you discover which database you're currently using in the session. What would happen if that logic was placed inside the stored procedure instead of left to the discretion of the developer writing a call to another stored procedure? Incorporating the DATABASE() function in the stored procedure would increase the utility of the stored procedure and hide the dependency on the current database.

It would also let you reposition a definer rights module as an invoker rights module. The beauty of implementing an invoker rights module is that you write it once for many different uses working against many different databases. This type of coding increases the reuse of stored procedures. This approach also requires a new step: You need to create a database to hold invoker rights programs, and, from my vantage point, only invoker rights programs. I would recommend you name the database something short and clear, such as lib. You can check back to Chapter 2 for the syntax required to create a new database and grant appropriate permissions to your student (or whatever you chose as a user name) account.

We can now create the dropForeignKeys procedure in the lib database. (There's no magic to the naming convention for the dropForeignKeys procedure, but if you're wondering about why it's that way, the procedure name follows the recommendation for Java methods.) As you recall, reset the DELIMITER to a $$ before running this statement (line numbers added to ease pointing to specific items of the program):

```
mysql> CREATE PROCEDURE dropForeignKeys
    2 -> ( pv_constraint_name   VARCHAR(64)
    3 -> , pv_referenced_table  VARCHAR(64))
    4 -> READS SQL DATA SQL SECURITY INVOKER
    5 -> BEGIN
    6 ->
    7 ->   /* Declare local statement variables. */
    8 ->   DECLARE lv_stmt VARCHAR(1024);
    9 ->
   10 ->   /* Declare local cursor variables. */
   11 ->   DECLARE lv_table_name       VARCHAR(64);
   12 ->   DECLARE lv_constraint_name  VARCHAR(64);
   13 ->
   14 ->   /* Declare control variable for handler. */
   15 ->   DECLARE fetched        INT DEFAULT 0;
   16 ->
   17 ->   /* Declare local cursor. */
   18 ->   DECLARE foreign_key_cursor CURSOR FOR
   19 ->     SELECT   rc.table_name
   20 ->     ,        rc.constraint_name
```

```
21 ->      FROM     information_schema.referential_constraints rc
22 ->      WHERE    rc.constraint_schema = database()
23 ->      AND      rc.referenced_table_name
24 ->        REGEXP CONCAT('(^|^.+)',pv_referenced_table,'(.+$|$)')
25 ->      AND      rc.constraint_name
26 ->        REGEXP CONCAT('(^|^.+)',pv_constraint_name,'(.+$|$)')
27 ->      ORDER BY rc.table_name
28 ->      ,        rc.constraint_name;
29 ->
30 ->   /* Declare a not found record handler to close a
31 ->      cursor loop. */
32 ->   DECLARE CONTINUE HANDLER FOR NOT FOUND SET fetched = 1;
33 ->
34 ->   /* Open a local cursor. */
35 ->   OPEN foreign_key_cursor;
36 ->   cursor_foreign_key: LOOP
37 ->
38 ->     FETCH foreign_key_cursor
39 ->     INTO  lv_table_name
40 ->     ,     lv_constraint_name;
41 ->
42 ->     /* Place the catch handler for no more rows found
43 ->        immediately after the fetch operation.        */
44 ->     IF fetched = 1 THEN LEAVE cursor_foreign_key; END IF;
45 ->
46 ->     /* Set a SQL statement by using concatenation. */
47 ->     SET @SQL := CONCAT('ALTER TABLE ',lv_table_name
48 ->                        ,' DROP FOREIGN KEY,lv_constraint_name);
49 ->
50 ->     /* Prepare, run, and deallocate statement. */
51 ->     PREPARE lv_stmt FROM @SQL;
52 ->     EXECUTE lv_stmt;
53 ->     DEALLOCATE PREPARE lv_stmt;
54 ->
56 ->   END LOOP cursor_foreign_key;
57 ->   CLOSE foreign_key_cursor;
58 ->
59 -> END;
60 -> $$
```

Line 4 includes a SQL SECURITY INVOKER phrase (not a clause, because it's standalone and changes behavior by its presence) that designates the procedure as an invoker rights module. Recall that invoker rights modules run with the privileges of the user calling the module, not the privileges of the module definer. Since the only table accessed is in the publicly accessible information_schema database, we only need to grant the user privileges to run the dropForeignKeys procedure, like so (as the root superuser):

```
GRANT EXECUTE ON lib.dropForeignKeys TO student;
```

Or, if you have restricted host access, you'd do it like this:

```
GRANT EXECUTE ON lib.dropForeignKeys TO 'student'@'localhost';
```

Check back to Chapter 3 for more on the GRANT options. The idea is that you only need to provide EXECUTE privileges to run the invoker rights stored procedure.

Lines 24 and 26 contain regular expressions that let the parameter value occur at the beginning, end, or anywhere in the referenced_table_name or constraint_name columns. The trick to that is in the *metasequences* within the parentheses; they allow for the start of a string or the start after any number of characters before the parameter value, or any number of characters before the end of the string or the end of the string. What won't work successfully is a null or empty string parameter value (see the "Hacking the Lack of Default Parameters" sidebar earlier in this chapter). Case sensitivity isn't at stake, because without the binary, keyword comparisons are case-insensitive matches (see the "String Comparisons" section in Chapter 6 for details).

Summary

This chapter has explained the purposes and uses of stored programs in the MySQL database. It has taught you how to define stored functions and procedures, and explained the sequence required for positioning elements, such as variables, containers, cursors, handlers, and executable statements.

The chapter also reviewed the NO SQL, CONTAINS SQL, READS SQL DATA, and MODIFIES SQL DATA modes of operation in functions and procedures. It also reviewed the conditional logic and iterative logic instruction used in the language, and concluded with demonstrations of prepared DDL and DML statements.

Mastery Check

The mastery check is a series of true or false and multiple choice questions that let you confirm how well you understand the material in the chapter. You may check the Appendix for answers to these questions.

1. **True** ☐ **False** ☐ MySQL stored procedures support only the IN mode for parameters.

2. **True** ☐ **False** ☐ MySQL stored function parameters support the IN, INOUT, and OUT modes for parameters.

3. **True** ☐ **False** ☐ MySQL requires that all assignments to local variables be made through the SET statement.

4. **True** ☐ **False** ☐ MySQL uses an ELSIF block like PL/SQL.

5. **True** ☐ **False** ☐ The value of a call parameter is always available inside a function or procedure regardless of the parameter's mode of operation.

6. **True** ☐ **False** ☐ MySQL supports a DO-WHILE loop statement.

7. **True** ☐ **False** ☐ MySQL supports simple and searched CASE statements.

8. **True** ☐ **False** ☐ Like Oracle, MySQL lets you parameterize CURSOR statements.

9. **True** ☐ **False** ☐ You can write a SELECT statement to echo variable content in any stored procedure but not in stored functions.

10. True ☐ False ☐ The LEAVE statement doesn't need to refer to a named block to exit a block.

11. Which of the following operators matches values and nulls?

    A. = comparison operator

    B. <> comparison operator

    C. != comparison operator

    D. <=> comparison operator

    E. None of the above

12. Which loop structure isn't supported in MySQL stored programs?

    A. The DO-WHILE loop

    B. The REPEAT UNTIL loop

    C. The WHILE loop

    D. The simple loop

    E. The infinite loop

13. What type of statements can't you run in prepared statements?

    A. A DDL statement when the SQL statement is concatenated

    B. A DDL statement with the USING clause for local variables

    C. A DML statement with the USING clause for local variables

    D. A DDL statement when the SQL statement is concatenated

    E. A DML statement with ? placeholders

14. What isn't a valid operational mode for a function?

    A. The NO SQL mode

    B. The CONTAINS SQL mode

    C. The READS SQL DATA mode

    D. The MODIFIES SQL DATA mode

    E. The CONTAINS SQL DATA mode

15. Which isn't a valid assignment model in MySQL stored programs?

    A. SET variable = value;

    B. SET variable := value;

    C. SELECT value INTO variable;

    D. SELECT column_name INTO variable FROM table_name;

    E. SELECT variable := 20;

CHAPTER
15

Triggers

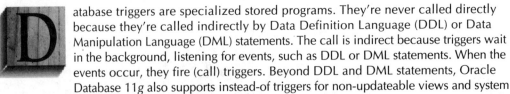atabase triggers are specialized stored programs. They're never called directly because they're called indirectly by Data Definition Language (DDL) or Data Manipulation Language (DML) statements. The call is indirect because triggers wait in the background, listening for events, such as DDL or DML statements. When the events occur, they fire (call) triggers. Beyond DDL and DML statements, Oracle Database 11*g* also supports instead-of triggers for non-updateable views and system or database event triggers. On the other hand, MySQL supports DML statement triggers only for the `INSERT`, `UPDATE`, and `DELETE` statements.

This chapter covers the following:

- Trigger architecture
- DDL triggers
- DML triggers
- Compound triggers
- Instead-of triggers
- System or database event triggers

You write database triggers in PL/SQL or SQL/PSM procedural programming languages. Oracle also lets you write trigger bodies in Java, while you define the trigger structures more or less the same way. This design lets you deploy database triggers against an Oracle database in C-callable programming languages.

Trigger Architecture

Triggers are specialized stored programs. They differ from stored functions and procedures because you can't call them directly. Database triggers fire when a triggering event occurs in the database. You can do the following things with triggers:

- Control and manage the behavior of DDL statements
- Control and change the behavior of DML statements
- Enforce referential integrity rules not supported by database constraints
- Audit system access and information
- Audit and record queries

Triggers can call SQL statements that in turn fire other triggers, and one of those triggers can fire another, and so forth. This is known as *cascading* triggers. Oracle 11*g* and earlier releases limit the number of cascading triggers to 32, after which an exception is thrown.

You can't generally sequence triggers, at least not in MySQL and most databases. Prior to Oracle 11*g*, that was true for Oracle, too. Oracle 11*g* introduced the `FOLLOWS` clause that now lets you sequence triggers.

The core role of database triggers focuses on how you insert, update, and delete data. These are typically known as DML triggers. Oracle and MySQL both provide DML triggers.

Oracle Trigger Architecture

Although Oracle 11*g* is the pinnacle of current trigger technologies, other databases continue to follow Oracle's lead. Oracle 11*g* offers five types of database triggers:

- **DDL triggers**   These triggers fire when you create, change, or remove objects in the database or schema. They let you control and manage the behavior of DDL statements. These triggers aren't implemented in MySQL.

- **DML triggers**   These triggers fire when you *insert*, *update*, or *delete* data from a table. They let you control and change the behavior of DML statements through row-level triggers, enforce complex referential integrity rules beyond what database constraints can do, and audit and record queries against the database by leveraging autonomous transactions. These are the types of triggers implemented in MySQL.

- **Compound triggers**   These triggers act as both statement- and row-level triggers when you *insert*, *update*, or *delete* data from a table. As a hybrid, this trigger lets you capture and work with data at four timing points: before the firing statement, before each row change from the firing statement, after each row change from the firing statement, and after the firing statement. There is no equivalent in MySQL.

- **Instead-of triggers**   These triggers let you stop performance of a DML statement against a view and redirect the DML statement to the underlying tables. Instead-of triggers are extremely useful in helping you write results when updating a non-updateable view. MySQL doesn't support an instead-of trigger.

- **System or database event triggers**   These triggers fire when a system activity occurs in the database, such as the logon and logoff event triggers. They let you track system events and link them to users.

The database trigger is a structure, while the trigger body is an anonymous block of PL/SQL code. Oracle stores the trigger logic in LONG columns inside the data catalog, but this behavior might change because Oracle has announced the deprecation of the LONG data type. These trigger

Privileges Required to Use Triggers

You must have the CREATE TRIGGER system privilege to create a trigger on an object that you own. If the object is owned by another user, you'll need that user to grant you the ALTER privilege on the object. Alternatively, the privileged user can grant you the ALTER ANY TABLE and CREATE ANY TRIGGER privileges.

You have definer permissions on your own schema-level components, but you must have EXECUTE permission when you call a schema-level component owned by another user. You should document any required privileges during development to streamline subsequent implementation.

bodies are stored in plain text and can be queried from the `ALL_`, `DBA_`, and `USER_TRIGGERS` catalog views, like this:

```
SET LONG 500000
SET PAGESIZE 9999
SQL> SELECT   trigger_body
  2  FROM     user_triggers
  3  WHERE    trigger_name = UPPER('trigger_name');
```

The maximum size of a database trigger is 32,760 bytes, and you can't wrap (or obfuscate) the trigger's code. You can, however, put the logic of the trigger in another stored program and obfuscate (hide) the code from prying eyes. The benefit of deploying logic to stored programs is that you can deploy larger logic units and hide that logic. There are risks when trigger bodies call other stored programs because they or their dependent database objects (tables and views) can be invalidated separately. More or less, a trigger that refers to tables or stored programs becomes invalid when you remove or change the definition of the tables or stored programs.

You have two options when you define database triggers: you can define them to run in the scope of the transaction that called them, or you can define them to run in an independent program scope. Triggers that run inside a DML statement's transaction scope can't set a `SAVEPOINT` or issue a `COMMIT` or `ROLLBACK` statement. Triggers that run as autonomous transactions must contain their own Transaction Control Language (TCL) commands. This means that an autonomous trigger may write changes to the database when the calling event and transaction scope simply fail without writing any changes.

You should use autonomous transactions to preserve an activity record when tracking the triggering event is critical. Triggers running in the same transaction scope are the more common practice, and they work in three scenarios:

■ The trigger raises an exception and stops the transaction.

■ The trigger lets the transaction proceed but logs the activity.

■ The trigger changes data to conform to business rules, and then logs the activity.

Obfuscating Means Hiding? Who'd Have Thought?

Oracle 11*g* lets you *wrap* or *obfuscate* your PL/SQL stored programs. Wrapping your code encapsulates the business logic of your applications, hiding the source code from prying eyes. Wrapping converts the clear text in the database to an unreadable stream of data. You can obfuscate the clear text by using the command line `wrap` utility or by calling the `CREATE_WRAPPED` procedure or `WRAP` function found in the `DBMS_DDL` package.

You wrap only the implementation details, such as functions, procedures, package bodies, and type bodies. You enable developers to use your code by leaving the package specification and type specification. This publishes the interface of your code without disclosing the logic and is an implementation of Interface Description Language (IDL).

Other developers don't know how the wrapped code performs tasks. They know only what actual parameters they can submit and what type of results to expect from functions or type methods. When you wrap packages, make sure you place reuse comments in the specification that help others reuse your code.

Triggers add complexity to your application solution and impact throughput. On occasion, triggers are deployed when other simpler solutions are available. You should avoid solving problems with database triggers unless you know they are the only way to solve the problem.

MySQL Trigger Architecture

MySQL supports only DML triggers when you insert, update, or delete data, and these are row-level triggers. There's no support for statement-level triggers in MySQL.

There are also restrictions on what you can put into database triggers, and they expand on those discussed in the "Stored Program Restrictions" section in Chapter 14. Moreover, trigger restrictions include all the restrictions for stored procedures and functions plus these:

- Foreign keys can't fire triggers.

- In row-based replication, triggers on the slave server aren't fired by events on the master server (key information, but beyond the scope of this text).

- Triggers can't return a value, and that means you can't use the RETURNS statement. You should use the LEAVE statement to exit a trigger.

- You can't define a trigger against anything in the mysql database catalog.

- Triggers don't detect external transactions that may change the data in a table, and triggers act on the current copy of the data from their transaction scope.

In all but the "DML Triggers" section, all that can be said about MySQL is that those features aren't yet implemented.

DDL Triggers

DDL triggers fire when you create, change, or remove objects from the database. These triggers aren't used frequently in production because of the nominal load on the database. When they are deployed, it's typically to monitor the GRANT and REVOKE privilege statements or the creation of tables where collections should be used.

Oracle DDL Triggers

Oracle supports DDL triggers, and Table 15-1 lists the data definition events that work with DDL triggers. These triggers support both BEFORE and AFTER event triggers and work at the database or schema level. (Oracle usage of database here means across the Oracle Server.)

You can leverage 27 different event attributes in DDL triggers. If you're interested in a broader coverage of possibilities, check Chapter 10 of the *Oracle Database 11g PL/SQL Programming* book.

Here is the prototype for building a DDL trigger:

```
CREATE [OR REPLACE] TRIGGER trigger_name
{BEFORE | AFTER | INSTEAD OF} ddl_event ON {DATABASE | SCHEMA}
[WHEN (logical_expression)]
[DECLARE]
  declaration_statements;
```

DDL Event	Description
ALTER	You ALTER objects by changing something about them, such as their constraints, names, storage clauses, or structure.
ANALYZE	You ANALYZE objects to compute statistics for the cost optimizer.
ASSOCIATE STATISTICS	You ASSOCIATE STATISTICS to link a statistic type to a column, function, package, type, domain index, or index types.
AUDIT	You AUDIT to enable auditing on an object or system.
COMMENT	You COMMENT to document column or table purposes.
CREATE	You CREATE objects in the database, such as objects, privileges, roles, tables, users, and views.
DDL	You use the DDL event to represent any of the primary data definition events. It effectively says any DDL event acting on anything.
DISASSOCIATE STATISTICS	You DISASSOCIATE STATISTICS to unlink a statistic type from a column, function, package, type, domain index, or index type.
DROP	You DROP objects in the database, such as objects, privileges, roles, tables, users, and views.
GRANT	You GRANT privileges or roles to users in the database on objects, such as objects, privileges, roles, tables, users, and views.
NOAUDIT	You NOAUDIT to disable auditing on an object or system.
RENAME	You RENAME objects in the database, such as columns, constraints, objects, privileges, roles, synonyms, tables, users, and views.
REVOKE	You REVOKE privileges or roles from users in the database on objects, such as objects, privileges, roles, tables, users, and views.
TRUNCATE	You TRUNCATE tables, which drops all rows from a table and resets the high-water mark to the original storage clause initial extent value. Unlike the DML DELETE statement, the TRUNCATE command can't be reversed by a ROLLBACK command. You can use the new flashback feature to undo the change.

TABLE 15-1. *Available Data Definition Events*

```
BEGIN
  execution_statements;
[EXCEPTION
  exception_statements;]
END [trigger_name];
/
```

The OR REPLACE clause is my favorite, because you don't have to drop the trigger before refactoring it, as you do in MySQL. The INSTEAD OF clause works only when auditing a creation event, and generally BEFORE or AFTER are more common.

This section's example requires a table in which the trigger can write output. If you want to work along with the example, you should create the `audit_creation` table and its accompanying sequence:

```
SQL> CREATE TABLE audit_creation
  2  ( audit_creation_id NUMBER
  3  , audit_owner_name   VARCHAR2(30)  CONSTRAINT audit_creation_nn1 NOT NULL
  4  , audit_obj_name     VARCHAR2(20)  CONSTRAINT audit_creation_nn2 NOT NULL
  5  , audit_date         DATE          CONSTRAINT audit_creation_nn3 NOT NULL
  6  , CONSTRAINT audit_creation_p1    PRIMARY KEY (audit_creation_id));

SQL> CREATE SEQUENCE audit_creation_s1;
```

Now you can create the `audit_creation_t` system trigger. This trigger shows you the behavior of a DDL trigger when dependencies become unavailable to the trigger. The `INSERT` statement includes two of those event attributes mentioned earlier, and they grab important information with little work on our end.

Following is the `CREATE TRIGGER` statement for the trigger. Notice that the name differs from the name of the table. You can name triggers with the same name as tables because triggers have their own namespace (separate from all other objects in the Oracle database). Although this is possible, it's discouraged, and this trigger uses a `_t` appended to the name of the table. When two or more triggers exist on a table, use a `_t1`, `_t2`, and so forth. If you follow this convention, it's easier to find and identify triggers when you look in the data catalog.

```
SQL> CREATE OR REPLACE TRIGGER audit_creation_t
  2  BEFORE CREATE ON SCHEMA
  3  BEGIN
  4    INSERT INTO audit_creation
  5    VALUES
  6    ( audit_creation_s1.NEXTVAL
  7    , ORA_DICT_OBJ_OWNER
  8    , ORA_DICT_OBJ_NAME
  9    , SYSDATE);
 10  END audit_creation_t;
 11  /
```

The following DDL statement triggers the system trigger, which inserts data from the trigger attribute functions. It creates a stray synonym that doesn't translate to anything real, but it does create an event that fires the trigger:

```
CREATE SYNONYM narnia FOR student.make_believe_land;
```

You can query the results of the trigger using the following SQL*Plus formatting and statement:

```
COL audit_creation_id FORMAT 99999999 HEADING "Audit|Creation|ID #"
COL audit_owner_name   FORMAT A6 HEADING "Audit|Owner|Name"
COL audit_obj_name     FORMAT A8 HEADING "Audit|Object|Name"
COL audit_obj_name     FORMAT A9 HEADING "Audit|Object|Name"
SELECT * FROM audit_creation;
```

The query returns the following:

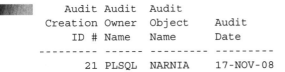

```
   Audit Audit  Audit
Creation Owner  Object   Audit
   ID # Name   Name     Date
--------- ------ --------- ---------
      21 PLSQL  NARNIA   17-NOV-08
```

MySQL DDL Triggers

MySQL doesn't support DDL triggers.

DML Triggers

DML triggers are the most frequently used triggers, and they're the only type of triggers supported in the MySQL database. DML triggers can fire *before* or *after* INSERT, UPDATE, and DELETE statements. You can define them as statement- or row-level triggers. Statement-level triggers fire and perform once per DML event. Row-level triggers fire and perform for every row touched by a DML event.

A *principal caveat* of triggers that manage data changes is that you cannot use SQL TCL in them, unless you declare the trigger as autonomous. Autonomous triggers are possible only in an Oracle database.

Most triggers run inside the scope of the transaction that fired the event that brought them to life. Triggers that run in the transaction scope of a DML statement disallow setting a SAVEPOINT or performing a ROLLBACK or COMMIT statement. Triggers also can't call any stored programs that contain TCL statements.

These rules apply equally in Oracle and MySQL databases for in-scope triggers. They don't apply to Oracle's autonomous transaction triggers. Unfortunately for MySQL developers, there is no way to create stored programs that run as autonomous transactions. As rule, simply remember not to use TCL (SAVEPOINT, ROLLBACK, or COMMIT) commands in MySQL.

Oracle DML Triggers

Oracle DML triggers provide statement- or row-level variations. Here's the prototype for an Oracle DML trigger:

```
CREATE [OR REPLACE] TRIGGER trigger_name
{BEFORE | AFTER}
{ INSERT [OR] |
 {UPDATE | UPDATE OF column1 [, column2 [, ...]] [OR] |
  DELETE} ON table_name
[FOR EACH ROW]
[FOLLOWS some_other_trigger_name]
[WHEN (logical_expression)]
[DECLARE]
  [PRAGMA AUTONOMOUS_TRANSACTION;]
  declaration_statements;
BEGIN
  execution_statements;
```

```
[EXCEPTION
  exception_statements;]
END [trigger_name];
/
```

You have the option of specifying when a trigger will fire—before or after the DML statement. Oracle lets you create a single DML trigger that fires for all *insert*, *update*, or *delete* events. When you omit the FOR EACH ROW clause, the trigger becomes a statement-level trigger, which means including FOR EACH ROW clause makes it a row-level trigger.

The FOLLOWS clause lets you position a trigger to follow another trigger. If all triggers are *on an event* but one uses the FOLLOWS clause, you can guarantee their sequential ordering. That's true from Oracle 11*g* forward but not true in prior releases of the product.

The WHEN clause lets you specify conditions that govern whether the trigger fires or not. It would be great if a WHEN clause were added to DML triggers in MySQL. This is extremely helpful in row-level triggers, because you can make determinations based on the values of *new* or *old* column values. The new column values are the values coming from the INSERT or UPDATE statement, and the old column values are those already in the table when you *update* or *delete* rows (see Table 15-2).

Including the PRAGMA AUTONOMOUS_TRANSACTION designates that a trigger will run in its own transaction context (or from the "Processes and Threads" sidebar in Chapter 4, they'll swim in their own swim lane as a concurrent process). The absence of the PRAGMA (precompiler instruction) means the trigger runs in the transaction scope of the DML event.

The DECLARATION block follows the same rules as any unnamed block, and you put the *declaration* in between the trigger's header block and the BEGIN keyword. As mentioned, the execution statements can't contain any TCL statements, such as SAVEPOINT, ROLLBACK, or COMMIT.

Statement-Level Triggers

Statement-level triggers are also known as table-level triggers because they're fired by a change event to the table. You can also restrict (filter) UPDATE statement triggers by constraining them to fire only when a specific column value changes.

Statement-level triggers don't let you collect transaction details, such as column values from rows processed. They do let you capture the inserting, updating, or deleting events against a table.

The example for statement-level triggers works on the premise that updates to the price_type column of the price table are batch programs, and the business needs to log those changes when

DML Statement	New Column Values	Old Column Values
INSERT	Available	Not available
UPDATE	Available	Available
DELETE	Not available	Available

TABLE 15-2.   *Trigger New and Old Column Availability*

they occur. To that end, you have the `price_type_log` table, as defined by this `CREATE TABLE` statement:

```
SQL> CREATE TABLE price_type_log
  2  ( price_id       NUMBER           CONSTRAINT price_type_log_nn1 NOT NULL
  3  , user_id        VARCHAR2(32)     CONSTRAINT price_type_log_nn2 NOT NULL
  4  , action_date    DATE             CONSTRAINT price_type_log_nn3 NOT NULL
  5  , CONSTRAINT     price_type_log_p1 PRIMARY KEY (price_id))
  6  /
SQL> CREATE SEQUENCE price_type_log_s1;
```

You would create a statement-level trigger to record any table change to the `price_type` column with this syntax:

```
SQL> CREATE OR REPLACE TRIGGER price_t
  2  AFTER UPDATE OF price_type ON price
  3  DECLARE
  4  BEGIN
  5    INSERT INTO price_type_log
  6    VALUES
  7    ( price_log_s1.NEXTVAL
  8    , USER
  9    , SYSDATE);
 10  END price_t1;
 11  /
```

The use of the `.NEXTVAL` pseudo column in an `INSERT` statement is a new feature of Oracle 11*g*. It isn't backward compatible in older releases.

You can fire the `price_t` trigger with this `UPDATE` statement:

```
UPDATE price p
SET     p.price_type = p.price_type
WHERE   EXISTS (SELECT NULL
               FROM   price q
               WHERE  q.price_id = p.price_id);
```

The following query shows that the trigger fired and wrote audit information to the `price_type_log` table:

```
SQL> COLUMN PRICE_ID    FORMAT 999 HEADING "Price|ID #"
SQL> COLUMN USER_ID     FORMAT A32 HEADING "User ID #"
SQL> COLUMN ACTION_DATE FORMAT A9  HEADING "Action|Date"
SQL> SELECT * FROM price_type_log;
```

You would see the following output (with the preceding SQL*Plus formatting):

```
Price
 ID # User ID #                          Action
                                         Date
----- -------------------------------- ---------
    1 STUDENT                           15-JUL-11
```

Backward Compatibility of .NEXTVAL

In prior releases, such as Oracle 10g, you would need to remove the call to the .NEXTVAL pseudo column from the INSERT statement. You would need to refactor it like this for the older releases:

```
SQL> CREATE OR REPLACE TRIGGER price_t
  2  AFTER UPDATE OF price_type ON price
  3  DECLARE
  4    lv_price_id NUMBER;
  5  BEGIN
  6    -- Retrieve sequence value and store in local variable.
  7    SELECT price_type_log_s1.NEXTVAL
  8    INTO lv_price_id
  9    FROM dual;
 10    -- Insert logging values.
 11    INSERT INTO price_type_log
 12    VALUES
 13    ( lv_price_id
 14    , USER
 15    , SYSDATE);
 16  END price_t1;
 17  /
```

The refactoring requires that you declare a local variable on line 4, then select a value from the sequence on lines 7 to 8, and then use the local variable inside the INSERT statement on line 13. Relatively speaking, it's a lot of work to move backward, but that's one reason why Oracle made it work inside DML statements in the current release.

Row-Level Triggers

Row-level triggers let you capture new and old values from each row. These values are available to you via two pseudo record structures: new and old. They're represented in the WHEN clause as simply new or old because that occurs within the scope of the DML statement, and it is part of the database trigger's structure. Inside the trigger body, they're :new or :old. This change can be confusing, but the following illustration highlights how trigger mapping works.

```
CREATE OR REPLACE TRIGGER contact_insert_t
BEFORE INSERT ON contact

                                    ┌──────────────────────────┐
                                    │ Checks the local         │
                                    │ transaction pseudo field │
                                    └──────────────────────────┘
FOR EACH ROW
WHEN (REGEXP_LIKE(new.last_name,' '))
BEGIN

  :new.last_name:= REGEXP_REPLACE(:new.last_name,' ','-',1,1);

END contact_insert_t1;
                              ┌────────────────────┐
                              │ Reads external     │
                              │ pseudo field       │
                              └────────────────────┘
  /   ┌────────────────┐
      │ Writes external│
      │ pseudo field   │
      └────────────────┘
```

The colon identifies a bind variable in the trigger body that points from its execution scope back to the event scope that fired the trigger. After creating the `contact_insert_t` trigger, you create an `INSERT` event with this statement:

```
SQL> INSERT INTO contact
  2  ( contact_id
  3  , member_id
  4  , contact_type
  5  , first_name
  6  , middle_name
  7  , last_name
  8  , created_by
  9  , creation_date
 10  , last_updated_by
 11  , last_update_date )
 12  VALUES
 13  ( contact_s1.NEXTVAL   -- contact_id
 14  , 1001                 -- member_id
 15  , 1003                 -- contact_type
 16  ,'Catherine'           -- first_name
 17  , NULL                 -- middle_name
 18  ,'Zeta Jones'          -- last_name
 19  , 3                    -- created_by
 20  , SYSDATE              -- creation_date
 21  , 3                    -- last_updated_by
 22  , SYSDATE)             -- last_update_date
 23  /
```

The `INSERT` statement uses comments after the values, which requires that a semicolon on the last line be dropped. It is replaced with a forward slash on the last line of the `INSERT` statement. Why? The semicolon must be the last character on the line to run a statement.

The trigger converts the last name to a hyphenated last name. To see the actual result, query the `last_name` from the `contact` table:

```
SELECT last_name FROM contact WHERE last_name LIKE 'Zeta%';
```

You should have the following results:

```
LAST_NAME
--------------------
Zeta-Jones
```

The only problem with the trigger is that a disappointed end user can simply update the column to remove the dash from the `last_name` column. You can prevent that by refactoring the trigger. You change it from a singular `INSERT` event to an `INSERT OR UPDATE` event. Here's the syntax:

```
CREATE OR REPLACE TRIGGER contact_insert_t
  BEFORE INSERT OR UPDATE OF last_name ON contact
  FOR EACH ROW
  WHEN (REGEXP_LIKE(new.last_name,' '))
```

```
BEGIN
  :new.last_name := REGEXP_REPLACE(:new.last_name,' ','-',1,1);
END contact_insert_t1;
/
```

The trigger is now fired on any INSERT statement and *only* for UPDATE statements that change the last_name column. It is always better to build triggers that work with multiple DML events when you take the same type of action. Unfortunately, this choice isn't available in MySQL.

MySQL DML Triggers

MySQL triggers work only in response to the INSERT, UPDATE, and DELETE statements. They're all row-level triggers, which gives them the ability to change values during *insert*, *update*, and *delete* actions.

Here's the prototype for MySQL triggers:

```
CREATE [DEFINER={user | CURRENT_USER}] TRIGGER trigger_name
{BEFORE | AFTER } {INSERT | UPDATE | DELETE} ON table_name
FOR EACH ROW
BEGIN
  statement_statements;
END;
```

Although Oracle lets you define a trigger that works on INSERT, UPDATE, or DELETE statements or any combination of those statements, MySQL lets you create a trigger that responds only to a distinct *insert*, *update*, or *delete* event.

You can designate whether you want the trigger to run before or after the DML statement. Choose BEFORE when you want to audit and change the value provided by the DML statement. When the BEFORE trigger fails, the DML statement fails and any AFTER trigger never runs.

Unlike Oracle, where you choose a statement- or row-level trigger type, MySQL supports only row-level triggers. Row-level triggers give you access to the values provided by the DML statement and the values in the tables themselves for UPDATE and DELETE statements. The values from the DML statements are the *new* values, and the values from the table are the *old* values. Inside a row-level trigger, you can change the new values before they're added to the table.

Here's the prototype to change the value of new column values:

```
SET new.column_name = value;
```

There is no other way to assign values to the new column values. If you were to try a SELECT-INTO statement, like this,

```
SELECT expression INTO new.column_name;
```

it would raise this error:

```
ERROR 1327 (42000): Undeclared variable: NEW
```

In general, MySQL is restrictive in how you use certain assignments. As you saw in Chapter 14, some assignments work for session variables but not local variables. This is apparently the case here, and only the SET statement appears in the MySQL documentation.

> **NOTE**
> *The new or old pseudo structure is exclusive to the SQL/PSM scope,*
> *and that's why you can't embed it in a SQL statement, as you can the*
> `SELECT-INTO` *statement.*

Although we'd like to make sure developers always write perfect code, they don't (you know, the other guys and gals). Triggers can help ensure that coding mistakes don't compromise data integrity. In the sample data model there is a `common_lookup` table, which is a table that contains many small tables. For example, here's the embedded table of lookup values for the `member_type` column of the `member` table:

```
+----------------------+----------------------+----------------------+
| common_lookup_table  | common_lookup_column | common_lookup_type   |
+----------------------+----------------------+----------------------+
| MEMBER               | MEMBER_TYPE          | GROUP                |
| MEMBER               | MEMBER_TYPE          | INDIVIDUAL           |
+----------------------+----------------------+----------------------+
```

Each row in the `common_lookup` table is uniquely identified by a table name, column name, and type value. Sets of rows are non-uniquely identified by a table and column name (like the set above). These non-unique sets define the lookup tables within the larger lookup table. This table will be instrumental in our example trigger, which will ensure that we have only a valid column value from our little table within a table (you can see more on the rationale for a `common_lookup` table in the Introduction).

Laying a bit more foundation for the coding example, foreign key constraints are great, but it's possible that a foreign key (constrained) column could hold a valid or invalid primary key value. That's because a foreign key constraint ensures only that the value is in the list of possible primary keys (every identifier column value in the table). A valid foreign key could point to the correct primary key column and row, while an incorrect foreign key would point to the correct column but the wrong row.

The example DML trigger makes sure that an `INSERT` statement can't insert the wrong value. Here are the correct values for the little table within the table:

```
+----+------------+-------------+------------+
| ID | TABLE_NAME | COLUMN_NAME | TYPE       |
+----+------------+-------------+------------+
| 5  | MEMBER     | MEMBER_TYPE | INDIVIDUAL |
| 6  | MEMBER     | MEMBER_TYPE | GROUP      |
+----+------------+-------------+------------+
```

Here's an `INSERT` statement that violates the business rule by trying to enter a value of *10* when the valid values are *5* and *6*. The syntax uses the `SET` clause (presented in Chapter 8), because it clearly maps the column names to the values, as you can see:

```
INSERT INTO member
SET member_type = 10
,   account_number = 'SJC-000005'
,   credit_card_number = '1234-5678-9012-3456'
,   credit_card_type = 8
,   created_by = 1
```

```
,    creation_date = UTC_DATE()
,    last_updated_by = 1
,    last_update_date = UTC_DATE();
```

This mistake would corrupt our data, but a trigger can prevent it from happening. The trigger evaluates the value submitted and substitutes a valid value based on a default assumption of an individual account.

Here's the CREATE TRIGGER statement along with those DELIMITER settings and a conditional DROP TRIGGER statement for a trigger (line numbers added for reference):

```
mysql> DELIMITER $$
mysql> DROP TRIGGER IF EXISTS member_type_t$$
mysql> CREATE TRIGGER member_type_t
  2 -> BEFORE INSERT ON member
  3 -> FOR EACH ROW
  4 -> BEGIN
  5 ->    /* Local control variable. */
  6 ->    DECLARE matched    INT DEFAULT 0;
  7 ->
  8 ->    /* Local data variable. */
  9 ->    DECLARE lv_type_id INT UNSIGNED;
 10 ->
 11 ->    /* Declare a handler variables. */
 12 ->    DECLARE fetched INT DEFAULT 0;
 13 ->
 14 ->    /* Declare a cursor to find valid identifiers. */
 15 ->    DECLARE verify_member_type CURSOR FOR
 16 ->      SELECT   cl.common_lookup_id
 17 ->      FROM     common_lookup cl
 18 ->      WHERE    cl.common_lookup_table = 'MEMBER'
 19 ->      AND      cl.common_lookup_column = 'MEMBER_TYPE';
 20 ->
 21 ->    /* Declare a not found record handler to close a cursor loop. */
 22 ->    DECLARE CONTINUE HANDLER FOR NOT FOUND SET fetched = 1;
 23 ->
 24 ->    OPEN verify_member_type;
 25 ->    verify_loop:LOOP
 26 ->
 27 ->      /* Fetch a record from the cursor. */
 28 ->      FETCH verify_member_type
 29 ->      INTO  lv_type_id;
 30 ->
 31 ->      /* Place the catch handler for no more rows found
 32 ->         immediately after the fetch operation.          */
 33 ->      IF fetched = 1 THEN LEAVE verify_loop; END IF;
 34 ->
 35 ->      /* Check value from insert against valid values. */
 36 ->      IF new.member_type = lv_type_id THEN
 37 ->        SET matched = 1;
 38 ->        LEAVE verify_loop;
 39 ->      END IF;
 40 ->
```

```
41 ->    END LOOP verify_loop;
42 ->    CLOSE verify_member_type;
43 ->
44 ->    /* Run when inserted MEMBER_TYPE is invalid. */
45 ->    IF matched = 0 THEN
46 ->      SELECT   cl.common_lookup_id
47 ->      INTO     lv_type_id
48 ->      FROM     common_lookup cl
49 ->      WHERE    cl.common_lookup_table = 'MEMBER'
50 ->      AND      cl.common_lookup_column = 'MEMBER_TYPE'
51 ->      AND      cl.common_lookup_type = 'INDIVIDUAL';
52 ->
53 ->      /* Replace value from the insert statement. */
54 ->      SET new.member_type = lv_type_id;
55 ->    END IF;
56 -> END;
57 -> $$
mysql> DELIMITER ;
```

The trigger definition is a *row-level* BEFORE INSERT ON trigger. The new.member_type column is compared against valid values from the little table (or data set) of possible values for the member_type column of the member table on line 36. The matched control variable is SET to 1, when the member_type column value equals one of the possible common_lookup_type values from the cursor on lines 15 through 19.

When the matched control variable is SET to 1, you use the lv_type_id value as a valid foreign key value in the member_type column of the member table. When the new.member_type value doesn't match the lv_type value from the cursor on line 45, a subsequent SELECT-INTO statement on lines 46 through 51 gets the foreign key value for an *individual* membership from the common_lookup table. The trigger assigns the common_lookup_id as the default member_type value on line 54, which occurs in an IF block that's runs only when necessary.

Sometimes you don't want to assign a default member_type value because you want to raise an exception. Raised exceptions help inform developers that they might have introduced an error in gathering the foreign key value (although our choice of an out-of-range foreign key value was intentional, their error isn't). It would be easy if MySQL stored programs supported a raise exception syntax like PL/SQL, but they don't.

You can engineer the logic into your trigger quite easily, however. The first thing you need to know is that stored procedures report errors on variable assignments as if they're column value errors in a DML statement (such as an INSERT, UPDATE, or DELETE statement). That means the first thing you need to do is modify line 9 and add a local variable with the same name as the column name in the table, like so:

```
9 ->    DECLARE lv_type_id, member_type INT UNSIGNED;
```

Hopefully, you remembered from Chapter 14 that you can declare multiple variables of the same data type on a single line, and if not, now you do. Next you need to change the logic inside the IF block on lines 45 through 55 with the following:

```
45 ->   IF matched = 0 THEN
46 ->     SELECT -1 INTO member_type;
47 ->   END IF;
```

The assignment of a negative integer to a variable that uses an unsigned integer data type on line 46 raises this error message:

```
ERROR 1264 (22003): Out of range value for column 'member_type'
at row 1
```

There's very little difference between DML triggers. The key to creating DML triggers is to define the trigger structure correctly and ensure that the body doesn't contain any invalid or unsupported elements. The restrictions on triggers are found earlier in the "MySQL Trigger Architecture" section of this chapter.

I suggest you test the logic in a stored procedure before you put it in a database trigger, because triggers have more moving parts and are more difficult to troubleshoot. You can do this by calling the procedure from the database trigger.

Compound Triggers

Compound triggers act as both statement- and row-level triggers when you *insert, update,* or *delete* data from a table. As mentioned earlier in the chapter, they have four timing points: before the firing statement, before each row change from the firing statement, after each row change from the firing statement, and after the firing statement. You implement statement-level triggers before or after the DML statement, and you implement row-level triggers before or after row events.

In the scope of compound triggers, the subordinate blocks can be considered *subcomponents* or *sequenced* trigger blocks. Although you only need to implement need one trigger block to write a minimal compound trigger, you can have up to four. The first trigger block would be a before statement-level trigger, the second trigger block is a before row-level trigger, the third trigger block would be an after row-level trigger, and the fourth trigger block an after statement trigger. Compound triggers are important and innovative because they facilitate exchanges of data between the individual trigger blocks.

Compound triggers are a new feature in Oracle 11g, and they don't exist in other commercial databases. MySQL falls into that other bucket and doesn't implement them.

Oracle Compound Triggers

Oracle implements compound triggers as if they're sequenced and threaded operations. However, you have one declaration section for the trigger as a whole, and each timing block section has its own local declaration sections. This means that the variables and structures declared in the compound trigger's scope are available to the nested trigger code blocks at each timing point—these are statement- and row-level trigger blocks. These nested trigger blocks can read from and write to the compound trigger's global structures.

The model of compound triggers resembles a multithreaded program with a discrete memory segment. When the program (process) starts, it creates a global memory area known as a *process control block (PCB)*. The process then spawns threads that in turn allocate memory for their private use in the same memory segment, and these are *thread control blocks (TCBs)*. Threads sometimes have the ability to read from and write to the PCB during execution. This concept of multithreaded programming mirrors the effective implementation of compound triggers.

Only DML statements, such as INSERT, UPDATE, and DELETE statements, fire compound triggers. The GOTO block exists and works in compound triggers, but it's restricted to a single timing block. That means you can't call between nested trigger blocks (or threads), which is very reasonable. The basic value of compound triggers arises from the fact that you can collect information at the row-level but insert it at the statement-level with a *bulk insert statement*. This minimizes the impact of row-level triggers that need to record logging information in a table other than the transaction table. The transaction table is the table in which the DML statement is inserted or updated, or from which data is deleted, and it's also the table that the trigger references in its definition.

Here's the compound trigger's prototype:

```
CREATE [OR REPLACE] TRIGGER trigger_name
FOR
{ INSERT [OR] |
 {UPDATE | UPDATE OF column1 [, column2 [, ...]] [OR] |
  DELETE} ON table_name
[FOR EACH ROW]
COMPOUND TRIGGER
[BEFORE STATEMENT IS
  [declaration_statement;]
 BEGIN
   execution_statement;
 END BEFORE STATEMENT;]
[BEFORE EACH ROW IS
  [declaration_statement;]
 BEGIN
   execution_statement;
 END BEFORE EACH ROW;]
[AFTER EACH ROW IS
  [declaration_statement;]
 BEGIN
   execution_statement;
 END AFTER EACH ROW;]
[AFTER STATEMENT IS
  [declaration_statement;]
 BEGIN
   execution_statement;
 END AFTER STATEMENT;]
END [trigger_name];
/
```

The example rewrites the insert event row-level trigger from the "Row-level Triggers" section as a compound trigger. The code follows:

```
CREATE OR REPLACE TRIGGER compound_connection_log_t1
    FOR INSERT ON connection_log
    COMPOUND TRIGGER
    BEFORE EACH ROW IS
    BEGIN
       IF :new.event_id IS NULL THEN
```

```
      :new.event_id := connection_log_s1.nextval;
    END IF;
  END BEFORE EACH ROW;
END;
/
```

You should note three key elements about compound triggers. You can't filter events in this type of trigger by using a WHEN clause. The :new and :old pseudo records are available only in the BEFORE EACH ROW and AFTER EACH ROW nested trigger blocks. Variables declared in the global declaration block retain their value through the execution of all timing blocks that you've implemented.

You can collect row-level information in either the BEFORE EACH ROW or AFTER EACH ROW timing points and transfer that information to a global trigger collection. Then you can perform a bulk operation with the collection contents in the AFTER STATEMENT timing point. If you don't write the data to another table, you could raise the maximum number of recursive calls error, ORA-00036.

Reading and Writing Session Metadata

The process of writing to and reading from the session CLIENT_INFO column requires you to use the DBMS_APPLICATION_INFO package. You use the SET_CLIENT_INFO procedure in the DBMS_APPLICATION_INFO package to write data into the 64-character CLIENT_INFO column found in the V$SESSION view. The following anonymous PL/SQL block assumes that the CREATED_BY and LAST_UPDATED_BY columns should be 3:

```
BEGIN
   -- Write value to V$SESSION.CLIENT_INFO column.
   DBMS_APPLICATION_INFO.SET_CLIENT_INFO('3');
END;
/
```

You can now read this value by calling the READ_CLIENT_INFO procedure. You should enable SERVEROUTPUT using SQL*Plus to see the rendered output when you run the following program:

```
DECLARE
   client_info        VARCHAR2(64);
BEGIN
   -- Read value from V$SESSION.CLIENT_INTO column.
   DBMS_APPLICATION_INFO.READ_CLIENT_INFO(client_info);
   DBMS_OUTPUT.PUT_LINE('[ '||client_info||']');
END;
/
```

User-defined session columns let you store unique information related to user credentials from your Access Control List (ACL). You assign a session column value during user authentication. Then the session CLIENT_INFO column allows you to manage multiple user interactions in a single schema. Authenticated users can access whole or partial rows from tables when their session CLIENT_INFO column value matches a striping column's value in the table.

The next example demonstrates collecting information in the row-level timing points, transferring it to a global collection, and processing it as a bulk transaction in the AFTER STATEMENT timing block. The first step requires that you create a log repository, which is done by creating the following table and sequence:

```
SQL> CREATE TABLE price_event_log
  2  ( price_log_id      NUMBER
  3  , price_id          NUMBER
  4  , created_by        NUMBER
  5  , creation_date     DATE
  6  , last_updated_by   NUMBER
  7  , last_update_date  DATE );
SQL> CREATE SEQUENCE price_event_log_s1;
```

The aforementioned compound trigger populates created_by and last_updated_by columns as part of the application's *"who-audit"* information. It assumes that you're striping the data, which means you need to set a CLIENT_INFO value for the session. (See the "Reading and Writing Session Metadata" sidebar for details on striping data.) The physical CLIENT_INFO section is found in the V$SESSION view.

The following sets the CLIENT_INFO value to 3, which is a valid system_user_id in the system_user table:

```
SQL> EXECUTE dbms_application_info.set_client_info('3');
```

The trigger looks at the session value of CLIENT_INFO before inserting that value in the table. When the value is null, the trigger replaces it with a -1.

The following defines the compound trigger with both BEFORE EACH ROW and AFTER STATEMENT timing blocks:

```
SQL> CREATE OR REPLACE TRIGGER compound_price_update_t1
  2  FOR UPDATE ON price
  3  COMPOUND TRIGGER
  4    -- Declare a global record type.
  5    TYPE price_record IS RECORD
  6    ( price_log_id      price_event_log.price_log_id%TYPE
  7    , price_id          price_event_log.price_id%TYPE
  8    , created_by        price_event_log.created_by%TYPE
  9    , creation_date     price_event_log.creation_date%TYPE
 10    , last_updated_by   price_event_log.last_updated_by%TYPE
 11    , last_update_date  price_event_log.last_update_date%TYPE );
 12    -- Declare a global collection type.
 13    TYPE price_list IS TABLE OF PRICE_RECORD;
 14    -- Declare a global collection and initialize it.
 15    price_updates  PRICE_LIST := price_list();
 16    BEFORE EACH ROW IS
 17      -- Declare or define local timing point variables.
 18      c        NUMBER;
 19      user_id NUMBER :=
 20      NVL(TO_NUMBER(SYS_CONTEXT('userenv','client_info')),-1);
```

```
21    BEGIN
22      -- Extend space and assign dynamic index value.
23      price_updates.EXTEND;
24      c := price_updates.LAST;
25      price_updates(c).price_log_id := price_event_log_s1.nextval;
26      price_updates(c).price_id := :old.price_id;
27      price_updates(c).created_by := user_id;
28      price_updates(c).creation_date := SYSDATE;
29      price_updates(c).last_updated_by := user_id;
30      price_updates(c).last_update_date := SYSDATE;
31    END BEFORE EACH ROW;
32    AFTER STATEMENT IS
33    BEGIN
34      -- Bulk insert statement.
35      FORALL i IN price_updates.FIRST..price_updates.LAST
36        INSERT INTO price_event_log
37        VALUES
38        ( price_updates(i).price_log_id
39        , price_updates(i).price_id
40        , price_updates(i).created_by
41        , price_updates(i).creation_date
42        , price_updates(i).last_updated_by
43        , price_updates(i).last_update_date );
44    END AFTER STATEMENT;
45  END;
46  /
```

The BEFORE EACH ROW timing block collects row-level data and stores it in a global collection, which can then be read from another timing block. The numeric index for the collection is dynamic and leverages the Collections API LAST method. If you'd like to check how that works, please refer to Chapter 13.

The AFTER STATEMENT timing block reads the global collection and performs a bulk insert of the data to the log table. The next time the trigger is fired, the global collection is empty, because the compound trigger implementation is serialized.

You can test the trigger by running the following UPDATE statement:

```
UPDATE price
SET    last_updated_by = NVL(TO_NUMBER(SYS_CONTEXT('userenv','client_info')),-1);
```

Then, you can query the price_event_log table:

```
SELECT * FROM price_event_log;
```

This example has shown you how to capture row-level data, save it in a global collection, and reuse it in a statement-level statement. This section has explained the new Oracle 11*g* compound triggers, and shown you how to implement them. They allow you to mix the benefits and operations of statement- and row-level triggers in a single trigger.

MySQL Compound Triggers
MySQL doesn't support compound triggers.

INSTEAD OF Triggers

INSTEAD OF triggers provide a means of writing data back to the source tables while working with non-updateable views. A non-updateable view occurs when the view contains any of the following:

- Set operators
- Aggregate functions
- CASE or DECODE statement
- CONNECT BY, GROUP BY, HAVING, or START WITH clause
- The DISTINCT operator
- Joins (with exceptions when they contain the joining key)

While MySQL doesn't support INSTEAD OF triggers, Oracle does. Oracle's implementation offers many advantages that make non-updateable views updateable.

Oracle INSTEAD OF Triggers

You can use the INSTEAD OF trigger to intercept INSERT, UPDATE, and DELETE statements and replace those instructions with alternative procedural code. Non-updateable views generally have INSTEAD OF triggers to accept the output and resolve the issues that make the view non-updateable.

Here's the prototype for building an INSTEAD OF trigger:

```
CREATE [OR REPLACE] TRIGGER trigger_name
INSTEAD OF {dml_statement }
ON {object_name | database | schema}
FOR EACH ROW
[WHEN (logical_expression)]
[DECLARE]
  declaration_statements;
BEGIN
  execution_statements;
[EXCEPTION
  exception_statements;]
END [trigger_name];
/
```

INSTEAD OF triggers are powerful alternatives that resolve how you use complex and non-updateable views. When you know how the SELECT statement works, you can write procedural code to update the data not directly accessible through non-updateable views.

You can deploy only an INSTEAD OF DML trigger against a view. There is no restriction regarding whether the views is updatable or non-updateable, but generally INSTEAD OF triggers are built for non-updateable views.

The following view is supported by the data model provided on the publisher's web site for this book (at www.mhprofessional.com/). It is also a non-updateable view because of the DECODE statement, as shown:

```
CREATE OR REPLACE VIEW account_list AS
  SELECT  c.member_id
  ,       c.contact_id
  ,       m.account_number
  ,       c.first_name
  ||      DECODE(c.middle_initial,NULL,' ',' '||c.middle_initial||' ')
  ||      c.last_name FULL_NAME
  FROM contact c JOIN member m ON c.member_id = m.member_id;
```

Without an INSTEAD OF trigger, a DML statement against this view can raise an ORA-01776 exception that says you're disallowed from modifying more than one base table through a join. You could also raise an ORA-01779 exception that tells you you're disallowed from modifying a column because it fails to map to a non–key-preserved table.

You can create an INSTEAD OF trigger that would allow you to update or delete from this view. However, the view doesn't have enough information to support INSERT statements to either base table. Without redefining the view, there is also no programmatic way to fix these shortcomings.

The following is an INSTEAD OF INSERT trigger. It raises an exception for any insertion attempt to the non-updateable view.

```
CREATE OR REPLACE TRIGGER account_list_insert
  INSTEAD OF INSERT ON account_list
  FOR EACH ROW
BEGIN
  RAISE_APPLICATION_ERROR(-20000,'Not enough data for insert!');
END;
/
```

After compiling the trigger, an INSERT statement runs against the view and raises the following exception stack:

```
INSERT INTO account_list
            *
ERROR at line 1:
ORA-20000: Not enough data for insert!
ORA-06512: at "STUDENT.ACCOUNT_LIST_INSERT", line 2
ORA-04088: error during execution of trigger 'PLSQL.ACCOUNT_LIST_INSERT'
```

The question here is, do you want to define three INSTEAD OF event triggers or one? A number of developers opt for multiple INSTEAD OF triggers as opposed to one that does everything. You should consider defining one trigger for inserting, updating, and deleting events.

Table 15-3 qualifies the INSERTING, UPDATING, and DELETING functions from the DBMS_STANDARD package. These functions let you determine the type of DML event and write one trigger that manages all three DML events.

Function Name	Return Data Type	Description
DELETING	BOOLEAN	Returns a Boolean true when the DML event is deleting
INSERTING	BOOLEAN	Returns a Boolean true when the DML is inserting
UPDATING	BOOLEAN	Returns a Boolean true when the DML is updating

TABLE 15-3. *DML Event Functions*

In this type of model, the view collapses columns into a single column. That means the trigger needs to reverse the process, parsing the previously concatenated column into two columns. SQL by itself can't do this for you. That means you must provide a programmatic way to fix the non-updateable characteristic of this view.

You can build a complete trigger for all DML statements by using the event function from Table 15-3. The following provides an example INSTEAD OF trigger, which parses the full_ name column into individual columns. As a side note, this trigger accommodates only a first, middle, and last name in the view; it would take a more complete regular expression to manage multiple middle or last names.

```
SQL> CREATE OR REPLACE TRIGGER account_list_dml
  2  INSTEAD OF INSERT OR UPDATE OR DELETE ON account_list
  3  FOR EACH ROW
  4  DECLARE
  5    -- Source variable.
  6    source account_list.full_name%TYPE := :new.full_name;
  7    -- Parsed variables.
  8    fname  VARCHAR2(43);
  9    mname  VARCHAR2(1);
 10    lname  VARCHAR2(43);
 11
 12    -- Check whether all dependents are gone.
 13    FUNCTION get_dependents (member_id NUMBER) RETURN BOOLEAN IS
 14      rows NUMBER := 0;
 15      CURSOR c (member_id_in NUMBER) IS
 16        SELECT COUNT(*)
 17        FROM contact
 18        WHERE member_id = member_id_in;
 19    BEGIN
 20      OPEN c (member_id);
 21      FETCH c INTO rows;
 22      IF rows > 0 THEN
 23        RETURN FALSE;
 24      ELSE
 25        RETURN TRUE;
 26      END IF;
 27    END get_dependents;
```

```
28   BEGIN
29     IF INSERTING THEN -- On insert event.
30       RAISE_APPLICATION_ERROR(-20000,'Missing data for insert!');
31     ELSIF UPDATING THEN -- On update event.
32       -- Assign source variable.
33       source := :new.full_name;
34
35       -- Parse full_name for elements.
36       fname := LTRIM(REGEXP_SUBSTR(source,'(^|^ +)([[:alpha:]]+)',1));
37       mname := REGEXP_SUBSTR(
38         REGEXP_SUBSTR(
39           source,'( +)([[:alpha:]]+)(( +|.+))',1),'([[:alpha:]])',1);
40       lname := REGEXP_SUBSTR(
41         REGEXP_SUBSTR(
42           source,'( +)([[:alpha:]]+)( +$|$)',1),'([[:alpha:]]+)',1);
43
44       -- Update name change in base table.
45       UPDATE contact
46       SET    first_name = fname
47       ,      middle_initial = mname
48       ,      last_name = lname
49       WHERE  contact_id = :old.contact_id;
50     ELSIF DELETING THEN -- On delete event.
51       DELETE FROM contact WHERE member_id = :old.member_id;
52
53       -- Only delete the parent when there aren't any more children.
54       IF get_dependents(:old.member_id) THEN
55         DELETE FROM member WHERE member_id = :old.member_id;
56       END IF;
57     END IF;
58   END;
59   /
```

Some tricks or risks are present in this type of trigger. You must ensure that triggers are foolproof. One potential flaw in *this* trigger is the assignment of the pseudo field :new.full_name in the declaration section. The database doesn't check when you compile the trigger if the size of the source variable is large enough to handle possible assignments. There wouldn't be any risk of a size mismatch when the first, middle, and last name variables are declared with an anchored data type, such as the source variable. That type of declaration on lines 8 to 10 would look like this when they're anchored to columns in the contact table:

```
8    fname   contact.first_name%TYPE;
9    mname   contact.middle_name%TYPE;
10   lname   contact.last_name%TYPE;
```

You would not need to worry if the variables inside the trigger are large enough at runtime, because any change to the table definition cascades to the trigger. However, this does create coupling between the trigger and the data catalog, or at least it formalizes the dependency. Having all four of these variables anchored to the data catalog ensures that you won't raise ORA-06502, ORA-06512, and ORA-04088 errors. The reason these types of errors would be raised in the declaration block of a trigger body is because the body is stored in the database and read on execution. The `DECLARE` block of a trigger body raises a runtime exception during statement parsing.

This trigger fires on any DML event against the non-updateable view and handles the insert, update, or deletion to the base tables where appropriate. As mentioned, there wouldn't be enough information to perform `INSERT` statements to the base tables. As is, the `account_list` trigger would raise a user-defined exception if someone attempted to insert a new record through the view. In fact, that's the only thing performed in the `INSERTING` block on line 30.

In the `UPDATING` block, there is enough information to *update* the name. As you can see, that wasn't a trivial task. The `DELETING` block statement touches only one table unless all dependent rows in the `contact` table have been deleted first. That's because you never want to leave orphaned rows in a dependent table. The `get_dependents` function in the trigger (lines 13 to 27) checks whether there are other dependent rows in the `contact` table. The call to this function on line 54 prevents removing a potential parent row and leaving orphan rows in the contact table.

You could remove the local function from the trigger and make it a schema-level function. That would make the trigger dependent on an external code block and would allow other programs to reuse the capability of the function. When triggers depend on external code blocks, they can become invalid when those components become unavailable, because the stored functions and procedures are dependencies for the trigger body.

This section has shown you how to write individual event and multiple event `INSTEAD OF` triggers. You should try to write all DML events in a single `INSTEAD OF` trigger because a single trigger is easier to maintain.

MySQL Instead-of Triggers

MySQL doesn't support instead-of triggers on views.

System Triggers

System triggers let you audit *server startup* and *shutdown*, *server errors*, and *user logon* and *logoff* activities. They're convenient for tracking the duration of connections per user and the uptime of the database server.

They're available only in the Oracle database because MySQL doesn't implement them.

Oracle System Triggers

Oracle system triggers are handy for administrative reasons and are the purview of the DBA. They provide the ability to track user behaviors and become predictive of ad hoc load behaviors when business entities enable query-only schemas on production servers. Query-only schemas support day-to-day reporting engines and are the way many businesses replicate their data sets to make them available to accounting, finance, and operations staff. System triggers can let a DBA track down users who run *nonperformant* (cool industry-specific word that means grossly inefficient) queries.

Here's the prototype for building a system trigger:

```
CREATE [OR REPLACE] TRIGGER trigger_name
{BEFORE | AFTER} database_event ON {database | schema}
[DECLARE
  declaration_statements;]
```

```
BEGIN
  execution_statements;
[EXCEPTION
  exception_statements;]
END [trigger_name];
/
```

The *logon* and *logoff* triggers monitor the duration of connections. The DML statements for these triggers are in the `user_connection` package. Both the `connecting_trigger` and `disconnecting_trigger` call procedures are in the `user_connection` package to insert *logon* and *logoff* information by user.

The `connecting_trigger` provides an example of a system trigger that monitors user logon to the database, as shown:

```
CREATE OR REPLACE TRIGGER connecting_trigger
  AFTER LOGON ON DATABASE
BEGIN
  user_connection.connecting(sys.login_user);
END;
/
```

The `disconnecting_trigger` provides an example of a system trigger that monitors user logoff from the database, as shown:

```
CREATE OR REPLACE TRIGGER disconnecting_trigger
  BEFORE LOGOFF ON DATABASE
BEGIN
  user_connection.disconnecting(sys.login_user);
END;
/
```

Both triggers are compact and call methods of the `user_connection` package. This package requires the `connection_log` table, which is shown here:

```
-- This is found in create_system_triggers.sql on the publisher's web site.
CREATE TABLE connection_log
( event_id            NUMBER
, event_user_name     VARCHAR2(30) CONSTRAINT log_event_nn1 NOT NULL
, event_type          VARCHAR2(14) CONSTRAINT log_event_nn2 NOT NULL
, event_date          DATE         CONSTRAINT log_event_nn3 NOT NULL
, CONSTRAINT connection_log_p1    PRIMARY KEY (event_id));
```

The package body declares two procedures: one supports the *logon* trigger and the other supports the *logoff* trigger. Here's the package specification:

```
CREATE OR REPLACE PACKAGE user_connection AS
  PROCEDURE connecting (user_name IN VARCHAR2);
  PROCEDURE disconnecting (user_name IN VARCHAR2);
END user_connection;
/
```

Here's the implementation of the `user_connection` package body:

```
CREATE OR REPLACE PACKAGE BODY user_connection AS
  PROCEDURE connecting (user_name IN VARCHAR2) IS
  BEGIN
    INSERT INTO connection_log (event_user_name, event_type, event_date)
    VALUES (user_name,'CONNECT',SYSDATE);
  END connecting;
  PROCEDURE disconnecting (user_name IN VARCHAR2) IS
  BEGIN
    INSERT INTO connection_log (event_user_name, event_type, event_date)
    VALUES (user_name,'DISCONNECT',SYSDATE);
  END disconnecting;
END user_connection;
/
```

You might notice that the `connection_log` table has four columns but the `INSERT` statement only uses three. This is possible because the `connection_log_t1` trigger automatically assigns the next value from the `connection_log_s1` sequence.

MySQL System Triggers

MySQL doesn't support system triggers.

Summary

This chapter has explored database triggers. It has taught you about trigger architecture and how you can implement DDL, DML, compound, instead-of, and system triggers. These tools and techniques round out your skills with building robust database-centric applications. You've also seen that MySQL supports only DML triggers.

Mastery Check

The mastery check is a series of true or false and multiple choice questions that let you confirm how well you understand the material in the chapter. You may check the Appendix for answers to these questions.

1. **True** ☐ **False** ☐ Database triggers are able to replace values submitted through `INSERT` and `UPDATE` statements with overriding values.

2. **True** ☐ **False** ☐ Oracle supports triggers on Data Definition Language (DDL) statements.

3. **True** ☐ **False** ☐ MySQL supports triggers on only some DDL statements.

4. **True** ☐ **False** ☐ A statement-level trigger lets you change the new value of a column on `INSERT` or `UPDATE` events.

5. **True** ☐ **False** ☐ An Oracle DML trigger can exist only for individual `INSERT`, `UPDATE`, or `DELETE` statements.

6. **True** ☐ **False** ☐ A MySQL DML trigger can exist only for individual INSERT, UPDATE, or DELETE statements.

7. **True** ☐ **False** ☐ MySQL lets you use the FOLLOWS keyword to sequence triggers that run on the same event.

8. **True** ☐ **False** ☐ The INSTEAD OF trigger works well when you want an alternative trigger approach for an INSERT statement to a table.

9. **True** ☐ **False** ☐ System event triggers are available in an Oracle database but not in a MySQL database.

10. **True** ☐ **False** ☐ Only Oracle supports autonomous transactions in database triggers.

11. Which of the following types of database triggers work in an Oracle database (multiple answers possible)?

    A. DDL triggers

    B. TCL triggers

    C. DML triggers

    D. Instead-of triggers

    E. Compound triggers

12. Which of the following types of database triggers work in a MySQL database?

    A. DDL triggers

    B. DML triggers

    C. System event triggers

    D. TCL triggers

    E. Instead-of triggers

13. You have pseudo new and old record structures for which triggers in an Oracle database?

    A. DML statement-level triggers

    B. DDL row-level triggers

    C. DDL statement-level triggers

    D. DML row-level triggers

    E. Compound triggers

14. Pseudo new and old record structures are available for which triggers in a MySQL database?

    A. DML statement-level triggers

    B. DML row-level triggers

    C. DDL statement-level triggers

    D. DDL row-level triggers

    E. Compound triggers

15. Oracle requires what syntax to access new column values from an INSERT or UPDATE statement in the code block?

   A. `new.column_name`

   B. `:new.column_name`

   C. `old.column_name.`

   D. `:old.column_name`

   E. None of the above

APPENDIX

Mastery Check Answers

his appendix contains the answer key to mastery check questions from the chapters in the book. Brief explanations supporting the answers follow each question. It is organized by chapter.

Chapter 1

Here are the questions and answers for Chapter 1.

1. ☑ **True** ☐ **False** Databases implement a two-tier client-server model.

   True. Databases implement client- and server-tiers, the client-tier manages the entry, parsing, and submittal of SQL statements to the server-tier that performs the physical access, change, and removal of data.

2. ☐ **True** ☑ **False** Client-software provides only an interactive method for running SQL statements.

   False. The client-software provides both interactive and batch processing.

3. ☑ **True** ☐ **False** SQL statements can be grouped into categories.

   True. Yes, SQL statements can be grouped into categories. They're organized in Data Definition Language (DDL), Data Manipulation Language (DML), Data Control Language (DCL), and Transaction Control Language (TCL).

4. ☐ **True** ☑ **False** You must interact with all databases across a network socket.

   False. No, most databases support both IPC (or a Operating System pipe) and TCP/IP connections, which is the case for Oracle and MySQL databases.

5. ☐ **True** ☑ **False** Distributed transactions occur by default in MySQL when you store data in two or more tables using different engines.

   False. No, most databases support both IPC and TCP/IP connections, which is the case for Oracle and MySQL databases.

6. ☐ **True** ☑ **False** You can connect to MySQL only through a network socket.

   False. You can connect to MySQL through a network socket or an operating system pipe, both of which are defined in the `my.ini` file.

7. ☐ **True** ☑ **False** You can connect to an Oracle database only through a network socket.

   False. You can connect to Oracle through an IPC socket or a TCP/IP socket, either of which is configured in your `listener.ora` file.

8. ☑ **True** ☐ **False** The MVCC model for Oracle Database 11*g* maps with some small exceptions to the MVCC model of a MySQL database transactional engine such as InnoDB.

   True. The MVCC models of the Oracle and MySQL database are similar, but Oracle's version has more configuration options.

9. ☑ **True** ☐ **False** Any Oracle user is synonymous with the schema of the same name.

   True. The Oracle user is synonymous with the private work area known as a schema.

10. ☑ **True** ☐ **False** Sequential log files are maintained by programs in MySQL databases as they are for Oracle databases, notwithstanding the engine of implementation.

True. Both Oracle and MySQL running with the InnoDB engine maintain sequential log files, which enable them to undo or rollback work.

11. Which of the following isn't a valid engine in a MySQL database instance?

   A. Blackhole

   B. CSV

   C. TSV

   D. Memory

   E. MyISAM

   C is correct. TSV is not a valid engine in MySQL.

12. Which of the following isn't a valid SQL category?

   A. Data Query Language (DQL)

   B. Data Control Language (DCL)

   C. Data Manipulation Language (DML)

   D. Data Definition Language (DDL)

   E. Transaction Control Language (TCL)

   A is correct. There is no Data Query Language (DQL) category in SQL.

13. Which of the following isn't a core background process for an Oracle Database 11*g* server?

   A. ARCn

   B. PMON

   C. SMON

   D. Checkpoint

   E. LGWR

   A is correct. There is an Archiver Process (ARCn) in the Oracle database, but it isn't one of the five core processes.

14. Which of the following isn't a property of an ACID-compliant transaction?

   A. Atomic

   B. Consistent

   C. Isolated

   D. Durable

   E. None of the above

   E is correct. All of the other choices are valid properties of ACID.

15. Which users have the same role and responsibility in Oracle Database 11*g* and MySQL 5.5, except for mapping to the data catalog?

    A. The Oracle SYSTEM and MySQL root users

    B. The Oracle SYS and MySQL root

    C. The Oracle SYS, SYSTEM, and MySQL root

    D. The Oracle SYS and MySQL super

    E. The Oracle SYSTEM and MySQL super

    B is correct. The Oracle SYS user is the same as the MySQL root user.

Chapter 2

Here are the questions and answers for Chapter 2.

1. ☐ **True** ☑ **False** You can set a session variable in Oracle outside of an anonymous PL/SQL block.

    False. You can set a session variable only inside an anonymous block PL/SQL programming unit. The same behavior is disallowed in named blocks. (See Chapter 13 for more details on PL/SQL programming.)

2. ☑ **True** ☐ **False** Customizing the SQL*Plus and MySQL Monitor prompts is possible.

    True. Both Oracle and MySQL support customizing the prompt. Oracle lets you do it by editing the `glogin.sql` file, which then resets it each subsequent time you start the SQL*Plus server. MySQL lets you modify the prompt but only for the duration of the session.

3. ☑ **True** ☐ **False** Oracle SQL*Plus maintains a buffer of the last SQL statement and allows you to edit its contents.

    True. Oracle SQL*Plus maintains an `afiedt.buf` file with the last statement processed by the SQL engine. It's possible for multiple `afiedt.buf` files to exist, because one is created in each directory where you sign-in to the server.

4. ☐ **True** ☑ **False** You run a script file in MySQL Monitor by using the `source` or `\.` command before the script name.

    False. This is false because a filename excludes the file type (if there is any) and the filename, a dot (.), and a file type are required to run most files.

5. ☐ **True** ☑ **False** You can edit the last SQL statement from a native buffer file in MySQL.

    False. You can edit the last SQL statement from a native buffer in an Oracle database but not in a MySQL database. MySQL doesn't maintain an editable buffer file.

6. ☑ **True** ☐ **False** You can connect to another database without exiting MySQL.

    True. This works because you can type `use database_name;` and switch to any database for which you have access privileges.

7. ☐ **True** ☑ **False** You can create log files by setting the ECHO environment in MySQL Monitor.

    False. There are no environment variables in MySQL Monitor; they exist only in Oracle SQL*Plus.

8.   ☑ **True** ☐ **False** You can run script files (collections of related SQL statements) from the SQL*Plus or MySQL Monitor client software.

    True. You can run script files from Oracle SQL*Plus or MySQL Monitor by sourcing and running the script files.

9.   ☑ **True** ☐ **False** You back-quote apostrophes with another apostrophe in both Oracle and MySQL.

    True. This is one of two ways to back-quote in Oracle and one of three ways to back-quote in MySQL.

10.   ☐ **True** ☑ **False** MySQL allows you to create log files and automatically overwrites any existing file with the same name.

    False. MySQL allows you to create log files with the TEE command, but if the file already exists, MySQL Monitor simply appends to the file. Oracle lets you write a new file by default and append it to an existing file.

11.   Which of the following lets you run a command in the MySQL Monitor?

    A. `mysql> @script_name.sql`

    B. `mysql> @script_name`

    C. `mysql> \. script_name`

    D. `mysql> \. script_name.sql`

    E. `mysql> source script_name.sql`

    D and **E** are correct. In MySQL, you must provide file extensions when they exist, which is almost always. In a nontraditional format, without a file extension, C would work. The `\.` or source lets you read and run files in MySQL; the @ symbol works only in Oracle.

12.   Which of the following lets you run a command in the Oracle database SQL*Plus?

    A. `SQL> @script_name.sql`

    B. `SQL> @script_name`

    C. `SQL> \. script_name`

    D. `SQL> \. script_name.sql`

    E. `SQL> source script_name.sql`

    A and **B** are correct. The @ symbol works only in Oracle SQL*Plus, and you can provide a script name with or without a file extension to read and run the program. SQL*Plus assumes a `.sql` file extension, but you can change that in the `glogin.sql` file.

13.   Which of the following isn't a supported data type in SQL*Plus?

    A. A `BINARY_DOUBLE`

    B. A `CHAR`

    C. A `STRING`

    D. A `REFCURSOR`

    E. A `VARCHAR`

C and **E** are correct. `STRING` and `VARCHAR` data types are not valid SQL*Plus data types. You can use any of the following data types: `BINARY_DOUBLE`, `BINARY_FLOAT`, `CHAR`, `CLOB`, `NCHAR`, `NCLOB`, `NUMBER`, `NVARCHAR2`, `REFCURSOR`, and `VARCHAR2`. `VARCHAR`, without the trailing 2, is used by MySQL and Oracle SQL as an alias for `VARCHAR2`.

14. Which of the following runs a function in an Oracle SQL*Plus environment (multiple possible answers)?

   A. A `CALL` statement

   B. An `EXECUTE` statement

   C. A `SELECT function_name() FROM dual;`

   D. A `SELECT function_name();`

   E. A `SOURCE` statement

   A and **C** are correct. The `CALL` statement lets you call a function into a session-level (bind) variable, and you can also query a schema-level function inside a `SELECT` statement.

15. You can use which special characters to back-quote in MySQL Monitor?

   A. The \

   B. The '

   C. The `q|some_character|`

   D. The "

   E. The /

   A is correct. The \ (backslash) character lets you escape the next character, which can make a special character act like a normal text character.

Chapter 3

Here are the questions and answers for Chapter 3.

1. ☐ **True** ☑ **False** You start securing security barriers by setting object privileges inside the database and working outward.

   False. Actually, you secure from the most outward-facing to innermost-facing system, such as network, operating system, and database.

2. ☑ **True** ☐ **False** The database stores encrypted passwords in the database.

   True. The database does store encrypted passwords.

3. ☑ **True** ☐ **False** Oracle validates only user name and encrypted password to start a database session.

   True. Oracle treats credentials as twofold pairs of text strings: the user name in clear text and the password in encrypted text.

4. ☐ **True** ☑ **False** Roles don't impede a hacker's discovery process after the hacker has connected to the database.

   False. Roles can impede hacker's progress by providing another layer of metadata that hides the real privileges.

5. ☑ **True** ☐ **False** You can grant ALL privileges on a database or a schema to a user.

   True. You can grant ALL privileges on a database or a schema to users in either Oracle or MySQL databases.

6. ☑ **True** ☐ **False** You can grant roles and privileges to a user.

   True. This is true in Oracle but untrue in MySQL. Fortunately, it asks the question without specifying a database. When it's true in one, it's possible in both, and that's why this is true. If you answered False, you probably took the approach if it's not true in both, it's false. The purpose of this question is to make you think about the differences and similarities because they're important.

7. ☑ **True** ☐ **False** Roles can contain one to many privileges.

   True. You can create roles with only one privilege, or more generally with more than one privilege. The collective privileges should let the user accomplish business tasks effectively.

8. ☐ **True** ☑ **False** The CONNECT and RESOURCE roles are recommended as best practices in Oracle Database 11g forward.

   False. These roles have been identified for deprecation in future releases and should be avoided.

9. ☐ **True** ☑ **False** Oracle MySQL 5.5 was the first version to support roles.

   False. MySQL doesn't support roles. You must grant individual privileges.

10. ☐ **True** ☑ **False** MySQL's inability to create synonyms prevents you from creating a definer rights model that isolates access from code and data.

    False. The lack of synonyms just means you must write updateable views or wrappers for functions and procedures.

11. Which of the following isn't a security barrier that you should secure?

    A. The network

    B. The intranet

    C. File system permissions

    D. Uniform Resource Indicator (URI)

    E. Operating system accounts

    D is correct. The URI is defined by specification, and not subject to change. You can suppress certain header information but that means browsers and routers may not serve your pages or allow them through the firewall.

12. Which of the following Oracle privileges are equivalent to the MySQL CREATE privilege (multiple answers possible)?

    A. CREATE ANY TABLE

    B. CREATE ANY SEQUENCE

    C. CREATE ANY DATABASE LINK

    D. CREATE ANY CLUSTER

    E. CREATE ANY COMMENT

A, **B**, **D**, and **E** are correct. Only the CREATE ANY DATABASE LINK doesn't map between Oracle and MySQL, because MySQL doesn't support database links.

13. Which of the following are Data Control Language (DCL) statements?

   A. A PRIVILEGE statement

   B. A ROLE statement

   C. A GRANT statement

   D. A REVOKE statement

   E. A PERMISSION statement

   C and **D** are correct. The GRANT and REVOKE statements are the only two DCL statements in SQL.

14. Which of the following are the two types of privileges?

   A. System privileges

   B. Database privileges

   C. Table privileges

   D. Object privileges

   E. Resource privileges

   A and **D** are correct. The system and object privileges are the two types of privileges in databases.

15. Which clause lets you grant the right to grant system privileges?

   A. The WITH ADMINISTRATOR OPTION

   B. The WITH GRANT OPTION

   C. The WITH GRANTOR OPTION

   D. The WITH ADMIN OPTION

   E. The WITH GRANTING OPTION

   B is correct. The WITH GRANT OPTION lets you grant rights to others on system and object privileges.

Chapter 4

Here are the questions and answers for Chapter 4.

1. ☐ **True** ☑ **False** An INSERT statement is always ACID-compliant.

   False. An INSERT statement is not always ACID-compliant. It is ACID-compliant in a transactional database, such as Oracle. An INSERT statement is also ACID-compliant in MySQL database when the table is defined using an InnoDB engine and the INSERT statement occurs inside the scope of a transaction. An INSERT statement is not ACID-compliant when the statement runs outside of a transaction scope or runs against a non-transactional engine, such as MyISAM.

2. ☐ **True** ☑ **False** An UPDATE statement runs in the second phase of a two-phase commit.

   False. The UPDATE statement runs in the first phase of a two-phase commit, and the COMMIT or ROLLBACK statement runs in the second phase.

3. ☐ **True** ☑ **False** A DELETE statement leaves deleted rows visible to all sessions until the COMMIT statement runs in another session.

   False. The DELETE statement can leave rows visible to other sessions where the DELETE statement ran and a COMMIT statement hasn't run in the same session. A COMMIT statement in another session has no impact on two-phase commit (2PC) statements. The removal of rows by a DELETE statement is immediate unless it occurs in a transactional scope, against a table defined and managed by a transactional engine, such as InnoDB. In a nontransactional database, deleted rows are not seen by any user after the DELETE statement.

4. ☐ **True** ☑ **False** You can create a single trigger that applies to multiple tables.

   False. Database triggers run against a single table and cannot run against multiple tables. In Oracle, a single trigger can manage an INSERT, UPDATE, or DELETE event, or any combination of those events. In MySQL, a trigger works against one table and event.

5. ☑ **True** ☐ **False** The industry uses 2PC as an acronym for two-phase commit.

   True. A 2PC is an acronym for a two-phase commit.

6. ☐ **True** ☑ **False** A SELECT statement isn't a DML statement because it doesn't lock or change any data in tables.

   False. A SELECT statement is a DML statement because it can lock rows inside the scope of a cursor, which runs in a PL/SQL or SQL/PSM program. (Chapter 13 covers PL/SQL and Chapter 14 covers SQL/PSM programming.)

7. ☐ **True** ☑ **False** You append the FOR UPDATE clause to DELETE statements when you want to lock the changes away from other sessions.

   False. You append the FOR UPDATE clause to a SELECT statement in the scope of a transaction to lock rows.

8. ☑ **True** ☐ **False** A MERGE statement provides INSERT or UPDATE behaviors.

   True. In an Oracle database, the MERGE statement provides INSERT or UPDATE behaviors, and the SELECT with an ON DUPLICATE KEY does the equivalent in a MySQL database.

9. ☐ **True** ☑ **False** MySQL supports a WAIT n seconds feature on SELECT statements used as cursors.

   False. MySQL doesn't support a WAIT n seconds feature; that's an Oracle feature.

10. ☐ **True** ☑ **False** A lightweight process is part of a thread.

    False. A lightweight process is the same thing as a thread and is a synonym for thread.

11. Which of the following lets you lock a subset of rows in a table in Oracle?

   A. The FOR UPDATE clause

   B. The LOCK TABLE SQL command

   C. The LOCK IN SHARE MODE clause

   D. The LOCK IN EXCLUSIVE MODE clause

   E. The FOR LOCK clause

   A is correct. In Oracle, the FOR UPDATE clause in a SELECT statement lets you lock a subset of rows in a table.

12. Which of the following lets you lock a subset of rows in a table in MySQL?

   A. The FOR UPDATE clause

   B. The LOCK TABLE SQL command

   C. The LOCK IN SHARE MODE clause

   D. The LOCK IN EXCLUSIVE MODE clause

   E. The FOR LOCK clause

   A is correct. In MySQL this is the same as in Oracle. The FOR UPDATE clause in a SELECT statement locks a subset of rows in a table.

13. Which isn't a valid Data Control Language (DCL) statement in Oracle or MySQL?

   A. COMMIT

   B. COMMIT IMMEDIATE

   C. SAVEPOINT savepointName

   D. ROLLBACK

   E. ROLLBACK TO savepointName

   B is correct. There is no COMMIT IMMEDIATE statement in Oracle or MySQL databases. The only place Oracle uses IMMEDIATE is in a database shutdown command, and MySQL doesn't use it at all.

14. Inside a stored program unit, what is the correct order for DCL statements?

   A. SAVEPOINT sName, COMMIT IMMEDIATE, ROLLBACK

   B. SAVEPOINT sName, COMMIT NO WAIT, ROLLBACK

   C. SAVEPOINT sName, COMMIT NOWAIT, ROLLBACK

   D. SAVEPOINT sName, COMMIT, ROLLBACK TO sName

   E. SAVEPOINT sName, COMMIT IMMEDIATE, ROLLBACK TO sName

   D is correct. Here is the correct sequence: (1) Sets a SAVEPOINT before attempting any DML statements; (2) performs a COMMIT statement when all statements complete successfully; and (3) performs a ROLLBACK statement when any statement fails.

15. You can use an UPDATE statement to perform which of the following things?

    A. Update any column not in a unique index

    B. Update any column regardless of its role in the design

    C. Update only columns that aren't in the surrogate or natural key

    D. Update only columns that are in the surrogate or natural key

    E. Update only columns that are numeric, text, or dates

    A and **B** are correct. The UPDATE statement can change any column regardless of its role in design, notwithstanding the harm it might do. This also means an UPDATE statement can change columns found in a unique index—at least if the update isn't violating the unique constraint.

Chapter 5

Here are the questions and answers for Chapter 5.

1. ☑ **True** ☐ **False** A database constraint can determine whether a column is mandatory or optional.

    True. A NOT NULL database constraint can determine whether a column is mandatory [1..1] or optional [0..1].

2. ☑ **True** ☐ **False** A database constraint can determine whether a row is unique in a table.

    True. A UNIQUE database constraint can determine whether a row is unique, and it builds an implicit index to ensure this behavior.

3. ☐ **True** ☑ **False** A database constraint can only accept or reject values for a column based on boundary conditions.

    False. A CHECK constraint can accept or reject values for a column based on boundary conditions, logical relationships, or combinations of such logic, as well as compare other values in related columns of the row. Unfortunately, this applies to the Oracle database only, because MySQL doesn't yet implement a CHECK constraint (other than provide for the keyword in the prototype).

4. ☐ **True** ☑ **False** You can't add any database constraint during a CREATE TABLE statement.

    False. You have the option of adding in-line and out-of-line constraints in a CREATE TABLE statement.

5. ☑ **True** ☐ **False** You can implement referential integrity through database constraints.

    True. You can implement referential integrity in the Oracle database and in the MySQL database. However, you must implement all participating tables using the InnoDB engine to effect referential integrity.

6. ☐ **True** ☑ **False** Creating a UNIQUE constraint is straightforward and doesn't create any other dependent structures in the database catalog.

    False. The process of creating a UNIQUE constraint is straightforward, but it creates a unique index to make it work. The index exists in the scope of the UNIQUE constraint and is thereby dependent on it.

7. ☐ **True** ☑ **False** A mutating table doesn't prevent a database trigger from changing the input values of an `INSERT` statement.

   False. A mutating table is the normal state of any table being inserted into or updated against. Both `INSERT` and `UPDATE` event triggers can change current values of the rows being inserted into or updated against. (See Chapter 15 for more details.)

8. ☑ **True** ☐ **False** Assigning an `ENUM` data type to a column acts like a check constraint.

   True. This is true, insofar that an `ENUM` data type can restrict values to a predefined list of values, which is one of the behaviors of a `CHECK` constraint.

9. ☐ **True** ☑ **False** MySQL supports referential integrity in the MyISAM database engine.

   False. The MyISAM database engine doesn't support referential integrity.

10. ☐ **True** ☑ **False** A foreign key works when it has a `signed int` data type while the primary key has an `unsigned int` data type.

    False. The data types of both primary and foreign keys must agree completely, which means if one is an unsigned integer or double, the other must be, too.

11. Which of the following behaviors is/are supported by a primary key constraint (multiple answers possible)?

    A. A column-level behavior

    B. A row-level behavior

    C. A table-level behavior

    D. A mutating table behavior

    E. An external relationship behavior

    A and **C** are correct. The answers are column- and table-level behaviors because a primary key can apply to one or more columns.

12. Which of the following behaviors isn't supported by a database trigger?

    A. A column-level behavior

    B. A row-level behavior

    C. A table-level behavior

    D. A mutating table behavior

    E. An external relationship behavior

    D is correct. A mutating table behavior is caused by DML statements, and a trigger can't touch tables that are in the midst of change(s) from the same DML statement that fired the trigger.

13. Which of the following constraints aren't supported in both Oracle and MySQL?

    A. A `NOT NULL` constraint

    B. A `CHECK` constraint

    C. A unique constraint

    D. An index constraint

    E. A foreign key constraint

    B is correct. The `CHECK` constraint is implemented only in an Oracle database.

14. Which of the following constraints are engine-dependent in MySQL (multiple answers possible)?

    A. A `NOT NULL` constraint

    B. A `CHECK` constraint

    C. A primary key constraint

    D. A foreign key constraint

    E. A unique constraint

    B is correct. The `CHECK` constraint is implemented only in an Oracle database.

15. What types of conditions aren't supported by `CHECK` constraints?

    A. A boundary condition

    B. A set membership condition

    C. A nullable condition

    D. A unique condition

    E. A complex business rule based on multiple columns in the same row.

    D is correct. A `CHECK` constraint can't change anything outside of its assigned column.

Chapter 6

Here are the questions and answers for Chapter 6.

1. ☑ **True** ☐ **False** A column can be made mandatory by using an in-line `NOT NULL` constraint in Oracle and MySQL databases.

   True. This is the only purpose of a `NOT NULL` constraint, and that makes this a true statement.

2. ☐ **True** ☑ **False** A `CHECK` constraint can be implemented in a MySQL database.

   False. A `CHECK` constraint cannot be implemented in a MySQL database (at the time of writing), but the syntax is there for some future use.

3. ☑ **True** ☐ **False** A `FOREIGN KEY` constraint can be implemented against only one column.

   True. You can implement a `FOREIGN KEY` constraint against any `PRIMARY KEY`. Because a `PRIMARY KEY` can reference many columns, so can a `FOREIGN KEY` constraint.

4. ☑ **True** ☐ **False** You can create tables with nested tables in an Oracle database.

   True. You can create tables with nested tables in an Oracle database, and you can implement nested tables within nested tables. These nested-inside-nested tables are known as a multiple-level nested tables.

5. ☐ **True** ☑ **False** You can use an `UNSIGNED INT` data type when creating a table in an Oracle database.

   False. Oracle doesn't implement unsigned integers.

6. ☑ **True** ☐ **False** Creating a unique index inside the `CREATE TABLE` statement is possible in MySQL.

   True. You can create a unique index inside the `CREATE TABLE` statement when it works against one or more than one column in the table.

7. ☐ **True** ☑ **False** A range partition uses the `VALUES IN` clause in an Oracle database.

   False. The `VALUES IN` clause works in MySQL list partitioning only.

8. ☑ **True** ☐ **False** An `ENUM` data type allows only one of a list of values to be stored in a column.

   True. The `ENUM` data type is an exclusive member type, which means only one element from a list of possible elements can be referenced in any column. This differs from the `SET` data type, which is an inclusive member type and allows a single column to refer to multiple items in the list.

9. ☐ **True** ☑ **False** MySQL supports composite partitioning.

   False. MySQL doesn't support composite partitioning, which is an Oracle feature. MySQL supports *range*, *list*, *hash*, and *key* partitioning.

10. ☑ **True** ☐ **False** A foreign key works whether the data type is a signed or unsigned integer.

    True. A foreign key works whether the data type is a signed or unsigned integer, which can occur only in a MySQL database. The only caveat is that the primary and foreign key columns must have the *same data types*—that is, unsigned or signed integers or doubles.

11. Which of the following data types isn't supported in a MySQL database?

    A. `BLOB`

    B. `MEDIUMCLOB`

    C. `TEXT`

    D. `DOUBLE`

    E. `FLOAT`

    B is correct. The `MEDIUMCLOB` would work only in some hybrid of an Oracle and MySQL database. The `CLOB` data type is supported by Oracle and the `MEDIUMTEXT` data type is supported by MySQL.

12. Which of the following data types isn't supported in an Oracle database?

    A. `CLOB`

    B. `BLOB`

    C. `NCHAR`

    D. `VARYING CHARACTER`

    E. `CHAR`

    D is correct. The `VARYING CHARACTER` is a synonym data type for the `VARCHAR` data type in a MySQL database.

13. Which of the following aren't date-time data types (multiple possible answers)?

   A. DATE in Oracle

   B. DATE in MySQL

   C. TIMESTAMP in either database

   D. TIME in MySQL

   E. YEAR in MySQL

   B and **E** are correct. The DATE and YEAR data types in MySQL are date-only data types and the others are date-time data types in Oracle and MySQL databases.

14. Which of the following syntax operations are prohibited in MySQL?

   A. Defining an in-line NOT NULL constraint

   B. Defining an in-line FOREIGN KEY constraint

   C. Defining an in-line UNIQUE constraint

   D. Defining an in-line PRIMARY KEY constraint

   E. Defining an out-of-line FOREIGN KEY constraint

   B is correct. MySQL doesn't support in-line syntax for a FOREIGN KEY constraint.

15. What data type is supported by list and range partitioning in MySQL?

   A. FLOAT

   B. CHAR

   C. VARCHAR

   D. DATE

   E. INT

   E is correct. The INT data type is required for list and range partitioning in MySQL.

Chapter 7

Here are the questions and answers for Chapter 7.

1. ☑ **True** ☐ **False** A *user* in Oracle is synonymous with a SCHEMA.

   True. The user is synonymous with a SCHEMA. A SCHEMA is a private work area for an individual user.

2. ☑ **True** ☐ **False** In an Oracle database, a user can change his or her password with an ALTER USER statement.

   True. Individual users can use the ALTER USER statement to change a password, but that discloses it on the console to prying eyes. Users should use the PASSWORD command to change their passwords.

3. ☐ **True** ☑ **False** You must know a user's password to change the user's password as a super user, such as SYSTEM, in an Oracle database.

   False. Any super user or administrative account with super user privileges can change a user's password without knowing the current value.

4. ☐ **True** ☑ **False** In a MySQL database a user can change his or her password with an `ALTER USER` statement.

   False. MySQL does not support changing passwords with the `ALTER USER` statement, as Oracle does. MySQL uses the `SET PASSWORD` statement and the `PASSWORD` function, like so:

   ```
   mysql> SET PASSWORD = PASSWORD('new_password');
   ```

   MySQL's approach is very different from the generic approach but very straightforward and consistent.

5. ☐ **True** ☑ **False** You can add a `NOT NULL` constraint to an existing column when it contains null values.

   False. You can't add a not null constraint to a column when there are rows that have a null value in that column.

6. ☐ **True** ☑ **False** You can `LOCK` and `UNLOCK` accounts in MySQL.

   False. No concept of locking or unlocking accounts exists in MySQL, because the concept applies to the database elements of a user in an Oracle database. You are effectively locking or unlocking the schema, not the user.

7. ☐ **True** ☑ **False** Oracle has deprecated tracing using the `DBMS_SYSTEM` package and replaced it with the `ALTER SESSION` statement.

   False. Quite the contrary; Oracle plans to deprecate `ALTER SESSION` for generating trace files, and you should use the `DBMS_SYSTEM` package for tracing.

8. ☑ **True** ☐ **False** Oracle lets you embed logic in your stored functions and procedures that is run only when you enable specialized session variables.

   True. Oracle 11*g* introduces the idea of conditional compilation, which lets you leave your debugging instructions in your code, and Oracle ignores them unless you set a session variable to enable them. This is extremely powerful when you distribute code to customers and they encounter a runtime error unique to their environment. You simply instruct them how to set the session variable and then the code collects debugging information. This eliminates your having to write customized debugging code for most problems and simplifies your release engineering issues with checking and debugging code on a branch of a release tree.

9. ☐ **True** ☑ **False** It's always best to define a `UNIQUE KEY` and `INDEX` when they work with the same columns in a MySQL database.

   False. You never want to have a `UNIQUE KEY` and `INDEX` on the same table and columns, because it means two unique indexes perform the same task. That's twice the overhead on inserts, updates, and deletes. You should ensure that either a `UNIQUE KEY` or `INDEX` is defined and implemented, but not both.

10. ☐ **True** ☑ **False** You can modify a column's data type when it contains data in an Oracle database but not a MySQL database.

    False. You can modify the data type in both, provided that the data can be implicitly cast from the old data type to the new data type.

11. Which of the following is not a valid constraint code in Oracle?

    A. A P

    B. A N

    C. A C

    D. A R

    E. A U

    B is correct. The P represents a PRIMARY KEY constraint, C represents a CHECK or NOT NULL constraint, R represents a FOREIGN KEY (naturally a referential integrity) constraint, and U represents a UNIQUE constraint. They're found in Chapter 7's Table 7-2 for reference. The N stands for nothing, or not one of the Oracle constraints.

12. Which rule applies in an Oracle database to changing the data type of a column?

    A. Any column can be changed when the table is empty.

    B. All columns can be changed except those that are members of a primary key whether the table contains data or not.

    C. All variable length string columns (VARCHAR2) can be changed to a DATE data type column regardless of the format mask involved when the table is full.

    D. All non-key columns can be changed when the table is full.

    E. None of the above

    A is correct. When a column contains data, it can be changed only when the database knows how to implicitly cast the data types. The most restrictive implicit casting rules exist for strings moving to dates, because the strings must conform to one of the two default format masks (they are 'DD-MON-RR' and 'DD-MON-YYYY'). When a table is empty, you can change any column data type to any other data type.

13. Which of the following isn't a keyword in an Oracle ALTER TABLE statement?

    A. An ALTER clause

    B. A CHANGE clause

    C. A MODIFY clause

    D. A DROP clause

    E. An ADD clause

    B is correct. MySQL lets you *change* columns but Oracle only lets you *modify* them.

14. Which of the following isn't a keyword in a MySQL ALTER TABLE statement?

    A. A CHANGE clause

    B. A MODIFY clause

    C. A DROP clause

    D. A DISABLE clause

    E. A READ ONLY clause

    D is correct. MySQL doesn't allow you to disable and enable constraints.

15. Which of the following constraints can't be added to a table in MySQL?

    A. The PRIMARY KEY constraint

    B. The FOREIGN KEY constraint

    C. The CHECK constraint

    D. The UNIQUE constraint

    E. The NOT NULL constraint

    C is correct. Although syntax does exist for a CHECK constraint, no implementation supports it (at the time of writing).

Chapter 8

Here are the questions and answers for Chapter 8.

1. ☐ **True** ☑ **False** An INSERT statement supports multiple row inserts through the VALUES clause in Oracle.

    False. Oracle lets you insert only a single row in the VALUES clause.

2. ☑ **True** ☐ **False** An INSERT statement supports multiple row inserts through the VALUES clause in MySQL.

    False. MySQL lets you insert one to many rows in the VALUES clause.

3. ☑ **True** ☐ **False** The list of columns in an override signature must match the number and data types of the list of values in the VALUES clause.

    True. That's true, but it might be better said that the list of values must match the override signature.

4. ☑ **True** ☐ **False** You can insert data into nested tables with an INSERT statement in an Oracle database.

    True. You can directly insert into nested tables when you insert into the container table.

5. ☑ **True** ☐ **False** In an Oracle database, you can use a .CURRVAL pseudo column in a VALUES clause provided the sequence has been placed in scope through an earlier .NEXTVAL pseudo column call.

    True. The .CURRVAL pseudo column has no scope in a session until the .NEXTVAL pseudo column has been called first.

6. ☑ **True** ☐ **False** A null value that maps to an auto-incrementing column in a MySQL database inserts the next number in the table's sequence.

    True. In MYSQL, a null value in an auto-incrementing column does insert the next value from the sequence.

7. ☐ **True** ☑ **False** In MySQL, you can use an override signature only when you want to insert sequence values.

    False. In MySQL, you can use an override signature only when you want to insert mandatory columns or you want to change the sequence of column values.

8. ☑ **True** ☐ **False** An INSERT statement that uses a query can insert one to many rows of data in both Oracle and MySQL databases.

True. An INSERT statement with a query can insert one to many rows in both an Oracle and a MySQL database.

9. ☐ **True** ☑ **False** MySQL supports the .NEXTVAL pseudo column.

False. MySQL doesn't support the .NEXTVAL or .CURRVAL pseudo columns. In fact, MySQL doesn't need them because sequence values are properties of tables.

10. ☑ **True** ☐ **False** Both Oracle and MySQL databases let you use subqueries in the VALUES clause of an INSERT statement.

True. Both databases let you use subqueries in the VALUES clause of an INSERT statement, provided they return only one column and row. These types of subqueries are called scalar subqueries or expressions.

11. Which of the following data types requires a built-in function call to put a long variable length character string in a VALUES clause of an INSERT statement?

   A. BLOB

   B. MEDIUMCLOB

   C. TEXT

   D. CLOB

   E. VARCHAR

   D is correct. The CLOB data type uses the DBMS_LOB package to accomplish the task. The MEDIUMCLOB is a make believe type combining the Oracle CLOB with the first half of a MEDIUMTEXT data type from MySQL.

12. In an Oracle database, how many rows can you insert through a VALUES clause?

   A. 1

   B. 2

   C. 3

   D. 4

   E. Many

   A is correct. You can insert only a single row with a VALUES clause in the Oracle database.

13. In a MySQL database, how many rows can you insert through a VALUES clause?

   A. 1

   B. 2

   C. 3

   D. 4

   E. Many

   E is correct. You can insert one to many rows inside a VALUES clause in the MySQL database.

14. When you use a query instead of a VALUES clause, which of the following is true about the query?

    A. The query can contain scalar subqueries.

    B. The query can return only one row at a time.

    C. The query must return a unique data set.

    D. The query can't be the product of a join between two or more tables.

    E. The query is independent of the table structure, which means you can return more columns than the table will accept.

    A and **B** are correct. The subquery can incorporate scalar subqueries, and it can be the product of a single table or join between tables provided it returns the same number and types of columns found in the database catalog. All queries return one row at a time, whether it's one or many rows is unimportant because INSERT statements based on a query can insert one to many rows.

15. Which of the following can't be put in a VALUES clause?

    A. 1

    B. 2

    C. 3

    D. Unlimited

    E. None of the above

    D is correct. All string literal values must be enclosed in single quotes for Oracle, and single or double quotes for MySQL.

Chapter 9

Here are the questions and answers for Chapter 9.

1. ☑ **True** ☐ **False** An UPDATE statement supports multiple row changes with only one set of date, numeric, or string literals.

   True. The SET clause in an UPDATE works against all rows in the table, unless the UPDATE statement is filtered by a WHERE clause or a correlated join.

2. ☐ **True** ☑ **False** An UPDATE statement supports DEFAULT values in Oracle databases only.

   False. The DEFAULT value is available only in a MySQL database, which means Oracle can't support it.

3. ☐ **True** ☑ **False** The SET clause must contain a list of all mandatory columns.

   False. Once a row has been inserted, the requirement of providing all the mandatory columns has been met. UPDATE statements can update one to many columns and they have only one restriction governing mandatory columns: They can't update the columns with a null value.

4. ☑ **True** ☐ **False** A multiple-table UPDATE statement in MySQL performs as a correlated UPDATE statement.

   True. A multiple-table UPDATE statement is just a different syntax equivalent to a correlated subquery.

5. ☐ **True** ☑ **False** MySQL supports a nested table UPDATE statement.

   False. MySQL doesn't support embedded objects and therefore can't create a table that holds a nested table.

6. ☑ **True** ☐ **False** A BLOB or CLOB requires the RETURNING INTO phrase to work with procedural programming modules.

   True. The BLOB or CLOB requires the RETURNING INTO phrase to work with external procedural programs. The RETURNING INTO phrase supports IN OUT mode for parameters in the USING subclause. These variables become sockets through which you can move segments of the BLOB or CLOB to the database.

7. ☐ **True** ☑ **False** The IGNORE keyword lets an Oracle or MySQL UPDATE statement run successfully even when it encounters errors.

   False. The IGNORE keyword is available only in MySQL, and it allows a statement to continue to completion when it encounters a failure.

8. ☑ **True** ☐ **False** A LOW_PRIORITY assignment lets an UPDATE statement run behind other DML statements in the database.

   True. MySQL provides the LOW_PRIORITY keyword that lets you defer UPDATE statement processing behind other priority tasks. There is no equivalent in the Oracle database.

9. ☐ **True** ☑ **False** MySQL supports the RETURNING INTO clause in UPDATE statements.

   False. MySQL doesn't support a RETURNING INTO clause in the UPDATE statement syntax.

10. ☑ **True** ☐ **False** A multiple column and row UPDATE is possible in either Oracle or MySQL databases.

    True. Yes, correlated UPDATE statements allow you to update multiple rows and columns. This is generally accomplished by putting the correlating statement inside a subquery of a multiple-row and column subquery.

11. Which of the following data types requires a RETURNING INTO phrase to interact with procedural programs?

    A. BLOB

    B. MEDIUMCLOB

    C. TEXT

    D. CLOB

    E. VARCHAR

    A and **D** are correct. Only the BLOB and CLOB data types require a RETURNING INTO clause to read and write to a BLOB or CLOB column in the database. The MEDIUMCLOB doesn't exist—it's a misleading answer that blends the MEDIUMTEXT and the CLOB data type.

12. In an Oracle database, what is the maximum number of rows that you can update through a SET clause when values are assigned by literals?

 A. 1

 B. 2

 C. 3

 D. 4

 E. Many

 E is correct. Many can be measured as all rows of the table, and without a filtering WHERE clause, that's what happens with an UPDATE statement.

13. In a MySQL database, what is the maximum number of rows that you can update through a SET clause when values are assigned by literals?

 A. 1

 B. 2

 C. 3

 D. 4

 E. Many

 E is correct. Many can be measured as all rows of the table, and without a filtering WHERE clause, that's what happens with an UPDATE statement.

14. When you use a correlated query instead of a SET clause in Oracle or MySQL, what filters the rows updated?

 A. The WHERE clause

 B. The SET clause

 C. The joins between the updated table and correlated subquery

 D. The ORDER BY clause

 E. The LIMIT clause

 C is correct. The join between the tables filters which rows are updated.

15. What can't you change with an UPDATE statement in an Oracle database?

 A. A collection of a UDT

 B. An element of a UDT

 C. A collection of a scalar data type

 D. An element of a scalar data type

 E. None of the above

 C is correct. You can't change an element of a scalar data type, such as a row in a single column VARRAY or nested table.

Chapter 10

Here are the questions and answers for Chapter 10.

1.   ☑ **True** ☐ **False** A DELETE FROM statement supports multiple-row deletes when more than one row matches the conditions of the WHERE clause.

     True. A DELETE FROM statement removes all rows found to meet a matching condition or all rows to meet a nonmatching condition.

2.   ☑ **True** ☐ **False** A DELETE FROM statement working against a single table has the same syntax in Oracle as MySQL when the WHERE clause uses values, subqueries or correlated subqueries.

     True. A DELETE FROM statement follows the same syntax requirements in both databases for a single table, but it differs for multiple-table deletes in MySQL.

3.   ☐ **True** ☑ **False** The deletion of rows is immediate in all cases.

     False. A deletion of rows is immediate only in a MySQL database when the engine is not InnoDB, or the DELETE FROM statement is not part of a transaction, which is started with a START TRANSACTION or BEGIN WORK statement.

4.   ☐ **True** ☑ **False** A TRUNCATE statement deletes rows similar to a DELETE FROM statement and writes pending changes to a redo log file.

     False. A TRUNCATE statement is immediate and doesn't write a redo log for recoverability. Oracle's *flashback technology* does allow recovery when previously enabled.

5.   ☐ **True** ☑ **False** In the scope of a transaction, the DELETE FROM statement has two phases when the table uses a MyISAM engine.

     False. All DML statements are immediate in the MyISAM engine.

6.   ☐ **True** ☑ **False** In the scope of a transaction, the DELETE FROM statement *always* has two phases when the table uses an InnoDB engine.

     False. The keyword is *always*, which makes this untrue, because two phases require you to start a transaction.

7.   ☐ **True** ☑ **False** Oracle databases support a multiple-table DELETE FROM statement that uses ANSI SQL-92 syntax with JOIN keywords.

     False. The Oracle database supports only correlated DELETE FROM statements.

8.   ☑ **True** ☐ **False** MySQL databases support a multiple-table DELETE FROM statement that uses ANSI SQL-89 syntax with JOIN keywords

     True. The MySQL database supports correlated and multiple-table DELETE FROM statements.

9.   ☐ **True** ☑ **False** Oracle and MySQL support multiple-column matches from subqueries.

     False. Only the Oracle database supports multiple-column (or record structure) matches.

10. ☐ **True** ☑ **False** A non-correlated subquery always returns a null value.

     False. A non-correlated subquery should generally return a value; otherwise, there's no way to match against the result. However, inside a scalar or single-row subquery, it may return a null value for a column value in an INSERT statement or the SET clause of an UPDATE statement.

11. Which of the following comparison operators work with a subquery that returns a single row with a single column?

    A. `=`

    B. `=ANY`

    C. `=ALL`

    D. `IN`

    E. All of the above

    E is correct. All of these comparison operators work because a value can equal another value, a value can equal any value when there's only one value, a value can equal all values when there's only one value, and a value can be found in a set of values.

12. Which of the following comparison operators work with a subquery that returns a single row with multiple columns (multiple answers possible)?

    A. `=`

    B. `=ANY`

    C. `=ALL`

    D. `IN`

    E. All of the above

    B, C, and D are correct. Only the equal (`=`) operator fails, because a left operand of one variable can't be *equal* to a set of things in the right operand; it can only be *equal* to one thing. It's important to recall that the `=ANY` and `=ALL` operators are specific to Oracle, and the `IN` operator is the generic solution across both platforms.

13. Which of the following comparison operators work with a subquery that returns multiple different rows with multiple columns?

    A. `=`

    B. `=ANY`

    C. `=NONE`

    D. `=ALL`

    E. All of the above

    B, C, and D are correct. This answer is *more or less* the same as the preceding question, except that this applies only to the Oracle database across the board. MySQL doesn't support a subquery that returns multiple columns.

14. A multiple-table `DELETE FROM` statement requires how many references to the target table?

    A. 0

    B. 1

    C. 2

    D. 3

    E. None of the above

    E is correct. The target table is the only one that doesn't support a reference (alias).

15. Which type of DELETE FROM statement doesn't support table aliases for the target table?

    A. A DELETE FROM statement that only performs value comparisons in the WHERE clause

    B. A DELETE FROM statement that uses value and expression (subquery) comparisons in the WHERE clause.

    C. A DELETE FROM statement that uses correlated subqueries in the WHERE clause.

    D. A multiple-table DELETE FROM statement that uses joins in the FROM clause.

    E. None of the above

    D is correct. The MySQL multiple-table DELETE FROM statement is the only one that disallows the reference (or alias).

Chapter 11

Here are the questions and answers for Chapter 11.

1. ☑ **True** ☐ **False** A SELECT statement can concatenate strings.

   True. In Oracle, you can concatenate with piped concatenation (with a double pipe symbol set [| |]) or with the CONCAT function. Oracle's CONCAT function doesn't use flexible parameter passing, and it only allows two values, and you must embed a call to the CONCAT function as a call parameter when you need three things, like this:

   ```
   CONCAT('thing_one',CONCAT('thing_two','thing_three'))
   ```

   In MySQL, you should use the CONCAT function, because it supports flexible parameter passing, which means you can send in any number of elements to glue together into a massive string. Piped concatenation can work in some cases when you set a MySQL Monitor parameter, but it fails inside function parameter lists. It's recommended that you don't use piped concatenation in MySQL.

2. ☑ **True** ☐ **False** A SELECT statement can add, subtract, multiply, and divide numbers to return derived results in the SELECT list.

   True. You can add, subtract, multiply, and divide numbers in the SELECT list or in the WHERE clause. Just make sure you're using the supported math operators. Results are returned as strings when you return them into an output file, and as numbers when you return them in a JDBC, ODBC, or OCI context in an external programming language from a cursor.

3. ☐ **True** ☑ **False** Date mathematics work the same way in both Oracle and MySQL databases, because you can get yesterday's date by subtracting one from the current date.

   False. Date math works differently in Oracle than in MySQL. Oracle allows you simply to add numbers to increment days to a date or subtract numbers to decrement days; it also lets you add fractional elements to change time. MySQL, on the other hand, requires that you use one of the date functions to add or subtract dates or times.

4. ☐ **True** ☑ **False** A scalar subquery returns one to many columns and only one row of data.

   False. A scalar subquery, also known as a SQL expression, returns only one column and one row. A scalar subquery is a specialized form of a single-row subquery that returns one to many columns and only one row of data.

5. ☑ **True** ☐ **False** An INNER JOIN can splice a set of columns from one table with a set of columns from another table based on a column that shares the same value.

   True. An INNER JOIN splices rows from two tables into one result set based on the resolution of a value match, or in a pseudo INNER JOIN where a value is found within a range of values. (Pseudo is used to describe it, because this syntax is really a filtered CROSS JOIN.)

6. ☑ **True** ☐ **False** A LEFT JOIN returns the INNER JOIN results plus everything in the left table of the join not found in the right table.

   True. A LEFT JOIN returns everything from the table on the left side of the join operator and splices on any rows that match from the right side of the join operator. The rows found in the table on the left that don't match anything from the table on the right are known as the relative complement of the table on the right.

7. ☑ **True** ☐ **False** In MySQL, you can use the IF function to perform conditional operations.

   True. MySQL does support the IF function, which performs equality and inequality comparisons and returns different values when the comparison is true versus false. You can nest IF statements within IF statements.

8. ☑ **True** ☐ **False** In Oracle, you can use the DECODE function to perform conditional operations.

   True. Oracle does support the DECODE statement, which allows you to perform only equality comparisons. You can also nest DECODE statement inside DECODE statements.

9. ☐ **True** ☑ **False** You use the UNION ALL set operator performs the exact same thing as a UNION set operator.

   False. You use the UNION ALL set operator when each query returns unique result sets; otherwise, it returns two copies of any non-unique results. You use the UNION operator when the queries returns non-unique result sets, because it filters out duplicate rows, like a DISTINCT operator.

10. ☐ **True** ☑ **False** You can't filter results in the WHERE clause on negation of a comparison.

    False. The WHERE clause lets you filter things that are found to be true or false, which means it supports negation, something that's not true or not false. Negation with comparative statements is *powerful but tricky*, so take care when you use it.

11. Which of the following returns a null and works as a subquery?

    A. A scalar subquery

    B. A single-row subquery

    C. A multiple-row subquery

    D. A correlated subquery

    E. None of the above

D is correct. A correlated query actually never returns a value, but it exists when the join between a row from the outer query finds a match inside the inner query (that's why this is sometimes called an outside to inside evaluation).

12. How many columns does a scalar subquery return?

    A. 1
    B. 2
    C. 3
    D. 4
    E. Many

    A is correct. A scalar subquery is by definition a specialized type of a single-row subquery and can return only one row.

13. What is the maximum number of rows you can update with a correlated subquery?

    A. 1
    B. 2
    C. 3
    D. 4
    E. Many

    E is correct. A correlated subquery can resolve for one to many rows and therefore the maximum number updated is many (naturally, dependent upon the individual statement's logic).

14. The MINUS set operator yields the symmetric difference in which of the following examples?

    A. The left join minus the right join
    B. The left join minus the inner join
    C. The right join minus the inner join
    D. The full join minus the cross join
    E. The full join minus the right join

    D is correct. A full join is required as the starting point, and it must subtract the CROSS JOIN or INNER JOIN to leave the symmetric difference. Those rows returned by a CROSS JOIN that aren't found in the INNER JOIN don't exist in a FULL JOIN, and as a result they're discarded by the MINUS operation.

15. Which clause holds the join between tables in ANSI SQL-92?

    A. The WHERE clause
    B. The GROUP BY clause
    C. The FROM clause
    D. The ORDER BY clause
    E. None, because the natural join principal always manages the process

C is correct. The `FROM` clause is where you place the `ON` or `USING` subclauses that contain the join condition in ANSI SQL-92. This differs from ANSI SQL-89, where the join is like any filtering condition of the `WHERE` clause. The benefit is that you know exactly where to find all your join conditions exclusively from filtering statements.

Chapter 12

Here are the questions and answers for Chapter 12.

1. ☑ **True** ☐ **False** In Oracle, you use external tables to import data from CSV files.

   True. Oracle uses external files as wrappers that let you access external files in virtual directories. Those files can be position-specific or CSV files.

2. ☑ **True** ☐ **False** MySQL supports external files with the `LOAD LOCAL DATA INFILE` statement.

   True. MySQL supports the `LOAD LOCAL DATA INFILE` and the `LOAD DATA INFILE` statements to read external files that are typically comma-separated value (CSV) files. You should avoid the `LOAD LOCAL DATA INFILE`, which can load files from remote sources and presents security risks. Also, you need to grant the global `FILE` privilege to any user issuing this statement. Those users with global `FILE` privileges should be administrator, special task, or super user accounts.

3. ☑ **True** ☐ **False** The definition of an external table relies on the ability to create virtual directories.

   True. Virtual directories are an Oracle 11*g* feature, and they're required before you can create an external directory. Any attempt to create an external file without pointing to a valid directory raises the following error:

   ```
   DEFAULT DIRECTORY unknown_virtual_directory
                             *
   ERROR at line 7:
   ORA-06564: object UNKNOWN_VIRTUAL_DIRECTORY does not exist
   ```

   After creating the external table, dropping the virtual directory invalidates the table.

4. ☐ **True** ☑ **False** You need to grant only `READ ON DIRECTORY` privileges to read external data and write error log files.

   False. Although you can create a virtual directory and access it with read-only privileges, it is unable to write log information. Log information is critical to your knowing whether any records weren't read.

5. ☐ **True** ☑ **False** The `ON` clause in an external table definition sets the criteria for whether or not you should insert or update records.

   False. There is no `ON` clause in an external table. The `ON` clause is part of the `MERGE` statement covered in Chapter 12.

6. ☐ **True** ☑ **False** You can update columns used to evaluate joins in the `ON` clause of a subquery.

   False. You can't update the keys used for resolving unique records inside the `ON` clause. The `ON` clause can refer only to non-unique keys and non-key columns.

7. ☐ **True** ☑ **False** You can load XML files with the LOAD DATA statement.

   False. MySQL doesn't support using the LOAD DATA statement for XML files.

8. ☑ **True** ☐ **False** You can load XML files with the LOAD XML statement.

   True. MySQL supports the LOAD XML statement in MySQL 5.5 forward to load XML files.

9. ☑ **True** ☐ **False** The INSERT ON DUPLICATE KEY statement supports a multiple row VALUES clause.

   True. The INSERT ON DUPLICATE KEY statement is supported only in MySQL database, and it works like any INSERT statement by supporting single- and multiple-row inserts with the VALUES clause.

10. ☑ **True** ☐ **False** The REPLACE INTO statement works only with a subquery.

   True. The REPLACE INTO statement syntax works only with a subquery. You can put a list of literals in a SELECT statement with or without reference to the pseudo dual table.

11. Which of the following isn't a valid option of the MERGE statement in Oracle?

   A. The OPTIONALLY ENCLOSED BY option

   B. The ACCESS PARAMETERS option

   C. The FIELDS TERMINATED BY option

   D. The ROWS IDENTIFIED BY option

   E. The DEFAULT DIRECTORY option

   D is correct. The ROWS IDENTIFIED BY is not a valid option of the MERGE statement.

12. Which of the following isn't a valid option of the LOAD DATA statement in MySQL?

   A. The LINES TERMINATED BY option

   B. The ENCLOSED BY option

   C. The FIELDS TERMINATED BY option

   D. The ROWS IDENTIFIED BY option

   E. The ESCAPED BY option

   D is correct. The ROWS IDENTIFIED BY is not a valid option of the LOAD DATA statement in MySQL. ROWS IDENTIFIED BY is the alternate naming convention for loading XML data and is an option of the LOAD XML statement.

13. Which of the following isn't a valid option of the LOAD XML statement in MySQL?

   A. The LINES TERMINATED BY option

   B. The ENCLOSED BY option

   C. The FIELDS TERMINATED BY option

   D. The ROWS IDENTIFIED BY option

   E. The ESCAPED BY option

   C is correct. The FIELDS TERMINATED BY is not a valid option of the LOAD XML statement in MySQL. FIELDS TERMINATED BY is an option of the LOAD DATA statement.

14. Which of the following options or clauses enables a LOAD DATA statement to replace the values of non-key columns?

    A. A REPLACE option

    B. An IGNORE option

    C. An IGNORE *n* LINES option

    D. An IGNORE *n* ROWS option

    E. An ESCAPED BY clause

    A is correct. The REPLACE option instructs the LOAD DATA statement to replace rows that match the unique key, and it changes any non-unique column values included in the loading process.

15. The target table of an INSERT ON DUPLICATE KEY statement requires which of the following?

    A. A primary key constraint

    B. A foreign key constraint

    C. An index

    D. A non-unique key

    E. None of the above

    E is correct. The table requires a unique index, which isn't in the list of choices.

Chapter 13

Here are the questions and answers for Chapter 13.

1. ☑ **True** ☐ **False** A basic block in PL/SQL must have at least a NULL; statement to compile.

    True. A basic block in PL/SQL must have at least one statement. Although a NULL; statement does nothing, it does provide the necessary statement to let the block compile successfully. The NULL; statement can be useful when you're blocking out logic and/or developing new logic for an existing program because it lets you validate the block structure before working with variables and cursors.

2. ☐ **True** ☑ **False** The ELSEIF lets you branch execution in an *if* statement.

    False. The ELSEIF is an invalid syntax in PL/SQL. You need to use the ELSIF in its place.

3. ☑ **True** ☐ **False** The DECLARE block is where you put all variable, cursor, and local functions and procedure implementations.

    True. The DECLARE block is where you put all variable, cursor, and local function and procedure implementations.

4. ☑ **True** ☐ **False** An EXCEPTION block is where you put handling for errors raised in the declaration block of the same anonymous or named program unit.

    True. The EXCEPTION block is where you put all error handling.

5. ☐ **True** ☑ **False** The colon equal symbol set (:=) is the only assignment operator in PL/SQL.

   False. The := is the only right-to-left assignment operator in the PL/SQL language, but you can also assign variables using the SELECT-INTO statement, like this:

```
SQL> DECLARE
  2    lv_target  VARCHAR2(10);
  3  BEGIN
  4    SELECT 'Wow!' INTO lv_target FROM dual;
  5    dbms_output.put_line(lv_target);
  6  END;
  7  /
```

   Although this is done routinely by many, it's a technique every developer should know.

6. ☑ **True** ☐ **False** You need to provide forward referencing stubs for local functions or procedures to avoid a not declared in this scope error.

   True. Although not required unless you make a call to a local function or procedure that follows the call, this is a best practice and will help you avoid compile time errors.

7. ☑ **True** ☐ **False** Oracle supports both simple and searched CASE statements.

   True. Oracle supports simple and searched CASE statements. The searched CASE statements work with an evaluation of true by default and false when you provide an overriding expression.

8. ☑ **True** ☐ **False** Oracle supports SQL and PL/SQL collections as parameter and return value data types.

   True. Oracle supports SQL and PL/SQL collections as parameters and return value data types. You can't call a function that returns a PL/SQL collection from SQL statement; and you can't call a function that has a PL/SQL parameter from a SQL statement. Where possible, you should use SQL data types as parameter and return data types.

9. ☑ **True** ☐ **False** Packages let you define overloaded functions and procedures.

   True. Packages are the only way for you to define a function or procedure name that takes different parameter lists, where the lists, uniqueness is determined by the sequential order of formal parameter data types.

10. ☐ **True** ☑ **False** Native Dynamic SQL (NDS) statements work with bind variables for table names in any type of DML statement.

    False. NDS doesn't support table names in statements as bind parameters. You should vet the authenticity of table names with the DBMS_ASSERT package before concatenating them into a statement for NDS processing.

11. Which parameter modes are supported in Oracle PL/SQL (multiple answers possible)?

    A. IN

    B. INOUT

    C. OUT

    D. IN OUT

    E. All of the above

A, **C**, and **D** are correct. The `IN`, `OUT`, and `IN OUT` modes are all valid. The `INOUT` is not a valid mode without an intervening white space in PL/SQL. Interestingly, as described in Chapter 14, the `INOUT` mode is valid in SQL/PSM stored programs.

12. Which of the following are valid loop structures in PL/SQL (multiple answers possible)?

    A. A simple loop

    B. A `FOR` loop

    C. A `WHILE` loop

    D. An `UNTIL` loop

    E. All of the above

    A, **B**, and **C** are correct. The simple, `FOR`, and `WHILE` loops are supported by PL/SQL. The `UNTIL` loop is supported by SQL/PSM but not PL/SQL.

13. A simple `CASE` statement works with which of the following data types (multiple answers possible)?

    A. A `TEXT` data type

    B. A `VARCHAR2` data type

    C. An `NCHAR` data type

    D. A `CHAR` data type

    E. A `DATE` data type

    B, **C**, and **D** are correct. The `CASE` statement supports the `CHAR`, `NCHAR`, and `VARCHAR2` data types in a simple `CASE` statement.

14. Which of the following isn't a keyword in PL/SQL?

    A. `RECORD`

    B. `REVERSE`

    C. `CURSOR`

    D. `LIMIT`

    E. `STRUCTURE`

    E is correct. `STRUCTURE` isn't a keyword in PL/SQL.

15. Which of the following isn't a cursor attribute?

    A. `%FOUND`

    B. `%ISOPEN`

    C. `%TYPE`

    D. `%NOTFOUND`

    E. `%ROWCOUNT`

    C is correct. The `%TYPE` isn't a cursor attribute but an anchoring technique that lets you inherit a type from a column. The `%ROWTYPE` can apply to the `SELECT` list returned by a cursor.

Chapter 14

Here are the questions and answers for Chapter 14.

1. ☐ **True** ☑ **False** MySQL stored procedures support only the IN mode for parameters.

   False. MySQL stored functions are limited to using only the IN mode for parameters. Stored procedures support the IN, INOUT, and OUT mode parameters.

2. ☐ **True** ☑ **False** MySQL stored function parameters support the IN, INOUT, and OUT modes for parameters.

   False. MySQL stored functions are limited to using only the IN mode for parameters.

3. ☐ **True** ☑ **False** MySQL requires that all assignments to local variables be made through the SET statement.

   False. MySQL requires that you use the SET operator or a SELECT-INTO statement, so SET is not the only assignment operator for local variables.

4. ☐ **True** ☑ **False** MySQL uses an ELSIF block like PL/SQL.

   False. MySQL uses an ELSEIF block, not ELSIF like PL/SQL.

5. ☐ **True** ☑ **False** The value of a call parameter is always available inside a function or procedure regardless of the parameter's mode of operation.

   False. The value of IN and INOUT mode variables are always available inside the function or procedure, but an OUT mode variable can't accept a call parameter value. OUT mode parameters only accept a reference.

6. ☐ **True** ☑ **False** MySQL supports a DO-WHILE loop statement.

   False. MySQL supports a WHILE, not a DO-WHILE loop.

7. ☑ **True** ☐ **False** MySQL supports simple and searched CASE statements.

   True. MySQL supports both simple and searched CASE statements.

8. ☐ **True** ☑ **False** Like Oracle, MySQL lets you parameterize CURSOR statements.

   False. MySQL can't parameterize a CURSOR statement with a parameter list, but you can mix local variables inside the SQL statements, and their values are substituted when you open them.

9. ☑ **True** ☐ **False** You can write a SELECT statement to echo variable content in any stored procedure but not in stored functions.

   True. MySQL supports SELECT statements in stored procedures but not in stored functions.

10. ☐ **True** ☑ **False** The LEAVE statement doesn't need to refer to a named block to exit a block.

    False. The LEAVE statement must refer to a named block to work at all.

11. Which of the following operators matches values and nulls?

    A. `=` comparison operator

    B. `<>` comparison operator

    C. `!=` comparison operator

    D. `<=>` comparison operator

    E. None of the above

    D is correct. The null safe comparison operator works with values and nulls. It returns true when it compares two equal values or two nulls and false when the values don't match or only one of the operands is null.

12. Which loop structure isn't supported in MySQL stored programs?

    A. The `DO-WHILE` loop

    B. The `REPEAT UNTIL` loop

    C. The `WHILE` loop

    D. The simple loop

    E. The infinite loop

    A is correct. The `DO-WHILE` doesn't exist in MySQL. An infinite loop can occur in a simple, `WHILE`, or `REPEAT UNTIL` loop when you forget or intentionally leave out the exiting statement.

13. What type of statements can't you run in prepared statements?

    A. A DDL statement when the SQL statement is concatenated

    B. A DDL statement with the `USING` clause for local variables

    C. A DML statement with the `USING` clause for local variables

    D. A DDL statement when the SQL statement is concatenated

    E. A DML statement with `?` placeholders

    B is correct. Prepared statements don't support DDL statements with the `USING` clause. You need to use concatenation when you want to manage them through prepared statements.

14. What isn't a valid operational mode for a function?

    A. The `NO SQL` mode

    B. The `CONTAINS SQL` mode

    C. The `READS SQL DATA` mode

    D. The `MODIFIES SQL DATA` mode

    E. The `CONTAINS SQL DATA` mode

    D is correct. There is no `MODIFIES SQL DATA` mode, and the other four are all supported.

15. Which isn't a valid assignment model in MySQL stored programs (multiple answers possible)?

    A. `SET session_variable = value;`

    B. `SET local_variable := value;`

    C. `SELECT value INTO session_variable;`

    D. `SELECT column_name INTO local_variable FROM a_table;`

    E. `SELECT local_variable := 20;`

    E is correct. This syntax doesn't work for a local variable but it works for a session variable. You can use the colon equal symbol set for assignment to a local or session variable when it's done in a `SET` statement.

Chapter 15

Here are the questions and answers for Chapter 15.

1. ☑ **True** ☐ **False** Database triggers are able to replace values submitted through `INSERT` and `UPDATE` statements with overriding values.

    True. DML row-level triggers can do exactly this by assigning the different value to the `new.column_name`. Other triggers can't perform this task. Both Oracle and MySQL implement row-level DML triggers.

2. ☑ **True** ☐ **False** Oracle supports triggers on Data Definition Language (DDL) statements.

    True. Oracle supports DDL triggers across all statements.

3. ☐ **True** ☑ **False** MySQL supports triggers on only some DDL statements.

    False. MySQL does not support DDL triggers at all.

4. ☐ **True** ☑ **False** A statement-level trigger lets you change the new value of a column on `INSERT` or `UPDATE` events.

    False. Statement-level triggers have no access to row-level values regardless of what event fires them.

5. ☐ **True** ☑ **False** An Oracle DML trigger can exist only for an individual `INSERT`, `UPDATE`, or `DELETE` statement.

    False. Oracle isn't limited to supporting DML triggers individually, and it is capable of working with triggers collectively by linking the individual events with `OR` clauses.

6. ☑ **True** ☐ **False** A MySQL DML trigger can exist only for an individual `INSERT`, `UPDATE`, or `DELETE` statement.

    True. MySQL triggers can support only individual DML events, and you must write separate triggers for `INSERT`, `UPDATE`, and `DELETE` events.

7. ☐ **True** ☑ **False** MySQL lets you use the `FOLLOWS` keyword to sequence triggers that run on the same event.

    False. MySQL doesn't have a `FOLLOWS` keyword. It is a new feature in Oracle 11*g* that lets you sequence triggers.

8. ☐ **True** ☑ **False** The INSTEAD OF trigger works well when you want an alternative trigger approach for an INSERT statement to a table.

False. INSTEAD OF triggers work well when you work with nonupdatable views, not tables, and they're limited to Oracle; they're not available in MySQL.

9. ☑ **True** ☐ **False** System event triggers are available in an Oracle database but not in a MySQL database.

True. Oracle supports system event triggers.

10. ☑ **True** ☐ **False** Only Oracle supports autonomous transactions in database triggers.

True. Oracle supports autonomous transactions in database triggers with the PRAGMA AUTONOMOUS_TRANSACTION statement.

11. Which of the following types of database triggers work in an Oracle database (multiple answers possible)?

   A. DDL triggers

   B. TCL triggers

   C. DML triggers

   D. Instead-of triggers

   E. Compound triggers

   A, C, D, and **E** are correct. Oracle supports DDL, DML, instead-of, and compound triggers. There is no such thing as a TCL trigger.

12. Which of the following types of database triggers work in a MySQL database?

   A. DDL triggers

   B. DML triggers

   C. System event triggers

   D. TCL triggers

   E. Instead-of triggers

   B is correct. MySQL supports only DML triggers.

13. You have pseudo new and old record structures for which triggers in an Oracle database?

   A. DML statement-level triggers

   B. DDL row-level triggers

   C. DDL statement-level triggers

   D. DML row-level triggers

   E. Compound triggers

   D is correct. The Oracle database supports only the new and old pseudo record structures in a DML row-level trigger.

14. Pseudo new and old record structures are available for which triggers in a MySQL database?

    A. DML statement-level triggers

    B. DML row-level triggers

    C. DDL statement-level triggers

    D. DDL row-level triggers

    E. Compound triggers

    B is correct. The MySQL database supports only the new and old pseudo record structures in a DML row-level trigger.

15. Oracle requires what syntax to access new column values from an `INSERT` or `UPDATE` statement in the code block?

    A. `new.column_name`

    B. `:new.column_name`

    C. `old.column_name.`

    D. `:old.column_name`

    E. None of the above

    B is correct. Oracle can only access a new pseudo record by using a bind variable, `:new`, from inside the trigger body. The reason is that the trigger body acts like a subshell and can only gain access to the new pseudo record structure's scope by referring outside of its scope. The prefacing colon (bind variable) lets the program refer to the DML statement's scope.

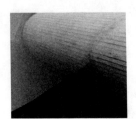

Index

GET YOUR FREE SUBSCRIPTION
TO *ORACLE MAGAZINE*

Oracle Magazine is essential gear for today's information technology professionals. Stay informed and increase your productivity with every issue of *Oracle Magazine*. Inside each free bimonthly issue you'll get:

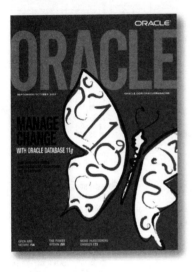

- Up-to-date information on Oracle Database, Oracle Application Server, Web development, enterprise grid computing, database technology, and business trends
- Third-party news and announcements
- Technical articles on Oracle and partner products, technologies, and operating environments
- Development and administration tips
- Real-world customer stories

If there are other Oracle users at your location who would like to receive their own subscription to *Oracle Magazine*, please photocopy this form and pass it along.

Three easy ways to subscribe:

① Web
Visit our Web site at **oracle.com/oraclemagazine**
You'll find a subscription form there, plus much more

② Fax
Complete the questionnaire on the back of this card
and fax the questionnaire side only to **+1.847.763.9638**

③ Mail
Complete the questionnaire on the back of this card
and mail it to **P.O. Box 1263, Skokie, IL 60076-8263**

ORACLE

Want your own FREE subscription?

To receive a free subscription to *Oracle Magazine*, you must fill out the entire card, sign it, and date it (incomplete cards cannot be processed or acknowledged). You can also fax your application to +1.847.763.9638. **Or subscribe at our Web site at oracle.com/oraclemagazine**

○ **Yes, please send me a FREE subscription** *Oracle Magazine.*   ○ No.

○ From time to time, Oracle Publishing allows our partners exclusive access to our e-mail addresses for special promotions and announcements. To be included in this program, please check this circle. If you do not wish to be included, you will only receive notices about your subscription via e-mail.

○ Oracle Publishing allows sharing of our postal mailing list with selected third parties. If you prefer your mailing address not to be included in this program, please check this circle.

If at any time you would like to be removed from either mailing list, please contact Customer Service at +1.847.763.9635 or send an e-mail to oracle@halldata.com. If you opt in to the sharing of information, Oracle may also provide you with e-mail related to Oracle products, services, and events. If you want to completely unsubscribe from any e-mail communication from Oracle, please send an e-mail to: unsubscribe@oracle-mail.com with the following in the subject line: REMOVE [your e-mail address]. For complete information on Oracle Publishing's privacy practices, please visit oracle.com/html/privacy/html

X	
signature (required)	date

name   title

company   e-mail address

street/p.o. box

city/state/zip or postal code   telephone

country   fax

Would you like to receive your free subscription in digital format instead of print if it becomes available? ○ Yes ○ No

YOU MUST ANSWER ALL 10 QUESTIONS BELOW.

① WHAT IS THE PRIMARY BUSINESS ACTIVITY OF YOUR FIRM AT THIS LOCATION? (check one only)

- ☐ 01 Aerospace and Defense Manufacturing
- ☐ 02 Application Service Provider
- ☐ 03 Automotive Manufacturing
- ☐ 04 Chemicals
- ☐ 05 Media and Entertainment
- ☐ 06 Construction/Engineering
- ☐ 07 Consumer Sector/Consumer Packaged Goods
- ☐ 08 Education
- ☐ 09 Financial Services/Insurance
- ☐ 10 Health Care
- ☐ 11 High Technology Manufacturing, OEM
- ☐ 12 Industrial Manufacturing
- ☐ 13 Independent Software Vendor
- ☐ 14 Life Sciences (biotech, pharmaceuticals)
- ☐ 15 Natural Resources
- ☐ 16 Oil and Gas
- ☐ 17 Professional Services
- ☐ 18 Public Sector (government)
- ☐ 19 Research
- ☐ 20 Retail/Wholesale/Distribution
- ☐ 21 Systems Integrator, VAR/VAD
- ☐ 22 Telecommunications
- ☐ 23 Travel and Transportation
- ☐ 24 Utilities (electric, gas, sanitation, water)
- ☐ 98 Other Business and Services _____

② WHICH OF THE FOLLOWING BEST DESCRIBES YOUR PRIMARY JOB FUNCTION? (check one only)

CORPORATE MANAGEMENT/STAFF
- ☐ 01 Executive Management (President, Chair, CEO, CFO, Owner, Partner, Principal)
- ☐ 02 Finance/Administrative Management (VP/Director/ Manager/Controller, Purchasing, Administration)
- ☐ 03 Sales/Marketing Management (VP/Director/Manager)
- ☐ 04 Computer Systems/Operations Management (CIO/VP/Director/Manager MIS/IS/IT, Ops)

IS/IT STAFF
- ☐ 05 Application Development/Programming Management
- ☐ 06 Application Development/Programming Staff
- ☐ 07 Consulting
- ☐ 08 DBA/Systems Administrator
- ☐ 09 Education/Training
- ☐ 10 Technical Support Director/Manager
- ☐ 11 Other Technical Management/Staff
- ☐ 98 Other

③ WHAT IS YOUR CURRENT PRIMARY OPERATING PLATFORM (check all that apply)

- ☐ 01 Digital Equipment Corp UNIX/VAX/VMS
- ☐ 02 HP UNIX
- ☐ 03 IBM AIX
- ☐ 04 IBM UNIX
- ☐ 05 Linux (Red Hat)
- ☐ 06 Linux (SUSE)
- ☐ 07 Linux (Oracle Enterprise)
- ☐ 08 Linux (other)
- ☐ 09 Macintosh
- ☐ 10 MVS
- ☐ 11 Netware
- ☐ 12 Network Computing
- ☐ 13 SCO UNIX
- ☐ 14 Sun Solaris/SunOS
- ☐ 15 Windows
- ☐ 16 Other UNIX
- ☐ 98 Other
- 99 ☐ None of the Above

④ DO YOU EVALUATE, SPECIFY, RECOMMEND, OR AUTHORIZE THE PURCHASE OF ANY OF THE FOLLOWING? (check all that apply)

- ☐ 01 Hardware
- ☐ 02 Business Applications (ERP, CRM, etc.)
- ☐ 03 Application Development Tools
- ☐ 04 Database Products
- ☐ 05 Internet or Intranet Products
- ☐ 06 Other Software
- ☐ 07 Middleware Products
- 99 ☐ None of the Above

⑤ IN YOUR JOB, DO YOU USE OR PLAN TO PURCHASE ANY OF THE FOLLOWING PRODUCTS? (check all that apply)

SOFTWARE
- ☐ 01 CAD/CAE/CAM
- ☐ 02 Collaboration Software
- ☐ 03 Communications
- ☐ 04 Database Management
- ☐ 05 File Management
- ☐ 06 Finance
- ☐ 07 Java
- ☐ 08 Multimedia Authoring
- ☐ 09 Networking
- ☐ 10 Programming
- ☐ 11 Project Management
- ☐ 12 Scientific and Engineering
- ☐ 13 Systems Management
- ☐ 14 Workflow

HARDWARE
- ☐ 15 Macintosh
- ☐ 16 Mainframe
- ☐ 17 Massively Parallel Processing

- ☐ 18 Minicomputer
- ☐ 19 Intel x86(32)
- ☐ 20 Intel x86(64)
- ☐ 21 Network Computer
- ☐ 22 Symmetric Multiprocessing
- ☐ 23 Workstation Services

SERVICES
- ☐ 24 Consulting
- ☐ 25 Education/Training
- ☐ 26 Maintenance
- ☐ 27 Online Database
- ☐ 28 Support
- ☐ 29 Technology-Based Training
- ☐ 30 Other
- 99 ☐ None of the Above

⑥ WHAT IS YOUR COMPANY'S SIZE? (check one only)

- ☐ 01 More than 25,000 Employees
- ☐ 02 10,001 to 25,000 Employees
- ☐ 03 5,001 to 10,000 Employees
- ☐ 04 1,001 to 5,000 Employees
- ☐ 05 101 to 1,000 Employees
- ☐ 06 Fewer than 100 Employees

⑦ DURING THE NEXT 12 MONTHS, HOW MUCH DO YOU ANTICIPATE YOUR ORGANIZATION WILL SPEND ON COMPUTER HARDWARE, SOFTWARE, PERIPHERALS, AND SERVICES FOR YOUR LOCATION? (check one only)

- ☐ 01 Less than $10,000
- ☐ 02 $10,000 to $49,999
- ☐ 03 $50,000 to $99,999
- ☐ 04 $100,000 to $499,999
- ☐ 05 $500,000 to $999,999
- ☐ 06 $1,000,000 and Over

⑧ WHAT IS YOUR COMPANY'S YEARLY SALES REVENUE? (check one only)

- ☐ 01 $500, 000, 000 and above
- ☐ 02 $100, 000, 000 to $500, 000, 000
- ☐ 03 $50, 000, 000 to $100, 000, 000
- ☐ 04 $5, 000, 000 to $50, 000, 000
- ☐ 05 $1, 000, 000 to $5, 000, 000

⑨ WHAT LANGUAGES AND FRAMEWORKS DO YOU USE? (check all that apply)

- ☐ 01 Ajax
- ☐ 02 C
- ☐ 03 C++
- ☐ 04 C#
- ☐ 13 Python
- ☐ 14 Ruby/Rails
- ☐ 15 Spring
- ☐ 16 Struts
- ☐ 05 Hibernate
- ☐ 06 J++/J#
- ☐ 07 Java
- ☐ 08 JSP
- ☐ 09 .NET
- ☐ 10 Perl
- ☐ 11 PHP
- ☐ 12 PL/SQL
- ☐ 17 SQL
- ☐ 18 Visual Basic
- ☐ 98 Other

⑩ WHAT ORACLE PRODUCTS ARE IN USE AT YOUR SITE? (check all that apply)

ORACLE DATABASE
- ☐ 01 Oracle Database 11*g*
- ☐ 02 Oracle Database 10*g*
- ☐ 03 Oracle9*i* Database
- ☐ 04 Oracle Embedded Database (Oracle Lite, Times Ten, Berkeley DB)
- ☐ 05 Other Oracle Database Release

ORACLE FUSION MIDDLEWARE
- ☐ 06 Oracle Application Server
- ☐ 07 Oracle Portal
- ☐ 08 Oracle Enterprise Manager
- ☐ 09 Oracle BPEL Process Manager
- ☐ 10 Oracle Identity Management
- ☐ 11 Oracle SOA Suite
- ☐ 12 Oracle Data Hubs

ORACLE DEVELOPMENT TOOLS
- ☐ 13 Oracle JDeveloper
- ☐ 14 Oracle Forms
- ☐ 15 Oracle Reports
- ☐ 16 Oracle Designer
- ☐ 17 Oracle Discoverer
- ☐ 18 Oracle BI Beans
- ☐ 19 Oracle Warehouse Builder
- ☐ 20 Oracle WebCenter
- ☐ 21 Oracle Application Express

ORACLE APPLICATIONS
- ☐ 22 Oracle E-Business Suite
- ☐ 23 PeopleSoft Enterprise
- ☐ 24 JD Edwards EnterpriseOne
- ☐ 25 JD Edwards World
- ☐ 26 Oracle Fusion
- ☐ 27 Hyperion
- ☐ 28 Siebel CRM

ORACLE SERVICES
- ☐ 28 Oracle E-Business Suite On Demand
- ☐ 29 Oracle Technology On Demand
- ☐ 30 Siebel CRM On Demand
- ☐ 31 Oracle Consulting
- ☐ 32 Oracle Education
- ☐ 33 Oracle Support
- ☐ 98 Other
- 99 ☐ None of the Above

08014904